THE RECORD SOCIETY OF LANCASHIRE AND CHESHIRE

FOUNDED TO TRANSCRIBE AND PUBLISH
ORIGINAL DOCUMENTS RELATING TO THE TWO COUNTIES

VOLUME CXLIV

The Society wishes to acknowledge with gratitude the support given towards
publication by

Cheshire County Council
Lancashire County Council

ISBN 978 0 902593 79 4

Printed in Great Britain by 4word Ltd, Bristol

WRENBURY WILLS AND INVENTORIES
1542–1661

Edited by Paul B. Pixton

PRINTED FOR THE SOCIETY
2009

FOR THE SUBSCRIPTION YEAR 2006 AND 2007

COUNCIL AND OFFICERS FOR THE YEAR 2007

President

J.R.H. Pepler, M.A., D.A.A., c/o Cheshire Record Office, Duke Street,
Chester CH1 1RL

Hon. Council Secretary

Dorothy J. Clayton, M.A., Ph.D., A.L.A., F.R.Hist.S., c/o John Rylands
University Library of Manchester, Oxford Road, Manchester M13 9PP

Hon. Membership Secretary

Maureen Barber, B.A., D.A.A.; *from September 2007* J.C. Sutton, M.A.,
F.R.I.C.S., 5 Beechwood Drive, Alsager, Cheshire, ST7 2HG

Hon. Treasurer and Publications Secretary

Fiona Pogson, B.A., Ph.D., c/o Department of History, Liverpool Hope
University College, Hope Park, Liverpool L16 9JD

Hon. General Editor

Peter McNiven, M.A., Ph.D., F.R.Hist.S., 105 Homegower House,
St Helens Road, Swansea SA1 4DN

Other Members of the Council

P.H.W. Booth, M.A., F.R.Hist.S.
Diana E.S. Dunn, B.A., D.Ar.Studies
M.R.V. Heale, B.A., M.Phil., Ph.D.
B. Jackson, M.A., D.A.A.
V. McKernan, B.A., D.A.A.

C.B. Phillips, B.A., Ph.D.
B.W. Quintrell, M.A., Ph.D., F.R.Hist.S.
D.A. Stoker, B.A., M.Ar.Ad.
D. Szechi, B.A., D.Phil., F.R.Hist.S.
T.J. Thornton, M.A., D.Phil.

CONTENTS

Foreword and Acknowledgements   vii

Introduction   ix

Index of Decedents   li

Index of Wills and other Probate Instruments   lvi

The Wills   1

Glossary of Parochial Terms   481

Bibliography   503

Index of Names   509

Index of Places   533

Index of Subjects   538

FOREWORD AND ACKNOWLEDGEMENTS

This collection of wills and other testamentary documents relating to the chapelry of Wrenbury began more than twenty years ago as the editor sought to establish the social context for the family of *Pexton* whose contours have been the object of a much longer search. Realizing that the parish registers for Wrenbury do not commence until the late sixteenth century, it became necessary for me to build that context out of other documents, primarily the manorial records of Newhall, found in the Cheshire Record Office in Chester, but also, importantly, the wills, inventories, administrations and inquisitions post mortem relating to the inhabitants of those villages which comprised the chapelry.

Needless to say, the project quickly outgrew its original purpose, so much so that we soon considered the benefit to others as well of the more than three hundred wills which we transcribed for the period 1540 to 1730. We had, after all, assembled wills and inventories of men and women whose lives had been played out in a rather remote corner of England, a region without any sizeable town or city, where agriculture was far and away the dominant economic factor. The rural nature of the region is obvious from the inventories found attached to many of the wills, and from the bequests made in the wills themselves. The collection seemed to be a valuable database not only for family history/genealogy, but for local and even micro-economic history as well.

The work of transcribing the wills has taken more than a score of years, aided by student research assistants at Brigham Young University. Some already had the necessary skills required for the task, being part of the Family History programme at the University, while others had to acquire the paleographic tools 'on the job', as it were. We express deep appreciation to Ryan Crisp, Amy Harris, Amanda Sims, Kristin Brandt, Nathan Murphy, John Clarke, Janae Lakey, John Young and Josh Perky for their valuable contributions in working from oft-times less-than-perfect microfilm copies of the documents found in the Family History Library of the Church of Jesus Christ of Latter-day Saints in Salt Lake City, Utah, and in the Harold B. Lee Library at Brigham Young University.

In addition to editing the wills and inventories, we have included inquisitions post mortem where these exist, since they shed significant details upon the wills themselves and/or provide information about the decedent which is totally lacking in the will. This is a departure from the format established for the parish of Stockport as published in volumes 124 and 131 of the Record Society, but we hope that the additional information they bring to bear on the decedent and his heirs and properties is a welcome addition.

We have also departed from the Stockport model in editing wills in that we have sought to provide genealogical pedigree tables for each decedent, extracting all possible information from the text of the will itself, and supplementing it with data drawn from parish registers and other local records. Since the transcribed wills will undoubtedly serve a variety of purposes, including providing a glimpse into the material culture of a rural Cheshire parish (i.e. chapelry) and also the needs and desires of family and local historians, we have made a concerted effort to place the testator within a family context. In many cases, this context seems limited, while in others, thanks both to the wealth of data contained in individual documents and to corroborating data found in the wills of other individuals, it is clearly significant.

We realize the risk in taking such a step, but we trust that the deep familiarity with the various families of Wrenbury chapelry which has resulted from this undertaking gives us a decided advantage. Extensive documentation of these tables provides support for our conclusions, which are generally well beyond the point of conjecture. Nevertheless, we welcome criticisms of our conclusions and reconstructions, but this collection of pedigrees may be unique, presenting the interrelationships of most families that resided within this religious, social and economic framework during almost a complete century.

The original wills are found in the Cheshire Record Office in Chester, and the editor extends his deepest appreciation to Mr Jonathan Pepler, Cheshire County Archivist, and to staff of the CRO, for their invaluable assistance rendered in 1996 and 2002 during extended visits to the document collections. Particular thanks are extended to Kate Tobias-Buick and Trevor Johnston for their repeated efforts to keep the supply of original documents flowing from the repository. Owing to a family health crisis, the editor's 2002 research visit was truncated. It is therefore with the greatest of thanks that we recognize the willingness of Mrs Elizabeth M. Green (likewise of the CRO) and the Rev. John Mitchell to act as our resident researchers and provide us with countless important details which we otherwise could not have acquired. Liz's own health challenges notwithstanding, she completed a long 'shopping list' for us which has been critical to this edition.

In 1996 the author spent a very pleasant afternoon visiting with Mr John R. Pound, resident of the Oak House, The Green, at Wrenbury. Pound was an architect by profession, but a local historian by passion, who shared with me his collection of materials accumulated over a lifetime of interest in this quiet and charming English village. It is to him that I dedicate this volume.

Above all, our thanks are extended to Dr Peter McNiven and the Record Society of Lancashire and Cheshire for accepting this collection of testamentary documents for publication. We have long been aware of the reputation of the Society among the county institutions of Great Britain, and we are deeply honoured to be included among its published authors/editors. We trust that our small contribution will meet the standard of those that have preceded it, and that its attempt at elucidating this small corner of Cheshire will prove beneficial to many others.

While acknowledging the countless contributions of others, the editor accepts full responsibility for the errors and shortcomings that remain, trusting, however, that they are minimal and of little significance when compared with the large volume of data contained in this fascinating collection.

Paul B. Pixton, Ph.D.
Provo, Utah, U.S.A.
March 2007

(a descendant of Richard Cotton, esq., of Combermere, father of George, Dorothy and Andrew Cotton, whose wills are published in this volume, and for whom an inquisition post mortem was held on 6 April 1605).

INTRODUCTION

Historical Setting

On 18 January 1586/87 one Edward Pexton, a yeoman of Harringay parish, Middlesex, declared his last will and testament. Among his bequests was the amount of ten shillings for the repair of the parish church at Wrenbury, Cheshire, 'where I was borne.'[1] Wrenbury lies deep in the southern portion of the county and diocese of Chester, near the extreme southwest border of the Province of York, four miles from the common border with Shropshire, and six miles from the Welsh border of Flintshire, near Whitchurch. In 1586/87 Wrenbury fell within Nantwich hundred, and despite Edward Peckston's reference to 'the parish church', it, together with the townships of Broomhall, Chorley, Smeatonwood, Dodcott and Woodcott, and with most of the townships of Newhall and Sound, comprised a parochial chapelry, rather than a parish *per se*, being part of the ancient parish of Acton.[2]

Several of these locations are mentioned in the *Domesday Book* of 1086 which attests to their Saxon or English origin, while others were Norman creations. We read in that ancient record that

> The same William de Malbanc holds Warenberie. Carle held it and was a free man. There is one hide and a half rateable to the gelt [i.e., are taxable]. The land is two carucates: one is in the demesne and there are two neatherherds [herdsmen] and one border [cottager]. There is a wood two leagues long and one broad with two hays [i.e., hags – forest hedgings or enclosures] and a hawk's eyrie. It was and is worth five shillings. The Earl found it waste.

Near *Warenberie* or Wrenbury was that spot later known as 'the Fryth', about which the king's officials declared the following:

> The same William de Malbanc holds Tereth. Lewin and Osmer held it for two manors and were free men. There is one virgate rateable to the gelt. The land is two carucates. Three villeins there have one carucate and there are four acres of meadow, and a wood half a league long and three furlongs broad. In King Edward's time it was worth seven shillings, now worth five shillings.

And a third property in this vicinity had come into the hands of William de Malbanc, as well, as a vassal of Earl Hugh Lupus, the nephew of the Conqueror:

> The same William holds Brunhalda, and Edric held it for two manors and were free. There is half a hide rateable to the gelt. The land is 1 carucate. Half a carucate is in

---

1   S.A. Smith, compiler, *Index of Wills Proved in the Prerogative Court of Canterbury*, vol. 4: 1584–1604, The Index Library, 25 (London, 1901; repr. 1968), p. 321.
2   On the more detailed history of Acton parish, see Frank A. Latham, ed., *Acton (Near Nantwich): the History of a Cheshire Parish and its Seventeen Townships* (Whitchurch, Shropshire, Local History Group, 1995).

the demesne with 1 neatherd. There is a wood a league long and half as broad and there is a hay. In King Edward's time it was worth 4 shillings and now two shillings. The Earl found it waste.

Northwest of *Warenberie* lay yet another hamlet – *Cerele* – *i.e.* Chorley, mentioned in *Domesday* where it also lay in the hands of William de Malbanc (previously an Aluric had held it):

> There are three virgates rateable to the gelt. The land is one carucate and a half. There are two villeins and one bordar with half a carucate.

Wrenbury, Frith, Broomhall, and Chorley were thus all villages of ancient origin which were enumerated by the royal agents in 1086.

Newhall, on the other hand, does not find mention in the survey itself, but a portion of it was surveyed under the name of *Essetune*, still known as Aston:

> The same William (de Malbanc) holds Essetune. Osmer and Oswin held it for two manors, and were free men. There are three virgates rateable to the geld. The land is 5 carucates. One is the demesne. Also there are 2 neatherds and 3 borders with one carucate. There is one acre of meadow. A wood one league long and half as broad. There are 3 leys and a hawk's eyrie. In King Edward the Confessor's time it was worth 20 shillings. Now 10 shillings. The Earl of Chester found it waste.[3]

Neither is Sound (sometimes spelled *Soond* or *Sonde*) mentioned in *Domesday Book*, but it was later part of the barony of Wich Malbank, that is, the barony of William de Malbanc and his descendants, and as such passed to the Audley family in the reign of Edward I.

Wrenbury, Broomhall, Frith and Aston were held in Norman times successively by William de Malbanc who died in 1093; by Hugh de Malbanc, his son, who died in 1135; and by William de Malbanc, his grandson, who died in the time of Henry II. During these three generations the Malbancs expanded the area around Aston: without disturbing the existing village and its inhabitants, they created new arable out of the forest or waste of the *Warmundestrou*, appropriately calling this improved manor New Hall. Newhall included within the township not only the ancient hamlet of Aston with its wood, but the wider moorland waste on both sides of the River Weaver, out of which copyholds were parcelled out among the villeins from time to time as dwelling houses were built for an increasing

---

3   On the *Domesday Book* descriptions of the area, see B.E. Harris, A.T. Thacker [and others], eds, *A History of the County of Chester*, Vol 1 (1987), Victoria History of the Counties of England (Oxford, Oxford University Press for the Institute of Historical Research, 1979–), i. 354, no. 154; *Domesday Book, vol. 26: Cheshire*, ed. Philip Morgan (Chichester, Phillimore, 1978), 265c no. 19. Further discussion of the relevant passages is found in H.A. Clarke, *The History of the Ancient Parish of Wrenbury (Including Combermere Abbey)* (Wrenbury, n.d. [1962/1989], pp. 2, 38; F.W. Norwood, *'Historic Notes'*, *The Wrenbury Church Monthly* (1900–1905), collected by John Parkin, Newhall Mill Farm, Aston, Nantwich, and made available to this writer by Mr John R. Pound, Oak House, The Green, Wrenbury; John R. Pound, 'St. Margaret's Church, Wrenbury: A Brief Account of This 900 Year Old Churchyard' [typewritten] (1993), p. 1.

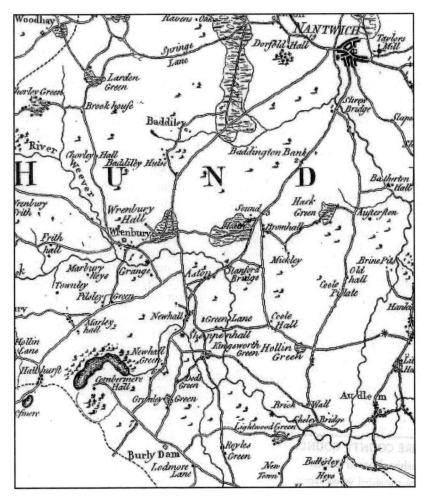

Area comprising Wrenbury Chapelry, as shown on 1777 P.P. Burdett Map.

population. Henceforth, Aston was included in the district of Newhall, and though the hamlet of Aston was of English origin the name given to the wider rural area – Newhall – was due to Norman enterprise. Thus, the township has even since been called, not Aston, but Newhall.[4]

Some indication of the economic importance of this new township can be seen from the fact that it was divided among the parishes of Wrenbury, Audlem and

4   Clarke, *Ancient Parish of Wrenbury*, pp. 40–5.

St Margaret's Church, Wrenbury, as sketched by John R. Pound
(used by permission)

Acton (perhaps even shortly after the establishment of Newhall), each of which shared in the woodland resources so vital to their wellbeing.[5]

The 'parish church' referred to by Edward Pexton in 1586/87, and which served the villages and hamlets noted above, was the chapel dedicated to St Margaret of Antioch, a third-century martyr and patron saint of expectant mothers who was a popular cult figure in the Middle Ages. It had existed at Wrenbury since the early part of the twelfth century, as a daughter chapel to Acton church, under a curate appointed by the priest at Acton. The structure itself was probably black-and-white half-timbered, similar to what is now characterized as typical Cheshire architecture.[6] Overlooking the village green, the tower of Wrenbury church remains a conspicuous feature. Dating from the early sixteenth century, it stands at the west end of the structure and contains six bells, two of which were inscribed and dated during the time-frame of this present volume:

---

5 N.J. Higham, *The Origins of Cheshire* (Manchester, Manchester University Press, 1993), pp. 142, 144, sees the division occurring about the time of the *Domesday Book*.

6 Cheshire Countryside and Recreation, *Cheshire Churches—Church of St. Margaret, Wrenbury* (Cheshire County Council, privately printed, 1988).

'1610. John Cheswith and John Cartwright, churchwardens.'
'1621. Robert Bancnes [Bankes] and Geo. Wright, churchwardens'.[7]

The very year that the third bell was cast, George Palyn, lately citizen and girdler of London, made a bequest in his last will and testament, the conditions of which were imposed upon those same two churchwardens at Wrenbury – John Cartwright and John Cheswys. The bond of obligation published by them contains the details of Palyn's bequest, as revealed in its complete form below:

> Know all people by these presents that we John Cheswys of Wrenbury in the county of Chester yeoman, and John Cartwright of Wrenbury aforesaid yeoman, now being wardens of the parish church of Wrenbury aforesaid are held and firmly bound to William Bonham citizen and vintner of London and to Richard Booth citizen and cloth-maker of London, executors of the testament and last will of George Palyn, lately citizen and girdler of London, deceased, in [the sum of] forty pounds of lawful money of England, to be paid to the same William Bonham and Richard Booth, or to either of them, or to their certain attorney, or to their executors or administrators. And that this payment may be well and faithfully made, we bind ourselves and each of us separately for the whole sum and for any part of it, and we bind our heirs, executors and administrators firmly by these presents, sealed with our seals. Given [?] in the eighth year of the reign of Our Lord James, by the grace of God, King of England . . . 1610

Thereupon follow the conditions of the bequest as set forth by George Palyn. From internal evidence, it seems likely that he had been born at Wrenbury, and that he had early on removed to London where he became reasonably successful. His intentions were that

> Whereas thabovenamed George Palyn deceased (in and by his last will and Testament) Willed and bequeathed unto the Wardens of the parish Churche of Wrenbury in the Countye of Chester the some of Thirtye Poundes wherewith his will and meaning was they should provide and hang upp (amongst the Belles of the same Church) ffyveth Bell tuneable with the rest of the Belles of the same Church Provided That if the Church Wardens of the said parish Church should not provide and hang up the same Bell Within one yere next after his decease that then the said guift should be voide, And not performaunce thereof in manner as aforesaid, he willed and bequeathed the said Thirtye Poundes unto his Brother James Palyn As by the said last will playnely appeareth Which said some of Thirtye Poundes thabove named William Bonham and Richard Booth Executors above named have paid unto the above bounden John Cheswys and John Cartwright Church Wardens of the said parish Church of Wrenbury To the intent that therewith they shall provide and hang upp (amongst the other Bells in the same Church) a ffyveth Bell tuneable to the rest of the Bells according to the will mynd and meaning of the said George Palyn deceased in and by his said last will expressed and declared, Nowe the Condicōn of this Obligacōn is such That if the said John Cheswys and John

---

7   Raymond Richards, ed., *Old Cheshire Churches, With a Supplementary Survey Related to the Lesser Old Chapels in Cheshire*, revised ed. (Didsbury, Manchester, E.J. Morten, 1973), pp. 369–73 (copy viewed 2002 at CRO). See also Clarke, *Ancient Parish of Wrenbury*, pp. 103–4.

Cartwright Church Wardens aforenamed or other the Church Wardens of the said parish Church of Wrenbury aforesaid doe and shall on this side and before the Twelveth Daye of October next ensuing the date within written with the said Thirtye Poundes provide and hange up amongst the [other Belles in the same Church a Fyveth] Bell tuneable with the rest of the Bells in the same Church according to the true intent and meaning of the said George Palyn deceased in his last will specified or declared without fraud or further delaye That then this Obligacion to be voyd and of none effect orelles [or else] it to stand and abyde in full force and virtue.[8]

It is not known whether the bell provided for by George Palyn's bequest is in fact the one bearing the inscription of 1610, or some other. Given the fact that this is the oldest extant bell in the tower, it seems most likely so. Those with later dates (nos 3–6) presumably replaced the four existing bells of 1610, while the one inscribed in 1621 was the last of the six bells added to the ring.

In addition to the significant addition of a new bell to St Margaret's tower, the church was the recipient of several bequests from testators whose wills are part of our collection, as well as those native to the parish who died elsewhere. These bequests suggest that at the turn of the sixteenth/seventeenth century the structure was badly in need of repairs:

Thomas Chessewes 1562	6s.	8d.
Edward Pexton (of Harringaye, Middlesex) 1587	10s.	–
Humphrey Wilson 1602	3s.	4d.

Interestingly, Thomas Chessewes was the father of John Cheswith, the above-noted churchwarden of 1610. The fly-leaf of the earliest parish register (commencing 16 September 1593) contains the notation, 'The chancel of the parish of Wrenburie was built at the costs and charges of the parish and some benefactors to the same in the year of Our Lord 1606',[9] again pointing to the time-frame of this collection of testamentary instruments as one crucial for the social and religious fabric of this rural chapelry.

In the Harleian MS 2176 there is a 'Catalogue of Such Charitable Gifts As Have Been Given to the Church of Wrenbury', subscribed in 1665 by the churchwardens, Robert Cudworth and Robert Bankes. It briefly describes the gifts and bequests made to the chapelry since the time of John Massey, the last abbot of Combermere, whose will is one of the earliest in this present collection:[10]

John Massey, † 1564/65:	non-specific legacies as related to Wrenbury;
Rafe Bulkley, † 1593:	by will bequeathed 200 marks to Wrenbury parish and directed that 13d. loaves be given

8 A copy of the original document was provided for this writer by Mr John R. Pound of Wrenbury in 1996. The transcription/translation is unattributed, but Elizabeth Danbury made critical comments on 10 January 1996. George Palin also provided a legacy to the Wrenbury school in 1610, as contained in a memorandum, a copy of which is included with a set of school rules, dated 1673; see CRO CR72/13/73.
9 Clarke, *Ancient Parish of Wrenbury*, p. 100.
10 Harleian MS 2176, fo. 64^, cited by Norwood, 'Historic Notes', no. xlii.

among the poor of Wrenbury and Marbury; each poor person at the same time was to receive 1d. in money; he also directed his executors to build a schoolroom near the church at Wrenbury and give £10 per year for seven years towards the maintenance of a schoolmaster;[11]

George Palyn, † 1610: by will bequeathed £30 to the Wrenbury church for the purpose of obtaining a new bell (as discussed above);

Richard Booth *[no will has been located in the CRO]*
Widow [Margaret] Ankers, by will bequeathed £10 to Wrenbury parish,
† 1609/10: in the hands of Thomas Tailer of Light-wood Green, the interest of which was to be paid out every year at the feast of St Thomas the Apostle before Christmas to the poor in perpetuity;

Widow [Anne] Bickerton, £10 to be divided equally between Audlem
† 1616: and Wrenbury parishes for relief of the poor, to be administered in the former by William Salmon of Coole Lane, and in the latter by the testator's son-in-law, William Bebbington; after their demise, this respon-sibility was to devolve upon the respective churchwardens;

John Cartwright, † 1631: £5 to the poor of Wrenbury parish;
William Babington, † 1630/31: £5 to the poor of Wrenbury parish;
Mary Evans;
Richard Cartwright, † 1693;
George Beckett, † 1662;
George Whittingham;
Roger Podmore, † 1676;
Elizabeth Podmore, † 1687;
George Cudwerth;
Robert Cudwerth, † 1665.

Remarkably, all the individuals who died before 1660 can be accounted for except Richard Booth,[11a] and although the wills of Rafe Bulkley and George Palyn have

---

11 A similar note is found on the fly-leaf of the earliest Register and written in the hand of William Prince, curate of Wrenbury: 'The scholehouse at Wrenburie was builded at the costs and charges of Mr. Rafe Buckley who in his last will and testament lefte the same to be builded with X^{li} for the marster and X^s to buy bookes for poore mens children to learne upon yearly during the terme of seven yeares. It was builded in the yeare of Our Lord 1605. The scolemaster entred to teach there at the feeste of the Annunciation.' See Clarke, *Ancient Parish of Wrenbury* p. 100.
11a Very likely the same as the Richard Booth who acted as executor for the will and testament of George Palyn, † 1610; Booth may thus have been a native of Wrenbury as well.

not been located, they can still be placed in context. The wills and bequests of those individuals from Mary Evans onward apparently belong to the time-frame beyond that covered in this volume. Surprisingly, however, there are other benefactors found among our group of testators whose names are not included in the 'Catalogue', including some whose generosity was quite substantial.

Some of the grants were one-time affairs, while others had extended – or even perpetual – durations. For example, in 1610 Roger Swann granted 4s. to the poor of the parish which, as a percentage of the entire value of his estate, was fairly insignificant. Roger Broome, on the other hand, in 1606, made a bequest of 6s. 8d.; George Kemp of Smeatonwood made a similar, one-time bequest of 6s. 8d. in 1614. Randle Povall, who served as parish clerk at Wrenbury until his death in 1593, not only designated that 20s. of his estate should go to the relief of the poor of Wrenbury, but that 6s. 8d. be given for a similar purpose to Marbury, and 4s. 4d. to Baddily parish. Henry Vernon of Coole Lane, whose personal fortune was quite substantial, and who appears to have loaned money to numerous individuals – often having to resort to legal processes in order to recover it – bequeathed a single sum of 10s. to the '*power* of Namptwich' – that is, to the poor of Nantwich. William Wilson of Wrenbury Frith, who styled himself 'Gentleman' at the time of his death in May 1639, left goods and chattels valued at £368 6s. 2d., from which £4 was to be given to the 'poore inhabetors of the parish of Wrenbury . . . .' William Cooper in 1611 established a bequest of 10s. to be awarded yearly for ten years, payable on Good Friday.

Very significant amounts of money were also granted by Thomas Palin in 1624 (£5), George Tenche in 1648 (£10), and George Hall, Jr in 1658 (£5). The latter also stipulated that '. . . the said sume of two pounds shall be paid in by my Executors hereafter named to the then present Churchwardens and overseers of the poore of the same parish, to be by them sett forth and imployed to the best benefitt, to the use of the poore aforesaid from time to time, And that the use and interest thereof shall be yearely distributed amongst the poore aforesaid, every St. Thomas day by the guarding Churchwardens, and overseers of the poore of the same parish as other charitable gifts formerly have bin.' Thomas Hamnett of the Grange in Smeatonwood, whose will was proved in 1635, not only made specific provisions for the poor of the parish, but he directed his executors to use whatever residue remained from the paying of his debts, legacies and funeral expenses to give to his 'poorest and neerest kindred'. Even Allis Pextonne of Newhall, a widow who died in 1632, stipulated that 'I would have you to give unto the poore at my buryinge one pennye to divyde' – the Biblical widow's mite, so to speak. In contrast, her neighbour, John Cartwright of Aston, who died a very wealthy man in 1604, left a single, one-time only sum – the somewhat standard 6s. 8d. – 'to the parishe church of Wrenburie'. As we shall see shortly, Cartwright's elder son and namesake was just as miserly as he, yet his other son, Richard Cartwright, became one of Wrenbury's most renowned benefactors.

On the other hand, in 1614 Thomas Ravenscroft of Newhall directed that 40s. per year be granted at Christmas-time to the poor of Wrenbury out of his estate, for a period of eight years – a total of £16. His widow, Ellen Ravenscroft, extended that generosity by her will made in 1627, bequeathing 20s. to the poor of Wrenbury, but directing her executors to give 2s. of that amount specifically to Robert Deverise. Unfortunately, Robert Deverise died about five days before her, so that he could not have benefitted at all from Ellen Ravenscroft's gift.[12] Andrew Cotton's perpetual bequest of 40s. annually, made in 1629, was to be distributed at the four quarterly Communions.

One of the most intriguing bequests is that of John Edgeley of Woodcott, a yeoman whose will was proved in 1637. Among the items noted is: 'my will is that my executors shall att my coste and charge free my said sonne out of all his troubles in the Spirituall Courte, if I doe not efecte it for him myselfe before my death'. We are not aware of the legal difficulties which John Edgeley Jr faced at this time, but the generosity of his father must have been most welcome.[13] The father also forgave this same son a debt of £10 16s., giving us some indication as to his personal qualities. On the other hand, as we will note below, frictions between fathers and children were not unheard of and undoubtedly created situations which had far-reaching consequences.

Equally telling is the bequest which Edmund Crewe made in 1632 of £28 'being in handes of George Orpe of Lightwood [Green] in the said County of Chester due me from the said George Orpe by bond att several dayes shalbe by the advise & oversight of my said Cosen Raphe Cardiffe and Richard Edgeley of Newhall aforsaid their heires executors and assignes to be imployed & sett forth For the benefitt & use of a reader or mynister at Burleydam Chappell for the mayntaynance of Gods word there from tyme to tyme for ever'. Such a bequest is significant not only because of what it tells us about Edmund Crewe's own piety, but also in the light of the fact that a few years later the inhabitants of Wrenbury chapelry sought relief of their burden in supporting their own curate. Obviously, the burden of such an essential person in the religious fabric of the community was not viewed equally by all the inhabitants.

The population of the chapelry in the period from 1550 until 1660 is not known with any exactness: Bishop Gastrell enumerated Chester Diocese in 1722, and the parish or chapelry of Wrenbury, including Burleydam, nearly all of Newhall, besides Chorley, Woodcott and Broomhall, was listed with about '1500 souls' – some 310 families of churchpeople (i.e. the Established Church) with one Quaker family.[14] A closer figure for our period can be obtained from an undated petition of about 1650/54 from the parishioners of Wrenbury to Parliament, seeking help in meeting the costs of maintaining a minister at their church: the document, found among the Cheshire

---

12   See CRO Mf 156/1–3, Wrenbury Parish Registers – Burials: 14 July 1640; Ellen Ravenscroft was buried 19 July 1640. Frances *Deavorise*, who must have been Robert's wife, was buried at Wrenbury in 1642; a daughter, Elizabeth *Deveres*, was baptized in 1621.

13   See will of John Edgeley of Moorehall, yeoman, pr. 1654, which reveals very little about his financial condition at the time of his death. Being a PCC will, it lacks an inventory from which we could reconstruct John's material world. His legacies probably amounted to about £15, plus two lambs, the value of which may have ranged between 2s. and 3s. each, based on a comparison with other contemporary inventories.

14   James Hall, 'The Manor of Newhall in Wrenbury Parish', CRO D4059/23, p. 6.

Composition Papers, indicates that there were some 600 communicants within the chapelry *cum* parish.[15] Until 1593 we are without the benefit of parish registers, but with the commencement of these critical records, we are able to reconstitute most of the families – great and small – whose lives were spent primarily within the boundaries of this rural Cheshire community.

———

In 1133, the second Baron, Hugh de Malbanc, gave lands in and around Wrenbury (including the manor of Wilkesley which was divided into four vills or hamlets, each with its own lands) to monks of the Cistercian Order who built Combermere Abbey two miles from Wrenbury. About 1180 Acton and its chapels (including Wrenbury village chapel) were taken as daughter chapels to the Abbey.[16] Little is known of Wrenbury or its chapel during the next three centuries: until the late fourteenth century (i.e. the time of Richard II), a family surnamed de Wrenbury held the vill from the Vernons. John de Wrenbury, son of Richard de Wrenbury, appears in various documents from the reign of Edward III; when he died without male issue, the estate was divided among his three daughters. From the eldest were descended the Starkeys who, in the sixteenth and seventeenth centuries, resided at Wrenbury Hall.[17]

John Starke/Starkey, esquire, married Douce Warburton, daughter to Sir John Warburton of Arley (Cheshire), knight; by her he had eight children. Starkey died in 1542 and his will was proved the following year at Chester, being the first in this present collection.[18] His young son Thomas Starkey married Katherine,

---

15 'The Parishioners of Wrenbury', *Cheshire Sheaf*, 3rd series, 10 (February 1913), pp. 75–6; also Clarke, *Ancient Parish of Wrenbury* p. 97.

16 Clarke, *Ancient Parish of Wrenbury*, pp. 3–7, provides an English translation of the foundation charter for Combermere, whereas pp. 8–30 give an excellent overview of the Combermere abbots and the documentary history of their abbey. See also Pound, 'St. Margaret's Church, Wrenbury', p. 1; *Cheshire Churches—Church of St. Margaret, Wrenbury*; Cheshire Federation of Women's Institutes, *Cheshire Village Book* (Newbury, Berkshire, Countryside, 1990), p. 246. *VCH Cheshire*, iii. 124–5 notes that Combermere was the first Cistercian house in Cheshire, and apart from Chester cathedral it was the only religious house in the county with substantial estates outside the shire. Further, see Latham, *Acton*, pp. 18–19.

17 George Ormerod, *The History of Cheshire* (1819; 2nd ed., 3 vols, revised and enlarged by Thomas Helsby; London, 1882), iii. 393–6, provides background on the Starkeys. The partition document of 1350 is found in CRO DDX 127. An inquisition post mortem (hereafter IPM) of 20 Henry VIII (TNA Ches 3/65) shows that Thomas Starkey of *Wrenebury*, esq. held [in his demesne as of fee] the manor and mill of Wrenburye, and other properties by [knight's or] military service. Thomas Starkey died 3 May 1529; his son and heir was John Starky, age thirty. A second IPM, 34 Henry VIII (TNA Ches 3/68), indicates that John Starkey, gent., held the mill and other properties at Wrenbury from Sir John Savage, knight, by military service; he died on 13 July, and his son and heir was Thomas Starkey. An IPM of 23 Eliz. (TNA Ches 3/80) states that Thomas Starkey [of Wrenbury] held the manor and mill of Wrenbury, and lands therein, from Sir John Savage; Arthur Starkey was his son and heir.

18 Indexed in W. Fergusson Irvine, ed., *An Index of the Wills, Inventories, [etc.]... at the Diocesan Registry, Chester [1487–1620]*, in *Miscellanies Relating to Lancashire and Cheshire*, RSLC,

daughter of Sir Richard Maynwaringe/Manwering of Ightfield, Shropshire, knight. Thomas, who was noted in the visitation pedigrees of 1566 and 1580, and who died in 1581, fathered Arthur Starkey (†1622); Arthur in turn married Mary, daughter of Thomas Billott (or Bellot) of Moreton (first wife and widow of Richard Minshull of Minshull Hall, north of Nantwich): they were the parents of Lawrence Starkey who died at Wrenbury Hall in 1611. Lawrence was the first of fifteen family members buried in the vaults beneath the chancel of Wrenbury chapel during the next century.[19]

Arthur married for a second time, to Mary Massey,[20] widow of John Massey of Codington by whom she was the mother of a daughter named Mary. Lawrence Starkey married his own step-sister, the younger Mary Massey, who bore him seven children – Margaret (ca. 1603), Mary (ca. 1604) Jane (ca. 1605), Frances (ca. 1606/07), Arthur (ca. 1608), Anne (ca. 1609) and Lawrence (ca. 1612). Lawrence also fathered a son by a woman whose last name was Clarke: the product of this adulterous union was baptized as John Clarke in 1610/11, but in 1630/31 he is simply referred to as John Starkey. Of these sons and daughters, Arthur (d. 1641) succeeded his grandfather at Wrenbury Hall about 1622 and perpetuated the family name; his wife, Mary, daughter of John Wicksted of nearby Nantwich, bore him four children

In an age when pretensions were important, the Starkeys employed the title 'Lord of the Manor' to the consternation of another family – the Cottons – who argued that Wrenbury had not legally been a 'manor' since the Middle Ages.[21] Reference to the 'manor of Wrenbury' was commonplace, however, and in life the Cottons and the Starkeys were involved in disputes over areas of land and

xxxiii (1896), p. xviii. Ormerod, *History of Cheshire,* iii. 395–6, gives the Starkey pedigree based on the Cheshire Visitation of 1663–64; cf. William Dugdale, esq., *Cheshire Visitation Pedigrees 1663,* ed. Arthur Adams, Harleian Society Publications 93 (1941), p. 104. Robert Glover, *The Visitation of Cheshire in the Year 1580...With...Additions and Continuations, Including Those From the Visitation...in...1566*[etc], ed. J. P. Rylands, Harleian Society Publications 18 (1882), p. 219, extends the pedigree of this John Starkey back three more generations to Thomas Starkey of Stretton and his wife Elenor, daughter and co-heiress of John Olton and his wife Margaret, daughter and co-heiress of Sir John Wrenbury. Thomas is also on the list of Cheshire county gentry resident in Nantwich hundred in the year 1580 (ibid., p. 8). He also appears in Richard and Henry St George, *Pedigrees Made at the Visitation of Cheshire, 1613,* ed. George J. Armytage and J.P. Rylands, RSLC, lviii (1909), pp. 226–7.

19   Glover, *Visitations of 1566 and 1580,* p. 219; also St George, *Visitation of 1613,* pp. 226–7. A letter patent issued 1566/69 grants to John Starkey, son and heir of James Starkey, licence to enter his lands upon reaching the age of twenty-one; see *Calendar of the Patent Rolls, Elizabeth,* vol. IV: 1566–1569 (London, HMSO, 1964), p. 61. The Inventory of Lawrence Starkey's personal property was exhibited at Chester in 1611/12; see below, no. 38, indexed in J.P. Earwaker, ed., *An Index to the Wills and Inventories Now Preserved in the Court of Probate at Chester, Vol. I, 1545–1620,* RSLC, ii (1879), p. 182. Further, see Pound, 'St. Margaret's Church, Wrenbury', p. 2. Lawrence Starkey is the first family member listed on the visitation pedigree made in 1663 during the Cheshire survey; cf. Dugdale, *Cheshire Visitation Pedigrees 1663,* p. 104.

20   Mary was herself the daughter of Charles Hughes of Hoult, co. Derby.

21   *Cheshire Churches—Church of St. Margaret, Wrenbury.*

over other rights, including the use of the chapel at Wrenbury as the family burial spot, and in the reservation of certain church pews for members of the respective families. In 1635 a dispute over seats at Wrenbury eventually drew the bishop of Chester, John Bridgeman, into the matter. Not until 1748 did an arbitration order settle their contentions.[22]

Like the Starkeys, the Cottons were descended through female lines from the Mainwarings – successors to the Malbancs – and rather than being friendly neighbours they were clearly 'rival dynasties' who for four hundred years vigorously opposed each other. There is no indication of marriages between the families, although each had ties through marriage with most of the other prominent families of the chapelry.

As noted above, the chapel at Wrenbury had belonged to Combermere Abbey since the twelfth century, but with the Act of Dissolution[23] the abbey and its lands reverted to the Crown which then sold it to George Cotton, of Cotton, Shropshire, as recorded in the records of King Henry VIII:

> [1541/42] George Cotton, and Mary, his wife. Grant, in tail male, of the house and site of the late monastery of Combermere, Cheshire, the church, steeple, and churchyard thereof, &c., and certain closes and woods (specified) in Wrenbury and Awdelem, Cheshire, the manor of Wilkesley, Cheshire, with lands called Heyfeldes, in Wrenbury and Awdelem, the lands called Dodcotte in the tenure of John Dodd, in Chyles Arkoll, Salop.; and the lands called Clyff in the tenure of John Hilles, in Drayton in Hales, Salop.; and the granges called Erled grange, now in the tenure of James Colyer, in Stafford; Wyncull grange, now in the tenure of Edm. Savage, in Presbury, Cheshire; Newton grange . . . all which premises belonged to the said late monastery; in as full manner as the last abbot held the same. The grantees to be discharged of an annual rent of 66s.8d. for the said lands called Heyfeldes.[24]

George Cotton, an esquire of the body to Henry VIII, apparently paid a price for Combermere which left him in debt for the rest of his life, despite his selling off the out-lying land.

Sir George Cotton was noted as being married at the time he acquired Combermere: his wife was Mary Onley of Catesby, Northamptonshire. Their three children – Richard (b. 1539/40), Mary (b. 1541) and Dorothy (b. 1543) – were

---

22 Pound, 'St. Margaret's Church, Wrenbury', p. 2; see also *VCH Cheshire,* iii. 34–5; Staffs R.O., D. 1287/18/2.

23 On the eve of the Dissolution, Robert Joseph Beecham, a monk at Evesham and a disciple of Erasmus of Rotterdam, wrote several letters to the Cistercians at Combermere, some of whom were old companions of the writer, or former students at Oxford; the letters to Combermere were carried by a fishmonger. See David Knowles, *Bare Ruined Choirs: The Dissolution of the English Monasteries* (Cambridge, Cambridge University Press, 1976), pp. 2–24.

24 *Letters and Papers, Foreign and Domestic, of Henry VIII*, 2nd ed., revised and greatly enlarged by R.H. Brodie (original edition London, HMSO, reprint, Vaduz, Kraus, 1965), XIV/2, 33, Nr 22. Del., Walden 24 Aug., 31 Henry VIII. S.B. Pat. p.1, m/2. Vacated on personal surrender by the said George and Mary, 1 February, 32 Henry VIII, in order that the grant might be made out in another form. See also Ormerod, *History of Cheshire*, iii. 404–5.

possibly born and raised at Combermere. Because Richard Cotton, who succeeded his father as lord of Combermere in 1545, was only five years of age at the time, his mother (Lady Mary Cotton) acted as his guardian and in his name paid off his father's debts as soon as possible. Knighthoods were not hereditary, so Richard did not succeed to his father's title. Soon after coming into his inheritance, he demolished the abbey buildings and built what is still part of the present family mansion house on the site.[25] An IPM of 2 Eliz. (1559/60) indicates that Mary, Lady Cotton (the widow of George and joint grantee with him of this dissolved abbey) died on 14 March of that year seised of Combermere, with its lands and tenements in the parishes of Wrenbury and Audlem, which she held of the queen *in capite* by military service; Richard Cotton was her son and heir.[26]

Richard Cotton died unexpectedly on 15 June 1602 – there is no will. In fact, it required some time following his death to set his affairs in order. The IPM, taken at Sandbach, Cheshire, on 6 April 1605, before Roger Puleston, esq., Henry Mainwaring, esq., escheator and Ralph Wilbraham, gent., feodary, produced the following deposition by a panel of fourteen men from various localities in and around Wrenbury parish:

> Richard Cotton on the day he died was seised in fee of a capital mess[uage] in Cumbermeyre & of a water mill, 1000 a. of land, 500 a. of meadow, 1000 a. of pasture, 200 a. of moor, 200 a. of wood & 200 a. of land covered with water in Combermeyre, Wrenbury & Aldelem [Audlem].
>
> He was also seised in fee tail, to him & his male issue, of the manor of Wilkesley. The said capital mess[uage] & lands are held of the King & at the time of Richard's death of Queen Elizabeth in chief, by 10th part of a knight's fee & rent of 53s. 4d. a year & worth yearly (clear), £12.
>
> The manor of Wilkesley held in like manner, by 20th part of a knight's fee & yearly rent of £4.12s.8d. & worth yearly (clear) £56.
>
> The said Richard died 15 June 44 Elizabeth [1602] & George Cotton, esq. is his son & next heir & now aged 40 years & more & since his father's death has occupied the said premises.[27]

Genealogical details of this inquisition can be sorted out with the help of Cheshire visitations from the years 1580 and 1613.[28] The George Cotton noted above was

25   *VCH Cheshire*, iii. 155; Pound, 'St. Margaret's Church, Wrenbury', p. 1.

26   TNA Ches 3/73 2 Eliz. no. 4; also CRO CR72/AppendixA/101 (dated 18 February 1561): special livery from the Queen to Richard Cotton of lands descended to him as son and heir of Sir George and Lady Mary; Richard reached the age of twenty-one on 26 August 1560. Cited in Ormerod, *History of Cheshire*, iii. 405.

27   TNA Ches 3/561 No. 1 19 Henry 7, no. 1; also CRO CR72/Appendix/127; printed in R. Stewart Brown, ed., *Cheshire Inquisitions Post Mortem: Stuart Period, 1603–1660, Vol. I A–D*, RSLC, lxxxiv (1934), p.146. CRO CR72/AppendixA/128 (dated 6 April 1605) is the record of the livery of the Combermere estate to George Cotton from the Court of Wards and Liveries.

28   See Glover, *Visitation of 1566 and 1580*, pp. 189–91, where Dorothy Cotton of Combermere is noted as the wife of Edward Tarbock; their children Edward, Thomas, and Mary all flourished in 1580 as well. Further, St George, *Cheshire Visitation Pedigrees 1613*, p. 66.

Richard's son from his first marriage to Mary Mainwaring – there were in all eight children born to Richard Cotton and Mary Mainwaring (of Ightfield, Shropshire) at Combermere – George (ca. 1560), Arthur (ca. 1562), Mary (ca. 1563), Andrew (ca. 1564), Frances (1565), Elizabeth (ca. 1566), Winifred (ca. 1568), and Dorothy (ca. 1572).[29]

George Cotton increased his inheritance by the purchase of both parts of the neighbouring manor of Newhall. From the time of King John until the death of Richard II, Newhall Manor was held by successive male heirs of the Audley family of Helegh, Staffordshire, and formed part of the Audley fee or barony of Wich Malbank.[30] The Audley inheritance had passed through the Touchets by attainder to the Crown, and in 1591 a two-thirds portion of the manor was acquired by Thomas Egerton, esq., solicitor-general to Queen Elizabeth I; he in turn sold it in 1605 to George Cotton of Combermere for £2,200. Newhall continued as a joint-manor until 1622 when George Cotton purchased the other one-third of the lord-ship of Newhall etc., in Aston, Newhall, and Coole, from William, Lord Fitzwarren and 3rd Earl of Bath, likewise an heir to the Audley inheritance, for £500, except-ing only 'Newhall Parkes' (80 acres), previously sold by him to Thomas Ravenscroft, with all his Wichhouses or Salthouses in Namptwich, and all the deeds and charters appertaining thereto.[31]

Chorley had also passed to the Audleys in the division of the Malbanc barony; and during the reign of Elizabeth I it was purchased by the lords of Cholmondeley whose seat lay but a few miles to the northwest of Wrenbury. The manor of Sound likewise became the property of the marquis of Cholmondeley, and he is men-tioned as landlord in several of the wills found in our collection.[32] The antiquity of certain families in that part of the chapelry is also attested to by a deed dated AD 1300, in which William, son of Thomas de Alstaneston, Lord of Sonde, con-firmed to his daughter Agnes

---

29   *VCH Cheshire*, iii. 155; Ormerod, *History of Cheshire*, iii. 406; for the family tree, see below, will no. 128. Technically speaking, the Cottons did not acquire the title Lords of Combermere until 1814. Ightfield Hall lies just over the Shropshire boundary, approximately fifteen miles south of Wrenbury.
30   Hall, 'Manor of Newhall', p. 18. Following page 26 of the MS. there is a major break, with the next section beginning with page 271, devoted to Ch. VIII, Newhall in the nineteenth century. The index to James Hall's works at the CRO in Chester indicates that at one time an entire MS. 'History of Newhall' existed, but that it is now missing. It would do well to see whether Clarke references the missing parts.
31   Hall, 'Introduction to a History of Combermere and Newhall', CRO D4059/15, pp. 56–8. The Egertons had previously been settled at Christleton. Ormerod, *History of Cheshire*, iii. 203, puts the transfer of Newhall at about 1625, without differentiation, noting that Sir Robert Cotton was possessed of it in 1666. See Harl. MSS 2010; William Webb, writing in late 1621, composed an 'Itinerary of Nantwich Hundred' which Daniel King then included in his *The Vale Royal of England*, published in 1656. Excerpts of King's work are scattered throughout Ormerod's *History of Cheshire*, in the case of Newhall, vol. iii. 203. See also Norwood, '*Historic Notes*', no. xxiv.
32   On the manor of Chorley, see Ormerod, *History of Cheshire*, iii. 400–1; on the manor of Sound, *ibid.*, 419–20.

A messuage with buildings and a croft at adjacent, which croft Thomas the Sergant formerly held in the vill of Sonde with a curtilage to the croft which John the Wode held of me. Fifteen selions below my fields of Sonde situated as set forth below:- Five selions in the fields between the vill of Sonde and the vill of Wrennebury, one of which is called Westo Wylond and another Irradelonde, two selions of which about on the cow pasture in length above the land of John of the Wode and my land and the fifth selion in length below Alvastbury and the moor. Five selions in the field between the vill of Sonde and the water of Wyvere and on the other side as far as the Midelyort, together with all waste below the said land. Five selions in the field between Sonde and Bromhale, two of which Thomas the Sergant formerly held, one selion lying in length between the croft of Henry Shepherd and my garden, one selion lying between my grange and the croft of Thomas the Sergant and one selion lying in Edlescroft.

A place of land which Roger Coole held in length as far as from the heath of Sonde to Battington rowe and in breadth from the land of William of Fouleshurst to the highway, with a certain croft called Lolegrove and a piece of land in Edlescroft. A place of land lying between the land of William Colenso and the land of Henry Shepherd and a place called Solumburner and a selion of land with hedge and ditch included.

I give also to Agnes and her heirs common of pasture for all her animals over my land at all times, and sufficient turbary on my marsh for all her men in respect of buildings erected.

Witnessing this grant were:

Richard, Lord of Wrenneburie
Robert of Harcourt
Peter de Stapeley
Robert de Wodecot
William de Praers
William le Chaner
James de Bromhale.

Descendants of James de Bromhale were among the yeoman class of inhabitants at Sound in the early seventeenth century, and well connected with other prominent families of the area.

It is clear from internal evidence that some of the residents of Sound and Chorley belonged to the parish of Acton, rather than to the chapelry of Wrenbury as did many of their neighbours. Elizabeth Sefton's will (proved in 1582) expresses her desire 'to be buried at Acton near my husband',[33] while Hugh Stockton of Chorley (will proved 1615) and Peter Walton of Sound (will proved 1618) also directed their executors to see to their burial in Acton churchyard.[34] In some cases, although we have not found evidence that the testator was in fact buried at Wrenbury, we have chosen to include them with the Wrenbury residents nonetheless.

---

33 There were Seftons at this time in Wrenbury chapelry, however, for the very first baptismal entry in the Wrenbury registers was that of 'Elizabeth Sefton 16 September 1593'; see CRO P172/1/1–4.
34 See the respective wills at CRO.

Among the most ancient families of Wrenbury chapelry was that of Griffin, first attested in the reign of Henry III in the person of Bertram Griffin, a tenant of James de Audley, of Haleigh Castle, near Madeley, who had inherited the Newhall part of the Malbank estates. Audley received dues from the said Bertram at Newhall, yearly at Michaelmas. And in 11 Edward I Geoffrey Griffin held at Batherton two carrucates of land of Nicholas de Audley, by the tenure of finding three foot soldiers in war time to guard 'Newhall Castle'.[35] The Griffins were well represented in the sixteenth and seventeenth centuries, even providing the rector for the local church, and the surviving wills show Griffin (later on, the Griffith form was most common) connections with several prominent families of the area.

The most extensive evidence for families in Wrenbury chapelry at an early date comes from the *inquisitio post mortem* of Sir John Lovell, knight, taken in the year 1408, which shows him with lands in Newhall and Aston. The tenants were:[36]

Richard Egynton	Richard Horry	Thomas Hughet
Richard Salmon	Richard le Taillior	William Horry
Thomas de Wordhull	John le Glover	Agnes Hoggedoghter
William atte Knolle	Johanna Body	John del Knolle
Malyn Bonde	Richard de Grendeley	Hugh Poystok
Margery le Parker	Richard del Fryth	William le Baxter
Alice Maynart	John le Glover	Richard Tenche
Richard le Mulward	William le Fyssher	William Malbon
William Redbert	Nicholas le Cartwright	Nicholas Daykin
John Wyrvyn	Mathilda de Crue	Thomas de Coneway
John Bernard	William de Blackhurst	John Shael
Hugh de Hampton	Richard de Grindley	Roger de Beston
Margaret del Vicaers		

Several of these same surnames appear on the court rolls of Newhall Manor during the fifteenth and sixteen centuries, and four of them – Taillor, Crue, Cartwright, and Tenche – find inclusion in the wills comprising this edition (1542–1660). A fifth family – that of Salmon – left testamentary documents, and, although their temporal affairs were associated with Newhall Manor, their ecclesiastical lives were split between Wrenbury and the parish of Audlem. For that reason only some of the residents of Coole Lane, which apparently divided the chapelry of Wrenbury from the parish of Audlem, are found in this volume.[37]

---

35 Norwood, 'Historic Notes', no. xvi; Clarke, *Ancient Parish of Wrenbury* [section 7], p. 48, sees this as some feudal fiction for some obsolete service. Webb's 'Itinerary of Nantwich', excerpted in Ormerod, *History of Cheshire*, iii. 203, cites this as well, referencing an inquisition of Edward I in 1283.

36 Hall, 'Manor of Newhall', p.14.

37 *Calendar of the Patent Rolls, Edward VI, Vol. III: 1549–51* (London, HMSO, 1925), p. 89, contains a grant of the tithes of grain, sheaves and corn within the lordship of Newhall (parish of Wrenbury) and Coolelane (parish of Audlem) and within the lordship of Wylkesley, Cheshire, lately in tenure of Humphrey Manwarynge, granted 21 December 1549 to Richard Venables and John Maynerde in return for a sum of £2,146. The will of Margaret Chester of Coole Lane,

'The Boke of the Tithe Calves of the Parish of Wrenbury A.D. 1574', preserved in the County Record Office at Chester contains the following entries, presumably written by the Cholmondeley steward:[38]

Elizabeth Broomhall had 6 last year and 3 this year, and we had one.

Thomas Breese had 6 last year and 3 this year, and we had one.

Robert Smyth had 4 last year and 4 this year. He said that he being new come into the parish might not count for the tythe until next Easter whereby calf we had none.

Robert Brereton had 7 last year and 2 this year and we had one last year and one this year.

Widow Shrewbridge had 4 last year and 1 this year.

Robert Shrewbridge had 2 last year and 2 this year.

The tithes in question had previously belonged to Combermere Abbey, which had fallen into the hands of the local gentry at the dissolution of the monasteries. Once again we encounter surnames which recur in the wills of our collection – Bromhall, Brees, Shrowbridge, the latter being connected with many of the more significant families of Wrenbury chapelry.

The most prominent family in the area of Coole was that of the Whitneys, who were associated with a gradual conversion of waste and wood into arable land on the eastern side of Newhall.[39] It is almost certain that the first Whitney to settle at Coole belonged to the ancient stock of Whitney of Whitney, on the upper Wye, at the north end of the Golden Valley, in the extreme west of Herefordshire. As early as 1383 a Whitney occupied land called Newland in Newhall township; he may have been a son or close relative of Sir Robert Whitney of Whitney, knt, if not the knight himself who, it is presumed, had landed interests in Cheshire, because his name occurs on several Cheshire recognizance rolls in the time of Richard II. Sir Robert married Constance, youngest of the three daughters of James, Lord Audley, who fell at Blore Heath in 1459. Sir Robert was a member of Parliament from Hereford on 3 November 1391, and he died on 12 June 1402 at the battle of Pilleth in Radnorshire.[40]

Howell de Whitney, a contemporary of Sir Robert, was the first to acquire property at Newhall and to reside in the township. He obtained from Nicholas de Audley 'an enfeoffment in fee-tail of 1 messuage, 60 acres of arable land, 4 acres of meadow, 20 acres of pasture, and 16 acres of wood in Coole and Aston, near Bromhall.' The date of the king's licence for this grant is 12 January 1389. Doubtless this was the nucleus of the Coole Hall estate.[41]

proved 1623, indicates her desire to be buried at Audlem; likewise the will of Richard Horton of Coole, proved 1607. Robert Hassall of Coole Lane, will proved in 1635, also identifies Audlem as his parish church (CRO WS 1635).

38 Cited in Clarke, *Ancient Parish of Wrenbury* pp. 41–2.

39 Clarke, *Ancient Parish of Wrenbury* pp. 46–7.

40 Hall, 'Newhall Families', CRO D4059/27, p. 284; Newhall Court Roll 1383; CRO Cheshire Recognizance Rolls 20 May 11 Rich. II (1388); 24 October 1393; 27 July 1394. Norwood, 'Historic Notes', no. xxxiii.

41 Hall, 'Newhall Families', p. 285; see Dr Henry Melville, *Ancestry of John Whitney* (New York City, De Vinne Press, 1896).

A few years after this event, Howell de Whitney, who had married Katherine, daughter of Vivian Serle, increased his freehold estate at Coole, Aston and Bromhall to '1 messuage, 100 acres of land, 6 acres of meadow, 10 acres of wood, and 10 acres of turbary.' However, between 1393 and 1396 both he and his wife found it necessary to defend in court at Chester their right to the same in a dower suit against Elizabeth Audley, widow of Sir Nicholas de Audelegh, of Helegh.[42]

Howell de Whitney is further mentioned between 1397 and 1430. There is for him, however, no inquisition post mortem; we do not know the date of his death, nor the name of his successor.[43] We are likewise uninformed as to his relationship to the Philip Whitney who flourished in 1427.

William Whitney, who appears in the Newhall Court Rolls in 1434, 1435, 1436, and 1479, also appears in inquisitions post mortem dated 1455 and 1459. He married Margaret, the daughter of Sir Adam Bostock of Bostock, knt, who died in 1459.[44] A Thomas Whitney flourished at Newhall on 30 July 1451.[45] His contemporary was a George Whitney whose wife Elizabeth survived him; between 1480 and 1487 she surrendered a messuage and five acres of land in Wildheath in Newhall to her daughter and heir, Margaret Whitney.

A Thomas Whitney, who in the time of Henry VII married Agnes Brooke[46] of Leighton, Cheshire, appears to have been the head of the family at Coole at that time. On 12 June 1504 he was appointed one of the collectors of a subsidy in Nantwich Hundred. It is impossible now to place all the foregoing names in a certain table of descent; but from the time of this Thomas Whitney, there is evidence sufficient for a pedigree of the family for the next two centuries. It is not known when Thomas died,[47] but his successor was Robert Whitney.

Robert Whitney, of Coole, married Anne, daughter of Richard Bird; she had been married twice before, firstly to Hamon Hocknell of Duddon, and secondly to Piers Bruin of Tarvin.[48] She also outlived her third husband, as Robert died on 3 December 1551. His son Robert was his heir, aged ten according to the IPM which was conducted on 1 May 1554. The jurors (none of whom were local men) declared upon their oath that

> the said Robert Whitney was seised in his demesne as of fee, of and in one messuage, 60 acres of land, 4 acres of meadow, 20 acres of pasture, and 16 acres of wood, with appurtenances in Coule and Aston near Bromhall in the co. of Chester [etc.] held of

42   CRO Cheshire Plea Rolls, *tempore Rich. II*; Norwood, 'Historic Notes', nos xxxiii–xxxiv.
43   Hall, 'Newhall Families', p. 286.
44   Hall, 'Newhall Families', p. 286; J. P. Earwaker, *East Cheshire: Past and Present; or A History of the Hundred of Macclesfield in the County Palatine of Chester*, 2 vols (London, pr. for the author by Wyman & Sons, 1877–80), i. 174n.; ii. 114.
45   CRO Cheshire Recognizance Rolls as cited by Hall; Hall, 'Newhall Families', p. 287.
46   In a seventeenth-century MS. Pedigree Book preserved at Dorfold Hall, she is called Anne Brooke, daughter of John Brooke, fifth son of Thomas Brooke of Leighton, co. Chester; see Hall, 'Newhall Families', p. 287.
47   Thomas occurs as a juror in IPM 1517; see Earwaker, *East Cheshire,*, i. 176n.
48   Hall, 'Newhall Families', p. 287; St George, *Visitation of 1613*, p. 50.

the Queen as countess of Chester *in capite* by military service, namely, by the tenth part of a knight's fee; and valued at £4 per annum in all issues beyond reprises [i.e., clear]. Also that the said Robert died seised in his demesne as of fee, of and in one messuage or burgage and 5 acres of land with appurtenances in Wich Malbank [Nantwich] which is held of Robert Corbet Esq. in socage by fealty as for all services and demands, and valued at 5s. per annum, in all issues beyond reprises;

Also, [etc.] of and in one messuage and 4 cottages, 40 acres of land, 10 acres of meadow, 20 acres of pasture, and 10 acres of heath with appurtenances in Coppenhall in the said county, held of the said Robert Corbet in socage etc.

Also [etc.] of and in one messuage, 20 acres of land, 6 acres of meadow, 10 acres of pasture and 3 acres of heath and moss with appurtenances in Leyhed[?] (Leighton) in said co. held of the said Robert Corbet etc.

Also [etc.] that the said Robert Whitney died possessed according to the custom of the manor of Newhall of and in one messuage, 10 acres of land, 3 acres of meadow with appurtenances in Coule lane and Wyldheth within the lordship of Newhall, which was held of Sir Richard Cotton, Knight, by copy of the court according to the custom of the manor of Newhall by the rent of 6s. per annum, and valued at 4s. per annum beyond reprises:

Also [etc.] the said Robert died possessed according to the custom of Newhall manor of and in 22 acres of wood in Newhall called Great Cole Wodde, which was held of the said Richard Cotton by copy of the court [etc.] in socage by the rent of 22s. and valued at 80s. per annum, beyond reprises.

And the jurors also say that the same Robert was not seised nor held on the day on which he died any other manors, messuages, lands or tenements of the Queen nor of anyone else in the said county.

Also [etc.] the said Robert died on the 3rd December in the fifth year of the reign of Edw. VI [1551]; and that Robert Whytney is his son and next heir and was 10 years old on the 6th October last past, and is not married: And that Anna Whytney, widow, Ralph Broghton, Thomas Clutton, Richard Hokenhull[49] and Geffrey Whytney have received the issues and profits of all the messuages, lands and tenements etc. from the time of the said Robert Whytney's death, but by what title or in what manner the said jurors are ignorant.[49a]

This inquisition is a critical document: It proves, first of all, that the capital messuage and lands called Coole estate in 1554 were the same property as that granted to Howel de Whitney in 1389; it further proves that Robert Whitney's copyholds in 1554 were held of Sir Richard Cotton, who had only become lord of Newhall

---

49   Richard Hokenhull of Duddon was the eldest son of Robert Whitney's widow by her first husband Geffrey, who was the brother of Robert; see Hall, 'Newhall Families', p. 289.
49a   As cited in Hall, 'Newhall Families', pp. 287–8, without provenance.

manor the year before[50]; and thirdly, that after Robert Whitney's death in 1551, the estate was left in a trusteeship during the minority of the heir.

Robert Whitney [Jr] was born on 6 October 1544. A record of a grant of 'livery' is not extant, which would have been granted after proof of majority age. In 1575 he married Mary, the daughter of Thomas Rutter, of Kingsley, gent. Their son, Hugh Whitney, lived to adulthood, but predeceased his father; their daughter, Elizabeth, married Hugh Massie. Robert Whitney, though styled *gentleman* in the record, did not appear before the herald at the Cheshire visitation of 1580 to prove his descent and the right to bear arms. Indeed, it is very remarkable that no large property owner residing in Wrenbury parish in the time of Elizabeth – not even Richard Cotton, esq. – entered his pedigree and arms, at either the visitation of 1580 or at that which preceded it, with the exception of Thomas Starkey, esq., of Wrenbury Hall.[51] Robert died in his seventy-second year (24 January 1616) and was buried at Wrenbury three days later. We have neither a will nor an inventory of his property, but the parish clerk wrote the word *generosus* beside his name in the burial register, undoubtedly because of his bequests to the poor of the local church during his lifetime. An inquisition post mortem was conducted following his death, and we have included this along with the testamentary documents of his wife.[52] His IPM is interesting mainly as showing how parts of his property were to be portioned out in jointure to his wife (who only survived him seven months) and to the wife of his son Hugh, pursuant to the two marriage articles quoted at length in the inquisition.

Hugh Whitney married Elizabeth Egerton on 21 August 1599; he died in 1611 and was buried at Wrenbury. His will is not extant either, but the inventory, taken by John Cheswis, John Cartwright, William Salmon and John Pichforde, is preserved in the CRO and included in this present collection (1611).[53] His family

---

50   See the letter patent of King Edward VI, issued 24 June 1523 to Richard Cotton, knight, confirming the exchange of several properties in Cheshire for lands he had held in Lincolnshire. Of special interest to this present volume are the following:

> . . . the lordship and manor of Tottenhall, Cheshire, which formerly belonged to John Tuchett, knight, lord Audley, lately in tenure of Peter Dutton, deceased; . . .
> . . . also the lordship and manor of Newhall, Cheshire, formerly of John Tuchett, knight, lord Audley, in tenure of Richard Cholmidley, the water mill called Newhall Mylle and the land called le Ryalles, le Courte, and le Ox Medowe in Newhall in tenure of Hugh Sterkye, late of the said Lord Audley, and of all kinds of appurtenances (long list) of Newhall manor in Newhall and Wrenburye, Chesh.; and the woods within the park of Newhall (58 ac.)
> Which manor of Newhall and mills and fisheries of Dee are extended at the clear yearly value of £112 15s. 2d.

These properties were held of the Crown by services of one-fortieth part of a knight's fee. See *Calendar of the Patent Rolls. Edward VI, Vol. V: 1547–53* (London, HMSO, 1926; reprint Kraus, 1970), pp. 15–16.

51   Hall, 'Newhall Families', p. 290.
52   See will of Mary Whitney, no. 51, below.
53   See below, will no. 34.

consisted of four sons and four daughters: all the sons died in infancy except Hugh, the eldest, who was ten years old when his father died, and fifteen when his grandfather Robert died and left him the Coole Estate. For the third time in the history of the family, the heir apparent was an only son; he was born in February 1601 and baptized at Wrenbury on 16 February.

The Hall of Coole was a timbered house, strongly moated, on the edge of Coole Forest, and had no manorial dependencies. The Whitney seat in the Wrenbury church was at the east end of the south aisle, where the more modern pew shows the Tompkinson coat of arms.[54]

Lying south from Aston was Aston Lane which turned eastward as Sheppenhall Lane and intersected the lane running south from Broomhall at Coole Hall. In this part of Newhall a branch of the Cartwright family formed a freehold farm, known as Sheppenhall, which appears as their residence from 1580 to 1680. The actual records of this creation are not extant, but there is likewise no evidence that it was the result of some clandestine encroachment. We can thus assume that it developed with the full knowledge and concurrence of other freeholders in the area.[55] Another branch of the Cartwrights designated itself de Aston, and it is obvious from the testamentary and parish records that they were clear and distinct dynasties.

Though these two families of Cartwright clearly were kinsmen, it is not known who was the common ancestor; nor is it possible now to trace with accuracy the earlier descents, because, like the Whitneys, the Cartwrights did not enter pedigrees at any of the Cheshire visitations, and early deeds relating to the family are not now extant. Thomas Cartwright of Aston appears as a juror in 1423 and as late as 1430; William Cartwright, of Aston, appears from 1423 to 1435; Edward Cartwright, a chaplain, was deceased in 1430; John Cartwright, apparently of Aston Hall, was a juror in 1479, 1480 and 1488. The fact that these occur long before the first mention in any record of the Cartwrights of Sheppenhall leads to the conclusion that the Cartwrights of Aston were the older line of the family.[56]

On the authority of family 'evidences', George Baker gives a pedigree of four generations commencing with Hugh Cartwright who, living in the time of Henry VII, was probably related to the above-mentioned John Cartwright. This Hugh Cartwright was the grandfather of John Cartwright of Aston who married Eleanor, the daughter of John Shrowbridge of the same place. They lived to be old and were buried at Wrenbury in the same year, 1604, leaving two sons, John and Richard, who both became wealthy men. Richard Cartwright, the younger brother, born ca. 1563, occurs as a juror on the Newhall Court Roll of 1585; but, leaving his native parish, he subsequently entered the Inner Temple, London, and in 1615–16 he purchased the manor of Aynho in Northants with its manor-house,

---

54 Norwood, 'Historic Notes', nos xxxiii–xxxiv.
55 Clarke, *Ancient Parish of Wrenbury*, p. 48.
56 Hall, 'Newhall Families', p. 307.

park and 2,245 acres of land from Shakerley Marmion, esq., and Sir Richard Tracy, knt., for the sums of £5,250 and £3,000.[57]

By his will (written before 28 November 1634), he left to the poor of Wrenbury an annuity of £4 6s. 8d., issuing from a rent-charge on his manor of Deddington in Oxfordshire, to be given in bread to ten aged or impotent people in Wrenbury parish every Sunday throughout the year, 'not for ostentation, but to incite and stir up the charity of others'. He had instituted this dole in his lifetime and continued it after his demise through his friend and agent George Cotton, esq., of Combermere, who received the money at Christmastime. Details of this arrangement are found in two letters preserved at the CRO, written by John Cartwright of Aynho to George Cotton, esq., of Combermere, in which he enclosed 'a coppie of soe much of [his] father's will as concerns the distribution to the poor of Wrenbury.' Dated 1 August and 25 December 1639, they explain the particulars of the bequest which was still being implemented in 1837.[58] The first, very brief note, is as follows:

> I have hereinlosed a Coppie of soe much of my dear Fathers will as concernes the distribution to ye poore of Wrenbury. I sent you about Christmas last foure pounds six shillings eight pence, which I have not heard yt you have received I desire you would be pleased to write me two words of ye receipt thereof which being directed to me at Mr. John Hallywells house Chancery Lane London ~~with~~ I shall certaynely receave. And soe with my best respects to my worthy Cosen your wife . . . .

The second letter reads:

> I have delivered according to a direcion in your last letter four poundes six shillings eight pence, . . . with a direct request that the same may not fayle to bee payde to your handes furthermore the like some I delivered to him about Cristmas last being this tyme twelve moneth, but I am a little troubled that I never heard of your receipt thereof. Therefore good Sir, let me entreate 2 words from you of your receipt of these two last somes at your next opportunity of writinge Sir synce you wrote to mee in your last letter that my father had charged his land with the payment of this releefe to the poor of Wrenbury. Now Sir, for your information I hold it needfull to let you know that upon some occasion (not long since) examyoning throughly how my fathers estate stood before his death, I did fynde cleerly that my father had noe power at the tyme of making his last will to charge that land out of which this releefe to Wrenebury poor by his sayd last will should issue with any payment or charge whatsoever but only during his own life: Which yet I am confident my father did never observe nor take any notice of

---

57   George Baker, *The History and Antiquities of the County of Northampton, Vol. I* (London, J.B. Nichols and Son, 1822), p. 548. In a 'Postscript re: Cartwright Family' written in 1946 by Walter J. Hall, the son of James Hall, the conclusions of Baker are rejected as suspect, since the Cartwrights appear at Aston earlier than Baker supposes: Margaret Cartwright's demise was recorded in the Court Roll of 1424 as the widow of William Cartwright – i.e., she was earlier than any of the four already mentioned by James Hall; also, the IPM of 1408 mentions a Nicholas le Cartwright as a tenant of Aston and Newhall.

58   CRO P172/12/2; cited in Norwood, 'Historic Notes', no. xlii; used by permission.

to his death. This I thought fitt to doe that you may know truly how things doe stand. Sir my best respects to your worthy self & my worthy cosin your wyfe. Presented I take leve & remayne

Your most assured loving kinsman & frend & servant till death.

Richard Cartwright had died in January 1637/38, leaving this single son, John Cartwright, of Aynho, esq., to continue the charity work at Wrenbury. He was a learned man, and he also gave to Brasenose College, Oxford a rent charge of £10 per annum out of lands in Bloxham, to found two scholarships for the natives of Cheshire, or Northamptonshire, but more especially for students to be chosen from the pre-grammar school of Aynho, or the parishes of Budworth or Wrenbury, in Cheshire.[59]

John Cartwright, of Aston Hall (near Wrenbury), gent., born ca. 1560, the elder brother of Richard Cartwright, and son of John Cartwright who died in 1604, is often mentioned in the Newhall Court Rolls. He added considerably to the paternal estate by the purchase of lands in other townships in Cheshire, and in Shropshire, and he died very wealthy in August 1630. There is nothing further to relate of him, except that his original will (dated 23 August 1630; proved 16 October 1630 at Chester), was a voluminous document of nearly fifty folios when James Hall examined it in the late 1890s; today, there is much less of the original document, but the accompanying inventory shows his personal fortune to have amounted to the impressively large sum of £2,061 3s. 2d., a personal fortune which clearly set him apart from virtually all of his neighbours, save only the Starkeys and the Cottons.

Yet his legacies to the poor of his native parish were apparently relatively small, for although he instructed his wife to 'bestowe some money on the poore of the parishe of Wrenbury as shee in her discrecōn shall thinke fitt', Mr Robert Nicholls, the contemporary preacher at Wrenbury, seems to have wanted to stress his niggardliness when, in the burial records, he wrote: 'John Cartwright *plousios* sepultus 27 Aug 1630!', rather than *generosus*.[60]

Sheppenhall Hall, with its moated mansion and surrounding lands situated about the centre of Newhall, was a freehold estate of the other line of the Cartwright family from the days of Queen Elizabeth I until the times of Charles II, the first possessor being 'John Cartwright de Sheppenhall the son of Geoffrey Cartwright', so named in the Newhall Court Roll of 1585. Geoffrey lived in Newhall, apparently in *Sutherdyne-lane* and near the *Styche-bridge* (cf. Court Roll 1580 and 1583). His sister Joan Cartwright married Geoffrey Whitney, of Lightwood Green, and became the mother of the emblem-writer Geoffrey Whitney who headed one of his emblems with the inscription 'To my uncle Geffrey Cartwright'.[61] Geoffrey Cartwright died and was probably buried at Wrenbury before September 1593, in

59 Hall, 'Newhall Families', pp. 307–8. See also Northamptonshire Record Office – C(A) Box 15/137.
60 Hall, 'Newhall Families', pp. 308–9.
61 See also *JSTOR: Review of English Studies*, new series 28, no. 112 (Nov. 1977), pp. 438–41: 'Geoffrey Whitney's "To Richard Cotton, of Combermere": an Early English Country-House Poem'.

which month the burial register there was commenced. The name of his wife has not occurred, but it may have been identical with 'Elizabeth Cartwright *anus sepulta* 11 Dec 1600.' (Parish Register).

John Cartwright de Sheppenhall died June 1596, leaving John his son and heir.[62] The origin of Sheppenhall Estate was probably due to the first enclosure of lands from the open arable fields of Newhall, in or shortly after the time of Henry VIII, for the purpose of grazing sheep, wool production being more profitable than wheat growing. The success of the venture is revealed in the fact that the mansion at Sheppenhall, at the time John Cartwright, Jr, wrote his will in 1634/35, had six rooms on the ground floor – the Hall, the Parlour, the Entry, the Kitchen, the Buttery and the Milk-house – over each of which was an upper chamber comprising the second storey. John Cartwright, Sr, of Sheppenhall was clearly one of the most active and most influential individuals within the chapelry of Wrenbury during the first quarter of the seventeenth century, and his involvement in the disposition of others' estates, as well as his son Arthur's marriage into the Starkey family of Wrenbury Hall, and his grandson's marriage into the Cotton family of Combermere, tended to give him a pre-eminence which anticipated the adoption of the title *gentleman* at Sheppenhall Hall by his successors.[63]

There were others as well who laid claim to the title 'gentleman' in Wrenbury records, whether rightly so or not – William Wickstead, Jr, of Wrenbury Frith (1629), John Egerton of Newhall (1619), Roger Hockenhull of Broomhall (1613), George Cudworth of Newhall (1624), Thomas Hamnett of the Grange in Smeatonwood (1635), William Wilson of Wrenbury Frith (1639), John Cheswis of Mickley Hall (1648) and Henry Griffiths the elder of Broomhall (1658). Significantly, however, only the pedigrees of the Cartwrights of Sheppenhall, the Cottons of Combermere and the Starkeys of Wrenbury Hall were recorded in the 1663 visitation of Cheshire.

Mickley Hall lay just east of Sound in Broomhall and was accessible by means of Mickley Hall Lane. From as early as the mid-sixteenth century, Cheswys family members had participated in the inner life of Wrenbury chapelry: e.g. in 1542/43 Thomas Chessewes, yeoman, was an executor of the will of John Starkye of Wrenbury, and in 1561 he made his own will.[64] Presumably, the John Cheswys the Elder, late of Mickley, who granted two pastures in Newhall Park on 4 January 1595 to Thomas Edgley of Newhall, was his son, and we have argued that this same John Cheswith is noted as one of the churchwardens on the bell installed in the church tower in 1610.[65]

---

62 CRO Newhall Manor Court Roll, View of Frankpledge, 12 October 1596; excerpted by Hall, 'Newhall Manor Court Rolls', p. 123; see also, Hall, 'Newhall Families', p. 316.
63 When Hall visited Sheppenhall in 1897, it was a run-down farm house, however; See 'Newhall Families', pp. 326–9.
64 See wills nos 1 and 3.
65 See above, pp. 12–14; see also Newhall Manor Court Rolls, CRO, as excerpted by Hall, 'Newhall Court Rolls', pp. 121–2. John Cheswys Sr, gen., was also excused from the Newhall Manor Court which met on 29 October 1599/CRO.

George Cudworth's claim to the sobriquet of 'gentleman' may have led to a series of legal proceedings between his son, William, and George Cotton. A tenant on the Cotton lands in Newhall, with a dwelling near the mill, Cudworth was presented at the Newhall manorial court held 10 April 1632

> for encroaching upon Cross Lane to the annoyance of the highway – fined 6s. 8d.
> for enclosing a garden place near to his house out of the common lane – fined 6s. 8d.

The following year he was again cited:

> for keeping his hoggs unringed and unyoked to the annoyance of his neighbours and fined 12d.
> for his encroachments in Newhall Lane – fined 4s. 0d.
> for not appearing at ye Court – fined 6d.

Cudworth, in fact, appears to have treated the authority of the local court with contempt.

The disagreement between the two gentlemen was further embittered by what the Rev. H.A. Clarke has called 'The Great Cudworth Pew Controversy'. In 1635 Cudworth wrote to the Bishop of Chester complaining that George Cotton had given one of his tenants, George Taylor, the right to certain seats in a pew which, since the re-pewing of the church in 1608 and indeed earlier, had belonged to the Cudworth family. George Cotton also wrote to the bishop alleging that Cudworth only had the right to some seats in the pew, not to all of it. He invited his lordship to send representatives to confirm this. The bishop delaying his decision, Cudworth appealed to the Archbishop of York, who wrote a long letter to the Bishop of Chester commanding him to deal with the matter at once.[66]

It seems remarkable that the Archbishop of York should have had to concern himself with the seating arrangement at Wrenbury church: there would even appear to have been echoes of this case in the bishop's consistory court which convened to hear evidence relating to a public brawl, apparently inside the church itself, between Cudworth and George Taylor over the issue of the pew. Cudworth said that Taylor had torn his (Cudworth's) stockings with his spurs, but he lost the case. In 1715 George Cudworth, gent. (obviously a grandson or great grandson of the aforesaid), and John Woolrich shared pew number VII on the north aisle of the church, while Cudworth shared pew number VIII as well with Thomas Whittingham, gent.[67]

In 1640 Cudworth was still refusing to pay the fines imposed by the manorial court or to relinquish his encroachment on the lanes. He now laid claim to a piece of land as his freehold which he and his father had held as copyholders. Ultimately, the differences between Cudworth and George Cotton came to an assize trial at Chester on 13 April 1640. The result was a clear victory for Cotton: Cudworth was ordered to accept the decision of the local courts which had already pronounced against him.[68]

66   CRO CR72/AppendixA/55.
67   Clarke, *Ancient Parish of Wrenbury*, p. 114.
68   Clarke, *Ancient Parish of Wrenbury* [section 10], pp. 78–9.

Among those prominent members of the chapelry who served as churchwardens was George Wright, whose name appears in 1621 with that of Robert Bankes on the new bell hung that year in the tower of St Margaret's church. Little is known of the family of Wright, other than the brief references to members in the parish registers. There were clearly several branches of the family in the period covered by this present volume – at least six other heads of households appear in the chapelry during the period 1611 to 1632, including the John Wright of Newhall whose inventory was exhibited in 1629. As with several other families of the chapelry, the Wrights may have been related to similarly-named inhabitants of Nantwich; however, in their case there is no direct evidence. Thus we are not able to say whether Sir Edmund Wright, who in 1640/41 served as Lord Mayor of London, did anything more than share a common surname. In his notes on 'Newhall Families', Hall makes Edmund Wright a native of Wrenbury and indicates that in the latter's will a bequest was made to Wrenbury. All of this seems curious, however, since Hall was also the author of *A History of the Town and Parish of Nantwich*, published several years earlier in 1883, in which he specifically states that Sir Edmund was the son of Rondull Wright, born at Nantwich and baptized there on 24 November 1573. Likewise, the monumental inscription for Edmund Wright establishes that he was born at Nantwich.[69] There were two separate wills for Sir Edmund Wright preserved at the Prerogative Court of Canterbury (now in The National Archives at Kew) in which it is noted that he established an almshouse at Nantwich, but the preponderance of his charity was directed towards the parishes of London, including St Lawrence, St Olave Jewry and St Peter near St Alban's. He also made gifts to Lincoln, Boston, Gainsborough, Beverley, Holden, Lynn and Lenton. Moreover, he remembered those incarcerated in various prisons – Ludgate, Newgate, King's Bench and others. But there is no reference whatsoever to Wrenbury church or chapelry.[70]

While clearly not from Wrenbury chapelry itself, Edmund Wright – like George Palyn and Edward Pexton before him – left the humble setting of southwest Cheshire for the greater opportunities of London. Having spent his earliest years in Nantwich, he then removed to the City where he became a successful tradesman (a grocer), and then rose to the offices of Sheriff, Alderman, and finally Lord Mayor.

The wills in this collection reveal that some of the more prominent members of the chapelry did indeed have extended contacts with London, whether in the capacity of sending their sons there to be apprenticed, or of engaging in business.

---

69   See James Hall, *A History of the Town and Parish of Nantwich or Wich Malbank, in the County Palatine of Chester* (Nantwich, printed for the author, 1883), pp. 367, 370, 486–7. The Wright pedigree appearing on pp. 492–3 and based on Harleian MS 2119, fo. 77 shows no wife for Sir Edmund, thus accounting for Hall's paragraph in *Notes and Queries* s9 IV: no. 91 (1899), pp. 247–8, asking for further information on the Lord Mayor. George Edward Cokayne, ed., *The Complete Baronetage* (reprint, Gloucester, Alan Sutton Publishing, 1983), shows Sir Edmund marrying, secondly, Jane daughter of William Mills, by whom he was father to Rebecca Wright, b. 5 June 1634 and baptized in St Olave's Jewry, London, that same day. A second daughter, Catherine, married Sir James Harrington, 3rd Bart of Ridlington, and died in 1675. In both cases, the information conflicts with that found in Harleian MS 2119, fo. 77.

70   TNA, PROB 11/191; PROB 11/201.

The examples of Richard Cartwright and Edmund Wright also demonstrate that boys of intellect and means could rise far above their parochial origins.

The will of Robert Tench of Newhall speaks of a kinsman – John Tench, late of London (though presumably a native of Wrenbury or nearby) – whose own will had established a legacy for a Wrenbury recipient. Edmund Crewe, whose will was proved in 1632, likewise had a kinsman – Arthur Crewe – living near London, while Thomas Hamnett in 1633 established legacies for both the son and the daughter of his niece, Hellen Skelhorne, who were living at London. Other wills merely make mention of the fact that the decedent had business dealings with the City, and in fact some of the more prominent individuals in the Wrenbury chapelry appear to have maintained substantial business contacts there. The accounting of expenses incident to the settling of Arthur Starkye's estate in 1542/43, for example, contains the entry of £3 11s. 4d., costs incurred by Thomas Starkey during two trips to London and two trips to Chester.

The most extensive account of ties with the Greater London area comes from the will of Thomas Hamnett of the Grange in Smeatonwood, proved in 1635. His moveable goods were valued at £629 150s. 65d., significantly less than those of John Cartwright of Aston, who died in 1630, and whose estate was valued at over £2,000. Hamnett, however, refers to a pension widow who held a tenement of him in the Long Woolstable of Westminster, as well as other tenants living in the same place; he makes a bequest to all his householder-tenants in the parish of Barking in Essex, and another to the poor of the parish of St Giles-in-the-Fields, in the county of Middlesex; he makes a third bequest to a resident of the parish of St Martin-in-the-Fields, as well as one to a citizen and cordwainer of London; he further establishes legacies for the wife and children of a resident of Eastcheap in London, and another for a waterman at Greenwich. All of this suggests that Hamnett had business dealings in various parts of Greater London, and that he held property there as well. He was thus far more than just a land-holder in rural Cheshire, engaged in raising sheep and producing cheese. In short, he was no stranger to the more complex world outside of south-east Cheshire.

Despite such evidence of contacts between this far corner of England and the capital, what is most striking about our collection of testamentary documents is the fact that most reflect the almost totally rural nature of this part of Cheshire in the sixteenth and seventeenth centuries. Of the 153 presented here – aside from those designated as 'clerk' – only three are those of persons who were not either a 'gentleman', that is, a property holder of some consequence, a yeoman farmer or a husbandman (or their wives or daughters), or the domestic servants of these individuals. The lone craftsman spoken of was Edward Powell of Newhall (1659), a *millener*, while the second individual was Richard Culliner alias Comber (1644), a labourer. Elinor Higson (will pr. 1597), a woman who was incarcerated at Chester at the time of her demise and speaks of her 'keeper', was apparently a woman of little social or economic standing – we are not told the reason for her imprisonment.

Within this rather homogeneous world of farmers great and small, there were nonetheless huge disparities of wealth. One need only contrast the inventories of John Cartwright of Aston, or one of the Cottons or Starkeys, with some of the humbler residents of Wrenbury chapelry to appreciate how large a gap separated the gentry from many lesser folk. Those inventories which give a breakdown of moveable property by room also help us build a mental image of significant differences in the dwellings occupied by people who attended the same parish church. We also get some sense of literacy levels among the members of the chapelry by the relatively few references to books in their bequests, and it does not surprise us that the greatest evidence of any sort of personal library comes from the will of Dorothy Cotton, who also appears to us as a woman of considerable piety.

> Mr Perkins works in 3 volumes;[71]
> Mr Grantam's works;
> The Doctrine of the Gospell;
> two of Dr Preston's books;[72]
> Mr Ball's treatise on faith.[73]

Andrew Cotton, her brother (will proved 1640) had a collection of Latin books (unspecified) and a large English Bible. This may well have been a copy of the fairly-recently published King James Bible of 1611, inasmuch as Andrew's prefatory comments to his will contain the following: '. . . for I know that my Redeemer liveth and that he shall stand the last upon the earth; and though after my skinne wormes destroy this body, yet in my flesh shall I see God' – an almost verbatim quoting of the Authorized Version rendering of Job 19:25–26.[74] At the least, this reference indicates that the person who prepared Andrew's will was familiar with that particular text. Andrew bequeathed the Bible to his cousin Thomas's new wife, Frances Cotton, 'in confidence that she will dayly bestow some time in reading and serious meditating thereon'.

Several other testators are also known to have possessed Bibles – William Cooper (1611); William Heighfield (1618); Randull Hare (1628); Edmund Crewe (1632); Thomas Hare (1639), who probably passed on the Bible inherited from

---

71   See William Perkins (1558–1602), *The Whole Treatise of the Case of Conscience, Distinguished Into Three Books*, the First Whereof is Revised and Corrected in Sundrie Places, and the Other Two Annexed. Taught and Deliuered by M.W. Perkins in his Holyday Lectures, Carefully Examined By His Owne Briefes, and Now Published Together for the Common Good (Cambridge, T. Pickering, 1606).

72   John Preston (1587–1628), doctor of divinity and chaplain in ordinary to the Queen, was a master of Emanuel College at Cambridge, and sometimes preacher of Lincoln's Inn. He wrote a number of works, including *The Brest-Plate of Faith and Love: A Treatise Wherein the Ground and Exercise of Faith and Love, As They Are Set Upon Christ Their Object, and As They Are Expressed in Good Works, Is Explained* (London, imprinted by R.Y. for Nicholas Bourne, 1634), and bound together with *Life Eternall: A Treatise of the Knowledge of the Divine Essence and Attribvtes. Delivered in xviii Sermons By the Late Faithfull and Worthy Minister of Jesus Christ* (London, printed by E.P., and are sold by Nicholas Bourne at the Royall Exchange, and by Ralpha Harford in Pater-Noster Row in Queenes-Head Alley, at the Signe of the Gilt Bible, 1634).

73   John Ball (1585–1640), *a Treatise of Faith: Diuided into Two Parts. The First Shewing the Nature; the Second the Life of Faith* (London, printed by George Miller for Edward Brewster, and are to be sold at the signe of the Bible, at the great north doore of Paul's, 1632).

74   This may also indicate the Bishops' Bible, presented to Queen Elizabeth I in 1568, the text of which was closely followed in producing the King James Version.

his father, Randull; Ralph Meakin (1645); and George Barnett (1649/50). John Massie, the former abbot of Combermere (1564/65) bequeathed 'all my bookes' without specificity to his brother William's son Rychard Massie; William Heighfield's bequest also included 'other [unidentified] books', while that of Crewe speaks of a 'service book'. Likewise, John Cartwright of Sheppenhall, gent., had a collection of 'Bookes' valued at 2s. at the time of his death in 1631, while that of George Tenche (1648) was valued at 10s. No value is attached to the 'bookes' belonging to Thomas Brees (1654) or to the 'booukes' which were mentioned in Jane Edgeley's will of 1657. Only in the instances of Dorothy and Andrew Cotton, therefore, can we enter more closely into their intellectual and spiritual lives. In Dorothy's case, several of the books were of fairly recent printing, and the works of prominent Anglican authors, suggesting that she took an active interest in the theological issues of her day; certainly she must have spent many an hour in private devotion, typical of women of her social standing. One wonders as well whether she had purchased the books herself during a visit to London, since we actually know where they were sold.

An obvious shift in the theological orientation of England is reflected in the wording of John Starkye's will in 1542 when compared with that of his descendant, Arthur Starkey, in 1622: the clear vestiges of Roman Catholicism in the former had given way to Calvinist sentiments in the latter. Since these expressions are often found in the most formulaic portions of any given will, however, we cannot know for certain the degree to which they truthfully reflect the feelings and faith of the testators. For instance, the will of Andrew Cotton (pr. 1640) contains a very lengthy prologue or preamble, followed by statements which seem more an expression of his innermost convictions: 'Wherefore abandoning (as strong delusions) all supposed meritorious workes of sinfull men; all fayned intercessions of Saints or Angells, or what else may derogate from that ever effectuall worke of our redemption, I repose myself onely upon the sufferings of my Lord and Saviour Jesus Christ'. We are not justified in dismissing such expressions as meaningless rubrics.

The intensity of religious feelings can also be sensed in the protest lodged against the will of Richard Edgeley of Smeatonwood, in that he had nuncupatively appointed his brother, Arthur, to be his executor on 26 December 1653, just a day before he died. This was challenged by Joseph Edgeley and John Peckston, however, who questioned Arthur's suitability to be the guardian of Richard's minor son, John – aged eight – and of his posthumously-born daughter, Elizabeth, primarily on the grounds that Arthur was not known to be a church-going man, and that during the English Civil War he had shown himself 'misloyal ... as a *sequestrator*'. The consistory court at Chester showed concern that John would be educated according to the teachings of the Established Church.

Many of the wills presented here were originally similarly contested. It is not uncommon to find the rubric *executum cum protestacōne* – executed with protest or challenge – in connection with the office endorsement appended to the will. In virtually all instances the reasons for such challenges have been lost with time, although it is often possible to infer from the distribution of a father's *goodes, cattels and chattells* among his children that one or more would have been disgruntled. For example, the will of Richard Cheswis of Wrenbury Frith, a husbandman whose moveable goods, cattles and chattels were valued at well over £200 when he died in February 1632/33, bequeathed to his son Thomas the amount of 10s., to be paid within a year of the proving of Richard's will 'in full satisfaccōn of his Childes part of my goods'. With the aid of the parish registers we learn that Thomas was actually the oldest son, born in 1598, but it was the second son, John, born in 1599, as well as his younger sons – George (b. 1609), William (b. 1611), and Hugh (b. 1614) – to whom Richard's various properties in Wrenbury Frith and Bickerton were granted, while the three youngest sons shared his moveable goods equally with their two sisters. In short, for reasons not now known to us, Thomas was virtually cut out of his father's will. We learn that Thomas owed his father a debt of £21 at the time of the latter's death, but whether that in itself was the cause of Thomas's exclusion we cannot say. We do not know why Richard Cheswis and other fathers withheld equal shares of their estates from their children, but one need only turn to the literature of the period to see how family members were estranged, and the whims of strong-willed family heads left children often nearly destitute. We can assume therefore that it was Thomas Cheswis who lodged the protest against his father's estate, but the details of its resolution are lost to us.

Of all the wills presented in our collection, none have more details than that of James Barnett of Aston in Newhall, a yeoman who died in 1610. A man of considerable piety by the standards of his day, he left a perpetual bequest of £10 to be paid annually on Good Friday to the churchwardens of Wrenbury for care of the poor who lived 'within the Newhall quarter'. His will, written on 12 May 1610, was modified by two codicils, the first written approximately three weeks after the will, the second about 21/22 June, since he was buried on 30 June 1610. In his will he established legacies totalling £161 320s. 12d. (or £177 12d.), of which the twelve pence was granted to his daughter Ellen[or] (her husband's name is not even mentioned in the will) 'in lue of her childs part of my goodes cattells and chattells'. Meanwhile, Ellen[or]'s sister, Isabel, the wife of the very prominent John Cartwright, Sr, of Aston, received £10 'in lue of such part or porcōn as she maie anie waie claime or chaling [challenge] of my goodes cattels or chattells.' Furthermore, to each of Isabel's three living children Barnett also granted legacies of £10 each. Even Barnett's servants received more in their legacies than did his daughter, Ellen[or].

James Barnett also granted a legacy of £40 to Elizabeth, late wife of Humfrey Barnett of Sound, and daughter of John Meredith, late of Kiddington, Cheshire. The significance of this bequest does not become clear until one reads the allegations filed in connection with the challenge brought against the will and the codicils by Ellen[or] and her husband. In Codicil 2, Barnett once again granted cash sums totalling £35 440s. 0d., distributed the rest of his goods moveable and unmoveable to his executors, and gave to 'Elizabeth late wife of Humfrey Barnett and daughter of John Meredith late of Kiddington deceased all my household goodes that she brought with her and one ioyned bedd standing in the parlor withall furniture therunto belonginge dureing her naturall life... '

The challenge lodged by Ellen[or] Barnett Shrowbridge and her husband, Richard Shrowbridge, seems to have been directed at the virtual exclusion of Ellen[or] from her father's estate, but also the seemingly unusual generosity shown towards Elizabeth Barnett, née Meredith. As a result, four men – Thomas Barnett, Thomas Gray, Thomas Burroughs and Robert Wright (the first three of whom witnessed the original will) – were summoned before an officer of the probate court and, under oath, deposed concerning the will and the various details associated with the decedent, especially with Elizabeth Barnett, daughter of the late Mr. Meredith.

Although there is an amazing degree of similarity in the depositions, there are details which surface in each which are lacking in the others – yet, in the end a rather complete picture appears. We do not know when the mother of Isabel and Ellen[or] died, but at some time around 1590 Elizabeth Barnett (wife of Humfrey Barnett, Sr) began to cohabit as man and wife with James, even though Humfrey Sr did not die until 1598. In moving into James's house, she brought with her certain household items which he then stipulated should remain for her use and benefit throughout her life. Even after James lost his eyesight, she continued to care for him, and it was because of this shared life and her service to him that James granted her the generous legacy of £40.

In none of the allegations does the reason for Ellen[or]'s niggardly treatment by her father become evident, but it is equally interesting that the deponents reveal that the will and the codicils were made in such a clandestine fashion that John Cartwright, a son-in-law, was not privy to what was transpiring either. One therefore forms a picture of this aging man who was generous to a fault with his estate so far as extended family members and even servants were concerned, but who was apparently totally alienated from one daughter and did not trust his other daughter's domineering (even scheming) husband. It is also worth noting that while Thomas Barnett, one of the original executors named in the will, renounced that responsibility, he also deposed that he favoured the challenge of the Shrowbridges. The other deponents tended to favour Elizabeth Barnett, née Meredith, yet all expressed a desire to see that the will and intent of the decedent be carried out, and that 'right' prevail.

Would that we had other such complete sets of testamentary documents, from which we could reconstruct a remarkably interesting and intertwined history of the denizens of this small chapelry. As it is, we catch only exquisite glimpses of their lives spread over decades of marrying and begetting, eking out a subsistence from the soil and from their flocks and small herds, or else enjoying a level of plenty and luxury consistent with their station in life. Obviously our collection of wills adds substantially to the source materials readily available to those seeking to do historical studies at both the local and family levels.

In the case of Joane Crewe's will, proved in 1641, we have an original will that was lost en route to the consistory court in Chester, and was later found. In the meantime, an attempt was made to reconstruct the sense of that will by means of taking depositions from the original witnesses. In the course of all this, it also became evident that Joane Crewe had made an even earlier will which had named a totally different executor – a man who claimed to be more closely related to her than the more recent nominee. All of this led to the will being challenged by two parties, with the implication that the second will was either a forgery, or that it was made under pressure from the most recent executor. Here again we come to realize that, although it was customary for the standard format of wills to include some such phrase as 'I revoke all previous wills and testaments', in some cases this was an actual fact and not merely formulaic. In the Crewe will and allegations we also get a rather complete set of questions or *interrogatories* posed to the witnesses and other deponents, whereas for James Barnett we simply have the responses and must infer the questions.

Wills such as that of James Barnett also illustrate extremely well the size of many of the extended families and kinship groups in early modern England. During the first distribution of his estate in his will, Barnett not only includes immediate family members and domestic servants who make up his close circle of associates, but he also provides legacies for children of other members of the extended Barnett family, whose exact relationship to him is not stated. From other Barnett wills, it is obvious that this was a rather large family with several branches living in Wrenbury chapelry in the seventeenth century. Such far-reaching family ties are also noticeable in the family of Hamnett, and best illustrated in the oft-noted will of Thomas Hamnett of the Grange, gent., who died in 1635. In addition to the large number of Hamnett family branches noted in the will, we can identify some thirteen other families to which he presumably had some kinship tie – those of Gray, Bradshaw, Bewmorris, Pextonne, Manning, Griffith, Macewen, Hartopp, Leeke, Skelhorne, Burroughs, Warner and Colling. Virtually all of these were resident within the chapelry of Wrenbury, suggesting how closely connected the social life of this community really was.

History

The first significant history of Wrenbury and its surrounding villages appears in J. Leland's *History of English Antiquities* published in 1634–43. Thereafter followed Daniel King's *Vale Royal*, in 1656, which included extensive portions of Sir Peter Leycester's *Antiquities of Cheshire*. George Ormerod's *History of Cheshire*, which he began in 1813 and published in 1819, was written while he was resident at Chorlton Hall in Bachford and had access to primary documents at Chester, supplemented by other original sources from the Public Record Office (now The National Archives) in London. The *Victoria County History* of Cheshire gives further details which have provided important assistance to local historians. More recently, volumes have appeared for Acton by Frank A. Latham, and for Nantwich by Jack Cockroft,[75] but as yet the best work on Wrenbury chapelry remains unpublished. James Hall (1846–1914), who served many years as a school teacher and local historian at Wrenbury, produced a manuscript history of the

---

75   See Jack Cockroft, transcr., *Transcriptions of Nantwich Wills and Inventories 1603–1688* (Crewe, South Cheshire Family History Society, 1999).

chapelry – and of the surrounding villages, together with many of the leading families – which is deposited in Cheshire Record Office.[76] Though undated, it can be attributed to the period 1890/1900. This is an indispensable source, since it contains extracts from Newhall Manor Court records dating back to the fourteenth century, transcriptions of countless documents relevant to both Newhall and the larger Wrenbury area, and an astute analysis of many technical aspects of late medieval/early modern English rural life. As can be noted from our own discussion above, we have relied on Hall's manuscript repeatedly in presenting details concerning some of the leading families of the chapelry as background to our collection of wills.

Heavily dependent upon Hall's work is the Rev. F.W. Norwood's 'Historic Notes' (1900–1905), though it does bring to the public documents which until then were buried in archives or in Hall's handwritten manuscript. Likewise, the Rev. H.A. Clarke's small *History of the Ancient Parish of Wrenbury* makes available for the first time to the general public many of the documents earlier worked through by Hall. Of some limited value to our study is also the small commemorative booklet, 'St. Margaret's Church Wrenbury: a Brief Account of this 900 Year Old Churchyard', compiled by John R. Pound on the occasion of the 1993 Flower and Craft Festival (Wrenbury; privately printed). Our debt to these more recent works is obvious, just as is their debt to the seminal works of the seventeenth century.

Wills and Testaments

A will is a legal transaction by means of which a person (called the testator) disposes of his/her property prior to death. While the history of will-making extends back to the ancient Greeks and Romans, in England a more or less standard format had evolved by about the thirteenth century which generally included the following parts:

> Introduction (usually invoking God or the Holy Trinity), which gives the name of the testator, his/her physical and mental state, etc.;
>
> Commendation of one's soul to God, an appeal to the mercy of Jesus Christ and some statement regarding the expectation of salvation through Christ's merits, some reference to funeral arrangements, and any bequests to the local church (to benefit the poor, etc.);
>
> Instructions for payments of debts;
>
> Bequests to individuals;
>
> Appointment of executors and overseers; list of witnesses; nullification of any previous wills.

Before 1540 one could not devise real property by will since this was determined by law; most often, land was inherited by the eldest surviving son (primogeniture), a practice in force since 1066. Over time, many landholders had sought

---

76 CRO D 4059/15.

to circumvent the strictures of law by transferring land to a person of their choosing during their own lifetime, resulting in a Parliamentary prohibition in 1535. The Statute of Wills in 1540 authorized the distribution of most land by will to anyone, and in 1661 all land could be devised by will.

Prior to the sixteenth century, will-making was not a general practice, being done primarily by wealthy landowners and burghers. It is estimated that between 25% and 33% of Englishmen made wills thereafter. Originally, the *will* was a separate and distinct document from the *testament*: while the former devised real property, the latter disposed of personal or moveable property. One-third of one's 'goods and chattels and cattles' went to one's wife or widow, one-third to their children, and one-third to whomever the testator designated. It is not uncommon from the sixteenth century to find the phrase 'last will and testament' used, even when the only property being disposed of is personal, and that is certainly true in the wills comprising this collection.

Before 1837, boys aged fourteen and older, and girls age twelve and older, could make wills, but in reality the only wills written by women before 1882 were of spinsters, widows, or married women with their husbands' consent. Twenty-seven of the present collection of wills were made by women, and of these six were spinsters; in twenty cases they were widows, while at least two of them – Emma Barnett (will pr. 1631) and Elizabeth Briscoe (will pr. 1637) – can be shown to have outlived two husbands. In eight instances, we possess wills and/or inventories from both the husband and the wife.[77] Only one of the wills in this collection was written by a woman whose husband was still living, however – that of Katherine Savage (proved 1641/42), whose husband John, was appointed her administrator.

A person desiring to make a will could do two things: 1) engage a scribe (usually the parish clerk), or 2) declare her/his will *nuncupatively* (an oral declaration of one's last wishes in the presence of three reliable witnesses).[78] Those who died without a written or nuncupative will were said to be *intestate*. When a will was first taken by the executor to the court of jurisdiction, it was recorded along with the pertinent information about the decedent, and the executor was given authority to carry out the wishes of the testator. From 1521 until 1750, the courts also generally required that an inventory of the testator's personal property be made by two or more reputable neighbours. In many cases the inventories have not survived, while in others the inventory is all that remains of the entire bundle of testamentary documents. Where no will existed, the court of probate appointed an administrator whose duties included providing an inventory of the decedent's moveable goods by a specific date.

Prior to 1858, the Church of England had jurisdiction in testamentary matters. In the case of the chapelry of Wrenbury, probate jurisdiction was in the hands of

---

77 Edmund and Joane Crewe; Emma and William Barnett; Edward and Elizabeth Baskerville; Elizabeth and Oliver Briscoe; Jane and Richard Edgeley; Anne and George Kempe; Ellen and Thomas Ravenscroft; Margerie and William Seavell.

78 See Giles Jacob, *New Law Dictionary: Containing the Interpretation and Defination of Words and Terms Used in the Law*, 6th ed. (London, pr. Henry Lintot for R. Ware [and others], 1750).

the Bishop of Chester. Occasionally, however, persons of means chose to have their estates probated at the Prerogative Court of Canterbury (PCC). There are three early instances of such wills, one from 1607/08 and the others from 1645 and 1646, but from 1653 to 1660, when all wills in England were probated at the PCC, there are thirteen.[79]

While the identities of some consistory court officials – such as Richard Kettle, clerk and dean, Thomas Stofford, bachelor of laws, and Edward Mainwaring, doctor of laws – remain unknown to us, that of David Yale, doctor of laws, is well established. Born about 1535 to John and Agnes (Lloyd) Yale, he died at Chester in 1626. He married Frances Lloyd, by whom he had fourteen children. He was the great grandfather of Elihu Yale, the major benefactor of Yale College (now University) in New Haven, Connecticut Colony. He served as rector of Llandegla (1564–73), prebendary of Y Faenol in St Asaph Cathedral (1578–1624), prebendary of Chester (1582–?), Chancellor of Chester (1587–1624), Justice of the Peace (1601–20) 'and of the Quorum' for the County of Chester (1603). A prominent landowner in Cheshire, he wrote his will on 15 August 1625, which was likewise proved in the consistory court of Chester following his death. He was kinsman to Dr Thomas Yale, Chancellor of Canterbury, whom he had succeeded in the prebend of Y Faenol in St Asaph Cathedral.[80]

Provenance of the documents

The probate records printed in this volume are largely to be found in Cheshire Record Office, the Diocesan Record Office for the Diocese of Chester. Microfilm copies of these records housed in the Family History Library of the Church of Jesus Christ of Latter-day Saints in Salt Lake City, Utah, U.S.A., served us during the first phase of research: these were searched, and transcriptions were made over a period of several years by the editor and by several student assistants at Brigham Young University in Provo, Utah, using as finding aids the printed indexes of wills published by the Record Society between 1879 and 1896. This was later checked against the online index which is now available through the Cheshire Record Office website. The editor benefitted greatly from a research leave supported by the university during the fall of 2002, which made it possible to check these transcriptions personally against the originals in the CRO. Those sixteen documents which have been preserved at the PCC have been viewed in microfilm copies only, however. So far as we have been able to determine, the inventories which originally accompanied the PCC wills have disappeared.

---

79 See Mark D. Herber, *Ancestral Trails: The Complete Guide to British Genealogy and Family History* (Stroud, Sutton in association with the Society of Genealogists 1977), pp. 173–99; Jeremy S.W. Gibson, *A Simplified Guide to Probate Jurisdictions: Where to Look for Wills*, 4th ed. (Birmingham, Federation of Family History Societies, 1994).

80 See Rodney Horace Yale, *Yale Genealogy and History of Wales* (Beatrice, Neb., pr. Milburn and Scott, 1908), pp. 86–91; Alfred Neobard Palmer, *History of the Thirteen County Townships of the Old Parish of Wrexham* (Hughes and Son, 1903; facsimile reprint, Wrexham, Bridge Books, 1983).

The following table shows the state in which these documents have survived, whether as a complete set of will and inventory, or as some portion thereof. In several cases (noted in the transcriptions), the condition of the will is such that portions are either missing or illegible. It would seem that in at least one instance, a late nineteenth-century user of one of the wills indicated a far greater number of folio pages than are presently extant. There are likewise a fair number of nuncupative wills, which may be an indication that death came suddenly and unexpectedly for some of our testators. On the other hand, the delay between the date of making the will and the actual date of death in some cases also indicates that the testator recovered from whatever illness had prompted her/him to set their affairs in order at the earlier date.

TABLE 1

Of the 153 testamentary documents in this present collection:

79 consist of both will and inventory.

11 consist of both will and inventory, together with a memorandum (e.g. a codicil or renunciation, allegations, etc.)

25 consist of the will only.

2 consist of the will only, together with a memorandum or codicil.

5 consist of nuncupative wills, 3 of which have inventories and/or administration, and 1 with allegations.

21 consist of inventory only.

6 consist of inventory, together with administration and account.

4 consist of administration only, 1 of which also has an account.

Since Wrenbury chapelry was comprised of several small villages, but lacked anything resembling a larger town, such as Nantwich or Whitchurch, this present collection of wills is not dominated by any single community: in fact, it reveals a rather remarkable distribution across the chapelry:

TABLE 2

[By dates of probate]

Wrenbury: Starkye (1542); Hare (before 1547); Pexton (1562); Woodfaine (1588); Povall (1593); Swane (1610); Davies (1611); Starkie (1611/12); Cowper (1613); Wilkinson (1615); Barnett (1616/17); Dodd (1619); Berrington (1619/20); Starkey (1623); Starkie (1626/27); Briscoe (1630); Barnett (1631); Graye (1632); Briscoe (1637); Savage (1641/42); Savage (1647); Tenche (1648); Savage (1648); Buckley (1649) – 24 wills.

Newhall: Massey (1584/85); Tenche (1594); Barnett (1595); Higson (1597); Fletcher (1607); Seavell (1609); Swann (1610); Sevell (1611); Fletcher (1611); Ravenscroft (1614); Bickerton (1616); Whitney (1617); Backhouse (1620); Egerton (1622); Cudworth (1624); Dickins (1626/27); Shrowbridge (1626/27); Wright (1629); Ravenscroft (1630/31); Crewe (1632); Pextonne (1632);

Tudman (1632); Hall (1636); Gray (1640); Crewe (1641); Malkin (1645); Sproston (1648); Lawrence (1649); Ravenscroft (1650); Wood (1653); Powell (1659) – 31 wills.

Aston in Newhall: Cartwright (1604); Barnett (1610); Brooke (1622); Cartwright (1630); Barnett (1633); Gray (1636); Hamnett (1646); Barnett (1647/48); Hall (1657); Hall (1658) – 10 wills.

Moore Hall: Edgeley (1654); Edgeley (1657/58) – 2 wills.

Royals in Newhall: Shrowbridge (1641); Shrowbridge (1659) – 2 wills.

Sheppenhall: Cartwright (1631); Cartwright (1635) – 2 wills.

Chorley: Bebbington (1592); Bebbington (1592); Patrick alias Wilson (1597/98); Wilson (1602); Flavell (1604); Broome (1606); Patrick (1611); Faulkner (1615); Taylor (1620); Rogers (1621); Patricke (1626); Hare (1628); Babington (1630/31); Bowdon (1638); Hare (1639); Jones (1639); Woodfen (1642/43) – 17 wills.

Wrenbury Frith: Bickerton (1594); Cooke (1604/05); Blackamore (1604/05); Tenche (1608); Tenche (1615); Palin (1624); Wickstead Sr (1629); Wickstead Jr (1629); Cheswys (1633); Wade (1633/34); Woollam (1635/36); Wilson (1639); Culliner alias Comber (1644); Woolrich (1647); Cheswys (1649/50); Twisse (1659) – 16 wills.

Smeatonwood: Hall (1606); Buckley (1607/08); Kemp (1616); Gray (1616/17); Kempe (1619); Hall (1630/31); Buckley (1630/31); Dodd (1637); Tenche (1639); Taylor (1649); Palin (1657); Edgeley (1660/61) – 12 wills.

The Grange in Smeatonwood: Hamnett (1635) – 1 will.

Broomhall: Ankers (1609/10); Lowe (1610/11); Hockenhall (1614); Bickerton (1616); Millington (1619); Heighfield (1620); Brees (1621); Whittingham (1622); Anckers (1641/42); Griffiths (1654/55); Brees (1655/56); Griffiths (1658) – 12 wills.

Mickley: Chessewes (1562); Cheswis (1648) – 2 wills.

Coole Lane: Vernon (1608); Whitney (1611); Whitney (1616); Salmon (1642) – 4 wills.

Sound: Bickerton (1611/12); Baskerville (1613); Cooper (1613); Baskerville (1617); Bickerton (1617); Bromhall (1630); Lowe (1637); Cowper (1637); Barnett (1649/50); Clark (1660) – 10 wills.

Woodcott: Edgeley (1637) – 1 will.

Combermere: Massie, late Abbot of Combermere (1564/65); Cotton (1640); Cotton (1647); Cotton (1648); Cotton (1648); Davies (1658) – 6 wills.

No place is recorded for Frances Ravenscroft (1658/59).

When all the various parts that comprised Newhall are added together, however, they clearly form the bulk of the wills for this particular period.

In some cases a will may be missing, as for example, in 1648 the prisers of Randle Sproston's goods and chattels make reference to a debt of £15 owing from the executors or administrators of John Cooke without specialty. The John Cooke in question is most likely he who was buried on 18 January 1615/16 at Wrenbury as *senex*,[81] but no testamentary document has survived. Nor can we offer even a rough guess as to how many others may have perished since their making.

EDITORIAL CONVENTIONS

The documents have been edited according to the format established in the Record Society's earlier Stockport probate material.[82] Documents are referred to by year of probate, either at Chester or at the Prerogative Court of Canterbury. The letters S. or I. indicate that the personal estates under consideration were valued either at £40 or more (*supra*), or less than £40 (*infra*). A third class of documents emerged at an uncertain date as a result of process in the consistory court (C.) which led to wills and inventories being filed with the court's papers. According to the editor of the index for this class, William Fergusson Irvine,

> It is not clear how the Wills came to be at the Diocesan Registry instead of at the Probate Registry, but they were probably wills about which some dispute had arisen, and were accordingly put aside while the case was pending in the Chancellor's Court, and have never been returned to their proper bundles, so that when in 1847 the Cheshire Wills were moved from the Diocesan Registry these were overlooked, and did not share in the removal.[83]

All the documents for each individual are printed in the order in which they were originally made: will, inventory, then any other. The arrangement of the volume follows the date of the grant of probate for each deceased's estate. There is an alphabetical list of decedents, with summary of documents and probate dates on pp. li–lv, below. Documents are printed according to the following conventions.

GENERAL

1. Documents have been numbered by the present editor for use in the format of this volume only.
2. Burial entries are from the unpublished parish registers of Wrenbury, copies of which were obtained by the present editor from the CRO; a microfilm copy exists at the Family History Library (film # 2106694, items 4–9).

81   See Wrenbury Parish Registers – Burials: 1615.
82   C.B. Phillips and J.H. Smith, eds, *Stockport Probate Records 1578–1619* and *1620–1650*, RSLC, cxxiv (1985); cxxxi (1992).
83   *Index of Wills*, RSLC, xxxiii (1896), iii.

3. Office Endorsements, where these survive, may record the person to whom probate was granted. The name of this person is recorded at the end of the decedent's entry.
4. Documents are in English unless otherwise stated.
5. Where documents are originals, it is indicated whether signatories sign or mark. On other documents it is noted where a mark is indicated.
6. Dates between 1 January and 24 March are rendered e.g. 1608/09. Where a date is in regnal years without an A.D. date the latter is given in [ ].
7. Place names in calendar conform to 1874 Ordnance Survey Map (6" 1st ed.) Personal names are given in the original spelling.
8. Standard extensions are silent.
9. All roman numerals have been rendered in arabic.
10. In lists of debts in wills, and in valuations and lists of debts in inventories, all values have been placed in columns for £ s d; other indications of £ or s or d have been omitted. Valuations have been left in the original denomination, e.g. 17d has not been altered to 1s 5d, nor has 30s been altered to £1 10s 0d. For valuations in whole numbers of shillings a 0 has been entered in the pence column.
11. In the texts of wills and inventories, sums of money expressed in words have been described as such, but such sums rendered in figures have been given as follows, retaining denominations: £17 125s 51d, £3 42s 36d, and £88 8s 9d.
12. All contemporary indications of totals, e.g. *summa totalis* have been left as such. Where necessary, however, corrected totals have been provided [*recte* £3 3s 3d], and where no total was given in the MS one has been supplied in [Sum – – –].
13. Erasures are indicated by *[erasure]*
    Gaps are indicated by [ ]
    Doubtful readings by [?]
    Interlineations by *[interlined]*
    Blank in MS – *[blank]*
    Gaps caused by damage – *[damaged]*
    Unable to read *[illegible]*
14. There is a separate sequence of footnotes for each document.

WILLS

1. In all wills the preamble, comprising date, identity, place, status, age and health has been summarized; within this summary exceptional statements are given in their original form. The standard forms are variations on 'sick in body but of sound mind' or 'aged in body but of perfect remembrance' and only significant departures from these forms are given.
2. Will and testament, or will, is indicated by the letters W.T., or W., before the date of the will.

3. In all wills the statements appointing executors and overseers or supervisors have been summarized.
4. Revocations of former wills have been omitted.
5. The records of witnesses have been summarized but include name, status and residence as and when given.
6. At the head of the preamble, on the right of the page of this text, the letters S., I., or C. are used to indicate to which class the documents belong. One of these letters prefixes the letters 'Pr.' which are followed by the probate date. Thus for John Millington, S.Pr. 28 July 1619 means that his documents are in the *supra* class and probate was dated 28 July 1619.
7. Where the testator states that he or she has set hand and seal, this is indicated at the appropriate point in the transcript by H. & S.
8. Those words in the will which indicate that the testator wishes to be buried at Wrenbury have been *italicized*, whereas those which simply leave the burial to the discretion of the executors have been left in non-italicized print. In several cases, while it seems obvious that the testator identifies with Wrenbury chapelry, no record of her/his burial at that place has been found; an attempt has therefore been made to locate the burial entry in the registers of adjacent parishes, often without success.

INVENTORIES

1. The preamble has been summarized, the summary giving the name, status and residence of the deceased, the date on which the inventory was taken and the place, where such information is given. The descriptive phrase, e.g. goods, cattells and chattells, is given in full. The name, status and place of residence of the prisers are noted, where such information is given.
2. *Imprimis* and *Item* are omitted throughout.
3. Where there is no will, the class in which the documents are to be found, and the probate date, are given at the right hand side of the preamble, using the formulae indicated for wills at Item 6, above.

The will of John Hall of Smeatonwood, yeoman (no. 22), proved in 1606, and the inventory of John Egerton of Newhall, gent. (no. 67), proved in 1622, are given in full below, with the calendared sections of the text rendered in *italics*. These full transcripts can be compared with the edited versions on pp. 56–7; 186.

In the name of almighty God Amen the third daie of December 1605 in the yeare of the raigne of our soveraigne Lord King James I off England France and Ireland the third and of Scotland the sixth I John Hall of Smeyton Wood in the countye of Chester yeoman beinge sick in bodie of good & perfect Remembrance thanks be to almighty god for the same do Ordayne and make this my last will and testament in manner and forme followinge that is to saie First, I doe moste humblye Comitt my soule into the hands of almightye god assuredlye trusting by thedeath and merritts of myne onelie Savior and Redeemer Jesus Christ and faith in him to be saved And My bodie to be buryed in the Church or Church yard of Wrenburye at the discrecōn of myne executors And as touching my worldly goods First I give and bequeath to Jane Hall my daughter £60 to be paied to her within two year-es next after my decease out of my whole goods Item I give and bequeath to Richard Hall myne oldest sonne my seacond best fetherbedd with the Coveringe blanquetts & other fur-niture to the same belonginge & two paier of sheets and also the moytye or one halfe of all my Carts timbrells yokes Cheynes plowes harrowes and other implements husbandry Item I give and bequeath to Elizabeth my welbeloved wyfe the other moytye or half of all my said Carts tumbrells yokes Chaynes plowes harrowes & other Implements of hus-bandrye Item whereas I did lend unto the right worshipfull and my verie good Mr. George Cotton Esqr. £3 13s. 4d. I doe forgive him the same And doe give and bequeath unto him more 10s. in gould, Item after my debts paied my funeral expenses discharged & my for-mer mencōned legacies performed my Will and mynd is that all the rest and residue of my goods Cattalls Chattalls and debts shall be devided into two equall moyties or parts the one moytye or halfe whereof I doe give and bequeath to the said Elizabeth my Wyfe And I doe further give and bequeath unto the said Jane Hall my daughter £10 to be paied to her out of the other halfe or moytye of the said rest & residue of my said goods Cattalls Chattalls and debts And the rest residue and Remnant of the same other half or moytye of the Rest of my said goods Cattalls Chattalls and debts I doe give and bequeath unto George Hall my sonne *And I doe ordeyne constitute and make the said Elizabeth my wyfe and Richard Hall my sonne my true and lawfull executors of this my last will and testament And doe most humblye desire my said Mr George Cotton be overseer of the same that everye thing touching the same be ordered disposed & done accordinge to the true meaninge hereof And I doe utterlye repell revoke and make voyde all former wills by me made And make this my last will and testament to be of force In wytnes hereof I have here-unto putt my hande and seale the daie and yeare first above wrytten.*

Debts which I owe

Whereas I have beene Charged with the goods of Mris Jane Cotton I have delivered twen-tye pounds thereof to my said Mr George Cotton Esqr whereof I humblye desire to see myne executors discharged Item I have more of her in my hands 13s 4d & 12s and also one Cowe.

Debts oweing to me vizt of

Thomas Ravenscroft of Newhall	£10	
William Higgenson	20s	
John Higgenson and Richard Higgenson which I forgive them	20s	
William Barnes	10s	
Roger Hamnett	13s 4d	
Richard Taylor my brother in law	£4	
whereof I forgive him	20s	
William Cappur of Poolecroft Heath	£7	
Alane Coxie the wyfe	10s	
John Taylor of Aston	28s	
John Evanson Humfrey Evanson & Richard Evanson one Cowe price	43s 4d	

Thomas Starkie the yonger   2s
William Lucas to the use of Richard Bowyer which
   he gave his word to paie   10s
 William Prynce Curat of Wrenbury   6s
                                                                  John Hall
                                                                      marke

Sealed signed publyshed & delivered in presence of the persons undernamed viz:
   Thomas Poole
   George Maynwaring
   Hugh Hopkin
   Thomas Babington
   George Coxies Marke
[On Wrapper] *Testamentum cum Inventorio John Hall dum vixit de Smeaton Woodd defuncti Probatum 29 die mensis Octobris Anno domini 1606 Commissaque fuit administratio bonorum ipsius defuncti executoribus in huiusmodi nominatis de bene et probatum. . . juratis etc. . . 1606*

A true inventorie of all the goods of John Egerton late of Newhall, gent., as it was prised by William Allen, John Pichford, Richard Hall and Thomas Bebington November the 18th 1619.

	£	s	d
Imprimis 4 oxen	16		
11 kyne and two Bulls	26		
3 Calves		40	
in Horsefleshe	11	6	8
in Swine	3		
in Poultrieware		17	
in necessaries of husbantrie	6		
in Corne	25	16	
in hay	5		
the estate of Deverton Dayth	80		
in Peavter	3	6	8
in Brasse	5	10	
in Iron ware belonginge to the kytchen		30	
in Treeneware		30	
in Tables with the formes Cheists Cheres			
and stooles with a liverie Cubboard and a Closse presse	5	6	8
for a little gylt Salte and ten silver spoones	4	13	4
in Carpetts and Quishens		46	8
in Beddinge	14	10	
in Bedsteeds	4	6	8
in Napperieware	8		
Beeffe Bakon Butter and Cheese	6		
in the Testators apparell	6	13	4

in Corne sowed		49	
in Fewell	3	6	8

Some tot:	244	9	4

Executum cum protestacōne

Endorsement: *Testamentum cum Inventorio bonorum Johannis Egertoni dum vixit de Newhall defuncti Probatum xxvii^{mo} Maij Anno domini 1622 et Commissa fuit administratio bonorum predicti defuncti Georgio Egerton uni executoribus in eodem nominato de bene &c personaliter Jurato potestate reservata altero executori Donec venerit salvo &c 1622*

PEDIGREE CHARTS

1. Unless otherwise specified, christening/baptism dates and burial dates are based on Wrenbury Parish Registers or Bishop's Transcripts.
2. Solid horizontal and vertical lines indicate clearly established family connection.
3. Dotted horizontal line indicates a presumed family connection, based on such words as 'cousin', 'brother', 'kinsman', 'god-son', etc.
4. ♀ indicates a union other than marriage, that is – adulterous.
5. Vertical dotted line indicated presumed line of descent.
6. Terms on pedigree correspond to those found in Parish Register, such as *senex, anus, generosus, filius, adulterius*, etc.
7. Abbreviations:
   = marriage
   † death
   bur. buried
   c. christened/baptized
   1), 2), etc. marriage order
   ca. (*circa*) about/approximately
   g.s. grandson

INDEX OF DECEDENTS

115. Anckers, John, of Broomhall, yeoman, W.I., S*upra?*, pr. 24 January 1641/42.
 28. Ankers, Margaret, of Broomhall, widow, W.I., *Supra*, pr. 13 March 1609/10.
 85. Babington, William, of Chorley, gent., W.I., *Supra,* pr. 1630/31.
 61. Backhouse, John, of Newhall, W.I., *Supra,* pr. 1 June 1620.
 87. Barnett, Emma, of Wrenbury, widow, W.I., *Supra*, pr. 24 October 1631.
135. Barnett, George, of Sound, *Supra*, administration granted 8 February 1649/50.
 29. Barnett, James, of Aston, yeoman, W.I., *Supra*, pr. 21 August 1610.
 94. Barnett, John, of Aston, yeoman, W.I., *Supra*, pr. after 26 October 1633.
 13. Barnett, Raffe, of Newhall, W.I., *Supra*, pr. 14 October 1595.
125. Barnett, Richard, of Aston in Newhall, yeoman, W.I., *Supra*, pr. 18 January 1647/48.
 52. Barnett, William, of Wrenbury, yeoman, I., *Supra*, pr. 1 February 1616/17.
 41. Baskerville, Edward, of Sound, I., *Supra*, pr. 10 June 1613.

55. Baskerville, Elizabeth, of Sound, widow, W.I., *Supra*, pr. 17 May 1617.
 8. Bebbington, Ellen, of Chorley, widow, W.I., *Supra*, pr. 1 August 1592.
 9. Bebbington, William, of Chorley, W.I., *Supra*, pr. 7 October 1592.
60. Berrington, Richard, of Wrenbury, I., *Infra*, pr. after 9 March 1619/20.
49. Bickerton, Anne, of Broomhall, widow, W.I., *Supra*, pr. 19 September 1616.
56. Bickerton, Edmond, of Sound, yeoman, W.I., *Supra*, pr. 10 July 1617.
12. Bickerton, Humphrey, of Wrenbury Frith, husbandman, W.I., *Supra*, pr. 28 June 1594.
48. Bickerton, John, of Newhall, yeoman, W.I., *Supra*, pr. 15 June 1616.
39. Bickerton, John, *the Soone of Edmond Bickerton of Sound*, I., *Infra*, pr. 27 January 1611/12.
20. Blackamore, Alice, of Wrenbury Frith, widow, W.I., *Infra*, pr. 23 February 1604/05.
106. Bowdon, Edward, of Chorley, I., *Supra*, pr. 18 April 1638.
141. Brees, Thomas, of Bromhall, W., *Supra* (PCC), pr. 8 March 1655/56.
 64. Brees, William, of Broomhall, yeoman, W.I., *Supra*, pr. 25 May 1621.
103. Briscoe, Elizabeth, of Wrenbury, widow, W.I., *Supra*, pr. after 19 July 1637.
 80. Briscoe, Oliver, of Wrenbury, husbandman, W.I., *Supra*, pr. 15 May 1630.
 82. Bromhall, John, of Sound, yeoman, W.I., *Supra*, pr. 1 November 1630.
 66. Brooke, James, of Aston, yeoman, W.I., *Supra*, pr. 15 May 1622.
 21. Broome, Roger, of Chorley, yeoman, W.I., *Supra*, pr. 12 August 1606.
132. Buckley, Alice, of Wrenbury, spinster, W., C., pr. 28 April 1649.
 24. Buckley, Robert, of Smeatonwood, yeoman, W., *Supra* (PCC), pr. 3 February 1607/08.
 84. Buckley, Timothy, of Smeatonwood, gent., I., *Supra*, pr. 10 March 1630/31.
 18. Cartwright, John, the elder, of Aston, W.I., *Supra*, pr. 24 November 1604.
 81. Cartwright, John, of Aston in Newhall, gent., W.I., *Supra*, pr. 16 October 1630.
 88. Cartwright, John, of Sheppenhall, gent., W.I., C., pr. 10 November 1631 [no documents for C.].
 96. Cartwright, John, of Sheppenhall, gent., I., *Supra*, pr. 28 August 1635.
  3. Chessewes, Thomas of (Mickley Hall) Wrenbury, yeoman, W., pr. 1562.
127. Cheswis, John, of Mickley, gent., W., C., pr. 28 August 1648.
 93. Cheswis, Richard, of Wrenbury Frith, husbandman, W.I., *Supra*, pr. 10 April 1633.
136. Cheswys, Margaret, of Wrenbury Frith, administration granted 5 March 1649/50.
152. Clarke, James, of Sound, yeoman, W., *Supra?* (PCC), pr. 16 July 1660.
 19. Cooke, Elizabeth, of Wrenbury Frith, spinster, W.I., *Infra*, pr. 7 February 1604/05.
 42. Cooper, William, of Sound, yeoman, W.I., *Supra*, pr. 15 July 1613.
111. Cotton, Andrew, of Combermere, gent., W.I., *Supra*, pr. 21 October 1640.
122. Cotton, Dorothy, of Combermere, spinster, W.I., *Supra*, pr. 5 June 1647.
126. Cotton, Elizabeth, of Combermere, widow, I., *Supra*, pr. 29 July 1648.
128. Cotton, George, esquire, of Combermere, W.I., *Supra*, pr. 21 September 1648.
 40. Cowper, Randull, of Wrenbury, husbandman, W.I., *Supra*, pr. 9 April 1613.

104. Cowper, William, the elder, of Sound, yeoman, W., *Supra*, pr. after 13 October 1637.

90. Crewe, Edmund, of Newhall, yeoman, W.I., *Supra*, pr. 4 September 1632.

113. Crewe, Joane, of Newhall, widow, W., Allegation, C.?, *Supra*, pr. 8 April 1641.

70. Cudworth, George, of Newhall, gent., I., *Supra*, pr. 2 October 1624.

119. Culliner alias Comber, Richard, of Wrenbury Frith, labourer, Nunc. I., C., *Supra*, pr. 29 October 1644.

146. Davies, Robert, of Combermere, yeoman, W., *Supra* (PCC), pr. 20 October 1658.

36. Davies, William, of Wrenbury, I., *Supra*, pr. 1 August 1611.

74. Dickins, George, of Newhall, W.I., *Infra,* pr. 8 March 1626/27.

59. Dodd, Phillip, of Wrenbury, I., *Infra*, pr. [ ] 1619.

101. Dodd, Richard, of Smeatonwood, yeoman, W.I., *Supra*, pr. 20 July 1637.

144. Edgeley, Jane, of Moorehall in Newhall, widow, W., *Supra?* (PCC), pr. 5 January 1657/58.

139. Edgeley, John, of Moorehall, yeoman, W., *Supra?* (PCC), pr. 13 August 1654.

102. Edgeley, John, of Woodcott, yeoman, W.I., *Supra*, pr. 26 July 1637.

153. Edgeley, Richard, of Smeatonwood, Nunc., *Supra*, pr. 10 January 1660/61.

67. Egerton, John, of (Eagle Hall) Newhall, gent., W.I., *Supra*, pr. 1622.

47. Faulkner, Thomas, of Chorley, yeoman, W.I., *Supra*, pr. 9 November 1615.

17. Flavell, Ellen, of Chorley, widow, W.I., *Supra*, pr. 27 July 1604.

37. Fletcher, Ellen, of Newhall, spinster, I., *Infra*, pr. 15 October 1611.

23. Fletcher, William, of Newhall, W.I., *Supra*, pr. 17 November 1607.

112. Gray, Thomas, of Newhall, yeoman, W.I., *Supra*, pr. 1 December 1640.

53. Gray, Thomas, of Smeatonwood, W.I., *Supra*, pr. 19 March 1616/17.

99. Gray, Thomas, the elder, of Aston in Newhall, clerk, W.I., *Supra*, pr. 3 June 1636.

89. Graye, Margaret, of Wrenbury, spinster, W.I., *Supra*, pr. 28 March 1632.

140. Griffiths, Henry, of Broomhall, clerk, W., *Supra?* (PCC), pr. 18 January 1654/55.

145. Griffiths, Henry, the elder, of Broomhall, gent., W., *Supra* (PCC), pr. 2 July 1658.

142. Hall, George, of Aston, yeoman, W., *Supra?* (PCC), pr. 29 September 1657.

147. Hall, George, jun., of Aston, yeoman, W., *Supra* (PCC), pr. 27 October 1658.

22. Hall, John, of Smeatonwood, yeoman, W.I., *Supra*, pr. 29 October 1606.

100. Hall, John, of Newhall, W.I., *Supra*, pr. 24 June 1636.

83. Hall, Richard, of Smeatonwood, I., C.?, *Supra*, pr. 13 January 1630/31.

121. Hamnett, Edward, the elder, of Aston in Newhall, yeoman, W., *Supra* (PCC), pr. 18 June 1646.

97. Hamnett, Thomas, of the Grange, in Smeatonwood, gent., W.I., *Supra*, pr. 26 October 1635.

76. Hare, Randull, of Chorley, W.I., *Supra,* pr. 20 September 1628.

108. Hare, Thomas, of Chorley, I., *Supra*, pr. 2 June 1639.

2. Hare, William, of Wrenbury, W., pr. ca. 1547.

62. Heighfield, William, of Broomhall, yeoman, W.I., *Supra*, pr. 20 June 1620.

14. Higson, Ellinor, of Newhall, spinster, W., *Infra?*, pr. 9 November 1597.

44. Hockenhull, Roger, of Broomhall, gent., W.I., *Supra,* pr. 10 July 1614.

110. Jones, Roger, of Chorley, W.I., *Supra*, pr. 2 July 1639.

50. Kemp, George, of Smeatonwood, yeoman, W.I., *Infra*, pr. after 2 October 1616.

57. Kempe, Anne, of Smeatonwood, widow, W.I., *Infra*, pr. after 10 May 1619.

133. Lawrence, Ralph, of Newhall, husbandman, I., *Supra*, administration granted 14 June 1649.

32. Lowe, Thomas, of Broomhall, husbandman, I., *Supra*, pr. 9 March 1610/11.

105. Lowe, Thomas, of Sound, husbandman, W., *Infra?*, pr. [ ] 1637.

120. Malkin [Meakin], Ralph, of Newhall, yeoman, W., *Infra?* (PCC), pr. 10 October 1645.

6. Massey, Thomas, of Newhall, W.I., *Infra*, pr. 10 March 1584/85.

5. Massie, John, late Abbot of Combermere, W., *Supra*, pr. 14 February 1564/65.

58. Millington, John, of Broomhall, W.I., *Supra*, pr. 28 July 1619.

143. Palin, Edward, of Smeatonwood, yeoman, W., *Infra* (PCC), pr. 2 October 1657.

71. Palin, Thomas, of Wrenbury Frith, yeoman, W., *Supra*, pr. 6 December 1624.

33. Patrick, William, of Chorley, W.I., *Infra*, pr. 6 June 1611.

15. Patrick alias Wilson, Elizabeth, of Chorley, widow, W.I., *Infra*, pr. 2 January 1597/98.

72. Patricke, John, of Chorley, Nunc. I., *Supra*, pr. 20 June 1626.

4. Pexton, Thomas, of Wrenbury, husbandman, W.I., C., *Infra*, pr. 23 October 1562.

91. Pextonne, Allis, of Newhall, widow, W.I., *Supra*, pr. 4 October 1632.

10. Povall, Randall, of Wrenbury, clerk, W., *Supra?*, pr. [ ] September 1593.

149. Powell, Edward, of Newhall, milliner, W., *Infra* (PCC), pr. 26 May 1659.

86. Ravenscroft, Ellen, of Newhall, widow, W.I., *Supra*, pr. after 11 March 1630/31.

148. Ravenscroft, Frances, W., *Supra* (PCC), pr. 21 January 1658/59.

137. Ravenscroft, John, of Newhall, I., C., *Supra*, pr. 2 July 1650.

43. Ravenscroft, Thomas, of Newhall, W.I., *Supra*, pr. 4 May 1614.

65. Rogers, Richard, of Chorley, I., *Supra*, pr. 25 June 1621.

117. Salmon, Rowland, of Coole Lane, yeoman, W.I., *Supra*, pr. 21 April 1642.

131. Savage, John, of Wrenbury, administration granted 10 November 1648.

116. Savage, Katherine, of Wrenbury, I., *Supra*, administration granted 16 March 1641/42.

124. Savage, Robert, of Wrenbury, yeoman, W.I., *Supra*, pr. 29 October 1647.

27. Seavell, William, of Newhall, W.I., *Infra*, pr. 19 April 1609.

35. Sevell, Margerie, of Newhall, widow, W.I., *Infra*, pr. 11 June 1611.

150. Shrowbridge, Robert, of Royals in Newhall, yeoman, W., *Supra?* (PCC), pr. 8 June 1659.

114. Shrowbridge, Robert, the younger, of Royals, yeoman, W.I., *Supra*, pr. [October?] 1641.

75. Shrowbridge, Thomas, of Newhall, yeoman, Nunc. I., *Supra*, pr. 10 March 1626/27.

130. Sproston, Randle, of Newhall, husbandman, W.I., *Supra*, pr. 24 October 1648.
69. Starkey, Arthur, esq., of Wrenbury, Nunc. I., *Supra*, pr. 25 April 1623.
38. Starkie, Lawrence, of Wrenbury, gent., I., *Infra*, pr. 16 January 1611/12.
73. Starkie, Randle, of Wrenbury, gent., W.I., *Supra*, pr. 8 February 1626/27.
1. Starkye, John, esq., of Wrenbury, W.I., *Supra*, pr. 1542/43.
31. Swane, Alles, of Wrenbury, widow, W.I., *Infra*, pr. September 1610.
30. Swann, Roger, of Dodds Greene (Newhall), husbandman, W.I., *Supra*, pr. 12 September 1610.
63. Taylor, William, of Chorley, I., *Infra*, pr. 28 October 1620.
134. Taylor, William, of Smeatonwood, husbandman, W.I., *Supra*, pr. 29 June 1649.
107. Tench, George, of Smeatonwood, yeoman, W.I., *Supra*, pr. 11 May 1639.
129. Tench, George, of Wrenbury, W.I., *Supra*, pr. 14 October 1648.
26. Tenche, John, of Wrenbury Frith, I., *Infra*, pr. 15 October 1608.
11. Tenche, Robert, of Newhall, W.I, *Supra?*, pr. 20 April 1594.
45. Tenche, Robert, of Wrenbury Frith, yeoman, W.I., *Supra*, pr. 23 August 1615.
92. Tudman, Robert, of Newhall, yeoman, W.I., *Supra*, pr. 13 December 1632.
151. Twisse, Ralph, of Wrenbury Frith, yeoman, W., *Supra?* (PCC), pr. 25 June 1659.
25. Vernon, Henry, of Coole Lane in the parish of Wrenbury, W.I., *Supra*, pr. 9 May 1608.
95. Wade, Robert, of Wrenbury Frith, yeoman, W.I., *Supra*, pr. 7 February 1633/34.
34. Whitney, Hugh, of Coole, gent., I., *Supra*, pr. 11 June 1611.
51. Whitney, Mary, of Coole, widow, I., *Supra*, pr. 25 October 1616.
54. Whitney, Michael, of Newhall, husbandman, I., *Supra*, pr. [ ] 1617.
68. Whittingham, Edward, of Broomhall, W.I., *Supra*, pr. 25 September 1622.
77. Wicksteed, William, sen., of Wrenbury Frith, gent., W.I., *Supra*, pr. 10 June 1629.
78. Wicksteed, William, jun., of Wrenbury Frith, gent., W.I., *Supra*, pr. 10 June 1629.
46. Wilkinson, John, of Wrenbury, husbandman, W.I., *Infra*, pr. 29 September 1615.
16. Wilson, Humphrey, of Chorley, W.I., *Supra*, pr. 27 November 1602.
109. Wilson, William, of Wrenbury Frith, gent., W.I., *Supra*, pr. 8 June 1639.
138. Wood, Thomas, of Newhall, (PCC), administration granted 31 August 1653.
7. Woodfaine, John, of Wrenbury, W.I., *Supra*, pr. 30 November 1588.
118. Woodfen, John, of Chorley, yeoman, I., *Supra*, administration granted 19 January 1642/43.
98. Woollam, Gilbert, of Wrenbury Frith, yeoman, W.I., *Supra*, pr. 14 February 1635/36.
123. Woolrich, Valentine, of Wrenbury Frith, yeoman, W.I., *Supra*, pr. 21 October 1647.
79. Wright, John, of Newhall, I., *Supra*, pr. 27 June 1629.

INDEX OF WILLS AND OTHER PROBATE INSTRUMENTS

1. John Starkye, esq., of Wrenbury — Pr. 1542/43
2. William Hare of Wrenbury — Pr. ca. 1547
3. Thomas Chessewes of Mickley Hall, yeoman — Pr. 1562
4. Thomas Pexton of Wrenbury, husbandman — Pr. 23 October 1562
5. John Massie, clerk, late Abbot of Combermere — Pr. 14 February 1564/65
6. Thomas Massey of Newhall — Pr. 10 March 1584/85
7. John Woodfaine of Wrenbury — Pr. 30 November 1588
8. Ellen Bebbington of Chorley, widow — Pr. 1 August 1592
9. William Bebbington of Chorley — Pr. 7 October 1592
10. Randall Povall of Wrenbury, clerk — Pr. [ ] September 1593
11. Robert Tench of Newhall — Pr. 20 April 1594
12. Humphrey Bickerton of Wrenbury Frith, husbandman — Pr. 28 June 1594
13. Raffe Barnett of Newhall — Pr. 14 October 1595
14. Ellinor Higson of Newhall, spinster — Pr. 9 November 1597
15. Elizabeth Patrick alias Wilson of Chorley, widow — Pr. 2 January 1597/98
16. Humphrey Wilson of Chorley — Pr. 27 November 1602
17. Ellen Flavell of Chorley, widow — Pr. 27 July 1604
18. John Cartwright the elder of Aston — Pr. 24 November 1604
19. Elizabeth Cooke of Wrenbury Frith, spinster — Pr. 7 February 1604/05
20. Alice Blackamore of Wrenbury Frith, widow — Pr. 23 February 1604/05
21. Roger Broome of Chorley, yeoman — Pr. 12 August 1606
22. John Hall of Smeatonwood, yeoman — Pr. 29 October 1606
23. William Fletcher of Newhall — Pr. 17 November 1607
24. Robert Buckley of Smeatonwood, yeoman — Pr. 3 February 1607/08
25. Henry Vernon of Coole Lane, in the parish of Wrenbury — Pr. 9 May 1608
26. John Tenche of Wrenbury Frith — Pr. 15 October 1608
27. William Seavell of Newhall — Pr. 19 April 1609
28. Margaret Ankers of Broomhall, widow — Pr. 13 March 1609/10
29. James Barnett of Aston, yeoman — Pr. 21 August 1610
30. Roger Swann of Dodds Green, Newhall, husbandman — Pr. 12 September 1610
31. Alles Swane of Wrenbury, widow — Pr. September 1610
32. Thomas Lowe of Broomhall, husbandman — Pr. 9 March 1610/11
33. William Patrick of Chorley — Pr. 6 June 1611
34. Hugh Whitney of Coole, gent. — Pr. 11 June 1611
35. Margerie Sevell of Newhall, widow — Pr. 11 June 1611
36. William Davies of Wrenbury — Pr. 1 August 1611
37. Ellen Fletcher of Newhall, spinster — Pr. 15 October 1611
38. Lawrence Starkie of Wrenbury, gent. — Pr. 16 January 1611/12
39. John Bickerton, the son of Edmund Bickerton of Sound — Pr. 27 January 1611/12

40. Randull Cowper of Wrenbury, husbandman   Pr. 9 April 1613
41. Edward Baskerville of Sound   Pr. 10 June 1613
42. William Cooper of Sound, yeoman   Pr. 15 July 1613
43. Thomas Ravenscroft of Newhall   Pr. 4 May 1614
44. Roger Hockenhull of Broomhall, gent.   Pr. 10 July 1614
45. Robert Tenche of Wrenbury Frith, yeoman   Pr. 23 August 1615
46. John Wilkinson of Wrenbury, husbandman   Pr. 29 September 1615
47. Thomas Faulkner of Chorley, yeoman   Pr. 9 November 1615
48. John Bickerton of Newhall, yeoman   Pr. 15 June 1616
49. Anne Bickerton of Broomhall, widow   Pr. 19 September 1616
50. George Kemp of Smeatonwood, yeoman   Pr. after 2 October 1616
51. Mary Whitney of Coole, widow   Pr. 25 October 1616
52. William Barnett of Wrenbury. yeoman   Pr. 1 February 1616/17
53. Thomas Gray of Smeatonwood   Pr. 19 March 1616/17
54. Michael Whitney of Newhall, husbandman   Pr. [ ] 1617
55. Elizabeth Baskerville of Sound, widow   Pr. 17 May 1617
56. Edmond Bickerton of Sound, yeoman   Pr. 10 July 1617
57. Anne Kempe of Smeatonwood, widow   Pr. after 10 May 1619
58. John Millington of Broomhall   Pr. 28 July 1619
59. Phillip Dodd of Wrenbury   Pr. [ ] 1619
60. Richard Berrington of Wrenbury   Pr. after 9 March 1619/20
61. John Backhouse of Newhall   Pr. 1 June 1620
62. William Heighfield of Broomhall, yeoman   Pr. 20 June 1620
63. William Taylor of Chorley   Pr. 28 October 1620
64. William Brees of Broomhall, yeoman   Pr. 25 May 1621
65. Richard Rogers of Chorley   Pr. 25 June 1621
66. James Brooke of Aston, yeoman   Pr. 15 May 1622
67. John Egerton of (Eagle Hall) Newhall, gent.   Pr. 1622
68. Edward Whittingham of Broomhall   Pr. 25 September 1622
69. Arthur Starkey, esq., of Wrenbury   Pr. 25 April 1623
70. George Cudworth of Newhall, gent.   Pr. 2 October 1624
71. Thomas Palin of Wrenbury Frith, yeoman   Pr. 6 December 1624
72. John Patricke of Chorley   Pr. 20 June 1626
73. Randle Starkie of Wrenbury, gent.   Pr. 8 February 1626/27
74. George Dickins of Newhall   Pr. 8 March 1626/27
75. Thomas Shrowbridge of Newhall, yeoman   Pr. 10 March 1626/27
76. Randull Hare of Chorley, yeoman   Pr. 20 September 1628
77. William Wicksteed, sen., of Wrenbury Frith, gent.   Pr. 10 June 1629
78. William Wicksteed, jun., of Wrenbury Frith, gent.   Pr. 10 June 1629
79. John Wright of Newhall   Pr. 27 June 1629
80. Oliver Briscoe of Wrenbury, husbandman   Pr. 15 May 1630
81. John Cartwright of Aston in Newhall, gent.   Pr. 16 October 1630
82. John Bromhall of Sound, yeoman   Pr. 1 November 1630
83. Richard Hall of Smeatonwood   Pr. 13 January 1630/31
84. Timothy Buckley of Smeatonwood, gent.   Pr. 10 March 1630/31

85. William Babington of Chorley, gent.   Pr. 1630/31
86. Ellen Ravenscroft of Newhall, widow   Pr. after 11 March 1630/31
87. Emma Barnett of Wrenbury, widow   Pr. 24 October 1631
88. John Cartwright of Sheppenhall, gent.   Pr. 15 November 1631
89. Margaret Graye of Wrenbury, spinster   Pr. 28 March 1632
90. Edmund Crewe of Newhall, yeoman   Pr. 4 September 1632
91. Allis Pextonne of Newhall, widow   Pr. 4 October 1632
92. Robert Tudman of Newhall, yeoman   Pr. 13 December 1632
93. Richard Cheswis of Wrenbury Frith, husbandman   Pr. 10 April 1633
94. John Barnett of Aston, yeoman   Pr. after 26 October 1633
95. Robert Wade of Wrenbury Frith, yeoman   Pr. 7 February 1633/34
96. John Cartwright of Sheppenhall, gent.   Pr. 28 August 1635
97. Thomas Hamnett of the Grange (in Smeatonwood), gent. Pr. 26 October 1635
98. Gilbert Woollam of Wrenbury Frith, yeoman   Pr. 14 February 1635/36
99. Thomas Gray the elder of Aston in Newhall, clerk   Pr. 3 June 1636
100. John Hall of Newhall   Pr. 24 June 1636
101. Richard Dodd of Smeatonwood, yeoman   Pr. 20 July 1637
102. John Edgeley of Woodcott, yeoman   Pr. 26 July 1637
103. Elizabeth Briscoe of Wrenbury, widow   Pr. after 19 July 1637
104. William Cooper the elder of Sound, yeoman   Pr. after 13 October 1637
105. Thomas Lowe of Sound, husbandman   Pr. [ ] 1637
106. Edward Bowdon of Chorley   Pr. 18 April 1638
107. George Tench of Smeatonwood, yeoman   Pr. 11 May 1639
108. Thomas Hare of Chorley   Pr. 2 June 1639
109. William Wilson of Wrenbury Frith, gent.   Pr. 8 June 1639
110. Roger Jones of Chorley   Pr. 2 July 1639
111. Andrew Cotton of Combermere, gent.   Pr. 21 October 1640
112. Thomas Gray of Newhall, yeoman   Pr. 1 December 1640
113. Joane Crewe of Newhall, widow   Pr. 8 April 1641
114. Robert Shrowbridge the younger of Royals, yeoman   Pr. [October?] 1641
115. John Anckers of Broomhall, yeoman   Pr. 24 January 1641/42
116. Katherine Savage of Wrenbury   Admin. granted 16 March 1641/42
117. Rowland Salmon of Coole Lane, yeoman   Pr. 21 April 1642
118. John Woodfen of Chorley, yeoman   Admin. granted 19 January 1642/43

119. Richard Culliner alias Comber of Wrenbury Frith, labourer   Pr. 29 October 1644
120. Ralph Malkin [Meakin] of Newhall, yeoman   Pr. 10 October 1645
121. Edward Hamnett the elder of Aston in Newhall, yeoman   Pr. 18 June 1646
122. Dorothy Cotton of Combermere, spinster   Pr. 5 June 1647
123. Valentine Woolrich of Wrenbury Frith, yeoman   Pr. 26 October 1647
124. Robert Savage of Wrenbury, yeoman   Pr. 29 October 1647
125. Richard Barnett of Aston in Newhall, yeoman   Pr. 18 January 1647/48

126. Elizabeth Cotton of Combermere, widow — Pr. 29 July 1648

127. John Cheswis of Mickley, gent. — Pr. 28 August 1648

128. George Cotton, esq., of Combermere — Pr. 21 September 1648

129. George Tench of Wrenbury — Pr. 14 October 1648

130. Randle Sproston of Newhall, husbandman — Pr. 24 October 1648

131. John Savage of Wrenbury — Admin. granted 10 November 1648

132. Alice Buckley of Wrenbury, spinster — Pr. 28 April 1649[8?]

133. Ralph Lawrence of Newhall, husbandman — Admin. granted 14 June 1649

134. William Taylor of Smeatonwood, husbandman — Pr. 29 June 1649

135. George Barnett of Sound — Admin. granted 8 February 1649/50

136. Margaret Cheswys of Wrenbury Frith, widow — Admin. granted 5 March 1649/50

137. John Ravenscroft of Newhall — Pr. 2 July 1650

138. Thomas Wood of Newhall — Admin. granted 31 August 1653

139. John Edgeley of Moorehall, yeoman — Pr. 13 August 1654

140. Henry Griffiths of Broomhall, clerk — Pr. 18 January 1654/55

141. Thomas Brees of Broomhall, yeoman — Pr. 8 March 1655/56

142. George Hall of Aston, yeoman — Pr. 29 September 1657

143. Edward Palin of Smeatonwood, yeoman — Pr. 2 October 1657

144. Jane Edgeley of Moorehall in Newhall, widow — Pr. 5 January 1657/58

145. Henry Griffiths the elder of Broomhall, gent. — Pr. 2 July 1658

146. Robert Davies of Combermere, yeoman — Pr. 20 October 1658

147. George Hall, jun., of Aston, yeoman — Pr. 27 October 1658

148. Frances Ravenscroft, widow — Pr. 21 January 1658/59

149. Edward Powell of Newhall, milliner — Pr. 26 May 1659

150. Robert Shrowbridge of Royals in Newhall, yeoman — Pr. 8 June 1659

151. Ralph Twisse of Wrenbury Frith, yeoman — Pr. 25 June 1659

152. James Clark of Sound, yeoman — Pr. 16 July 1660

153. Richard Edgeley of Smeatonwood — Pr. 10 January 1660/61

1. JOHN STARKYE, ESQ., OF WRENBURY

S. Pr. 1542/43
W.T. 16 [ ] 1542/43

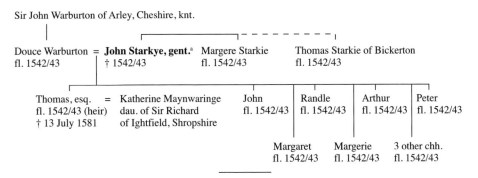

Sir John Warburton of Arley, Cheshire, knt.

Douce Warburton = **John Starkye, gent.**[a] Margere Starkie Thomas Starkie of Bickerton
fl. 1542/43   † 1542/43   fl. 1542/43   fl. 1542/43

Thomas, esq. = Katherine Maynwaringe John Randle Arthur Peter
fl. 1542/43 (heir) dau. of Sir Richard fl. 1542/43 fl. 1542/43 fl. 1542/43 fl. 1542/43
† 13 July 1581 of Ightfield, Shropshire

Margaret Margerie 3 other chh.
fl. 1542/43 fl. 1542/43 fl. 1542/43

Will, 'of gud health'.

I give my soule unto almyghtye god my creator and redeemer & ladie saynt Mare & to ye celestiall company of heaven *my bodie to be buried within ye chancell or cherch of Wrenbury* Item I geev for my mortuarie according to ye kings graces statuts Item I will yt my sonne & here shall have for ye *mone* of his year *[heir]* lombes first the hall hangyngs bords & forms Item in ye parlor 2 beds one cupbord all coffres except one of my wifes Item my best gowne my best jacket & my best dublet my payr of hossens 8 silver spones with knoxtts one silver salt set a cover one of my best bord clothes 4 napkens one gret pott or panne one godyche the leydl in ye coyrkr ye best broche with one parre of gobbarch ye best weyne one bull one bore one ploughe one harrow one aumare *[ambry]* in ye seller over ye parlere one horse my best sword my best bowe with all my arrows & harnes also all manor of tymbr with all others ordened for occupacions. Also I will yt John Starky my yonger sone have my second sword ye residue of my apparell I will shalbe devided emongest my yongest children & I will yt my detts & saverals be payed & mad of all ye rest of my goods and cattels which payed so done & that ye residue of my goods & cattels be devided in thre parts by my executors & over sears whereof I will yt my wife shall have ye one parte & all my children except myn here another parte & yt my executors shal have ye other parte and yt to be devided by my executors or overseers imongest my yonger children . . . & I will yt my executors have all ye ordenearie cost over my whole goods as well as ye probacion of this my testament as all other reasonable causes . . .

---

[a] The names of John Starkye's children are given in Glover, *Visitations of 1566 and 1580,* p. 219; cf. also St George, *Visitation of 1613*, pp. 226–7. A 'Pedigree of the Starkey Family from the 15th Century to 1663' is found in CRO DDX/16.

Executors: Thomas Starky of Bickerton, Sir John Tench capleyn & Thomas Cheswisse.

Overseers: Thomas *[surname omitted]* esquire & Thomas Maystersonne of Nantwich, gent.

Witnesses: Thomas Maistersonne of Nantwich, gentilman, Sir John Tench chaplen with others John Desley, David Hoffeld.

Debts yt I John Starkie ougheth:

to Mary Starkie my sister} 40 marks
to Hankyn Yure of Minshull Vernon}

Which I have receved of 2 yeres rente}   £8   13s   4d
For the rent of twentie akarreas [acres]

These are ye detts expencis & debts payed of us Thomas Starkie Thomas Chewise & Sir John Tench executors of ye testament & last will of John Starkie of Wrenbury esquire decessed frome ye first daye of December anno domini 1592 *[sic]* unto ye 17th June anno domini 1550.

	£	s	d
For ye probacion of ye testament & our costs	11	10	0
To ye vicar of Acton for ye mortuare	3	4	0
To Richard Shrowebridge for debts		8	0
For ye reparlyng *[sic]* of Margaret Starkie & bryng hir To my Ladie Tervell	23	11	0
Alis Gryndley Katherin Fleccher Raf June Randull Garrett John Sewell Annis Harper Anne Hurleton Richard Starkie Katrin Slare Thomas Barnet & Rauff Westbroke for ye Severall Wagis as hit appereth by ye particulers	34	3	0
To Mr Vicare of Acton for 2 tithe clues	6	8	0
To Sir Richard Manwering for ye bord of Thomas Starkie	13	4	0
To ye buttler for 2 peyre of showes a purse & a girdell		13	0
Ye coste of Thomas Starkie 2 tymes to London & twise to Chester with chargis [be]longinge to same	3	11	4
to William Manwering of Eightfield		35	0
To Edward Smith for Thomas Rynshawe		10	0
Costs thes tymes yt we had witacōns [visitations] & agreed with Roger Brok & his wife		4	8
To Randull June	8	13	3
To Mr Dolten gold silver goods	11	0	0
To Margaret Starkie	26	16	0
More to Margaret Starkie	2	0	0

To Thomas Shrowbridg for his wages	5	0
Funerall expensis	30	0
To Randull Venables for his pene	3	4
To David Molocke	6	0
More to Edward Twise for Thomas Renshawe	6	8
To Alis Renshaw for dett		22
To Edward Janyon	25	0
To William Starkie	3	4
A cupbord	3	4
To David Hoffeld for det	8	0
To Thomas Dod for det	13	4
To Thomas Barnet		22
Ye repariling of Margery Starkie	39	7

To my sonne Thomas Starkie for his heirloms	16	8	0
Spend sence candilmas was twelmoneth labour			
Or visitations & other business		11	7
Ye costs of aniversarie 5 yeres		8	0
For meyt drynke & cloths for Thomas Starkie & Maria			
Starkie 5 yeres	11	0	0
To Robert Woodward for dets		3	0

Summa totalis	93	13	6
[*recte*	260	334	103]

Inventory: John Starkie of Wrenbury, esq.

Taken: 2 January 1542/43

Prisers: John Bromall Edward Bikerton John Hampnet & John Edgley.

	£	s	d
apparell 3 sheats one peticote one bonete		9	0
one velvet coyffe one Saten quoffe price			4
one Dublet of blake sarcenet one of white fustian one			
of canvis		7	4
one jacket of blake Satten one of valans one of blak cloth		20	0
one gowne of cherabet one gaberdine of medley color			
garded with velvet	4	0	0
3 payre of hossen 3 payre of shoes one clocke of marbull		10	0
in silver		4	4
2 swords one buclere one dagar price		10	0
4 sallets 4 rackes one payre of splentes		40	0
2 polloxes 2 billes one payre of brickyudars		28	4
four bowes two chefes of arrowes		11	8
one grete bord in ye hall 2 forms one screne		5	0
3 bord cloths 9 napkens 3 towels		4	0
sixteen brod arrowes eleven shaftes		4	0
one bassen of masslen one yewer of pewter one pewter bassen		4	0

	£	s	d
ye hengyngs in ye hall 6 coveryngs of carpet for cusshyns		13	4
in ye parloure one fether bed price		10	0
2 blankets 2 payre of canvers shetes		6	8
one bed coveryng one coverlet one twell schete		6	8
saye & paynted clothes to heng about ye bed		3	4
2 coffers one cubbard 2 bedcases 2 littill formes		16	0
one matres 2 bolsters 4 pillowes		17	0
3 coveryngs for beds 2 blankets price		13	8
2 coverlettes 3 bedcases pented clothes to hang to bed with		12	0
one armare 2 formes price		6	0
one grete potte 3 smale pottes one possenet		33	4
2 panes 2 skelletes price		5	0
3 brochis one payre of gobbarts		4	0
3 dreping pannes one brendreth one frieng pan		3	0
2 chaffing dishes 2 pott hengulles with one rod of iron		4	0
foure chandellers one videor [?] 9 chargers		13	4
9 pottynggers 6 facers 8 conterfettes		5	0
2 salts 3 pipes 2 barrels one coffer		4	0
2 combes 8 storindes with bastying dishes with other trene ware		12	0
one tun of salt fleshe in ye price		16	0
2 twill schetes one blanket one bedcase		3	0
one coverlet one under cloth one twill shete 7 bedcases		10	0
Glerio [?] tymber price		3	0
2 payre of plughe irons price		2	0
4 chenes 2 cope souls one turwich		4	0
2 Spades one mattock			16
3 naugars one boye 2 chessels		14	0
a payre of pincorr one spoycks schayff *[spoke shave]* one wimble one how			8
one hatchat one axe one nele parsell			8
chese & butter		10	0
2 yrons boynde waynes with bodies & exenayalls *[externals?]*		33	4
2 mucke tumbrels 2 forkes with one payre of other weylls		6	0
4 plowes price		20	0
9 yocke price		4	6
Tymber for carts & plowes		2	4
2 harrowes price			16
whette price		25	0
Rie		40	0
barlie		40	0
ottes		35	0
heye in ye oxe house price		20	0
heye in ye house price		40	0
3 fatte oxen	4	0	0

13 drought oxen		21	0	0
18 kyne		21	0	
4 twynter besse price	20 Marks (=		260	80)
5 heffers in caulfes		3	16	0
10 stirks price	5 Marks (=		65	20)
10 caullfes price			40	0
11 capulles price		6	0	0
2 stacks in heye price			5	0
Sayd bords & other tymbr			10	0
On coffer one grid iron one cresset price				12
[Sum		38	1081	238]

Endorsement: None but the year 1542.

2. WILLIAM HARE OF WRENBURY

Pr. ca. 1547

William Hare = [   ]
† ca. 1547

Ralph Hare
fl. ca. 1547 (executor)

Rondell Hare = Elizabeth [   ]
† 1606 *senex* | † 1602 *anus*

Randull Hare = Elizabeth [   ]   William Hare = Ellen Manninge
1593-1626/27   † 1633   fl. 1597-1628   md. 1597
† 1628[a]

a. See the will of Randull Hare, pr. 1628. The correspondence of the names William and Ralph/Randull leaves little doubt that we are dealing with the same family, and that the William and Randull Hare who flourished in Wrenbury chapelry after 1593/97 are direct descendants either of William Hare (ca. 1547) or an unknown brother. The Rondull Hare *senex* who died in 1606 could conceivably be the same as the executor of William Hare's estate in 1547, but that would make him seventy-nine years of age in 1606 at the youngest: this is itself not implausible.

Will: near death.

[NOTE: document frayed to varying degrees down left hand side]

... George Wilmesley, Bachelor of Laws, for deciding ecclesiastical causes ... of
our Lord Henry the eighth by the grace of God of England, France and Ireland ...
under Christ Supreme Head, upheld, by the Reverend Father in Christ and Lord
...Vicar General in Spirituals and Official Principal of his Consistory Court or your
[Commissioner?] ... of the honest persons Philip Grey and James Rowe
Churchwardens of the Church ... [Ralph] Hare of the said parish and William
Belingham of the parish of Rostherne, executors ... and of your Jurisdiction, and
also who and whosoever other is before you for the same ... in these writings pro-
pounds in law jointly and severally and articulately as follows

[paragraph] ... last wills and of whatsoever of the deceased, by a fraud, deceit,
spite or malice ... justice they hinder, to be hindered or they provide that they
ought not to distribute ... and in/to/by injuries [according to] canonical sanctions
duly revised and corrected

[paragraph] ... near death, of sound mind and memory, rightly and lawfully composed his ... will in the presence of trustworthy witnesses in which a certain testament or last ... his ... and he has named, ordered, appointed William Belingham his
true and lawful ... he sets out jointly and severally and concerning whatsoever.

[paragraph] ... the said William Hare before a competent Ordinary to have proved,
approved and brought in ... in writings [they] have received and held, sworn in
due form of law, and the selfsame executors of the said testator and justly exe-
cuting and implementing the last will of the same deceased [they] have sworn and
taken the corporal oath; and he says as above.

[paragraph] ... whilst he lived, to pay the debts and legacies of the same deceased
and to implement ... notably have reached or at least are to reach the hands of the
said executors.

[paragraph] ... deceased in his aforesaid testament has bequeathed, left and given
to the parochial Church of Wrenbury aforesaid ... of his goods to pay as in the
content of his testament or last will has been made manifestly clear to which the
party of the said Philip Grey and James Rowe, Churchwardens of the same Church
relates as far as ... in manner. And he posits as above.

[paragraph] ... of William Hare deceased to hand over and release to the aforesaid Churchwardens, in law and in the name of the said ... he bequeaths six shillings
and eight pence on behalf of and on the part of the said Churchwardens ... were
... and appealed to. And he states as above.

[paragraph] ... [Ralph Hare and William] Belingham executors abovesaid thus as
before related it is premissed, requested and appealed ... [they] were willing to hand

over and release to the said Churchwardens (as they are bound to) but have express-
ly refused ... [they] have delayed and delay in the present in grave peril of their
souls and of other ... of the said Churchwardens and parishioners of Wrenbury, no
small injustice & grievous

[paragraph] ... William Belingham executors aforesaid were and are of the
Archdeaconry of Chester in the diocese of Chester ... [by reason of which they
are] under and subject to [our jurisdiction], and he states as above.

[paragraph] [That all and singular the premises] were and are true, public, notoriously manifest and reputed and of and concerning the same in the parish ... in
public [places] to the same neighbourhoods and surrounding areas, public voice
and fame has worried and in the present are worrying. [Whereof with the proof
lawfully] required in this regard having been made, the party of Philip Grey and
James Rowe pray right and the fullness of justice [to be done and ministered to
him and his party], and the aforesaid Ralph Hare and William Belingham to hold
and pay [to the parochial church] of Wrenbury aforesaid as in the content of the
testament of the said William Hare is declared and contained ... and in like manner to be canonically forced and compelled to payment transfer and release. And
also in expenses [in lawful expenses] of the said Philip & James in this part made
and being declared to be made over and above to be condemned. And ... to force
and compel with effect by you and your definitive sentence or final [decree] ...
aforesaid, and furthermore to be done, established and decreed in the premises
and those concerning whatsoever in them [shall have been of law and reason,
which premises] the party of the said Philip Grey and James Rowe [propounds]
and prays to be done jointly and severally, not obliging himself to [proving all
and singular the premises nor] to the burden of a superfluous proof, concerning
which he protests, but in so far as he shall have proved in the premises [so far as
he may obtain in the petitions], saving always the benefit [of law] in all things,
humbly imploring, O wise Judge aforesaid, ... to correct, revise and emend this
libel for a fitting and suitable place, time & cause agreeable and opportune.

Executors: Ralph Hare and William Belingham.

3. THOMAS CHESSEWES OF (MICKLEY HALL) WRENBURY, YEOMAN

Pr. 1562
W.T. 18 August 1561

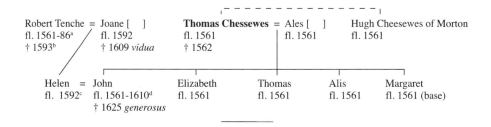

Robert Tenche = Joane [   ]   **Thomas Chessewes** = Ales [   ]   Hugh Cheesewes of Morton
fl. 1561-86[a]   fl. 1592   fl. 1561   fl. 1561   fl. 1561
† 1593[b]   † 1609 *vidua*   † 1562

Helen = John   Elizabeth   Thomas   Alis   Margaret
fl. 1592[c]   fl. 1561-1610[d]   fl. 1561   fl. 1561   fl. 1561   fl. 1561 (base)
† 1625 *generosus*

Will, sick.

First I bequeath my soule to almyghtie god my creature & redemer & *my bodie to be buried in ye church of Wrenbury in ye forme which belongith to my house* Item I geve to ye wardens of ye said church for my buriall & to be prayed for toward ye repairs of ye said church 6s. 8d. Item I geve to Elisabeth Chessewes my dowghter over & besyde hir childs parte of goods £30 [?] yer is in ye hand of Richard Wright of ye Bell in Nantwich £15 due to be payed at ye tyme it Is asket Also in the hand of Richard Stanley of ye parishe of Bunbury £14 due at ye feast of Saynt Mychell Tharchangell next Insuing the date here of Also in ye hands of Ellin Fisher 20s. due at ye present tyme Item I gieve to Ales Chessewes my dowghter over & besyde hir childs parte of goods £20 Item I gieve to Thomas Chessewes my sonne over & besyde his childs parte of goods £110 of ye which £30 remenethe in ye hands of Rauf Pagets £5 due to be payed at ye feast of Saynt Mychell Tharchangell next Insuing ye date hereof Item it is due at this present tyme in ye hands of John Twise servant to Mayself Personally 20s. Item in ye hands of Nicolas Goldsmyth 20s. Item In ye hands of Hugh Griffyn 53s. 4d. Item In ye hands of Roger Walthall gentilman for ye hynmost payment for ye marriage of my sone John Chessewes £3 6s. 8d. & ye rest to be mad of my whole goods Item I geve to Margeret Chessewes my base daughter 40s. Item I gieve to Ales Cheswes my wiffe ye third parte of all my lands duryinge hir naturall life & lyvyng sole & if she marrye then there I will my sone John Chessewes shall paye to hir 40s. yerely durying hir naturall life in ~~mon~~ money in ye name of hir

[a]   Noted as juror on CRO Newhall Manor Court Roll, 1586.
[b]   See will of Robert Tench, pr. 1594 (will no. 11).
[c]   See will of Robert Tench, pr. 1594.
[d]   Fl. 1595 at Mickley Hall, Newhall (CRO Newhall Manor Court Rolls); 1610, churchwarden at Wrenbury.

Joynt & dowrie & she to be excluded from any parte of my lands durying hir lyff
Item I will my wiff shall have ye house yt I dwell in with thapurnancs & ye cotage
in Broomhall which ye Widowe Poole dwelleth in with all ye ground yerto longy-
ing if she live sole durying ye minoritie of my dare *[i.e. daughter]* & also yt my
wife & my yonger cheldren not married shall occupie ye parte of ye Newhall parcel with Raffe Tenche*[&]* Robert Tenche as I have done in my tyme to all pro-
fyts to them ~ ~ ~ ~ ~ ~ ~ ~ ~ ~ ~

Item I geve to Thomas Chessewes my yonger sone 13s. 9d. to be payed to hyme
yerely durying his naturall lif if my lease do Indure soe long out of my parte of ye
Newhall parcel be my wif or John Chessewes my sone or whether of them it shall
thanc to have ye occupacion yerof & for lack of payment at ye tyme there usuall
yt is to saye at ye feast of Saynt Mychell Tharchangell & thanunciacion of our ladye
to enter into ye on half of my parte & occupie it durying her naturall liff if my lease
Indure so long Item I will my wiff shall take & receve of my tenement in there unto
yerely 20s. in parte of of *[sic!]* hir third parte of my lands & the rest to be made
out of my other lands acordyng to right & justice Item I gieve to Ales Chessewes
my wife all my sheepe Item I will my wife shall have ye orderyeng of my children
not married & there goods tyll ye be married or tyme discresion to order them there
selfs Item If chance any of my thre chyldren not married to die under ye age of 21
yeres not married then ye parte of goods of yt child so daying so daying *[sic!]* to
remene to ye other twone not married or to which of them is not married & so to
ye longest lives of the thre Item I gieve to John Chessewes my sone on gret pote
& all my harness yt is to saye on bow on shev of arrowes 2 racks one longe sword
on shorte sword with own bucler and sallet on stoole on payer of splenets on
bevylling bill on glese bill one morris pike with all boy[r]eds & bed casis in my
house except one bed case for my wiff & boirds to make 2 coffers for my 2 doughters
Item I gieve one hyve of bees/ The residue of my goods both movable & not movable my debts & funerall expensis beyng payed I gieve & bequieth to Ales Chessewes
my wiff Thomas Chewes my sone Elisabeth & Alis my doughters equally to be
devidid ye on half to my wiff & ye other to my sayd children.

Executors: Richard Stanley of Bunbury parish, in the county of Chester, yeoman,
and Thomas Brester of Broomhall in the same county husbandman.

Overseers: John Newton of Coole Lane & Rauf Paget of A[?] gentilman.

Witnesses: John Tenche Clerk William [ ]esons
James Griffiin Homfrie Bynse with others.

Detts owing to the Testator:

	£	s	d
the good Wiff Bolton & Randull her sone		8	4
Item Hugh Chessewes of Morton	6	0	8
[Sum	6	8	12]

Endorsement: Date 1562 only.

4. THOMAS PEXTON[a] OF WRENBURY, HUSBANDMAN

C.(I).Pr. 23 October 1562
W.T. 5 June 1562

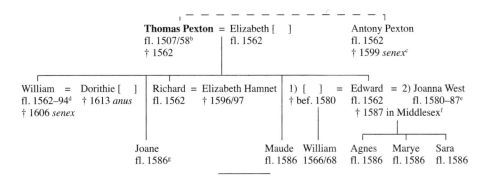

Will, sicke in bodye.

First I bequeth my soule to almyghtye god, my creator and redemer, and *my bodye to be buryed in the churche yard of Wrenbury,* Item, I Wyl my moveable goodes shalbe devydet in to thre parts, Wherof I Wyl on part to bryng me hoyme, pey

[a]   Indexed at CRO as *PIXTON*, following William Fergusson Irvine, *Index of Wills*, RSLC, xxxiii (1896) p. 67, but the spelling is clearly *PEXTON* on the wrapper and in the text of the will itself. Its being included in the Diocesan Registry wills indicates that it was a contested will, but the details of that contesting are no longer evident. An early attempt to reconstitute the Pexton family at Wrenbury is found in: Paul B. Pixton, 'Wrenbury, Cheshire, and the Pixton Family', *Journal of the South Cheshire Family History Society* (Crewe, Cheshire), 19 (Spring 1995), pp. 13–20; 20 (Summer 1995), pp. 15–23; 22 (Winter 1995) pp. 11–14.

[b]   TNA Ches 15/1/127: a Bill of Debt brought by Thomas *Pexstons* of co. Chester and his wife, Elizabeth, against Roger Parleby, for 35s. The dating is uncertain – during the reigns of Henry VIII, Edward VI or Mary Tudor, though the last decade of that time-frame seems most reasonable.

[c]   Wrenbury Parish Registers – Burials: 18 June 1599 *Antoine* Pexton *senex*. Unless otherwise stated, all baptisms, marriages and burials hereafter will have reference to Wrenbury Parish Registers.

[d]   Appears as a witness for the will of Humphrey Bickerton, pr. 1594 (will no. 12).

[e]   Edward Pexton obtained a licence to marry Joanna West of St Martin le Grand parish, at St Leonard's parish church, Westminster, on 20 March 1580/81; see George J. Armytrage, ed., *Allegations for Marriage Licences Issued by the Dean and Chapter of Westminster 1558–1699*, Harleian Society Publications, 23 (1886), p. 7.

[f]   See S.A. Smith, comp., *Index of Wills Proved in the Prerogative Court of Canterbury*, vol. 4: 1584–1604, The Index Library, 25 (London 1901; repr. 1968), p. 321: will of Edward Peckstons of Harringay parish, Middlesex, pr. 1587: '10s. for the repair of the church roof at Wrenbury where I was born'.

[g]   The names of Edward's sisters, Joane and Maude, as well as his children, derive from Edward's will.

my detts and my bequethes, and the rest of that parte, yf any be over, to William
Pexton, my sonne, Item, I gyve of this parte to Antony Pexton, on coffer and 10s.
in sylver, Item, Where yt was covenantet at the makyng up of my sonne Rychard
Pexton to his wyff that John Hampnet shuld gyve with his doghter to hym fyve
marks, and that I shuld gyve to my sayd sonne Rychard fyve marks, wherof I have
delyvered to my sayd sonne on koo and on stuere whycche were better then 20s.,
Item, I Wyll he shall have peyd to hym by my executores 26s. 8d. in ful recompense of his fyve marks as his ful chyldes parte of my goods, and that he shall
not vex nor trowbull his mother nor his brethyrne nor my executors for any more
of my goods, Item, the seconde parte of my goods, I wyl my wyff shal have, and
the thyrd parte my too sonnys, Edward and William, Equaly to be devydet betwyxt
them,

Executors: testator's wife Elisabeth Pexton, David Hofeld and John Graye.

Witnesses: John Tenche parysch clerke, and Thomas Tenche, with otheres.

Dettes oughyng to this testator

	£	s	d
Raff Henbere		6	0
Willam Hurdluston		5	0
[Sum		11	0]

Dettes that this testator doyth ough

	£	s	d
To Rychard Pexton, his sonne, for parte of mylne stonne		20	0
to Edward Pexton, his sonne,		20	0
to Thomas Cockesee,		5	0
to Rychard Weytfelde		7	11
to Randul Wade		2	0
to Margaret Hassall,		11	0
to Nicolas Acson			6
to David Hofeld		3	9
[Sum		68	26]

Inventory: Thomas Pexton.

Taken: 20 October 1562

Prisers: Thomas Tenche, Richard Hall, Thomas Cocsee and Thomas Gray.

	s	d
apparell for his bodye, the price	13	4
beddyng, 3 mattrasse, the price	15	0
2 coverlettes, the price	10	0

2 twyll schetes and on coerse coverlet, the price		6	0
3 bolsterres, the price		5	0
3 pars of schetes, the price		10	0
2 towelles, on meat cloyth, the price		2	0
2 *[interlined]* pottes, 2 pannys, the price		10	0
on mastulyn panne, on chaffyng dyshe,			
2 fryeng pann(es), the price		4	0
5 chandelerres, the price		3	4
12 peycys of peuter, the price		6	8
on brendart, on broythe, 2 goberdes, on gryd iren, a pare			
of pot hoycks, on tressel, the price		5	0
2 combys with other treene wayr, the price		10	0
2 boyrdes, 3 cheyres, on forme, 3 bedstockes, the price		4	0
on peynyte cloyth, 2 bed hengynges, the price		2	0
on yron bonde weyne, 3 youkes, on cheyne, on cop solle,			
on byll, 2 nagares, 2 worthyng yewes, the price		26	8
20 schepe, the price		30	0
4 capulles, the price		50	0
4 stueres, the price	5	0	0
4 kyne, the price	4	13	4
3 hefferres, 2 styrkes and 2 weynyges, the price	4	6	8
barle and hey, duckes and geese, the price		10	0
an old plogh with yrons, the price		2	0

Sum	29	0	4
[*recte*	13	242	36]

Endorsement: Probated 23 October 1562; administration to the executors named in the will.

5. JOHN MASSIE, CLERK, LATE ABBOT OF COMBERMERE

S?Pr. 14 February 1564/65
W.T. 5 February 1564/65
Buried: February 1564/65 at Chester

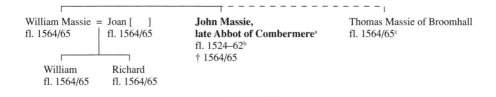

William Massie = Joan [ ]	**John Massie,**	Thomas Massie of Broomhall
fl. 1564/65 fl. 1564/65	**late Abbot of Combermere**[a]	fl. 1564/65[c]
	fl. 1524–62[b]	
	† 1564/65	

William   Richard
fl. 1564/65   fl. 1564/65

Will, sick.

First I bequeth my sowle unto almightie god the father the sonne and the holye gost three persons and one god and *my body to be buried in the north aisle of Christes Churche*. Item I bequethe to the whole quyer to bury me fourtie shillings Item my will is that if John Shawe do receave my pencōn that then my fyve porre beyde women shall have cloth to make every of them a gowne of blake Cotton and every of them in money 12d. Item, I bequeth unto Thomas Massie of Broomhall my clothe gowne which is furred with Conye two table clothes and a quylte. Item I bequeth unto William Massie the yonger my Russett ou[r]styd *[i.e. worsted]* gowne, And also my beed which is *[in]* the hawle with all things therunto belonginge and apperteyninge. Item I bequeth unto Joan Massie wief unto my brother William Massie my short cloth gowne. Item I bequethe unto Randall Cotgreve a payre of flaxen sheetes. Item I bequethe unto Rychard Massie sonne of William Massie all my bookes and my best beed wherin I have lyen with all things therunto belonginge and apperteyninge. Item I bequeth unto the seid Richard Massie tenne pounds in redy money (if my pencōn be gotten and receyved) to be bestowed and delyvered hym at the oversight of his father &

[a] Cf. *Cheshire Sheaf*, 3rd series, x, p.15, where John Hewitt attributes John Massie to the family of Massey at Broomhall.
[b] John Massey is first mentioned as sub-prior at Combermere in 1524; he first appears as abbot 26 Henry VIII (1535). Three years later (on 27 June 30 Henry VIII) he surrendered the abbey into the hands of the king, receiving for himself and his monks royal pensions. Records show him receiving his pension of £50 per year as late as 1562. See Clarke, *Ancient Parish of Wrenbury*, pp. 31–7; further, Ormerod, *History of Cheshire*, iii. 210. The will is in The Rev. G.J. Piccope, ed., *Lancashire and Cheshire Wills and Inventories from the Ecclesiastical Court, Cheshire*, Part II, Chetham Society, 51 (1860), pp. 56–7, where the date of probate is erroneously given as 4 February 1564/65.
[c] This is presumably a different Thomas Massie from the one who flourished in 1584 at Newhall (will no. 6). That makes problematic the identity of the Thomas Massie who in 1593 is noted as the father-in-law of Randle Povall, the Wrenbury parish clerk (will no. 10).

brother William Massie every one of them. Item I bequeth unto William Kelso my servant a gowne that is furred with foxe And the bed that he hathe lyen on with the fetherbeed matteres two blancketts and fourtie shillings in money And if my pencōn be recyved to Lend hym fyve pounds for one yere upon suerties by hym bounde for repayment thereof at one yeres ende to my other executors or one of them. Item I bequethe unto porre Ellin the Trucklebeed with Matteres and coveringe. Item I bequeth unto Mawde Carver a payre of sheetes and a gowne. Item I bequeth unto Robert Moseleys wief a coverpane and the London pynte. Item I bequeth unto John Flecher the Chaffer and the grete Pewter pottell pott, Also there is to be receyved of Mr Rychard Lye fyftie pounds for my pencōn for one hole yere ended at Mychelmas Last Anno Regni domine Elizabeth dei gratia Anglie Francie et Hibernie Regine &c Sexto *[1564]*. My will is that if John Shawe receive the same he shall delyver yt unto my brother William Massie or his certen attorney, And that after my debts payd legacyes performed and funeralls discharged my seid brother to delyver the rest to my other executors to be by hym & them disposed accordinge to their discreccōns. Moreover my will is that if John Shawe receave my seid pencōn that £3 therof shalbe delyved unto hym for is paynes els not.

Executors: testator's brother William Massie, William Massie the yonger his cousin, William Kelso his servant, and Rychard Massie.

Overseers: testator's friends John Meyre clerke & John Taylor.

Witnesses: John Meyre clerke, John Taylor.

Debts owing to testator: Thomas Sanders alias Steward is indebted unto me by bill of his hand in the some of 40s.

Endorsement: *[badly faded]* Probated 14 February 1564; administration to William Massie, brother of the testator, and to William Kelsey.

6. THOMAS MASSEY OF NEWHALL

I.Pr. 10 March 1584/85
W.T. 3 September 1584

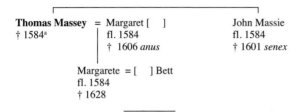

Thomas Massey = Margaret [   ]   John Massie
† 1584[a]   fl. 1584   fl. 1584
          † 1606 *anus*   † 1601 *senex*

    Margarete = [   ] Bett
    fl. 1584
    † 1628

Will, sick.

First, I commende my soule to almightie god my creatorre & redimer trustinge that I shalbe one of that number which shalbe saved, And *my body I comitte to the earth to be buried in the Churche yarde of Wrenbury* aforesaid Item I will that all such debts & duties which I owe ether of right or conscience to any manner of persone or persones be well & truly satisfied & paid By my executors hereafter named or els ordained for soe to be paid withoute fraude or contradicton Item I give & bequeath to Margarete Bett my doughter the bedd which shee lieth in with the appurtenances there to belonginge. Item I give to the said Margarete one hefer calfe of color Blacke and all the rest of my goods cattells & debtes my bodye beinge honestlye brought home upon the whole & my debts & legacies beinge paid & discharged. I give & bequeth to Margarett my wife & Margarete Bett my doughter Equally to be devided betwixte them.

Executors: testator's wife Margarete, and testator's brother, John Massie.

Overseer: testator's friend William Chester of Coole Lane.

Wittnesses: John Twisse, Richard Morres, Randulphe Povall clerke.

Debts owed by testator	£	s	d
to Godfraye Minshall merser	3	3	0
to Thomas Grindleye		4	0

[a] We have argued above that this is probably not the same individual as the Thomas Massie of Broomhall noted as a kinsman of John Massie in 1564. His relationship to the Thomas Massie who fl. 1593 as the father-in-law of Randle Povall, Wrenbury parish clerk, cannot be established with any certainty.

to John Bicarton tealor			21
to Anne Fysher			10
to William Wickestide shoomaker			8

[Sum	3	7	39]

Debts owinge to testator: | £ | s | d

John Massye my brother & executor		6	0

Inventory: Thomas Massye of the parish of Wrenbury.

Taken: 7 October 1584

Of: goodes & cattells.

Prisers: Randle Cartwright, Richard Cartwright Richard Chester & Thomas Grindley.

	s	d
his apparell	6	8
in corne	13	4
in haye	20	0
heffer calfe price	12	0
three shote pigges price		12
Brasse & Pewter price	46	8
Beddinge & napperye ware price	23	4
Iron ware price	2	0
two spinninge weeles price		16
one coffer Two stoundes one chorne	3	4
one table one dysheboarde one forme & one cheare	3	4
in pulterye		16
mucke or worthinge price	2	0

[Sum	0	118	64]

Endorsement: Probated 10 March 1584; administration to Margaret Massy, one of the executors named in the will, with power reserved to the other executor until he comes.

7. JOHN WOODFAINE[a] OF WRENBURY

S.Pr. 30 November 1588
W.T. 5 May 1588

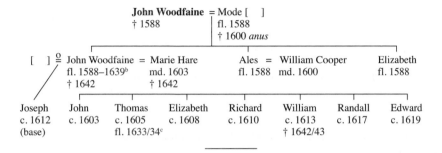

Will, sick.

Firste I commende my soule to almightye god my creatorre and redeemer and *my body to be buried in the church yearde of Wrenbury* aforesaid. Item I will that all suche debtes and duties yt I oughte of ~~duty~~ right or conscience ~~of right or conscience~~ to any person or persons be well and truely contented and paide or els ordayned by my executores hereafter named soo to be payde without fraude or contradiction. Item I give unto Mode my wife all my householde goodes which nowe I am possessed with. Item I give & bequeath unto Mode my wife the one halfe of all the residue of my goods and the other halfe of my goods (my houshould excepted) I give to John my sonne Elizabeth and Ales my daughters to be equally devided betwixte them by even portions. There is due to me of righte by John Sevill 15s. beinge parte of a cowe price due longe paste Item there is due to me of righte by Hughe Stondeley 18s. beinge parte of the price of a nagge due longe paste.

Executors: John Halle, Thomas Halle and Mode Woodfaine, the testator's wife.

Overseers: Henry Price.

Witnesses: Henry Bebington, Thomas Bebington, William Pattricke with others.

---

[a] Indexed at CRO as John *Woodfin*; in printed Indexes as John *Woodfen*.
[b] John Woodfyne was owed 25s. by Hugh Broome, son of Roger Broome, 1606; see Roger Broome's will, pr. 1606 (will no. 21); John Woodfen was priser for Richard Rogers, 1621 (will no. 65) and for Roger Jones, 1639 (will no. 110).
[c] Thomas Woodfen was witness for Robert Wade of Wrenbury Frith 1633/34 (will no. 95).

Inventory: John Woodfaine.

Of: goods & cattells.

Prisers: William Bebington Senior, William Bebington Junior, Henry Price with others.

	£	s	d
4 oxen the price	8	6	8
five kine with 2 calves	11	0	0
2 heaffers	3	0	0
2 mares	10	0	0
6 yewes with theire lambes and another odd sheep [*damaged*]			0
3 swine		15	0
poultrie ware		5	0
all manner of husbandry wares Iron wares thereunto appertaininge		13	4
all manner of houshoulde stuffe as beddinge brasse pewter naperie ware bords formes & querns of corne and all manner of trine wares with whitemeats	6	0	0
his apparill		10	0
Summa totalis	37	10	0
[*recte*	38	49	12]

Endorsement: Probated before George Tatnall, dean of the deanery of Nantwich, 30 November 1588; administration to the executors named in the will.

8. ELLEN BEBBINGTON OF CHORLEY, WIDOW

S.Pr. 1 August 1592
W.T. 22 August 1591
[† ca. 1 Sept 1591]

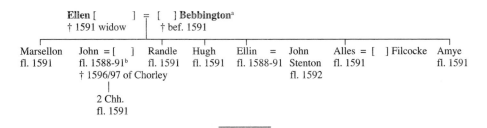

Will, sick.

First I bequeth my soule to almighty god & to all the holy company in heaven and my body to the earth whence it came. I give to my daughter Marsellon Twenty wolles and to my Sonne John Bebington 12d. and to my Sonne Randle Bebington 12d. and to my Sonne Hugh Bebington 12d. and to my daughter Ellin Stenton 12d. and to my daughter Alles Filcocke 12d. and to my sonne Johns two children ether two shillings. Also my will is that my debts be paide my legacies discharged and I beang honestly brought home the residue of my goods I give to my daughter Amye Bebington.

Executors : testator's son John Bebington of Chorley, William Wrighte of Chorley.

Overseer: George Wright of Chorley.

Witnesses: Richard Bickerton, Richard Downe.

Inventory: Ellin Bebbington of Chorley, widow.

---

[a] While there is some temptation to identify this Ellen Bebbington with the wife of William Bebington of Chorley, named as Ellen in 1588, there is very little other congruence between the two families, and thus no compelling evidence that they are identical: while both have a daughter Ellen, and both have a son Randle/*Randulphe*, there are no other equations, and the married children in the one family do not find mention at all in the other. The most likely possibility is that they were agnate families, which fact explains the son of Ellen (John) being witness for William in 1588/89 (will no. 9), and the son of William (William Jr) being a priser for Ellen in 1591: William Bebington mentions a cousin, William Bebington, who also resided in Chorley in 1588, and there were presumably others.

[b] Witness for will of William Bebington of Chorley, pr. 1592 (will no. 9).

Taken: 2 September 1591

Of: goods.

Prisers: William Bebington, John Stenton, Richard Downe and George Wright.

	£	s	d
for two oxen	5	13	0
for two steeres	3	13	4
for one odde Bullocke		28	0
for foure Kyne	7	10	0
for two Twenter heffers	3	0	0
for Two stryke black cavles [*sic*]		33	4
for Tow weaning calves		20	0
for A mare		40	0
for six swyne		36	0
for A bounde weane		40	0
for implements to husbandry		18	8
for corne	13	15	0
for hay	4	0	0
for mucke		8	0
for wodde		6	8
for hempe flaxe		6	8
for Treen ware		33	4
for Brasse		40	0
for pewter		20	0
for bedding		40	0
for shettes & nappery ware		26	8
for chese & bakon		15	0
for powtry		2	0
for moug pots and cups		2	0
for apperell		13	4
[Sum	35	487	48]

Endorsement: Probated 1 August 1592 in the presence of David Yale doctor of laws; administration to the executors named in the will.

9. WILLIAM BEBBINGTON OF CHORLEY

S.Pr. 7 October 1592
T. 30 January 1588/89(?)

NOTE: The top third of the will is badly damaged, resulting in gaps in the text which can in places be conjectured.

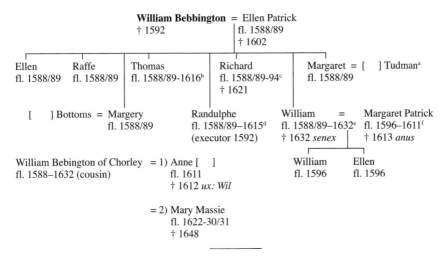

Will, sick.

First, I do commend my Soule unto the mercifull hand [of almightie god not] doubtinge but by the merits of his deere sonne Jesus Christ my onely [Rede]mer I shalbe one of that blessed [number in the kingdom of Heaven, And *my bodie]* *I doe committ to the earth to be buried in the Churche of Wrenbury* [afore] said. Item I will & it is my minde that [any debts] which I doe owe of Right or consience

---

a   There are two apparent possibilities for this unnamed Tudman: see will of Robert Tudman, pr. 1632 (will no. 92).

b   1588 witness for will of John Woodfaine (will no. 7); witness for will of William Patrick of Chorley, 1611 (will no. 33); priser for goods of George Kemp, 1616 (will no. 50).

c   Owed debt of 20d. to Humphrey Bickerton 1594; see will of Humphrey Bickerton, pr. 1594 (will no. 12).

d   Owed a debt by Thomas Faulkner 1615 'for the cariage of hay' (will no. 47).

e   Noted as the grandson of Elizabeth Patrick alias Willson 1596; see will of Elizabeth Patrick alias Wilson, pr. 1597/98 (will no. 15); made inventory for Roger Broome, 1606 (will no. 21); owed debt of £20 by, and priser of the goods of, Thomas Faulkner, 1615 (will no. 47); executor of will of William Patrick of Chorley, 1611 (will no. 33); priser of the goods of Anne Bickerton, 1616 (will no. 49); priser of the goods of Richard Rogers, 1621 (will no. 65).

f   See will of William Patrick, 1611 (will no. 33).

to any person or persons whatsoever they be well and trulye satisfied and payed by my executor here[after] named without fraude or contradiction. Item I will and it is my verye minde that my funeralle debts and legaces shalbe made and payed out and of my whole goods. Item I geve and bequeth to Ellen Bebingtone my daughter Tene pounds good and lawfull money of England in full satisfaction of all her childs parte of goods. Item I give to Margery Bottoms my daughter 13s. 4d. in satisfaction of her childs parte of goods. Item I geve & bequeth unto Raffe Bebington my sone 40s. of currant money of England in full payment and satisfaction of his childs parte of my goods. Item I geve and bequeth unto my sonne Randulphe Bebington 12d. in full recompence and satisfaction of his childs part of my goods. Item I geve to Thomas Bebington my sone 12d. of good & lawfull money of England in full recompence and satisfaction of all his childs parte of my goods. Item I geve and bequeth to Richard Bebington my sonne 12d. of good and Lawfull money of England in full recompence and satisfaction of all his childs parte of goods. Item I geve and bequeath to William Bebington my sone 12d. of good and Lawfull English money in full payment and satisfaction of his chylds parte of my goods. Item I geve and bequeth to Ellen Deaks one stirke heffer and all the rest and Residue of my goods Cattels chattels and debts moveable and not moveable my body beinge honestly brought to christian buriall and my debts and Legacies contayned in this my present Testament payed and discharged out and of my whole goods I geve and bequeth whollye to be devided betwixt Ellen my wyffe and Margarete Tudman my daughter eaquallye.

Executors: Raphe Davemport of Baddiley yeoman, the testator's cousin William Bebington of Chorley.

Overseer: the testator's son Randulphe Bebington.

H.

Witnesses: Randulphe Powall, John Bebington, Thomas Hurlebutt, Richard Findelaye.

Inventory: William Babington of Chorley.

Taken: 28 February 1592/93

Of: goods & Chattels.

Prisers: Roger Brome, John Babington, Richarde Rogers, and Richard Doonne.

	s	d
in butter and cheses	4	0
yorne and towe	12	0
marke [warke?]salet splenets and a bill		5
one matres	5	0
3 bolsters and a pillow	3	0
2 coverletts and twilshete	4	0
2 bedstocks	2	5

one flocke bed		5	0
one fether bed		16	0
2 boulsters and a billowe		6	3
2 coverletts		8	0
2 blanckets		1	0
one pare of bedstockes		2	0
one matres		4	0
one fetherbed		20	0
2 boulsters and 2 pillowes		6	0
3 coverletts and towe twilshets		12	0
a parre of ould bed Stockes			8
3 Flaxen shets		45	0
7 payres of tere of hempe shetes		35	0
a longe burde clothe and a square burdclothe		2	6
4 towells		6	0
6 towell table napkins		3	0
2 pillow beeres		2	0
2 greatt Chests		6	8
one ould chest			6
one longe burd with trestles			16
one square table		2	6
one little burd			12
one cubborde		10	0
2 ould chers			6
2 ould wheles	2	0	0
3 fletches of beffe		6	0
6 fletches of bacone		24	0
4 formes		12	0
tow great pannes		33	1
4 litle pannes		2	8
2 great potts		16	0
2 litle potts		6	0
one chafinge dishe			8
2 brasse candlestickes			8
3 potts		4	0
a gridyrone a payre of pothockes a pare potracks a pare of tongues a handyron		2	4
13 pewter dyshes		13	0
one maselen bason			12
2 sawsers and pewter bole			12
2 Barrels		2	8
4 stounds		2	8
a Chorne a close bowk and a tournell		2	4
dyshes trenchers and pegons			12
6 erthen potts			6

Item	£	s	d
3 powkes			12
4 Quyssions and a benche clothe		2	0
one tornell		2	0
one cowmpe			12
a knedinge troughe and melding burd			8
a musterd whirle			12
4 fenes			6
3 bowrdes			6
4 paynted clothes		2	4
the paynted cloths in the house		2	0
a muck wyane bodie and the cop		2	6
a wayne bodie a payre of boundes whelles with the furniture & 3 yokes		30	0
one Sploid with yron and one snike		2	8
one harrowe			12
one copsole & one chaine			20
an axe a mattock a spade, 4 byls 2 hatchets two nagers a wimble a hammer		5	0
Wanne Timber and ploughe timber		3	4
all the fyrewoodde			12
Two ladders			12
3 pykels			6
corne in the house and in the barne	5	3	4
a buz and a Stryke of wintercorne sowed uppon the grounds		20	0
all the haie in the barne		6	8
one shovell		[	]
two Oxen	4	6	0
six kyne	12	0	0
4 heaffers	4	13	4
one old mare		10	0
one tagged bullock		20	0
three calves		20	0
three buz of barlie malte		15	0
a buz of ote malte		4	0
Two swyne		10	0
foure hens and a cocke		20	0
his purse and his apparell		20	0
Sum	56	[00]	22
[recte	47	641	324]

Endorsement: Probated 7 October 1592; administration to the executors named in the will.

10. RANDLE POVALL OF WRENBURY, CLERK

S?Pr. [   ] September 1593
W. 16 August 1593

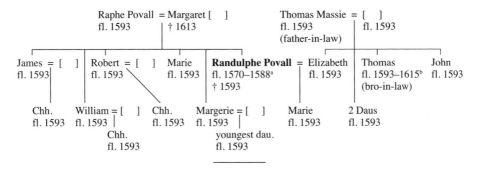

Will, sick.

I geve and bequeath 20s. to the poore of the parish of Wrenbury to be devided amonge them bie my executors hereafter named. Item I geave and bequeath 6s. 8d. to the poore of the parish of Marbury and to the poore of the parish of Baddiley 4s. 4d. Item I gieve and bequeath to everie one of my godchildren 12d. a persone. Item I gieve and bequeath to the right worshipfull Sir Hughe Chomeley thelder a Kinge Henry Angell the eight in token of my own full good will desiringe him as hee hath stood my good master that he will so stand to my wife and daughters Item I gieve to Edward Bradford 5s. and a booke Item I gieve to James Povall my brother 20s. Item I gieve to William Povall my brother 20s. Item I gieve to my father Raphe Povall 40s. a yeare duringe his naturall life Item I gieve to my brother Robert and his children 10s. Item I give to my brother in law Edward Hinnes[c] and his children 10s. Item I give to my brothers children viz James and William De[?]ie one twinterheiffer a peece. Item I gieve to my sister Margerie and her youngest doughter 5s. Item I gieve to Mr Lawrence Starkie Esquire £10 per annum Item I gieve to Mr Thomas Minshull the younger a bull calf Item I

---

[a] Clerk at Wrenbury, fl. 1570–84; see will of Thomas Massey, 1584 (will no. 6) where he appears as a witness; witness to will of William Bebington, pr. 1592 (will no. 9).
[b] Either this Thomas, or his father, is the Thomas Massie thelder noted 1611 in the inventory of John Bickerton (no. 39); in 1615 Thomas Massie is noted as owing a debt of 15s. to John Wilkinson (will no. 46).
[c] The manner in which Edward Hinnes (of whom there is no further mention in the sources) was related to Randle Povall as his brother-in-law is not clear: while Randle could have been married previously, there is no reason to assume that Elizabeth Massie, daughter of Thomas Massie, was his second wife, making a deceased sister of Edward Hinnes Povall's first wife. Less strain is placed on the sources if we assume that Hinnes was the husband of either Randle's sister Margerie, his sister Marie, or a third, unnamed sister.

gieve my father in law Thomas Massie thelder 3s. 4d. Item I gieve to my brother in law Thomas Massie and his sonne 3s. 4d. Item I gieve to Agnes Farington and her Children 3s 4d. Item I gieve to my mother in lawe and her too daughters 3s. Item I gieve to my brother in law John Massie 3s. 4d. and a pere of hose. Item I gieve to John Wickstedds children a ewe ~~lambl~~ lambe Item I gieve to Thomas Hurlestons children another ewe lambe Item I gieve to Margaret Hurleston widow and her three children 8s. to bee devived equallie amoungst them Item I gieve to Joane Reade the finchte [?] Item I gieve to Thomas Graie 3s. 4d. and a peare of black hose. Item I gieve to Margerie Spenser my servant a twinter hieffer. Item I reserve to John Seavill and his sonne Thomas one yeare in revertion of all the ground that I hold of hers others of them ~~others~~ Item I reserve to William Spenser and his children one yeares proffitt in revertion of those 2 closes that I hold of him Item I reserve to Richard Fisher one yeare proffitt in revertion in the ground that I hold of him Item I gieve and bequeath all the rest of my goods cattels and chattalls [?] moveable and unmoveable whatsoever I gieve wholie to Elizabeth my wief and Marie my daughter.

Executors: William Bebington, Edmond Bickerton, Thomas Graie, Edward Bradford.

Overseer: Hugh Cholmley, Knight.

Debts that the testator doth owe:

	£	s	d
I owe Thomas Graie		16	0
To Randle Hare		10	0
To William Dickins		8	6
To William Church according to his note		[	]
To [E]d[wa]rd Babington		2	2
To Thomas Lanmarke			4
To John Finnie			12
[Sum		36	24]

Debts oweinge the testator:

	£	s	d
Thomas Johnson due at Bartholomew daie nexte		10	0
Thomas Cooke due at Martinsmas daie nexte		3	4
John Shrowbridge of Newhall due at the same daie		3	4
Raphe Barnett due at the same daie		3	0
Ales Cartwright [?] due at the [same] daie		5	4
Richard Massie due at Michaellmas daie nexte			20
Richard Tailor of Dodcott due at Michaelmas daie nexte		10	0
William Phillipps late of Whitchurch chesemonger	3	15	0
[Sum	3	49	32]

NOTE: The top of the will is damaged, limiting what we can make of the record of the probate.

Endorsement: Probated [ ] September 1593; administration to William Bebington and Edmond Bickerton, two of the four executors named in the will; the other two executors, namely Edward Bradford and Thomas Graie, having utterly renounced the burden personally by oath.

11. ROBERT TENCH OF NEWHALL

S?Pr. 20 April 1594
W.T. 27 August 1592
Died: 5 April 1593
Buried: 5/6 April 1593

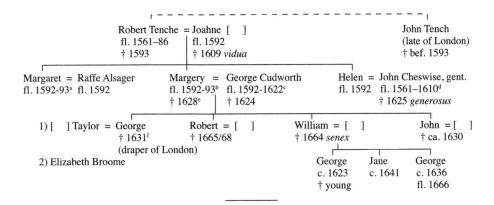

[a] Aged 52 plus.
[b] Aged 40 plus.
[c] See note 'd' to inventory of George Cudworth, 1624 (no. 70).
[d] On 4 January 1595, John Cheswis the elder late of Mickley, co. Chester, gentleman, issued a declaration showing the devolution of Newhall Park from 1555 to 1595. Cheswis himself had purchased all the pastures etc. in Newhall Park by deed on 14 July 1593 from Randull Stanley. He then declared: 'Now know that the said John Cheswis in consideration of £3 7s. 8d. paid to him by Thos Edgeley, of Newhall, yeoman, hath granted and assigned to the said Thos Edgeley the aforesaid two pastures, and the aforesaid pasture, springe or parcell of ground and one meadow in Newhall Park during all the continuance of the foresaid severall terms etc.'
[e] Fl. 1625 as *widow Cudworth* in CRO Newhall Rentals.
[f] Harleian MS, as cited in Norwood, *Historic Notes*, no. li.

Will, sick.

First I committ my soule to almightie god my maker and redeemer & *my bodie to be buried within the church of Wrenbury* Item I geve and bequeath 33s. 4d. of money which is in the hands of my daughter Helen Cheswise to be Imployed & bestowed upon my funerall expenses & upon poore people by the discretion of my executors hereafter named. Item I geve and bequeath unto my daughter Helen Cheswise and to the heires of hir bodie lawfully begotten and to be begotten all that half & moitie of of *[sic]* all my lease hold land messuage tenemente medowes leasowes feedings pasturs & all other hereditaments with theire [appurtenances] situat and beinge in Newhall in the countie of Chester aforesayde as they shalbe now devyded and nither *[damaged]* of John Cheswise gentleman and the sayde Helen or their assignes to have and to hold all that moitie of [my lease hold etc.] to my sayde daughter Helen Cheswise and to the heires of her bodie lawfullie begotten & to bee begotten accordinge unto the effect lymitacōns & true meaninge of one peare of Indentures bearinge date the seconde daye of Aprill in the neenteenth yeare of the queenes maiestie that nowe is confert and made betwixt me the saide Robert Tenche upon thone partie and Richard Edgley deceased uppon thother partie and to none other intent or intents use or uses purpose or purposes. Item I gieve and bequeathe thother half or moitie of all my sayde freeholde lands messuage tenements meddowes leasowes feedings pastures and all other hereditaments to the same belonginge with their appurtenances scytuat lyinge and beinge in Newhall aforesayde in the sayde countie of Chester and in thoccupacōn of me the sayde Robert Tench or my assignes unto Joan Tenche my wyfe for and duringe hir naturall lyfe for & in the name of her Jointure or dowere and after her decease be remayninge and come unto my daughter Margerie Cudworth and to the heires of hir bodie lawfullie begotten & to be begotten for ever Accordinge unto the effect lymytacōns and true meaninge of the saide peare of Indentures bearinge date and made betwixt me the saide Robert Tench uppon thone partie and the said Richard ~~Edley~~ Edgley deceased upon the other partie and to noe other use or uses intent or intents. Item I will that this my last will and testament be a confirmacōn and a sure establishinge of the sayde recyted peare of Indentures and of everie article conclusion condicōn and agreement contayned in the same Indentures. Item I geve and bequeath unto my sayde daughter Helen Cheswise one great pan and one ~~pan~~ pott which I lond unto her when she came to the Newhall Park to dwell. Item I geve and bequeath unto my saide daughter Helen Cheswise twentie shillings for and in consideracōn of her childs parte of all my goods cattells, & chattells. Item I geve and bequeath unto my sonne in lawe George Cudworth all my armour and harneis. Item I geve and bequeath unto my sayde daughter Margerie Cudworth one beetinge comnpe & one garnett. Item I geve and bequeath unto the foure sonnes of my sayde sonne in lawe George Cudworth unto everie one of them 6s. 8d. Item I give and bequeath unto my sonne in lawe Raffe Alseger and unto Margreate his wyfe twentie shillinges for theire childs parte of all my goods, cattells & chattells. Item I give and bequeath unto Raffe Tench my best cote. Item I give and bequeath unto John Barnes the wryter heres three shillinges foure pence Item I give and bequeath unto the twoe youngest daughters of my cosen William Tench of Nantwich unto either of them three shillinges foure pence Item I geve and bequeath unto my sayde wyfe Joan Tench and unto my sayde sonne in lawe George Cudworth all my tythe terme of peares and interest which I have of and in anie parte of the Newhall Park And I will that after the decease of my saide wyfe Joane all my tythe terme and interest shall come unto my sayde sonne in lawe George Cudworth for and duringe all the whole terme accordinge to the effect and true meaninge of an assignment thereof made by me to the sayde George Cudworth. Item I geve and bequeath unto the twoe youngest daughters of my cosen John Tench of Nantwich to either of them 3s. 4d. Item I geve and bequeath all the rest of my goods cattells and chattells unbequeathed whatsoever after my funerall expenses expenses [sic] performed my debts payde and legacies discharged unto my sayde wyfe Joane Tench to be disposed at hir pleasure.

Executors: Wife, Joane Tench, loving neighbour John Cartwright, Thomas Swanne and John Barnes.
Overseers: cousins John Tench of Nantwich and William Tench of Nantwich.

H & S.

Memorandum: that the intent and meaninge of the testator is that Synswood and Synsmedowe shall not passe unto George Cudworth by the within bequeathed legacie of Newhall Park except yt be conseyned and conveiyed unto the sayde George Cudworth by the within nominated assignenement [sic!] made from the sayde Robert Tench unto the sayde George.

Memorandum: that the sayde testator hath bequeathed unto Ellen Edgeley the widow of Richard Edgeley deceased twentie pence.

[damaged] unto the within named Joane Tench John Cartwright and John Barnes in the sight of John Cheswys & George Cudworth.

Debts that this testator is nowe indebted this daye beinge the 5th day of Aprill in the 35th yeare of the queenes majesties Raigne that nowe is.

	£	s	d
To master John Cheswis for heye		38	4
For one fliche of Bacon		5	0
For butter and cheese		20	0
For a hoope of wheat			20
To William Johnson		13	4
Ker' of Richard Barnett as afore rent for grounde		21	0
Ker' of William Evanns as afore rent for grounde		16	8
The rent of Syns woodde		9	0
To Ellen Edgley for wages		2	0

To Robert Shrowbridge his wages	3	4
To Geffrey Cartwright in rent	11	8
Paid the funerall expenses of this testator and his wyf	56	8
For breakinge the church flowre for there 2 burialls	6	8
In rent for the Newhall Parkes	4	11
For the tythe of Newhall Parkes		20
Geven Lawrente Wryght for his payns	*[damaged]*	
Spent that daye we weare at cyted before the deane	6	[ ]
For a copie of the will & Inventorie Indented	12	[ ]
[Sum	222	95]

Inventory: goods and cattells.

Taken: 13 April 1593

Prisers: John Orpe Robert Tench and Geffrey Cartwright.

	£	s	d
His wearinge apparell priced to		16	8
Three heffers priced unto	4	6	8
Twoe kyne priced unto	4	0	0
Seesteene sheepe and six lambes	4	6	8
Rye uppon the grounde pryced		40	0
One crofte called Grindleyes feeld		16	0
Three bushells of barlie in the hande of			
Helen Cheswis pryced unto		12	0
Twoe hyves of bees the half of them		3	4
One axe, one Bill, one hatchet & one Iron wedge praysed unto		2	0
In the hande of Helen Cheswys which should have bin payed			
toward the funerall expenses		33	4
One legacye given unto the testator by one one			
[sic!] John Tench late of London		50	0
Summa totallis	21	6	8

Endorsement: Probated 20 April 1594; administration to the executors named in the will.

Inquisition Post Mortem: for Robert Tench, lately of Newhall.
Taken at Nantwich 27 August 40 Eliz. (1598).

The jurors found that Robert Tench was seised in fee of one messuage with appurtenances in Newhall, of 15 acres of arable land, 2 of meadow, and 15 of pasture, also in Newhall; in all, a fief held by military service, as one one-hundred-and-fourth part of a Knight's fee; and that, being so seised, in consideration of a marriage between a certain George Cudworth and Margery, one daughter of the said Robert Tench, and in consideration of his paternal love towards Margaretta, another daughter of the said Robert, he enfeoffed George Cudworth and Margery his wife with the aforesaid messuage and lands, to be by them had and held, with remainder to their heirs of their bodies legitimately begotten, and with further remainder to Margaretta.

Thereafter, on April 5th, 35 Eliz. [1593], Robert Tench died at Newhall. His nearest heirs were found to be Margery and Margarette his two daughters, of whom the former was, at the time of the holding of the Inquisition, aged 40 and more, and the latter 52 and more.

The Jurors moreover found that, since the decease of Robert Tench, Cudworth had received half the profits of his estate, and one Elena Eggeley, a widow, the remainder.[a]

12. HUMPHREY BICKERTON OF WRENBURY FRITH, HUSBANDMAN

S.Pr. 28 June 1594
W. [bef. 28 April 1594]
Buried: 28 April 1594

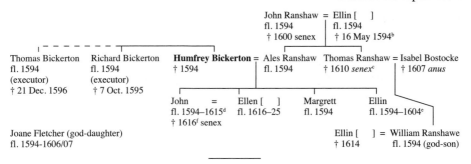

Will, sick.

First, I give my sole into the hands of almightie god my Creator & maker & *my bodye to be buried in the parishe churche yarde of Wrenbury* At the discretion of my frends where my elders have bene accustomed to be buried. Item I geve

---

[a] Inquisition no. 11, 40 Elizabeth, excerpted in Norwood, *Historic Notes*, no. li.
[b] Or 8 July 1606: no clear indication which; she was alive when the will was made.
[c] Though there is no direct evidence, this is most likely Ales's brother, who served as a priser of Humphrey Bickerton's goods in 1594 (will no. 12). It also explains the connection with William Ranshawe, Humphrey's god-son. See will of Thomas Ravenshaw of Broomhall, pr. 1610 (CRO).
[d] John Bickerton appears 1609, 1611, 1615 in CRO Newhall Manor Court Rolls.
[e] Received repayment from John Cartwright of Aston in Newhall, 1604 (will no. 18).
[f] See will of John Bickerton of Newhall, yeoman, pr. 1616 (will no. 48).

towards the reparation of the said church 12d.. Item I geve to my sonne John all Iron ware and all Implements belonging to husbandrey and one tow yere old heffer and one 3 yere old bullocke. Item to my Daughter Margrett a three yere old heffer. Item to my Daughter Ellin £6 13s. 4d. and a yere old Calfe and 4 lambs and which of the wenches soever dyeth before they be maried her portion to remaine to the sister remeininge and yf bothe Die before mariage then ther portions to Remayne to John my sonne Item I give to John Ranshaw my father in law my best upparends of my hose and to him & my mother in lawe 6s. 8d. wherof the have recived 3s. Item I give to Rondull Fleet 2s. Item I geve to William Ranshawe my god sonn 12d. Item I geve to Joane Flecher my god Daughter 12d. and for all the Rest of my goods Cattels moveable and unmovable my Debts legacies and funerall expences discharged uppon the whole my will is that the be distributed in three parts whereof Ales my wyfe to have one and the other tow parts to be devyded equally amonge my three Children John Margaritt and Ellin.

Debts owing to Testator:

	£	s	d
Thomas Minshall		27	4
Henrye Garfferth & John his sonne	6	0	0
Thomas Moyle		13	4
William Wollam		28	0
Raphe Gest		2	8
John Sevill		4	0
John Alcock and Thomas his sonn		13	4
William Ranshaw & Thomas Ranshaw	6	3	4
Thomas Sevill Richard Salmon and Richard Lane	5	12	0
Richard Venables			5
Roger Brome		5	0
James Coxton		5	0
Humphrey Palin		5	4
Richard T[?]	3	0	0
Richard Babington			20
[Sum	20	117	53]

Executors: the testator's brother, Richard Bickerton, John Cartwright, Thomas Bickerton.

Overseer: Thomas Minshall of Erdswick.

Witnesses: Simon Savage (his marke), Robert Tenche, William Pexton, Thomas Ranshaw, with others.

Inventory: Humphrye Bickerton of Wrenbury Frith, husbandman.

Taken: 1 May 1594

Of: goods and Cattalls.

Prisers: Robart Tenche, James Barnitt, Randle Tenche and John Massie.

		s	d
his apparill price		10	0
salte meate at the house		4	0
haye price		5	0
twoe oxen	5	10	0
4 steers	11	0	0
fyve kyne & three Calves	9	6	8
4 yonge heffers	3	6	8
2 stearks		26	8
one horse & one mare	3	0	0
three swine		13	4
cart plowe & all such husbandrye ware		16	0
[Sum	31	96	28]

Debts owing to Testator:

	£	s	d
Thomas Minshall		27	4
Henrye Greffith & John his sonne	6	0	0
Thomas Moyle		13	7
William Wollam		28	0
Raphe Gest		2	8
John Sevill		4	0
John Alcocke & Thomas his sonne		13	4
Willim Ranshaw & Thomas Ranshaw	6	3	4
Thomas Sevill Richard Salmon & Richard Lane	5	12	0
Richard Venables		5	0
Roger Brome		5	0
James Croxton		5	0
Richard T[?]		3	0
Greffen Heath		5	4
Richard Babington			20
[Sum	17	125	51]

Endorsement: Probated before [ ] on 28 June 1594; administration to Richard Bickerton and John Cartwright, executors named in the aforesaid will.

13. RAFFE BARNETT OF NEWHALL

S.Pr. 14 October 1595
W.T. 7 June 1595
Buried: 26 June 1595

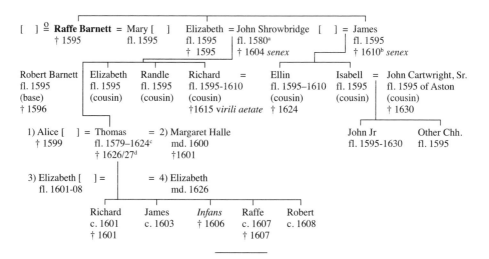

Will, sick.

First, I geve and bequeth my soule unto almighty god my maker and Redeemer and *my body to be buried in the parishe Church of Wrenbury.* Item I geve unto the said Church 3s. 4d. Item I geve unto Robert Barnett my base sonne £13 6s. 8d. Item I geve unto my sister Elizabeth Shrobridge 26s. 8d. Item I geve unto my Cozen Elizabeth Shrobridge 10s. Item I geve unto my Cozen Ellen Barnett 20s. Item I geve unto every one of my god Children 12d. a peece Item I geve unto Thomas Barnett 30s. Item I geve unto William Barnett 30s. Item I geve unto other of the Children of John Cartwright 6s. 8d. a peece Item I geve unto Elizabeth Whittingham 20s. Item I geve unto John Barnett 3s. 4d. Item I geve unto my Cozen Isabell Cartwright 10s. Item I geve unto John Sale 20s. Item I geve unto Margery Parker 10s. Item I geve unto my Cozen Richard Shrobridge Thomas and

---

<small>
a Since the name of Elizabeth Shrowbridge's husband is not given, she may well be the widow Shrowbridge who appears in 1595 in a presentment. Her husband may thus have been the John Shrowbridge who appears in 1580 as a juror in CRO Newhall Manor Court Rolls; the Richard Shrobridge who owes a debt to Raffe Barnett in 1595 (see below) is then his son.

b See will of James Barnett of Aston, yeoman, pr. 1610 (will no. 29).

c Flourished 1598 as tenant at Newhall with Richard Shrowbridge, his brother (see Newhall Court Roll/CRO).

d See will of Thomas Shrowbridge, pr. 1626/27 (will no. 75).
</small>

Randle 12d. a peece Item I geve unto Ellen Wright and Robert Wright 20s. Item I geve unto John Barnett a yowe sheepe, Item I geve unto the poore 20s. att the oversight of my executors Item I geve all the rest of my goods moveable and unmoveable after my Legasies performed and my funerall expencs discharged unto my wief Mary Barnett.

Executors: the testator's wife Mary Barnett, the testator's cousin John Cartwright senior, the testator's brother James Barnett, and the testator's cousin John Cartwright.

Debts owinge to the Testator:

	£	s	d
Jeffrey Cartwright	4	6	8
Thomas Cartwright		20	0
William Hampton		26	8
Peter Onley		31	0
Randle Bucley	4	10	0
John Shrobridge	3	0	0
Thomas Baker		33	4
William Johnson		33	4
John Whittingham		40	0
John Cartwright	5	0	0
Robert Henbury		3	4
Thomas Barnett		20	0
William Barnett		30	0
Richard Shrobridge		20	0
John Morrey	5	14	0
my brother James Barnett	4	0	0
for an oxe wich I geve to Robert Barnett my base sonne			
[Sum	25	286	28]

Inventory: Raphe Barnett.

Taken: 30 June [1595], 37 Elizabeth

Of: goods.

Prisers: John Cartwrighte of Aston, John Barnet, Arthor More, Thomas Kelsoe.

	£	s	d
for his Apparell		20	0
for Ten kyne	18	6	8
for twoe twinters		40	0
for twoe stirkes		26	8
for one weininge Calfe		10	0

for shipe		42	0
for swine		13	4
for pultrie ware		5	0
for one mare		33	4
for all husbandrieware		3	0
for all Iron ware and edge toules		5	0
for Brasse and pewter		3	4
for Cowpry ware and trine ware borde formes dishbordes and stooles		40	0
for Beddinge and Napry ware		10	0
for Corne and Maulte within the house	3	0	0
for Butter and Cheese and Baken		33	4
for Wolle		10	0
twoe Coffers and the pented Clothes		4	0
for Corne on the grounde	6	13	4
more to be taken and had in debts as the will speaketh of the sume of	36	11	0
[Sum	63	326	36]

Endorsement: Probated in the presence of David Yale Doctor of Laws lawfully appointed Commissary of Archdeacon Matthew 14 October 1595; administration to Mary widow of the deceased, James Barnett and John Cartwright, three executors named in the will, with power reserved to the aforesaid John Cartwright named as the other executor in the aforesaid will until he shall come.

14. ELLINOR HIGSON OF NEWHALL, SPINSTER

I?Pr. 9 November 1597
W.T. 27 August 1597, anno Regine Elizabeth 39
Buried: probably at Chester

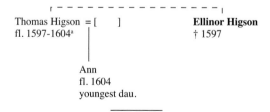

Thomas Higson = [   ]   **Ellinor Higson**
fl. 1597-1604[a]   † 1597

Ann
fl. 1604
youngest dau.

---

[a] See Alice Blackamore's will, 1604/05 (will no. 20).

Will, sick and imprisoned at Chester (Castle).

First, I commend my soule to the lord fully assuringe my self that I am one of the elect and my body to proper buriall Item I geve and bequeath unto Thomas Sutton my keeper all my goodes cateles debts retes and creditts whatsoever which I am either possed of or entiteled unto In consideracon that he hath bene good unto me duringe the tyme of my ymprisonment, and that I am indebted unto him for meate and drincke that I have had of him.

Executor: Thomas Sutton.

Witnesses: Thomas Minkas, John Smith.

Debts owinge to the Testatrix:

She bought a Cowe of Thomas Hurleston and delived him 40s. and yf the cowe had proved with calf she was to geve him 10s. more, the cowe was still in his possion and proved not to be with calf, she demamdes the 40s. againe   40s.

Roberte Fleete of Cholmondley had a cowe to hyer for 8s. a yeare Att Martinmas next he is behinde for one yeare, the cowe is seysed by Sir Hughe Cholmondley for the Queenes use.
Thomas Hickson of Sutton nere Middlewich hath a gowne and a peticoate and divers other goodes of the testators.

Thomas Hurleston hath a hatt of the testators.

Endorsement: Probated 9 November 1597; administration to the executor of the same, together with the deposition of the witness Higgson.

The said testimony about and upon the validity of the will of Elenore Higgson was taken before the venerable David Yale Doctor of Laws the 9th day of November 1597

John Smithe of the City of Chester of the age of [?] or thereabouts, having been sworn, said that he was with the said deceased when he heard her geve & bequeath as in the will is contained and that he this deponent did write the same will with his owne hand & therefore knoweth the same to be the true will of the said deceased.

15. ELIZABETH PATRICK ALIAS WILSON OF CHORLEY, WIDOW

I.Pr. 2 January 1597/98
W.T. [ ] July 1596
Buried: 23 December 1597

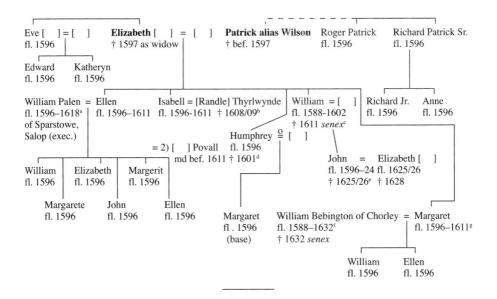

Will, sick.

First, I bequethe my sowle to allmightie god assuredlie trustinge by the merits of Iesus Christ to be saved & *my boddie to be buried at the parishe churche Wrenbury* by the discression of my Executors Also my mynd & Will is that my Executors shal bestowe 40s. for my funeralls that is to say towardes the brynginge of me whome & yf this said some of 40s. be not sufficient then to make it forth then upon the rest of my goodes by there discression: Also I gyve & bequeth unto William Palen my sonneinlawe the fourme in the howse with the woodwaint &

---

[a]   Witness for will of Anne Kempe, pr. 1619 (will no. 57).
[b]   Presumably the Randle Thyrlwynde who was buried 6 March 1608/09 at Audlem (see Parish Register at CRO).
[c]   Witness for John Woodfaine's will, 1588 (will no. 7); see will of William Patrick, pr. 1611 (will no. 33).
[d]   See will of Humphrey Wilson of Chorley, pr. 1602 (will no. 16).
[e]   See will of John Patricke, pr. 1626 (will no. 72).
[f]   See will of his father, William Bebbington of Chorley, pr. 1592 (will no. 9); 1606 made inventory for Roger Broome (will no. 21).
[g]   See will of William Patrick, pr. 1611 (will no. 33).

the longe shelfe in the buttrie over the ale borde Also I gyve & bequethe unto Ellen Palen my daughter, wyfe of the said William one coffer at my bedsyde in the parlor one fidderbed one bedstydde in the loft one peere of pathookes one chayne over the fyre one payre of Iron goberts: one grete stounde one drepyng-panne one table clothe one gray wemtell & one brasse panne of 2 gallans Item I gyve & bequethe unto William Palen my granndson 2s. 6d. Also I gyve & bequethe unto Margrete Palen sister to the said William 2s. Item I gyve & bequethe unto Margerit Palen sister unto the said Margaret & both daughters unto Ellen Palen my doughter one kettle: Also I gyve & bequethe unto Elizabeth Palen doughter to Ellen Palen my doughter one arke in the butrie & one greate skellet Also I gyve & bequethe unto John Palen my granndson 2s. Item I gyve & bequeathe unto Ellen Palen doughter unto Elyn Palen my doughter one candelstick & one pottynger: Also I gyve & bequeth unto ~~Elizabeth~~ Issabell Thyrlwynde my daughter my best fryeing pan & one gray coverlet: Also I gyve & bequethe unto Elizabethe Whitesyde 12d. Item I gyve & bequethe unto Elizabethe her doughter 12d.: Item I gyve & bequethe unto William Pattrick my sonne one coppe yock one draught yock one fowrme one benche in the parlor one stounde with eares one copsoule without pynne one great turnell one pewter dishe & one beddstydd under the steares also I gyve & bequethe unto John Pattrik my granndsone all the payntyd clothes in the howse onely one wheleplowe with wheles one sack one borde called the aleborde one other bord next therunto: one beddstidd at the greesehedd & one hoope of barley whiche I lente hym to repare the howses yf neede requere: Also I gyve & bequethe unto Richard Pattrick the yonger 3s. 4d. Also I gyve & bequethe unto Anne Pattrick one pewter dishe: Item I gyve & bequethe unto Richard Pattrik thelder 6s. 8d. Item I gyve & bequethe unto Roger Pattrik brother unto the said Richard 13s. 4d. yf he come for it & if he come not then I gyve & bequeth the same unto Issabell & Ellen my doughters & unto Margrete Patrik doughter unto Homnfree my son to be equalie devided betwixt them Item I gyve & bequethe unto William Bebbyngton my granndson 3s. 4d. & unto Ellen Bebyington hys sister 3s. 4d. Item I gyve & bequethe unto my sister Eve 12d. & unto Edward & Katheryn her children eyther of theme 6d. Also I gyve & bequethe unto John Burton 3s. 4d. Item I gyve & bequethe unto Jone Allixanders one over warne coverlet: Item I gyve & bequethe unto Richard Foundelynge one hoope of corne: Item I gyve & bequethe unto William Telior 12d. Item I gyve & bequethe unto Margrete Penket 6s. 8d. & one pewter dish & one canvasshete Also my ful mynd & will is that if it fortune that Margrete Pattrik alias Wilson base begotten doughter of Homnmfre Patrick alias Wilson to lyve untill she have fullye accomplished the age of 21 yeres then I gyve & bequethe unto the said Margrete one black cowe with a star in the forhed one bedsted one fetherbed whereon I lye one bolster one tikk pillowe 2 coverlets the one red & blewe the other white one blanket 2 peere of shetes the paynted hangyngs about the the [*sic!*] same bedd 2 brasse potts the one of 3 gallons the other almost 2: 2 candelstiks the one of brasse the other of pewter the coffer at the bedsfeete one gryd Iron one tabelclothe one towell one brasse chafying dishe one broche one spynnynge whele one brasse panne of 4 gallons: one brend Iron the better peere of pothookes one chene over the fore & fyve pewter dishes 2 counterfetts at the hall of Chorley in the custodie of John Bebington

2 counterfetts one depe potynger a saltceller & one new cheese: & yf it fortune the said Margrete Pattrik alias Wilson to decesse & dye before she have accompished the full age of 21 yeres that then I gyve & bequeth unto William Pattrik: Issabell Ellen & Margrete my children all these parcells of goodes for said & my sonneinlaw William Palen to have the custodie of the same goodes untill the said Margrete have accomplyshed the age of 21 yeres also I gyve & bequeth my goodes movable and unmovable unbequethed unto William Issabell Ellen & Margrete my sonn & daughters equally to be devyded between them.

Executors : William Palen of Spurstowe in the countie of Chester husbandman, John Burton of Preece, in the countie of Salop yeoman.

H & S

Witnesses: Richard Rodgers, Randull Hare.

Debts which the testator doth owe at the houre of her death:

	s	d
Isabell Cooke	23	4
to Margaret Pownall	22	0

Inventory: Elizabeth Pattrick of Chorley alias Wilson.

Taken: 29 December 1597

Of: goods and Cattells.

Prisers: Roger Broome, Randull Hare, Richard Rogers, Thomas Pollett, with others.

	£	s	d
3 kine price	12	14	4
2 threeyeware bullock price	4	13	4
haye and Corne price	7	8	0
brasse and pewter price		20	0
Iron ware price		2	6
cowprie ware price		8	0
beds formes trestelles and shilfes price		4	0
4 payre of bedstocks		2	0
butter & Cheese price		16	0
one hogge in salte price		10	0
beddinge and napprie ware price		40	0
shoote pigg price		3	4
pultrie ware hennes & geese price		5	0
her wearinge apparell price		26	8
paynted Clothes price			12
Corne sowen upon the grounde beinge bladdes		26	8
Summa	31	19	10
[recte	33	00	10]

Endorsement: Probated 2 January 1597; administration to William Palen, the executor named in the will.

16. HUMPHREY WILSON OF CHORLEY

S.Pr. 27 Nov 1602
W.T. 24 July 1602
Buried: 25 July 1601[!]

[NOTE: either the Parish Register is inaccurate as to the year of burial, or else the dates in the will are incorrect].

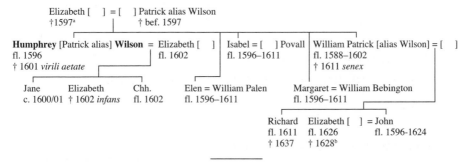

Will, sick.

First, I bequeath my soule into the hands of almightie god And *my bodie to bee buried in the parishe Church of Wrenbury* accordinge to the discreacōn of my executors Item my will is that all my goods moveable and immoveable bee devided into three parts equallie whereof my will is that Elizabeth my wife shall have the one parte and my Children one other parte and the third parte to discharge my debts and Funerall expences and that which doth remaine the saide debts and Funerall expencs discharged I give and bequeath amonge my saide Children Item my will is that my saide wife shall have the goverment of all the saide goods and Children so longe as shee doth keepe her Widdowe Item I give and bequeath unto the Children of my brethern and Sisters in this shier *[i.e. shire]* & 12d. a peece Item I geve to the repaire of Wrenbury Church 3s. 4d.

Executors: John Hall, and the testator's brother William Wilson.

Debts owing by the Testator:

	£	s	d
To Edward Minshall		40	4
To William Prince clerk		*[damaged]*	
To [John or William Pattericke]		*[damaged]*	
To *[damaged]* Hall		*[damaged]*	
[Sum		40	4]

ᵃ See will of Elizabeth Patrick alias Wilson of Chorley, widow, pr. 1597/98 (will no. 15).
ᵇ See will of John Patricke, pr. 1626 (will no.72).

Debts owing to Testator:

	£	s	d
John Patricke	10	6	8
John Griffith	3	20	0
William Pattricke		10	0
John Simcone	4	6	0
[Sum	17	42	8]

Witnesses: William Prince clerk, John Pattricke, John Hall.

Inventory: Humphrey Wilsonn.

Taken: 13 August 1602

Of: goods and Cattells.

Prisers: Roger Broome, Richard Dune, John Patricke, and Raphe Preane.

	£	s	d
14 kyne and a bull	28	0	0
2 oxen	6	0	0
foure younge beasts	4	0	0
a mare		46	8
fowre swyne		40	0
sixe sheepe		26	0
all haie and corne	12	0	0
all husbandrie ware and plowes Carts harrowes yoaks Cheanes and other Instruments thereunto belonginge		30	0
one Father bed six coverletts and a blankett		46	8
all linnens and naperieware		30	0
all brasse and pewter		20	0
all bedstocks bords and formes Chests and all treene ware		20	0
his apparell		26	8
Some totallis	50	284	24
[*recte*	64	6	0
for butter and Cheese the rente together and funerall expenses beinge dishchargede		20	0

Debts that are owinge mee: [*repeat of above with small variations*]

	£	s	d
John Patricke	9	6	8
John Griffith	3	19	0
William Pattricke		10	0

John Simcone	4	6	0
[Sum	16	3	8]

Endorsement: Exhibited 27 Nov 1602, and because the executors named in the same utterly renounced the burden of execution of the same, as is asserted by Elizabeth the relict of the said deceased, administration was granted to the same Elizabeth sworn in person.

17. ELLEN FLAVELL OF CHORLEY, WIDOW

Pr.S. 27 July 1604
Buried: No record at Acton or Wrenbury[a]

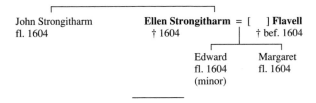

Will, sick in body.

I give my brother John Strongitharm 20s. To Robert Eccles in Sound 5s. to Thomas Swane 2s. to Henrie Swane 2s. to Randulff Swane 1s. to Aleys Swane 1s. to my sonne Edward Flavell I give towe hefers & one cowe. My will is that my daughter Margaret Flavell have the halfe of the housse tyll hir brother Edward be 21 yeares of age. I give my sonne Edward all my husbrandry ware I give to my sonne Edward one bedd. And for all the rest of my goods whatsoever I give to my daughter Margaret Flavell.

Executors: the testator's brother, John Strongitharm, and her daughter, Margaret Flavell, and Henry [Heigh]field

Inventory: Ellyn Flavell.

Taken: 20 July 1604

---

[a] There are no Parish Register entries bearing either the name of Flavell or Strongitharm, leaving highly questionable whether or not this will rightfully belongs in this collection. Of the other surnames noted in the will, only Swann, Wright and Falkener occur in Wrenbury records, but none of the individuals here noted can be identified.

Prisers: John Wright, Thomas Whytycars Thomas Strongitharm.

		£	s	d
one cowe that was the heryote	7 nobles =			
7 kyne		15	0	0
4 heyfers		5	8	4
4 styrkers		3	4	0
2 calves			20	0
3 mares		7	0	0
2 swyne			20	0
in pullyn			2	0
3 bushels of rye			30	0
2 bushells of barley			12	0
7 houpes of ottes			7	0
in corne upon the grounde		6	0	0
the husbandry ware			20	0
in pot brass & pane brass		3	0	0
in pewtter			18	0
in cannvres[ ]ules and wooden ware			27	0
drynking pots and glasses			4	0
Cresetts Goberts & Iron ware			4	0
bedsteads cowpery bords formes			14	0
her apparell & nappery ware		4	0	0
in lynine cloth			23	0
in beddynge			44	0
in cheyse and bacone			30	0
in a tacke of ground		3	10	0
debts William Colfall [?]			30	6
Margaret Norbury		3	2	0
the said Margaret			6	7
Edward Swane			51	11
Edward Chantler & Edger Chantler			50	0
Rodger L[yes] of Denton			15	0
the executors of Edward Falkener			17	4
Thomas Swane			5	0
Thomas Strongitharm			2	9
Anne [Dalle]			6	4
George [Burgen]			7	0
[Sum		49	488	45]

Endorsement: Probated 27 July 1604; administration to the executors named in the will.

18. JOHN CARTWRIGHT (THE ELDER) OF ASTON

S.Pr. 24 Nov 1604[a]
W.T. 19 August 1604
Buried: 15 September 1604

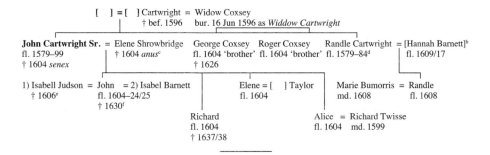

NOTE: *The condition of this will in 2002 was extremely poor, necessitating imme-diate attention by the preservation specialists at the CRO; rather than indicate with [damaged] throughout the transcription,* we have inserted words in brack-ets where the meaning seems indisputable, but otherwise left the brackets empty to indicate the damaged portions of the will.

Will, sick.

I bequeath my soule to the almightie god my maker [and] redeemer and *my bodie to be [burie]d in Wrenbury [C]hurch.* Item I give & bequeath [to] the righte wor-shipfull Mr. G[eorge] Cotton Esquire one Ang[el]l of gold for a remembrance of my good will to his worshipfull. Item I give unto my wife Elene Cartwrighte duringe her lief the beste bed in the parlor and the furniture to itt and after her lief ended then I give the same bed & the furniture to itt to my sonne Richard Cartwrighte [Item I] give to my wief Elene C[ar]twrighte the one half of my pewter and thother half of my pewter I give to my sonne Richard Cartwrighte. Item I give [more] to my wief Elene Cartwright the great Cheste in the parlor and all her linnen Clothes and one Mattres and the best Coverlett & one white

---

a   Date of probate is based on James Hall's notes of ca. 1890, since the Endorsement is no
    longer extant; see 'Newhall Families' (CRO).
b   Acton parish registers (CRO) contain a badly damaged marriage entry dated between 1609
    and 1617 for Randle Cartwright and Hanna Barnett. While this could be either Randle sen-
    ior or junior, it is most likely the elder, given the recent (1608) marriage of Randle junior to
    Marie Bumorris.
c   Buried 5 December 1604 as *Elline* Cartwright *anus.*
d   Juror at Newhall Court 1579; noted in will of Thomas Massey, pr. 1584/CRO.
e   Buried 13 May 1606 *Elizabeth* Cartwright.
f   See will of John Cartwright of Aston, pr. 1630 (will no. 81).

ticke bo[lst]er. Item I give more to wief Elene Cartwrighte and to little William
Cartwrighte [ ] hose sheepe [ ] are [ ] give I take them to Bee [ ] ht [ ] in [ ] m[ ]
er to be equalie devided betwixte ha[ ] t[ ] Item I give to my daughter [A]lice
Twis[se] the . . .

[p. 2] . . . moveable or unmovable. I give unto my sonne John Cartwrighte recon[]
in [ ] my debts. Item I give to Frances Cartwrighte 40s. Item I give [my sonne]
John Cartwrighte 25s. 8d. and my dager and knyves. Item I give to my brother
George Coxsey 10s. Item I give to the parish church of Wrenbury 6s. 8d. Item I
give to Randle Bathoe my beste sute of apparell & the second sute of my apparell I give to George C[oxs]ey also my will is that my sonne John Cartwrighte shall
paie the rent for the grounde hee holds of [me] after my decease And I doe leave
my sonne John Cartwrighte and my brother Roger Coxsey [to have my body]
brought home att their discracōns Item I give to John Jackson twoe sonnes 3s. 4d.
a piece. Item I give to my daughter Elene Taylor 12d. for her childs parte of good.
Item I doe [give] unto my sonne John Cartwrighte 28s. nowe which I have owinge
unto mee [which he] oweth. Item my sonne John Cartwrighte oweth mee that is
due nowe £24. Item ~~Mr. Richard Clutton~~ the same John Cartwright oweth mee
more that is due at mid somer nexte to come [t]he some of £24 Item Mr Richard
Clutton hath [agr]eed to paie mee that [which is] owinge to mee by Thomas
Minshall the some of £3. Item [vi]ker of Act[on] [ow]eth due [M]artinmas nexte
[ ] Richard Johnson owe[th] mee £1 due [ ] John Barnett oweth mee 6s. 8d. [fr]om
[ ] Richard Cartwright [ ] my will is [to] bee discharged [ ] inter [ ] all the whole
[ ] ee [ ] legasies [ ] harriott & funerall [expenses] my debts of he[ ] discharged
and [ ] have disch[arged] hees th[ ] my mon[eye] [ ] debts [My s]onne Richard
[John?] Wright . . .

[p. 3] Twyfort what you will bestowe upon them for the reste of your freinds &
last of all . . .

Executors: the testator's sons, Richard Cartwrighte and John Cartwrighte of all.

Overseer: the right worshipfull George Cotton.

I hast forgotten one thinge that I am to paie to Elene Bickerton what is said to
bee due unto her to have of mee in my booke of Accompts in her [ ] I have owinge
mee more money by W[illiam?] T[aylor?] for [ ] the some of 26s. 8d. due [y]earlie
[ ].

Witnesses: George Coxsie Randull Bathoe.

The [total] some of my debts that I [have owing] unto mee is as is above written
is in all [ ].

Debts that I doe owe my self to my sonne John as above saide is 28s.

No more to nobodie in all the world but what is found due for mee to paie to [Elene] Bickerton daughter of Humphrey Bickerton deceased.

Inventory: John Cartwright thelder of Aston in Newhall.

Taken: 13 November [1604]

Of: goods [cattells & Chattells].

Prisers: George Coxsey, Geoffrey Cartwright and Richard Shrobridge.

his wearinge apparell		£	33	8
in beddinge and naperie ware		[2]	10	0
in Brasse & pewter			60	0
in treene ware		[	]
one cubbord		[	]
[ ] bedstockes beds coffers		[	]
[ ] and Shilves		[	]
[ ] and Sheepe		[	]
in debts owinge unto		[	]

[badly damaged lower third of page 3]

Endorsement: *[The date of probate has been preserved in the historical notes of James Hall, cited above; presumably, administration was granted to the executors named in the will.]*

19. ELIZABETH COOKE OF WRENBURY FRITH, SPINSTER

I.Pr. 7 February 1604/05
W.T. 2 January 1604/05
Buried: 6 January 1604/05

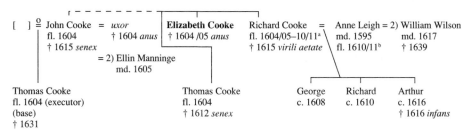

^a Executor for Alles Swane, 1610 (will no. 31); priser for William Davies, 1611 (no. 36).
^b Witness for Alles Swane, 1610 (will no. 31).

Will, sick.

I bequethe my bodie unto Allmightie god my maker & Redimer Trustinge by Faythe to be saved in Christ Jesus & *my bodie to be buried in Wrenbury Churchyard* & my funerall to be at the descretion of my Executors.

	s	d
I geve to my brother Thomas Cooke	20	0
I give unto Margret Fillcocke	20	0
I give unto Alles Savage	20	0
I give unto John Whittingham	5	0
I give unto Marrie Grindley	5	0
[Sum	70	0]

All the Rest of my goods movable or unmovable quicke or dead of what kynde or quallitie soever the be I give unto Thomas Cooke a basterd of John Cooke of Newhall.

Debts owing to the Testatrix:

	£	s	d
Thomas Backhowse of Canfeth Green	6	0	0
Richard Taylor of Burleydam		30	0
John Taylor of the Chappell house		20	0
Thomas Grindeley and John Collines of Woodhouses		40	0
John Greene of Grindleys Green		10	0
Allen Clarre of Grindleys Green		40	0
Richard Batte of Inillon		20	0
Richard Shawe of Burleydam		50	0
[Sum	6	210	0]

Executors: Thomas Cooke (a bastarde of John Cooke), and Richard Hamnet of the Fellees.

Wittnesses : John Prowdman, John Cooke, Thomas Weebe.

Inventory: Elizabeth Cooke of Wrenbury Frith.

Taken: 6 February 1604/05

Of: goods.

Prisers: Richard Cooke, Allen Clarre.

	£	s	d
in Readie money and Debt	18	10	0
one pyde Cowe price		30	0
3 sheepe price		10	0

brasse and pewter price	6	0
5 hives of beese price	20	0
beddinge and napprie ware price	20	0
2 Cofferes price	2	0
her wearinge apparall price	13	4
[Sum	18 111	4]

Endorsement: Probated in the presence of Richard Kettle clerk, dean and [ ] man 7 February 1604/05; administration to Thomas Cooke one of the executors named in the said will.

20. ALICE BLACKAMORE OF WRENBURY FRITH, WIDOW

I.Pr. 23 February 1604/05
W.T. 1604
Buried: 9 November 1604

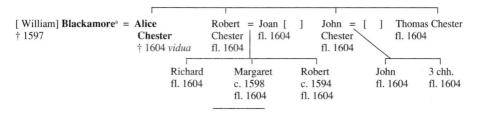

Will, sick.

First, I bequeath my sole to Almightie God my maker and Redemer by whose death I hope to have forgevnes of all my sinnes and *my bodye to be buried in the Churchyard of Wrenbury,* Item I give and bequeth to my brother Robart Chester and Johne his wyfe all my whole korne in on field called Hitchins Field to theme & ther Assignes Duringe the lyfe of Ales Wright wyfe of John Wryght Item I give and bequeath to John Chester sonne of John Chester my Brother one cubbord and that his father shall have the use thereof Duringe his lyfe Item I give & bequeath to my Brother Thomas Chester the bed which I doe use to lye on with all the aportnences thereto belonginge Item I give & bequeath to Hughe

---

[a] A Robert Blackamore and a William Blackmore were both buried at Wrenbury in 1597. Except for Alice, the next burial entry is that of Robert Blackamore, *senex*, in 1609. It thus seems likely that the Robert of 1597 was a younger person, perhaps even a child, while the William was Alice's husband.

Blackamore my greatest pan Item I geve unto Margarett Chester Doughter of Robart Chester my second pann Item I give & bequeath to my brother John Chester 10s. Item I give & bequeath to my brother Thomas Chester an Iron pot Item I give & bequeath to Richard Chester and Robart Chester sonnes of Robart Chester other towe potts Item I give to my brother Robarts three Children everyon a Coffer Item I give to John Chester and Thomas Chester my bretheren eich of theme A stricke of barlie Item I give to my brother Thomas his three children 6s. Item I give to Anne Higson yongest of Thomas Higson 12d. All the Rest of my goods Cattelles and Debts my debts beinge paid my legasies and my funerall Expenses discharged I give and bequeath to my brother Robart Chester and this my present will.

Executors: William Cartwright and the testatrix's brother, Robert Chester.

Overseer: John Bickerton.

H. & S. (no signature)

Witnesses: Thomas Chester, Richard Morres.

Debts owed by Testatrix:

	s	d
John Ferrer	27	8
Jasper Priese	7	0
Robart Tudman	6	8
John Barnet milliner	3	4
John Bickerton	22	0
William Cartwright	5	0
Roger Hockenhill	13	4
Thomas Edgley	6	8
[Sum	89	32]

Inventory: Alles Blackamore of the parishe of Wrenbury.

Taken: 10 November 1604

Of: goods & Cattles.

Prisers: John Bickerton, Robert Fisher, Robert Henberie & Thomas Chester.

	s	d
her wearinge Clothes praysed to	6	8
wood praysed	2	0
6 geese & 6 hennes on cocke on cappon	5	0
beddinge & naprie ware	10	0
brasse & pewter praysed to	5	0
Iron ware preysed	2	6
Cheese & Butter with the potts the butter is in with other earthen poots prased to	6	8

one Cubbord with bordes formes with other treenware prased to	10	0
three Coffers preysed to	3	0
three kyne on little mare prased to	5 10	0
on Hogge praysed	8	0
Corne & hay prased to	33	4
towe prased to	20	0

Suma Totalis	10	8	10
[*recte*	5	120	26]

Endorsement: Probated in the presence of Richard Kettle dean, 23 February 1604; administration to the executors named in the will.

21. ROGER BROOME OF CHORLEY, YEOMAN

S.Pr. 12 August 1606
W.T. 6 August 1606
Buried: 10 August 1606

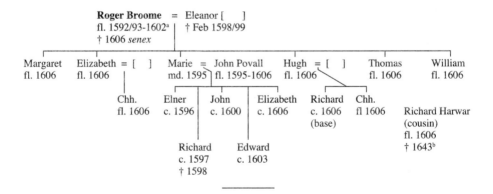

[a] Made inventory for William Bebbington 1592/93 (will no. 9); owed debt of 5s. to Humphrey Bickerton, 1594 (will no. 12); priser for Elizabeth Patrick alias Wilson, 1597 (will no. 15); priser for Humphrey Wilson 1602 (will no. 16).
[b] Buried at Wrenbury (see Bishop's Transcripts – Burials); resident of Nantwich.

Will, sick.

First, I bequeath my soule into the hands of almightye god my maker and onelie Redeemer trusting onelie to be saved by the merritts and bloodsheeding of Jesus Christ my onelie saviour And my bodie to be buryed in Christian buriall according to the discrecōn of myne executors Item my will is that all my Debts which I shall owe at the tyme of my decease and my funerall expences shall be paied out of my whole goods Item I give and bequeath unto my sonne Hughe Broome the longe table standing in the howse with the frame thereunto belonginge with the form and benche and stylinge work upon the bentche exceptinge a border of Cuttwork upon the said styling and the painted Cloath upon the beantche with all the glass about the howse Item: I give unto my said sonne Hughe Broome 12d. in moneye in full satisfaccōn of his Child parte of goods Item I give and bequeath unto my sonne Hugh his two Children 6s. 8d. a peece Item I give unto my daughter Elizabeth Children 6s. 8d. a peece Item I give and bequeath unto my daughter Marie Children to eache of them £4 apeece in moneye and if anie of her said Children Doe dye that then the said legacie of £4 to be equallye devided amongst the Rest of the said Children Item I give unto the said Children of my daughter Marye all my tytle estate and interest of one Crofte belonging to Henrye Healinshowse as by all asseyment doeth appeare, and my will is that my sonne in lawe John Povall shall have the good interest of the said money and Crofte for the use and behoofe of the said Children puttinge in securytie unto myne executors for the payement of the same at what tyme or tymes all myne executors shall demande the same Item I give unto my daughter Margarett 12d. in moneye in full satisfaccōn of her Childs parte of goodes Item I give unto my Cosin Richard Harware 10s. in gould Item I give unto my sonne William Broome that £30 which my sonne Thomas Broome is Covenanted by on assignement to paye unto him Item I give unto my said sonne William fortie shillings in consideracōn of a heffer which I gave unto him when she was a Calfe Item I give unto my sonne William a two yeare ould Coulte Item I give unto my sonne William 20s. in full satisfaccōn of his Childs parte of goods Item I give and bequeath unto my sonne Thomas Broome three plowes a Cupp yoke a draught yoke, a geare a Copp sole & a coppine Item I give unto my sonne Thomas a longe Chest Item I give unto my sonne Thomas one black Cowe with a whyte elder Item I give unto my sonne Thomas two Cart bads a Coppe a sett of spoaks & a sett of fellyes Item I give unto my sonne Thomas a ioyned bedstead standing in the lower Chamber the better of the two that are therein Item I give and bequeath unto my daughter Marye Povall the greatest brasse pott and the greatest brasse panne and fower of the greatest Chargers and alsoe a pewter flagen Item I give unto my sonne Thomas the fourth parte of all the rest and residue of the brasse and pewter Item I give unto my daughter Marie Povall all the lynnans Item I give unto my sonne Thomas the fourth parte of all the bedding whith one harrowe and a paier of ploweirons in full satisfaccōn of his Childs parte Item I give towards the Releefe of the poore of this parishe of Wrenbury 6s. 8d. All the Rest of my goods and Cattells moveable and unmoveable my debts being paied and my funerall expenses discharged I give and bequeath unto my sonneinlawe John Povall and Marie his wife.

Executors: my wilbeloved in Christ William Hassall of Alkinton within the Countie of Salop gent., and Raphe Davenport of Blackhurst within the Countie of Chester yeoman.

H.&S.

Debts owing by Testator:

	s	d
To Raphe Davenport	24	4
To John Povall	40 for a mare	
To John Povall	40 for a cowe	
I have given my worde to John Woodfyne for my sonne		
Hughe for a debt of	25	0
[Sum	89	4]

Debts owing to Testator:

	£	s	d
Thomas Broome my sonne	6	0	0
Hughe Broome my sonne		10	0
Robert Connyes		8	0
Wyddowe Motterham		7	0
which I paied her husband for a bussell of Rye and never had it delivered			
[Sum	6	25	0]

the mark X of
Roger Broome

Witnesses: William Prince Clerke [at Wrenbury], Edward Bradford C.

Inventory: Roger Broome of Chorley.

Taken: 15 August 1606

Of: goodes and Cattels.

Prisers: William Bebington, Richard Davenport, John Patterick and Richard Rogers.

	£	s	d
6 oxen	25	0	0
9 kyne & one calfe	20	10	0
fower twinters & 4 yerlinge stirkes	14	0	0

2 marres	4 marks: (=	52	16)
3 & twenty sheep	3	40	8
for 4 swyne		40	0
the poultry ware		5	4
all the Corne growinge	8	0	0
all the hay		50	0
An ould bound Cart and a muck Cart		40	0
plowes Harrowes yokes chaynes Capsoules with other implements belonginge		20	8
Cart timber & plow timber also Bordes		20	0
the mucke		10	0
wood & turves		26	8
a ladder & towe swine troughes			20
for hemp growinge		3	4
for butter & cheese		50	0
for all the molte & Corne within ye house		45	8
wole Yearne & towe		24	0
seven flyches of Bacon & a Beefe		42	0
all the Brasse	8	0	0
all the pewter	3	10	0
towe washne dishes & 3 ticknals one glasse Charger		5	0
6 silver spoones		40	0
a firegrate broches & gobartes dripinge pans Brunderd with other implements of Iron		30	0
a hammer & ymsons & other ieron tewels		5	0
the best ioyned Bedsted	4 marks: (=	52	16)
one truckle Bed		3	4
Chestes & Boxes with one little [?]press in the lower Chamber		30	0
bedstockes with a matarese one tub in the loft towe in the house		13	4
3 payre of bedstockes with other bordes and Implements in the lower loftes		13	4
3 ioyned bedsteades standinge in the 2 lower Chambers and 3 chestes in the same		22	4
tables ioyned stoyles Syting Cheres benches formes shelfes in the butteries		40	0
a Cuphord in the house		20	0
Cupes glasses & earthen potts		2	0
a Cheespresse & frame		5	0
all the treene ware & tow spininge wheles		35	0
the Beddinge in the towe lower chambers and in the said loftes over the said Chambers	7	0	0
18 yeards of wollen Cloth at dressinge		30	0
all the nappery ware	4	13	13

the Beddinge in the higher Chamber & the loft over the same	3	13	4
a plate Colt a head peace 2 polayens		10	0
a Cross bowe towe gaffes a sword and dagger & towe bucklers		20	0
one pictures & paynted clothes		2	0
one Carpet & 6 quiches		20	0
his wearinge apparrell		40	0

Some is	142	27	4
plus 8 marks:	(	104	32)
[*recte*	142	131	36]

Prisers: (repeated) William Bebington, Richard Davenport, John Paterick, Richard Rogers.

Endorsement: Probated 12 August 1606; administration to the executors named in the will; they have to exhibit an inventory at Michaelmas next. The inventory was exhibited 27 September 1606.

22. JOHN HALL OF SMEATONWOOD, YEOMAN

S.Pr. 29 October 1606
W.T. 3 December 1605
Buried: 7 December 1605

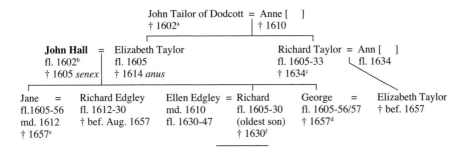

[a] See will, pr. 1602, Audlem parish/ CRO.
[b] Executor for Humphrey Wilson's will, pr. 1602 (will no. 16)
[c] See will of John Tailor of Dodcott, pr. 1602/CRO; further, will of Richard Tailor of Dodcott, pr. 1634/CRO.
[d] Bequeathed 12d. as god-son of George Kemp, will pr. 1616 (will no. 50); noted in will of Richard Tailor of Dodcott as his son-in-law, will pr. 1634/CRO; see will of George Hall of Aston, pr. 1657 (will no. 142).
[e] See will of Jane Edgeley of Moorehall, pr. 1657/58 (will no. 144).
[f] For documentation, see below, no 83, note a.

Will, sick.

First, I doe moste humblye Comitt my soule into the hands of almightye god assuredlye trusting by the death and merritts of myne onelie Savior and Redeemer Jesus Christ and faith in him to be saved And *My bodie to be buryed in the Church or Church yard of Wrenbury* at the discrecōn of myne executors And as touching my worldly goods First I give and bequeath to Jane Hall my daughter £60 to be paied to her within two yeares next after my decease out of my whole goods Item I give and bequeath to Richard Hall myne oldest sonne my seacond best fetherbedd with the Coveringe blanquetts & other furniture to the same belonginge & two paier of sheets and also the moytye or one halfe of all my Carts timbrells yokes Cheynes plowes harrowes and other implements of husbandry Item I give and bequeath to Elizabeth my welbeloved wyfe the other moytye or half of all my said Carts tumbrells yokes Chaynes plowes harrowes & other Implements of husbandrye Item whereas I did lend unto the right worshipfull and my verie good Mr. George Cotton Esqr. £3 13s. 4d. I doe forgive him the same And doe give and bequeath unto him more 10s. in gould Item after my debts paied my funeral expenses discharged & my former mencōned legacies performed my Will and mynd is that all the rest and residue of my goods Cattalls Chattalls and debts shall be devided into two equall moyties or parts the one moytye or halfe whereof I doe give and bequeath to the said Elizabeth my Wyfe And I doe further give and bequeath unto the said Jane Hall my daughter £10 to be paied to her out of the other halfe or moytye of the said rest & residue of my said goods Cattalls Chattalls and debts And the rest residue and Remnant of the same other half or moytye of the Rest of my said goods Cattalls Chattalls and debts I doe give and bequeath unto George Hall my sonne.

Executors: the testator's wife Elizabeth and the testator's son Richard Hall.

Overseer: Mr. George Cotton.

H. & S.

Debts owed by Testator:

Whereas I have beene Charged with the goods of Mistris Jane Cotton I have delivered twentye pounds thereof to my said Mr. George Cotton Esqr. whereof I humblye desire to see myne executors discharged Item I have more of her in my hands 13s. 4d. & 12s. and also one Cowe.

Debts owing to Testator:

	£	s	d
of Thomas Ranscroft of Newhall	10	0	0
William Higgenson		20	0
John Higgenson and Richard Higgenson which I forgive them		20	0
William Barnes		10	0
Roger Hamnett		13	4

	£	s	d
Richard Taylor my brother in law	4	0	0
whereof I forgive him		20	0
William Cappur of Poolecroft Heath	7	0	0
Alane Coxie the wyfe		10	0
John Taylor of Aston		28	0
John Evanson, Humfrey Evanson & Richard Evanson one			
Cowe price		43	4
Thomas Starkie the yonger		2	0
William Lucas to the use of Richard Bowyer which he gave			
his word to paie		10	0
William Prynce Curat of Wrenbury		6	0
[Sum	21	182	8]

John Hall (marke)

Witnesses: Thomas Poole, George Maynwaring, Hughe Hopkin, Thomas Babington, George Coxsie (marke).

Inventory: John Hall of Smeatonwood.

Taken: 13 December 1605

Of: goods and Cattalls.

Prisers: Thomas Grene, Thomas Swane, Thomas Babington and George Coxsie.

	£	s	d
eight drawen beasts & one old bullock	25	0	0
17 kyne and one bull	45	0	0
11 three yeare olds and twynters	15	0	0
5 yeare ould Calves	3	13	4
one bullock and two heffers fatt	5	0	0
two mares and one fillye	5	10	0
24 sheepe	4	10	0
foure rearing swyne & one hogg	33	4	0
in wheat and Rye	2	6	8
in barlie	5	0	0
in oates	2	10	0
all the haye	6	0	0
in malt 18 bushells	5	0	0
three fetherbedds with theire furniture	5	6	8
foure mattresse bedds & one chaff bedd with theire furniture		46	8
Lynens and napperie ware	9	0	0
eight bedsteeds		26	8
a press and six Coffers		20	0
a Cupboard & boards formes and stooles		16	0

shelves and all treene Ware		26	8
brass and pewter	3	13	4
plowes and Carts yokes and cheanes harrowes and all other			
Implemnts of husbandrye	4	0	0
Iron Ware within the house		6	8
sacks and baggs		2	6
butter and Cheese	3	16	8
hopps		13	4
hempe flaxe and yarne		10	0
[damaged top of page]		3	4
bacon	2	10	0
poultrie		6	8
painted Cloathes		2	0
bees		6	8
his apparell		26	8
one ould heirs Cloth		2	0
sawed boards & Reales and other broken tymber		13	4
six silver spoones		30	0
in readie money	42	12	0
in debts oweinge as maye appeare by the ~~bill~~ will	27	2	8

More unsett downe in the will as followeth

Mris Kathren Poole wyfe of William Poole of Marley	4	0	0
George Kempe	4	0	0
Thomas Bernett	4	0	0
Allen Coxsie		40	0
Randall Buckley		20	0
John Taylor of Aston		20	0
Roger Hamnett		20	0
John Phillipps		20	0
Thomas Massye of Wrenbury		10	0
[Sum	262	49	112]

Endorsement: Probated 29 October 1606; administration to the executors named in the will.

23. WILLIAM FLETCHER OF NEWHALL

S.Pr. 17 November 1607
W.T. 11 February 1606/07
Codicil: 12 March 1606/07

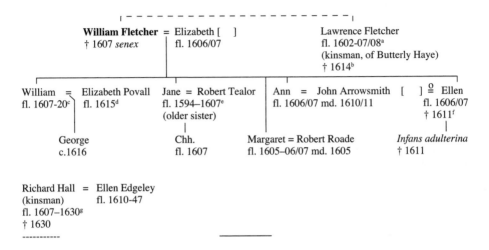

Will, sick.

First, I bequeath my soule to Almightie god my maker hopeinge all onelie to be saved by the merritts of Jesus Christ my onelie Saviour & Redeemer and *my bodie to be buried in the parishe Churchyard of Wrenbury* in the place accustomed for buriall Item I give and bequeath all that my messuage and tenement wherein I dwell with all the lands meadowes lessowes pastures woods and withall and singuler, the appurtenances to the same belongeinge or in anie wyse apperteyninge sett lyeing and beinge in Newhall in the Countie aforesaid and nowe in the occupacōn of me, the saide William or my assignes unto William Fletcher my sonne and to the heirs of his bodie lawfullie to be begotten for ever and for want of heires of my saide sonne William my will intent, and meaninge is and I doe give

---

a   Made inventory for John Tailer, 1602.
b   See will of Lawrence Fletcher of Butterly Heys (pr. 1614/ CRO).
c   Made inventory for John Backhouse, 1620 (will no. 61); 1615 married Elizabeth *Povey* (Povell) of Wrenbury parish: Wrenbury Bishop's Transcripts – Marriages.
d   William Fergusson Irving, *Chester Licences*, ii.193, at Wrenbury.
e   Noted 1594 as the god-daughter of Humphrey Bickerton.
f   An inventory of the goods etc. of Ellen Fletcher of Newhall, spinster, was made in 1611 (no. 37).
g   Richard Hall married Ellen Edgeley 1612 at Wrenbury; see also inventory of Richard Hall of Smeatonwood, 1630 (no. 83).

all my said landes, tenement, and other my hereditament before expressed unto Margaret Fletcher Ellen Fletcher and Ann Fletcher my Daughters to equallie to be devided amongst them and if soe it happen that it Doe fall and Come to them for want of heires of my said sonne my will is that my saide three daughters being possessed of my said tenement and lands shall give unto theire oldest sister Jones children ten pounds of Currant moneye of England equallie to be devided amongst them within one half yeare after that they shallbe possessed of the same Item my will intent and meaning is that after my decease Elizabeth now my wyfe shall have & enioye half of all my tenements lands and other my hereditaments During her naturall lyfe and my sonne William to have the other half against her and after her decease then to have hould and enioye yt all to him and all his heires as afore for ever provided alwaies that my said sonne William shall paye or Cause to be paied unto Margaret Fletcher Ellen Fletcher and Ann Fletcher my daughters to everye one of them severallie a peece tenn poundes of Currant moneye of England to be paied unto them my said daughters within one half yeare after it shall please god my said sonne William to marrie and take a wyfe or els within two years after it shall please god to take me out of this transitorie world & to departe this life Item I give and bequeath unto Elizabeth my wyfe and unto William my sonne all ymplementes whatsoever I have belongeinge unto husbandrie equallie to be devided betwixt them Item I give & bequeath unto Elizabeth my wyfe half of all my goods within my house except the bords sawes settells and shelves which I will my sonne William shall have and not to be removed out of my howse from hime Item I give unto my said wyfe three of my best kyne and my mare, and all the rest of my goodes my funerall expenses discharged I give and bequeath unto Margaret, Ellen, and Ann my daughters equallie to be devided amongst them in full satisfacion of all their childs parte of goodes whatsoever Item I doe forgive my daughter Jone 12s. which she borrowed of me and I doe give her 12d. of moneye in full payment and satisfacion of all her Childs parte of goodes.

Executors: Elizabeth, the testator's wife, and William Fletcher, his son.

Overseers: the testator's 'goode friends' Thomas Manwaring of Nantwich gent: Richard Hall of Smeatonwood, and Lawrence Fletcher of Butterly Hey, his kinsmen.

H. & S.

Witnesses: Thomas Manwaring John Hall John *[surname omitted]* Lawrence Fletcher John Backhouse.

A Codicell: added 12 March [1607].

Whereof I have given by my will within written unto Margaret Fletcher Ellen Fletcher and Ann Fletcher my Daughters tenne pounds apeece for their porcōns and for want of heires of my sonne William, my lande to goe to them three my will intent and meaning nowe is notwithstanding whatsoeever within wrytten is that inasmuch as my said daughter Margaret is now preferred by me in my life tyme to marriage shee shall accept and take that which I have given her & her husband for her full porcōn and satisfaccōn of her childs parte of goods and that hereafter that beinge paied & discharged she shall not make Clayme or Challenge to anie parte of my lands or goods but for ever to be frustrated and voyde from the same.

H. & S.

Witnesses: Thomas Manwaring, John Backhouse, Richard Hall, John Bickerton.

Inventory: William Fletcher of Newhall.

Taken: 29 July 1607, 5 James I

Of: goodes and Chattells.

Prisers: John Backhouse, John Bickerton Richard Hall & James Carter.

	£	s	d
in Cattell fyve kyne	13	0	0
towe twnter Bullocks	4	13	4
three sterke heffers	3	13	4
towe wayning Calves		20	0
one mare		40	0
one nagge		13	4
one sheepe		3	0
three swyne		30	0

In the house

	£	s	d
in Brasse and pewter	10	0	0
in Bedding & in nappery	10	0	0
in boordes formes & shelves		10	0
in Bedsteeds		3	4
towe Cuppords		20	0
in treene ware		30	0
in husbandry ware		40	0
towe pack saddles		10	0
all Iron ware		10	0
toe Cloth and yarne		1	0
in threshed Corne in the house		20	0
in Corne growing in the ground	2	0	0
in Cheeses	3	12	0
in Bacon		13	4
in hay and strawe		4	0
in Coffers & one greate chest		6	8
fewell		3	0

timber	3	4
towe ladders	2	0
three Cheers	2	0
foure Cushions	2	8
a payre of stocke Cards & Ripponcombe Well Cards		
& a hatchowe	2	0
in Broches	2	0
his wearing apparrell	26	8
toe growing uppon the ground	6	8
in paynted Clothes	5	0
in mucke	5	0
in Geese piggs and hens	5	0

Sum is	66	16	8
[recte	63	18	8]

Endorsement: Probated 17 November 1607; administration to the executors named in the will.

24. ROBERT BUCKLEY OF SMEATONWOOD, YEOMAN

S.Pr. PCC 3 February 1607/08
Nuncupative will of 11 and 30 December 1607
Buried: 31 December 1607

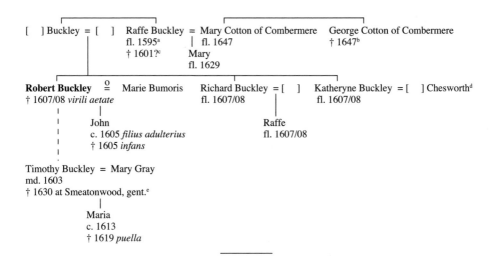

The laste will and testament of Roberte Buckley late of Smeatonwood in the countie of Chester yeoman deceassed as yt was delivered by him in words unto the personns whose names are under written the eleventh daye of December anno domini 1607 First I gyve and bequeath unto George Lester tenne pounds towards the buildinge of his howse Item I give and bequeath unto my Master a cupp like to that was geven him by John Taylor Item I give unto my Mistress my seale Ringe to be altered at her pleasure and to notaryze yt for me Item I give unto Mr Thomas Cotton tenne pounds Item my will is that my sister Katheryne Chesworth

---

[a] Randle Buckley owed Raphe Barnett a debt of £4 10s. in 1595; see will of Raphe Barnett, pr. 1595 (will no. 13).
[b] See will of George Cotton, pr. 1648 (will no. 128).
[c] Ralph Buckley 'by will in 1601 bequeathed 200 marks and directed thirteen penny loaves to be given among the poor of Wrenbury and Marbury; each poor person at the same time was to have one penny in money. He also directed his executors to build a schoolroom near the church of Wrenbury and give ten pounds a year for seven years towards the maintenance of a schoolmaster'. See Cheshire Federation of Women's Institutes, *Cheshire Village Memories*, p. 127; also Clarke, *Ancient Parish of Wrenbury*, p. 97. This is in turn most likely the Ralph *Bulkley* noted as the husband of Mary Cotton of Combermere.
[d] Given the peculiarity of the surname, this is probably identical with the *Cheswith/Cheswes* family which flourished within the chapelry at Mickley Hall.
[e] See will of Timothy Buckley, pr. 1630/31 (will no. 84).

shall have the threescore and tenne pounds beinge a remaynder of a legasye so lefte her by my unckle Raffe Buckley lastlye I give unto my brothers sonne Raffe Buckley one hundred pounds.

Witnesses: George Lester, Margaret Whitney[a].

Executor: Richard Buckley, brother of the testator.
There speeches heerunder written were confirmed by the saide Roberte Buckley the thirtith daye of December in the presence of those personnes whose names are under written, anno domini 1607 Item I give and bequeath unto my master five pounds to buy a cupp like to that John Taylor gave Item I give my seale Ringe to my Mistris to be altered into a ringe for her Item my will is that my sister Katheryn Chesworth shall have the threescore and tenne pounds in my hand remaynder of a legacye lefte her by my unckle Raffe Buckley Item I give unto Mistrises Elizabeth and Martha Cotton eyther of them twentie pounds Item I give to Mister Thomas Cotton tenne pounds Item I give unto Margery Whitney for her paynes tenne pounds.

Witnesses: George Lester, George Bickerton.

Endorsement: Probated at London before John Bennett knight of the laws, in the Prerogative Court of Canterbury, 3 February 1607; administration to Richard Buckley, brother to the deceased and the executor named in the said will.

---

[a] This otherwise unidentified woman is perhaps the unnamed wife of Michael Whitney of Newhall, whose will was pr. 1617 (no. 54).

25. HENRY VERNON OF COOLE LANE IN THE PARISH OF WRENBURY

S.Pr. 9 May 1608
W.T. 26 February 1607/08
Buried: 1 March 1607/08

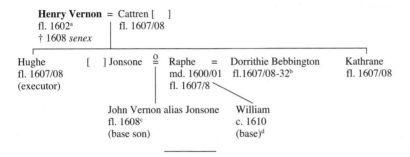

Henry Vernon = Cattren [ ]
fl. 1602[a]   fl. 1607/08
† 1608 *senex*

Hughe   [ ] Jonsone ≗ Raphe = Dorrithie Bebbington   Kathrane
fl. 1607/08   md. 1600/01 fl.1607/08-32[b]   fl. 1607/08
(executor)   fl. 1607/8

John Vernon alias Jonsone   William
fl. 1608[c]   c. 1610
(base son)   (base)[d]

Will, sick.

First, I comende my soule and life in to the hands of allmyghtye god trustinge to be savfed by the deathe and passion of his sonne Jesus Christe: and by the faithe in him I truste to be savfed And to be in the number of the Elleckte: & my bodye I Comite unto my Executors: to be Conveyed unto the Christian buriall at his descreshion: Item I geve and bequeath unto my wyfe Cattren Vernhone: the third parte of my goodes Cattles and Debts Item I geve and bequeath unto my Daughter Kathrane Vernhone Five pounds to be payed yerlye by my Executores at towe payementes dewringe her naturall life in full satisfaxshone of her Chiles parte and portion of my goodes Allso my will is that my sonne Hughe Vernhone shall asshew over her by good and suffeshante securetye: upon her demawnd or within on halfe yere after my deseace and the afforsaid payement to begine at mydsomer or Martinmas next after whether it shall happaine to faull firste after my deseace Item I geve and bequeath unto my sonne Raphe Varnhone twentye pounds in full satisfaxion of his Chides parte and portion of my goodes Item I geve & bequeath unto John Vernhone allious Jonson the reputed sone of my sonne Raphe Vernhone fortie shillinges to be payed unto hime within a monthe after my deseace that it maye be put forth for his prefermente, And further my will is that my Executores shall kepe hime the afforsaid John Vernhon allious Jonsone tull hee Com to be

---

[a] In 1602 the Welson family surrendered Pinnacle House in favour of Henry Vernon as sub-tenant; see CRO Newhall Manor Court Roll.
[b] A Dorothie Vernon is noted as the daughter of William Bebbington of Nantwich, 1632 (CRO).
[c] A John Vernon witnessed the nuncupative will of Richard Edgeley 1653 (will no. 153).
[d] William Pa[lin or -trick] *adulterius Rad.* Vernon.

twentie on yeres of age with good and suffesyente meate drincke & Apparell and that hee shalbe kepte unto skolle for a time at the defenshs of Mr. William Sallman my nighbore And I geve and bequeath unto my sonne Hughe Vernhone the Resedue of all my goodes and Cattles movfabell & unmovfabell and the Reste and Resedue of my debtes It my will is that If anye matters of Conterversie shall arise Conserninge the true meninge of this my laste will that then it shalbe devided by Mr. Robart Whitnaye and Mr. William Sallman.

Executor: testator's son Hughe Vernhone.

Witnesses: Jhone Vernhon, Hughe Vernhone clarke, Thomes Brocke, Raphe Venables.

Debtes owing unto the Testator:

	£	s	d
Robert Browne dothe owghe unto me of his owne debt the some of	28	0	0
Yt the same Robert Browne oweth unto Mr Lawrance Monckas of London I beinge his shewerty	22	10	0
William Gilbert of All[ert]on for charges of shewete in lawe		36	5
the same William Gilbert for rente of grownde	6	0	0
more hee owethe by shewetie for Hugh Woodlaye the clarke of All[ert]on	10	0	0
Raphe Venables his debte	4	0	0
John Blantoone for among [?] more	5	6	10
William Tayeller Chapman indebted unto me	[?]	5	0
Thomas Safton indebted unto me for a housse	3	6	8
Thomas Calles his debte in all unto me is	4	16	8
Thomas Monckas oweth unto me of a debt wich I borrowed of hime in the Cowntie Cowrte with ye charges of anterest		14	10
Wiliam Linghame of Sandbyge parish oweth unto me as maye appeare by a bill of his Hande & Mr Bromes	10	16	8
Thomas Bromes gentullmon owethe me	4	4	0
Hugh Dale late of Littull Hashall owethe me as maye appere by a bill	8	13	4
Raphe Cardy[f]e gentullmon oweth me lente monaye	4	4	0
Thomas Monchkas did receve more full his dewe of Mr Thomas Malbane for charges		6	0
Thomas Venables & John Ranshall oweth unto me as maye appere by there bill	15	15	4
more Thomas Venables oweth me recovred in the countie Cowrt	5	9	0
Robert Tenche oweth me that hath bine recovred by lawe the the debt is	30	1	2
more the charges in lawe dewe me	8	0	0

Johne Loe of Burleydam Chapell oweth unto me the some of	20	0	0
Ser Thomas Smythe Esquire oweth me the some of	5	8	4
wich debt I doe geve unto Margerye Darlington the dowghter of Gorge Darlington			

Total	188	165	72

Other debts:

John Tarnher of Buerton oweth unto me		6	1
more for a pacsadell		6	8
George Borrowes part of ye Racke his debte is	15	0	0
the same ?[ ] of Hendrye Gandye of Walkerton	12	0	0
Wiliam Browne of Buerton for rente	3	5	7
William Reiffe of Doddington oweth me the debte of		7	0
Charles Brocke late of Walkerton		16	10
John Jones butcher of Nantwich	9	10	0

[Total	46	44	17]

Ralphe Venables in debted unto me the some of £4 to be payed yerlye by 13 shillings and 4 pence. And the same Raphe Venables to geve unto the power *[poor]* of Namptwich 10 shillings to be payed at the discretion of my executors Mr Robert Whitnaye and Mr William Sallman.

wich to debtes I give and bequeth unto my brother John Vernhone as may appeare by a letter of attorney made and sealed by me.

Witnesses: Robert Whittingham, gent.

William Salmon, gent.
Robert Podmore
William Heifilld

Debita	224	19	6

Inventory: Henry Vernon of Coole Lane.

Of: good and chattels.

Taken: [before 24 March] 1607/08

Prisers: Roberte Whitnaye, William Sallman, Robert Podmore, William Heifilld.

	£	s	d
on ox wich went for the principall	7	0	0
4 oxsone praysed at	19	0	0
7 ould oxen praysed at	6	8	4
4 kine praysed at	10	0	0

	£	s	d
2 milk heaffers praysed at	5	0	0
2 other heifers praysed at	3	6	8
7 barrane cowe praysed at		40	0
2 bollockes praysed at	3	6	8
5 cawefes praysed at	4	0	0
6 shepe and 4 lambes praysed at	10	6	8
on owld mare praysed at	4	0	0
1 fillye coolt praysed at	3	8	4
on littull baye nage praysed at		26	8
on graye coolt praysed at		8	4
a parsell of Barly in the barne praysed at	10	5	0
riee in the same barne praysed at		26	8
wheate in the same barne praysed at		13	4
stocke in the same barne at		6	8
sartane hee in the barne praysed at		30	0
in the heehowes more hee praysed at		3	0
2 Ieren *[iron]* bownd cartes praysed at	4	8	4
2 mocke cartes praysed at		20	0
2 whiell ploues and 2 foote plowes at		4	0
some 40 lodes of mucke about the howse		23	4
2 shedes praysed at			12
all stex and other wode gotten for ye fier		2	0
2 harrowes praysed at		2	0
2 yelfes and on howe praysed at			18
3 pacsadles praysed at		10	0
2 hacknaye sadles praysed at with bridles		6	8
5 picklifes praysed at		2	0
all terrene ware with yockes and chaines at		35	0
on seithe and the sweathe praysed at			12
2 brackes praysed at			12
in the backhowes on tornell 1 combe 1 sokinge pipe and 2 chornes 2 stowndes praysed at		3	4
in the lofte over the homes 3 skore cheises at		33	4
in the same lofte 3 hopes of wheate		13	4
in the same lofte 20 parye of shites and 1 canves shit	4	10	0
more in the same chamber 5 flaxson shites		20	0
3 bordclothes napkins and other linens praysed at		4	0
1 crache to set in chieses			6
on cornes basket a heichowe bordes and small basketes		2	0
in the chamber over the parller 2 paryes of bedshites		2	0
2 flockebedes forneshed praysed at		20	0
on great sawe to sawe stox with at and 3 wedges		4	0
in the same chambers 4 boshells of otes		24	0
5 shipinges of yearne and 9 sackes		5	0
in the parller on paryer of bedstides and a feather bed			

praysed at	3	6	8
1 cubboard on tabell 2 coffers 1 forme praysed at		13	4
on barrel of varyies *[various]* praysed at		3	4
in the howes 1 longe tabell 1 forme 1 benche 2 cheares and shelves		13	4
6 quishenes upon the benche praysed at		15	0
8 hopes of wheate sowne in the grounde		40	0
in the loft over the cutrye 2 bedes		20	0
all brase and pewter praysed at	3	6	8
6 fletches of backhone *[bacon]* praysed at		40	0
potracktes and golbordes broches a gridieren 1 grate a fersholle 1 paryer of tonges and all iron ware		20	0
2 swine praysed at		20	0
2 potes of butter praysed at		12	0
more 1 combe and 1 tornell at		6	8
the paynted clothes praysed at			12
4 balles of flax praysed at		20	0
1 piece of howline cloth in the soo praysed at		15	0
the monaye in the there kepinge after the fewnrall	3	8	4
the wene rope and other th*[damaged]*htes		2	6
all the shelves stondes [?] and other treenen ware		13	4
on frine pane praysed at			6
his wayeringe apperill praysed at	[?]	3	4
[Sum	130	8	8]

Endorsement: Probated 9 May 1608; administration to the executors named in the said will.

26. JOHN TENCHE OF WRENBURY FRITH

I.Pr. 15 October 1608
Buried: 1 May 1603

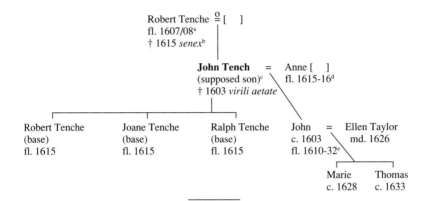

```
                    Robert Tenche ⚲ [    ]
                    fl. 1607/08ᵃ
                    † 1615 senexᵇ

                    John Tench    =   Anne [    ]
                    (supposed son)ᶜ      fl. 1615-16ᵈ
                    † 1603 virili aetate

Robert Tenche    Joane Tenche    Ralph Tenche    John    =    Ellen Taylor
(base)           (base)          (base)          c. 1603      md. 1626
fl. 1615         fl. 1615        fl. 1615        fl. 1610-32ᵉ

                                                Marie    Thomas
                                                c. 1628  c. 1633
```

Inventory: John Tenche of Wrenbury Frith.

Taken: 6 October 1608

Of: goods & Cattalls Chattalls and debts.

Priser: Robert Tenche, his father.

	£	s	d
a lease of a certaine peece of ground sett lyeing and being within the towneshipp or Lordshipp of Wrenbury Frith aforesaid valued unto the some of	33	6	8
according as was paidd for the same which the said deceadent died possessed of and noe more			
the some is	33	6	8

Endorsement: Inventory: of the goods of John Tench late of Wrenbury Frith deceased . . . by Robert Tenche his father having been duly sworn &c. 15 October 1608.

ᵃ See debts owed to Henry Vernon of Coole Lane, will pr. 1608 (will no. 25).
ᵇ See will of Robert Tenche of Wrenbury Frith, yeoman, pr. 1615 (will no. 45).
ᶜ So described (deceased) by Robert Tenche in 1615 (see will no. 45).
ᵈ This is undoubtedly the Anne Tench, widow, who occupied one of the tenements in Wrenbury Park belonging to Thomas Minshull of Erdswick (see R. Stewart Brown, *Cheshire Inquisitions Post Mortem*, ii. 207).
ᵉ Owed debt to James Barnett 1610; see latter's will, pr. 1610 (will no. 29); John Tench had a licence to marry Ellen Taylor of Marbury parish 1626 at Wrenbury or Marbury (see William Fergusson Irvine, *Chester Licences*, iii. 68); he was a priser of the inventory for Richard Cheswis 1632/33 (will no. 93).

NOTE: The reason for the long delay between the death of John Tench and the probate of his simple will cannot be ascertained with existing documents. One may wonder at the various claims to his estate, however, given the number of bastard children he sired. To complicate things, he was the 'supposed son' of Robert Tenche who administered his will.

27. WILLIAM SEAVELL OF NEWHALL

I.Pr. 19 April 1609
W. Anno domini 1607
Buried: 23 February 1608/09

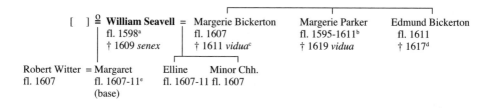

Will, sick.

First, I give & bequeath my soul to allmightee god my creator & redemmer & *my bodie to be buryed in the parish Church yard of Wrenbury*. . . . Item I give & bequethe to my doughter Elline my best pane but one & one Coffor & husbandrey [ware] and my bedestede Item the rest of my goodes I give & bequeth to my wife & Children payinge the debbtes which I owe to bringe me home.

Debts owed by the testator:

I owe to Robart Witter which maried my base doughter which I am behind with him for mariage good 20d. Item I give & bequeth to my Base doghter Margeret one shafeing dish.

Executors: the testator's wife, Margaret, and the testator's daughter, Elline.

S.

---

[a] Cottager of Newhall, 1598 Court Roll.
[b] Received 5s. as bequest from Raffe Barnett 1595; see will of Raffe Barnett (will no. 13).
[c] See will of Margerie Sevell of Newhall, widow, pr. 1611 (will no. 35).
[d] See will of Edmond Bickerton of Sound, pr. 1617 (will no. 56).
[e] Both Margaret and Elline appear as beneficiaries of Margerie Sevell in 1611 (will no. 35).

Witnesses: Richard Edgley, Robart Wright.

Inventory: William Sevell of Newhall.

Taken: 23 March 1608/09

Of: goods.

Prisers: Thomas Edgley, Robart Wright, John Massy, Richard Edgley.

	£	s	d
all his wearinge cloths praysed to	6	8	0
all his Befe praysed to	7	16	0
whereof the harriot was praysed to	2	13	3
all the poultrie praysed to		2	6
the Bedinge praysed to		2	0
shetes bordcloths & othar napprie ware with weringe cloths praysed		1	0
Brase & pewter praysed to		3	0
whereof he lefte one pare to his doughter Ellin Sevell which was praysed to		10	0
all Impellments of Iron other howse hould or husbandtrie prised to		3	4
cubord Dishbord & all bords formes cheres & stoweles		10	0
stoundes bouckes & all other trine ware in the howse		6	8
Chestes & Bedstockes prised to		10	0
Chushines & pinted clothes		2	6
tole & woole prised		10	8

	£	s	d
The whole somme is	19	7	8
whereof he was indebted fiftie shilliings			
[recte	15	96	35]

Endorsement: Probated before Richard Kettle 19 April 1609; *[no indication as to whom administration was granted].*

28. MARGARET ANKERS OF BROOMHALL, WIDOW

S.Pr. 13 March 1609/10
W. T. 27 July 1605
Buried: 24 December 1609

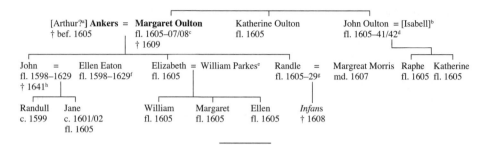

Will, sick.

First, I doe bequeath my soule to the hands of almightie god my maker saviour and redeemer by whose precious blood sheeding I trust to be saved and *my bodie to be buried in Christian buriall of the parishe Church or Church yarde of Wrenbury* afforesaide Item I geve and bequeath unto the poore people of the parishe of Wrenbury the sume of ten poundes of currant Englishe money which is in the hands of Thomas Tailer of Lightwood Green And the interest of the said ten pounds to be dealt everie yere at the feast of St Thomas the apostle before Christmas to the poore people aforesaid for ever Item I geve and bequeath to John Ankers my eldest sonne the great pott the bentch board and forme and halfe the Cheanes and yoakes and cart and plowes gotten upon the grounde and two shillinges of lawfull Englishe money in full satisfaccōn and paiement of all his parte and porcōn of his childes parte of all my goods and Chattells whatsoever Item I geve to Johan Ankers daughter of John Ankers my sonne 5s. Item I geve

---

a   An Arthur Ankers appears in 1602 as a debtor in a Tailor will.
b   The inventory of John Bostocke (1607/08) shows a debt of £2 15s. 6d. which he owed to Isabell Oulton: she fits extremely well within the timeframe of Margaret Ankers's will, and the fact that Margaret Ankers is also named in the Bostocke inventory suggests close association of them all. On the other hand, she could be the Katherine Oulton noted as the daughter of Oliver and Elizabeth Briscoe 1624–32; see will of Oliver Briscoe, made 1624/25, pr. 1630 (will no. 80); will of Elizabeth Briscoe, made 1632, pr. ?1637 (will no. 103).
c   The inventory of John Bostocke of Coole Lane, exh.1607/08/CRO, shows her owing 6s.
d   Priser of the inventory of John Anckers, pr. 1641/42 (will no. 115).
e   The given name, William, is deduced from the William Parkes who is one of the witnesses to the will, and also from the name of the oldest son (1605).
f   Noted as wife of John Anckers in his will, made 1629, pr. 1641/42 (will no. 115).
g   Noted in will of his brother, John Anckers, made 1629, pr. 1641/42 (will no. 115).
h   See will of John Anckers, pr. 1641/42 (will no. 115).

to Elizabeth Parkes my daughter three pounds for her childes parte of all my goods as aforesaid incase she survive and overlive me the said Margaret Ankers Item I geve to William Parkes Margaret Parkes and Ellen Parkes my daughters Children to everie of them 20s. apeece Item I geve to my brother John Oulton 13s. 4d. Item I geve to Raphe Oulton my brothers sonne 6s. 8d. Item I geve to Katherin Oulton my brothers daughter 20s. Item I geve to my sister Katherin Oulton 3s. 4d. Item I will and it is my full minde and entent that after my debts being paid and my funerall expences discharged, That then all such goods and chattells of myne as shall remaine moveable in what handes or what place soever the same shalbe shall remaine to the use behoofe and benefitte of Randle Ankers my sonne.

Executor: the testatrix's son, Randle Ankers.

S. and X

Wittnesses: William Prince, minister, Richard Plant, William Parkes, John Ankers, William Cudworth, Margaret Pemberton.

Inventory: Margaret Ankers of Broomhall.

Taken: 5 January 1609/10

Of: goods and Cattells.

Prisers: Robert Whitney gente, William Brees, Michael Hope, John Ankers, and John Myllinton.

	£	s	d
her apparell		40	0
thirtie kyne	70	0	0
foure yonge beasts	4	6	8
one horse and one mare	5	0	0
two swyne		6	8
poultrie		2	0
bedding and napperie	6	0	0
butter and Cheese	6	0	0
brasse and pewter		46	8
beefe and bacon		40	0
Iron ware		10	0
treene ware		10	0
boords formes shelves Cheares and stooles & bedstocks		13	7
Carts plowes harrows and such ymplements for husbandrie		10	0
Cushions baggs syves and basketts		20	0
haye and Corne sowen and unsowen		11	0
paynted clothes		12	0
all her fuell		5	0
seaven Coffers		10	0
in Debts oweinge or there abouts	12	0	0
two Cratches two ladders one sleade & swine troughes		20	0

a Cheese presse			18
a brake			12
two spyninge wheeles		2	0
a gryndlestone & the stock			6
a sleade vumade [*i.e. some part of a sled*]			8
a Crab troughe			12
a heyre clothe		2	0
more in Debts oweing	17	11	4
[Sum	120	264	103]

Endorsement: Probated 13 March 1609; administration to the executors named in the will.

29. JAMES BARNETT OF ASTON, YEOMAN

S. Pr. 21 August 1610
W.T. 12 May (1610)
Buried: 30 June 1610

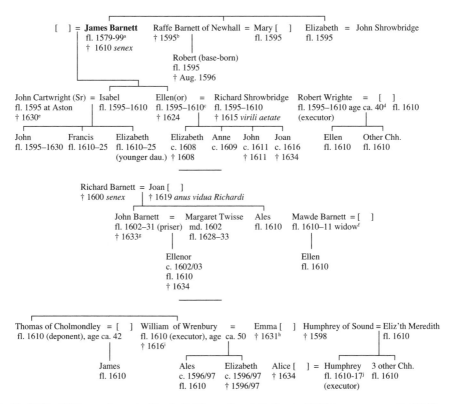

---

^a Fl. 1579, 1580 as a juror in Newhall Manor Court Rolls; in 1595 he appears with William Barnett as joint tenant of one messuage and a tenement and 6 acres of customary land in Newhall, held by Sir Hugh Cholmondeley, Sr, of Sir Thomas Egerton, Keeper of the Seal for Queen Elizabeth; appears also 1596–99 as James Barnett of Aston/CRO.

^b James was an executor of his will in 1595 (will no. 13).

^c Fl. 1595 as 'Cozen' of Raffe Barnett of Newhall (will no. 13).

^d Appears with an Ellen Wright (presumably his sister rather than his daughter) as recipient of a legacy from Raffe Barnett, 1595 (will no. 13).

^e See will of John Cartwright (will no. 81).

^f Appears as a widow in 1611 when she was fined 3s. 4d. at Newhall Manor Court for not scouring her ditch/CRO.

^g See will of John Barnett of Aston, yeoman, pr. 1633 (will no. 94).

^h See will no. 87 below, pr. 1631.

ⁱ See will no. 52, below, pr. ca.1616/17.

^j Priser of inventory of William Cooper of Sound, yeoman, 1613 (will no. 42) and of Edmond Bickerton of Sound, yeoman, 1616/17 (will no. 56).

Will, sick.

First, I comend my soule to god my maker assuredlie trusting that through the death and passion of my lord and savior Christ Jesus to have free remisson of all my sinnes and *my bodie to be buried within the parish churchyard of Wrenburie* Item my will is and I geve and bequeath to the use of the poore which dwell and heerafter shall dwell within the Newhall quarter £10 which my will is shalbe putt forth yeerlie by my executors and the survivor of them, and after their death by the churchwardens of the said parishe church of Wrenbury, and the profetts thereof to be yeerlie distributed amoungst the same poore upon Good Fridaie by my said executors and the survivor of them, and after by the said church wardens at their discrecōns. Item I geve to my daughter Isabell Cartwright £10 in lue of such part and porcōn as she maie anie way claime or chaleng of my goodes cattels or chattells. To John her sonne £10. To Francis her daughter £10. To Elizabeth her younger daughter £10. Item I geve to Ales Barnett daughter of Richard Barnett deceased 40s. To Ellenor Barnett daughter of John Barnett 40s. Item I geve to Robert Wright of Newhall his wief and children £10 amoungst them. Item I geve to Ellen Barnett daughter of Mawde Barnett £10. To Ales Barnett daughter of William Barnett of Wrenbury £3. To Humfrey Barnetts foure children £5. To Elizabeth Whittingham daughter of John Whittingham 20s. Item I geve to James Barnett sonne of Thomas Barnett of Chorley £4. Item I geve to Thomas Edgley William Barnett and Humfrey Barnett whom I make executors of this my last will £40 to be divided amoungst them equallie. Item I geve to Elizabeth late wief of Humfrey Barnett and daughter of John Meredith late of Kiddington deceased £40: Item I geve to Robert Ravenscrofte and his children 40s. Item I geve to Ellen my daughter in lue of her childs part of my goodes cattells and chattells 12d. To Oliver Acson and his wief 20s. Item I geve to James Acson their sonn 40s. Item I geve to Ellen, Johan, Thomas, Alice Barnett and John Ravenscrofte my servants 40s. a peece. Item I geve to Thomas Grey 40s. Item I geve to the widow Bathow, widow Blackmore, Ellen Cartwright daughter of Jeffrey Cartwright and Maud Fisher daughter of John Fisher £4 to be equallie divided betweene them. Item I geve to Elizabeth Whittingham wief of John Whittingham 40s. Item I geve to Richard Acson sonne of the said Oliver Acson £5. Item I geve to the children of William Barnett of Apsdall 40s. Item my will is that my funerall expences shalbe discharged out of my whole goodes.

Executors: the said Thomas Edgley dwelling in Newhall, the said William Barnett dwellinge in Wrenbury, and the said Humfrey Barnett dwelling in Sound.

S.

Item I geve to John Barnett of Pillston £10 and all such Debts as are owing to mee in Wynnall and Lutterworth.

Witnesses: Thomas Grey, Thomas Barnett, Thomas Burroughes.

Codicil 1 [written about 3 weeks after original will] Item I geve to Isabell Cartwright my daughter £10 more. To John her sonne £10 more. To Francis her daughter £10 more. To Elizabeth her younger daughter £10 more. Item I geve to my executors above named £20 more. Item I geve to Robert Paline 40s. Item I geve to Thomas Graie £3 more. Item I geve to Elizabeth Bewmariss 40s.

signum Jacobi X Barnett

Codicil 2 [written about 1 week before decedent's death] Item I geve to Margarett Henberrie 40s. Item I geve to John Parker 40s. Item I geve to John Massey 20s. Item I geve to Thomas Chester 40s. Item I geve to Thomas Turner 40s. Item I geve to Richard Turner 40s. Item I geve to Oliver Acson and his wief 20s. more. Item I geve to Hugh Hall 40s. Item I geve to Richard Evanson 40s. Item I geve to Humphrey Evanson 40s. Item I give to Thomas Evanson 40s. Item I geve to William Hurlbutt 40s. Item I geve to my executors above named £5 a peece more Item I geve and bequeath all the rest of my goodes moveable and unmoveable to my executors above named. Item I geve to Elizabeth late wife of Humfrey Barnett and daughter of John Meredith late of Kiddington deceased all my houshould goodes that she brought with her and one ioyned bedd standing in the parlor withall furniture therunto belonginge dureing her naturall lief and after her decease to Ales Barnett daughter of William Barnett, and for want of issue of the said Ales Barnett daughter to Ellen Wright daughter of Robert Wright: All the rest of my houshould goodes I geve the one half to Ezabell Cartwright and the other half to William Barnett. Item I geve to my executors above named 20s. a peece more. Item I geve to Isabell Cartwright 20s. more. Item I geve to my executors abovenamed £20 more. Item I geve to Robert Wright £5 more.

Inventory: James Barnet of Aston, yeoman.

Taken: 2 July 1610

Of: goodes and Cattells.

Prisers: John Bromehall, William Cooper, John Barnet, and James Beckett.

	£	s	d
his aparell		40	0
one oxe due for a heriot to Mr. Cotton	3	13	4
one steere due for a heriot to Richard Shrobridge	3	6	8
Two oxen twilve kine five twinter bestes three stirkes one Barraine Cowe one twinter Bull and five waineinge cavles	59	5	0
Two twinter Coultes	4	6	8
fore Swine		40	0
Sheepe	4	16	8
Two Cartes and an ode wheele		40	0
Two plowes three yokes and one harrowe		13	4
one Cheine and all Iron ware		15	0
fore bushele of otes		13	4
Two bushell of Rie		16	0

three strick of barlie	9	0
one Bushell of wheat	11	0
Three bushell of malt	29	0
Bedinge and naperie	7	0
All brase and pewter	7	0
Trene ware Couperie bedsteds Chestes bordes formes shilefes		

Cheares one Cupborde stockes and other smale impellments	4	0	0
Walkers erth		7	5
Bife and bacone		20	0
new wollen Cloth		20	0
painted Cloths		2	6
poulterie		6	8
Muck		10	0
Timber and fier fuell		20	0
A Bargaine of ground of Mr. Grovener untill our ladie day			
cum tuilve mounths		10	0
A bargaine of ground of William Twyfforde untill candellmas			
cum tuilve mounths		10	0
A reversion of yearelie rent from Thomas Taylor for fore yeares			
and above six poundes a yeare the which somme unpaide is		27	0
A reversion of a lease of Acsones ground for two yeares from the			
first day of St. John Baptist next cuminge untill that day		30	0
A reversion of ground cauled Sucknales		2	10

	[77	450	65]

Debtes that wer oweinge to the testator:

	£	s	d
William Barnet		33	0
John Orpe		22	0
Thomas Starkie		11	0
Roger Sparke of Apsdall		22	0
Thomas Tench John Tentch John Church		11	0
John Cartwright	30	0	0
Thomas Shrobridge	6	13	0
Robart Shrobridge	5	10	0
John Edgley	4	13	8
Robart Whitney gent and James Skelton	6	12	0
Thomas Groverner and Michill Hope	2	6	0
Nicolas Cartwright	5	10	0
Jone Hall Widowe	10	0	0
Roger Hockenhull gent	5	0	0
Richard Cartwright	9	13	4
Randull Becket	2	0	0
Thomas Sparke	10	0	0
William Jonesone	5	0	0

John Cartwright of Aston	5	0	0
Thomas Birch smith		30	0
John Cartwright smith	3	6	8
John Sale		13	4
Mr Prince		30	0
Thomas Ranshall		12	0
Richard Taylor		32	0
Thomas Bickerton		56	0
Richard Shrobridge		10	0
Thomas Torner		4	8
John Ranschrofte	6	13	4
Widdowe Blackmore		10	0
Raph Henberie		40	0
the Hollinlane house and ground to the same belonginge beinge a tacke for yeares yett in beinge and praysed to the sume of		38	0

[113 470 36]

Endorsement: Probated 21 August 1610; administration to Thomas Edgley and Humphrey Barnett two of the executors named in the will, the third executor fully renouncing the duty of administration; they have to exhibit an inventory by the feast of St. Michael the Archangel next; the inventory was exhibited 28 September 1610.

Depositions of witnesses concerning the validity of the will and allegations of James Barnett deceased taken 7 July AD 1610.

Thomas Barnett of the parish of Malpas 42yrs of his age or thereabouts, having known well the said deceased, examined concerning the aforesaid testament and allegation says that about a month or five weeks since to this deponents nowe remembrance of the tyme there came a messenger to Nantwich for this deponent and his brother from the decedent for them to come rel speake with him the decedent And this deponent & his brother came to him the decedent imediatly And upon his oath and his brothers saide concerning the decedent did declare unto him that [hee] much feared him self and that hee thoughte hee should nott continue longer in this world and that hee had a desier to sett his estate in order and to make his will whereupon this deponent by thappointment of the decedent sente for one Thomas Burroughs to will him come write the decedents will, which Burroughs came and broughte with him penne Inke and paper and did rite the decedents will as the saide decedent did give him direccōns And when the saide Burroughs had written the saide will his Thomas Graie did reade the same over to the decedent and hee liked well of the same and putt his marke to the same, sealed the same, and delivered the same for his laste will And testament: to his Executors named in the same and appointed Thomas Edgley to keepe his saide will present at the makeinge signeinge sealinge and deliveringe of the saide will

Thomas Graie Thomas Burroughes Robert Wright Thexecutors & named in the will and this deponent: And saith that the decedent was of good and sound memorie att the makeinge of the saide will and delivered his mynd of his owne accordinge withoute the moveeinge or instigacōn of anie man And haveinge the will exhibited shewed to this deponent and read over to him saith that hee this deponent was presente att the sealinge & writing of the will exhibited from the beginninge of the same untill the legasie of £10 and debts viis given to John Barnett of Pillston was written all which was written by the saide Thomas Burroughes And after the will was finished & soe farre written then the same was signed sealed and delivered as This deponent hath formerly deposed And saith that nowe upon the seeinge and hearinge of the will exhibited read saith hee remembreth all the legasies conteyned in the same soe farr as was written by Burroughes and knoweth the decedents marke putt to the same And is fully perswaded in his conscience this is the verie self same will for soe much as Burroughes did write this the decedent did signe seale and deliver as this deponent hath predeposed and further cannott depose.

Ad Interrogatoria: (Responses to the Questions).

To the first [question]: hee referreth himself to the statements set downe in his deposicōn and saith hee was present att all the plaintiffs predeposed by him.

To the 2nd: declares hee is a husbandman and liveth by husbandrie and hath lived in Cholmondley thes ten yeares and hath knowne the parties litigant and the decedent thees 20 yeares att the leaste.

To the 3rd: declares hee liveth upon a racke rente & is worth £40 of debtles goods.

To the 4th: hee denies any further knowledge.

To the 5th: hee is a kinne to Humphrey Barnett and saith theire fathers were brothers children otherwise hee knows nothing.

To the 6th: hee favoreth Shrowbridge & his wief more then thexecutors yett hee wisheth the decedents will maie bee performed.

To the 7th: hee denies any further knowledge.

To the 8th: hee cometh att the requeste of William J Barnett his brother who was named an executor in the decedents will otherwise he knows nothing.

To the 9th: hee denies any further knowledge.

To the 10th: hee declares hee hath knowne James Barnett theese 30 yeares before his death and did knowe him to make the will predeposed by this respondent and saith the same was made in a parlor in the decedents howse, (he does not know the day of the month) in this yeare of o[u]r lord nowe current the decedent then lyeing in his bed in the parlor aforesaide.

To the 11th: hee declares for soe much as this deponent sawe written by Thomas Burroughes ~~wh~~ was the decedents originall will butt saith hee cannott write otherwise he refers himself to his deposition given above.

To the 12th: hee declares that soe farre as this deponent hath deposed concerninge the will which was written all att one tyme otherwise he knows nothing.

To the 13th: hee declares that the decedent att the makeinge of the will exhibited said hee had manie more legasies to give and hee would sett them downe afterwards as they should come to his mynd And saith hee was nott urged by anie one saveinge ~~the said~~ Elizabeth Meredith moved the decedent that hee would give her all his howshould goods butt the decedent would not yeeld to the same otherwise he denies any further knowledge.

To the 14th and 15th: hee declares that hee cannott further answeare then hee hath deposed to the will.

To the 16th and 17th: hee declares and denies that hee hath anie legasie given unto him by the decedent and saith the reason that induceth this deponent to believe the decedent was in good memorie att the tyme of the makeinge of the will predeposed by this deponent is because that the decedent spoke sensiblie and understanding and gave a good reason to anie question demanded of him and declared his mynd of his owne accorde, And one in the companie asked the decedent what hee would give to this deponent & the decedent said [*damaged, – what*] shall I give to him hee hath as little neede as I.

To the 18th: hee remembreth all the severall legasies in the will predeposed by this deponent butt cannott tell them legacie by legasie And that in the ~~fie~~ w[*damaged*] this deponent was att the makeinge of the saide Elizabeth Meredith hath fortie pounds given to her ~~als~~ att one tyme and rendringe a reason why the decedent gave her soe large a legasie saith hee beleaveth it was because shee had lived with him the decedent as man & wife for the space of 20 yeares or thereabouts.

To the 19th: hee declares that hee this respondent did take the saide Elizabeth Meredith for the decedents wife [*interlinear — in his lief tyme*] for hee called her wief and shee him husband untill the tyme of his death, and cannott depose for the same, Butt saith shee was thoughte and generally reputed and taken to bee the wife of Humphrey Barnett of Newhall whyleste hee lived.

Thomas Graie of the parish of Wrenbury, 47yrs of his age or thereabouts, having known well the said deceased, examined concerning the exhibited writings for the testament of the selfsame deceased and the allegations annexed to the same, saith that the daie specified in the will exhibited this deponent was sente for to come to the decedent to write his will and when this deponent came there was Mr Thomas Burrowes whoe beinge a better clerke then this deponent hee this deponent did requeste the saide Mr Burroughes to undertake the writeing of the saide decedents will, whoe did take penne Inke and paper and did write the decedents will as hee the decedent declared the same and when Mr Burroughes had finished the saide will hee this deponent did reade the saide will to the saide decedent distinctly and playnely and [*interlinear* – the decedent] liked well of the same & putt his marke to the same and delivered itt for his laste will and testament to the executors named in the same and appointed that Thomas Edgley should have the keepeinge of the saide will the saide decedent beinge of good and perfecte memorie for hee spoke sensiblie orderly and declared his mynd and will with his owne mouth of his owne accord aga and answeared with good understandinge to anie question demanded of him: presente att the writeinge signeinge and selinge and delivering of the saide will Mr Thomas Burrowes Roberte Wrighte Thomas Barnett this deponent and the three executors named in the will And haveinge the will exhibited shewed to this deponent and perused by him saith itt is the verie self same will the decedent then made signed sealed and delivered withoute anie alteraċon and saith all that was written att that tyme was written by Mr Thomas Burrowes vizt: from the beginninge of the will untill the end of the legasie given to John Barnett of Pilston, and after the writeing thereof the decedent did signe seale and deliver the will exhibited for his laste will and testament [which hee declared was] true for hee this deponent knoweth his owne hand writinge subscribed as a witnes to the same and read the will to the decedent imediately after the same was written.

Concerning the first codicil, he saith that aboute three weeks or a moneth after the originall will of the decedent was made this deponent was sente for to come to the decedent and upon this deponents comeinge the saide decedent tould this deponent that hee had sente for him to write downe more legasies which hee would have written & added to his will will and then the will was broughte to this deponent and this dept. and this deponent did write downe the legasies severally as the same were delivered by the decedent and firste this deponent began att thees words: Item I gieve to Isabell Cartwright and writt att that tyme to the end of thees words my Executors above named and saith the legasie in the margen was written att the same tyme And when this deponent had written the saide legasies hee did reade the same to the legasies decedent and the decedent did like well of the same and did acknowledge them for parte of his will Present att the same tyme all the three executors Elizabeth the late wife of Humphrey Barnett deceased and this deponent.

Concerning the second codicil, hee saith that aboute a weeke or more before the decedent dyed after the decedent had added the legasies predeposed by this deponent the saide decedent sent for this deponent a second tyme and requested this deponent to write downe more legasies which hee was intended to give ~~to the~~ and the will beinge broughte this deponent did write downe the legasie as the saide decedent delivered the same to this deponent: beginninge att thees words Item I give to Elizabeth late wiefe of Humphrey Barnett and endinge to Roberte Wrighte £5 more: which when this deponent had written hee this deponent did reade the same over unto the decedent and hee liked well of the same and did acknowledge them for parte of his will beinge both then and att the firste settinge downe of legasies after the makeinge of the originall will in good & sound memorie for hee spake with good understandinge & declared the severall legasies from his owne mouth Presente att this second tyme of Addinge the three executors nominated in the originall will Roberte Wrighte Elizabeth late wief of Humphrey Barnett and this deponent and haveinge the will exhibited shewed to this deponent and perused by him saith the saide legasies were given by the decedent as they are settdowne in the will exhibited withoute anie alteracōn [which hee declared was] vera for this deponent saith they are everie word this deponents owne handwritinge which hee knoweth verie well.

To the first [and 2nd questions]: hee declares that hee referreth himself to the reasons sett downe in his deposicōns to the will and codicills: aged aboute 47 and saith hee is parishe clarke att Wrenbury, getteth his liveinge by his place & writinge bills ~~and~~ bounds & wills & hath dwelled in this saide parishe about 10 years and hath knowne the decedent & plaintiffs & defendants about 20 yeares.

To the 3rd: hee is worth 20 nobles of debtles goods.

To the 4th: hee denies any further knowledge.

To the 5th: hee denies any knowledge as far as this is concerned.

To the 6th: hee favours the parties equally and would direct Justice to having the victory and wisheth the will maie take place accordinge to the testators mynd.

To the 7th: hee denies completely.

To the 8th: hee comes at the request of the parties acting [Plaintiff], otherwise, hee says no [denies].

To the 9th: hee knows nothing, Saveinge hee did thinke before hee came that itt was aboute the decedents will that hee this deponent should testifie.

To the 10th: hee knewe James Barnett about 20 yeares before his death and knoweth hee made the will exhibited on the daie sett downe in the same in his bedchamber within his owne house the saide testator lyinge in his bed in the same chamber for soe much as Mr Thomas Burroughs writt att one tyme as this deponent hath formerly deposed to the will.

To the 11th: declares: the will aforesaid is the true originall will which the decedent made And saith hee writt the severall legasies predeposed by him and receaved instruccōns for the saide legasies from the decedents owne mouth.

To the 12th: Upon interrogation, hee declares that with reference to the deposed codicills and allegacōns, that they are true And saith further the originall will was written all att one tyme and then the severall legasies att two severall tymes afterwards And saith hee cannot tell [wh]at daie of the moneth the codicills were written butt saith both were written in the ~~after~~ nyghte tyme *[damaged]* daies wherein they were written in the said [dece]dents bedchamber presente as hee hath predeposed an[d] [giveinge] a reason saith hee is an eie witness of all the *[damaged]* in the same *[damaged]*.

To the 13th: hee declares that when the originall will was written signed sealed & delivered the decedent saide hee had more legasies to sett downe butt saide hee would take an other tyme for the same And saith hee was nott urged att anie parte of his will.

To the 14th: hee dwelleth within 20 roods of the decedents howse & dwelleth from the plaintiffs in this sute aboute three quarters of a myle / And saith hee was sente for the two severall tymes att writinge of the codicills by the decedents meanes as this deponent beleeveth butt saith hee cannott sett down the precise daie of the month butt referreth him self to his former deposicions for the places & tymes.

To the 15th: the decedent neither subscribed nor sealed the codicills predeposed.

Replying to the 16th [question] about the rationality of the memorie of the said deceased hee saith that hee the decedent did call everie man by his name that was present att the tyme of the makeinge of the will and codicills and delivered both his will and codicills from his owne mouth and said when hee gave the executors theire laste legasie in the ~~laste~~ later codicill I will give you some what more for you shall find itt troublesome & you shall have enoughe to doe with itt all.

To the 17th: hee saith hee hath a legasie or two given by the will to the value of fyve pounds butt hath nott received anie parte thereof and thinketh there is noe reason to the contr[ar]ie butt that hee should receve the same if othermen receve theires accordinge to the decedents will.

To the 18th: hee declares hee cannot ~~remember~~ repeate all the legasies butt upon vewe of the will doth perfectly remember them all, And saith, there is a legasie of £40, ~~half parte~~ all of the decedents howsehold stuffe which shee broughte with her & one standinge bedd firnished and given unto Elizabaeth Meridith duringe her lief, and saith these given att several tymes And cannot Imagōn the reason of these freake legasies given to the saide Elizabeth excepte itt was because shee tooke w*[damaged]* with the decedent hee beinge a blynd man & kept his howse and lookeing to his goods.

To the 19th: hee declares that the decedent did keepe the saide Elizabeth Meredith as his wife and ~~hee called~~ they called one another husband and wief and carried them selves one towards an other as man and wief and saith there was & is a report in Wrenbury that the saide Elizabeth could nott bee the decedents wief *[interlinear]* if she Elizabeth had beene Humphrey Barnetts wief before, And hath heard they have beene presented to the ordinarie, And saith shee was reputed & taken for Humphrey Barnetts wief of Newhall soe longe as hee the saide Humphrey lived otherwise he knows nothing.

Called to Mind before a Justice (of the Court)   Thomas Graie

Robert Wrighte of the parish of Wrenbury, 40yrs of his age, having known well the said deceased, examined concerning the exhibited writings for the testament of the selfsame deceased and the allegacōn annexed to the same, saith that aboute seaven weeks since as this deponents remembrance of the tyme this deponent came to the how[s]e the decedent did, hee beinge this deponents uncle and after this deponent had staide a space with the decedent hee the decedent bad this deponent goe home and come againe presently and bring his neighbor Thomas Edgley with him for the decedent saide hee intended to make his will that eveninge and when this deponent & Thomas Edgley came againe to the decedents there came Thomas Burrowes whom the decedent desiered to write his will and the saide Burroghes tooke pen Inke and paper and did write the decedents will as the saide decedent gave him direccōns and when the same was written itt was read publiquely to the decedent and hee liked well of the same putt his marke [on the] same, sealed the same and acknowledged [as] his laste will & testament & delivered it to his executors: beinge then [of good and perfecte memorie] for hee spake verie understandingly *[damaged]* and answeared reasonably to anie questions [demanded] of him Presente att the same tyme [of the writinge signeinge and selinge of the said will] the three executors named in the will Thomas Burrowes, Thomas Graie, Thomas Barnett Elizabeth late wief of Humphrey Barnett of Newhall deceased and this deponent: And haveing this will exhibited shewed to this deponent and read unto him saith hee remembreth all the contents of the same ~~and saith~~ for soe ~~fard~~ farre as hee saide Thomas Burrowes did write att the tyme of the signeinge sealinge and deliveringe of the will abovesaid and saith itt agreeth with the saide decedents mynd then delivered and beleeveth in his conscience itt is the verie self same will the decedent made att the tyme predeposed written by Thomas Burrows Butt saith there is more added unto the saide will since whereunto this deponent cannott depose certainly.

Ad Interrogatoria

With reference to the first question, he has been deposed.

To the 2nd [question]: hee is a husbandman and liveth upon his tenement: hath dwelled in his owne howse ever sinse hee was borne And hath knowne the plaintiffs and defedants ~~thees~~ & the decedent about 20 yeares paste.

To the 3rd: hee declares hee is worth £20 everie man paid.

To the 4th: hee knows nothing thereof.

To the 5th: hee declares Humphrey Barnett is something a kynne to this respondent butt cannot tell in what degree.

To the 6th: hee favoreth both parties alike and wisheth the decedents will maie bee performed according to his true meaninge.

To the 7th: hee denies further knowledge.

To the 8th: hee came att requeste of the decedents executors, otherwise, he denies further knowledge.

To the 9th: hee denies further knowledge saveing hee thoughte hee should bee examined concerning the decedents will, otherwise he knows nothing.

To the 10th: hee was presente when the will exhibited was made by the decedent written by Thomas Burroughes as hee hath formerly deposed he knows not what day of the month for certain, butt saith itt was written signed sealed & delivered in the decedents bed chamber in the saide decedents howse the decedent lyeinge in his bedd.

To the 11th: hee declares the decedent gave instructions for the will written by Thomas Burroughes with his owne mouth ~~as~~ & saith hee is perswaded in his conscience this is the originall will.

To the 12th: hee states for soe farre as this deponent hath deposed all the will was sett downe att one tyme in one place by one person otherwise he knows nothing, unless as previously deposed.

To the 13th: hee states that att the tyme the will predeposed by this respondent was made the decedent saide hee was wearie & desierd reste and saide hee would consider further with him self & then hee would send for his executors and sett downe such further legasies as shold seeme good to him otherwise, he knows nothing.

To the 14th: hee dwelleth about half a myle and some what more from the decedents howse and came to bee presente att the makeinge of the decedents will by the decedents requeste otherwise he knows nothing for certain.

To the 15th: the decedent putt his hand to the saide will predeposed by this deponent otherwise, he knows nothing.

[To the 16th: declares that] hee the decedent declared his [will] of his owne accorde and named both *[damaged]*dents and made choise of what [persons] hee would have presente att the makeinge [of the will] which was a signe of his good memorie.

To the 17th: hee hath five pounds given him by the ~~will~~ codicill or one of them and saith if the will prove according to the testators mynd hee looketh for his legasie.

To the 18th: hee cannot name all the severall legasies in the will butt hearinge the will read hee doth remember all that were written by Thomas Burroughes and saith hee was present also att all the legasies given by the decedent in the later codicill and saith itt was the decedents will and mynd to have the same soe sett downe and saith there is £40 *[interlinear]* given to Elizabeth Meredith, a bed furnished duringe her lief and all the howsehould goods shee broughte butt cannott tell what the reason was that hee the decedent gave her the legasies saveinge this respondent beleeveth the decedent did accepte of the saide Elizabeth as his wief.

To the 19th: hee cannott judge of thees matters butt saith the saide decedent did take the saide Elizabeth as his wife & called her soe & shee him husband, and saith there was a publique speeche the saide Elizabeth could nott bee the decedents wief, And saith they have beene trubled for soe living together And saith she was reputed And taken for Humphrey Barnetts wief of Newall dureing his life.

Repeated before a Justice (of the Court).

(X – his mark)

19 July 1610

Thomas Burroughes of the parish of Malpas, 38yrs of his age, having known well the said deceased, examined concerning the exhibited writings for the testament of the selfsame deceased and the allegaccōn annexed to the same, saith that hee this deponent was sente to come to the selfsame deceased upon a Saturdaie beinge the 12th daie of Maie laste paste and this deponent came accordingly and after this deponent comeinge there was a place prepared for this deponent to write in And saith the decedent did deliver his mynd to Thomas Grey this deponents precontest when the decedent intended to have written his will and the saide Grey delivered the same againe to this deponent butt this deponent saith hee heard every particulier legasie that the saide decedent gave att that tyme and this deponent beinge prepared did write the saide decedents will as hee the decedent declared the same from his owne mouth and when the same was written and finished hee the saide Grey did reade the same out distinctly and audiblie to the decedent who lyked well of the same and acknowledged the same, putt his marke onto the same and delivered itt to his executors or some of them they all beinge presente for his laste will and testament beinge then of good & sound memorie for hee spake sensiblie and understandingly and delivered his mynd with his owne mouth of his owne accord ~~inge~~ withoute the instigacōn of anie, presente att the same tyme the three executors nominated in the saide will Thomas Barnett Thomas Grey and this deponent ~~beinge presente~~ And haveinge the will exhibited shewed to this deponent and perused by him saith itt is the verie self same will from the beginninge of the same untill thees words In Wynnall and Lutterworth which the saide decedent signed sealed and delivered for his laste will and testament ~~all~~ withoute anie alteracōn [And he declared that the will is] true for this deponent saith hee ~~know~~ [did] write the same *[damaged]* soe farre as hee hath deposed and nowe seen the will exhibited knoweth his owne hand writing very well.

With respect to [(Codicill 1)*damaged*] he does not know what to depose.

[damaged to bottom of membrane]

Ad Interrogatoria

To the first question he answers, it has been explained as far as the penalty for false witness &c.

To the 2nd: declares hee is a servinge man and is imployed in his masters affaires in sollicitinge his sute and such like and saith hee hath dwelled att Cholmondley thees ten yeares and hath knowne ~~knowne~~ Thomas Edgley and ~~William~~ Humphrey Barnett about ~~fore~~ two yeares and hath nott knowne the decedent before the tyme of the writinge of the predeposed will to this deponents remembrance neither doth hee knowe Shrobridge his wief, butt hath knowne him for some certeine yeares laste paste.

To the 3rd: hee does not know what to depose.

To the 4th: hee denies further knowledge.

To the 5th: hee denies further knowledge.

To the 6th: hee answers hee wisheth the will maie take place because itt was the testators mynd and otherwise he would direct Justice to having the victory.

To the 7th: hee denies further knowledge.

To the 8th: hee went at the asking of Thomas Edgley one of the executors of the said deceased.

To the 9th: hee denies further knowledge.

To the 10th: hee knows nothing except as previously stated and Saith hee the decedent made the will predeposed by this deponent in the decedents bedchamber the daie & yeare predeposed hee the decedent lyeing in his bed.

To the 11th: hee cannot answeare more to this question than hee hath predeposed to the will.

To the 12th: for soe much as this deponent hath formerly deposed concerninge the will exhibited was written all att one tyme, otherwise, he knows nothing, except as he has previously deposed.

To the 13th: declares the decedent did saye att the makeing of the will exhibited that hee for the reste of his goods which hee had to bestowe hee would ta[ke] tyme to bethinke him self howe to bestowe *[damaged]* same hereafter or words to that effecte to this dep[onents] remembrance.

To the 14th: he answers hee Thomas Barnett & this deponent dwell both in a towne & saith this deponent is some 3 [miles] from the reste of his contests dwellings as much or thereabouts as the *[damaged]* decedents house otherwise he knows nothing to declare except as previously deposed.

To the 15th: hee knows nothing to declare except as previously deposed.

Replying to the 16th [question] about the rationality of the memory of the selfsame deceased saith that someone in the companie moved the decedent to give some thinge to Thomas Barnett one of this deponents precontests and the decedent answeared that hee meaninge Thomas Barnett had as much neede neede of anie thinge as hee him self or words to that effecte And saith hee was moved by his wief (as this deponent did take her) to give some thinge to a god doughter sonne of hers one of the saide Thomas Barnetts doughters sonnes which the decedent refuseed to doe and spake to this deponents judgment as though hee had nott beene sicke att all & did seeme to lye in his bed with greate ease & answeared to anie questions demanded of him with good understanding.

To the 17th: hee denies any further knowledge.

To the 18th: he refers himself to his own deposition concerning the will made above.

To the 19th: hee does not know anything more to depose.

Tho: Burroughs

William Barnett of the parishe of Wrenburie, 50yrs of his age or thereabouts, having known well the said deceased, examined concerning the exhibited writings for the testament of the selfsame deceased and the Allegation and Codicil annexed to the same, saith, by force of his oath, that aboute 8 or 9 ~~wei~~ weekes since or thereabouts the decedent was mynded to make his will and tould the same to some of his friends who caused Thomas Burroughes to come to the decedents house who did write the same as the saide decedent delivered the same from his owne mouth butt saith the decedent declared his mynd to Thomas Grey who ~~was~~ in the hearinge of Thomas Burroughes and when the saide Thomas Burroughes had written the decedents will soe farre as the saide decedent was disposed then to proceede then the saide Thomas Gray did reade the same over very playnely to the decedent and hee liked well of the same and acknowledged the same for his laste will [&] testament and putt his marke and seale to the same and deli[vered] the same to this deponent and the reste of thexecutors named in the same and appointed that Thomas Edgely should have the keepe[inge of] the saide will, the decedent beinge then of good & sound [mind] for he spake understandingly & delivered his will & mynd of [his owne] accord present at the same tyme all this deponents precontests the decedent *[damaged]* [the plaintiffs] in this sute and this deponent and haveinge the will delivered and read to this deponent saith this is the verie self same [will which the] decedent made and delivered att the tyme [?] predeposed by this deponent written from the beginninge thereof untill the end of the legasies gaven to John Barnett of Pulleston by the saide Thomas Burroughes and imediately after signed sealed and delivered by the saide decedent for this deponent saith hee remembreth every severall legasie speciall and given in the same upon the readinge of the will aforesaide.

Concerning the codicill he saith that about ~~a weeke~~ a fortnighte after the decedent had made his will predeposed by this deponent hee the decedent sente for thexecutors named in the will and Thomas Gray who came all accordingly and then the decedent did desier the saide Thomas Gray to write downe certeyne legasies which hee would add unto his will and the saide Gray took penne Inke and paper and did write as the said decedent appointed him and when hee had written the same hee the saide Graie did reade them over to the decedent and hee the decedent liked well of the same and acknowledged the same for p̄ parte of his will And saith further that aboute a week or somewhat more before the decedent dyed hee the decedent caused thexecutors aforesaide and the saide Thomas Gray to come to him againe and did add more legasies to the fore saide will which the saide Gray did sett downe as the decedent did deliver the same and when the same were finished the saide Gray did reade the same to the decedent and hee liked well thereof & did acknowledge them for parte of his will beinge both severall tymes of good memorie to all mens Judgment presente and delivered the legasies from his owne mouth of his owne accorde presente att the makeinge of the former codicill or addicōn to the will predeposed by this deponent: thexecutors ~~Thomas~~ Thomas Gray, And att the later codicill or Addicōn there were presente Roberte Wrighte, thexecutors aforesaide, Thomas Graie and Elizabeth Barnett alius Meredith and haveinge the severall codicills shewed & read to this deponent saith hee remembreth them ~~Inter all~~ verie well and every severall legasie and saith ~~of them~~ they were parte of the decedents will & mynd.

Ad Interrogatoria

To the 1ˢᵗ question: hee answers, it has been explained as far as the penalty for false witness &c.

To the 2ⁿᵈ: hee saith hee is a husbandman and [dwelleth upon] his tenemente and hath dwelled upon the same thees 10 years and hath knowne the decedent plaintiffs and James Barnett thees 40 yeares & *[damaged]* & his wief from heire infancie.

To the 3rd: hee is worth an hundreth marks everie man paide.

To the 4ᵗʰ: hee denies further knowledge.

To the 5ᵗʰ: hee is cosine German to Humphrey Barnett and is somethinge allged *[i.e. alleged]* to Edgley butt cannot tell in which degree.

To the 6ᵗʰ: hee favoreth the truth of the will which is true and wisheth right maie take place.

To the 7ᵗʰ: hee denies further knowledge.

To the 8ᵗʰ: he comes at the request of the parties acting [Plaintiff].

To the 9ᵗʰ: hee denies further knowledge.

To the 10ᵗʰ: declares the will exhibited and the codicills predeposed by this respondent were made by the decedent hee cannott tell the daie of the moneth ~~whereof~~ butt saith itt was upon a Saturdaie when the originall will under seal was made declared and written and saith the same was written in a chamber in the decedents hows (hee the decedent lyeinge in his bed) upon a cheste [stan]dinge neare the bed syde.

To the 11ᵗʰ: declares the will exhibited is the originall will that the decedent made as this deponent hath predeposed and saith hee that writt the originall will did heare the decedent declare the same from his owne mouth.

To the 12ᵗʰ: the originall will was all written att one tyme butt saith the Addicõn of the legasies were written att two severall tymes afterward, as this respondent hath formerly deposed.

To the 13ᵗʰ: hee declares that ~~the decedent saide~~ att the makeinge of the originall will the decedent said lett us take heede that wee doe not overshoote ourselves butt rather [?]de unto the legasies then take anie thinge awaie and Then [saide?] hee the decedent that he woulde pause upon the further *[damaged]* this will otherise he denies completely.

To the [14th: hee dwelleth] aboute half a myle and more from the de[cedents howse] And saith the contests in this cause fro*[damaged]* were all broughte together by the d[ecedents] saveing Thomas Buroughes whoe was sent *[damaged]* Barnett to write the will because hee is a good *[damaged]* cannot remember the daies and howers wherein the saide will and codicills were made butt saith theye were all written in one place the decedent beinge still in bed and further cannott depose more then hee hath predeposed.

To the 15th: when the originall will was made and written the decedent sealed & signed the same butt nott the codicills otherwise he knows nothing except as he has previously deposed.

To the 16th: hee declares that the decedent did shewe manie signs of his good remembrance all the tyme of the makeing and writeing of the will and codicills and rendering a reason saith the saide decedent would have and had both the will and codicills written by nighte to the end that his sonne in lawe John Cartwright should nott bee acquainted with his doings for the decedent saide that if John Cartwrighte should knowe hee would keepe a great coyle to knowe howe hee had disposed of his goods which the decedent would not acquaint him withall And this much the decedent told to this respondent.

To the 17th: declares hee hath renounced both the will and the codicills and the benefit there.

To the 18th: declares hee cannott repeate all the whole legasies butt hearinge them read hee knoweth the same to bee true And saith there is £40 given to Elizabeth Meredith by the will and by the later codicill all her howsehould stuff which shee broughte with here and one standing bedd in his parlor during her lief, the reason is because the decedent toke the saide Elizabeth for his wief.

To the 19th: hee knows nothing saveinge there was a m[ean?]inge in Wrenburie parishe that this saide Elizabet was nott the decedents wief and hath heard that *[damaged]* [?]ne beene predeposed otherwise hee does not know And saith [she was reputed?] to bee Humphrey Barnett of Newhall his w[ief]*[damaged]*hee lived and that they were contracted *[damaged]* together as this deponent hath heard reported *[damaged]*.

30. ROGER SWANN OF DODDS GREENE (NEWHALL) HUSBANDMAN

S. Pr. 12 September 1610
W. T. 20 August 1610
Buried: 29 August 1610

```
William Swanne     =    [   ]
fl. 1595–1611 at Newhallᵃ
              |
    1) [   ] = Roger Swan      =   2) Elene [   ]
            |  † 1610 virili aetate        fl. 1610
            |
    John Swan = [   ]
    fl. 1610–14 |
              |
           Martha
           c. 1614
```

Will, sick.

First, I give and bequeath my self both body and soule into the hands of Almighty god that hath made mee and Jesus Christe my only Lord and Saviour that hath redeemed mee by his death and bloody pasion unto the greate ioy of my soule And as Concerninge *my body I give and bequeath the same unto the earth to bee buried in Wrenbury Church :* ~~Church~~ *yard* trustinge in my mercifull Lord that he will raise upp the same att the laste daie & to raigne with my god for ever. ffirste I give & bequeath unto my nowe wief Elene Swan £40 within her owne Custodie Item I give & bequeath unto my sonne John Swan £20 by specialty Item I give the saide John Swan my great pott & his mothers pann with a Cloute on the syde And as Concerninge all the reste of my goods both Cattall & Chattall both moveable and unmoveable both bills bounds and speciltyes whatsoever to bee equally devided betwixte them both my wief & my sonne.

Debts owing to Testator:
by Specialty that I have to showe for

	£	s	d
Thomas Taylor of Lightwood Green	3	6	0
Richard Bate of Lodmore Lane	2	15	0
Richard Plante of the Walke value heifer	1	9	4
Richard Plante	3	6	0
Richard Plante	2	4	0

ᵃ CRO Newhall Manor Court Rolls, 1595 and 1611.

Richard Plant	5	10	0
Thomas Backhowse	3	13	4
Edward Chapman two speciltyes	3	8	4
whereof received 10s.			
Randle Ravenscrofte	2	13	4
Richard Edgley and Thomas Edgley	7	14	0
William Hamlett		5	10
to bee paied att Maie Daie next Comeinge more to			
the said William Hamlett one Debte of	4	8	0

	[35	111	26]

Debts oweinge to the estate that are due in my very Conscence:

Anne Bickerton of Broomhall widowe	3	4	0
John Hamblett of Coole Lane	2	4	0
Thomas Grindley	3	0	0
Thomas Taylor for foure kyne hyer		28	0
Thomas Taylor of ould debte		40	0
John Taylor of the Capellhowse		6	8
Phillipp Dod		20	0
Edward Hamlett		6	8

[Sum	43	221	32]

Executors: Richard Hamlett, Richard Cooke.

I give to my Executors 2s. 6d. a peece.

S.

Witnesses: Richard Allen, John Bickerton, William Hamblett, Richard Cowper.

Inventory: Roger Swann of Dodds Green, husbandman.

Taken: 30 August 1610

Of: goods Cattell and Chattell.

Prisers: William Hamlet, George Gouldsmithy, Raphe Crosby, Richard Allen.

	£	s	d
16 kine praysed at	35	0	0
one Cowe more taken for a harryot praysed at	2	0	10
two stirkes praysed at	3	0	0
two mares and a filly praysed at	6	6	7
Corne praysed at		20	0

hay praysed at	5	0	0
two swine praysed at	2	0	0
Powltry ware praysed at		3	4
a Carre, a Plowe & 2 harrowes		10	0
Cole & wood praysed at		13	4
Boordes praysed at		10	0
Baken praysed at		6	8
Iron ware & tooles praysed at		13	4
a Cubbarte & Coffers praysed at		13	4
bedsteddes, shelves & stooles praysed at		5	0
treene wares, praysed at		6	8
Butter praysed at		12	0
a peece of Cloth praysed at		12	4
Cheeses praysed at	2	0	0
beddinge and naprye ware praysed at	3	0	0
Brasse and pewter praysed at		30	0
one peece of wollen cloth praysed at		29	0
the testators wearinge apparell		10	0
one tacke of ground of Robert Lodmore	5	0	0
money given to his wife in his life time	40	0	0
[Sum	103	198	53]

Debtes owinge to Testator by specialty:

	£	s	d
Thomas Taylor of Lightwood Green	3	6	0
Richard Bate	2	15	0
Richard Plante	1	9	4
Richard Plante	3	6	0
Richard Plante	2	4	0
Richard Plante	5	10	0
Randulphe Ravencrofte	2	13	4
Edward Chapman whereof received 10s.	3	8	4
Thomas and Richard Edgeley	7	14	0
William Hamnet	5	0	0
William Hamnet	4	8	0
[Sum	37	93	12]

Debtes owinge to Testator that he charge noe specialties to shewe for, that in my very conscience are due:

	£	s	d
Anne Bickerton of Broomhall	3	6	0
John Hamnet of Coole Lane	2	4	0
Thomas Grindley	3	0	0

Thomas Taylor for 4 kyne hyre		28	0
Thomas Taylor of old debte		11	0
John Taylor of the Chappellhouse		6	8
Phillipp Dodd		20	0
Edward Hamnet		6	8
Richard Plante		12	0
Richard Bate		5	0
the herbriche of the grounds		10	0
Richard Plante for one Cowe price	2	12	0
Thomas Grindley for one packet of Cheeses	2	0	0
Anne Fletcher for money lent		20	0
Roger Sadler for 3 measures of wheate		10	3
for kyne hire			
first Anne Bickerton for one Cowe hire		6	8
John Hamnet for the like		6	8
Thomas Backhowse for the like		6	8
[Sum	12	168	43]

Debtes owinge by Testator:

		s	d
first to the poore of the parishe		4	0
to Richard Bate			20
[Sum		4	20]

Endorsement: Probated 12 September 1610; administration to the executors named in the will.

31. ALLES SWANE OF WRENBURY, WIDOW

I. Pr. September 1610
W.T. August 1610
Buried: 30 August 1610

Alles Swane = Christopher[a] Swann   John Swane
† 1610 *anus*   † 1604 *senex*   fl. 1610 (cousin)

Randull Wixsted alias Swane
fl. 1610

---

[a] Alles Swane's husband could also have been Robert Swanne *senex* who was likewise buried in 1604.

Will, sick.

First I give and bequeath [my s]oule unto allmightie god by whome I hope to be saved *a[nd my] bodie to be buried In the churchyarde of Wrenbur[y – damaged]* Item I give unto my Cossin John Swane my greate brasse pane 6 yards of black clothe [?] flaxen sheete and my best coffer Item I give unto Margret Holline a wolbede that lyethe under me a sheete a pillow a coverlet and all my apparrell except my best peticote Item I give Elizabethe Bostocke my meate bordes my great bacen my turnell and all my best peticots Item I give unto everie one of Elizabeth Bostocks children 12d. and to her son William 2s. Item I give unto Ales Grindley the bede that she lyeth in one nother all that belongethe unto that all the yarne and towe that is in this house my swyne a bo[ ]cke and a stande Item I give unto my executor Richard Cooke my rede cowe to bringe me whome and discharge provinge of my will Item after my deptes be payd my legacies performed and my funnerall expences discharged I doe give all the rest of my goods that are unbequeathed moveable and unmoveable quicke and deade unto my laste sone Randull Wixsted alias Swane to his owne use and behoufe.

Executor: my lovinge friend Richard Cooke.

Witnesses: Margerie Grindley Margerie *[illegible]* Ane Cooke.

Inventory for Alles Swane.

Taken : 31 of August 1610

Of: goodes.

Prisers: John Watkys and Richard Shawe.

	£	s	d
her wearinge apparrell		10	0
3 kyne	5	0	0
haye		20	0
beddinge		13	4
napperie ware		5	0
brasse and pewter		13	4
Iron ware			12
a pew of wollin cloth		10	0
in chesses		5	0
in Swyne		10	0
bedstides shillvfes chistes and all other treenen ware and woddenware		6	8
yarne and towe		3	0
Some is	9	17	4

Endorsement: Proved September 1610; administration to the executor named in the will.

32. THOMAS LOWE OF BROOMHALL, HUSBANDMAN

S. Pr. 9 March 1610/11
Buried: 13 September 1608

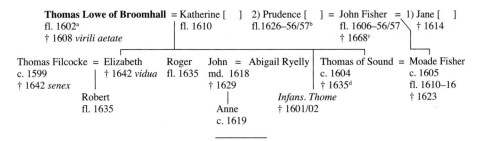

Inventory: Thomas Lowe of Broomhall, husbandman.

Taken: 21 February 1610/11

Of: goodes and Catteles.

Prisers: Thomas Sefton, Thomas Hill, John Paraphet and Richard Davie.

	£	s	d
towe oxen prased Att	7	6	8
towe Steares prased to	6	5	0
Fowre kine prased to	10	0	0
towe Heffers prased to	4	13	4
towe bullockes prased to	3	13	4
one twinter bullocke to		30	0
towe yeare ould Cavles to		26	4
towe weaninge Cavles		20	0
one mare and An ould Nadge to	3	0	0
Fowre Shote pidges prased to		16	0
towe gysse and a gandar to		6	8
12 Hennes and a Cocke to		6	0
Barlye estimated to 25 busshiles	5	13	4
Five busshilles of Rye		33	4
Beans pees friches [?] and Oates		35	6
Fyve busshilles of Maulte		30	0
Haye prased to		20	0
plowes Harrowes Cartes And other Impulmentes belonginge to husbandrie	7	0	0

ᵃ Thomas Lowe owed debt of 4s. to the estate of Thomas Tailer of Dodcott, 1602.
ᵇ Witness to will of Thomas Shrowbridge of Newhall, yeoman, pr. 1626/27 (will no. 75).
ᶜ Executor of will of Thomas Shrowbridge (will no. 75); priser of the inventory of Oliver Briscoe, 1629 (will no. 80); also inventory of John Fisher, pr. 1668/CR0.
ᵈ See will of Thomas Lowe of Sound, pr. 1637 (will no. 105).

poote and panne brasse prased to and pewter	5	0	0
towe and yarne to		6	8
napperrie ware to		23	4
beddinge prased to		46	8
trene ware and bordes Formes Cheares and stowles		22	8
Sattlerye prased to		26	8
his wearing aparill to		20	0
three Coffers		6	8
poughtes Sackes and a windowe		4	0
Corne Sowen on the ground		22	0
worthinge about the house and Fuele		15	4
The whole some is	72	9	2

Endorsement: Exhibited 9 March 1610; administration, with the agreement of Katherine relict widow of the said deceased, to John Lowe son of the said deceased and to Bartholomew Towers.

33. WILLIAM PATRICK OF CHORLEY (WITHIN THE PARISH OF WRENBURY)

I.Pr. 6 June 1611
W.S. 2[ ] 1600
Buried: 14 May 1611

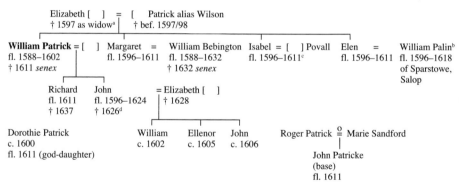

a   See will of Elizabeth Patrick alias Wilson, pr. 1597/98 (will no. 15).
b   Of Sparstowe, Shropshire; fl. 1596–1618. Executor and beneficiary of Elizabeth Patrick alias Wilson, 1597/98 (will no. 15).
c   Ca. 1597/98 Isabel appears as the wife of Randle Thyrlwynde; see will of Elizabeth Patrick alias Wilson (will no. 15).
d   See will of John Patricke, pr. 1626 (will no. 72).

Will, *[very illegible]* (no statement regarding health).

I bequeathe my soule into the hands of Almyghtye god my maker and onlie Redemer and my bodie to the earth from whense ytt came to bee buried in Christian buri-all att the discreshon of my executors. Item I give and bequeathe unto my sonne Richard Patrick 3s. 4d. In full satisfaction of his childs parte of my goods. Item I give to my sonne John Patrick 12d. for his childs parte. Item I give to my god-daughter Dorothie Patrick 12d. Item I give and bequeath to John Patricke sonne of Roger Patricke and Marie Sandford 40s. Item my will is that . . . brasse potte . . . brasse pannes 8 pewter dishes. . . a payre of Iron Goberts . . . one leatherbill one bolster one coverlette and a blancett a bed pa[nne] . . . of . . . and a . . . chiste. Item I give and bequeath unto my said sonne John my plowes carts harrowes yokes cheanes and all the reste of my husbandry ware and a combe and a [?] framinge Tawe [and yarne] . . . Item I give and bequeath to my servant Margerie Rall the least pott three pewter dishes the worsted [?] & the other coverlett and all the reste of my trillene ware . . . Item all the [remaynder] I leave to bee devided betwixte the same Margerie and the said sone John equallie. Item I bequeath to my three sisters: Margaret Bebington, Isabel Povall & Elen Palin 12d. [apeece] . . . All the reste of my goods moveable and unmoveable I give and bequeath unto the said Margerie and the said John equallie to all . . . Item I give unto Sara Wilson 12d.

Name & seal

Executors: William Bebington, Richard Davenport.

Witnesses: William Prince, Thomas Bebington.

Inventory: **William Pattrick of Chorley.**

Taken: 14 May 1611

Of: Goods, Cattles and Chattles.

Prisers: Richard Rogers, Richard Millington, Randull Millington, Raphe Orton.

	£	s	d
Butter & Cheese praised to		6	0
On kow praised to		53	4
Other tow ky[ne]	4	0	0
Tow yong swyne		9	0
Pot brass		17	6
Pan brass		5	3
Pewter praised to		9	8
On payre of gobarts & on brace		2	4
Tow iorn wedges		18	0
On paiere of plow forms		18	0
Other form wares		2	2
Tow axes on bill tow nagers on hand saw with other od things			4
Tow drawing knyves		10	0

Tow sycthes on hoop tow handles tow pykels	12	0
On brendreth on paier of tongs on paier of pot rackes on gridle on frying pan	2	0
Bedding praised at	40	0
Four paiere of course sheets	3	0
Backon praised to	9	0
Mault praised to	6	0
Old s[h]eets and on course winow sheete	2	0
Coffers	3	4
On cart rop	14	0
One heirsive on peck & tow riddls	3	0
[?] praised to	15	0
barh[?] praised to	19	8
on paiere of waiene whiels with an axeltrei and on foot plow	20	0
on kneading turnill and swyne tob		12
hey and strawe	3	4
a flock of geese	7	6
tow harrows	4	0
on draught yoake	16	0
on weeting kombe	2	6
trene ware	2	0
on cock and tow hens	14	0
muck praised to	4	0
cropwood	2	6
on grindle stan		6
stock for the f[?] and an old nagg	2	6
corne groing on the ground	3	4
money in his purse	6	0
His apparrell	6	7

Endorsement: Probated in the presence of David Yale doctor of laws 6 June 1611; administration to the executor named in the will; they have to exhibit an inventory within the next month; the inventory was exhibited 19 June 1611.

Allegations: Wrenbury, dated 6 January 1611.

Dicta testium super validitate testamenti Willelmi Patrick defuncti capta die vj mensis. Januarij 1611.

William Prince Clerk, curate of Wrenbury [now] in the 53rd year of his life, has known the said deceased for 12 years before his death. In the above considered writings furnished on behalf of the will and by the allegation/representations [made] in the writings of the remaining official record, he [William Prince] asserts that aboute five or six weekes before the deathe of the sayd deceadent he sent for this deponent to make his will & this deponent came to hym and found hym sicke in his bedd and hee willed this deponent to wryte his will & this deponent tooke penne forth & paper & dyd wryte the will exhibited legasie by legasie after the Deceadents will and mynd for the deceadent dyd deliver ~~hym~~ everie legasie to this deponent and when this deponent had written the said will this deponent saith that hee dyd read the same to the said deceadent & hee lyked well of the same and dyd putt his seale [to ytt &] the *[sic]* signed the same with his marke and dyd deliver the will exhibited for his last will & testament beinge then of good & perfect memorie for hee spake sensiblie and dyd deliver [& pronounce] this said will hym selfe beinge present Thomas Bebington & the deponent.

William Prince

Thomas Bebington of the parish of Wrenbury in the 23rd yeare of his life, has known the decedent during the ten weekes before his death. In the above considered writings furnished on behalf of the will of the deceased (and by representation) he asserts according to the power of his oath that the said Deceadent sent for this deponent to come to hym about 5 or 6 weekes before the deceadent dyed and this deponent found his præcontest Mr Prince with the deceadent whoe had wrytten then the said decadents will and the said decadente after this deponent came willed the said Prince to read his will & the said Prince dyd read the said will to the *[crossed through]* nowe exhibited to the said decadente and hee lyked well of ytt and dyd seale the same signed the same and dyd delived the same for his last will & testamente beinge of good & perfecte memorie for hee spoke senseblie & freelie and this deponent saith the will exhibited ys the same the said decadente dyd seale signe & deliver in the presence of this deponente & his præcontest Prince.

Thomas Bebington.

34. HUGH WHITNEY OF COOLE, GENT.

S.Pr. 11 June 1611
Buried: 11 March 1610/11

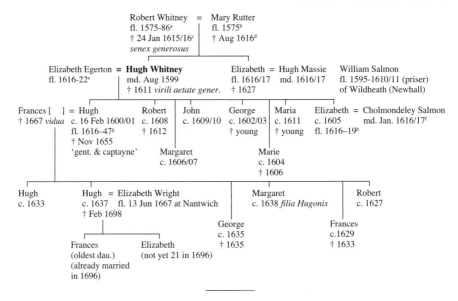

---

 a   Date of marriage (Hall, 'Newhall Families', p. 290); appears in CRO Newhall Manor Court Rolls 1579, 1580, 1585, 1586.
b   Daughter of Thomas Rutter of Kingsley, gent. (Hall, 'Newhall Families', p. 290).
c   See IPM taken for Robert Whitney 2 April 1616 (R. Stewart Brown, *Cheshire Inquisitions Post Mortem*, iii. 169–71). Noted 1602 in CRO Newhall Manor Court Roll with Hugh, son and heir apparent. On Whitney family origins, see Ormerod, *History of Cheshire*, iii. 389; see also Paul C. Reed, 'Whitney Origins Revisited: John Whitney of Watertown, Massachusetts, and Henry Whitney of Long Island and Norwalk, Connecticut', *The American Genealogist*, 69 (1994) 9–14, which discusses some of the fraudulent documentation of early Whitney genealogists.
d   See administration of the estate of Mary Whitney of Coole, widow, 1616 (no. 51).
e   See administration of the estate of Mary Whitney of Coole; will of James Brooke, pr. 1622 (will no. 66).
f   William Fergusson Irvine, *Chester Licences*, i. 82: 7 July 1610, to Cholmondeley Salmond of Audlem parish, and Elizabeth Whitney, spinster of Wrenbury parish; bondsman, Thomas Chester of Coe Lane; at Wrenbury. A marriage entry at Wrenbury for 4 July 1610 would suggest that the licence was in fact used, but a second licence, issued 21 January 1616/17 to Cholmely Salmon, of Audlem parish, and Elizabaeth Whitney, spinster of Wrenbury parish, suggests that the first marriage was annulled; the second licence was addressed to Mr William Prince, curate of Wrenbury; bondsman, Robert Sproston, feltmaker of Chester; see *Chester Licences*, ii. 23. The Parish Registers record the marriage the following day, i.e. 22 January 1616/17. The necessity for a third licence, issued 14 June 1618 to Cholmondeley Salmon, of Audlem parish, and Elizabeth Whitney, of Wrenbury parish (see *Chester Licences*, ii. 60) is unclear; it too was intended for use at Wrenbury; bondsman was Richard Egerton, gent.

Inventory: Hugh Whitney of Coole, gent.

Taken: 4 June [1611]

Of: Goods and Chattells.

Prisers: John Cheswis, John Cartwright, William Salmon and (the marke of) John Pichforde.

	£	s	d
his Aparelle	3	6	8
sheetes and naperie ware	6	0	0
bedinge in the chamber over the hall	4	0	0
bedinge in the chamber over the buttrie	4	0	0
two standinge beds and three trocle beds		40	0
foure coffers and a troncke		15	0
tables formes stoles and chears		13	4
corne and malt in the house	7	0	0
beefe and bakon		26	8
butter and cheese	4	0	0
two peeces of linen cloth and one of wollen		40	0
Englishe bookes		10	0
halfe a dosen of quishions		10	0
halfe a dosen of silver spones		40	0
brase and pewter	4	0	0
in trine ware and straw baskets		26	8
goberts, spits, rackes, fireshoo, tonges & bellows		3	0
corne in the barne unthressed	7	0	0
hay in the new barne		40	0
corne that was lately soeed	5	0	0
carts, plowes, yokes, chaines, harrowes and other husbandrie ware, or implements thereto belonginge	8	0	0
compas and strae at the new barne		10	0
8 olde sheepe and 4 lambes		45	8
two nages and three mares	15	0	0
7 beafe in the great mosse	16	0	0
a yoke of oxen	9	0	0
9 kine	22	10	0

footnotes for no. 34 continued

[g] Juryman for the IPM held 18 January 1624/25 for John Wicksted at Nantwich (see R. Stewart Brown, *Cheshire Inquisitions Post Mortem*, iii. 171). Obtained livery of the estates on 25 November 1622 (value was £3 19s. 0d/CRO document, an amount increased by 6s. by the survey of the Feodary of Chester); took oath on 1 January 1623, about the time he md. Frances; present at the skirmish at Market Drayton 28 May 1643 (Malbon, *Memorials of the Civil War in Cheshire*, pp. 129–30); 1647 in will of John Tenche of Wilkesley (CRO); 1642 tenant of Newhall, excused; 1648 tenant; 1647 tithe.

[h] The will of John Egerton, pr. 1622 (will no. 67) mentions his Whitney grandchildren; IPM refers to two children of Hugh (deceased), naming only his oldest, Hugh, born 1600/01.

4 calves		30	0
two swine		20	0
Railes, montans and pannells	3	6	8
4 ladders		6	8
bricke		50	0
boords bases and other timber		30	0
fewall for the fire about the house		6	8
27 trees in Wrenbury Wood		11	10
two quarter of woode	3	13	8
poultry		5	0
bills, bands, and debts owing to him		63	11
leases of the Great Mosse and Woods feelds now lownd the Springyard man feelde the pingath valued at ten pounds a yeare	10	0	0

Some is	246	7	8
[*recte*	159	1	5]
The funerall expences and debts owinge by him to others	37	7	10
the remainder is	208	19	10
[*recte*	121	1	5]

Endorsement: Exhibited 11 June 1611; administration to Elizabeth his widow.

35. MARGERIE SEVELL OF NEWHALL, WIDOW

I.Pr. 11 June 1611
W. [bef. 2 April] 1611
Buried: 15 March 1610/11

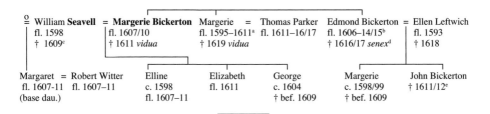

ọ̱ William **Seavell**	= **Margerie Bickerton**	Margerie	= Thomas Parker	Edmond Bickerton	= Ellen Leftwich
fl. 1598	fl. 1607/10	fl. 1595–1611[a]	fl. 1611–16/17	fl. 1606–14/15[b]	fl. 1593
† 1609[c]	† 1611 *vidua*	† 1619 *vidua*		† 1616/17 *senex*[d]	† 1618

Margaret	= Robert Witter	Elline	Elizabeth	George	Margerie	John Bickerton
fl. 1607-11	fl. 1607–11	c. 1598	fl. 1611	c. 1604	c. 1598/99	† 1611/12[e]
(base dau.)		fl. 1607–11		† bef. 1609	† bef. 1609	

Will, sick.

First, I bequeth my sole to almightie god my *bodie to the Church yarde of Wrenbury*. . . . I desier that my land lord shall have the best good I have. Item then I beqeath to Margeret Witter the best of my goodes when it is devided, then to my Syster Margerie Parker one goune one pettecote one partelit one smocke and one Croscloth: And then to my brother Yedmonde one shirt of the cloth that is now in makeing. Then to my doughter Elline my best gowne and hate. Then doughter Elizabeth my best petecote and band Then the Rest of my goods to be ecole devide moungest them.

Executors: Robart Witter and Robart Wright.

---

[a] Received 10s. as bequest from Raffe Barnett 1595 (will no. 13).
[b] There is no direct internal evidence which identifies the brother *Yedmond* of both Margerie Seavell and Margerie Parker as the Edmond Bickerton who flourished at Sound and died 1616/17 (will no. 56), but there is strong circumstantial evidence: 1) the casual reference to 'our brother Yedmond' without any sort of surname allows the conclusion that this particular Edmund was familiar to the inhabitants of Newhall; 2) there is only one other person with that given name found in the records of Wrenbury at this time, namely, Edmund Crewe († 1632) whose burial entry actually shows *Yedmon* Crewe, but there are no other indications of any association between him and the two women who were Yedmond's sisters; the name is rare enough to help us limit the possibilities; 3) Edmond Bickerton had property in Nantwich which was occupied by one Thomas *Parker*, and here we have the hoped-for connection between Margerie Parker and a brother named Yedmond: Thomas Parker could as easily be Margerie Parker's son as her husband, thus explaining why she is living in Wrenbury parish when she dies.
[c] See will of William Seavell, pr. 1609 (will no. 27).
[d] See will of Edmond Bickerton, pr. 1616/17 (will no. 56).
[e] See will of John Bickerton, pr. 1611/12 (will no. 39).

Witnesses: Robart Wright Roger Goosteloe.

Inventory: Margerie Sevell of Newhall, widow.

Taken: 2 April 1611

Prised: Thomas [Parker ?], Robart Hall, Richard Edgley yeomen.

	£	s	d
her Apparell	*[erasure]*	10	0
one Cowe due for a heriot to Mr. Chitwoode	2	3	4
her part of Cattell	1	3	4
the forthe parte of A Swine		1	8
brase and pewter			5
brdes [*sic!*] formes shilefes bedsteds and all coperie & coffers		3	4
bedinge and naperie and all other linan cloths		3	6
painted cloths			6
hempe and yorne spone in the howse			1
Corne in the house and upon the ground		10	0
all the poulterie		3	4
[Sum	4	39	46]

Endorsement: Probated 11 November 1611; administration to the executors named in the will.

36. WILLIAM DAVIES OF WRENBURY

I.Pr. 1 August 1611
Buried: 18 June 1611

William Davies = Alice [   ]
† 1611 *senex*   fl. 1611

Inventory: William Davies of Wrenbury.

Taken: 24 June 1611

Of: goods and Cattells.

Prisers: John Cartwright of Aston, Arthur Hussie, Richard Cooke and Robert Whittingham.

	£	s	d
his wearinge apparell		10	0
one Cowe price	10	11	8
the beste sterke beaste price		26	8
two sterke beastes		50	0

4 shotts	16	0
poultrie ware	4	0
brasse and pewter	30	0
beddinge and naperie	53	4
whytmeate	26	8
baken	6	8
bedstids Chists tables formes shillfes and all other Cowprie ware and woodden ware Cobbords and trennen ware	40	0
Iren ware	5	0
Corne and Mallte	6	0
Corne growinge upon the ground	30	0
husbandrie ware	5	0
2 weaninge Caulfes	13	4

Some is	18	9	4
[*recte*	26	3	6]

Endorsement: Inventory of the goods of William Davies was exhibited 23 June 1611; administration granted 1 August 1611 to Alice his widow who was sworn personally before Mr Prince the Curate of Wrenbury.

37. ELLEN FLETCHER OF NEWHALL, SPINSTER

I.Pr. 15 October 1611
Buried: 20 July 1611

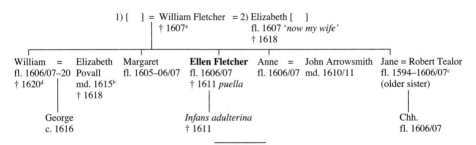

[a] See will of William Fletcher of Newhall, pr. 1607 (will no. 23).
[b] William Fergusson Irvine, *Chester Licence*s, i. 193: 1615 William Fletcher to marry Elizabeth *Povey* (Povell) of Wrenbury parish at Wrenbury.
[c] Joane Fletcher mentioned 1594 as god-daughter in will of Humphrey Bickerton (will no. 12); married 1601.
[d] William Fletcher noted as witness to will and priser of the goods of John Backhouse of Newhall, will pr. 1620 (will no. 61).

Inventory: Ellen Fletcher of Newhall, spinster.

                                    Taken: 1 October 1611, 9 James I

Of: goods and Cattells.

Prisers: John Bickerton, John Backhowse and Robarte Hall.

	£	s	d
her Weringe Apparell presed at	4	0	0
in Redye monye	21	0	0
howsehould goods presed at	2	10	0
one Cowe presed at	2	13	4
Some is	30	4	4
[*recte*	29	3	4]
more 2 fliches of backon presed at		16	0
Some totall is	30	19	4
[*recte*	29	23	4]

Endorsement: Exhibited 15 October 1611. *[No indication as to whom adminis-tration was granted].*

38. LAWRENCE STARKIE OF WRENBURY, GENT.

I.Pr. 16 January 1611/12
Buried: 8 December 1611

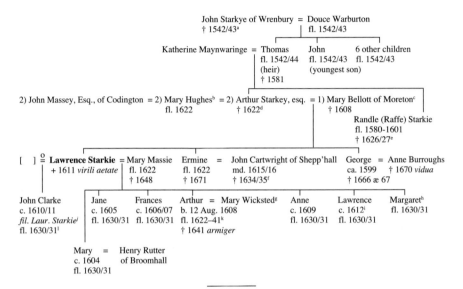

John Starkye of Wrenbury = Douce Warburton
† 1542/43[a] | fl. 1542/43

Katherine Maynwaringe = Thomas   John   6 other children
fl. 1542/44   fl. 1542/43   fl. 1542/43
(heir)   (youngest son)
† 1581

2) John Massey, Esq., of Codington = 2) Mary Hughes[b] = 2) Arthur Starkey, esq. = 1) Mary Bellott of Moreton[c]
fl. 1622   † 1622[d]   † 1608

Randle (Raffe) Starkie
fl. 1580-1601
† 1626/27[e]

[ ] $\stackrel{\circ}{=}$ **Lawrence Starkie** = Mary Massie   Ermine = John Cartwright of Shepp'hall   George = Anne Burroughs
+ 1611 *virili aetate*   fl. 1622   fl. 1622   md. 1615/16   ca. 1599   † 1670 *vidua*
† 1648   † 1671   † 1634/35[f]   † 1666 æ 67

John Clarke   Jane   Frances   Arthur = Mary Wicksted[g]   Anne   Lawrence   Margaret[h]
c. 1610/11   c. 1605   c. 1606/07   b. 12 Aug. 1608   c. 1609   c. 1612[i]   fl. 1630/31
fil. Laur. Starkie[j]   fl. 1630/31   fl. 1630/31   fl. 1622–41[k]   fl. 1630/31   fl. 1630/31
fl. 1630/31[l]   † 1641 *armiger*

Mary = Henry Rutter
c. 1604   of Broomhall
fl. 1630/31

Inventory: Lawrence Starkie of Wrenbury, gent.

Taken: 10 December 1611

Of: goods and Cattells.

Prisers: William Willson, William Barnett, John Fisher and Thomas Hurleston.

[a] See will no. 1, above. Glover, *Visitations of 1566 and 1580, p.* 219; St George, *Visitation of 1613*, pp. 226–7.
[b] Daughter of Charles Hughes of Hoult, co. Derby.
[c] Daughter of Thomas Bellot of Moreton and relict of Richard Minshull of Minshull.
[d] See will of Arthur Starkey of Wrenbury, esquire, pr. 1623 (will no. 69).
[e] See will of Randle Starkie of Wrenbury, gent., pr. 1626/27 (will no. 73).
[f] See inventory, etc. of John Cartwright of Sheppenhall, pr. 1635 (no. 96).
[g] Daughter of John Wickstead of Nantwich.
[h] See Ormerod, *History of Cheshire*, iii. 396.
[i] Ormerod, *History of Cheshire*, iii. 396, shows him dying unmarried.
[j] This is possibly the John Starkey, citizen of London, noted on Ormerod's chart, *History of Cheshire*, iii. 396.
[k] Identified as the next of kin and heir of Arthur Starkey, IPM, ?1622; see will no. 69; owed John Cartwright of Aston £1 in 1630 (will no. 81); received bequest of 20s. from William Babington, 1630/31 (will no. 85); owed debt of 10s. to Richard Cheswis, 1632/33 (will no. 93); noted in will of Elizabeth Briscoe, pr. 1637 (will no. 103). A monument in the chancel at Wrenbury contains the inscription: *Arthur Starkey son of Lawrence buried 19 July 1641*; see Ormerod, *History of Cheshire*, iii. 207.
[l] As John Starkey.

	£	s	d
his apparell	3	0	0
one tacke of one howse lyinge and beinge in Wrenbury for two yeares to Come	14	0	0
foure kyne and two Calves	8	13	4
one ould mare and a coulte		26	8
five younge swyne		20	0
haye		40	0
two silver spoones		10	0
brasse and Pewter		10	0
Lynnens or naperye		20	0
two Chests two boxes and one truncke and one deske		20	0
books		15	0
treene ware Coopes and glasses		10	0
fyre fuell		3	4
Iron ware		5	0
Bacon Cheese and such lyke provision for the howse		26	0
one stryke of twylve Corne		5	0
one Loockinge glasse and twoe brushes		2	0
in powltrie		3	4
one paire of bedstocks			12
Brooke grasse *[i.e. broken glass]*		3	4
[Sum	25	231	36]

Endorsement: Exhibited 16 January 1611; administration to Edward Lapworth.

39. JOHN BICKERTON, THE SONNE OF EDMUND BICKERTON OF SOUND

S.Pr. 27 January 1611/12
Burial: None recorded at Wrenbury or Acton[a]

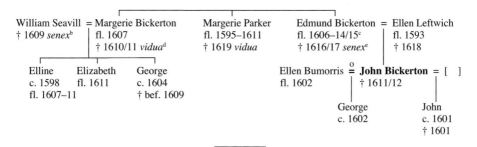

Inventory: John Bickerton 'the sonne of Edmund Bickerton of Sounde that we doe know within the county of Stafford yeoman lately deceassed the 20th day of August and his goods in the county of Chester and Sallopp'.

Taken: 20 August 1611

Of: goods and chattells & debts moveable.

Prisers: Richard Sanemp, John Bebinton, John Evanson, George Beckett.

	£	s	d
Oweing by Edmund Bickerton to his sonne		20	0
More remaining in the hande of the said Edmund being left of the funeral expence		4	1
On cowe in the hande of Thomas Massie thelder price		46	8
The hier of the same cowe		6	8
His wearing apparell	6	10	0
Chest		10	0
Money found in his purse to discharge his funerall		27	1
Owing him by William Hampton and Richard Clarke	7	4	0
More owing him by John Beckett	6	12	0

---

[a] The fact that John's father, Edmund Bickerton, was buried at Wrenbury may also argue for John's unrecorded burial there. The Wrenbury Parish Registers are of no help in establishing a family for him which would be further proof that he identified with Wrenbury, and not Acton, as did some of his neighbours at Sound.
[b] See will of William Seavell of Newhall, pr. 1609 (will no. 27).
[c] For arguments regarding the larger family relationships of Edmund Bickerton, see will no. 35, above.
[d] See will of Margerie Sevell, pr. 1611 (will no. 35).
[e] See will of Edmond Bickerton, pr. 1617 (will no. 56).

More by Richard Cowper	3	6	0
By Randle Blackhurst		44	0
By Thomas Corey		22	0
By William Allin		22	0
On sword		6	8
[Sum	22	239	26]

Endorsement: The inventory of John Bickerton 'the sonne of Edmund Bickerton of Sounde county of Stafford *[sic!]* yeoman' was exhibited 27 January 1611. *[No indication as to whom administration was granted].*

40. RANDULL COWPER OF WRENBURY, HUSBANDMAN

S.Pr. 9 April 1613
Will [last day of February] 1611/12
Buried: 5 April 1612

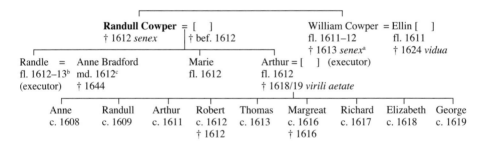

Will, sick.

First and principally I Comend my soule into the hands of almighty god hopeinge by the merits and bloodsheding of Jesus Christe to bee one of the number of those that shall bee made partakers of everlastinge Joy and felicitie and *my bodie I Comitt to the earth to bee buried in the Church yard of Wrenbury* Item my will and mynde is that all such debts as I owe of righte or conscience will and truly Contented to be paide by my Executors hereafter named Item I give and bequeath

---

a See will of William Cooper of Sound, pr. 1613 (will no. 42).
b Made inventory for William Cooper 1613 (see will no. 42).
c William Fergusson Irvine, *Chester Licences*, i. 119: 1 May 1612, Ralph Cowper of Wrenbury and Anne Bradford of Baddiley; bondsman, Arthur Cowper; at Baddiley.

to Elene Stringer one yeare ould Calf All the reste of my goods moveable and unmoveable (exceptinge my workinge tooles my bodie beinge honestly brought-paide by home, my funerall expenss and my debts beinge paide and discharged I give and bequeath to Randle Cowper my sonne and Marie Cowper my doughter to bee equally devided betweene them Item I give my saide workinge tooles to Arthur Cowper and Randle Cowper my sonnes to bee equally devided betweene them.

Executors: the testator's brother, William Cowper, and the testator's son, Randle Cowper.

Overseer: John Bebington.

Randull Cowper
his marke

Witnesses: Thomas Graie, John Mosse, Thomas Mosse, and John Evanson.

Debts owing to the testator:

	s	d
by John S[avage]	20	0

Debts owed by the Testator:

	£	s	d
to John Savage		44	0
to Oliver Briscoe	3	0	0
more to John Savage		17	6

all other debts to bee discharged as are due by speciallty

Inventory: Randulph Cooper of Wrenbury.

Taken: 23 April 1612, 10 James I

Of: goods Cattells and Chattells.

Prisers: John Bebington, Thomas Sparke, John Savage and Olyver Bruscalle.

	£	s	d
Eleaven kyne and heiffers with theire values price	27	10	0
three twinter heiffers with a bulle calf	6	13	4
three calves		40	0
other three calves		12	0
one mare price	3	0	0
one nagg price		50	0
sheepe price		14	0
Brasse price	3	6	8
pewter		20	0

Trinde ware		20	0
one presse with boords, formes shelves coffers cheyres & stooles		20	0
fower bedstydds price		20	0
Beddinge and Napery ware	3	0	0
his owne wearinge apparrell		20	0
wollen clothe		5	0
corne on the grounde		30	0
Timber		26	8
Fleshe		5	0
Hennes ducks geese & other poultry		3	4
his workinge tooles		12	0
Carts plowes harrowes horse geares and other implements of husbandrye		13	4
all the Iron ware		6	8
sawed boords		2	0
Cushens			6
the mucke		3	4
one grindleston			12
[Sum	42	350	58]

Endorsement: Probated 9 April 1613; administration to the executors named in the will.

41. EDWARD BASKERVILLE OF SOUND

S.Pr. 10 June 1613
Burial: None recorded at Wrenbury or Acton

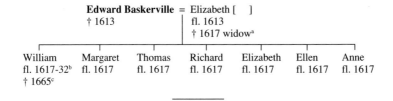

Edward Baskerville = Elizabeth [ ]						
† 1613	fl. 1613					
	† 1617 widow[a]					
William	Margaret	Thomas	Richard	Elizabeth	Ellen	Anne
fl. 1617-32[b]	fl. 1617	fl. 1617	fl. 1617	fl. 1617	fl. 1617	fl. 1617
† 1665[c]						

[a] See will of Elizabeth Baskerville, pr. 1617 (will no. 55).
[b] Noted as god-son of William Bebington of Nantwich, will pr. 1632/ CRO.
[c] See nuncupative will and inventory of William Baskerville, pr. 1665/ CRO.

Inventory: Edward Baskerfild of Sound.

Taken: 3 February 1613

Of: goods and Cattell.

Prisers: Edmunde Bickerton, Robert Pownall, Peter Walton and John Watson.

	£	s	d
wereinge apparell	3	0	0
Beddinge	15	0	0
Bedstockes	3	0	0
Napperie and sheets	7	0	0
one Cobbord & a presse & 3 Chests	2	0	0
Tables formes & Chers		6	8
one Corstet		26	8
Brasse and pewter	3	0	0
Trine ware		20	0
Irone Ware tooles & Instruments of husbandrie	3	0	0
Corne unthreched & hay	3	0	0
[blank]			
Corne and malt in the house	4	0	0
Beefe and Bacon		30	0
Butter and Cheese		20	0
yarne and towe		20	0
apece of wollen Cloth		12	0
tow sadles		10	0
Poultrie		6	8
fore harriots	40	0	0
one Mare	3	3	4
4 kine	9	6	8
3 bullocks	4	6	8
2 heffars	2	8	4
1 Cow and Calfe	3	6	8
2 swine		16	0
1 sheepe		3	4
5 pounds of woll		7	6
for bees		14	4
spining whiles		2	0
one here Cloth		6	8

[Sum   ]

Debts owing by Edward Baskervild of Sound dececed:

	£	s	d
to John Broumole *[Bromhall]*	1	0	0
the same John Broumole	2	0	0

Thomas Orpe	40	0	0
The same Thomas Orpe	4	6	8
Widdow Leftwich	2	0	0
William Leay	6	0	0
Peeter Wolton		18	0
Edward Fletcher		19	11
[Sum	55	43	19]

Endorsement: Exhibited 10 June 1613; administration to Elizabeth his widow.

42. WILLIAM COOPER OF SOUND, YEOMAN

S.Pr. 15 July 1613
W. 29 May 1611
Buried: 9 June 1611

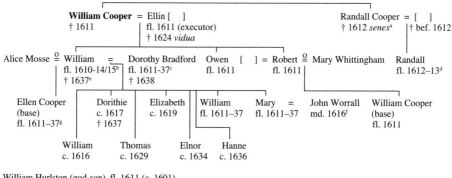

William Hurlston (god-son), fl. 1611 (c. 1601)
William Brees (god-son), fl. 1611 (c. 1601)
William Bathoe (god-son), fl. 1611

---

[a] See will of Randull Cowper of Wrenbury, husbandman, pr. 1613 (will no. 40).
[b] Priser 1610 for James Barnett (will no. 29)..
[c] William Fergusson Irvine, *Chester Licences*, i. 179: 20 Feb. 1614/15, to William *Cowper* of Wrenbury parish and Dorothy Bradford of Wrenbury parish, spinster, at St Oswald's Chester.
[d] See will of his father Randull Cowper of Wrenbury, pr. 1613 (will no. 40); made inventory for his uncle, William Cooper, 1613 (see below, this will).
[e] See will of William Cowper the elder of Sound, 1637 (will no. 104).
[f] William Fergusson Irvine, *Chester Licences*, ii. 12: 29 August 1616 to Mary *Cowper* (no parish listed)/ John Worrall of Baddily parish, at Wrenbury; bondsman: John Plant.
[g] See will of William Cowper (will no. 104), where she is noted as Ellene Mosse *alias* Cowper.

Will, sick.

First and pryncipally I doe Comitt my sole into the handes of Allmightye god my maker and onlye redeemer hopinge Assuredlye through the death and passion of Jesus Christ to have Forgivnes of my synnes and inherytance in the Kingdome of Heavenn And as towching *my bodye I will that It be buryed in the parishe Churchyarde of Wrenbury,* where yt shalbee thought good by the discretion of mine executors Item I doe give and bequeath unto and amongest the poore people in habytinge within the parishe of Wrenbury yerelye for duryng the tearme of tenne yeres next after my deceasse, the yearlye some of tenne shillings of lawfull money and to be distributed yerely uppon Good Fryday by the discretion of my executors and the overseers for the poore within the sayde parishe for the tyme beeinge or any twoe of them. Item I doe give and bequeath unto William Cooper the supposed sonne of my sonne Robert begotten of on Mary Whittingham the somme of Tene pounds to be payd unto the sayd William whithin one whole yeare next after the deceasse of Ellen my wife. Item I doe give and bequeath unto William Cooper and Marye Cooper Children of my sonne Robert to either of them the some of five pounds to bee payd unto them in like manner within on yeare next after the deceasse of my sayd wife Item I doe give and bequeath unto my sonne Robert Cooper the somme of five pounds Item I doe give and bequeath unto Ellen the supposed doughter of my eldest sonne William Cooper begotten on Allice Mosse the some of Ten pounds, to bee Likewise payed unto her within on yeare next after the deceasse of the sayd Ellen my wiefe, All which sayd severall Legacyes and sommes of money my will and meaninge is shallbe payde by my sonne William Cooper in full satisfaction of £40 which the sayd William my sonne is lymited and Charged to pay in respect and Liewe of the lease of the Hobbfieldes in Wrenbury Frith which I have hearetofore Assigned to his use. Item I doe give devise and bequeathe unto the sayd William Cooper my eldest sonne All that my free Lands tenements medowes Leasowes pastures and Commons with thappurtenences and hereditaments scituate Lyinge and beinge in Sound within the sayd Countye of Chester now in the tennure and occupation of John Barnett thelder. To have and to hould the same with thapputenances to him the sayd William his heires and Assignes for ever, uppon this Condicion and soe as hee the sayd William Cooper my sonne shall and doe well and trulye Content satisfye and paye unto Owen Cooper my sonne the somme of Twenty pounds of Lawfull money of Englande within three monethes next and Immediatlye after the end and determinacōn of an Indenture of lease made of the premisses by John Preslande gent deceased unto the sayd John Barnett for dyvers yeares yett enduringe And if yt happen the sayd Owen Cooper my sonne to deceasse before the end and determinacon of the sayde Indenture of leasse made by the sayd John Prestlande, that then my will is that my sayde sonne William shall in noe wise be Charged with payment of the sayd somme of £20. Item I doe give and bequeath unto my sayd sonne William All my seylinge and wainscote now Remayninge in my house, three table boords, the best bedstockes one Presse one Cubboorde the Furnice Panne and the greate Brasse pott which I will and my meaninge is that they and

Every of them shall Remaine and bee unto him as standerds and heireloomes, (savinge that my will is that my sayd wiefe shall have the use and occupacōn of them duringe her naturall lief.) Item I doe give and bequeath unto William Hurleston, William Brees, and William Bathoe my god children to every of them 3s. 4d. Item The rest and Residue of all and singuler my goodes and Chattells houshould stuffe and Implements not before given nor bequeathed my debtes beinge payd and fully satisfied and Likewise I being honestlye brought home and my funerall expences discharged I doe give and bequeath the same wholly to Ellen my wife.

Executors: the testator's wife, Ellen Cooper, and the testator's son, William Cooper.

H. & S.

Inventory: William Cooper of Sound.

Taken: 15 June 1613

Of: goodes and Chattels.

Prisers: John Beeckett, Peter Paltonne, Humfrey Barnett, Randull Cooper.

	£	s	d
For all his apparrell		33	4
For tow oxen	8	0	0
For nine kine and a bull	26	0	0
For eighteene yonge beasts	25	0	0
For tow mares	5	6	8
For sheepe	3	10	0
For three Calves		30	0
For swine		26	8
For Poultrye		5	0
For Bees		10	0
For weanes plowes harrowes yookes, Cheanes and all other Ironware		40	0
For Brasse and pewter	4	0	0
For Beddinge and nappery ware	10	0	0
For seylinge Bedstockes tables Formes and al other treinware	5	0	0
For silver spoones		8	0
For on gould Ringe		8	0
For on Bible booke		6	0
For saddels and Brydles		2	0
For wooll		13	4
For Butter and Cheese and Fleshmeate		40	0
For wood and tymber and Fyerfuell		10	0
For mucke		3	4

For Corne within the house and growinge on the ground	13	13	4
For hempe and flaxe		5	0
Summa totall	112	10	8

Endorsement: Probated 15 July 1613; administration to the executors named in the will.

43. THOMAS RAVENSCROFT OF NEWHALL

S.Pr. 4 May 1614
W.T. 19 Jan 1613/14
Buried: 23 January 1613/14

Thomas Ravenscroft = Ellen [ ] Jane = Richard Dodd of Smeatonwood Anne Ravenscroft = William Heighfield
fl. 1605-11ᵃ fl. 1614-25ᵇ fl. 1613/14 † 1636/37ᶜ fl. 1618 (testator's kinsman)
† 1613/14 *virili aetate* † 1630/31ᵈ † 1633 fl. 1613/14
† 1619

John = Elizabeth [ ] Thomas = Eleanor [ ] Anne John Booth = Elizabeth James
c. 1593 † 1637 c. 1598 c. 1604 fl. 1626/27–30 c. 1608 fl. 1613/14
(elder son) fl. 1609–36ᵉ fl. 1613/14–26/27 fl. 1613/14
fl. 1614-35/36ᶠ (younger son) Elene † 1630
† 1649 (4 Nov.) † 1645/46 c. 1601 John
fl. 1613/14-26/27 c. 1628

Thomas Anne John George (not yet aged 16)
c. 1617 c. 1620 c. 1626 c. 1628 † 1634
fl. 1626/27 fl. 1626/27 fl. 1626/27

Anne Elizabeth
† 1614/15 fl. 1626/27
† 1640

ᵃ Wrenbury churchwarden 1605; Thomas Ravenscroft *Afferer* 1611/CRO. Owed debt of £10 in 1605 to John Hall (see above, will no. 22).
ᵇ CRO Newhall Rentals, 1625.
ᶜ See will of Richard Dodd of Smeatonwood, pr. 1637 (will no. 101).
ᵈ Earwaker, *Index to Wills at Chester*, ii. 158: see will of Ellen Ravenscroft of Newhall, widow, pr. 1630/31 (will no. 86).
ᵉ Thomas Ravenscroft of Newhall Park noted with son Thomas 25 Sept. 1609; Newhall Rentals 1625; Thomas Jr was priser with his brother John for George Dickins of Newhall 1626/27 (will no. 74); witness with his brother, John, to the will of John Hall of Newhall 1635/36 (will no. 100).
ᶠ Owed debt of £6 13s. 4d. to James Barnett 1610 (will no. 29); priser for William Heighfield (kinsman of Thomas Ravenscroft and overseer of his will) 1620 (will no. 62); priser with brother Thomas Ravenscroft of goods of George Dickins of Newhall 1626/27 (will no. 74); priser 1626/27 for Thomas Shrowbridge of Newhall (will no. 75); priser for Richard Hall of Smeatonwood 1630 (no. 83); witness and overseer for will of John Hall of Newhall pr. 1635/36 (will no. 100).

Will, sick.

First, I doe comend & comitt my soule into the hands of allmaightie god & of Jesus Christ his onelie sonne my onelie redeemer by whose death & passion I hope & by faith in him am assured to be saved & redeemed from that death which my sines have deserved & now resting in that hopefull assurance I doe thus dispose of my temporall goods & estate. I give & bequeth & by these presents I doe assigne & settover unto my younger sonne Thomas Ravenscrofte & to his Assignes all my estate Claymed tytle & interest which I have or may have in or unto a certen farme lands or tenements comonlie knowne called Finny Wood lying in Darley or neere unto Darley within the foresayed Countie of Chester being parcell of the inheritaince of Henrie Starkey of Darley Esquire with all profitts & comodities there unto belonging hee my sayd sonne Thomas yelding paying & doing all such rents duties & service as in the same lease are specifide Provided & my will is that my older sonne John Ravenscrofte shall have the use & disposall of the sayd lands & tenements for the terme & space of seaven yeares now next coming Provided that he paye & performes these rents & condicōns following *videlicit* that this next yeares full profitts & comodities be whollie dispossed towards the paymente of my detts & such legacies as I shall hereafter bequeath & for the six yeares then following he shall yearlie paye unto my three daughters Elene Ravenscrofte Anne Ravenscrofte & Elizabeth Ravenscrofte ~~fourtie~~ twentie pounds yearelie the first ~~two the first~~ towe of the six yeares payments to be made to the use of my older daughter the next towe yeares profitts to the use of my second daughter & the ~~lastes~~ laste towe yeares profitts to the use of my youngest daughter Also upon condicōn that my sayd sonne John shall doe ~~p[aye]~~ build in & upon that tenemente & acowement dwelling house within the terme of foure yeares now next Coming And alsoe my will is that my sayd sonne John doe yeld & paye the benefitts & profitts of the last three yeares which shalbe over & besides that [£]20 yearelie to be payd unto my three daughters wch shall arise out of the sayd tenemente unto & towards the discharge of my detts legasies & towards the further prefermentes of my three daughters & att the end of the foresayed seaven yeares my will is that then my foresayd sonne Thomas shall then enter upon have & enioye to his owne proper use profitt & occupacōn ~~of~~ all the whole & ~~[sew all]~~ onlie parte of the sayd tenemente called Fenny Wood for & during all the whole terme which then shall remayne unexpired Alsoe my will is & I doe give & bequeath & further by theise presents I doe assigne & settover unto John Ravenscrofte my oldest sonne & to his Assignes all my estate tytle & interest which I have or may have in or unto a certen parcell of landes & tenements in Newhall within the Countie of Chester Comonlie knowne & ~~known~~ called by the name of Newhall Park now in the Houlding of mee or of my Assignes being parcell the inheritance of the right honorable the Earle of Bathe with all howses there to belonging Alsoe my will is & hereby I doe give & bequeath unto my foresayd three daughters Elene Anne & Elizabeth so much more out of all my goods bargaines & estate as will make upp the forenamed somes of fourtie pounds apeece to be payd theym from Finny Wood the some of £100 apeece to be payde them

when they & eich of theym respectivelie shall attayne to the age of sixeteene yeares & yf all my goods with ~~mh~~ my other leases & the forenamed some of £20 from
Finny Wood shallbe ~~inbe~~ insufficient to discharge this with other legacies then my
will is that my eldest sonne John shall out of the profitts of the forenamed Newhall
Park lands make upp so much as shalbe wanting unto my sayd daughters the full
some of a hundred pounds apeece to be payd unto theym as before when they
shall respectivelie attayne to to the age of 16 yeares Also I give & bequeath unto
my welbeloved wyfe £40 and 4 such of my kyne as shee her selfe shall make
chayse of Alsoe I give unto my sonne James £10 to be payde or allowed out of
such wages as I am to receive from him & his partner Alsoe I give unto my sister Jane Dodd £4 Also I give unto my master Mr. Cotton of Combermere 40s. &
to everie of his children unmarried 20s. apeece Also I give unto everie one of my
godchildren 10s. apeece lastlie I give & bequeath unto the poore of the parishe of
Wrenbury for the terme of eight yeares the some of 40s. yearelie to be payd yearelie by my executor att the feast of Christmas & to be distributed as shall seeme
fittest by the gent. & *Church wardens of the sayd parishe of Wrenbury where I
desire my bodie may be buried* Yet further my will is that my bargains with
Lodmore for his lands with backhouse & all such lyke estates be disposed & be
converted unto & towards the paymente & discharge of my detts legacies &
towards the prefermente of my three daughters.

Executors: the testator's wife, and the testator's son, John Ravenscrofte.

Overseers: Mr. Cotton of Combermere, and the testator's kinsman William
Heighfeild of Broomhall.

H. & S.
Thomas Ravenscrofte
marke

Witnesses: George Graye, John Taylor and William Heighfeilds marke.

Inventory: Thomas Ravenscroft of Newhall.

Taken: 31 January 1614/15

Of: goods & Cattels.

Prisers: Richard Taylor, Thomas Edgley, William Heyhfeild and William Tench.

	£	s	d
his wearing apparell	5	0	0
eight oxen	10	0	0
nyneteene kyne & heffers with calfe att three pounds sixe shillings eight pence a cowe	63	6	9
three stirke heffers foure calves & one Bull	12	0	0

three mares & a nagg	8	0	0
fyve Swyne and a pigg		33	4
fyve lambs		16	8
corne in the barne	23	2	8
hey in barnes & stacks	*[illegible]*		
beding cowerings & such lyke	10	0	0
lynons sheetes table clothes & napperie	5	0	0
three standing beddes three tubbs & three chests			
cheeres & shelves	4	10	0
Brasse verdelt[?] potts & Pans	5	0	0
Pewter & Candesticks		25	0
treeneware with combes barrels stannds Eshenns & such lyke		20	0
carts ploues yokes cheynes & all impements of husbandrie	3	6	8
all Iron ware in the house spytts Goberts tongs fyre shovell			
dreeping pans Racks & And Iernens		13	4
Beefe & Bacon	3	0	0
poultrie		2	0
bricke readie made	5	0	0
corne upon the grounde	3	0	0
wood coles tornes & a fouling peece		20	0
Butter & Cheese		40	0
a payre of waights of halfe ahundred waight		3	4
one cowe more	3	6	8
six silver sponnes	30	0	0
Towe & yarne		20	0
three spinning wheeles		3	0
Cushens		2	0
pictures paynted clothes heyre & such lyke		3	4
hempeseede & lynseede		5	0
[Sum	192	235	57]

Endorsement: Probated 4 May 1614; administration to the executors named in the will.

44. ROGER HOCKENHULL OF BROOMHALL, GENT.

S.Pr 10 July 1614
W.T. 10 September 1613
Buried: 13 December 1613

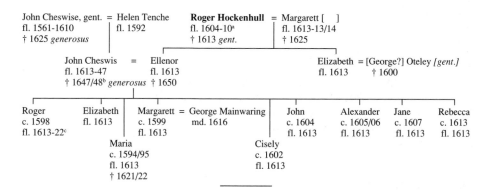

John Cheswise, gent. = Helen Tenche	**Roger Hockenhull** = Margarett [ ]
fl. 1561-1610 fl. 1592	fl. 1604-10[a] fl. 1613-13/14
† 1625 *generosus*	† 1613 *gent.* † 1625

John Cheswis = Ellenor
fl. 1613-47   fl. 1613
† 1647/48[b] *generosus* † 1650

Elizabeth = [George?] Oteley *[gent.]*
fl. 1613   † 1600

Roger	Elizabeth	Margarett = George Mainwaring	John	Alexander	Jane	Rebecca
c. 1598	fl. 1613	c. 1599 md. 1616	c. 1604	c. 1605/06	c. 1607	c. 1613
fl. 1613-22[c]		fl. 1613	fl. 1613	fl. 1613	fl. 1613	fl. 1613

Maria
c. 1594/95
fl. 1613
† 1621/22

Cisely
c. 1602
fl. 1613

Will, sick & weak.

First, I bequeth my soule into the hande of almighty god Trustinge only by the death and bloudsheedinge of Jesus Christ my alone Saviour to have free pardon and remission of all my sins. And *my body to be buried in the parrishe Church of Wrenbury* accordinge to the discreation of my Executors. Item I give and bequeath unto my grandchild Roger Cheswis my silver salt parcell guilt with six of my best silver spoones and my silver Boule. Item I give & bequeath unto the sayd Roger Cheswis forty poundes of Currant money for and towardes his education and bringinge upp. Item I give and bequeath unto the sayde Roger Cheswis all my Armor and the rest of my weapons, and all my bookes. Item I give and bequeth unto my daughter Ellenor Cheswis the on halfe of my heath sheepe. Item I give and bequeth unto my sayde daughter Ellenor Cheswis my other six silver spoones And my mazer cupp furnished with silver & guilt. Item I give and bequeth unto my daughter Elizabeth Oteley eight Angels of gould in consideration of her chyldes part of my goodes. Item I give and bequeth unto seven of the Children of my sonne in lawe John Cheswis *videlicit* To Elizabeth, Margarett, Cisely, Jane, Rebecca, John and Alixander to eitch on of them foure pounds of currant monie

---

[a] Owed debt of 13s. 4d. by Alice Blackamore in 1604 (see will of the latter, no. 20); juryman in the IPM taken for Richard Cotton, esq., of Combermere, at Sandbach 6 April 1605 (see R. Stewart Brown, *Cheshire Inquisitions Post Mortem*, i. 146) as Roger *Hocknell*; Roger Hockenhull, gent., owed £5 to James Barnett, 1610 (will no. 29).
[b] See will of John Cheswis, pr. 1648 (will no. 127).
[c] Roger Cheswis owed £11 to James Brooke of Aston, yeoman, 1622 (see will no. 66).

to goe forwardes with them. All the rest of my beastes and Cattell I give and bequeth unto my wyfe Margarett Hockenhull. Item my will is that my wyfe shall have the use & occupation of all my househould goodes dureinge her naturall lyfe except those houshould goodes which I have alreadie bequeathed And at the decease of my sayd wyfe Then my will is that my grandchyld Mary Cheswis shall have the on halfe of my sayde houshould goodes And the other halfe to be at the disposinge of my sayde wife. Item if it happen that my wyfe do marry, Then my will is that my grandchyld Maria Cheswis shall have the fore sayd on halfe of my houshould goodes delivered unto her within three dayes next after the sayd marriage Item I give and bequeth unto Margarett my wyfe All my Hay and Corne as well groen as growinge at the tyme of my decease. Item I leave the use and occupation of all my husbandree ware unto my wyfe dureinge her lyfe And after her decease I give and bequeth all the sade husbandry ware unto my grandchild Roger Cheswis. Item I give and bequeth unto my Sonninlawe John Cheswis tenn pounds of Currant monie. All the reste and residue of my goodes moveable and unmoveable my debtes and legasies beinge payde and my funerall expences discharged I give and bequeth unto Margarett Hockenhull my wyfe.

Executors: the testator's wife, Margarett Hockenhull, his son-in-law, John Cheswis, and his daughter, Elizabeth Oteley.

H. & S.

Witnesses: William Prince minister, John Greenowlers.

Inventory: Roger Hockenhull of Broomhall, gent.

Taken: 13 January 1613/14

Of: goods and Cattels.

Prisers: Robart Whitney, Thomas Starkey, Thomas Swaine, John Broomhall, Henrye Rutter and William Brees.

	£	s	d
One yocke of oxen	7	0	0
Tenne kyne and Three Heafers	21	13	4
Five Twynter beasts	8	10	0
Two Calves		20	0
Two mares	6	0	0
Sheepe	3	0	0
Three shotes		10	0
Poultry		4	0
All Corne	6	13	4
Hay		40	0
Brasse and Pewter	5	0	0
Beddinge Bedsteds and nappery	10	0	0
In Plate	6	0	0
Boords formes Cheares stooles & Cushions		40	0

Coffers and Chests		13	4
Treene ware and Cowpery ware		20	0
Beefe and Bacon		20	0
Butter and Cheese		20	0
yarne wooll hempe and flaxe		13	4
One Corslet furnished & a Plate Coatt	5	0	0
His apparrell	5	0	0
Cartes plowes harrowe yockes and all other Implements of Husbandry		13	4
All Iron ware and Tooles		13	4
Bookes		10	0
Fire fuell		6	8
In money & goulde at the tyme of his desceased	34	0	0
In debtes oweinge by specialtyes or there abouts	82	0	0
In debte oweinge by Mres Elizabeth Otley without specialty	4	0	0
One swarme of Bees		2	0
Painted clothes sives baskets sarches and Hoopes		3	4
[Sum	197	283	36]

Endorsement: Probated 8 July 1614; administration to Margaret his relict and John Cheswis two executors named in the will; Elizabeth Oteley, the other executor named in the will fully renouncing the same burden.

45. ROBERT TENCHE OF WRENBURY FRITH, YEOMAN

S.Pr. 23 August 1615
W.T. 13 June 1615
Buried: 8 July 1615

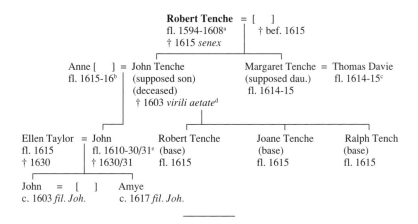

Will, sick.

First, I commend my soule into the hands of almightie god hoping onelie by the bloodsheeding of Jesus Christ my alone Savior to have pardon and remission of all my sinnes And *my bodie I committ to the earth to be buried in the parishe Church of Wrenbury* Item I doe geve and bequeath unto Thomas Stoke sonne of John Stoke the elder 40s. Item I doe geve and bequeath unto John Stoke the yonger 40s. Item I doe geve and bequeath unto Randle Stoke 40s. Item I doe geve and

---

ᵃ Made inventory for Humphrey Bickerton, May 1594 (will no. 12); owed debt to Henry Vernon 1607/08 (will no. 25).
ᵇ This is presumably the Anne Tench, widow, who occupied one of the tenements in Wrenbury Park belonging to Thomas Minshull of Erdswick (see R. Stewart Brown, *Cheshire Inquisitions Post Mortem*, ii. 207).
ᶜ William Fergusson Irvine, *Chester Licences*, i. 61: granted 11 June 1614 to Margaret Tenche of Wrenbury and Robert Davis of Marbury at Marbury. The substitution of names — Robert for Thomas – undoubtedly resulted from a confusion of Margaret's father with her prospective husband.
ᵈ See inventory of John Tenche, pr. 1608 (no. 26).
ᵉ John Tench, Thomas Tench and John Church owed James Barnett a debt of 11s. in 1610; see will of latter, pr. 1610 (will no. 29). The identity of the John Tench who made the inventory for Richard Cheswis in 1632/33 (will no. 93) must be established if this John died in 1630/31.

bequeath unto Sara Stoke £3 Item I doe geve and bequeath unto Robart Tenche bastard sonne of Johne Tenche deceased the supposed sonne of me the said Robart £3 Item I doe geve and bequeath unto Raphe Tenche bastard sonne of the said John Tench deceased £3 Item I doe geve and bequeath unto Joane Tenche bastard daughter of the said John Tenche 40s. Item I doe bequeath and geve towards the repairinge of the horse pavemente in Baddiley Lane 13s. 4d. Item I doe geve and bequeath unto Alice Graie 3s. 4d. Item I doe geve and bequeath unto Thomas Graie my fustian dublet Item I doe geve and bequeath unto John Tenche of Nantwich gent. and Richard Davenport of Blackhurst gent. whome I meane hereby And name my executors of this my Will 40s., that is to saie unto either of them 20s. toward their paines to be taken in the execucōn of this my Will Item I doe geve and bequeathe unto John Tenche my granndchilde sonne of the said John deceased all my goods and implements belonging to husbandrie That is to saie Carts plowes yokes Chaines harrowes and other husbandrie tooles and implements together with broches golborts pothookes linkes and all Iron Ware in and aboute my house Item I doe bequeath and geve unto my said grandchilde John Tenche my greateste brasse panne and sixe silver spoones, the table bord in the house with the forme thereunto one presse one Cupbord my two biggest Chests and one gardiner to put corne in standing in the lower loft All which goods as well houshold goods as husbandrie goods and implements my will and mind is that Anne Tench my daughter in lawe late wife of the said John Tenche deceased and mother to the said John my grandchilde shall have the use and occupacōn of them untill he the said John shall accomplish and be of the full age of 20 one yeres, she the said Anne then leaving and yelding up the same goods and implements to her said sonne in as good reparacōns as they are now at the time of my decease Item I doe geve and bequeath unto the said John Tenche my grandchild all my part of Corne Which I now have growing upon John Wicksteads ground in Wrenbury Item I doe geve and bequeath unto Anne Tenche my daughter in lawe late Wife of my said supposed sonne John Tenche deceased three swine, all the poultrie that is about my house all my corne and mault all my fleshemeate and whitmeate all my wooll my great brasse pott together with all my corne on the ground growing upon my tenement and also all the her and her grasse which I shall have growing at the time of my decease All the rest and residue of my goods and Cattells aswell quicke as dead not before geven nor bequeathed (as well the three kyne, which I lent unto Thomas Davie as other goods Cattells and debtts my bodie being first honestlie brought home of the whole and my legacies and funerall expences being first paid satesfied and discharged) my mind is that they shalbe devided and parted into two equall parts, The one equall part Whereof I geve and bequeath unto the said Anne Tenche my daughter in lawe and to John Tenche her said sonne to be equallie devided betweene them And the other equall part thereof I doe geve and bequeath to Margaret Davie wife of the said Thomas Davie my suppossed daughter.

Executors: John Tenche of Nantwich and Richard Davenport of Blackhurst, aforesaid.

Overseers: William Bebington of the Hall of Chorley and William Tenche of Wilkesley.

H. & S.
Signed [dci] Roberti Tenche
Testator

Wittnesses: Thomas Palin, Gilbert Wollam, William Whicksteed, William Whicksteed Junior.

Inventory: Robart Tench of Wrenbury Frith, yeoman.

Taken: 11 July 1615

Of: goods & Cattells.

Prisers: William Wilson, George Edgeley, Thomas Palin and Valentine Woolriche.

	£	s	d
Three oxen	10	10	0
one oxen ressed for a heriott	4	10	0
two heffers	4	13	4
two Bullockes	3	6	8
foure yereling caulfes	5	10	0
five wayning caulfes	3	0	0
one Mare	3	0	0
seventeene kine	46	0	0
six sheepe		26	8
three swine		33	4
Bees		16	0
poultrie		2	0
his wering aparell		26	8
beding blanckets Coverletts Caddowes boulsters & pillowes	3	6	8
Naparie		50	0
fire fuell		6	8
Cart timber & plowe timber		6	8
one haire clothe		8	0
bords swine troughes & whele borowe		8	0
bedstocks	13	4	0
sacks baggs & sives hope & peake		5	0
Chese bords all shelfes cheres stooles & one chest		6	8
treene ware		10	0
Corne growing at Sound		20	0
brass & pewter		30	0
one spining wheele carts lyin & lanterne one brake & a chese press		5	0
corne growing upon the tenement	12	0	0

hay growing upon the tenement		5	0
corne & maulte in the house butter chese bacon & wooll	7	10	0
hay at Sound		30	0
one pott		17	0
Cartes plowes harowes yokes chaines billes axes mattockes & all other Implements Belonging to husbandrye	4	0	0
one press		13	4
one pann a mastin discharging pan		35	0
two Chests & one long table with the frame one whiche & one forme		26	8
six silver spoones		30	0
broches pot rackes land Irnes tongues fire forke bellowes & all other such houshould Irne ware		6	8
one Swine		2	4
corne growing at Wrenbury		33	4
a sadle & bridle		3	0
in debts		40	0
rent owing from William Spencer	3	6	8
Whitton crest		16	0
a debt which Thomas Breese owes	22	0	0
John Axson	12	13	4
William Twiss	11	0	0
John Axson	11	0	0
the executors of John Tench decessed		40	0
Oliver Braye		40	0
[Sum	176	681	100]

Alsoe for Wildriges grounde wee refer our selves to the note, wee Can make nothinge of it.

[Editor's note: on a separate sheet the following was written, two items of which may be a repeat of the last two entries in the Inventory; if not, they are to be added to the total value of Robert Tench's estate.]

Debts owing to the testator without specialtie:

	£	s	d
The executors of John Tenche deceased		40	0
Oliver Braye		40	0
Raphe Twise of Chorley		10	0
[Sum	176	771	100]

Endorsement: Probated 23 August 1615; administration to the executors named in the will.

46. JOHN WILKINSON OF WRENBURY, HUSBANDMAN

I.Pr. 29 September 1615
W.T. 1615
Buried: 29 August 1615

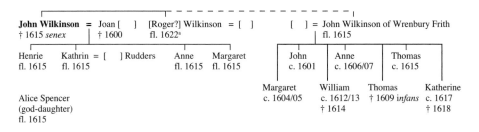

Will, sick.

First, I Commende my soule into the hands of almightye god hopinge only by the blood Sheedinge of Jesus Christe my alone Savior to have free pardon and remission of all my sinns and *my body I Comitte to the earthe to bee buried in the Church yard of Wrenbury* in sure and certaine hope of the Joyfull resurreccōn Item I give and bequeath to Henrie Wilkinson my brothers sonne 2s. Item I give and bequeath unto Kathrin Rudders my brothers daughter 2s. I give and bequeath unto Anne Wilkinson my brothers daughter 2s. Item I give and bequeath unto Margaret Wilkinson my brothers daughter 2s. Item I give and bequeath unto the Children of John Wilkinson of Wrenbury Frith the somme of 15s. which Thomas Massie doth oe unto me to bee equally devided amongste them. Item I give and bequeath unto Richard Seyvil my servante 6s. 8d. Item I give and bequeath to Alice Spencer my goddaughter 12d. Item I give and bequeath unto Joane Orten alias Wyen 2s. All the reste of my goods moveable and unmoveable my legasies funerall expences and my bodie beinge honestlie brought home and the execution of my will and of Chargs payd I give and bequeath unto theabovesaid John Wilkinson of Wrenbury Frith

Executors: William Barnett and Humfrey Barnett of Wrenbury.

H. & S.
John Wilkinson his marke

Debts owing to the Testator:

	£	s	d
Thomas Massie . . . as is abovesaid		15	0

---

[a] Roger Wilkinson owed 11s. to James Brooke, 1622 (see will no. 66).

Witnesses: Thomas Gray, Edward Bathowe and Henrie Griffin.

Inventory: John Wilkinson of Wrenbury, husbandman.

Taken: 31 August 1615

Of: goodes and Cattell.

Prisers: William Wilson, Thomas Hurleston, John Fisher and George Cleaton.

	£	s	d
his apparell		3	4
Two little kyne	3	6	8
Two hennes			13
Beddinge and nappery		10	0
Brasse & Pewter and all Iron ware		20	0
Treene ware Cowpery ware & one Cupeboord		10	0
Boords formes shelves cheares stooles Coffers & bedstocks		20	0
Corne		13	4
Hay and mucke		6	8
one spynninge wheele sives riddle and ladder & other finale Implements		2	0
Paynted Clothes and fire fuell		2	0
A debte oweing to the Testator by Thomas Massie as may appeare by his wil		15	0
[Sum	3	107	37]

Endorsement: Probated 29 September 1615; administration to the executors named in the will.

47. THOMAS FAULKNER OF CHORLEY, YEOMAN

S.Pr. 9 November 1615
W.T. 14 March 1614/15

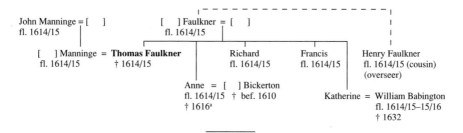

ᵃ See will of Anne Bickerton, pr. 1616 (will no. 49).

Will, sick.

I comend my soule to my true and faithfull Savior Christ Jesus whoe hath redemed me with his most presious bloud and my body to the earth from whence it came. Item I give to my honest true frend Mr Roberte Weyver my birdinge peece Item I give to my brother Richard my best stuffe sute my riding Coate my sword & dager with silver bucle a paire of bootes and spures and a paire of wuulsted stockings. Item I give to my Cosen Henry Faulkner my saddle and all the furniture to it and a paire of bootes & spuirres. Item I give to William Good one cut Fustian doublet a paire of Cloth breches a paire of Cloth stockings and a paire of shooes and to his wife 12d. in money. Item I give to my sistere Francis 12d. Item I give to my [servant] John Whininge my graven ringge. Item I give to my sister Anne Bickerton my three foule gould ringe. Item I give to my father a payre of new gloves which are in my trunke at Cholmeley. Item I give to Thomas Burroughes my hatcht sword and dager and the rest of my goods these legaxies paid and my funerall discharged I give them all to my wyf whatsoever moveable and unmoveable quick and dead whatsoever.

H. & S.

Debts Owed By Testator:

	£	s	d
to Richard Weaver of Povlle	30	0	0
to William Bebington	20	0	0
to Thomis Pollitt	4	0	0
to Randle Bebington for the cariage of hay	*[blank]*		

Debts Owed to the Testator:

	£	s	d
Stanley Burroughes to be pad at his marriage	1	3	0
John Maninge my father in lawe	1	5	0
my sister Francis	1	10	0
Hughe Roe Jun	1	16	8
Randle Weever	3	10	0
Rauffe Bostocke	7	8	4
James Hutton	1	0	0
Fardinande Wyn		10	0
Francis Rodes	1	0	0
Mr George Davenport of the Chefe	1	3	0
Thomas Parr and [ ]Flite either of them 7s. apeese		14	0
Mr Clarke which was Mr Mynshulls man		5	0
Josua Greatbatch at his marridge or death	2	0	0
James Woodealle	2	0	0
Henry Torner	1	0	0

[Sum   ]

Executors: the testator's wife, and Thomas Burroughes.

Overseers: Randle Wickstead and Henry Falkner.

Inventory: of Thomas Falkner of Chorley, yeoman.

Taken: 27 October 1615

Of: Goods, Cattells & Chattells.

Prisers: Thomas Pollitt, William Bebington, Richard Rogers & Randle Croxton.

	£	s	d
twelve kine	30	0	0
three twinters	4	0	0
Sevon Whynynge Calves	4	0	0
one Mare	3	6	8
one Coulte		30	0
twoe fatt hoggs	2	0	0
foure shoetts		20	0
Corne and hey	11	0	0
one Iron bound wayne one harrowe one payre of ploughe Irons twoe Collers and twoe payre of treyses	3	7	6
brasse and pewter	4	4	0
bedinge nappye ware & three bedsteds	5	3	8
broches goulberts & other iron ware		16	0
trunckes Chests & boxes		21	0
treene ware Coupieware and twoe spninge wheles		29	8
one longe table a little table with formes Cheires sheilves & stooles		30	0
butter Cheise bacon & poultry ware	3	15	4
one birdinge peece a crosse bowe & a stone bowe with furniture Therunto belonginge		30	0
twoe swords and daggers with furniture therunto belonginge		43	4
his wayringe apparell with saddels bridles bootes and spures	5	0	0
bookes		13	4
twoe paire of boules		5	0
Six yards of fussian within lineing and other furnitur for the making of one payre of breches		15	0
Corne on the ground		41	0
Sume totall	138	19	6

Endorsement: Probated 9 November 1615; administration to the executors named in the will.

48. JOHN BICKERTON OF NEWHALL, YEOMAN

S.Pr. 15 June 1616
W.T. 6 March 1616
Buried: 8 May 1616

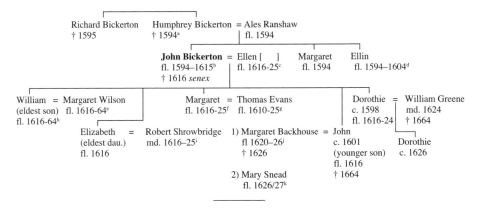

Will, sick.

First I bequeath my soule to almightie god my maker and redeemer and *my bodie to be buried in the parishe church of Wrenbury* afforsaid Item my will is that my eldest sonne William Bickerton shall paie to my yonger sonne John one hundred pounds to be paid yerelie by £10 a yere forth of my lande and if it fortune that the said William Bickerton shall marrie before the said £100 be paid by £10 a yere to the use of the said John Bickerton then the remainder which at his said marriage shalbe unpaid my will is that William Bickerton shall paie at his daie

ᵃ See will of Humphrey Bickerton, pr. 1594 (will no. 12).
ᵇ Noted in will of Humphrey Bickerton 1594 (will no. 12); witness to will of Roger Swann, 1610 (will no. 30); priser for Ellen Fletcher, 1611 (no. 37); John Bickerton appears 1609, 1611, 1615 in CRO Newhall Manor Court Rolls.
ᶜ See CRO Newhall Rentals, 1625.
ᵈ See will no. 12.
ᵉ See will of John Bickerton, pr. 1664/CRO.
ᶠ William Fergusson Irvine, *Chester Licences*, iii. 29: 18 May 1625 to Margaret Bickerton and Thomas Evans, at Wrenbury; bondsman Richard Moore.
ᵍ Received bequest of 40s. from James Barnett, 1610 as Thomas *Evanson* (will no. 29).
ʰ William Fergusson Irvine, *Chester Licences*, ii. 16: 30 September 1616 to William Bickerton of Wrenbury parish and Margaret Wilson of Audlem parish, spinster, at Audlem, Newhall Rentals, 1625; see will of John Bickerton, pr. 1664/CRO.
ⁱ See CRO Newhall Rentals, 1625.
ʲ William Fergusson Irvine, *Chester Licences*, iii. 64: 1226 – John Bickerton and Margaret Backhouse.
ᵏ William Fergusson Irvine, *Chester Licences*, iii. 85: 1626/27 – John Bickerton and Mary Snead; at Acton or Wrenbury.

of marriage the halfe of that, that then shall remaine unpaid: and the other halfe
to paie within one twelve month next after his said marriage Item I geve and
bequeath to Elizabeth Bickerton my eldest daughter fiftie and one pounds thirteene shillinges which I have paid for a lease for the said Elizabeth Item I geve
to the said Elizabeth one brasse panne and my Wil is that she shall have one fether
bed Item I geve and bequeath to my other two daughters Margaret and Dorothie
Bickerton fortie pounds a peece to be paid forth of my bills bonds and specialties
and debts and my will is that they shall have either of them one brasse panne and
either of them one feather bed provided that Ellen Bickerton my wife shall have
the use of them till they be preferred in marriage Item I geve and bequeath to
Ellen my wife and William Bickerton my sonne all my Carts ploughes and all
other Implements of husbandrie to use betwixt them Item I geve the said William
Bickerton my sonne one twinter heiffer Item I geve to my sonne John Bickerton
one Twinter heiffer in lue of his childs part Item I geve ~~the said William Bickerton
my sonne one twinter heffer~~ to Katherin Sivill daughter of John Sivell one heffer
Calfe Item I geve and bequeath all the rest of my goods Chattells and Cattell
moveable and unmoveable the one halfe to my Wife Item my Will is that the other
moitie or halfe of the said goods I geve to my daughters Margaret and Dorothie
Bickerton to be equallie devided betwixt them . . . . Item I geve my said executors 10s. a peece Item my Will is that my wife and my sonne Willim shall
keepe house this yere and my Will is that they shall have ten pounds forth of the
remainder of my debts to paie the first ten pounds to my yonger sonne John
Bickerton and my Will is that if my sonne John Bickerton doe die within the yeres
then the payments after to cease but onelie to paie ten pounds a peece to my two
daughters Margaret and Dorothie Bickerton.

John Bickerton his marke
S.

Executors: George Gray and Richard Hall.

Taken: 15 May 1616

Witnesses: William Prince minister, Robert Tench and Richard Edgley.

Inventory: John Bickertonn of Newhall.

Of: goods Cattall and Chattells.

Prisers: Thomas Edgley, John Backhouse, Richard Edgley and William Flecher
of Newhall in the Countie aforesaid yeoman.

	£	s	d
fyve kine prised to	10	10	0
three kyne Due for hariots prised to	8	0	0
two Incalf heffers and foure stirke Calves prised to	9	0	0
three twinter heffers prised to	4	10	0
one stub ox and a nagge and a coult prised to	5	0	0
two wayninge Calves and two swyne prised to	2	0	0
one Cow at hyer at John Sales prised to	2	6	8

	£	s	d
poultrie prised to		3	4
Beeife and bacon		20	0
six bushell of Barlie		3	0
three strickes of Malt and three measures of Rye and two bushells of oats prised to		35	0
Corne upon the ground prised to	6	0	0
Brase and pewter prised to	6	0	0
Beddinge and Naperie prised to	10	0	0
bedstockes and Chests and ~~nap~~ Coffers prised to		20	0
bords formes and shilves prised to		25	8
Cowprie and trene ware prised to	10	0	0
Cheares stoules and Chusshens prised to		3	4
Broches and all Iron ware in the house prised to		6	8
Carts Chaines yokes ploughes harrowes and all other Implements of husbandrie prised to		3	0
mucke prised to		6	8
timber and fier fuell and a cheese presse prised to		2	0
his wearinge apparrell saddles brydles with sword and other furniture for a horse prised to		20	0
spinninge wheles and hempe and flaxe prised to		2	0
two quarter of wood prised to	3	3	4
Thomas Buckley and Hugh Higginson a debte by bound Doe michellmas prised to	7	17	0
Randell Bruerton and John Cartwright a debt by bound doe at 7th Daie of Aprill 1617 prised to		11	0
John Patricke a debte due by bond prised to		5	0
Thomas Starke and Thomas Orp a debt by bill due the 16th of June 1616 prised to		11	0
John Orpe and John Sheeime a debt prised to	4	13	4
George Capper Raphe Ankers and James Bodall a debt due by bound the 16th of June 1616 prised to		11	0
John Whild of Market Drayton a debte Due prised to	10	10	0
John Sheeine and John Sale a debte due for a mare prised to	37	0	0
Ellis the Butcher a Debte Due prised to		20	0
William Dode a debte due prised to		28	0
Mris Whitney thelder a debte of her husbande prised to		4	6
Readie money in the house	2	0	0
William Hughson a Debt Due the first Daie of Maie 1617 prised to	9	18	0
a Revercion of a lease with William Hughson seven yeares yett Remaininge £6 a yeare prised to		42	0
[Sum	144	325	54]

[Exhibitum fuit Inventorium cum & protestacōne de addend si'.]

The inventory with protestation was exhibited . . .

Endorsement: Probated 15 June 1616; administration to the executors named in the will.

49. ANNE BICKERTON OF BROOMHALL, WIDOW

I. Pr. 19 September 1616
W. T. 22 February 1615/16
Buried: 13 May 1616

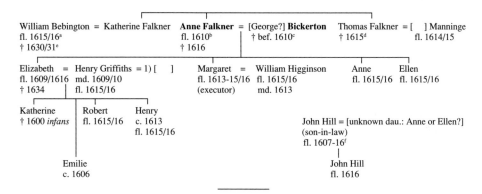

Will, sick.

First I bequethe my soule in to the hands of almightie god reposing my whole trust and Confidence in the merrits of Christ Jesus, and by his Death and bloode shedinge to have remission of all my sines And *my bodie to bee buried in the parish church of Wrenbury* at the discrecōn of myne executors Item I give and bequeath unto my foure daughters Elizabeth, Ellen, Margaret and Anne to eache of them 12d. a peece for and *[struck out]* consideracōn of there Childs parte of

---

ᵃ Made inventory for William Barnett, 1616 (no. 52).
ᵇ Noted 1610 as owing a debt of £3 4s. 0d. to Roger Swann of Dodds Green (Newhall); see will of Roger Swanne, pr. 1610 (will no. 30).
ᶜ See will of Henry Griffiths of Broomhall, pr. 1654/55 (will no. 140), note 'b', where we argue the case for George Bickerton, who was buried at Wrenbury in 1596.
ᵈ See will of Thomas Faulkner of Chorley, yeoman, pr. 1615 (will no. 47).
ᵉ See will of William Babington of Chorley, gent., pr. 1631? (will no. 85).
ᶠ John Bostock owed John Hill £4 8s. in 1607 (see will of John Bostock/CRO). John Hill is undoubtedly related to the family of Rowland Hill that flourished at Coole Lane and appears in CRO Newhall Manor Court Rolls from 1599 to 1623.

my goods. Item I give unto my grandchild Robert Griffies 22s. of money beinge in the hands of Edward Hamnett of Aston Alsoe I give unto the same Robert a Weetinge Combe Item I give unto my grandchild John Hill 22s. which is in the hands of the said Edward Hamnett Item I give unto my grandchild Henrie Griffies myne Annuitie of 8s. which I receave yearlie of the kings magistrats to bee imployed for the benifite of the said Henrie duringe his natural lief and after the decease of the said Henrie then to the right heires Item I give and bequeath unto the parishes of Wrenbury and Audlem the some of £10 of Lawfull money to either of the said parishes £5 to bee putt out to interest at the end of halff a yeare next after my decease and the use and proffits a risinge thereof to bee imployed for and towards the relief of the pore in the said paryshes and my will is that William Salmon of Coole Lane shall have the orderinge and governinge of the said £5 belonginge to the parishe of Audlem and bestowinge of the interest that shall arrise thereof upon the poore of the said parishe duringe his naturall lief and after his decease then it to remaine to bee disposed by the church wardens of the said Parrishe to the poore as before said for ever Item my will is that my brother in lawe William Bebington shall have the orderinge and governinge of the other £5 and the use thereof to bee imployed by him unto the poore of the parish of Wrenbury duringe his naturall lief and after his decease then to the ordering of the Church wardens of the parishe of Wrenbury for the tyme beinge and the exsise thereof to bee by them distributed upon the poore of the said parishe for ever Item I give unto everie one of my good Children 6d. a peece Item I give unto unto Anne Shingleton a gowne and a peticoate and a measure of Corne at the discrecōn of Moade my daughter all the rest and residue of my goods and Cattalls moveable and unmoveable my debts and legacies beinge paid and my funerall expenses discharged I give and bequeath unto my daughter Moade Bickerton.

Executrix: Moade Bickerton.

H. & S.

Witnesses: William Prince minister, Thomas Taylor, Henrie Griffith, William Higginson.

Debts owing the Testator:

	£	s	d
my sonne in Lawe John Hill	3	6	8
Thomas Needham esquire		40	0
[Sum	3	46	8]

Inventory: Anne Bickerton of Broomhall, widow.

Taken: 16 May 1616

Of: goods and Cattalls.

Prisers: William Bebington, Thomas Taylor, William Higginson and William Brees.

	£	s	d
in plate		30	0
4 kyne price	10	0	0
two weaninge Calves		20	0
Rye growinge one the ground		27	0
oats growinge one the ground		7	0
Barlie and French wheate		16	0
7 sheepe and 4 lambes		45	0
one swyne		5	0
4 yonge beasts	5	0	0
Carts and plowes and harrowe		15	0
hempe and flaxe		2	0
all the Iron ware		13	4
in brasse		46	8
in pewter		16	0
in treene ware		10	0
a table forme wenscott and bench		15	0
three Cheares stooles and a little table		4	0
bedsteeds		20	0
4 Coffers spinninge wheeles Cards and hettchells		4	0
one Roape crease and collers		2	0
all the beddinge	4	0	0
all the napperie ware	2	0	0
boards sheelves and a safe		3	0
Cheses Corne in the house and baken		30	0
painted clothes Cheese presse and musterd mill		2	6
Cupes glasses Baskets measures and syves		2	0
pultrie		2	0
her wearinge Clothes		20	0
lent to Mr Thomas Needhame esquire	2	0	0
in John Hyll his hands	3	6	8
[Sum	26	362	26]

Endorsement: Probated 19 September 1616; administration to the executors named in the will.

50. GEORGE KEMP OF SMEATONWOOD, YEOMAN

I. Pr. [n.d.], after 2 October 1616
W.T. 14 July 1614
Buried: 22 September 1616

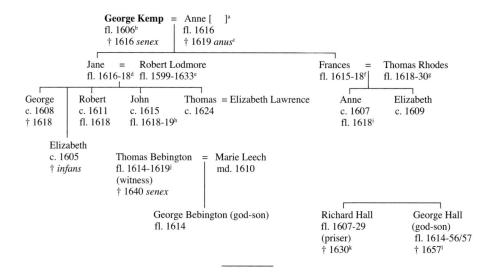

---

^a Since Halls were involved with both George Kemp and his wife, Anne, and since George
    Hall was George Kemp's god-son, Anne Kemp was possibly a Hall. On the other hand, it
    may simply be that they were close neighbours at Smeatonwood, and that this – as in the
    case of the Bickertons – led to George Kempe serving as god-father at George Hall's bap-
    tism. George Bebington, the other god-son noted in George Kemp's will, was probably the
    son of Thomas Bebington, one of the witnesses in 1614; Thomas Bebington, in turn, is referred
    to as 'my good neighbour' by Anne Kempe in 1618 (will no. 57), who appointed him one
    of her executors.
^b George Kempe received £4 in the will of John Hall, 1605 (will no. 22).
^c See will of Anne Kempe of Smeatonwood, pr. 1619 (will no. 57).
^d See will of Anne Kempe.
^e Robert Lodmore owed £12 2s. with two others to James Brooke in 1622 (will no. 66).
^f Frances Rhodes owed Thomas Faulkner £1 in 1615; see Faulkner's will, pr. 1615 (will no.
    47); see will of Anne Kempe, pr. 1619 (will no. 57).
^g Thomas Roades leased a parcel of land to Richard Hall; see inventory of Richard Hall, 1630
    (no. 83).
^h The will of Anne Kempe , pr. 1619 (will no. 57) refers to the *children* of her daughter Jane,
    without names or the number: presumably this includes at least two of the three shown here
    as born before 1619.
ⁱ See will of Anne Kempe.
^j Witness for George Kemp's will, 1614; co-executor of Anne Kemp's will, pr. 1619.
^k See inventory of Richard Hall of Smeatonwood, 1630 (no. 83).
^l See will of George Hall of Aston, pr. 1657 (will no. 142).

Will, sick.

First I bequeath my soule into the handes of almyghty god trusting by the death and bloodsheedinge of Jesus Chrust my alone saviour to have free pardon and remission of all my sinnes: And *my bodye I Comitt to the earth to be buried in the churchyard of Wrenbury* in sure and Certaine hope of a joyfull resurrection. Item I give and bequeath to the poore of the parishe of Wrenbury 6s. 8d. to be disposed to them at the oversight of the churchwardens minister & parishe Clarke of the said parishe. Item I give & bequeath to the Ryngers which shall Rynge at my buriall 3s. 4d. Item I give and bequeath unto Jane Lodmore my daughter 12d. in full satisfaction of all her Childes parte of my goodes to be paide out of my goods. Item I give and bequeath unto Frances my daughter 12d. in full satisfaction of all her childes parte to be paid her out of my goodes. Item I give and bequeath unto George Bebinton my god son 12d. I give and bequeath unto George Hall my god son 12d All the rest of my goodes, Cattels, Chattels & debtes of what sort or qualitye soever they bee, moveable and unmoveable (my debtes Legasies and funerall expences being first discharged and paid) I give and bequeath unto Anne Kempe my wife.

Executor: the testator's wife, Anne Kempe.

H. & S.

Witnesses: Thomas Graie 1614, Thomas Bebinton.

Inventory: George Kemp of Smeatonwood, yeoman.

Taken: 2 October 1616

Of: goodes Cattels and Chattels.

Prisers: Thomas Bebinton, Richard Halle and Thomas Swanne.

	£	s	d
One Cowe and one farrowe heaffer	4	13	4
Another Cowe which went for a heriott		53	4
one three yere old heaffer & two twynters	4	0	0
his apperrell		20	0
Corne and hay in the barne		40	0
Beddinge and lynnens		50	0
Brasse and Pewter		30	0
Iron ware and Implements of husbandtrey		3	4
Bordes formes stooles bedstocks Coffers and all other treene ware		30	0
two swyne and a pigge		10	0
Poultree ware		2	0
Three silver spoones		10	0
mucke or worthinge		4	0
[Sum	8	265	12]

Endorsement: [NOTE: Wrapper is badly stained and the Office comments are barely visible. No other date than the year, written by a later hand]. Administration to Anne Kemp widow of the deceased, and the executrix named in the will.

51. MARY WHITNEY OF COOLE, WIDOW[a]

S.Pr. 25 October 1616
Administration granted 13 and 14 September 1616
Buried: 29 August 1616

Thomas Rutter of Kingesley, gent.   = Margery, dau. of John Spurstowe of Spurstowe, esq.
fl. 1574/75
† 9 Nov, 22 Eliz[b]

Mary Rutter   =   Robert **Whitney**, gent.
fl. 1574/75   fl. 1574/75-1606[c]
† Sept. 1616   † Jan 1615/16[d]

Hugh Whitney = Elizabeth Egerton   Elizabeth = Hugh Massie
md. 1599   fl. 1616-22[e]   md. 1616/17 fl. 1616/17
† 1611 *virili aetate*   † 1627   † 1620

Hugh Whitney   7 other Chh.
c. 1600/01
fl. 1616-1624/25[f]

Inventory: Mary Whitney late wife of Robert Whitney of Coole, gent.
Taken: 2 September 1616

Of: goodes cattells, and chattels.

Prisers: John Cheswis gent., Edward Bressie gent., Thomas Dikes and John Pichford.

	£	s	d
tew oxen the price	9	0	0
sixe kyne	15	0	0

---

[a] The two sets of documents relating to Mary Whitney are filled separately at the CRO: The first, containing the inventory and the letter of administration is in WS 1616 (Mary Whitney of Wrenbury); the second, containing the accounting given by Humphrey Page, is in WS 1617 (Mary Whitney of Coole, Wrenbury, gent.)

[b] Ormerod, *History of Cheshire*, ii. 94.

[c] Robert Whitney married Mary Rutter on 12 February 1574/75 according to his IPM; jury-man for the IPM for Geoffrey Minshull taken at Sandbach, 4 September 1604 (see R. Stewart Brown, *Cheshire Inquisitions Post Mortem*, ii. 203); also 16 June 1606 at Nantwich for Jasper Rutter (see *Cheshire Inquisitions Post Mortem*, iii. 31). Ormerod, *History of Cheshire*, ii. 94 has Mary Rutter's husband as *Thomas* Whitney of Coole Lane alias *Cowley*!

[d] See IPM taken for Robert Whitney 2 April 1616 (*Cheshire Inquisitions Post Mortem*, iii. 169–71); CRO Newhall Rentals, 1625.

[e] Owed debt of £5 to William Heighfield in 1618; see will, pr. 1620 (will no. 62). Received bequest from James Brooke, 1622 (will no. 66).

[f] Hugh Whitney of Coole was a juryman in the IPM for John Wicksted, esq., taken at Nantwich 18 January 1624/25 (see *Cheshire Inquisitions Post Mortem*, iii. 171).

sixe young bullocks	15	0	0
a young sterke & tow calves	2	13	4
an olde nagge	2	6	8
a younge coulte	1	6	8
sixe & fortie thrave of rie		9	4
for barley in the house & fielde		4	0
20 loads of haye		8	0
for oates uppon the grounde		3	0
Cartes, wheeles, and all husbandrie ware	2	0	0
3 swyne	2	13	4
all the brasse	3	0	0
all the iron ware	1	3	4
all the coperie and treane ware	1	6	8
White meate		5	0
towe and yarne		13	4
the bedd over the parlor	1	13	4
in the same chamber, a woole bedd & bolster		13	4
all the beddinge over the halle	4	0	0
in the same chamber, the chest, presse & an bedsteede	1	6	4
the beddinge over the kitchine	3	6	8
the cheste & table in the same chamber	6	3	4
all her wearing apparell	5	0	0
a bedd over the Intrey & other implements in the same roome	1	6	8
the beddinge in the parlor	2	0	0
the naperie in the cheste standinge there	3	0	0
sixe silver spoones	2	0	0
on cheste, tow boxes, and a table in the parlor		10	0
in the hall chaires, stooles, quishions & little tables		15	0
for pewter and other fine naperie	2	0	0
Count is	113	2	0
[*recte*	91	7	6]
Mr Wright debts owing For wood	1	10	0
19 geese, hennes, turkies, & such like		17	8
baskets & sackes for corne			8
a bedsteede that men did lye in			1
stone troughes			5
timber in the barne			2
hempe and flaxe			7
Some is	116	13	0
[*recte*	92	17	1]

Administration:

13 September 1616

Upon the receipt of a commission out of his Majesty's Court of Exchequer of Chester to us and others dyrected for the hearinge and deteremyninge of dyvers Contencōns and Controversies nowe dependinge between Hughe Massye gent and Elizabeth his wife on the one parte And Elizabeth Whytney wydow late wyfe of Hughe Whitney gent deceased on the behalfe of her twooe yonger Children upon the other parte. We have mett accordinge to the tenor of the Commission And by the consent of the parties on boeth syds wee doe order that Hughe Massye above shall said take lettres of Administracōn of the goods of Marye late wyfe of Robt Whyney gent. deceased without the interrupcōn or Contradictōn of the above named Elizabeth Whytney or any other by her procurement.

And it is further ordered that if there shalbe any surplusage debts and legacyes discharged of the goods and Chattels of the ~~said~~ said Marye Whytney that the same shall remeyne and be due to the twooe yonger doughters of the said Elizabeth Whytney.

And it is lastly ordred that the appell of the said Mary Whytney shalbe disposed of by the said Hughe Massye accordinge to the true meaninge of her the foresaid Marye Whytney And adednotion to be made out of the inventorye for the said apparell.

The Commissoners names whoe made this agreement: Richard Lee, George Cotton, Edward Bressye and John Cartwright[a].

Righte Worshipfull, our dueties most humblie remembered &c. For as much as it hath pleased god to take to his mercie Marie Whytney of Coole widdw, late wyfe of Roberte Whitney late of Coole affore said gent deceased, dyed intested, And that Elizabeth Massie Wyffe of Hugh Massie of Denfield gent in the County of Chester, Beinge the onelie and naturall daughter of the said Marie Whitney and not anie other Shalbe livinge Theis are therefore humblie to crave yor Worshipps favour, That for as much has the said decedent dyinge intested, and not anie to whom the administration of the goods and chattels doth belonge But onlie to the said Elizabeth Massie wyffe of Hughe beforsaid for as much as the said Hughe Massie, beinge a gent. full of infirmities (As at is Well known) And therefore not able to travell And that Elizabeth Massie his wyffe beinge a gent. Altogeather unexperiece in those matters. Therfore we humlie crave yor worships favoure that it may please you to grante yor lettres of Administracōn of the goods and chat-telles of the said decedente, to his trusted and welbeloved frende Humfrey Page

---

[a]   This declaration is found on a separate sheet of paper with the note on wrapper: 14 Sept. To the Right Worshipfull Doctor Yale, Chancellor of Chester, at Chester. Two seals (now missing) were attached.

of Eardssall Gent whom we doe by theis presents ordeyne constitute and make our true and lawfull Atturney & doe preforence fulfill and accomplish her and averie thinge and things what soever, which shall or maie [and should] concerne the goods and Chattels of the said decedente: Thus craving pardon for our bouldnes, prayinge to god for yor worshipps happie fortune we humblie take or leave Denfeilds this 14the of September 1616.

Yor worshippes to Commande
Hugh Massie (signature)
Elizabeth Massie (+ her mark)

Witnesses: Hugh Gandy, John Cheaddocke.

Endorsement: Inventory was presented to Humphrey Page of Yerdshawe, gent.; administration to Hugh Massie, gent., and to Elizabeth, his wife, natural daughter and heir of the said deceased ; the inventory with the addendum was exhibited 25 October 1616.

Accounting: Accompting of Humphrey Page of Yerdshaw, gent., in the County of Chester, administrator of all and singular goods rights credits and c[h]attels of Mary Whitney, widow, while she lived of Coole in the parish or chapelry of Wrenbury, diocese of Chester, deceased, concerning his administration of the rights credits and c[h]attels of the said deceased given in the presence of the venerable David Yale, doctor of laws, deacon of Chester and episcopal vicar in matters general and spiritual in the Episcopal Consistory Court of Chester, the 25th day of November AD 1617.

First the accomptant acknowledges that the named and specified goods rights credits and c[h]attels of the aforesaid deceased found in the annexed Inventory are true and that he is satisfied with the value and price assigned to them of £116 13s. 0d. His expenses have been as followeth:

	£	s	d
This accomptant saith that he hath satisfied and paied unto			
Jane Massy which she had formerly lent to paye and defraye			
the Charges of the funeralls of one Robert Whitney deceased			
whereof he Craveth allowing the some of	27	0	0
paid by this accomptant to Hugh Massye for the one halfe of			
Mr Robert Whitney his woods which amounted to	139	13	4
the one half whereof is	69	16	8
and yet contented to take by agreement the some of	50	0	0
paid for the funeralls and other Charges for the foresaid			
Mistreis Mary Whitney deceased as by a note of particulers			
appeareth the some of	18	7	8

		£	s	d
paid for the one halfe amount Comission out of the [?]chey the some of			15	0
paid for lettres of adiuracōn of the goods of the said deceadant & other Charges about the same			2	8
paid John Bowden in full for his wages the some of			7	6
paid Margery Davies in full for her wages the some of			5	0
to John Hampton in full for his sonnes wages the some of			5	0
paid to widow Rutter which was owing to her			6	6
for a Coppie of Recognizature and charges of his accomptant att Chester the some of			4	10
for a tyeth Calfe to the vicar of Acton the some of			10	0
paid to Jane Massie which shee lend out in the sicknes of Mris Whitney aforesaid deceased the some of		13	0	0
paid Mr Newall for puttinge in the Answeres of Mr Hugh Massie & his accomptant ~~the some of~~ at the sathe *[i.e. sayeth]* of Margery Orten and spent at Chester			30	0
paid Mr Grosenor for husbandry ware being formerly due by Mr Whitney			22	0
paid Mr Barker a dyer at Nantwich the summe of			5	0
paid widowe Whitney in full satysfaccōn of a bill the sume of			40	0
paid Hughe Hamnet for weavinge of linnen cloth			5	0
to the vicar of Acton for a yeres rent for hempe the sume of			20	0
paid a debt due to Edward Massie being the summe of			13	0
paid to Ellen Wolley in full satisfaccōn of her Wages			7	0
paid to Mr Tomas Brooke of Leighton a debt due to him by bond the sume of			13	6
paid to Mr John Slade in full satisffaccōn of an obligacōn for Mr Gascoyne the sume of		3	0	0
paid and spent by this accomptant in travellinge to Chester about the busines of the forsaid decedent			3	4
paid to Ellen Gandie in full satisfaccōn of her wages the sume of			10	0
this accomptant desireth of the husbandriee ware belonging to the forsaid decedent which never came unto this accomptants hands but was by agreement delivered to senior Hugh Whitney which husbandrie ware according to the Inventorie afforsaid extendeth to the sume of			40	0
his accomptant doth not charge himselfe with the wearing apparell of the forsaid Marie Whitney deceased which came not to his accomptants hands but was otherwise disposed by Commissioners being the sume of		5	0	0
his accomptant doth not charge himselfe with the linnen and pewter of the said decedent because the same came not to his accomptants hands but was by agreement delivered to Jane Massie granndchilde of the decedent extending to the sume of			40	0

paid a debt due unto the executors of Mr William Lecester late alderman of Chester deceased the sume of	26	7
paid for drawinge of these accompts	3	4
for proctors fees	2	0
For exhibitinge of the same		4
for lettres of Acquittaince or quietus est	14	0
and for the copie of the accompts	2	0
in toto	21	8
disbursed and spent by this accomptant in travellinge to Chester to procure the said lettres of acquittance the sume of	5	0
Summa Inventorii	116	13	0
Summa expenditures et allocacōns	135	7	3
Expensis et allocacōns	18	14	4

Endorsement on Computus: Accounting of Humphrey Page of Yerdshaw administrator of the goods of Mary Whitney widow while she lived of the chapelry of Wrenbury deceased exhibited &c. 21 November 1617.

EDITOR'S NOTE: Because of its bearing on our understanding of the testamentary instruments associated with Mary Whitney of Coole, we have here included the Inquisition Post Mortem of her husband, Robert Whitney, as well.[a]

Inquisition taken at Middlewich, 2 April, 14 James I [1616] before Henry Mainwayring esq., the King's escheator, by virtue of the King's writ to enquire after the death of Robert Whitney gent., by the oath of Edward Cotton, esq., Thomas Baskerville of Withington, Thomas Brooke of Leighton, Humphrey Page of Yerdshawe, John Cheswis of Mickley, John Aston of Aston, Ralph Bostock of Moulton, Thomas Deane of Churchulme, Thomas Woodcocke of the same, James Bradshawe of Allstocke, William Venables of Sproston, Phillip Downes of Tofte, Edmund Howe of Ollerton, John Ravenscroft of Ocleston, Hugh Venables of Wimbaldsley, William Austen of Stanthorne & Oliver Vernon of Middlewich, gentlemen.

They say that the said Robert Whitney was seised in fee of a messuage, 60 a. of land, 4 a. of meadow, 20 a. of pasture, 16 a. of wood in Coole & Aston by Bromhall & so being seised on 12 February, 17 Eliz. [1574–75] on his marriage with Mary, daughter of Thomas Rutter of Kingesley, he enfeoffed Ralph Bryne, Richard Hocknell, Thomas Grymsdich & Thomas Rutter, the younger, son of said Thomas, gentleman, of the said premises, to the use, as to the New Lands, the Wardes

[a] See R. Stewart Brown, *Cheshire Inquisitions Post Mortem*, iii. 169–71.

Fields, the Great Mosse, the Calvers Croft & the Gardiners Field, being about 34 a., of the said Mary for life & as to the moiety of the said messuage, barns &c., also to her, with remainder to said Robert & his issue by said Mary, in default to his issue, in default to his right heirs; the residue to said Robert, his issue by said Mary, &c.

They had issue, Hugh Whitney, now deceased.

On a marriage to be had between the said Hugh Whitney & Elizabeth Egerton, the said Robert & Hugh enfeoffed Edward Cotton, Richard Clutton, Jasper Rutter & John Moulson of the premises, to the use, as concerned the New Lownes, containing 4 a., of Hugh Massye, & as concerned a pasture in Coole called the Great Mosse, of 20 a. & 2 pastures called the Wardes Fields, of 7 a., to the use of the said Hugh Whitney & Elizabeth Egerton, as dower of said Elizabeth, with contingent remanders to said Hugh & his male issue by Elizabeth, to him in tail male, to the issue of Hugh & Elizabeth, to the issue of Hugh, to Elizabeth, daughter of said Robert Whitney, wife of the said Hugh Massye & their issue; & as to Dovehouse Fields, Beggars Fields, Hurdemans Feild, Sheppcroft & the Lower End of the Lane, about 30 a., to the use of the said Robert Whitney, for life, with contingent remainders to the said Elizabeth Egerton during the life of the said Mary, wife of Robert & after Mary's death, to the use of the said Hugh Whitney & his male issue by Elizabeth Egerton, the male issue of Hugh, his issue, to the use of Elizabeth, wife of the said Hugh Massye & their issue, the right heirs of Robert Whitney for ever; & as to the kitchen & the loft or chamber over the same, & the milk house, to the use of the said Elizabeth Egerton, for life, & as to the Little Weever Meadow, in Coole, being $1/_2$ a., to the use of the said Elizabeth Egerton, for life, with remainder to said Hugh Whitney.

The said Hugh Whitney married Elizabeth Egerton & had issue Hugh Whitney the younger, now surviving & afterwards Hugh the elder died & Elizabeth, his wife, survived & still survives & dwells at Coole.

The said Robert Whitney died at Coole, 24 January last past & Mary his wife survives & dwells at Coole & Hugh Whitney the younger, son & heir of Hugh senior, son & heir apparent of Robert Whitney, is next of kin & heir of said Robert & is now aged 15 years, 1 month, 18 days.

The said premises are held of the King, as Earl of Chester, by 20th part of a knight's fee & are worth yearly (clear) £3 19s.

52. WILLIAM BARNETT OF WRENBURY[a], YEOMAN

S.Pr. 1 February 1616/17
Buried: 2 September 1616

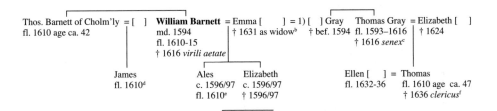

Thos. Barnett of Cholm'ly = [   ]   **William Barnett** = Emma [   ] = 1) [   ] Gray   Thomas Gray = Elizabeth [   ]
fl. 1610 age ca. 42   md. 1594   † 1631 as widow[b]   † bef. 1594   fl. 1593–1616   † 1624
                                         fl. 1610-15   fl. 1616 *senex*[c]
                                         † 1616 *virili aetate*

James   Ales   Elizabeth   Ellen [   ] = Thomas
fl. 1610[d]   c. 1596/97   c. 1596/97   fl. 1632-36   fl. 1610 age ca. 47
                         fl. 1610[e]   † 1596/97   † 1636 *clericus*[f]

Inventory: William Barnett of Wrenbury, yeoman.

Taken: 6 September 1616

Of: goodes and Cattels.

Prisers: William Bebinton, William Taylor, John Graie and Thomas Spencer.

	£	s	d
his apparrell		40	0
Two oxen	7	10	0
Three Twynter bullocks	5	16	8
Two bulles	3	10	0
Sixteene kyne	45	0	0
Sixe Twynter heaffers	11	0	0
Two Calves		30	0
one mare		46	8
another oulde mare			12
Eleven swyne	3	0	0
In Poultrey		3	0
Corne and haye	*[damaged]*		

NOTE: The bottom half of the inventory is missing, resulting in our having just the top portions of both pages 1 and 2.

[a] Executor of will of James Barnett, pr. 1610 (will no. 29); deponent for allegations to that same will, 1610, wherein he is noted as the brother of Thomas Barnett of Cholmondeley, age 42 or thereabouts.
[b] See will of Emma Barnett, pr. 1631 (will no. 87).
[c] See will of Thomas Gray of Smeatonwood, pr. 1616/17 (will no. 53).
[d] Received bequest of £3 from James Barnett, 1610 (will no. 29).
[e] Received bequest of £4 from James Barnett, 1610.
[f] See will of Thomas Gray of Aston in Newhall, pr. 1636 (will no. 99).

mucke and one swyne trough of stone		6	8
Two peeces of bacon			2
Paynted Clothes		3	4
one saddle brydle pillowe & packelant		5	0
Sixe silver spoones		30	0
In goulde		22	0
In money		2	0
[Sum	74	223	42]
debtes oweinge John Shrowbridge	14	1	8
John Phillippes	8	0	0
Elizabeth Allyn	6	0	0
John Cartwright	3	0	0
William Prince Clerke		3	6
Thomas Hurleston		5	0
Thomas Woollam		7	0
Standley Burrowes		7	0
William Prince of Buerton		33	0
Thomas Gray for Rent due at Martins next		23	4
[Sum	31	79	18]

Endorsement: Exhibited 1 February 1616. *[No indication as to whom adminis-tration was granted].*

53. THOMAS GRAY OF SMEATONWOOD

S.Pr. 19 March 1616/17
W.T. 4 June 1613
† 7 November 1616
Buried: 8 November 1616

2) William Barnett = Emma [ ] = 1) [ ] Gray		**Thomas Gray** = Elizabeth [ ]				
md. 1594 † 1631 *vidua* † bef. 1594		fl. 1593–1616[a] fl. 1613-16 (executor)				
fl. 1610–15		† 1616 *senex* † 1624				
† 1616 *virili aetate*						
Timothy Buckley = Mary		Thomas = Ellen [ ]		Elizabeth	Jane	
fl. 1603-30 md. 1603		fl. 1610-16 fl. 1632–36		c. 1595	c. 1601	
(executor) fl. 1613–30/31		(executor) † 1644		fl. 1613	fl. 1613	
† 1630[b] † 1636/37[c]		† 1636 *clericus*[d]		† 1638	† 1638	
Maria	George = Jane Swan					
fl. 1613	fl. 1607–16[e] md. 1607[f]					

Will, sick.

First I bequeathe my soule to Allmightie God my only maker and redeemer and *my bodie to bee buried in the church yard of Wrenbury*. Item I Will and bequeathe my tenement wherin I now dwell to Elizabeth Grey my wife for the terme of my lease or the acres which I have of my Landlord if shee soe longe live. Item I give unto my sonne George Grey the pasture of ground called Scrateley for his whole Childs parte of goods. I give unto Timothie Boulcley and Mary his wiffe and my daughter the one halfe of my Tenement wherin I nowe dwell and which I have made him a signeature of heere afore after my wives decease In a full recompencce of here whole Childs parte of goods Item I give unto Thomas Gray my sonne the other halfe of my Tenement or holdinge wheerein I now dwell and the whole Tenement to bee devided betweene my sonne in Lawe Timothie Boulcley and his wiffe and my sonne Thomas Gray in an equall division betweene them

---

[a] Witness 1614 to will of George Kemp of Smeatonwood (will no. 50); owed rent of 23s. 4d., due at St Martins Day next after 6 September 1616 to estate of William Barnett of Wrenbury (see will no. 52).

[b] Timothy Buckley owed John Bromhall £24, payable in four sums of £6 each over four years; see will of John Bromhall, pr. 1630 (will no. 82); also inventory of Timothy Buckley of Smeatonwood, exhibited 1630/31 (no. 84).

[c] Mary Buckley fl. 1630 as *widdow Buckley*, owing 4s. 3d. to John Bromhall (will no. 82).

[d] Witness for John Wilkinson, 1615 (will no. 46); see will of Thomas Gray of Aston in Newhall, pr. 1636 (will no. 99).

[e] Witness for Thomas Ravenscroft, 1613/14 (will no. 43); executor for John Bickerton, 1616 (will no. 48).

[f] William Fergusson Irvine, *Chester Licences*, i. 21: 4 July 1607, George Grey and Jane Swan, both of Wrenbury parish; bondsman Thomas Swanne of Smeatonwood; at Wrenbury.

Item I give unto my sonne Thomas Gray my Carts plowes yoakes Chaines harrows and Slead for his whole Childs parte of goods and then to remaine att the house as longe as his mother lives. Item I give unto Elizabeth Gray my wiffe the one halfe of my goods both moveable and unmoveable and the other halfe of my goods to my two daughters Elizabeth Gray and Jane Gray and to bee equallie devided betweene them Item I give unto Elizabeth Gray my daughter fower silver spoones of the best manner of spoones Item I give unto Joan Graye my daughter one sillver spoone. Item I give unto Mary Boulcley my daughter one sillver spoone Item I give unto Thomas Gray my sonne my Coulte Item my will is that if god Call for my sonne Thomas Gray before my lease bee ended that then my two daughters Elizabeth Gray and Jane Gray shall have the one halfe of my said tenement or lyvinge with there brother Thomas Inioyed duringe the said Tearme of yeares which I had of my Land lord and soe to have itt Joyntly betweene them Item my will is that my bodie shall bee honestly brought home of the whole.

Executors: the testator's wife, Elizabeth Gray, the testator's son-in-law, Timothie Boulcley, and the testator's son, Thomas Gray.

H. & S.
By mee Tho: Gray

Inventory: Thomas Gray of Smeatonwood 'who left this liffe November vii 1616'.

Taken: [n.d.], after 7 November 1616

Of: goodes, Cattells and Chattells.

Prisers: William Mainwaringe and Thomas Bebington.

	£	s	d
Cattell	69	10	0
Corne and Haie	17	0	0
Carts ploughtes and other Implements for husbandry	5	0	0
timber	1	9	8
brasse and pewter	5	6	0
spitts pottracks and other Iron ware in the house	1	0	0
tables Cupbords Coffers and other wooden and treene ware	4	18	0
beddinge and naperie	11	0	0
butter Cheese and Bacon	8	5	0
honie and Bees		15	0
poultrie ware		16	8
hemp and flaxe	1	0	0
fewell		3	4
a muskett	1	0	0
lease goods	16	0	0
debts plate wearinge Cloathes and money in his purse	39	0	0
Some is	182	3	8

Endorsement: Probated 19 March 1616; administration to Timothy Buckley and Thomas Gray two of the executors named in the will; Elizabeth his widow one of the executors named in this will came and [renounced the burden].

54. MICHAEL WHITNEY OF NEWHALL,[a] HUSBANDMAN

S.Pr. [no closer date given] 1617
Buried: 14 November 1616

Margery [   ] = [   ] Whitney
fl. 1607-16[b]
† 1617 *anus*

    Michael Whitney = Jone Morris
    md. 1610   fl. 1610-16[c]
    † 1616 *virili aetate*

Inventory: Michaell Whitney of Newhall, husbandman.

Taken: 22 November 1616

Of: goodes Cattels and Chattels.

Prisers: Randull Bryan, John Hamnett, Richard Cartwright and John Fisher.

	£	s	d
Foure kyne	10	0	0
one heaffer and a stirke		53	4
one mare and one twynter Fillie	3	6	8
In Poultrey		4	0
Corne hay and strawe		53	4
one trough for one horse a plowe harrowe and furniture belonginge to them		6	0
wood for fyer and three ladders		3	4
All Iron ware		6	0

a   Incorrectly labelled as Michael Whitney of *Henhall* by a later hand.
b   This may be the person noted 1607 in the will of Robert Buckley (will no. 24) as Margery Whitney, a name which is unknown in the Whitney family of Coole; Mistress Whitney the elder is noted in the inventory of John Bickerton of Newhall, 1616 (will no. 48) as being obligated for a debt of her husband amounting to 4s. 6d.
c   This may be the Mistress Whitney referred to in the inventory, who might, however, be the otherwise unaccounted-for Margery Whitney noted 1607 in the will of Robert Buckley (will no. 24).

Cowpery and Treene ware	5	0
Brasse and Pewter	31	0
Beddinge and Napperye	45	0
His apparrell	20	0
Chese and bacon	46	8
Corne and Mault in the house	16	0
Flaxe and yarne	10	0
Foure Coffers	8	0
sives Riddles & strawe baskets	2	0
one olde Cupebord bedstocks Cheares formes stooles shelfes		
tables one spyninge wheele & one safe		8

debtes oweinge by specialties	52	17	4

Debtes oweinge without specialties		
Richard Cartwright	20	0
Roger Sadler	10	0
Richard Curriar and Richard Shore his suertie	[ ]	
James Eaton	[ ]	
Thomas Meddens	13	4
Thomas Gryndley and John Sale his suertie		6
one Cowe which Mistres Whitney had for a heriott		50
five peeces of tymber		5
one house and grownde threre unto belonginge for three yeares if		
Margarett Morrey[a] Doe soe longe live foure marks a yeare and		
one hoope of barlie		[ ]

[Sum	65	374	105]

Endorsement: Exhibited 1617. *[No closer date; no indication of to whom admin-istration was granted].*

---

[a] Margaret *Morrey* is presumably related to Jone *Morris*, Michael Whitney's wife. Thomas Palin refers to Margaret *Morrey* as his god-daughter when bequeathing 10s. to her; see will of Thomas Palin, pr. 1624 (will no. 71). *Margerie Morris*, who may be the same individual, received a legacy of 2s. from Ellen Ravenscroft, ca. 1631 (see will no. 86).

55. ELIZABETH BASKERVILLE OF SOUND, WIDOW

S.Pr. 17 May 1617
W.T. 2 September 1616
Burial: None recorded at Wrenbury, Audlem or Acton

Edward **Baskerville**	=	**Elizabeth [ ]**
† 1613[a]		fl. 1613
		† 1617 as widow

William	Thomas	Richard	Margarett	Elizabeth	Ellen	Anne
fl. 1617–32	fl. 1617	fl. 1617	fl. 1617	fl. 1617	fl. 1617	fl. 1617
(eldest son)		(youngest son)				
† 1665[b]						

Will, sick.

First I Comende my soule to almyghtie God my maker and redeemer, and my body to the earth from whence it was formed Item I give and bequeath to my yongest sonne Richard Baskervilde the some of £30. Item I give & bequeath to William Baskervilde my eldest sonne the some of 3s. 4d. Item I give and bequeath to my daughter Anne Baskervilde one brodde Chest, Item my will is: That all the rest & residue of my goodes & Cattell whatsoever moveable and unmoveable shalbe equally devided amongest Thomas Baskervilde Richard Baskervilde my sonnes, Margarett Baskervilde, Elizabeth Baskervilde Ellen Baskervilde and Anne Baskervilde my daughters, (my Legasies & funerall expenses & other charges first discharged).

Executors: my welbeloved in Christ Raphe Cheynie and Thomas Orpe.

Overseer: my welbeloved in Christ William Cheynie and John Orpe.

H. & S.
Elizabeth Baskervilde

Witnesses: Thomas Bebington, with others.

Inventory: Elizabeth Baskerfild of Sound.

Taken: [before 17 May 1617]

Of: goods and chattels.

Prisers: Thomas of the Preses, William Bebington, Thomas Bebington, John Judson and John Bebington.

[a] See inventory of Edward Baskerville of Sound, 1613 (no. 41).
[b] See nuncupative will and inventory of William Baskerville of Sound, pr. 1665/CRO.

	£	s	d
in money		6	0
4 buloks and a cow		14	0
3 calves	1	6	8
a mare and a coult	3	6	8
a cow and 2 calve	5	6	8
a mare which was the heriot	2	13	4
in beding		14	0
in Naprie ware			6
a cobord a pras and 2 chests	1	10	0
in tabls forms chers and stons		6	8
a costlet	1	0	0
in brasse and peuter	3	0	0
a cather a brake a chiste pres and al other treen ware	1	0	0
in iron and all other husbandtree ware	3	0	0
in yarne and tow	2	16	8
2 fliches of bacon		16	0
in hony		2	0
in malt	1	16	0
in wheat		9	0
in pes		6	8
in rie	3	0	0
in barli	1	16	0
in sadle and feathers		5	0
in plankes		10	0
2 hives of bees		13	4
in poultri		10	0
in fuel		8	0
in bedstids	2	0	0
in corne upon the ground	3	0	0
in wearing aparel	3	6	8
The whole sum is	88	8	9

Endorsement: Probated 17 May 1617. *[Nothing is noted on the wrapper regarding administration].*

56. EDMOND BICKERTON OF SOUND, YEOMAN

S.Pr. 10 July 1617
W.T. 14 January 1616/17
Buried: 23 March 1616/17

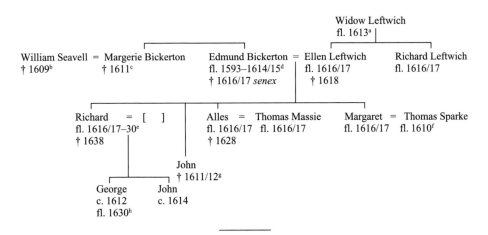

Will, 'weak in body by reason of old age'.

First I Comend my Soule in to the hands of Almighty god hopeinge assuredly by the merritts and bloodshedinge of Jesus Christ my onely saviour and Reedemer to be made partaker of life everlasting And *I Comyt my body to the earth to be*

---

a Owed £2 by Edward Baskerville of Sound; see his inventory, 1613 (no. 41). Leftwich is not a name found in Wrenbury parish records, however.
b See will of William Seavell, pr. 1609 (will no. 27).
c See will of Margerie Sevell, pr. 1611 (will no. 35), where note 'b' argues that she was the sister of Edmond Bickerton.
d The IPM for John Chetwoode taken 16 January 1615/16 at Middlewich declared that long before the death of the said John, Thomas Chetwoode, his father, was seised of three messuages, 20 acres of land, 22 acres of meadow, 30 acres of pasture, 3 acres of wood, and 10 acres of heath in Sound, in the tenure of Edmund Bickerton, John Barnett sen. & jun., and Humphrey Barnett (see R. Stewart Brown, *Cheshire Inquisitions Post Mortem*, i. 120-1, 123). The lands at Sound were held of the heirs of Thomas de Alstaston by fealty only and worth yearly (clear) thirty shillings. Edmund Bickerton was a juryman for the IPM of Richard Cotton, esq., of Combermere, taken at Sandbach 6 April 1605 (see *Cheshire Inquisitions Post Mortem*, i. 146); he also made the inventory for the estate of Edward Baskerville, 1613 (no. 41). Edmond Bickerton was an executor of the will of Randle Povall, 1593 (will no. 10).
e Priser for the goods of Richard Hall, 1630 (no. 83).
f Thomas Sparke owed £10 to James Barnett, 1610 ; see will of James Barnett, pr. 1610 (will no. 29).
g See inventory of John Bickerton, son of Edmond Bickerton of Sound, 1611 (no. 39).
h See inventory of Richard Hall, 1630 (no. 83).

buried in the parishe Churche of Wrenbury. Item as Concerninge my messuage & Tenementes in Sound wherein I Dwell and all houses barnes buildinge orchard gardens Lands Tenements meadowes Leasowes pastures woods waters & Comones thereunto belonginge with theire appurtennts I doe geve Devise and bequeath the one half and full moyetie thereof unto Ellen Bickerton my wife and her assignes To have and to hould the same one half or full moyety of the said messuage Tenemente and premisses with thappertennts for & duringe all such tearme and nomber of yeares as I the said Edmond Bickerton have in one Indenture of Lease thereof made by Thomas Chettwood Deceassed yf the said Ellen doe soe longe live & keepe her self sole & unmarried the said Ellen and her assignes payeinge the one half of the Rents Dueties and servics reserved in and by the said Indenture of lease And after her Decease or marriage I Doe give & bequeath the Remainder of these yeares of and in the said moyetie unto Richard Bickerton my sonne his executors and assignes Item I Doe give Devise and bequeath unto the said Richard Bickerton my sonne the other moyety of all and singuler the said messuage & tenemente & primisses with thappurtenance in Sound aforesaid for & duringe all my whole tearme in the said lease paieinge likewise the moyetie of the Rents and service as aforesaid Item I doe give grannte Devise and bequeath unto Ellin my wife all these my Foure messuags or dwellinge houses & gardens with thappertenance scituate lying and being in Nantwich in the said County of Chester in a certaine streete there Called the Hospellstreete and now in the occupacōn of Margret Horobin widow Richard Clubbe John Dale and Margret Wright widow To have and to hould the same foure messuags ten(emen)ts & gardens with Thapurtenancs to the said Ellen Bickerton my wife for and Duringe her naturall life keepinge her self sole and unmarried And after her Decease or Marriage Then I Doe give grannte bequeath & Devise the same foure messuags or Tenements & gardens with thappertenancs to the said Richard Bickerton my sonne To have and to hould the same to him and to the heires of his bodye lawfully begotten and to be begotten and for Default of such yssue then to the right heires of me the said Edmund Bickerton and of theire heres & assignes for ever Item I doe give grannte Devise and bequeath unto the said Richard Bickerton my sonne All that my messuage or Tenemente and garden with thapputtennce in Nantwich aforesaid now in the occupacōn of Thomas Parker And also one wiche house of six Leads with wood Rownes bryne wallinge occupacōn & Makinge of Salt the same wiche house scituate lyinge and beinge in Nantwich aforesaid & under a roofe or Cover with one other six leads and now in the occupacōn of Hughe Manwaringe and the bryne Wallinge occupacōn and makynge of Salt now beinge in the occupacōn of Harry Bickerton To have and to hould the said messuage or Tenemente & garden wiche house wood Rowines Wallinge bryne occupacōn & makinge of salt with theire appurtenancs unto the said Richard Bickerton my sonne and to the heires of his body lawfully begotten and to be begotten And for Default of such yssue Then to the right heires of me the said Edmond Bickerton & of theire heires & assignes for ever Item I doe like wise geve and bequeath to Ales Massie my Daughter wife of Thomas Massie 10s. in full satisfaccōn of all her Childs parte or filiall porcōn of my goods Item I Doe likewise geve and bequeath to Margret

Sparke my daughter wife of of *[sic]* Thomas Sparke 10s. in full satisfaccōn of all her Children parte or fillial porcōn of my goods Item I Doe give Devise and bequeath the Residue of all my goods and Cattell quick & dead houshould stuffe Jewells plate Implements and Corne & all other my goods cattells and Chattells whatsoever (not before given nor bequeathed my debts & legacies beinge first paid and my funerall expences Discharged) To Ellen my wife & Richard Bickerton my sonne to be equally parted and devided betweene them.

Executors: the testator's wife, Ellen, and the testator's son, Richard Bickerton.

Overseer: the testator's brother-in-law, Richard Leftwich.

Witnesses: William Whicksteed, Richard Leftwiche, Jasper Whicksteed and William Whicksteed (the) younger.

Inventory: Edmund Bickerton of Sounde, yeoman.

Taken: 24 March 1616/17

Of: goods cattells and Chattells.

Prisers: James Beckett, Humphrey Barnett, William Cowper, and George Barnett.

	£	s	d
his apparell		40	0
two bullocks	4	0	0
foure kine and two Calves	12	13	4
two yeare old Calves		40	0
three mares and one horse	12	0	0
7 yewes and 7 lambes		46	8
two goates		20	0
in poultrie		10	0
Corne hay and strawe		53	4
two carts		46	8
plowes harrows yocks and Cheanes		20	0
all Iron ware		10	0
brasse and pewter	3	6	8
Beddinge and naperie	12	0	0
two Silver Spoones		8	0
treene ware and Cowperie		14	0
all bedsteedds		40	0
tables formes cheares stooles and shelves		40	0
one old Cupboard and foure Chests		20	0
Wood mucke and coales		10	0
two standes of beese		8	0
Foure laddars		4	0
beefe and bacon		20	0

Butter and cheese	30	0
sives sacks spinninge wheeles and all other smale implements	10	0
[Sum	43 308	32]

Endorsement: Probated 10 July 1617; administration to Richard Bickerton, son of the deceased and one of the executors named in the will, with power reserved to Ellen [Bickerton] his widow when she comes.

57. ANNE KEMPE OF SMEATONWOOD, WIDOW

I.Pr. [n.d.], after 10 May 1619
W.T. 14 April 1618
Buried: 7 April 1619

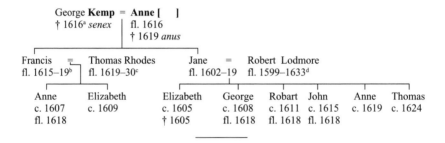

Will, sick.

First, I Comende my soule in the handes of almyghty god hopeinge by the merits & bloodsheddinge of Jesus Christ, my alone Saviour, to have free pardon & remission of all my sinnes: And *my bodye I comitt to the earthe to be buried in the Churchyarde of Wrenbury* abovesaide in sure & certaine hope of a ioyfull resurrection. Item I give and bequeath unto Frances Rhodes my daughter 40s. and one silver spone in full satisfaction of her Childes parte of all my goodes. Item I give and bequeath to the saide Franices Rhodes to the use of her daughter Anne Rhodes one ioyned bedstedd one boulster, one peare of Flaxen sheetes, one bourdclothe, one Flaxen towell, two pillowe beares, one longe Chest, one silver spoone, and 40s. in money which 40s. Thomas Rhodes her father doth owe unto mee. All

---

^a See will of George Kemp of Smeatonwood, 1614 (will no. 50).
^b Frances Rhodes owed £1 to Thomas Faulkner in 1615; see his will, no. 47.
^c Thomas Roades leased a parcel of land to Richard Hall; see inventory of Richard Hall, 1630 (no. 83).
^d Owed debt to James Brooke,; see the latter's will, pr. 1622 (will no. 66).

the rest of my goodes moveable an unmoveable Cattles and debtes (my bodie beinge honestly brought home an my funerall expences discharged) I give and bequeathe unto Jane Lodmore my daughter and to her Children.

Executors: Thomas Swanne and Thomas Bebenton 'my good neighboures'.

H. & S.

Witnesses: Thomas Graie, John Wright (seal) and William Palin (seal).

Debts owing to the Testator:

	£	s	d
John Woolley	5	10	0
Thomas Gryndley		17	10
[Sum	5	27	10]

Inventory: Anne Kemp of Newhall, widdowe.

Taken: 10 May 1619

Of: goods and Chattels.

Prisers: George Cudworthe and Thomas Hall.

	£	s	d
Two oulde kyne	4	0	0
Brasse Item in severall parcels of Brasse	1	2	0
Pewter Item in severall parcels of Pewter		4	6
Beddinge Item one bedsteed with a tester & one little bedsteed one little table 2 formes & 3 Cheares		15	0
Treenware Item in severall parcels of Treenware		3	4
Beddinge Item one oulde Feather bed 2 Coverings 2 blankets one olde woolbed 2 boulsters and 2 pillowes with oulde Apparell	1	0	6
Iron Item in severall parcels of Iron ware		2	10
Plate Item 3 silver spoones 2 with gilt heds & one playne		13	4
Nappery Item one table Clothe one peare of sheets 2 pillowe beeares & one towell all of fyne flaxen		19	10
one rounde table Clothe 3 olde Course paire of sheets of readings; pillowe beeare, & 4 ould napkins		8	6
one faire greate Chest, little Chest & 2 boxes		10	0
Suma totalis	9	19	10
specialties Item a bill of debt	6	0	0
a Swarme of bies		5	0

Endorsement: Probated [1619]; [administration to] Thomas Swanne and Thomas Babington executors named in the will.

58. JOHN MILLINGTON OF BROOMHALL

S.Pr. 28 July 1619
W. T [parchment]. 6 February 1618/19
Buried: 11 February 1618/19

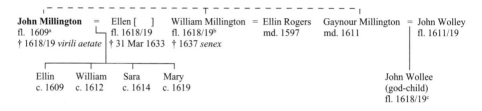

John Millington = Ellen [   ]   William Millington = Ellin Rogers   Gaynour Millington = John Wolley
fl. 1609ᵃ   fl. 1618/19   fl. 1618/19ᵇ   md. 1597   md. 1611   fl. 1611/19
† 1618/19 *virili aetate* │ † 31 Mar 1633   † 1637 *senex*

Ellin   William   Sara   Mary   John Wollee
c. 1609   c. 1612   c. 1614   c. 1619   (god-child)
                                                                                     fl. 1618/19ᶜ

Will, sick.

First and principally I bequeath my soule into the hands of almightye god, trustinge onelye by the death and bloud sheedinge of Jesus Christ my alone saviour, to have free pardon and remission of all my sinnes; And *my bodye to be buryed in the Churchyoard of Wrenbury* Item my mynde is that my debts and funerall expencs shalbe discharged out of my whole goods: And after my debts paid and my funerall expences discharged, my will is that all my goods Cattells and debtes shalbe wholye to Ellen my wife, towards the educacōn and bringinge upp of my Children, duringe the tyme that she doe keepe her sole and unmaryed; And att such tyme that she doth marye agayne, my will is that my Children shall have theire portions as by the Inventorye thereof may fall to theire parts beinge equallye devided amongst my wiffe and Children: Item I geve and bequeath to John Wollee my godchild one yooe lambe.

Executrix: Ellen my wife.

Overseer: John Bromhall the yonger.   H.
                                                    John Millington O marke

Witnesses: William Breesse, William Millington, John Wollee and John Bromhall.

ᵃ Priser of the goods of Margaret Ankers, 1609/10 (will no. 28).
ᵇ The William Millington who witnessed John's will is quite probably the same who married Ellin Rogers at Wrenbury 20 January 1597/98; his burial is recorded at Wrenbury on 4 March 1637/38 as *senex.*
ᶜ A John Wolley was baptized at Wrenbury 1612; the parents' names are not given, but they may have been the John Wolley and Gaynour Millington who married at Wrenbury in 1611, thus accounting for the god-father/god-son relationship noted in the above will. Since John Millington himself had minor children in 1618/19, the god-son, John Wollee, was probably the son of John Wollee the witness.

Inventory: John Millington.

Taken: 24 February 1618/19

Of: goods Catles and debts.

Prisers: Henrye Rutter, William Brees, Robert Heath and Michell Hope.

	£	s	d
his aparell		20	0
15 kyne	40	0	0
in yonge Cattell	13	6	8
three horses and one Colte	6	0	0
in Sheepe		40	0
Two swyne		16	0
in Poultry		4	0
hey and other Fother		3	0
Corne in the howse and in the fyeld		50	0
in Baken, Chees, And Butter		20	0
in woole, Tawe and yearne		20	0
in Beddinge and Napryware		50	0
Bedsteedes, Treaneware, Coffers Boords, Cheeres, stooles, spinninge wheeles		13	4
in Brasse and Pewter		20	0
Edgtoomes, Brand rate and pothangers		6	0
Carts, plowes, and other implements belonginge to husbandrye		13	4
wood and other fuell for the fyer		2	0
mucke in the meedinge		3	4

debts that the said John Millington owed To William Brees 4 2 6

Debts owing to Testator:

	£	s	d
in the hands of Richard Brester		48	0
in the hands of Robert Grinley	17	0	0
in the hands of Phillipp Grinley		19	0
Summa totalis	80	8	8
[*recte*	95	18	2]

Endorsement: Probated 28 July 1619; administration granted to the sole executor named in the will.

59. PHILLIP DODD OF WRENBURY

I.Pr. 1619
Buried: 30 March 1611[a]

Phillip Dodd = Christian [   ]
fl. 1592-1610   † 1610/11 *ux: Phil.*
† 1611 *senex*[b]

William
fl. 1619
† 1642

Inventory: Phillip Dodd of Wrenbury.

Taken: [ ] 1619

Of: goods Cattels, & Chatteles.

Prisers: Richard Hamnett Senior and Richard Hamnet Junior.

	£	s	d
In haye		32	0
brass & pewter		14	0
in beddinge, & napperie ware		14	0
bords & formes		5	0
in trene ware		2	0
one Cobbord & one Chest		4	0
geese & hens		2	0
iron ware			2
his wearing Clothes		6	0
[Sum		79	2]

Endorsement: [1619 – No date on wrapper]. Administration to William Dodd natural son [of the deceased].

----

[a] The date on the inventory is faint but clearly 1619, but there is no date at all on the wrapper; thus, unless the entry in the Parish Register is incorrect, Phillip Dodd *senex* died about 29/30 March 1611 and was buried 30 March 1611, but his estate was not probated until 1619. While there may have been a younger Phillip Dodd who died in 1619, there is no record of his burial at Wrenbury and we have therefore assumed that the testator was identical to he who was buried in 1611.

[b] Owed debt of 20s. to the estate of Roger Swann of Dodds Green (Newhall); see will of Roger Swann, pr. 1610 (will no. 30). The IPM for Roger Bickerton, held 31 March 1619, declared that George Bickerton bequeathed by will on 29 August 1592 to his wife Margery a messuage in Newhall called Dodds House and all thereunto belonging, in the tenure of the said George Bickerton and Phillip Dodd, for her life, and after her death to his younger sons, Richard and Arthur Bickerton; see R. Stewart Brown, *Cheshire Inquisitions Post Mortem*, i. 16-20. Through reversion, the property came into the hands of Roger Bickerton who held the premises in Newhall of the king in chief by a hundredth part of a knight's fee; it was valued at twenty-two shillings (clear) yearly.

60. RICHARD BERRINGTON OF WRENBURY

I.Pr. [n.d.], after 9 March 1619/20

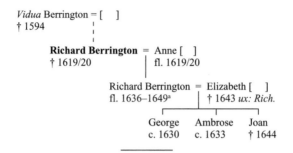

Inventory: Richard Barrinton of the parish of Wrenbury.

Taken: 9 March 1619/20

Of: goods.

Prisers: Thomas Taylor and William Barnes.

	£	s	d
his Wearinge apparell praysed unto		13	4
beddinge sheyts Coverlets and napperieware		26	8
brasse and pewter praysed to		20	0
Chestes coffers shilfes tables bourds frames and tressels & Cheares praysed unto		13	4
bouks and all other treyne ware praysed to		8	0
tow spinninge wheeles praysed to		3	0
Iron ware praysed unto		10	10
poulterie ware praysed unto		3	4
Som is	4	18	6

Ann Berrington relic[ta] . . . *[nothing further]*.

Endorsement: *[no wrapper and no probate date]*.

---

^a Richard Berrington appeared 1635/36 as a priser for John Hall (will no. 100); 1636/37 as a priser of the goods of Richard Dodd of Smeatonwood (will no. 101); 1647 he owed John Tench money (see inventory of the latter); priser of the goods of John Ravenscroft, 1649 (no. 137).

61. JOHN BACKHOUSE OF NEWHALL

S.Pr. 1 June 1620
W.T. 6 February [1619/20], 6 James I
Buried: 18 March 1619/20

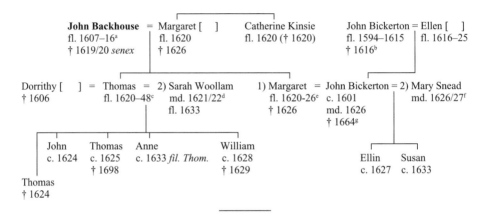

Will, sick.

Fyrst, I doe give and bequeath my Soule unto Almighty god my maker and redeemer by whom I hope to be saved, and *my body to be buried in the Church of Wrenbury*: Item I doe give and bequeath unto my wife that now is Margreate Backhouse my beste brase pan, two of the best Chests, the lesser Turnell a little Table boarde, Item I doe give and bequeath unto my sonne Thomas Backhouse al the Implements of husbandry and a presse of sylinge worke, the best Table and

---

^a Witness to will and priser of goods of William Fletcher, 1606/07 (will no. 23), served as juror 1611 at Newhall Manor Court; priser for John Bickerton, 1616 (will no. 48); appeared 18 April 1620 at Newhall Manor Court/CRO.
^b See will of John Bickerton, pr. 1616 (will no. 48).
^c Identified as the heir of John Backhouse, deceased, at Newhall Manor Court 1620; noted on 1623 Suit Roll for Newhall Manor Court/CRO; made inventory for George Cudworth, 1624 (no. 70); appointed overseer by (1626/27), and priser for (1630/31), Ellen Ravenscroft (will no. 86); priser for the goods of John Wright, 1629 (no. 79); object of a presentment at the Newhall Manor court 1631; he owed a debt of £20 16s. to Randle Sproston, 1648 (will no. 130). The Thomas Backhouse whose will was proved 1698 must be his son, as was the John Backhouse whose will was proved 1700/ CRO.
^d William Fergusson Irvine, *Chester Licences*, ii. 152: 19 January 1621/22 to Thomas Backhouse and Sarah Woollam.
^e *Chester Licences*, iii. 64: Margaret Backhouse of Wrenbury parish and John Bickerton of Wrenbury parish, at Acton or Wrenbury.
^f *Chester Licences*, iii. 64: 2 February 1626/27, to John Bickerton and Mary Snead, spinster; at Acton or Wrenbury.
^g See will of John Bickerton, pr. 1664/CRO; see also will of John Bickerton, pr. 1616 (will no. 48).

the frame, and the best Turnell my Cloake: Item I doe give and bequeath unto my wiffe Margrette Backhouse and unto my sonne Thomas Backhouse to be equally devided these parcsells followinge all my Tymber other sawinge Tymber or Clifte tymber, except the bordes that be in use aboute the house and barne the which I leave and give to my sonne Thomas Backhouse Item I doe give unto my sister in law Cathren Kinsie 5s. Item my will is that al the rest of my goodes moveable and unmoveable quicke and dead shalbe equally devided into three partes, the one parte whereof I doe give unto my wiffe Margrette Backhouse, the second parte I give unto my sonne Thomas Backhouse and the third parte I doe give unto my daughter Margrette Backhouse. Item my will is that my debts shalbe payd out of the whole my funerall expences and my legaces.

Executors: the testator's wife, Margrette Backhouse, and the testator's son, Thomas Backhouse

H. & S.

Witnesses: Richard Cooke, William Flecher.

Inventory: John Backhouse of Newhall.

Taken: 21 March 1619/20

Of: goodes and Cattels.

Prisers: Richard Hamnett, Robert Darlington, William Flecher and John Ravenscrofte.

	£	s	d
his wearinge apparrell		20	0
Two Oxen	9	0	0
nyne kyne	25	10	0
Two incalfe heffers & two bullockes	10	0	0
Two lesser heffers & two Calves	4	6	8
one nagge and a Colte	5	10	0
Hay and straw	2	0	0
one hogge		9	0
hard Corne in the house	2	10	0
malte		14	0
Oates		20	0
Cartes plowes Yoakes & Chaynes with al other implements of husbandry	2	10	0
Corne sowed on the grounde		20	0
one bargayne of grounde houlden of Mary Davie	12	0	0
pannell & muntanes with other timber		6	0
fewell for the fyre		4	0
boards and goysts		20	0
Brasse and pewter	3	10	0

	£	s	d
Beddinge and nappery	12	0	0
one presse and one table boarde		30	0
Bedstockes Chestes & Coffers benches & formes Cheires & stooles with other shylves	2	0	0
Combes stoonde & al other tryne ware		20	0
Yarne & Tooe		10	0
three spinning wheeles		3	0
three straw baskets & one Cradle		3	0
Bacon at the roofe Butter & Cheese		30	0
paynted Clothes		3	4
poultry ware		3	0
one grate one fryinge pan potrackes and tonges with al other houshould Iron ware		6	8
quishens		1	0
one brake one ould heare & a Chese presse		3	4
mucke		10	0

Debtes owinge to the testator:

	£	s	d
Richard Meakin		7	0
Rondull Greene		6	0
Thomas Cooke		1	6
Thomas Proudman		1	6
Raphe Powfall		1	0
[Sum	88	0	0]

Wrapper: 'a coppie of the last will & testament of John Backhouse of Newhall deceased'.

Endorsement: Probated 1 June 1620; administration granted to the executors named in the will.

62. WILLIAM HEIGHFIELD OF BROOMHALL, YEOMAN

S.Pr. 20 June 1620
W.T. 9 December 1618
Buried: 13 June 1619

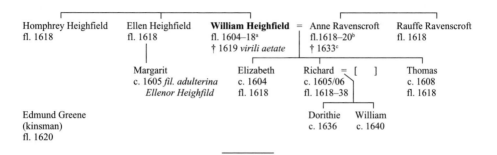

Will, sick.

First therefore, I geve and bequeath into the handes of Almightie god my maker trustinge assuredlie through the merites and bloudsheadinge of Jesus Christe my alone redeemer to be made partaker of lief everlastinge, and *I Comyt my bodie to the earth whence it Came to be buried in the parishe churchyard of Wrenbury* where it shalbe thoughte fittinge by my Executors Item as Concernynge my daughter Elizabeth Heightfeild who must have a speciall Care of, I therefore geve and bequeath unto her for her Childes parte and filiall porcōn of all my goodes and Cattels and chattels the full some of one hundred and twentie poundes which my will is shalbe paid unto her at the end of thirteene monethes nexte after the tyme of my decease Item I doe geve and bequeath unto Margerie Ravenscrofte my servante maide six poundes soe that she doe Contynewe and abide in service with my wief for the space of two yeres next ensueinge after my deceasse which some of £6 my will is shalbe paid her at the end of the said two yeres by myne executors Item I doe geve and bequeath unto Richard Heighfeild my eldest sonne one bay Colte and a peece of gould of Eleavon shillings. Item I doe geve and bequeath unto Thomas Heighfeild my yonger sonne Eleavon shillings in gould. Item I doegeve and bequeath unto Elizabeth Heighfeild my said daughter Eleavon shillinges in gould Item I doe geve and bequeath unto Henrye Griffithes five shillings six pence in gould Item I doe geve and bequeath unto William Brees

---

[a] Kinsman, witness and overseer of will, and priser of goods, of Thomas Ravenscroft of Newhall, will pr. 1614 (will no. 43).
[b] Anne Heighfield owed William Brees a debt of 4s., 1620 ; see will of William Brees (will no. 64).
[c] See will, pr. 1633.

the elder 5s. 6d. in goulde Item I doe geve and bequeath unto Anne my wief Eleavon shillinges in goulde. Item I doe geve unto Thomas Heath 12d. Item my will is that yf my wief doe Contracte or marie with any man within the space of fyve yeres next ensueinge after my deceasse Then doe I ordaine geve and bequeath unto Thomas Heighfeild my said sonne the some of one hundred poundes to be due and paid unto him by my said wief at the tyme of her mariage or at the ende or expuracōn of the said fyve yeres which of either of the said tymes shall first Come Item I doe geve and bequeath unto Homfrey Heighfeild my brother fortie shillings to be paid unto him at the end of twelve monethes next after my deceasse Item I doe further geve and bequeath unto Ellen Heighfeild my sister the like some of 40s. to be paid unto her at the end of twelve monethes nexte after my deceasse Item the residue of all my goodes and Cattells as well moveable as unmoveable quicke and deade goodes not before geven nor bequeathed my legasies beinge paid and my funerall expencs beinge discharged I doe geve and bequeath unto Anne my wief To have hould occupie and enioye the same for and duringe the terme of her naturall lief, and after her deceasse, I doe wish my said wief to bequeath her goodes or the most parte of them to Thomas Heighfeild my said sonne he behavinge himself towardes his said mother as a duetifull Childe oughte to doe which I hope she will performe.

Executors: the testator's wife, Anne, the testator's neighbour, Henrye Griffithes and Wiliam Brees.

Overseers: the testator's brother-in-law, Rauffe Ravenscroft, and the testator's kinsman, Edmond Greene.

H. & S.
William Heighfeild his marke

Witnesses: Thomas Brees, Thomas Heathe, Elizabeth Heighfeld, with others.

Inventory: William Heighfield of Broomhall.

Taken: 14 June 1620
Of: goodes Cattells and debtes.

Prisers: Edmond Greene, John Ravenscroft, John Ankers and Roberte Heathe.

	£	s	d
his apparell	5	0	0
six oxen	32	13	4
fifteene kyne and a Bull	48	0	0
fyve stirks and one two yere old heiffer	8	0	0
three waynyng Calves	1	0	0
one mare price	3	16	0
the wynter Corne one the grounde	3	13	4
the Lenten seedenes	2	3	4

fower swyne price		32	0
hempe and flaxe dresses		6	8
in poultetrie price		7	0
wooll and yarne			20
beefe and bacon		26	8
Corne & Maulte in the howse	2	3	4
Cheese & other victualles	6	0	0
beddinge price	8	0	0
sheets towells bordclothes & other napperie ware	6	10	0
bed steedes tables Cubbords Coffers & stooles	3	13	4
treen ware price		13	4
Brasse & pewter price	8	0	0
Carts & ploughes harrowes Cheynes yokes axes billes nagers			
& other ymplements of husbandrye	3	8	0
one Bible & other books		10	0
in money and gould	7	0	0
half dozen of silver spoones	3	0	0
painted Clothes & Cushions		5	0
fewell & Coales for the fire	1	10	0
the mucke in the Myddinge		10	0
debts by specialtie as may appeare by the same are	100	0	0
debts with out specialtie			
in Mrss Elizabeth Whytnes hand	5	0	0
in John Hamptons hand		16	0
in John Massies hande		30	0
in Rondull Hares hand		50	0
in Ellen Ravenscrofts hand		20	0
[Sum	260	9	0]

Endorsement: Probated 20 June 1620; administration granted to Anne Heighfield widow of the deceased, [one of the executors] named in the will, with power reserved to the other two executors when they come.

63. WILLIAM TAYLOR OF CHORLEY

I.Pr. 28 October 1620
Buried: Not noted at Wrenbury or Marbury

William Taylor = [   ]
† 1620
_____

Inventory: William Taylor of Chorley.

Taken: 25 March 1618/19

Prisers: none named.

		s	d
one mare	4	0	0
his apparrell		40	0
the reversion of on feelde of gresse		31	8
ould heye in the bottom of the stack		10	0
one oulde chest		3	4
one pare of ould Bootts		2	0
receyved of John Mottershed and Edwarde Mottershed one debte due by them unto the said William Tailier	7	10	0
receyved of Edward Fyndlowe	4	13	4
in money founde at the decedants death	7	0	0
Summa	27	4	0
[*recte*	22	109	16

Computus calculus: Account calculation and reckoning of Edward Royley one of the executors named in the last will and testament of William Taylor, while he lived, of Chorley, lately deceased and of and on his administration of the goods, rights, credits and chattels of the aforesaid deceased, returned and made on the strength of his oath sworn in person on the holy gospels of God taken in the presence of the venerable Master David Yale doctor of laws lawfully appointed Official Principal of the Consistory Court of Chester 24 October AD 1620.

The Charge

Firstly the accountant aforesaid acknowledges and admits that all and singular the goods, rights and credits of the aforesaid deceased contained and specified in the inventory of them annexed to these presents have come into his hands and possession. The which inventory annexed as aforesaid amount to the sum of £27 5s 4d.

Whereof he says that he has paid satisfied and contented and seeks to be allowed
to him as follows:

Discharge

Firstly the accountant aforesaid says that he has paid for the funeral expenses of
the aforesaid deceased   £6   9s   0d.
Item he says that he has paid for the citation, for entering the cause, for making
the allegation and exhibiting it together with the last will of the aforesaid deceased,
for the production of witnesses and copies of their depositions, for the proctor's
fees, for various legal fees, for making the sum and for *[damaged]* of the same
and for other necessary fees and *[damaged]* concerning the proving of the aforesaid will and approval of the same, the sum of   £3   0s.   0d.

The aforesaid accountant also says that *[damaged]* and settled the sums of money
below owed by the said deceased to the persons below and recovered from this
accountant in various courts as follows:

	£	s	d
Firstly paid to one John Walker		7	14
Item to Richard Davenport		12	10
Item to Margery Preston widow	4	18	4
Item to Laurence Birtles		46	0
Item to Radulph Lingart		33	0
Item to Richard Bancroft		32	0
Item to Henry Orwele		42	2

Item *[crossed through – no amount]*
Item the aforesaid accountant says that he himself lent the aforesaid deceased in
his lifetime the sum of   £6   10s

Therefore he seeks the said sum to be allowed to him namely   £6   10s

Item he says that he paid the sum of 20s. for medicines and other necessities for
the deceased during his illness and therefore he seeks to be allowed the said sum
                                                                        20s
Item he says that he paid for making this account 34s. 4d., for a copy of the same
3s. 4d., for the making of letters of quittance 3s. 4d., for the sealing of the same
7s. -d., for exhibiting the inventory 15*[damaged]* and for proctor's fees 2s.—
                                                                  20s   0d

Endorsement: Inventory of [the goods of] William Taylor while he lived of
Chorley deceased probated the 28th of October 1620 returned and made in the
presence of the venerable David Yale doctor of Laws etc.

64. WILLIAM BREES OF BROOMHALL, YEOMAN

S.Pr. 25 May 1621
W.T. 16 May 1620
Buried: 20 May 1620

William Brees	=	Dorothye [Cooper?]				John Brees		Thomas Brees
fl. 1606-20[a]		fl. 1620				fl. 1606–20[b]		fl. 1620[c]
† 1620 *senex*		† 1633				(cousin)		(cousin)

William	Robert	Jane	=	Edward Bowdon	Thomas	=	Elizabeth [ ]
c. 1601	fl. 1606[d]	c. 1607		fl. 1613–26	fl. 1615–20[e]		fl. 1654
fl. 1613–20[f]	† 1613 *adolescens*	md. 1626		† 1638	† 1655/56[g]		† 1666/67 *vidua*
† 1637/38							

Elenor	Henrie				Thomas	Elizabeth	Susan	Marie
c. 1599	c. 1604				c. 1624	c. 1628	c. 1632	c. 1636
† 1600	† 1607 *puer*							

Will, sick.

First I Comend my soule to almighty god my maker assuredly trusting by the meritts of his sonne & my savyour Christ Jesus to have free remission of all my sinnes & to be inherytor of the kingdom of heaven, And for my body I comitte yt to the earth whereof yt was made, and to be buried at the discretion of my executor, Item (my debts beinge payd & funerall expencs discharged) I give & bequeath unto Dorothye my wyfe the moytye or one halfe of all my goods Cattells & Chattells, And my will is that the said Dorothye my wife shall pay to William my sonne and Jane my daughter Fortye shillings a peece. Item I give & bequeath to Thomas my sonne the other halfe or moytye of all my said goods, Cattells & Chattells, And my will and mynde is That the said Thomas shall give & pay unto the said William his Brother Fortye pounds of lawfull money of Englande within the terme & space of foure yeares none next ensuinge the Date of theis presents,

---

[a] Executor for estate of Robert Ravenshaw, 1606/CRO; priser of goods of Margaret Ankers of Broomhall 1609/10 (will no. 28); priser for Roger Hockenhull, 1613/14 (will no. 44); made inventory for Anne Bickerton 1616 (will no. 49); witness and priser for John Millington, who owed him £4 2s 6d., 1618/19 (will no. 58); executor of estate of William Heighfield of Broomhall and received bequest of 5s. 6d., will pr. 1620 (will no. 62).
[b] Made inventory for Robert Ravenshaw, 1606/CRO.
[c] Witnessed will of William Heighfield, 1618 (will no. 62).
[d] Noted as the god-son of Robert Ravenshaw (will pr. 1607). That he belonged to this family might be argued from the fact that both William Jr and Thomas, his brother, named sons Robert.
[e] Thomas Breese owed £22 to Robert Tenche in 1615 (see will of Robert Tenche, pr. 1615).
[f] William Brees noted 1611 as god-child of William Cooper of Sound (will no. 42).
[g] See will of Thomas Brees of Broomhall, pr. 1655/56 (will no. 141).

And my further will & mynde is that the said Thomas shall (within the space and terme of five yeres) pay to the said Jane my Daughter Fourty pounds of like law-full money of Englande, And in case the the said William doe dye & departe this transitory life before the ende and expyracōn of the said terme of foure year-es, Then my will & mynde is That the said Thomas my sonne shall pay & give the said Jane Twenty pounds more parcell of the Legacy bequeathed to the said William within the said terme of five yeres. And in case alsoe the said Jane doe dye & departe this life before thende & expyracōn of the said terme of five yeres & the said William then lyvinge my will & mynde is that the said Thomas shall pay to the said William £20 more, to be paid him at thend and expiracōn of the said terme of five yeres. Item my will is that my sonne Thomas shall pay to Margarett my servant 20s. Item I give & bequeath unto my Cosin John Breese 13s. 4d. Item I give & bequeath unto Thomas Breese brother of the said John 13s. 4d.

Executor: the testator's son, Thomas Breese.

Witnesses: Henrye Rutter, George Mainwaringe, John Bromhall and Thomas Bowker.

Debts owing by the Testator:

	£	s	d
to Henrye Rutter	4	0	0

Debts owinge to the Testator:

	£	s	d
John Breese	4	0	0
Richard Wilson		40	0
John Seyvell		40	0
Thomas Massye		40	0
Anne Heighfeilde		4	0

Inventory: William Breese of Broomhall.

Taken [about 20 May] 1620

Prisers: Henrye Rutter, William Huxley, Randull Bryan and John Bromhall.

	£	s	d
His weareinge Clothes	5	0	0
Nyne Kine	27	0	0
Foure twinter heaffers & two bullocks	6	0	0
Three yeare old stirkes		30	0
Three Calves		30	0
Two mares, one horse, one Coult	11	0	0
Eleven sheepe	2	16	0
Two swyne		12	4
Gise and hennes		13	4

Nappery ware	7	13	0
Beddinge	11	10	0
Brasse and Pewter	3	8	0
Corne and mault	10	0	0
Beefe and bacon	2	0	0
Cheese		20	0
Bedsteeds Coffers bords Cupebords shilves wenescott Cheares and stooles	6	0	0
Treene ware		25	0
yarne and towe	2	0	0
woole	1	3	4
one haire Clothe		20	0
Carte plowes harrowes horse geares bills shules and picheforkes	4	0	0
Coales and wood	2	0	0
mucke		20	0
Debts oweinge which is due for Katheren Shrowbridge to pay	2	11	0
wheeles sives & all other implements which we may leave out		2	4
Corne on the grounde	2	0	0
Sume totall is	114	16	0

Endorsement: Probated 25 May 1621; administration granted to the sole executor named in the will.

[*later hand of cataloguer wrote*: William Breese of Bramhall].

65. RICHARD ROGERS OF CHORLEY

S.Pr. 25 June 1621
Buried: 8 May 1621

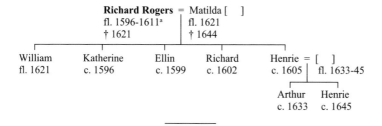

ᵃ Witness for Elizabeth Patrick alias Wilson, 1596, and priser of her goods, 1597 (will no. 15); priser for Roger Broome, 1606 (will no. 21); priser for William Patrick, 1611 (will no. 33).

Inventory: Richard Rogers of Chorley.

Taken: 22 May 1621

Of: goods & Chattells.

Prisers: John Bebington, William Babington, John Woodfen, Thomas P[len]kett.

	£	s	d
12 kine with 3 calves with them price	32	0	0
4 oxen price	13	0	0
4 twinters price	6	0	0
4 yerelinge calves price		48	0
2 mares price	5	0	0
one yewe & 2 lambes price		10	0
9 swine price		45	0
wood & kiddes price		20	0
one Iron bound weane price		40	0
all manor of Implements of husbandry		26	8
Pewter in the house price		30	0
pott brasse & pan brasse price	4	0	0
all manor of trien ware or cowperie ware		16	0
beddinge price	4	0	0
all manor of napperie ware price	6	10	0
Lynen yarne price		33	4
hempe and flaxe price		15	0
Chestes a presse & bedstocks price		15	0
Corne in the house price		10	0
towe twil shites & sacks price		10	0
one borde with a frame under hit one Cubborde with formes Cheeres stowles & dishbords price		30	0
4 flittches of bacon price		26	8
one hundreth weight of Cheise price		16	0
all manor of Iron ware spitts pottracks brendreth and like price		10	0
all manor of pultrie ware price		8	0
his wearinge apparell price		20	0
Corne upon the grounde sowen price		3	4
one outer peer price		3	4
one principall or harriott price	3	0	0
one outer *seddell* price		3	4
mucke price		3	4
[Sum	73	440	36]

Debts due to the testator 1621

Mres Marie Mottersthed	8	0	0
Thomas Mottersthed	9	20	0

Endorsement: Inventory exhibited 25 June 1621; administration granted to Matilda widow of the deceased, and to William Rogers his son.

66. JAMES BROOKE OF ASTON, YEOMAN

S.Pr. 15 May 1622
W.T. 8 April 1622
Buried: 15 April 1622

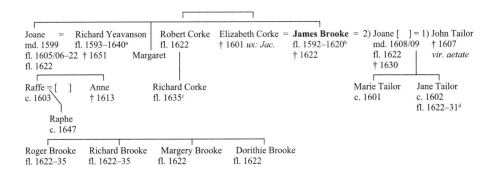

Will, sick.

First I commende my soule into the handes of Almightie god hopinge by the bloud sheedinge of Jesus Christ my alone Saviour to have pardon and remission of all my sinnes, And *my body I committ to the earth to be buried in the Churchyarde of Wrenbury* abovesaide in sure and certeyne hope of a joyfull resurrection. Item I give to my sister Joane 11s. in goulde. Item I give to my sister Margaret 11s. in goulde. Item I give to Elizabeth Kinsey 22s. Item I give to Anne Hooline 22s. Item I give to Elizabeth Ranshall 7s. 8d. Item I give to Elizabeth Whitney 10s. Item I give to James Heath my godsonne one Ewe and one lambe, and to the rest of my godchildren 12d. a peece, Item I give to Amy Williams sister to Randall Maddocke 26s. 8s. to be payde her by the saide Randall Maddocke out of the debt he oweth me and the rest which he oweth me I give to the children of the saide Randall Maddocke. Item I give to Ellenor Eddowes 10s. Item I give to Margaret

---

^a In 1605 Richard *Evanson*, John *Evanson* and Humphrey *Evanson* (apparently brothers) owed John Hall the debt of a cow; see will of John Hall, pr. 1606 (will no. 22). That *Yeavanson* and *Evanson* are identical seems self-evident, just as in some cases *Edmond* is spelled *Yeadmond*. In 1639/40 Richard *Yeavans* appears as 'cousin' of Thomas Gray of Newhall; see latter's will, pr. 1640 (will no. 112).

^b Noted 1592 and 1611 as *burleyman* in CRO Newhall Manor Court Roll; 1615 as Newhall Manor tenant/CRO.

^c Made inventory for Gilbert Woollam, 1635 (will no. 98).

^d Since her mother, Joane/Jane Brooke, died in 1630, the Jane Brooke who was a witness for Emma Barnett in 1630/31 (will no. 87) was presumably the step-daughter of James Brooke, generally now known as Jane Brooke.

Maddocke 10s. Item I give to Thomas Weston his children to either of them 5s. Item I give to Richarde Whitney 10s. and my Jerkin and breeches which were made last Item I give to Roger Brooke my best cloke Item I give to Richarde Brooke my greene breeches and Jerkin. Item I give to Margery Brooke £3. Item I give to Randall Tunnall 10s. Item I give to Jane Tailor my wyves daughter my new feather bed and boulster & one payre of new flaxen sheetes. Item my mynde and will is, that my bodie shall be honestly brought home and my funerall expences discharged out of my whole goods, and that Joane my wife shall have all such houshoulde goods as were hers before I marryed her, accordinge as we were agreed, and the rest of my houshoulde goods my mynde is that Richarde Brooke Roger Brooke and Margery Brooke their sister shall have them to be equally divyded amongst them. Item I give to Robert Corke my brother in law 20s., requestinge him to take the paynes to be one of my Executors. Item I give to Elizabeth Hooline daughter of Raphe Hooline 5s. Item I give to Edwarde Kinsey his two daughters either of them 5s. Item I give to Elizabeth Wollam my servant mayde one Ewe and one lambe And further my mynde is that all the rest of my goods moveable and unmoveable shall be divyded into two equall parts, the one equall part whereof I give and bequeath unto Joane Brooke my wife and the other equall part to discharge my legasies and to pay the debt which I owe unto Jane Taylor my wyves daughter, and the residue of the remaynder thereof I give and bequeath unto Dorothie Brooke, Richarde Brooke, Roger Brooke and Margery Brooke to be equally divyded amongst them.

Executors: the testator's wife, Joane Brooke, and the testator's brother-in-law, Robert Corke.

H. & S.
James Brooke
his mark

Debts owinge to the Testator without specialties:

	£	s	d
Roger Cheswis	11	0	0
George Gouldsmith		18	6

Witnesses: Thomas Graye, Robert Parker, William Taylor.

Inventory: James Brooke of Aston yeoman.

Taken: 18 April 1622, 20 James I

Of: goods cattells and chattels.

Prisers: John Cartwright, William Cartwright, John Judson and John Lawton.

	£	s	d
two oxen the one beinge seized for the decedents herriott	7	0	0
fyve kyne and calves	15	10	0

	£	s	d
seaven other kyne	16	6	8
three incalfe heyffers	8	0	0
two twinter heyffers		53	3
8 cooples and 18 other sheepe	5	4	0
a nagge and a mare	5	0	0
two swyne		20	0
poultrie		6	8
an yron bounde payre of wheeles & carte & a mucke wayne		4	4
ploughes harrowes yokes chaynes and other implements of husbandrie		20	0
a grindlestone a framinge Sawe, shoovells mattocks pykells bills axes, and other edgetooles and implements		20	0
Rye on the grounde	3	0	0
Oates on the grounde	16	0	0
Corne in the barne unthreshen	3	0	0
Hay and strawe		26	8
mucke		10	0
fewell and timber		40	0
turnells and treeneware in the Bakehouse		10	0
the decedents apparrell	5	0	0
Beddinge	7	0	0
Sheetes and other naperieware	6	13	4
Brasse and pewter	10	0	0
Spitts or broches, golberts potracke grate Reapinge hookes, tongs & other yron ware in the house		10	0
Stoonds, barrells and other treeneware in the house		13	4
bordes formes trestles, Chayres, stooles, Coshions and sheelves in the house and other roomes		16	0
one Cupborde, bedstede, Cheste and payntted clothes		33	0
Corne and malt in the house		50	0
linnen cloth yarne and towe		30	0
wollen cloth		6	0
beefe and bacon	3	0	0
butter and cheese		10	0
a hoope, a hopper, a winnowe sheete, bagges sieves basketts and flasketts		10	0
Saddles brydles and other furniture		5	0
Glasses cuppes and earthen potts			12
a lanterne hetchells, cardes and other little implements in and about the house		5	0
in money or Coyne	10	8	10
a debt owinge by Roger Cheswis specifyed in the will	11	0	0

Debts owinge to the decedent by Specialties:

	£	s	d
Timothie Buckley and George Gray	11	0	0
John Sale Thomas Grindley and Robert Lodmore	12	2	0
Gilbert Wollam	4	8	0
George Gray	4	0	0
John Evanson		44	0
Richarde Gorstilowe		22	0
Robert Greene		22	0
Robert Mundew		11	0
Robert Mundew more		11	0
Roger Wilkinson (11s. beinge payde)		11	0
Richarde Hall		22	0
John Sale		40	0
John Wollen	3	6	0
Raphe Tomise and William Wright		22	0
Raphe Tomise and William Wright more		22	0
Raphe Tomise and William Wright (10 s. beinge payde)		12	0
Raphe Tomise more		16	0
Summ	185	18	2
[*recte*	201	4	1]

NOTE: Badly water-stained on outside of parchment wrapper, making it impossible to read all of the endorsement without the aid of UV light.

Endorsement: Probated 15 May 1622; execution and administration granted to Joan Brooke, widow, one of the executors, Robert Corke, the other executor having utterly renounced the burden in person.

67. JOHN EGERTON OF (EAGLE HALL) NEWHALL, GENT.

S.Pr. 1622
W.T. 14 October 1619
Buried: 16 November 1619

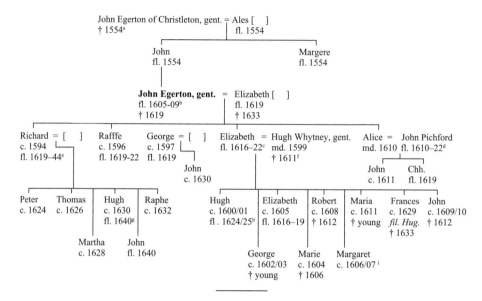

Will, sick.

First and principally I bequeath my sole in to the hands of almighty god trusting
to be saved and have the full pardon of all my sines for the merritt of Jesus Christ
my alone saviour & redeemer And *my bodie to bee buryed in the parish church
of Wrenbury* according to the disposing of myne Executores. Item my will is that

[a] See will of John Egerton of Christleton, gent., pr. 1554 /CRO.
[b] John Egerton was a juryman for the IPM held 6 April 1605 for Richard Cotton, esq., of
Combermere (see R. Stewart Brown, *Cheshire Inquisitions Post Mortem*, i. 146); John
Egerton, gent., was a copyholder in 1609 for 'Hall of Eagle'; Raffe Egerton was a freehold-
er 1609. Newhall Manor Court records declare for 1619: 'we find John Egerton gen' deceased
since last court & Rich Egerton his son next heir'.
[c] Received bequest of 10s. in will of James Brooke of Aston, pr. 1622 (will no. 66).
[d] Inventoried estate of Hugh Whitney of Coole, gent., 1611 (no. 34)..
[e] Made an indenture in June 1630 with John Bromhall and others; see will of John Bromhall,
pr. 1630 (will no. 82). In 1644 Richard Egerton surrendered Eagle Hall to Thomas
Cholmondeley of Cholmondeley.
[f] See inventory of Hugh Whitney, 1611 (no. 34).
[g] Hugh Egerton and his brother, John Egerton, are noted in the will of Thomas Manning, pr.
1640.
[h] Hugh Whitney of Coole was a juryman for the IPM for John Wicksted, esq., taken at Nantwich
18 January 1624/25; see R. Stewart Brown, *Cheshire Inquisitions Post* Mortem, iii. 171.
[i] Two younger daughters (without names) are noted in the administration of the estate of Mary
Whitney of Coole, widow, 1616 (no. 51).

Elizabeth my wife shall have the use and occupation of my goods what soever moveable and unmoveable during her naturall life and after the decease of my wife, my will is that George Eggerton my sone shall have the halfe of my sayd goods And the other halfe I leave to the diposing of my wife at her pleasure Item I give and bequeath unto my sone Richard Eggerton after the decease of my sayd wife the greatest brasse pott all the glasse and wainescott in my house: all my armor, all my husbandry ware as plooes, Carts, Cheens yokes, harrowes with such other appurtenances as doe belonge to such husbandry ware. Also I leave unto my soone Richard Eggerton one Chest wherin my Evidences doe lie, allsoe I bequeath unto my sone Richard Eggerton the longe Table in the parlor with the formes ther unto belonging Item I give & bequeath unto my sone George Eggerton foure Closes or parcelles of land in *Chrisleton*ᵃ, lying in the longe lowinds now in the teanure & occupation of Mr Sparke of Chester. Item I give & bequeath unto George Eggerton my sone the teythe of Tearton in the parish of Bunbury payinge unto my Cozen John Albersey the accustomed Rent. Item I give and bequeath unto my sone George Eggerton my wich house in the Nantwich with all the profetts and Comodityes there unto belonging To have, hould, and enioy, the fore sayd: Closes, Teith, and wichhouse, for and untill such tyme as the sume of tow hundreth pounds shalbee rune up & discharged unto the sayd George and after I leave them all to my sone Richard Eggerton. Item I give and bequeath to my sone George Eggerton one tenement lying in Cauden, within the parish of Tilston after the expiration of a lease now in the hands of Thomas Bebington. To have, hould, and enioy the same during the naturall life of the sayd George and noe longer. Item I leave unto my sone George Eggerton one Chamber in my house at Chrisleton wherin Richard Emeswouth now dwelleth, to have, hould, occupie and use the same during the naturall life of the sayd George. Item my will is, that my sone George Eggerton shall have meate, drinke and lodging with his mother and with his brother Richard, during his life if hee keepe him selfe sole and unmarryed. Item I give and bequeath unto my sone Raffe Eggerton two hundred pownds to be payd unto my sayd sone Raffe at such tyme as he shall set up his trade. And if the sayd two hundred pownds bee not payde unto my sayd sone Raffe at the sayd time when he shall ~~set~~ set up his trade Then I leave unto my sayd sone Raffe Eggerton three ten-nements which I purchased lying in Rowton and in Chrisleton. That is to say Thomas Pullfords, Hugh Culkin and John Hassellwalles, To have, and to hould, the three sayd Tennements. If the sayd some of Tow hundred pownds bee not payd at the tyme by mee set Downe unto the sayd Raffe and his heires for ever. Item I give and bequeath unto every one of my Grandchildren both of my daugh-ter Whytnay and my daughter Pichford to Each one of them a Crowne of gould. All the Rest and Resedeu of my goods moveable and unmoveable my debtes being payed, and my funerall expences discharded. I give and bequeath unto my wiffe and my sone George. Item I give and bequeath unto every one of my servants that have dwelled with mee one yeare at the tyme of my decease 10s.

Executors: the testator's two sons, Richard Eggerton, and George Eggerton.

ᵃ Original has *Chrislington*.

Debts owing to the Testator:

	£	s	d
Randle Holbrook	13	6	8

H. & S.
John Egerton

Witnesses: William Prince minister, Elizabeth Goughe.

Inventory: John Egerton late of Newhall, gent.

Taken: 18 November 1619

Prisers: William Allen, John Pichford, Richard Hall and Thomas Bebington.

	£	s	d
4 oxen	16	0	0
11 kyne and two Bulls	26	0	0
3 Calves		40	0
in Horsefleshe	11	6	8
in Swine	3	0	0
in Poultrieware		17	0
in necessaries of husbantrie	6	0	0
in Corne	25	16	0
in hay	5	0	0
the estate of Deverton Dayth	80	0	0
in Peavter	3	6	8
in Brasse	5	10	0
in Iron ware belonginge to the kytchen		30	0
in Treeneware		30	0
in Tables with the formes Cheists Cheres and stooles with a liverie Cubboard and a Closse presse	5	6	8
for a little gylt Salte and ten silver spoones	4	13	4
in Carpetts and Quishens		46	8
in Beddinge	14	10	0
in Bedsteeds	4	6	8
in Napperieware	8	0	0
Beeffe Bakon Butter and Cheese	6	0	0
in the Testators apparell	6	13	4
in Corne sowed		49	0
in Fewell	3	6	8
Some tot:	244	9	4

Executum cum protestacōne

Endorsement: Probated 28 May 1622; administration granted to George Egerton one of the executors named in will, with power reserved to the other executor until he comes.

68. EDWARD WHITTINGHAM OF BROOMHALL

S.Pr. 25 September 1622
W.T. 13 April 1612
Buried: 8 June 1622

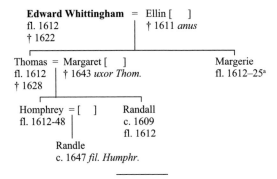

Will, sick.

First I bequeath my soule into the handes of Almightie god trusting by the merittes and bloudshedinge of Jesus Christe my alone Saviour to have remyssion of all my synnes And *my bodie to be buried in or at the parish Church of Wrenbury* according to the descrecon of myne executors. Item I geve & bequeath unto my sonne Thomas Whittingham one Cowe which is at hyre with John Whittingham or els 40s. of money whether he will Item I geve unto my said sonne Thomas ~~Whitingham~~ three Ewes and three lambes, my dun nagge, my Carte, plowes, harrowes and all the rest of my husbandrie ware as yokes Chaynes & all other such like tooles belonging to husbandrie, Item, I geve unto my said sonne Thomas the table standing in the howse with benches bemes shelves dishbord, one paire of bed stocks, a great Chest in the upper Chamber with Chaires & stooles Item I geve unto my said sonne Thomas one pott of brasse which is daylie used in the howse, and the least brasse pan of the three, one kettle, and skellett, and the one half of all the trayne ware and pewter Item I geve unto my said Sonne Thomas the one half of all my Corne both of that which is growinge and of that which I have bothe in the howse and barne with the one half of a Shoate and one half of all my bacon and half of all my poultrye ware and the one half of all the Iron ware. Item I geve unto my grandchildren Homfrey Whittingham and Randall Whittingham one browne twynter heyffer to be set to goe forward equallie betwixt them. Item I geve unto William Prynce Curate at Wrenbury one lambe the best that I have at his owne Choosing. All the rest and residue of my goodes moveable and unmoveable both within howse and without my debtes being paid I geve and bequeath unto my daughter Margerie Whittingham.

---

[a]   CRO Newhall Rentals, 1625.

Executors: the testator's son, Thomas Whittingham, and the testator's daughter, Margerie Whittingham.

H. & S.

Witness: William Prynce, mynister, Henrie Rutter.

Debts owed by the Testator:

	s	d
unto my sonne Thomas Whittingham	13	4

Inventory: Edward Whittingham of Broomhall.

Taken: 12 May 1622

Of: goodes Cattells & Chattells.

Prisers: John Cheswis gent., Henrye Rutter, Henrie Griffyths and Thomas Farres.

	£	s	d
two oxen price	10	0	0
two kyne	5	6	8
one mare and a nagge		33	4
15 sheepe		44	0
one swyne		8	0
the Poultrey		5	0
the Cartes ploughes yokes Chaynes harrowes working tooles and other things belonginge to husbandrie		40	0
Corne in the Barne and in the howse	7	0	0
Corne growing in the grounde	6	0	0
one stacke of old hey		5	0
all the brasse and pewter	3	13	4
gobiring Broches tongues & other Iron ware		10	0
the trayne or Cowperie ware		10	0
one great Chest in the howse		6	0
the bedding		20	0
sheetes & other napperie ware		20	0
twill sheets & sackes		5	0
ware and other fewell about the howse		20	0
towe in the howse		2	0
Cheese bacon & other victualls		23	0
one painted Cloth			6
his apparell		10	0
Some is	44	16	10

Endorsement: Probated 25 September 1622; administration granted to Thomas, son of the deceased, the executor named in the will.

69. ARTHUR STARKEY ESQUIRE OF WRENBURY

S.Pr. 25April 1623
Nuncupative will 28 September 1622
† 29 September 1622
Buried: 1 October 1622

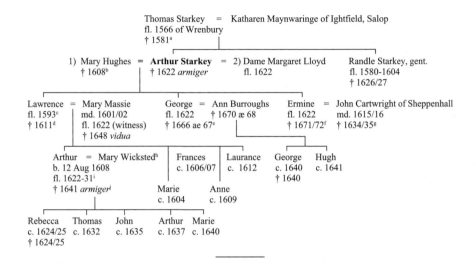

^a See Glover, *Visitations of 1566 and 1580*, p. 219; St George, *Visitation of 1613*, pp. 226-7. IPM 23 Eliz. No. 6 (TNA Ches 3/80).
^b Daughter of Charles Hughes of Hoult, co. Derby.
^c Received £10 per annum from estate of Randle Povall of Wrenbury, clerk, will pr. 1593 (will no. 10).
^d See inventory of Lawrence Starkie, exh. 1611/12 (no. 38).
^e Died 15 August 1666; buried at Wrenbury. A volume of notes found in Harleian MS 2151 (cited in Ormerod, *History of Cheshire*, iii. 207) gives the following inscription: 'Here lyeth the body of Geo. Starkey, youngest son of Arthur Starkey, esq., and Anne his wife, daughter to Thomas Burrough of Bickley, by whom he had issue six sons and two twine daughters. He died 15 Aug. 1666, aged 67 years. His said wife died 11 Nov. 1670, aged 68.'
^f Died 8 February 1671/72; buried at Wrenbury: see Harleian MS 2151 (cited in Ormerod, *History of Cheshire*, iii. 207) where the inscription is found: 'Jo. Cartwright of Sheppenhall, gen. died 16, and was buried 18 of Jan. 1634, and Ermine his wife died 8 Feb. and was buried 12, both in this place; she being the daughter to Arthur Starkey of Wrenbury, esq. anno Domini 1671.'
^g See inventory of John Cartwright of Sheppenhall, 1634/35 (no. 96).
^h Mary was the daughter of John Wicksteede of Nantwich, who was a witness to the will of Arthur Starkey and figured prominently in his Inquisition Post Mortem.
ⁱ Indicated as next of kin and heir of Arthur Starkie in the IPM; received bequest of 20s. from William Babington, 1630/31 (will no. 85); owed 10s. to Richard Cheswis, 1632/33 (will no. 93); bequeathed 3s. 4d. by Elizabeth Briscoe, 1632 (will no. 103).
^j A monument in the chancel at Wrenbury contains the inscription: *Arthur Starkey son of Lawrence buried 19 July 1641*; see Ormerod, *History of Cheshire*, iii. 207.

Will, 'his bodie much diseased and in verie weake estate'.

Memorandum:

That Arthure Starkie esquier late of Lankhayder in Kynnierch did upon the 28th daie of September Anno domini 1622 call certaine of his neerest and deerest frendes unto him and signified unto them that he founde his bodie much diseased and in verie weake estate and therefore said it was his will and mynde beinge fully resolved for the setlinge of his worldly estate to declare and utter before them his last will and Testament and desired them to beare testimonie thereof and then by wordes without writinge published his last will in Manner and forme followeinge First he Comended his soule into the handes of Allmightie God and his bodie to Christian buriall. Item It was his will and Mynde That his wiefe dame Margaret Lloyd should have all his goodes whatsoever And he did give them wholly unto her and said he was sorry he was not able to doe better for her And further it was his will and mynde that his debtes should be paied out of his landes in Shetton to which purpose he made a Lease for one Thousande yeares of the said Landes in Shetton to Roger Bellot and John Wicksteed to that use Wittnesses present at the utteringe publishing and Declaringe of his said last will the said John Wicksteede and Marie Starkie widdowe.

Inventory: Arthur Starkey Esquier of Wrenbury.

Taken: 9 November 1622

Of: goods Cattells and Chattells.

Prisers: John Edgeley, William Cartwright, John Bebington and Andrew Bebington.

By vertu of letters of administracōn given to dame Margeret Loyd (the Relict of the said decedent Arthur Starky esquier) from the Consistory Couert, the 25th daye of October 1622 authorizing her thereunto &c.

At the mansion house of the sayd decedent at Wrenbury in the diocease of Chester, in the parlor of the said house the stuffe and goods therin weare prayzed and valued as followeth

	£	s	d
one leaved table or drawing table and forme		12	4
one other little square table		8	0
one livery table			12
4 Cheyrs seated and backet with black leather		22	0
3 framed stooles Covered with blacke leather in the seat		10	0
4 low framed stooles covered with green cloth and needle worke of Cruell		16	0
6 framed ioynt stooles			13
one Iron grate of 4 barrs a fier shovell and a payer of tongs		5	0
on throwed Cheyre			20

2 womens pictures	4	0
3 frame with paynted armes	6	8
a table and chessmen		6

they doe estimate every Foote of Glasse in the saide roome at 5d.
the foote, and every yard of the said waynscoat at 20d. the yard,
but they stand in suspence wheather the saide waynscote and
glasse be moveble good or not

one iron rodd, rings and ould Curteynes		18

In the Closett within the sayd parlor

one great cupboord		20	0
one little cupborrd		5	0
one payer of bellows			14
one frame and 3 shylfes		3	0
one payer of table and men		3	0
18 venic Glasses		9	0
2 bells a great one and a lettle one		10	0
9 earthen paynted pannes and dishes		*[illegible]*	
2 Cases or Cupboords for wine Glasses		4	0
fouer Canns			8
one payer of snuffers			8
2 wax Candles			4
2 stone muggs			13
one Dusson of painted frute trenchers and theire box		3	4
3 Dussen and a halfe of trenchers		18	0
one panninge morter of allablaster		12	0
2 brasse weights in caseis	2	0	0
one payer of scales for gould weights in a brasen case		6	0
one brasen dustbox a leaden standish and a leaden diall		12	0
a payer of dubbing shers		12	0
one searer		18	0
on iron ringe a little Brandart and an iron hooke and some other ould iron			4
one wicker hamper			4
01*[sic; prob. 10 reversed]* books whereof som be very ould and little worth		10	0

In the loft or sellar above the parlor

the beddcase	4	0	0
one Arras hylling at	1	13	3
one white blankett		8	0
2 downe featherbedds two bowlsters one ould blanket two pilloes and one flockbedd	6	13	0

the testerne valens and Curteyns of the said beddcase	4	0	0
on livery cupboord and Carpett thereon		8	0
2 large cheyrs		26	0
one little cheare		5	0
2 buffett stooles		10	0
a little iron Grate of 3 barrs a fire shovell and a payre of tonges		5	0
for the waynscoat and Glasse in the said rome they estimate the same as formerly in the parlor			

In the closett in the sayd chamber

one little cupboord one deske one little frame to keepe books	4	0

In the Chamber over the buttery

one payer of Gould weights and an iron ladle		4	0
one standinge beddcase	10	0	0
one payer of Curleyes of stuff readd and white mixt		10	0
one Couerlett and and a blankett		6	8
one featherbedd and bolester		33	4
one trucklbedd		2	6
one hilling redd and yealew and a blanket		10	0
one other featherbedd and a bolster		13	4
one larder chest and cupboord together		10	0
one throwed cheyr		2	0
one ould stracon cheyr			6
for the Glasse in the said Chamber as formerly			

Item in the Chamber over the pantry

the bead of Canepey and Curteyns	2	13	4
one Arras bedd hylling		30	0
one featherbedd 2 bowelsters and a stockbedd and a pillow		50	0
one livery cupboord and a Carpett		3	4
one larder cheyre		4	0
2 little cheyrs and 2 buffett tooles		12	0
2 ould landirons			6
for the glasse and waynscott as formerly in other roomes at the same rate.			

In the upper garret above the loft over the parlor

2 ould chests	5	0
one ripple come		6

In the pantry

one table and frame	10	0
one cupboord	5	0
one binge and a chipping knife	2	6

one Dussin of varisht trenchers		12
one squar of waynscot beinge a cover of a chymneys harth	3	6
2 barrell frames	2	0
8 beere barrells and 2 hogeseads	10	0
one sheelfe		2

In the loft over the haule

one beddcase with Curteyns and valens of greene say		30	0
2 ould Irish Cadows and a blankett very ould		10	0
one fetherbed 2 bowlsters and an ould woolbedd	10	6	8
one little narrow truckelbedd one featherbedd one owld hillinge and one blankett		24	0
one lardge cheyre sealed and backed with green cloth		3	4
one other throwed cheyre			16
2 low little frame stooles			12
2 longe window Cushins		26	8
2 new Cushons of Arras		13	4
2 Cushens more of needle woorke		8	0
6 Cushens of Thrivin woorke		18	0
8 Cushens more thrivin woorke		13	4
3 ould Cushens more			12
one lardge arras carpett	5	0	0
one ould lardger lookinge glasse		3	4
one greene carpett of broadecloth		26	0
one other Greene Carpett of hoom worke		3	0
2 cupboord cloaths		6	0
2 fringed for windows, of stuffe		5	0
one presse or wyne chest		13	4

the lynen

11 payer of rounde or sumwhat worst sheets whereas some bee farr wearen	3	0	0
4 payer of flaxen sheets	3	0	0
5 table cloathes of some 5 yardes long flaxen		36	8
2 square table cloathes		10	0
3 lynen cupboord cloathes		5	0
11 towells		11	0
4 dusson of table napkins		10[£]s	0
5 pillow beers		11	0
a little square table and frame		3	0
3 trunks		26	8
3 Chests 2 greate ones & a little one		10	0
one little deaske		2	0
one little wicker baskett		6	0
one warming pan and a chandler of brasse		6	0

3 brushes 2 of brissills and an other of lent		18
one owld beaner		6
one blacke leathern box with scalle barrs of Iron		6
one payer of bellows an iron grate and a payer of twongs	2	0
2 pictures	2	0
one white wax candell		4

In the myddle chamber

one beddcase and bolstern	10	0
one ould featherbedd an ould bouwlster and an ould blanktett	8	0
one little trucklbedd	2	6
one other beddcase without a testern	6	0
one other featherbedd a bowelster a blankett and a Coverlett	26	8
one other featherbedd and an ould bowelster	51	0
one oulde Caddow and 3 owld couerletts	10	0
one presse	16	0
3 Curteyns	2	0

The pewter

4 lardg voyders	20	0
4 basens and 4 ewers	26	0
a dussen and a halfe of milling podege dishes	33	4
one dussen of platters of a lardger size	26	8
a dussen and a half of lesser size	20	0
56 salett dishes plates and broad sawcers	26	8
13 sawcers of a lesser size	3	4
a dussen of the smalest sawcers		18
8 podege dishes	2	8
4 pye plates	2	8
3 small basyns and a Colander	3	4
6 Chamberpotts	7	6
one gallepottlpott *[sic!]*	6	0
2 smaler gallepotts and a Jill	5	0
one ould quart pott without a lidd 2 lardge pynts and a salt	4	6

Brass

in the kitchen 4 lardge brass potts	8	0	0
2 of a lesser size		[ ]	0
2 possnetts		8	0
one brewing pan		13	4
4 panns of a lesser size		20	0
one lardge kettle		3	4
3 Chaffen dishes		10	0
one Skimer			18
one brasse pott lidd			4

one brazen ladell very lardge		18
one dobnett to warme water in	2	0
one other little brazen ladell		6
12 brazen kandilsticks of severall sorts	24	0
2 basters of brasse		6
one little kettell of brasse		16
one little pann		16
one little chamdler of brasse		6
3 drippinge panns	15	0
6 spitts		14
one payer of iron racks	20	0
2 payer of potthooks and 2 chayns and an iron barr across	6	6
one griddiron		12
2 frying panns a new one and an ould	3	0
2 skeletts very ould		16
one kleeuer		6
2 hackinge knifes		8
3 bradarts	3	0
one bread grater		12
one chandler of tyein *[tynne]*		6
one barr of iron used by the fier before drippinge panns		10
one morter	6	0
2 land Irons	4	0
one lantern		10
on flesh forke and a payer of tonngs	3	0
one beeff tubb	6	8
one ould Cupboord in the larder	10	0
4 sheelffs in the larder		12
5 Chestatts a salting basyn	3	4
4 Tubbs and 2 turnells very smale	5	0
one ould Churn and a Churn staff		12
2 droppers one longnette and ashins cheestandler	2	0
3 treen dishes 3 pottlidds and a little cann		12
one Past piele		6
one Trestle		8

In the haule

one Table and frame and two Forms	12	0
the long hall Frame and Foorms	16	0
one still to distill waters	2	0
3 spyns wheels or wooll wheels	5	0
1 Iron rake		6
3 iron wedges and an ax	3	4
one ould badd stead under stares	2	0

In the chamber over the kichen

one payer of valans and a standing beddcase		30	0
3 lardge chears and 2 buffett stooles		10	0
one little square table		2	0
one Cupboord and Cupboord cloth		10	0
one wicker skreene		2	6
6 payer of armor	10	0	0
2 drums		12	0
one owld desk		2	0

In the day house

one presse		6	8
one furnace		13	4
one owld beddstead			12
one cheese press with a stone			20
one ould Jacke for a Iorn spitt			6
one applgrate one owld saw a fire forke and a wreking iron		5	0
a great brons waight		6	8
a lardge longe chest		10	0
2 beddcasses		5	0
3 iron cheyns		6	0
one Lynbeck for distillinge		10	0
2 buckett irons a ty with for a wheel plow of iron a Copsow and a Copp pyn		20	0
a long table above the brewhouse		4	0
3 sheelves		2	0
4 pownd stones of lead			8

In the brew house

one furnace		20	0
one cooler and 2 bruinge coumes		20	0
one beeffe coume a turnell and a kneeding trough		12	4
7 hundred of quarrell bricks		14	0
the chickin trough and an owld brak			12
an ould mattock			6
2 swine troughes			12
14 thowsand of Bricke	7	14	0

In the kylln

2 Coulters and a hand saw		2	0
3 ould ploughs			18
3 payer of horscheynes		7	0
one payer of owld wheels with iron snetts		2	0
2 steeping Comes		26	8
the heyr very ould		3	4
one presse and ripple come		7	0
one loome to weave cushons		2	6

In the barn

9 score thrawe of Barly	at forty markes		
7 and fifty thrawe of Oates	at 17 nobles		
in peace a bushell			8
3 thrawe and a halfe of wheat		36	0
all the ry at a bushell		20	0
4 sett of spoaks for wayns		12	10
2 payer of little plough wheeles		3	6
3 axell trees		2	6
2 plough beames			8
9 fellies for carte wheels			18
16 planks or bass		5	4
5 syling nayles		10	0
2 rayles shorte in length			12
other finale clowen tymber of severy sorts		10	0
a Carte body and wheels		10	0
an owld wayne body and owld tunbrell and a slead		5	0

The Cattell

6 Bullocks	10	0	0
7 Heyfers	11	0	0
one Cow and a bull	3	16	8
one yonge filly	10	0	0

at Mrs Starkeys

one feather bedd and a bowlster	30	0
2 blanketts and on pillow	8	0
one other ould featherbedd one boulster and 2 blanketts	20	0
on cheyr throwed and a tornt *[turned]* forme	4	6
one brasse pott one bruing pann, a frying pann	21	0
one spitt 1 pottrak 1 payer of potthooks	2	0
2 pewter dishes very ould	2	0
one barrell		6
one little square table	2	0

the waynscoat is 6 score and 17 yardes the chaffe is 17 score
  and 19 foote, which was me asured by Richard Pigitt Clerke
  and Andrew Bebington.

[Sum   99 1918 912]
                     plus 40 marks & 17 nobles

Endorsement: Probated 25 April 1623.

Memorandum: [Nuncupative] Will of Arthur Starkie esquire deceased exhibited 29 October 1622; administration granted to Lady Margaret Lloyd widow of the deceased because no executor was named in the will; an inventory to be certified and exhibited by 1 January next [1622/23].

Inquisition Post Mortem[a].

Inquisition Post Mortem taken at Nantwich before Sir Richard Wilbraham knt. & bart., Hugh Mainwaring esq., escheator & Peter Danyell esq., feodary, to inquire after the death of Arthur Starkey who died on 29 September 1622.

Long before his death, the said Arthur Starkie was seised in fee of the manor of Wrenbury & of 20 mess., a watermill, 200 a. of land, 40 a. of meadow, 200 a. of pasture, 100 a. of wood, 300 a. of turbary & 16*d*. rent in Wrenbury; of 2 cottages, 20 a. of land, 20 a. of pasture in Woodcott; of a watermill, 200 a. of land, 40 a. of meadow, 200 a. of pasture in Stretton & a yearly rent of 108*s*. 4*d*. issuing from certain lands in Codington, Churton, Barton, Clutton, Farndon, Cardon, Hanley & Cuddington.

By his deed dated 18 August [1617] he enfeoffed John Cartwright gent. of the premises in Woodcott, to be void on repayment of £300 on 1 September 1623 by the said Arthur.

Being seised of the said watermill & premises in Wrenbury, by his deed of 23 September [1617] he demised to Mary Starkie, widow, late the wife of Lawrence Starkie, late son & heir of the said Arthur, the said mill, a close in Wrenbury called the New Ridding, & another there called the Little Casy Meadow for 60 years & the said Mary survives & dwells in Wrenbury.

On 24 September [1619] he enfeoffed John Wicksteed of the said manor of Wrenbury & the other premises there, to be void on payment of £200 on 1 February, 1621 or 1624 or 1631.

By indenture of 29 September, last past, he granted the manor of Stretton & premises to Roger Bellot & John Wicksteed for 1000 years.

The said manor of Wrenbury & premises there are held of Sir Thomas Savage kt. & bart. by knight service & 12*d*. rent & worth yearly (clear) £5.

The premises in Woodcott are held of George Cotton esq., service unknown & worth nothing because of the said enfeoffment.

The manor of Stretton & premises there held of Sir William Brereton kt., in socage, by fealty only & worth nothing for 1000 years for the same reason, & after worth yearly 40*s*.

The said Arthur Starkie died 29 September last past & Arthur Starkie gent., is his next of kin & heir & was aged 14 years on 12 August last past.

[a] R. Stewart Brown, *Cheshire Inquisitions Post Mortem*, iii. 80-2; 21 Jac 1, No. 12 (TNA Ches 3/98).

70. GEORGE CUDWORTH OF NEWHALL, GENT.ᵃ

S.Pr. 2 October 1624
Buried: 26 March 1623/24

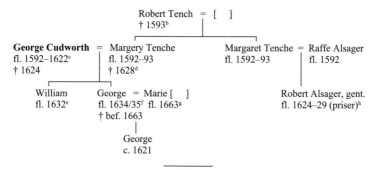

Robert Tench = [   ]
† 1593ᵇ

George Cudworth = Margery Tenche   Margaret Tenche = Raffe Alsager
fl. 1592–1622ᶜ   fl. 1592–93   fl. 1592–93   fl. 1592
† 1624   † 1628ᵈ

William   George = Marie [   ]   Robert Alsager, gent.
fl. 1632ᵉ   fl. 1634/35ᶠ fl. 1663ᵍ   fl. 1624–29 (priser)ʰ
              † bef. 1663

George
c. 1621

Inventory: George Cudworth, gent.

Taken: 27 March 1624, 22 James I

Of: goods Cattells and Chattells.

Prisers: Robert Alsager gent., Thomas Hamnett, Thomas Backhowse and Thomas
Madeley yeomen.

	£	s	d
two Oxen two steeres Three kyne with Calves and five other kyne	31	16	8
two heffers three stirks and a bull	9	1	4
a mare A nagge and two Colts	5	0	0
Three Swyne		15	0
in Pullen and poultery		6	0

ᵃ Cudworth's claim to gentry status was clearly based on his acquisition of property formerly
   belonging to his father-in-law, Robert Tench, whose IPM (1598) is given above (will no. 11).
ᵇ See will of Robert Tench, 1594 (will no. 11).
ᶜ George Cudworth figures prominently in the will and other testamentary documents of Robert
   Tench (will no. 11); in 1619 he made the inventory of Anne Kempe's goods etc. (will no.
   57); 1619 also a member of the IPM jury for Roger Bickerton, R. Stewart Brown, *Cheshire
   Inquisitions Post Mortem*, i. 17; 1622 on IPM for Robert Crockett (see ibid., i. 147); juryman in IPM for Richard Cotton, esq., of Combermere taken 6 April 1605 (ibid., i. 146); also
   the IPM for Hugh Massie of Denfield, gent., taken 4 January 1620/21 at Nantwich (ibid., ii.
   184); 1604 for Geoffrey Minshull (ibid., ii. 203); 7 October 1613 at Nantwich for John Starkey
   of Darley (ibid., iii. 84).
ᵈ Wife, Margery Tenche Cudworth, was aged 40 plus in 1593; fl. 1625 as widow; † 1628 as
   widow.
ᵉ TNA Ches 3/101: Livery 7 Car. 1, No. 3: William Cudworth, son of George, received livery
   of his father's properties.
ᶠ The George Cudworth who was a juryman in 1634/35 IPM is doubtless the son of George.
ᵍ Noted as widow of George Cudworth in will of Robert Cudworth of Newhall, pr. 1663.
ʰ Noted 1630 in will of John Bromhall of Sound as a party to an indenture entered into in June
   1630 by Bromhall (will no. 82).

	£	s	d
in Corne in the howse and uppon the ground	3	2	8
in hay	3	0	0
in Cartes waynes yokes plowes Iron bound wheeles wayne and plowe tymber husbandryware and ymplements of husbandryware	4	12	4
in hoole squared Tymber		10	0
A stand of bees		3	4
in muck and fuell		13	4
a weavers loome		4	0
a haire for the kyll		6	8
in Feather Bedds and Beddinge and Bedcloths and bedsteeds and the syled bed	8	19	4
in lynnen cloth and naperie ware & a peece of Kersie	3	5	2
in Brasse and pewter	4	12	10
A Cubbord and an Arke		8	8
in Iron ware about the fyre and in old Iron in the howse		12	6
in Treene and Cowperie ware and in Earthen potts cuppes and glasses		18	0
a muskett with furniture and the decedents Armour a crosse bowe & a stone bowe & other Artilery and two swords and staves		20	0
in Ioyned tables and frames formes Cheires stooles shelfes and loose bords		31	6
in Chests truncks and boxes		15	0
in Bacon beefe and whitmeate		33	4
in Becks measures sives and basketts		5	0
in wollen Cloth		6	0
Thomas Chester in debted by byll		24	0
Robert Podmore indebted by byll	4	15	10
John Tudman in debted by bond £3 6s. 8d. whereof is unpaid		26	4
Thomas Pursell by bond indebted	2	10	0
William Tench indebted by bond £10 whereof is unpaid	6	0	0
George Jenkinson and Thomas Jenkinson indebted by bond	5	17	4
silver spoones and silver Buttons		28	4
the decedents Apparrell and rydinge furniture	3	11	2
in money and gould in his purse	24	9	0
[Sum	114	412	100]

In desperate *[disparate]* debts which this Administrator will be accountable for as he receaveth and ad to this Inventorie as they come to his hands beinge Two hundred pounds or thereabouts.

Exhibitum cum protestacōn &c.

Endorsement: Exhibited 2 October 1624. *[No indication as to whom administration was granted].*

71. THOMAS PALIN OF WRENBURY FRITH, YEOMAN

S.Pr. 6 December 1624
W.T. 8 October 1624
Burial: None recorded at Wrenbury or Marbury

[Note: some moisture damage on outer edges of the document].

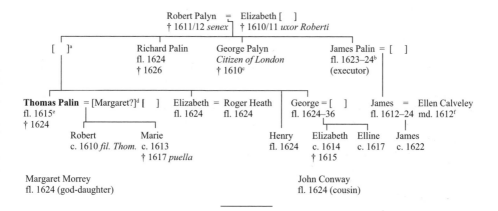

Will, sick.

First I Commytt and Commend my Soule into the hands of Allmightye God my maker and of Jesus Christ his onelye Sonne my alone Saviour and Redeemer in and by whose Death and passyon And by noe other meanes I hope to be saved and bee made partaker of his heavenly kingdome, And my bodye I Commytt to the Earth to be buryed in such a place and in such sorte as to my Exexutor here- after herein named shall seeme fitting And touchinge the disposall of such Worldly goods as yt hath pleased god of his goodnes to bestowe upon me I give Devyse and bequeath the same as hear after followeth Imprimis I give and Bequeath to my lovinge and kind Master Mr Thomas Cholmondleye Esquier the

---

ᵃ Wrenbury Bishop's Transcripts – Burials show a Thomas Palin on 23 May 1623 who may be the father of the testator, if it is not he himself with an incorrect date.
ᵇ James Palyn of Wrenbury Frith, gent., made an indenture with Wiliam Wicksteed in 1623, see IPM with will no. 78.
ᶜ See Introduction pp.xiii-xv, where George Palyn makes a bequest to the church at Wrenbury.
ᵈ Although Thomas Palin's wife is not mentioned by name, the fact that Margaret Morrey is noted as his god-daughter might argue for her given name being Margaret as well.
ᵉ Thomas Palin was a witness to the will of Robert Tenche in 1615 (will no. 45).
ᶠ William Fergusson Irvine, *Chester Licences*, i. 129: 26 October 1612, James Palen of Wrenbury and Ellen Calveley of Bunbury; at Harthill.

Some of six pounds to buy him a nagge Item I give and Bequeath to Mr Nicholls Preacher att Wrenbury the Some of Fyve pounds Item I give & bequeath to my loveinge Sister Elizabeth Heath the wief of Roger Heath the Some of £10 if he the said Roger Heath bee Cast or overthrowne in the Suyte wherein my uncle Richard Palyn now Doeth prosecute and sue him the sayed Roger Heath in the Exchequer of Chester, But if my said Brotherinlaw Roger Heath Doe overthrowe my said uncle Richard Palyn in the said Suyt then yt is my mynd and Will and I Doe give and Bequeath unto my said uncle Richard Palyn the Some of Fyve pounds and then the sayed Elizabeth my Sister to have but £5 insteed of the said Some of Tenne pounds Item I geve and Bequeath to the poore people of Wrenbury Parishe the some of fyve pounds to be payed by my Executor within halff a yeare after my Deceasce to be Distrybuted by the Discrecōn of my Executor Item I give and bequeath to Thomas Llewellyn of Whitchurch Wollen draper the some of £3 Item I geve and Bequeath to Robert Richardson of Whitchurch Shoemaker the some of 10s. Item I give and Bequeath to my goddaughter Margarett Morrey Tenne shillings Item I give and Bequeath to William Hall of Nantwich 12d. over and above the Debte which I owe him, to be Druncke in Wyne Item I give and Bequeath to Raphe Twisse of Wrenbury Frith Tenne shillings Item I give and Bequeath to Robert Massye of Nantwich Felt maker the Some of Tenne shillings whereof I truelye owe him 6s. 6d. Item I give and Bequeath to William Blooer of Baddiley Park Fower shillings. Item I give and Bequeath to my twoe Brothers Henrye Palyn and George Palyn to Eyther of them Fyve pounds if my uncle James Palyn thincke yt fittinge Item I geve and Bequeath to my lovinge Frend Robert Jones Cooke to my ladye Cholmondely one plaine Ruffe band and to Mr Hollford my Sword and my best Ruffband and to Ellis and Robert Dod all the rest of my Apparell that are there att Hollford Item I give and Bequeath to Richard Minshall 10s. And of this my Last Will and Testament I Doe nomynate ordaine and Appointe my loveinge uncle James Palyn my true and sole Executor Desyringe him to see the same truelye performed as my trust is hee will And I Doe leave unto him 20s. to make him a Ringe And alsoe I Intreate my said Executor to bestowe out of my goods the Some of Tenne pounds att my Buryall And all the rest and residue of my goods whatsoever my debts beinge payed and the legasies hearby geven and Bequeathed and my Funerall Expences beinge all payed and Discharged I give and bequeath to my lovinge Cosin James Palyn sonne of the said James my uncle and executor.

H. & S.
Thomas Palin

Witnesses: Ellen Damold her marke, Randle Dawson.

Executor: Testator's uncle, James Palyn.

Debts owed by the Testator:	£	s	d
To Robert Dod		10	0
To my Cosin John Conway		20	0

Endorsement: Probated 6 December 1624; administration granted to the sole executor named in the will.

72. JOHN PATRICKE OF CHORLEY

S.Pr. 20 June 1626
Nuncupative will dictated about 16 March 1625/26
Buried: 18 March 1625/26

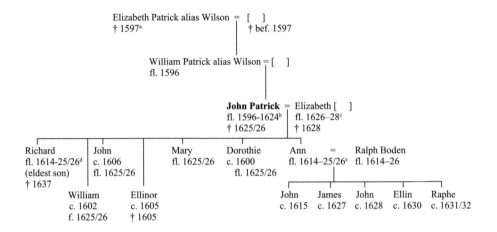

Allegation:

20th June 1626

Testamentary business or probate of the nuncupative testament or nuncupative last will of John Patrick, deceased, promoted by Elizabeth Patrick, widow, relict of the said deceased, and John Patrick his son.

On which day Barkley, by name Proctor, and as lawful Proctor of the said Elizabeth Patrick and John Patrick by every better way, method and form of law to which, according to law he was and is bettere and more effectively able and bound in whatsoever manner to follow and to every sound effect of law and fact whatsoever in accordance with the underwritten, says, alleges and in these writings in law propounds jointly, severally and articulately as follows.

[a] See will of Elizabeth Patrick alias Wilson, pr. 1597/98 (will no.15).
[b] Witness to will, priser of goods, and debtor of Humphrey Wilson, 1602 (will no. 16); priser for Roger Broome's estate, 1606 (will no. 21); noted as owing Oliver Briscoe £3 6s., due at midsummer, will proved 1630 (will no. 80).
[c] Noted as a widow in inventory of Randull Hare, 1628; Hare had lent her two hundred [weight] of hay (will no. 76).
[d] Richard Pattrick was bondsman for the marriage of his sister Ann to Ralph Boden in 1614.
[e] William Fergusson Irvine, *Chester Licences*, i. 172: 10 November 1614 to Ralph Boden of Over parish, Cheshire, and Ann Pattrick, spinster, of Wrenbury parish, at St Bridget's, Chester.

1. Firstly, namely, this party propounds and it is articulated that the aforesaid John Patrick being of sound mind and perfect memory, on or about the seventeenth day of March AD 1625 last past, with a mind of testifying nuncupatively, in words and or in writings, made and declared his last testament containing in it his last will and, concerning his goods rights and credits, fully willed bequeathed and disposed in all things and for all as is contained in a certain document annexed to these presents and acknowledged and recognised for his testament and last will in the presence of several trustworthy witnesses specifically sought and requested for that purpose; and afterwards he died. And he propounds jointly, severally and concerning whatsoever.

2. Item that all and singular the premises were and are true, public, well known, manifest and equally renowned and of and concerning the same public speech and opinion has been, and is, troubled. And he propounds as above.
Whereof proof being made &c. this party prays right and justice to be done and administered to him with effect and also for the assets and value of the said nuncupative testament or nuncupative last will annexed to these presents to be pronounced, judged and declared and also to grant and allow Letters of Administration of the goods, rights and credits of the same, together with nuncupative testament which is annexed to the same and according to the effect of the same, to the aforesaid Elizabeth Patrick and John Patrick according to the demand of law in this manner: And furthermore what shall be of law and reason to be done, the premises propounding &c. but in so far as &c. hitherto &c. with the benefit of law in all things always safe, humbly imploring, O Lord Judge, your office in this regard.

Endorsement: Allegation dated 20 June 1626, with nuncupative testament of John Patrick deceased annexed to the same.

Witness Statements:

Randull Hare of the chapelry of Wrenbury, aged 54 years or thereabouts, having known well the deceased before his death, was examined concerning the allegation and the nuncupative testament annexed to the same, about which he is being produced, and says that upon or about the sixteenth day of March last past, this deponent was sent for by the deceadent to come unto him which he accordingly did, & imediately after he came to the deceadent he the said deceadent tould him this deponent that he had sent for him to bee a witnes att the declaringe of his will to theme that hee might heere after of occasioned served testifie the same, and then the deceadent beinge of perfec memory & good understandinge, did nuncupatively in words without wrytinge utter & declare his will & minde as followeth or the like in effectt viz: he did give & bequeath unto his eldest sonne Richard Pattricke, and to his daughter Anne wife of Raphe Boden 12d. a peece And he did will & leave that all the rest of his goods Creditts & Cattalls whatsoever his debts beinge first paid & discharged should bee equally divided into two parts, the one part whereof he did give & bequeath unto Elizabeth his wife, and the other part or halfe he did give & bequeath to his fower younger Children William, John, Mary & Dorothie Pattricke to bee equally devided amongest them. Present at the primisses this deponent, the deceadents wife, Mary Pattricke one of his the deceasts daughters & Alice Grindley of the age of 27 years. To the second [article] he says that the [statement] predisposed by him was true.

Randull Hare

Maria Pattricke of the chapelry of Wrenbury, 27 years of her age or thereabouts was examined concerning the allegation and nuncupative testament aforesaid, and says that upon or about the sixteenth day of March last this deponent was present, when the deceadent her late father beinge of [sane?] memory & understandinge did nuncupatively in words without wrytinge utter and declare his last will & testament in manner & forme followeinge or the same in effect viz: hee did give & bequeath unto his eldest sonne Richard Pattricke & Anne wife of Raphe Boden 12d. a peece, And all the rest of his goods Cattalls & Chattells (his debts beinge first paid and discharged) hee did will & bequeath to bee devided into two equall parts, one parte whereof he did give & bequeath unto Elizabeth his wife, And the other halfe part he did give & bequeath unto his fower younger Children videlicet William John, Mary, and Dorothy Pattricke to bee equally devided amongst them. Present at the primisses this deponent, her precontest Randle Hare, the deceadent, his wife beinge mother to this deponent, and Alice Grindley of the age of 27 years. To the second [article] she says that the [statement] predisposed by her was true.

Memorandum That upon Thursday being the 16th day of March last Anno domini 1625 John Pattricke late of Chorley within the Chapellry of Wrenbury in the county of Chester deceased being visited with sicknes but yet being of perfect mind and memory did by words without writing make & declare his last will concerning his goods and chattels and did will, give bequeath and dispose of the same as followeth, viz: Imprimis hee did give & bequeath unto his eldest sonne Richard Pattrick and to his daughter Anne wife of Raph Boden 12d. apeece And all the rest and residue of his said goods and Chattells, his debts and the charge of his buriall being first paid and discharged hee did will to bee devided into two equall parts, The one halfe or part hereof hee did give and bequeath unto Elizabeth Pattricke his wife, and the other halfe or part hereof hee did give and bequeath to William John Mary and Dorothy Pattricke his younger Children to bee equally devided betweene them. And the premisses were spoken and done in the presence of certen Credible witnesses whom the said decedent had sent for or requires to bee present at the same.

Witnesses: Randull Hare, Marie Patricke.

Inventory: John Pattricke of Chorley, yeoman.

Taken: 27 April 1626, 2 Charles I

Of: goods Cattells and Chattells.

Prisers: William Bebington, William Hare, John Woleftodfen, Randull Hare and Thomas Frenche.

	£	s	d
Eight kine	24	0	0
foure bullocks	11	6	8
four twinter heffers	7	13	4

twoe stirke Calves	2	0	0
one twinter bulloke	3	0	0
foure swine		25	0
Poultrie		11	3
one silver Cupp and sixe silver spoones	5	0	0
in beddinge	8	10	0
new wollen Cloth	2	0	0
twoe table Carpetts		10	0
three Cushines		3	0
in clappery ware	3	3	4
bedsteeds	2	0	0
one presse and Chest twoe boxes & three ioyned cheares	2	0	4
one Cubbard		7	0
foure tables		22	0
bench sileinge Cheares and stooles		12	0
three Coffers		6	8
pott brasse and pann brasse	2	10	0
in Pewter		2	0
a morter a pestell and twoe Candlesicks		5	0
in Corne		2	0
in Coperie ware & erthen ware	2	0	0
in yarne and toe		18	0
in bacon		20	0
in Cheese		3	0
three corne basketts		3	0
Cheese bowel dishbords shilves cheese presse & waigths		20	0
spinninge wheeles		3	0
Iron ware	2	0	0
in sacks		2	0
Cartropp packillant cart saddle		3	0
Carts plowes Cart tymber ladders forme tooles grindlestones			
all the tymber about the howse and fewell	2	10	0
mucke		5	0
debts due to the testator	3	0	0
books & his weareing appell		30	0
	—	—	—
[Sum	80	264	31]

Endorsement: Nuncupative testament together with an Inventory of the goods of John Patrick deceased, of Chorley, whilst he lived, exhibited 20th day of September AD 1626 and because no executor was named in the same therefore Letters of Administration were granted of the goods of the aforesaid deceased with the aforesaid testament to the same annexed, to William and John Patrick sons of the said deceased . . .

73. RANDLE STARKIE OF WRENBURY, GENT.

S.Pr. 8 February 1626/27
W. 2 July 1624
Buried: 9 February 1626/27

```
Thomas Starkey  =  Maud, dau. of Sir John Maynwaringe
  of Wrenbury Hall

        John Starkey   =   Dorothy (nicknamed Douce), dau. to Sir John Warburton of Arley
          of Wrenbury Hall
          † 1541ᵃ

              Thomas Starkey   =   Katharen Maynwaringe of Ightfield, Salop
                fl. 1566 of Wrenbury
                † 1581

Jane Williamson alias Wade  ⚲  Randle Starkie  =  Elizabeth Barke = 2) John Sheen    Arthur Starkey, esq.
fl. 1604                         fl. 1580-1604      md. 1601      md. 1629ᵇ      † 1622 armiger
                                 † 1626/27          fl. 1626/27
                            Joseph Starkie
                            c. 1604
                            fl. 1626/27
                            (base)
```

Will, sick.

First, [I commend my] soule into the hands of almighty god, trusting onely by thee meritts & precious blood sheeadinge of Jesus Christ my alone Saviour to have remission of all my sinnes and *my bodie to bee buried in the parishe Church of Wrenbury* accordinge too the discrecōn of myne Executors Item I give & bequeath unto Joseph my servant now dwellinge with mee begotten of the bodie of Jane Williamson alias Wade 6s. 8d. of Currant money to bee paid unto the said Joseph by my executors within one twelve moneth next after my decease Item I give & bequeath unto Margarett Bromhall daughter of Elline Spencer 3s. 4d. to bee paid her within one halfe yeare next after my decease, All the rest & residue of my goods Cattells & Chattells moveable & unmoveable debts & whatsoever is or may bee due to mee (my debts beinge paid & my funerall expencs discharged) I give & bequeath unto Elizabeth Starkie my wife.

Executor: the testator's wife, Elizabeth Starkie.

ᵃ IPM: TNA Ches 3/68.
ᵇ William Fergusson Irvine, *Chester Licences*, iii. 163.

Witnesses: Thomas Harwar, Thomas Graye.

Randle Starkey
(his signature)

Inventory: Randull Starkey of Wrenbury, gent.

Taken: 15 August 1626

Of: goods & Cattells.

Prisers: William Cowper, Thomas Taylor and Randull Weaver.

	£	s	d
fower kyne	8	0	0
one stirke heifer		20	0
two Calves		20	0
two marres & one nagg	4	0	0
one hogg		10	0
poultrie		5	0
hay		30	0
Corne groweing in the Milne feild rye oats & filches	3	6	8
Corne groweinge in George Claytons feild rye		13	4
Corne groweinge in the long sandy Crofte rye barlie & french wheate		20	0
Corn groweinge in the other sandy Crofte pease & oates		8	0
Corne groweinge in the other sandye Crofte barlie		40	0
Corne groweinge in Margarets Wolls Crofte barlie		13	4
three feather bedds		20	0
three boulsters & pillowes		6	8
6 blanketts & Coveringes a paire of greene Curtaines & Ireon rodds		13	4
two standinge bedds		10	0
three paire of bedstocks		5	0
ten paire of sheets		30	0
table Clothes napkines a dosen & halfe pillowe beares		10	0
2 brase potts one bigger clothe lese		10	0
one pan 2 posnetts a skellett a brasen morter and a pestle a skinner two Chafeinge dishes 2 Candlestickes 2 rydinge stirropps		14	0
a paire of brasen skalles & waights		5	4
gould weights			12
one bigger pan which Margarett Fleete laid to pawne		9	0
a basen & Ewer		2	6
15 peece of pewter 2 salts 2 Candlesticks & eight spoones		10	0
two Cofers of Tinn		5	0
5 other Cofers a deske a box fower small boxes & a shelfe which they stand on		13	0
one long table with a frame		6	8
6 ioyned stooles of walnutt tree		8	0

one square table with a frame	3	4
one other table		12
one long table without a frame	2	6
one forme		6
one tresle		6
another forme		4
4 shelves	2	0
one frame to sett Cheeses on with 5 shelves	5	0
for hanginge bords	2	6
two planckes to make a table		12
fower bords & 2 tresles in the milke house loft		16
12 other bords for necessarie uses	3	4
one standinge Cuppord		20
one kneadinge troughe with a Cover	3	4
one kneadinge turnell & a boullinge pipe		20
one Cheese presse	2	6
2 barrells one fir kine & three stonnes	4	0
one Closse bouke & a little Close bouke & 2 priggens	2	0
7 milke basens & one eshen	3	0
eight Cliespitts [?] one turninge dishe & one presinge bord	5	0
5 noggens 4 Cannes 2 booles & 5 dishes		16
two lond Ireones a fire shovell & an aple grate	3	4
one payre of tongs potracks pothooks 2 fryinge pans & a Cresselt	2	6
one paire of goberts 2 piltts a hackinge knife & a shreadinge knife	5	0
2 billes one hatchett one axe one shovell one mattocke a turfe spade a gorese axe & hopp h*[damaged]*	4	0
one rake with Ireon teeth one trovell & one Chese forke	9	0
3 nogers one plane one square one spoake shave 3 Chisells one gourge one markeinge Ireon 3 hamers 2 hand sawes a paire of pinsorres & 3 wimble bitts	5	0
one pol axe a dagger & a locke	3	4
a paire of tables & table men	2	6
one lanthorne		8
one old sithe a muck yelve [?] 2 harrowes one plowe a paire of plowe Ireons two horse Combs	3	4
one Carte a mucke Cart 2 bushells & 2 Clipps	20	0
Cheeses	20	0
6 basketts & 6 earthen potts		12
one Churne & a Churne staffe		6
4 paire of horse geares & a paire of tuggs	2	0
3 halters one Coller a packlent a pillin & a Cart rope	3	4
fower Ireon wedges		16
a grid Ireon a ticknall drippinge pan & 3 dishes		10

2 pickyelves & one short ladder		6
one Cheare 4 stooles & 2 dishbords	3	0
measure hoppes		12
a dishrate [?] a payre of bellowes & a ladre		7
2 potlidds		2
4 Cushiones		6
one brondrett a hetchell a ripple Combe		20
3 spininge wheeles & a reele	2	0
3 paire of Cards		9
hempe & Flaxe	5	0
yarne beinge but round	2	0
2 pound of woolen yarne	2	0
fire fuell	2	6
mucke	6	8
one bottle & 2 glase bottells		3
a paire of wooden waights & a brake		6
5 plowe beames & 4 throcks	2	0
4 old sacks		12
my apparell	20	0
the whole sume is	41 12	1

Witnesses hereof: Thomas Graye, 1626, William Cowper, Thomas Taylor and Randull Weaver.

Endorsement: *[Very badly damaged]* Probated 8 February 1626; administration granted to the sole executrix named in the will sworn in person by Master [ ] . . .

74. GEORGE DICKINS OF NEWHALL

I.Pr. 8 March 1626/27
W.T. 27 May 1625
Buried: 28 January 1626/27

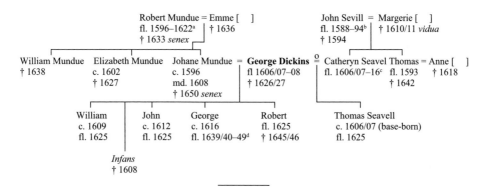

Will, sick.

First I comitt and bequeath my soule into the hands of allmighty god my maker and redeamer and *my body to be buried in the parish church yard of Wrenbury* Item I give and bequeath all my goods and Chattles moveable and unmoveable unto Johane Dickins my wyfe the one halfe yf shee keepe her selfe wydow and unmarried and the other parte to my two sonnes John Dickins and William Dickins

---

ᵃ Owed two separate debts of 11s. to estate of James Brooke, will pr. 1622 (will no. 66).
ᵇ Noted as owing debt of 15s. to John Woodfaine, will pr. 1588 (will no. 7). In 1593, Randle Povall stated that he held land of John Seavill and his son, Thomas (will no. 10). Owed Humphrey Bickerton debt of 4s., will pr. 1594 (will no. 12).
ᶜ J.H.E. Bennett and J. C. Dewhurst, compilers and editors, *Quarter Sessions Records, with Other Records of the Justices of the Peace for the County Palatine of Chester 1559-1760*, RSLC, xciv (1940), p. 59, contains a letter dated 27 April 1607, from George Cotton and Arthur Starkey to Robert Whytebye, clerk of the peace at Knutsford:
> Mr. Whytby, there was a recognizance acknowledged before us by Thomas massye and John Sale for the dischargeing the parish of Wrenburye of a bastard childe supposed to be gotten by George Dicken upon the bodye of Catherine Sevell which recognizance together with examinacon is returned unto the Sessions, and since the sending thereof, the parties bound have brought before us the father of George Dicken who hath together with certaine friends entered into newe recognizances to discharge the said parish of the childe if it be lawfully fathered upon Dicken or else to bring in George Dicken to appeare at the next Sessions after this Sessions, therefore wee desire that the said Massye and Salle may be released of their recognizance, and have sent money by this bearer for their discharge, whereof praying you not to ffayle. Combermere 27 April 1607.

Katherin *Sivill*, daughter of John *Sivell*, received a heifer calf in 1616 as a bequest in the will of John Bickerton (will no. 48).
ᵈ George Dickins was witness to the will of Edmund Bower of Chorley, pr. 1649.

equally to be devided betweene them moreover I Constitute and ordaine that my said wyfe Johane shall have the goverment and oversight of my said goods & Cattalls and also of my two children untill the come to the age of one and twen-ty yeres and then my said children to receive their said porcōns as aforesaid Further I ordaine that yf my wyfe Johane Dickins doe marry that my goods shalbe dev-ided into three equall parts & my said wyfe to have but one parte theirof and my said sonnes William and John to have the other twoe eaich one a parte equally devided Item I give and bequeath out of theise my goods unto my sonne Roberte Dickins 18d. and to my sonne Thomas Seavell 12d.

Executors: the testator's wife, Johane Dickins, and John Ravenscroft.

Overseer: Thomas Taylor.

H. & S.

Witnesses: Peter Ledsame, Richard Gueste.

Debts due to the Testator & unpayed:

	s	d
Richard Meakin for a Cowhyer	9	0
Richard Bucher		12

Debts owed by Testator:

	£	s	d
to Douse Hall	2	10	0
to Elizabeth Simson	1	6	0

Inventory: George Dickins of Newhall.

Taken: 6 March 1626/27

Of: goodes & Cattells.

Prisers: John Ravenscrofte, Thomas Tealor and Thomas Ravenscrofte.

	£	s	d
his wearinge Aparrell		6	8
all his Beddinge	1	2	8
Sheetes & Linnen		12	0
new Cloth in the house		12	8
Brasse & pewter		18	0
Butter & Chese & bacon		6	8
Tryne ware		6	0
Bedstockes boards formes shelves stooles & an old cubboard a cheire		9	0
ticknall ware			6
toe & yarne		4	0
Iron ware		4	4

two wheeles & two quishins		1	0
corne in the house		1	0
a cocke & a hen		1	0
a packsadle wountye & a brake		2	0
hey & mucke		5	0
an old mare		13	4
two kyne & a stirke heffer calfe		7	0
a bill of debt & money oweing him & money in his purse	2	3	6
the totall somme is	15	8	4
[*recte*	8	16	4]

Endorsement: Probated 8 March 1626; administration granted to Joan, widow of the deceased, one of the executors named in the will, with power reserved to the other executor until he shall have come.

75. THOMAS SHROWBRIDGE OF NEWHALL, YEOMAN

S.Pr. 10 March 1626/27
Nuncupative will made 1 March 1626/27
Buried: 3 March 1626/27

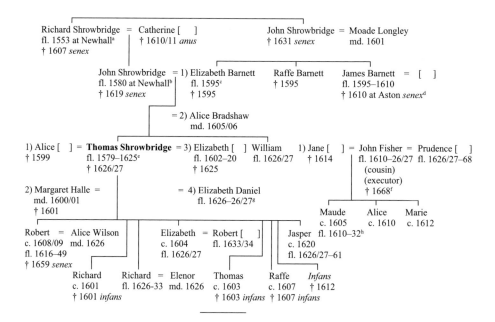

Allegation: 6th day of March (in the style of the English Church) AD 1626.

Before the venerable Mr Thomas Stofford, Bachelor of Laws, Official Principal of the Consistorial Court of Chester lawfully deputed.

Business of the proving of the testament or nuncupative last will of Thomas Shrowbridge, deceased, of Newhall in the parish or Chapelry of Wrenbury.

---

[a] CRO Newhall Manor Court Rolls.
[b] CRO Newhall Manor Court Rolls.
[c] See will of Raffe Barnett, pr. 1595 (will no. 13).
[d] See will of James Barnett, pr. 1610 (will no. 29).
[e] Thomas Shrowbridge fl. 1579 and 1586 as juror at Newhall Court; Richard and Thomas Shrowbridge fl. 1598 as tenants of Newhall Manor; CRO Newhall Manor Court Rolls.
[f] See will of John Fisher, pr. 1668/CRO.
[g] William Fergusson Irvine, *Chester Licences*, iii. 73: 29 September 1626 to Thomas Shrowbridge and Elizabeth Daniel, spinster of Wrenbury parish, at Wrenbury; bondsman was John Fisher. The fact that Elizabeth is noted as Thomas's relict is a clear indication that the marriage did indeed occur.
[h] See will of James Barnett, pr. 1610 (will no. 29); 1616 as *Margaret* Fisher.

On which day Humphreys by name Proctor, and as lawful Proctor of John Fisher, one of the executors named in the testament or nuncupative last will of the aforesaid deceased, by every better way, method and form of law to which, according to law he was and is better and more effectively able and bound thence in whatsoever manner to follow and to every sound effect of law and fact whatsoever, says, alleges and in these writings in law propounds **That** the said Thomas Shrowbridge being of sound mind and perfect in his memory, the day, month and year specified in the writings affixed to these presents, or thereabouts, with a mind of testifying and distributing his goods, rights, credits and chattels, composed, declared, *[damaged]* and expressed his testament, containing in it his nuncupative last will, in which concerning his goods and assets, in speech and by writings, he gave, willed, bequeathed and nuncupatively disposed in all things and for all as is described and contained in the writings annexed to these presents, or similar in effect; and afterwards he died. **Which** allegation this party propounds jointly and severally and prays the same to be admitted and for the value and meaning of the testament or nuncupative last will exhibited to be pronounced, judged and declared [and also] to grant and allow execution of the same and administration of all and singular the goods, rights, credits and chattels of the aforesaid deceased to John Fisher one of the executors named in the same testament and last will (the other executor completely renouncing for himself the acceptance of the burden of execution) **And furthermore**, whatever shall be of law and reason in the premises and in whatsoever concerning them, to be done, determined and judged, **Which** premises this party propounds and prays to be done jointly and severally not obliging himself to proving all and singular the premises nor to the burden of surplus proof, concerning which he protests, but insofar as he shall have proved in the premises hitherto he may obtain the benefit of law in everything always preserved, humbly imploring your office, O Lord Judge, in all things.

Memorandum That upon the First daie of March Anno domini 1626 Thomas Shrowbridge of Newhall in the County of Chester yeoman beinge in perfecte sence and memorie did by wordes without writinge utter and declare his last will and Testament in manner and forme following Imprimis he did give and bequeath unto his sonne Robert Shrowbridge those seaven kine that bee at Richard Edgleys and £3 of that money for Consideracōn of £20 Item he did give to Elizabeth his wieffe two kine called Filboule and Bendeboe and one Calfe with a white face and the Canopie bedd that stands in the lofte Item he did give to his sonne Richard Shrowbridge three kine and one Calfe and the best Mare Alsoe all the husbandrie goodes, Also the bedd that the testator then laid in and the table in the house and all the bourds and shilfes in or aboute the house. Item he did give unto his daughter Elizabeth the Ioyned bedd in the Chamber and one silver spoone. Item he did give unto his doughter Mary one Cowe called Faireheade Item he did give unto Ellenor his doughter in lawe one silver spoone. Item he did give unto the said Elizabeth his wief 50s. to be paid unto her yearely by his sonne Richard soe longe as she keppe herselfe sole unmarried and in his name Item All the rest of his goodes (his debtes beinge paid, his Legacies beinge discharged and his funerall expences fulfilled) he did give and bequeath to be devided equally amongst Roberte Shrowbridge Elizabeth Shrowbridg Mary Shrowbridge and Jasper Shrowbridge his Children.

Executors: the testator's brother, William Shrowbridge, and the testator's cousin, John Fisher.

Wittnesses at the uttering: Robert Shrowbridge, Richard Barrowe, Prudence Fisher, Alice Shrowbridge and Richard Shrowbridge.

Witness statements: Statements of witnesses taken and exhibited the 6th day of March AD 1626 concerning the nuncupative testament or last will and allegation affixed to the same of Thomas Shrowbridge, deceased, of Newhall in the parish or Chapelry of Wrenbury.

Robert Shrowbridge of the parish or Chapelry of Wrenbury, 36 years of age or thereabouts, produced as a witness, sworn and examined of and concerning the aforesaid allegation and the writings relating to the nuncupative testament or last will of the aforesaid deceased exhibited, says that Thomas Shrowbridge the deceadent beinge of perfect and sane memory yett being visited with sicknes did upon Thursdaie last past being the first daie of this instant moneth of March Dispose of his goods and Chattells of his owne accord without the interogacōn or Mocōn of any one as in the will exhibited annexed to the allegacōn or taken in effect vizt his expressed first hee did give & bequeath unto his sonne Robert Shrobridge seaven kyne that were at Richard Edgleys of the Hall of Moore & £3 of Money in Consideracōn of £20 pounds that were due unto him the said Roberte from him the deceadent Item hee did leave & bequeath to his wife two kyne one Called Feelbowe & the other Benbowe & one Calfe with a white fase a Canopie bed that stood in the lofte & out of two peeces of Cloth eyther peece, three yards & one silver spoone and 50s. a yeare soe longe as she kept his name And to his sonne Richard three kine & one Calf & the best Mare & all his husbandrie goods & the bedd he then laye in & the table in the house & all the bords and shelves in or about the house to his daughter Elizabeth one Ioyned bed in the Chamber & a silver Spoone unto his daughter Mary one Cowe Called Fayrehead to his daughter In lawe Elenor one silver spoone And All the rest & residue of his goods hee Did give devise & bequeath (his debts Legacies & funerall expences beinge discharged) To his fowre Children Roberte Elizabeth Mary & Jasper Shrowbridge equally amongst them to be devided and did appoint executers of the same will his Brother William Shrobridge & his Cosine John Fisher beinge as he hath deposed of good & perfect memory for hee spake orderly & sensibly as ever hee did in his last present at the publishinge & declaringe of the will & deposed this deponent and Richard Shrowbridge this deponent Contest and alsoe Richard Barrow Prudence Fisher & Alice Shrobridge and otherwise knows nothing to depose with certainty.

Signum Robert X Shrobridge marke

Richard Shrowbridge of the parish and Chapelry of Wrenbury 23 years of age or thereabouts, produced as a witness, sworn and examined of and concerning the testament and allegation aforesaid, says that the deceadent Thomas Shrowbridge beinge visited with Sickness did upon Thursdaie last past of His owne accord utter & declare his will & mynde concerninge the disposall of his goods & Chattells as followeth or the like in effect vizt First hee the deceadent did give & bequeath unto Roberte Shrobridge his the deceadents sonne seaven kyne that were at Richard Edgleys of the Hall of Moore & £3 of Money in consideracon of £20 pounds he had in his hands of the said Robertes Unto his wife Elizabeth two kyne one Called Filbowe & the other Benbowe & one Calfe with a white face & out of two peeces of Cloth either peece three yards one silver spoone & 50s. a yeare soe longe as shee kept her in his the deceadents name to this deponent three kyne & one Calfe & the best mare & all the husbandry goods the bed he lay in the table in the house & all the bords & Shielfes to his daughter Elizabeth one Ioyned bed in the Chamber & one silver spoone unto his daughter Mary one Cowe Called Fayrehead to his daughter in lawe Elenor one silver spoone And all the rest & residue of his goods hee did devise give & bequeath to his foure Children Roberte Elizabeth Mary & Jasper Shrowbridge (his debts legacies & funall expences payd) equally to be divided amongest them & did appoynt executors of his said will his Brother William Shrobridge & John Fisher beinge then of good Memory sence & understandinge as ever hee was to this deponents knowledge present at the utteringe & declaringe of the Will predeposed this deponent & his precontest Roberte Shrowbridge Richard Barrow Prudence Fisher & Alice Shrowbridge And otherwise knows nothing to depose with certainty.

Richard Shrowbridge

Inventory: **Thomas Shrowbridge of Newhall, yeoman.**

Taken: 5 March 1626/27

Of: goods and Cattells.

Prisers: John Ravenscrofte, Richard Cartwright, George Hall and Thomas Taylor.

	£	s	d
seaven kine at the hall of Moore	22	3	4
Twentie eight kine at home		81	17
foure heaffers	7	13	4
foure Calves	3	0	0
one Calfe		19	0
tenn sheepe		9	0
foure swyne		18	0
two mares one nagg and one Coulte	12	0	0
hay	2	0	0
Corne in the Barne		55	0

Cartes plowes and husbandrieware		25	0
Timber		13	3
fire fuell and swyne troughes		5	0
Corne and malt in the house	5	17	0
Rie sowen on the grounde		10	0
mucke		15	0
bedding and napperie	9	15	0
Brasse and pewter	4	13	4
beefe and bacon	4	0	0
Butter and Cheese		20	0
yarne toe and wooll		30	0
Cushons		5	0
bedstocks bords formes stooles coffers and shilfes	3	15	0
treene ware and Cowperie		23	8
Pultrie		3	6
Iron ware		10	0
painted clothes and ticknall ware		4	0
Sacks and bagges		5	0
baskette		4	0
his apparrell	3	10	0
Saddles		2	6
pees		5	0
three silver spoones		15	0
readie money	4	16	2
debts as may appeare by specialties	34	4	6
in debtes without specialties	19	7	0
a debte oweing by John Egley of		7	0
[Sum	131	496	56]

Exhibitum cum protestacōne.

Endorsement: Probated 6 March 1626; administration granted to John Fisher, one of the executors named in the will; the other executor utterly renouncing the burden.

Allegation and witness statements included and action registered in the book of the Consistory Court on the same day 1626.

76. RANDULL HARE OF CHORLEY

S. Pr. 20 September 1628
W.T. 31 May 1628
Buried: 8 June 1628

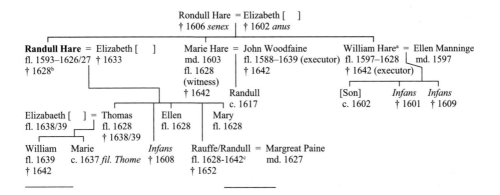

Will (parchment), sick in body.

First I give & bequeath my soule into the hands of god my creator & to Jesus Christ my only Savyor & redemer, by whose death & passion I hope to be saved thereby & by no meryts of myne owne & my body to christian buryall 1628 Inprimis I give and bequeath to my sonne Thomas Hare a peese of syleing standing in the house & the joyned bedsteed that he lyth in & all the yokes & ploughes Item I give & bequeath to my sonne Rauffe Hare 10s. Item I give & bequeath to my daughterinlaw my best brasse pot but two in the house & on pewter dish Item I give & bequeath to my daughters Ellen & Mary the two best brasse pots and to my sonne John Hare the fourth brasse pott, all the rest of my goods moveable & unmoveable I give unto my daughter Mary the one half, and the other half unto my sonne John and my daughter Ellen Equally to be devyded betwixt them — My debts & funerall expenses being discharged out of the whole.

S.
Rondull Hare

[a] Given the roles which William Hare, John Woodfaine and Mary Woodfaine, née Hare, played in connection with Randull Hare's will, it is reasonable to conclude that William and Mary were his siblings. This is further supported by the fact that John Woodfaine named his son, born in 1617, *Randull*.

[b] Randull Hare was one of the deponents for the nuncupative will of John Pattrick, 1625/26 (will no. 72); witness and priser for Elizabeth Patrick alias Wilson, will pr. 1597 (will no. 15); owed 10s. by Randle Povall, the parish clerk, in 1593 (will no. 10).

[c] Randle Hare, yeoman made inventory for John Woodfen 27 December 1642 (no. 118); witness to the will of Thomas Manning, pr. 1640.

Executors: William Hare and John Woodfaine.

Witnesses: Mary Woodfaine, Thomas French with others.

Debts that are owing unto me as followeth of theis persons:

William Chapman of London that he received by a letter of Attorney from
   Mr Dainton.
Josua Taylor that I sent him 22s.
William Bathoe of Duckington and Josua Taylor for two cheeses that Bathoe did
   buy of me to send to his wyves [ ] Mr Wixsted and for the carriage of them to
   London by William Barnes 6s 10d. that was 5s. for two cheeses and 22s. that
   I did lay out for the carriage and I now had peny for neither yet.
Randle Weaver 4s. that he was to give me to take my nagg againe.
William Callye unpayd 4s. 1d. of his rent due to me.
Mr Cholmdley of Pencrage that did serve at Cholmondeley oweth me eight or thre
   shillings that I did pay to John Wylls of the Nantwich for shertyship for him.
James Wooddall unpayd of the price of a calf 18s.
Thomas Spragg that I lent him 3s. 4d. & 9 hundred of hay that I lent him to paye
   at Easter next.
Richard Lacy of Chester for a cheese that I did sell him at 3s. prise when his wife
   lay in whereof I received 12d. of Humfrey sone & Richard said he would pay
   me the rest, so here is due 2s.
Mary Churton 14s.
Thomas Bebington 42s.

Debts that I owe:

	£	s	d
To Richard Spencer	5	8	0
Christofer Greson	5	0	0
William Millington	4	13	4
William Bebington	8	0	0
Richard Damport	3	0	0

Inventory: Randle Hare of Chorley.

Taken: 11 June 1628

Of: Goods and cattells.

Prisers: Rauff Orton, Thomas Willson, Roger Johnes, Thomas French.

	£	s	d
Two Bullocks	4	10	0
Foure cowes	11	13	4
Two heffers	4	6	8

Foure styrks	4	6	8
Two ytarmy[?] Calves		20	0
On mare		20	0
Two swyne		13	4
Foure geese		4	0
Three hens & chickens			18
In twelue ould sheepe & five lambs	3	15	0
On wayne		23	4
On cupboard		26	8
A paire of gobarts & two Broaches		5	0
Two iron chaynes		2	0
On turfespade on ax & two bills on shovell on pudding plate & on hacking knyfe	2	6	0
On frying pan			12
On Brundret, two paire of potracks with hooks & a landiron		2	0
On iron rake on hayhooke & a drale of iron ware			12
Three reaming hooks			8
On potting stick			2
On presser		20	0
On kneading turnell		4	0
On bedd stedd		11	0
On hoppet on wheele & an ould saddle		2	6
On bedsted		8	0
On forme		2	6
On featherbed two boulsters three pillowes on Caddowes on blanket on ould flockbed & on chafboulster		40	0
On coffer		4	0
On paire of bedstocks two coverlets two blankets on featherbed on chaffbed on flockbed & on boulster		28	0
On paire of stockcards			12
On hoope			12
On Turnell & two closetubbs		2	6
On coffer			12
In feathers		4	0
On paire of waighes			12
Two flaskets		2	0
On paire of bedstocks two featherboulsters two blankets & on woollbedd		13	4
On search & a hayre sive			20
On coffer		2	6
On shilfe two tressles & a lantherne			12
All the earthen ware			12
On churne on barrell five stounds three boraks on bottle two cans on Scoch & on cheese ladder		10	0
On dishcrate trenchers dyshes & piggins			8

On Bible		6	0
On long table		13	4
On square table		4	0
Three joynt stooles		2	0
Tenn measures of barly		13	4
Foure chayres			18
On coffer			18
On sive & a riddle			2
All the nappery ware		13	4
On hetshall			3
Two pounds & a half of flaxen yarne		6	8
Hempe unbrak [*i.e. unbroken/unseparated*]		4	0
Ten measures of seede barly		30	
Six measures of oates		7	6
In hempe seede sowen			12
Two kettells two little brassepots two little pans 7 a skellet		35	0
Three brasse pots		53	4
An other brasse pot		10s	0
Three brasse candlesticks			12
On hanging candlestick			1
All the pewter		36	0
On copyoke & a draught yoke & a harrow		4	0
Two ploughes		4	0
On chafeng dish a brasse morter & pestell		2	6
Two hundred weight of cheese		32	0
All his wearing apparell		20	0
In a tack of ground	10	0	0
Left by Mary Churton		20	0
Thomas Wollam		46	0
A rooke of wood		34	0
Lent to Josua Tayler		22	0
Randle Weaver		4	0
James Wooddall			18
Thomas Spragg		3	4
Thomas Bebington		42	0
On bedsteed		14	0
On peece on syling		5	0
Two axletrees on sleade & a cheesestone			16
All the fewell		2	0
On ring			3
Two joyne trees & a paire of bellowes		3	0
Two sacks		2	0
For an ould cart			16
For two iron wedge			12
For on grindlestone			2

For two paire of horsegeares	2	0
Turfs & fyrrewood	5	0
Foure hundred of hay	3	4
Lent to Thomas Spragg six hundred of hay —		
Lent to Elizabeth Pattrick widow two hundred of hay —		
Lent to Roger Johnes on hundred of hay —		
The herryott taken by the [?] —-		

[Sum	38	824	397]

Endorsement: Probated 20 September 1628; administration granted to the executors named in the will.

77. WILLIAM WICKSTEED[a] (SENIOR) OF WRENBURY FRITH, GENT

S.Pr. 10 June 1629
W.T. 9 February 1627/28
Burial: 13 February 1627/28
Renunciation: 20 March 1628/29

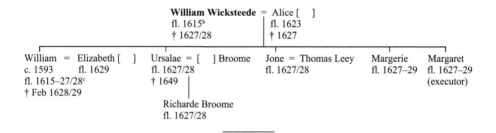

Will, sick.

First I doe bequeath my soule to the protextion of the almightie god And *my body to bee buryed in the Church att Wrenbury* Itim I give and bequeath unto William Wicksteede my sone my longe table in the howse and tow formes and the side table I alsoe give him my Cuborde in the parler and the Cubborde that hath my Evidences in and the bed steides standinge in the same (seinge me well and

---

[a] Filed at CRO as William *Wickstead* WS 1629; file contains wills of both William Sr and William Jr.
[b] Witness for will of Robert Tenche 1615 (will no. 45).
[c] Witness for the will of Robert Tenche.

sufficienty brought home) for his Childes parte of all my goods whatsoever. Itim I give and bequeath unto Ursalae Broome my daughter £12 Itim I give and bequeath unto Jone Leey my daughter wife wife *[sic]* of Thomas Leey my least heaffer Item I give and bequeath unto Richarde Broome my GranChilde to bynde him to some trade 40s. Itim I give and bequeath unto my tow daughters Margerie and Margeret all the rest of my goods and Cattell movable and unmovable to be Equally devided betwixte them.

Executors: the testator's son, William Wicsteede, and the testator's daughter, Margerte.

Overseers: William Wilson and John Tench.

William Whicksteed *[signed with seal]*

Witnesses: the marke of Lawrence (L) Mores, Lawrance Wilson.

Inventory: William Wicksteed gent.

Taken: 11 March [1628/29]

Of: goods and Catls.

Prisers: William Wilson, Thomas Wicksteed, Valentyne Wouldrich and John Tench.

	£	s	d
All his wearinge apparell		40	0
The beadsteeds in the parler		8	0
Two Cubbords in the same		20	0
Sixe stooles and a forme		8	0
A table in the same		3	4
A Joyned Cheere		2	0
All his books		5	0
Two tables in the hall and two formes		16	0
One table in the loft over the halle		6	8
One table in the lofte over the parler		5	0
One Coffer in the same		3	4
One ioyned beade in the same		6	8
A glade nett		3	4
A straine flaskett			6
Three sacks		2	0
Two truckle beads		5	0
A ioyned beade in the kitchin lofte		6	0
A little table in the same		2	6
A ioyned forme			18
All the beadinge in the same		50	0
All the beadinge in the lofte over the parler		36	0
A peece of Stuffe		12	0
All the Linnens and Napperie	5	10	4

The bead in the lofte over the butterie One boulster and two Coveringes		30	0
The servants beade		3	4
All the Brasse	4	13	4
All the Pewter	4	9	4
Broaches goulbords a dreppinge panne A fryinge panne a grate a paire of Toungs pottracks and potthooks		9	0
A litle Cubbord in the kitchin		7	0
A borde a forme a tressell a litle stoole		2	6
A litle Boorde in the Butterie and all the Traine warre in the house		10	0
A Carte		26	8
Three yoakes a plough & 2 paire of Irons		6	0
A Copsowe pine and Chaine		2	0
A Carte rope and sawe		2	0
Two spads two pikes a muckyelfe and a wedge		3	0
Fower kines and two heffers	14	0	0
A horse		3	4
A harrowe a Bill and a nager			3
[Sum	27	382	95]

Endorsement: Exhibited 10 June 1629; administration granted to Margaret, daughter of the deceased, and to Elizabeth, widow of the deceased son William.

Renunciation: Knowe all men by these presente That whereas William Wicksteed late of Wrenbury Frith in the Countie of Chester by his last will and testament in writinge gave and bequeathed unto Margarett Wicksteed his daughter diverse goods Cattls and Chattls as well moveable as unmoveable and to others diverse Legacies and by the same will did nominate and appointe William Wicksteed his sonne and the Margarett Wicksteed to be his executors as in and by the same will beareinge date 9th February 1627 more at lardge appeareth and for as much as the said William Wicksteed the sonne is since alsoe deceased Nowe knowe yee that I the said Margaret Wicksteed executrix of the last will of the said William Wicksteed the father for diverse good Causes and Consideracons me hereunto spetiallie movinge have freely resigned renounced and refused and by these presents doe for me and my assignes utterly Resigne Renounce and Refuse to take any advantage benefitt or profitt of the said Testators will or at any tyme hereafter to have Challenge or pretende any Clayme Right title or interest of in or to the premisses or to any parte or parcell thereof In wittnes whereof I have to theise presents put my hand and seale the Twentieth daie of March Anno domini 1628.

Margreat Wicksted (her mark M)

Witnesses: William Willson, John Tench, Edward Readinges.

78. WILLIAM WICKSTEED (JUNIOR) OF WRENBURY FRITH, GENT.

S.Pr. 10 June 1629
W.T. 3 February 1627/28
Died: 4 February 1628/29
Buried: No record at either Wrenbury or Malpas (within which parish lies Puddington)

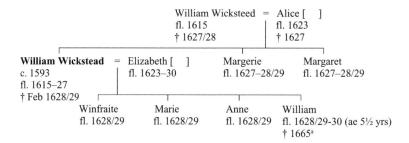

Will, sick.

First I Comend my Soule into the hands of Jesus Christ my saviour hopeinge through his pretiouse bloodd and passion to make itt partaker of lyfe everlastinge, and for my bodie I Comitt it to the earth from whence it Came. Item I give and bequeath unto Elizabeth Whicksteed my deare wyfe all my goods Cattles and Chattles whatsoever moveable and unmovable quicke & dead, to the end that she the said Elizabeth shall Carfullie truely and honestly as I doubte not satisfie and pay all and every my debts whatsoever that I owe to anie person by spetialltie or without spetiallty without hinderinge anie bodie a pennie that I owe Item the over-pluse and reasidue of my said goods Cattles and Chattles my debts beinge paid as aforsaid, If anie overpluse ther bee, I give and bequeath whollie unto Elizabeth my wyfe to her only proper use and behooffe Item my will and mynd is that my sweete wyfe Elizabeth Whicksteed shall have and enioy wholy to her selfe to bringe upp her Foure Children videlicett her one boy and three Girles all my man-tion or dwellinge house, and all the lands therunto belongeinge called & knowe by the names of the leven Acres situate in the Frith aforesayd for the terme and space of ten yeares next ensuinge shee the sayd Elizabeth or some other for her use payinge unto my Sisters Margerie and Margarett the sume of Twentie markes yearly att every Michaellmasse for and duringe the space of six yeares Enssuinge Item my will is that after thexpiracōn of the sayd terme of tenn yeares my said wiffe Elizabeth Whicksteed shall Contente her selfe with the moetie or one halfe of the sayd dwellinge house and lands with the apurtenances afore sayd and the

---

[a]   See will of William Wicksteed gent. of Wrenbury Frith, pr. 1665/CRO.

other moetie or one halfe of the sayd dwellinge house and lands with the appurtenances shee the sayd Elizabeth her Executors Administrators or assignes shall
sett lett or imploy for the reasinge of porcions for my three daughters *videlicet*
Winfraite Marie and Anne which shalbe payd unto theym in maner followinge
videlicet to my eldest daighter Winfraite the sume of Fortie pounds to be imployd
for her best use and profitt and the sume of Fortie pounds for my daughter Mary
next to be payd for her best use & profitt and lastly the sume of Fortie pounds to
payd unto my yongest daughter Anne and with her to bee imployed to her best
use and Bennefitt And in Case anie of my said daughters shall die before she
receave her sayd whole portion then the portion of her dyinge shalbee equellie
devyded upon the others Item I give divisse and beqweathe unto my sonne William
Whicksteede ~~my lease~~ all the reaseadue and remayneder of my lease of Twoo
thousand yeares of and in the Tennement Called Dunns Tenement situate in the
Frith afore sayd and late in occupation of mee the sayd William Whicksteed my
under tennate or under tennats to have & to hould the same to ~~say~~ his heares &
assignes as freely Clearly and absolutly as I the sayd William Whicksteed Could
or might have held or enIoyed the same.

Executor: the testator's wife, Elizabeth.

Overseer: the right worshipfull Mr Sir William Massie of Puddington knight to
be heade overseer; my deare frend Mr John Cottingham of At le Nesten to be an
overseer.

William Wicksteed

Witnesses: John Cottingham, Edward Kniveton.

Inventory: William Wicksteed of Wrenbury Frith.

Taken: 23 February 1628/29

Of: goods Catle and Chatle.

Prisers: William Wilson, Valentine Wouldrich, John Tench.

	£	s	d
all his wearinge apparell	6	13	4
The beadsteeds standinge in the Parler		8	0
Two Cubbords in the parler		20	0
Sixe stoules and a forme		8	0
A table and Joyned Cheers		5	4
All his bookes		10	0
A longe table in the hall a litle table and two formes		16	0
An other table		6	8
A table in the loft over the parler		5	0
A Coffer		3	4
A Joyned beade		6	8

A saltinge turnell		5	0
A glade Nett		3	4
A strayne flaskett			6
Three sacks		2	0
Two truckle beades		5	0
A Joyned beadde		6	0
A litle table		2	6
A Joyned forme			18
A Feather beadde a boulster a Pillowe and a Cover		36	0
All the Lynnens	5	10	8
All the Beaddinge in the kitchin lofte	4	3	4
A Coveringe Curtens and Ballance		26	8
A Feather Beadd Pillows and Boulster		53	4
Curtens Ballance and other Linnens		20	0
A Feather Beadde Ticke and boulster		14	0
Two Chaffinge dishes		5	4
Two Brasse Panns		33	4
Fower Potts and a Posnett		40	0
Seaven Candlesticks a brasse pann a skimer pestle malter and a skellett		13	0
All the Pewter	4	6	0
Broches goulbards dreppinge Pann greate tonges fire shovell and Pottracks		9	0
A litle Cubborde		7	0
A Borde a forme a tressell & stoule		2	6
All the treyne warre		15	8
A Carte		26	8
Three yoakes		3	0
A Copsowe pine Cartrope & sawe		3	0
Two spades two pickles a muckyelfe and wedge		3	0
A harrowe Bill and nager		3	0
All the pictures in the parler		6	8
A payre of tables		3	4
woole and woollen yarne		13	4
Two silver spoones		9	0
three dozen of trenchers			12
One dozen of Bedstaves			12
Sixe Cushens		6	0
Fower Truncks sword and Belt		24	8
A loockinge glasse			18
Thirteene over sea dishes 2 Counter fetts and seaven glasses		5	0
Half a hundred of Cheese		10	0
A spinninge wheele?			20
Three pounde of yarne and flaxe		4	6
A paire of Bellowes			12

Sixe fliches of Baccon		20	0
A sarch			6
Corne and hey in house and Barne		36	8
One swyne		3	4
A geldinge	5	0	0
Three Calfes		20	0
Five younge Beasts	6	13	0
Seaven kyne	15	13	4
Five poles		10	0
A feilde of wheate	4	13	4

Sum Total	83	4	6
[*recte*	83	1	6]

Endorsement: Probated 10 June 1629; administration granted to Elizabeth widow of the deceased, sole executrix named in the will.

Inquisition Post Mortem[a].

Taken: 29 March [1630], 6 Charles I

Inquisition taken at Northwich, 29 March, 6 Charles I [1630] before Hugh Maynwaring, esq., escheator in co. Chester, by virtue of the King's writ to enquire after the death of William Wicksteede gent., by the oath of Paul Wynyngton of Berches, Henry Pickmeare of Hulse, Robert Holford of Lostocke Gralam, George Bradford of Shipbrooke, Randall Wrenche of Moulton, Arthur Symcocke of Leftwich, John Winyngton of the same, Arthur Joynson of Wareton, Thomas Neild of Shurlach, Andrew Burton of Over, Richard Whittingham, Thomas Barker & Ralph Maddocke of the same & Ralph Blease of Shipbrooke, gentlemen.
They say that William Wicksteed, father of the said William, & Alice, his wife, were seised in fee of a mess., 30 a. of land, 10 a. of meadow, 30 a. of pasture & 5 a. of wood called Eleven Acres in Wrenbury Frith, & by indenture of 25 April [1623] made between William Wicksteed the father and Alice, his wife, of one part & Hugh Wicksteed of Marbury, gent., & James Palyn of Wrenbury Frith, gent., of the other, he settled the said premises on the said William, the elder, for life, with remainder to the said Alice, for life, & a moiety of the said remainder to the said premises, including the Orchard Croft, Kitchin Croft, Middle Field & Two Barn Crofts, after their deaths, on the said William Wicksteede, the younger & Elizabeth, his wife, & the heirs of their bodies & the other moiety, including Rough Crofts next Eleven Acres Lane, Eleven Acres Meadow, Great Eleven Acres, to the use of the said William the younger & the heirs of his body.
The said William Wicksteed, the father, by indenture of 9 February [1626/28] granted to his daughters Margery & Margaret Wicksteed the pastures called Great Leaven Acres, Leaven Acres Meadow & Rough Croft next Little Lane for 21

---

[a] See R. Stewart Brown, *Inquisitions Post Mortem*, iii. 172–3.

years, at a yearly rent of 8s.

The said premises are held of the King, as Earl of Chester, by 200th part of a knight's fee & worth yearly (clear) 20s.

The said William Wicksteed died at Puddington 4 February [1628/29] & William Wicksteed is his son & heir now aged 5 ½ years; Elizbeth wife of William aforesaid survives at Puddington & has taken the issues, &c., since her husband's death. . . .

79. JOHN WRIGHT OF NEWHALL

S.Pr. 27 June 1629
Buried: 5 May 1629

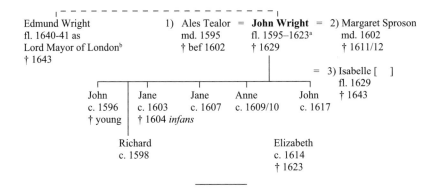

Inventory: John Wright of Newhall in the parish of Wrenbury.

Taken: 7 May 1629

Of: Goodes and Cattells.

Prisers: Thomas Hamnet, Thomas Backhouse, Richard Hassall, John Greene, Rowland Bates.

	£	s	d
his wearing Apparell	1	0	0
one stone of woole		12	0
yarne and Towe		16	0
Nappery ware	3	0	0

---

[a] Fined 1595 at Newhall Manor Court; also at the 1623 Newhall Manor Court/CRO.
[b] See above, p. xxxiv of the Introduction, where we discuss the documents and literature relevant to Sir Edmund Wright, Lord Mayor of London and his connections to Cheshire.

All manner bedding boulsters blankets and Coverlets	2	6	8
Three Cushions		1	6
Three small Coffers & one strawe basket		4	0
Treene ware		16	8
Brasse and pewter	2	0	0
One Carte with Chaines, Collers, and homes	1	13	4
Bils Axes mattocks shovels and other Iron ware		10	0
Corne	1	8	0
Butter and Cheese		2	0
Bacon		10	0
Ticknall vessels		1	0
One Table with formes boards shelves chaires and stooles		13	4
Three swine		15	0
Nine keyne four heiffers And twoe mares	29	13	4
spinning wheeles		3	0
painted cloathes			6
Mucke and Fuell	1	0	0
Money as in possession	8	13	4
debts due to the deceased		11	6
haye		6	8
One Packsaddle twoe Packelants with a winnow Sheet			
Bagges and a winnowe sheete & a grinding stone		5	0
Sume tot	57	2	10

Endorsement: Exhibited 27 June 1629; administration granted to Isabelle his widow.

80. OLIVER BRISCOE OF WRENBURY, HUSBANDMAN

S.Pr. 15 May 1630
W.T. 10 March 1624/25
Buried: 4 November 1629

NOTE: The will exists in both the original and a copy.

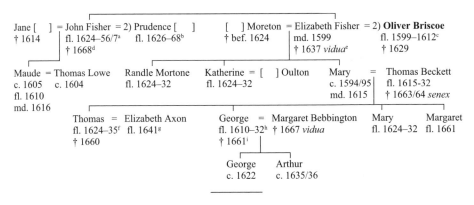

Will, sick.

First I comende my soule into the hands of allmightie god hopeing by the meritt and bloud sheding of Jesus Christ my alone Savior to have free pardon and remission of all my sinnes and *my body I Comitt to the earth to be buryed in the*

ª For John Fisher as executor for his sister Elizabeth Briscoe, see will of Elizabeth Briscoe, pr. 1637 (will no. 103). Executor for Thomas Shrowbridge, 1626/27 (will no. 75). John Fisher resided at Aston and owed John Bromhall £2 per annum for seven years by bond; see list of debtors to John Bromhall, 1631 (will no. 82). John Fisher owed Alice Buckley £4 10s. in 1646; see will of Alice Buckley, pr. 1649 (will no. 132). He was a witness for George Hall Sr, 1656/57; see will of George Hall, pr. 1657 (will no. 142).
ᵇ Witness to nuncupative will of Thomas Shrowbridge, pr. 1626./27 (will no. 75).
ᶜ Randull Cowper of Wrenbury owed Oliver *Bruscalle* £3 in 1612; see will of Randull Cowper, pr. 1613 (will no. 40). Oliver *Bruscalle* was also one of the appraisers of the goods and chattels of Randull Cowper in 1612 (will no. 40).
ᵈ See will of John Fisher, pr. 1668/CRO.
ᵉ See will of Elizabeth Briscoe, widow, pr. ca. 1637 (will no. 103).
ᶠ Thomas Beckett is noted as the god-son of Thomas Hamnett and was bequeathed 5s. in his will, pr. 1635 (will no. 97).
ᵍ William Fergusson Irvine, *Chester Licences*, iv. 88: 27 May 1641, to Thomas Beckett of Wrenbury, and Elizabeth Axon, spinster of Audlem; at Wrenbury, Audlem and Acton; bondsman Thomas Poole.
ʰ *Chester Licences*, i. 83: 25 July 1610, George Beckett of Wrenbury parish, Margaret Bebbington of Baddily parish.
ⁱ See will and inventory of George Beckett of Sound, pr. 1661.

Churchyarde of Wrenbury abovesayde in sure and certayne hope of a joyfull resurrection Item I give and bequeath unto Thomas Beckett the yonger 15s. Item I give
unto George Beckett 15s. Item I give unto Marie Beckett the yonger 15s. Item I
give unto Randle Moreton 20s. Item I give unto Kathereine Oulton 20s. Item I give
and bequeath unto Elizabeth Briscoe my wife my house wherin I now dwell dureinge
her life and after her decease the remaynder during the lease I give and bequeath
unto Mary Beckett wife of Thomas Beckett Item I give unto the sayde Thomas
Beckett my other little house All the Rest of my goods moveable and unmoveable
Cattells and Chattels I give and bequeath unto the sayde Elizabeth my wife.

Executors: the testator's wife, Elizabeth, and William Willson.

H. & S.

Witnesses: Thomas Harwar, Thomas Graye, Andrew Bebington.

Debts owing to the Testator:

	s	d
John Patterick due att midsumer	3	6	0
Hugh Burrouges due att midsomer	3	6	0
Arthure Hurleston	3	0	0
John Cartwright	11	0	0
Andrewe Bebington	9	0	0
James Baker		38| 0
The same James due the second Day of march next		40| 0

Inventory : Oliver Briscoe of Wrenbury Husbandman.

Taken: 12 November 1629

Of: goods Chattels and Cattle.

Prisers: John Sheen, John Fisher, Thomas Spencer, Andrew Babington.

	£	s	d
in ready money	8	0	0
In bills and bounds	17	0	0
Debts beside	17	15	0
A featherbed 2 boulster with other bedding	3	0	0
six payer of sheets and other nappery		30	0
Bedsteeds coffers Tables forms		14	4
chayres stooles and shelfes		2	0
Brasse		30	0
Pewter		20	0
Iron ware		6	0
Cowpery ware		26	0
Two kine	5	0	0
A mare		50	0
Two swine		30	0

Hay		11	0
A pott of Butter		7	0
Fewel: muck: an old carte		11	10
A lease for 21 yeares	15	0	0
His wearing apparel		26	8
Sum total		73	19	2

The Inventory was exhibited 25 November 1629. Thomas Stofford, bachelor of laws, being vicar general in spiritual matters with the godly permission of Lord John, Bishop of Chester and Reverend Father in Christ, and the lawfully appointed principal Official of the Episcopal Consistory Court of Chester, sends Greetings to our beloved in Christ Thomas Beckett Marie Marie *[sic]* Beckett, also known as Burscoe, the natural and legitimate daughter the recently deceased Oliver Burscoe of Wrenbury. Since the said deceased Oliver Burscoe recently departed this life without composing any Will, at least any that has been displayed in our presence, in accordance with the terms of which the Administration and Performance of the Administration regarding all & singular goods, privileges, credits, and chattels, both jointly & individually, of the deceased person (might be effected), it has been established that this task & responsibility is now indubitably devolved upon us. Therefore, in order to administer the collection, levying, recovery, reclamation and exaction of the goods, privileges, credits and chattels, both jointly & individually, which belonged to the deceased during his life and at the time of his death, and repay any debt, by which the deceased was under an obligation to any person or to a creditor to whom he was indebted, and to make satisfaction for any legacies which he had made, we entrust to you, in whose honesty we have the greatest confidence, our power & authority. And first and foremost, in respect to administering the same matters well & honestly, and in respect of drawing up a true & full inventory of the same & an accurate computation, calculation or reckoning, and concerning the rendering of an account in respect to the aforegoing to us or another judge who is competent in this field, whoever he be, when and whensoever you shall be lawfully requested to do so, we appoint, order and, through the present document establish you to be the Administrator and Receiver of the goods, privileges, credits and chattels of this kind, once you have personally sworn an oath on the holy Gospels of God, always providing the rights of every party are not infringed.

Issued under the seal which we use in this (legal) area, on the third day of November Anno domini 1629.

Thomas Stofford

John Bickerton, Notary Public

Endorsement: Probated 15 May 1630; administration to Elizabeth relict of the said deceased and one of the executors named in the said will, with power reserved to the other executor until he comes.

81. JOHN CARTWRIGHT OF ASTON IN NEWHALL, GENT.

S.Pr. 16 October 1630
W.T. 13 May 1625
Codicil: 23 August 1630
Buried: 27 August 1630

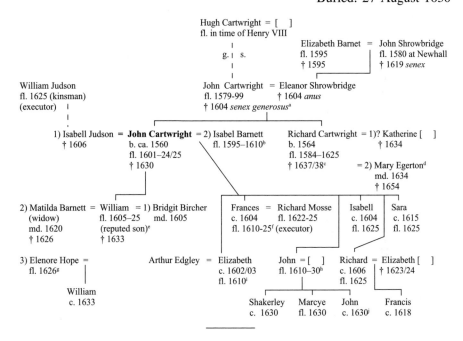

a See will dated 19 August 1604; pr. 24 November 1604 (will no. 18).
b Daughter of James Barnett; see a codicil to the latter's will, pr. 1610, which indicated that she was married to John Cartwright by that time (will no. 29).
c Richard Cartwright of Aynho, co. Northants., member of the Inner Temple, died 13 January 1638, aged 74; he was buried at Aynho 15 January 1638. Priser for Thomas Massey, 1584 (will no. 6).
d Daughter of Sir John Egerton of Egerton.
e William Fergusson Irvine, *Chester Licences*, ii. 107: 14 February 1620, William Cartwright *alias Cowper* and Matilda Barnet, widow, parish of Wrenbury, at Wrenbury.
f Bequeathed £20 by grandfather James Barnett, 1610 (will no. 29); licence to marry issued 24 September 1622 for Wrenbury (William Fergusson Irvine, *Chester Licences*, ii. 166); marriage took place 26 September 1622.
g *Chester Licences*, iii. 69: 1626, William Cartwright and Elenore Hope of Wrenbury, at Nantwich or Wrenbury.
h Bequeathed £20 by grandfather James Barnett, 1610 (will no. 29). John Cartwright of Aston, gent., succeeded his father and was duly admitted to his deceased father's copyholds at Newhall manorial court 11 October 1631.
i Bequeathed £20 by grandfather James Barnett, 1610 (will no. 29); married Arthur Edgley after 1630; their son was the Rev. Samuel Edgley, vicar of Acton (1675-1721).
j Baptized at Wrenbury on 12 September 1630, this John was presumably just weeks old when John Cartwright of Aston bequeathed £5 annually for the education of his grandson John, son of John, in the codicil to his will dated 23 August 1630.

Will, sick.

First I comend & bequeath my soule to the mercyfull hands of Almightie god hopinge stedfastly by the merritts & passion of his deere sonne our Lord & Savior Jesus Christe to bee one of the number of his elect & to have a Joyfull resurreccōn at the dreadfull daye of Judgment *And my bodie I bequeath to the earth to bee decently buried in the parishe Church of Wrenbury* aforsaid at the discrecōn of my Executors hereafter herein named And as touchinge the disposicōn of my wordly goods and substance I doe first give & bequeath to Isabell my lovinge wyfe all my kine oxen horses Nages Mares Colts yonge beasts swyne & pulleyne and all other my quick cattaill of what kind qualytie or propertie soever the same bee (excepte twoe kine which I give and bequeath to my reputed sonne William Cartwrighte, & excepte all such other oxen kine or horses shalbee lawfully claymed & taken for herriotts after my death. Item I give & bequeath to my said wyfe all my Corne & hey aswell in the howse as in the barne & all my corne growinge upon the ground & all other my provision of victuall. Item I give & bequeath to my said wyfe the use & occupacōn of all my beddinge and bedds furnishings & of all my napery & Lynnens and of all my brasse pewter broches gobetes Cowperie & treene ware Chests fawcetts boards Formes Cheres stooles shelfs and all other my utensills & houshould stuffe whatsoever, to use and occupie the same duringe her naturall lyfe, if shee soe longe keepe herselfe sole & unmaried and soe as that if she happen to marrye agayne after my death that then the same shalbee devyded betweene her & my three daughters that are unmarried in foure equall porcōns & that if shee keepe herselfe sole and unmarried duringe her lyfe, that then my said wyfe may dispose thereof at her pleasure (excepte my twoe best bedstedes twoe table boards with frames my best pot & best pan & my greatest broache, twoe livye Cupboards, the weetinge malte combe in the kilne & my best Chere) of all which my said last excepted goods my mind & will is that my said wyfe shall have the use & occupacōn (keepinge them in good reparacōn) for and duringe the terme of nyne yeres next after my death (if shee soe longe doe live and keepe herselfe sole & unmarried) & that from and after thend & expiracōn of the said terme of nyne yeres or death or marriage agayne of my said wyfe which soever shall first happen, then my mind & will is & soe I doe devyse that the same goods soe excepted shalbe and remayne with my howse in Aston aforsaid, to myne heyres of the same howse as heire loomes soe longe as the shall endure or continue Item I give & bequeath to my said wyfe all my Towe yarne & newe of both, And my mind and will alsoe is that my said wyfe shall have the use & occupacōn of all my Carts ploughes yokes Cheynes & all other my implements & instruments whatsoev belonginge to husbandrye & shee to keepe theim in good reparacōn for & duringe the terme of nyne yeres nexte after my death (if shee soe longe doe live & keepe herself sole and unmarried) and that after thend & expiracōn of the said terme of nyne yeres or death or marriage agayne of my said wyfe whichsoever shall first happon, then I will that the same shalbee & remayne to my righte heyre to use & dispose of the same with my dwellinge house in Aston aforsaid. Item I give dvyse & bequeath to my wyfe all my Customarye or Copyhould messuage Lands tenements & heredytamts whatsoever with there appurtennces scituate

lyinge or beinge within the Towneshipp of Aston aforesaid within the mannor of
Newhall in the said Countie whereof or wherein I the said John Cartwright now
live to the custome of the said mannor To have & to hould the same to my said
wyfe & her assignes imeadiatlye from & after my death unto the full end & terme
of three yeres & soe from three yeres to three yeres untill the terme of nyne yeres
nexte after my death bee fully expired and determined if she the said Isabell shall
& doe soe longe live and after my death doe keepe herselfe sole and unmarried
upon trust & confidence that shee will discharge my funall expencs & to the intente
that shee shall & will with the rentes yssues & profitts thereof Educate bringe up
keepe & mayntaine all my yonger children that are or shall continue soe longe
unmarried with meate drink apparell lodginge & all other things necessary for and
duringe the said terme And if it happen my said wyfe doe die & depte this transitorie lyfe or to marrie agayne after my death and before the said terme of nyne
yeres be fully expired & determined then my mind & will is & soe I doe devyse
& bequeath that my worthie & worshipfull good friends Sir Richard Wilbraham
of Woodhey knight & Barronett & George Cotton of Combermere in the said
Countye Esquire & my lovinge brother Richard Cartwrighte Esquire & the sorvivors or sorvivor of theim & theire heyres shall have take & receive the rents
yssues & profitts of all & singler the said Mesuages lands tents & heredytamts &
the same shall converte & imploy to the best use benifitt & profitt of all or such
& soe manye of my Children & in such sorte as they or the sorvivors & sorvivor
of theim & theire heyres or the greater number of theim shall thinke meete & convenient for & duringe all the rest & residue & continuance of the ymeadyallye
from & after thend & expiracōn of the said terme of nyne yeres my mind & will
is & soe I doe devyse and bequeath that all the said mesuages lands tenements &
heredytaments & all myne estate & interest therein & in everye parte thereof
respectivelye shall wholly be & remaine to my righte heires for & duringe the
said severall estate & interests therein. Item I doe give devyse & bequeath to myne
executors hereafter herein named all the rest and residue of my Copyhould or
Customarye lands tents & heredytaments whatsoever with theire appurtenancs
within the severall Mannors of Newhall aforsaid & Whitchurch in the Countie of
Salop or elswhere whereof or wherein I have anie estate of inheritance or other
estate or terme accordinge to the customes of the mannors severally & respectivelye To have & to hould all & singler the said rest & residue of my said
Copyhould or customarie messuages lands & heredytaments with theire appurtenancs to my said executors for & duringe the terme of three yeres & soe from
three yeres to three yeres duringe the terme of nyne yeres nexte & imediatlye
ensuynge my death Att for & under the yerelye rents duties and services due for
the same to the lords of the said Mannors severally and respectivelye. And I alsoe
give devyse & bequeath to my said executors & there heyres forever; All that my
tenemente in Wrenbury Frith called Dunnes Tenemente and all howses edyfics
buildings orchards gardens yords lands tents & heredytaments whatsoever thereunto belonginge or therewith occupied which I have of the givfts & feoffement
of William Wicksteed yeoman & the Mortgage money that lyeth upon the same
beinge an hundred pownds or more whatsoever upon due accompte it shall happen to bee incase the same shall happon to bee reddeemed & all deeds chares &

evidences which I have concerninge the same & my will & true meaninge as concerninge the same lands is that neither my said executors nor myne heyres shall take any advantage of forfeyture or breath of Condicōn touchinge the redempcōn of the said lands, soe as the said William Wicksteed or his heyres doe paye the said sume of £100 and all accerages or rents due for the same upon iust accomts to my said executors upon any feast daye of the anuncyacōn of the blessed Marie the virgin which shalbee within twoe yeres nexte after my death And I doe further give devyse and bequeith to my said executors all & singler my chattells rears leases taxes termes of yeres and Annuities for yeres whatsoev which I nowe have & am possed of or lawfully entitled unto what or wheresoever the are within the severall Counties of Chester Salop or elswhere. And whereas by one Indenture of assignement beiringe date the eighte and twentieth day of Aprill last past before the date hereof confect and made betweene me the said John Cartwrighte upon the one parte, And the said George Cotton of Combermere in the said Countie of Chester Esquire & Andrewe Cotton gent. brother of the said George Cotton upon the other parte, I have demised granted & assigned to them the said George Cotton and Andrewe Cotton, All that my mesuage or tenemente howses buildinges barnes orchards gardens clausures of Arable land meddowe & pasture & all other heredytaments with there appurtenancs scytuate & beinge in Wettenhall in the said Countie which heretofore I had by the demyse & assignement of Walter Webbe gent. for the terme of the naturall lives of the said Walter Webb & of Eustace Webb & Thomas Webb sonnes of the said Walter. To have & to hould the said Messuage or tenemente & all other the premisses last above mencōned to theim the said George Cotton and Andrewe Cotton theire executors administratores & assignes imeadiatly from and after the daye of the date of the said Indenture of assignement unto the full end & terme of Fourescore & nyneteene yeres from thence nexte followinge and fully to bee complett and ended (if they the said Walter Webb Eustace Webb & Thomas Webb or any of theim should & did soe longe live) upon speciall trust & confidence nevertheles in theim the said George Cotton & Andrew Cotton expressed by me & to the tenemente that they the said George Cotton & Andrewe Cotton and the Survivors & Survivor of theim there executors administrators assignes ymeadyatlye from and after my death should & would permitt and suffre the said last mencōned mesuage or tenemente & all other the heredytaments & premisses last aforsaid with theire appurtenancs & everye parte thereof respectivelye to bee had occupied and enioyed and the rents yssues & profitts thereof & of everye parte thereof respectivelye to bee had and taken by such person & persons to whom or to whose use & in such sorte as I the said John Cartwrighte by anie writinge or writings by me hereafter to bee signed & sealed before three witnesses or more or by mie last will & testament in writinge to bee by me signed & sealed before three wittnesses or more should give grante assigne limitt devyse or bequeath the same & everye parte thereof respectivelye at for & under the yerely rent of £3 6s. 8d. & other the reservacōns In the Indenture of leas thereof reserved as in & by the said Indenture of assignement more fullye & a large it doth & maye appere, Nowe I the said John Cartwrighte after full & deliberate consideracōn beinge fullie minded & resolved to use & putt in execution the power soe in trust to me reserved & belonginge for & as concerninge the

said last mencōned mesuage or tenemente & premisses in Wettenhall aforsaid doe
by this my present last will & testament in wrytinge give devyse and bequeth all
the said last mencōned mesuage or tenemente & all other the premisses in
Wettenhall aforsaid to my said executors To hould to theim & theire assignes for
& duringe all the continuance of the said terme of fourescore & nynteene yeres
And I will & devyse That they the said George Cotton and Andrewe Cotton and
the Survivors of theim theire executors & assignes shall permitt & suffre my said
executors & theire assignes to have hould occupie & enioye the same duringe all
the continuance of the said terme of fourescore & nynteene yeres as yett to come
and unexpired And I doe lastly give and bequeath to my said executors all my
reddye money & gould & all such debts creditts and sumes of money whatsoever which at the tyme of my death shalbe due or oweing unto me by bound bill
specialtie simple contracte or otherwyse howsoever And my will & full mind is
& soe I doe devyse lymitt and appoynt that my said executors out of all my said
severall estats tacks farmes Chattells Annuities Lands tenements debts creditts &
other the premisses to theim herein & hereby formly bequeathed or lymitted &
with the same & the rents yssues & profitts thereof shall well & truelye satisfie
and paie all such debts & sumes of money as I owe or stand indebted in to anie
person or persons whatsoever as the same shall severally & respectively become
due & shall well & honestly exonerate acquite discharge or otherwyse save &
keepe harmeles all & everye such person & persons as in any sorte stand bound-
en or engaged as my suertie or suerties by bound bill specialtie or promis in my
wyse howsoever for any debte or demannd whatsoever. And my will & mind further is & soe I doe alsoe devyse lymitt & appoint that my said executors alsoe
out of all my said severall estats tackes farmes Chattells Annuitites Lands tenements debts creditts & other the premisses soe to theim hereby formerly
bequeathed & with the same & the rents yssues & profitts thereof shall alsoe paye
to my daughters hereafter herein named the saverall summes of money or porcōns
hereafter alsoe herein severally & reespectively to eche of theim lymited viz: to
my daughter Francis Mosse nowe wyfe of Richard Mosse the full sume of £200
of lawfull money of England & the same to bee unto her payd & satisfied first
of all before any other of my daughters Legacies in this my will mencōned. Item
to my second daughter Elizabeth Cartwrighte the full sume of £200 of like lawfull money Item to my third daughter Sara Cartwrighte the like sume of £200 Item
to my fourth & yongest daughter Isabell Cartwrighte the like sume of £200 of
lawfull money of England which said severall sumes my will & true intente &
meaninge is, shall be unto everye of theim respectivelye in full satisfaccōn & barre
of everye of there childs parts & porcōns of my goods And my will & true
meaninge is & soe I doe devyse that if anye of my said three daughters last named
doe happon to die & departe this transitorie lyfe befure shee be married or have
receyved her said full porcōn that then & in such case the porcōn or porcōns of
her or theim soe dyinge or soe much thereof as shalbe soe unreceyved shall wholly bee & remayne & bee payd to the Survivors or Survivor of theim. And my
mind & will alsoe is that the said porcōns soe formly lymited to my said three
last named daughters shalbee payd unto everye of theim or to theire lawfull Tutors
to bee putt fourth & imployed to theire best profitt severally & respectivelye as

they are in senioritie of birth viz: theldest to be first payd & the yongest last soe soone as the same sumes, togeither with my debts soe to bee payd can bee levyed & raysed out of the yerely profitts of the premisses as aforsaid And my further will & mind is & soe I doe alsoe devyse bequeath lymitt & appoynt that my said executors shall conveye over & deliver to Richard Cartwrighte my yonger sonne, all the rest residue and remaynder of my said severall estats tacks termes Chattells annuities lands tents debts creditts & other the premisses soe to theim therein form-ly bequeathed which shall or may bee spared & bee remaynge over & above the payement & full discharge of my said debts & porcōns to my said daughters excepte such estats tacks termes & Chattells as are scytuate and beinge within the severall mannors of Newhall in the said Countye of Chester & Whitchurch in the said Countie of Salop To have & to hould the said severall estats tacks termes Chattells Annuities Lands & tenements (excepte before excepted) to the said Richard Cartwrighte my said sonne his heyres executors administratores & assignes for & duringe the severall & respective continuances of the said severll estats tacks termes chattells & Annuities (if the said Richard Cartwrighte my said sonne or anye woman which hee the said Richard shall hereafter marrie or take to his wyfe or any yssue of the bodye of the said Richard Cartwrighte my sonne lawfully begotten shall & doe soe longe live) at for and under the severall rents reservacōns & servics severally & respectively due for the same. And soe as that if it happen the said Richard Cartwrighte my sonne to die & departe this transi-torie lyfe before all the said estats tacks termes Chattells Annuities (excepte before excepted) be fully expired ended or determyned, and havynge neither wyfe or anye yssue of his bodie lawfully begotton then livinge or if anye such woman as he shall hereafter lawfully marrye & take to his wyfe or anye yssue of his bodie law-fully begotton be lyvinge at and after the tyme of his death, & yett neverthelesse doe all of theim die before thend & expiracōn of all the said severall estats & ter-mes that then ymeadyatly from & after the death of the last decedent of theim the same severall estats tacks termes Chattells Annuities Lands and tenements (excepte before excepted) or such &c soe manye of theim as shall not be then expired ended or determined shall & may whollye be remayne & continue to such yonger sonne as at that tyme shall happon to bee the second sonne of the bodie of John Cartwrighte my sonne lawfully begotton & to his executors admrators & assignes & for defalte of such second sonne then to John Cartwrighte my Cosen his execu-tors admirators & assignes To have hould occupie & enioye the same & everye of theim severally & respectively with there appurtenancs & the rents yssues & profitts thereof to have & take to his & theire owne use & behoofe without accompte rendringe for and duringe all the rest & residue & continuance of the said severall estats and termes & of everye of theim respectively at for and under the severall rents reservacōns & servics severally & respectively due for the same Item my will alsoe is & soe I doe further devyse bequeath lymitt and appoynte that all my Copyhould or Customarye lands & all other my lands leases tacks & farmes of what kind qualitye or nature soever the same bee scytuate lyinge and beinge within the severall Mannors or Lordshipps of Newhall in the said County of Chester & Whitchurch in the said Countie of Salop (after the opticuler estates thereof and therein ended which before in these presents I have devysed or bequeithed to any person or persons whatsoever) shall wholly be & remayne or be conveyed by my said executors to be remayne & continue to my sonne John Cartwrighte his heyres & assignes for and duringe all such severall & respective estats as I have in the same & everye parte thereof respectivelye And lastly my mind & will is & soe I doe devyse & appoynt that if anye doubt question ambiguitie or controversie doe hereafter happen to arise or growe betweene or amongst my said wyfe children & executors or any of theim for or concerninge anye guifte legacie bequest or any other matter or thinge in this my presente will contayned, that then the same shall from tyme to tyme bee hard ordered & determined by the overseers of this my present will, hereafter herein named & by the Survivors & Survivor of theim & theire heyres & if any of theim refuse to stand to obey & performe such said order that then he shee or they soe refusinge shall take noe benefitt at all by this my present will moniewyse.

Executors: the testator's son-in-law, Richard Mosse, and his kinsman, William Judson.

Overseers: the testator's good friends, Sir Richard Wilbraham knighte & Barronett, and George Cotton of Combermere Esquire, and the testator's brother, Richard Cartwrighte Esquire.

I doe lastly give & bequeath to my said executors & overseers viz: to either of theim the said Sir Richard Wibraham & George Cotton five pownds a peece to make either of theim a ringe or a Cup wherein I desire that my name maye be engraven & to my said sonne in law Richard Mosse £20 & to my said kinsman William Judson five marks to make him a ringe wherein I alsoe desire my name maye be engraven Item I give & bequeath to Mr Nicholls our preacher at Wrenbury 20s. & I wishe & desire that my said wyfe shall bestowe some money on the poore of the parishe of Wrenbury as shee in her discrecon shall thinke fitt. In wittnesse whereof I have hereunto putt my hand & seale the daye & yere first abovewritten.

Memorandum that this presente will written & conteyned in foure sheets of paper was signed sealed & published by the testator in presence of Mind that at the sealinge & publishinge of this presente will the testator aforsaid expressed his meaninge to be, that soe soone as his debts weare paid & discharged that then his sonne John & his heyres should enter upon & have his hands in Burghall to his & theire owne use in presence of Geoge Cotton Rauffe Egerton. Andrewe Cotton. Randle Wylson. George Cotton. Rauffe Egerton. Andrewe Cotton. Randle Wilson.

23 die August anno 1630.

Memorandum that the daye & yere abovewritten John Cartwrighte of Aston gentleman did declare himselfe & willed, that this should bee added as a Codicell to this his will That his sonne John Cartwrighte should after his decesse have such parte & porcōn of his estate fourth of his wyfes parte of his estate lymited unto her as at the ovsighte of Sir Richard Wilbraham George Cotton & Richard

Cartwrighte Esquires should be thought fitt, And that his sonne John Cartwrighte should have £250 as a porcōn fourth of his personall estate to bee paid by his executors. And I give £20 to Shakerley Cartwrighte[a] my sonne John Cartwright his youngest sonne And that his will & mind is that William Judson nominated as his executor shalbe altered & that John Judson to bee putt in his place with his sonne in lawe Richard Mosse In Consideracōn of these legacies & bequests to John Cartwrighte his sonne hereby givon his sonne is to acquitt & discharge the executors of this his will of all actions fites and demannds which hee maye have or pretended to have for any cause or Coller of cause touchinge his fathers estate agaynst the executors Item I give to my sonne in lawe Mosse his second sonne £40 Item I give to Marcie Cartwrighte my sonne John Cartwrights daughter £20 & my mind & will is that if either of theim the said Shakerley or Marcye Cartwrighte depte this lyfe that the sorvivor of theim shall have the whole £40 Item I give to Thomas Felton £20 to bee paid within three yeres after my decese, Itm I give to John Twyford £4 which is my Lord Nedhams hand Item I give to Thomas Teylor £5 Item I give unto John Cartwrighte my sonne Johns sonne £5 yerelye to kepe him to schole Item I give to John Judson five marks for the paines hee is herein to take.

Witnesses: George Cotton, Arthur Cartwright, Richard Cartwright.

Debts owinge to the Testator without Specialtie:

	£	s	d
John Hall oweth me for rente	10	0	0
Arthure Cartwrighte for rente	2	0	0
Clemence Fisher oweth me for seaven hundred of Cheese at the rate of 19s. 6[d]. the 100. sume of	6	16	6
Arthure Starke Esquire oweth me	1	0	0
Rauffe Tomis oweth mee for three loads of faggotts		13	0
widdowe Elcocke oweth mee for carriage of twoe quarter of wood from Handley Parke	3	6	8
Thomas Wicksteed oweth me	1	0	0
Roger Wrighte Richard Wicksteed & Thomas Wicksteed doe owe me 10s. for three quarter & a halfe of wood to bee paid at Candlemas nexte	40	10	0
John Mason oweth me lent money	4	0	0
Richard Axson oweth mee for a mare	4	0	0
Thomas Cheswis of the Frith oweth mee	1	5	0
Owen Davie oweth mee	1	0	0
Richard Bathoe oweth me £8 Rent which when hee payes it my will is that hee shall have fortie shillings of itt given him agayne.			
	83	11	2

[a] Shakerley Cartwright was christened on 22 August 1630, just one day before this codicil was made!

Renunciation of John Judson:
Mr John Bickerton my best love unto you with many thankes for yor love all wayes towards mee, &c: This is to Certiefie you that I Am Content to leave of beinge Exequitor for Mr John Cartwright & that Mr Richard Mosse his sonn in law shall undertake it his one sealf & this much to Certifie this unto you, & for I Rest & will Remayne yor lovinge frend.

John Judson Nantwich this 16th October 1630.

Richardus Mosse [attested] that John Judson did renounce.

Memorandum of John Cartwright Jr.

Mr John Bickarton I did a Caveat in the Cowart to stay my fathers will for beinge proven but now I am Contented that it shall be proven by the Executor & this shalbe your suffitient warrant with my best love to you remembered I rest
your ever lovinge frend
John Cartwright
Richardus Mosse [attested] that Mr Cartwright wrote this marke.

Inventory: John Cartwrighte of Aston, gen.
Taken: 2 September 1630, 6 Charles I
Of: goods cattells & chattels.

Prisers: Henrye Griffithe, John Ravenscrofte, John Fisher and Thomas Taylor.

	£	s	d
his apparell	10	0	0
12 Oxen & steeres	32	0	0
25 yonge bullock & heifers & one bull	44	0	0
5 steeres more	16	13	4
one horse	3	6	8
6 Naggs, mares & Coults	10	0	0
18 kine & 2 Calves	45	0	0
14 sheepe	2	0	0
Corne upon the ground	11	0	0
Corne in the Barnes	6	0	0
Hey in the house	8	13	4
One Corslet with it furniture	2	10	0
In the ground chamber by the parlor			
One standinge bedd, feather beds, boulsters Coverings & curtaynes	4	6	8
one table & one chest		5	0
In the Chamber over the porche			
Two beds	1	0	0

Goods in the chamber over the parlor
one bedd with it furniture one table one cort
    cupboard, & 2 chests   7   10   0

In the little chamber over the ground chamber by the parlor.
One bedd & one cheste   3   0   0

In the chamber over the butterie.
one bedd   2   0   0

In the store chamber
Cheese, butter, beefe bacon & other things   14   0   0

In the kitchin chamber.
Twoe bedds with theire furniture 12 chests & one Cupboard   4   0   0
foure silver spoones   2   0   0
Towe, wool, & yarne   4   0   0

In the loft over the Entrye.
One bed   10   0
Sheetes table clothes Napkins & all other Nappie Ware   10   0   0

In the backhouse or kilne
two peere of woollen clothe   3   0   0
Brass   5   0   0
Pewter & treene ware   6   10   0
Iron ware spitts goubborts & tongs & other things belonginge
to the kitchin   2   0   0
Tables stooles formes & shelves & other things in the kitchin
& kitchin buttrie   10   0
One hayre clothe one cheese presse other things   10   0
Iron bound Carts & one Mucke Wayne   4   10   0
Plowes harrowes yoaks cheanes horse geares & the furniture
    belonginge to 2 Cartes   2   0   0
one stocke sawe, billes, Mattocks shovells & all other Iron
    ware & ymplements of husbandrie   7   0   0
Carte & Plowe tymber   100   0
3 hoggs   2   0   0
Cartes & Wood for the fire   2   0   0
Mucke   1   0   0
Poultrie   13   4
Bees   10   0

[Sum   277   19   4]

Good debts due by specialties: 565   0   8

desperate debts by specialties: 250   6   0

Good debts due without specialties:		53	26	2

due upon leases, Mortgaugs & others bargaynes of lands or grounds		454	0	0

[Sum		1399	51	14]
		2061	3	2

Endorsement: Probated 16 October 1630; administration granted to Richard Mosse, one of the executors named in the will, the other executor, to whit, John Judson, having renounced according to his letter written from Nantwich to that effect.

82. JOHN BROMHALL OF SOUND, YEOMAN

S. Pr. 1 November 1630
W. T. 13 July 1630
Buried: 29 September 1630

```
John Bromhall the Elder = Anne [   ]    Ellin Bromell  =  Richard Harr[ould]     William Harrould
fl. 1613-18/19ᵃ          | † 1621      md. 1600         fl. 1600              fl. 1630
† 1633 senex            |                                                      (witness)

John Bromhall  = Elizabeth Edgeley   George Edgeley   Thomas   Robert Bromhall   Richard Tailer
fl. 1618–29ᵇ     md. 1624            fl. 1630         fl. 1630  fl. 1630          fl. 1630
† 1630           fl. 1630            (of Marley)      (of Baddiley)              (of Birmingham)
                                                                                 (brother [-in-law?])

Ellen      Sara        John        Marye      Thomas
c. 1617    c. 1619     c. 1625     c. 1629    c. 1630
fl. 1630   fl. 1630    fl. 1630–47ᶜ  fl. 1630–40ᵈ  fl. 1630
(eldest daughters)     (eldest son)              † 1672ᵉ
                       † 1672ᶠ
```

ᵃ Edward Baskerville owed debts of £1 and £2 to John *Broumole* in 1613; see inventory of Edward Baskerville of Sound, 1613 (no. 41).

ᵇ Noted as John Bromhall *the yonger*, overseer of will of John Millington, pr. 1619 (will no. 58); witness for the will of William Brees, pr. 1621 (will no. 64). Also in will of Peter Walton of Sound: witnesss and recipient of a bequest, also made the inventory (see will of Peter Walton, pr. 1618, Audlem parish/CRO). As John *Bramhall* he was a witness for the will of Andrew Cotton of Combermere, made in 1629, pr. 1640 (will no. 111).

ᶜ Witness for John Cheswis's will, pr. 1648 (will no. 127).

ᵈ Noted as the *cousin* of Thomas Gray of Newhall, who bequeathed £4 to her in 1639/40 (will no. 112).

ᵉ See inventory for Thomas Bromhall, pr. 1672/CRO.

ᶠ Thomas Manninge's will, pr. 1640, mentions property leased from him by John Bromhall; see also administration & inventory of Thomas Bromhall, 1672/CRO.

Will, sick.

First I comend my soule to almightye god my mercyfull Creator & redeemer trusting by faith in his bloud to receive remission of all my sins & I comitt my bodie to the earth whence it was in hope of a glorious change at the resurection of the just, As touchinge my worldly goods and chattells it is my will that my debts & funerall expences togeither with an herriott to the lord of the tenament wherein I dwell shall in the first place be satisfied & discharged Item I give & bequeith unto Henry Watson my servant £5 Item I give & bequeith to Elizabeth Davies my late servant £2 Item I forgive to William Sergeant a debte of 12s. which hee oweth to me Item I give & bequeith to my twoe oldest daughters Ellen Bromehall & Sara Bromehall foure paire of flaxon sheets, three paire of sheets of teere of hempe, one paire of sheets of flaxon reedings, eight pillowe beeres, twentiefoure napkins, sixe table cloths, five whereof are flaxon & on diapre twoe round table cloths, twoe towells too dozen of round napkins four paire of round sheets, twoe round towells, to witt to Ellen Bromhall such of the said linnens as are marked with the first letters of her name, & to Sara those that are marked with the first letter of her name And all the rest of my linnens & napperye I give and bequeith to my deere wyfe Elizabeth Bromhall Item I give & bequeith to my said daughters Ellen & Sara twoe feather bedds with blew Inkle about them, twoe bolsters of the same like Inckle alsoe about theim foure pillowes, one orringe coloured coveringe one redd beddhillinge, twoe white caddows twoe banketts twoe flocke bedds to bee in differrently & equally devided betweene them by my executors, Item I give to my said daughter Ellen Bromhall one silver salte over guilded & foure silver spoones whereof twoe are newe and twoe are warne Item I give & bequeith to my said daughter Sara my best silver cupp & foure silver spoones whereof twoe are newe & twoe are worne Item I give & bequeath to either of my said daughters one chest. Item I give to my said daughters Ellen Bromhall & Sara Bromhall £90 pounds to be equally devided betweene them Item I give & bequeith to my beloved wyfe abovenamed twoe newe feather bedds twoe bolsters, foure pillowes twoe bed hillings, twoe blankett twoe caddowes, twoe paire of curtaynes, one silver cupp, seavon silver spoones whereof one is over guilded, Item I give & bequeith to my eldest sonne John Bromhall all the glass and wainscott belonginge to the dwellinge house wherein I live, twoe bedsteeds whereof one is in the upper & the other in the lower chamber of the newe buildinge, the longe table, and formes in the house, one cupboard in the buttrie my best silver cupps & sixe silver spoones, Item I give and bequeith to my daughter Marye Bromhall £70. Item I give & bequeith to my sonne Thomas Bromhall £70, Moreover I give to my said deere wife 75s. And my will is that (if it please god) any of my children die before the age of 21 yeres & before that tyme be not married that then the portion of him or her soe dying shall be equally devided amonge them survivinge Item I give & bequeith to my undernamed executors 40s. to bee equallie devided amonge them, the residue of all my goods cattells & chattells I give & bequeith to my said wyfe, my sonne Thomas and daughter Marye to bee into three parts equally devided amonge them moreover whereas by my deed Indented beiringe date the 12th day

of June last past, made betweene me of the one parte & my beloved freinds Richard
Egerton of Newhall in the said countie gent Roberte Alsager of Alsager in the
said countie & George Mainwaringe of Badington in the said countie of the other
parte I have granted unto the said Richard Egerton Robert Alsager & George
Mainwaringe all that mesuage or tenament wherein I now dwell situate & beinge
in Sound aforsaid & all lands tents & heredytmts thereunto belonginge To have
& to hold the said mesuage & other the premisses from the making thereof for
all the rest & residue of the terme which I then had in the same upon special trust
& to the severall uses in the said recited deed indented mentioned In which deed
indented there is a provisoe that it shall be lawfull tax for me the said John
Bromhall at anye time & from tyme to tyme at my pleasure, duringe my naturall
lyfe by my writynge indented by mee sealed before three or more witnesses or by
my last will & testamt in writinge in like sort wittnessed to alter determine, dimin-
ish, Change or enlarge all or any use or uses conditions or intents comprized in
the said Indenture And that after such alteration determination diminishinge or
enlarginge lymitage or appoyntinge, any use or uses conditions or intents of the
said premisses or of any part or parcell thereof as is aforsaid The use onely of soe
much of the premisses whereof any alteration determination dyminishinge or
enlarginge shall be so had & made shalbe to such person & persons uses intents
& conditions as shalbe mentioned specified or declared in that writing indented
or last will & testament & to none other person or persons uses intents nor provisions in anywyse, as by the said deed indented more at large appereth Nowe I
the said John Bromhall doe by these presents declare my last will & testament to
be that if it please god to offer my said friends partye to the said deed indented
theire executors administrators or assignes or any of them a fitt oporunitye upon
termes to theire likinge of takinge the said mesuage or tenemente wherein I live
& lands tenements & hereditamts thereto belonginge for the live of my twoe sonnes
or incase she or either of them be dead of such other child or children of mine as
she shall make choyce of, soe that she take the said mesuage lands tenaments &
other the premisses for the lives of three or at least of twoe of my children That
then the my said freinds parties to the said deed indented the survivors or survivor of them theire or his executors administrators or assignes shall have lawfull
right to surrendre the lease by which I now hould to my honored lord & Mr Sir
Richard Wilbraham knight & Barronett his heyres or assignes & to paye to him
or them for such other lease as is aformenconed out of such of the rents yssues
& profitts of the said mesuage & after the premisses as are formerly by my said
deed appoynted to bee by them employed to the use of John Bromhall my sonne
& to bee to him delivered when hee shall come to the age of 21 yeres & if hee
die before that age then to the use of my sonne Thomas to bee delivered to him
when hee shall come to the age of twentie & one yeres & if hee die before that
age then to the use of the other persons to whom it is by the said deed respectively appointed And my will is that my said freinds theire executors & administrators shall bee discharged of & from the payement of soe much of the said rents
issues & profitts (as shall be so paied for such lease as aforsaid) unto my said
sonne John or any other to whom by the said deed they are appointed to paye the

same. And that incase the said rents yssues & profitts so appointed to be employed to the use of my said sonn or sonnes or other persons respectivelye doe not amount to soe much as shall bee soe payed for such lease as aforsaid before the same shall bee due & payeable to my said sonne John or to such other person or persons to whom by the said deed it is appointed Then my will is That my said sonne John shall within twelve monthes after hee shall attaine to the age of 21 yeres paie to my said freinds Richard Egerton Roberte Alsager & George Mainwaringe or the survivors of them his or theire executors administrators or assignes the rest of such summe & summes as hath bin so by them paid togeither with all such damage as the have susteined by the forbearance of the same and shall alsoe paie to Thomas my sonne, the summe of £30 if the said Thomas be then lyvinge or incase the said John die before he come to the age 21yeres, that then such other person or persons to whom by my said deed the use & trust of the said mesuage & other the premisses is lymitted shall within twelve moneths after hee or they shall attayne to the age of 21 yeres paye to my said freinds theire executors or assignes the rest of such summe or summes as hath bin soe by them payd togeither with all such damage ass the have sustained by the forbearance of the same And in defalte of such payement my will is that my said freinds Richard Egerton Roberte Alsager & George Mainwaringe theire executors administrators & assignes shall receive and take the moytie of the rents issues & profitts of so much of the said mesuage lands & tenaments as should or ought otherwise have come to the person or persons soe makinge default of paiement untill such time as such summe or summes soe by them paid togeither with such damage as aforesaid and alsoe the said summe of £30 to my sonne Thomas, if the same fall to be due, bee fully discharged. Moreover whereas by the said deed it is provided, That if Elizabeth my wyfe doe refuse to keepe & maintaine my children, or to yeild an indifferrent rent for anye such parte of the premisses as may upon the determination of any former estate by me made revert to the said Richard Egerton Roberte Alsager & George Mainwaringe by vertue of the said deed or doe marrie or die before anye sonne of mine doe come to the age of 21 That then they the said Richard Egerton Roberte Alsager & George Mainwaringe there executors & assignes shall out of the yssues & profitts of the said mesuage lands tenaments & other the premisses (those formerly conveyed for the joynture of the said Elizabeth onely excepted) levie & raise sufficient meanes & the same faithfully expend & employe accordinge as by the said provisoe is appointed Nowe my will is that they the said Richard Egerton Roberte Alsager & George Mainwaringe theire executors & assignes shall after anye of the said contingencies, out of the issues & profitts as well of those lands tenaments or hereditaments formerly conveyed for the joynture of the said Elizabeth as of anye other contayned in the said deed levie & raise sufficient meanes & the same faithfully expend & employe in the same manner & forme & to the same use & purpose as for the meanes levied & raised out of the rest of the said mesuage lands tenaments & other the premisses is & are by the said provisoe lymited & appointed in like manner as if the said lands tenaments or heredytaments formerly conveyed to the said Elizabeth for the Joynture had not at all bene excepted nor foreprized by the said provisoe Alsoe whereas in the said deed it is lymited & appointed that they the said Richard Egerton Roberte Alsager & George Mainwaringe theire & everye of theire executors administrators & assignes shall permitt & suffre the said mesuage lands tenaments & all other the premisses thereby granted to be houlden & enjoyed & the profitts thereof to bee received & taken by John Bromhall my sonne & his assignes to his & theire owne use & behoofe so soone as he shall accomplish the age of 21yeres from thencefourth for fortie yeres & if my sonne John die before hee come to the age of 21yeres then the same to be houlden & enjoyed in like manner by my sonne Thomas & his assignes when hee shall accomplish the age of 21yeres & if hee die before he come to the age of 21 yeres, then the same to bee houlden & enjoyed by diveres other persons severelie as by the said deed at large appereth Nowe my will is & I doe hereby lymitt & appoint that the said John Bromhall my sonne & his assignes soe soone as he as he shall accomplish the age of 21 yeres or if hee die before that age, then the said Thomas Bromhall my sonne & his assignes so soone as hee shall accomplish the age of 21 yeres & if hee die before that age then everye of such person or persons to whom the same is by the said deed lymited & appointed shall hould & enjoye the said mesuage lands tenaments & other the premisses & the profitts thereof shall take & receive to there owne use & behoofe not onely for the said terme of fortie yeres by the said deed mentioned, but alsoe for & duringe all the terme by mee by the said deed to the said Richard Egerton Roberte Alsager & George Mainwaringe granted & assigned & then not expired, And in all other things my will is that as well the said recyted deed Indented made to my said freinds Richard Egerton Roberte Alsager & George Mainwaringe as alsoe such lease soe bee by them taken shall be to the same uses intents & purposes as in the said before named deed indented.

Executors: my deere & beloved brothers Richard Tailer of Burmingham in the Countie of Warwicke, Thomas Bromhall of Baddiley in the said Countie of Chester, Roberte Bromhall of Nantwich in the said Countie of Chester & George Edgley of Marley in the said County of Chester.

H. & S.

Memorandum that before the ensealinge & publishinge of this to bee the last will of the said John Bromhall, the worde foure was enterlyned & three strucken out in the eighteeneth lyne in the legacie given to Ellen & Sara Bromhall & some other words of lesse moment were enterlyned with the same hand & then the said John Bromhall published & declared this as his last will.

Witnesses: William Kinge, George Mainwaringe, William Couper, Thomas Noden, William Harrould, John Bromhall.

Inventory: John Bromehall of Sound yeoman.

Taken: 6 October 1630

Of: goods debts cattells & chattels.

Prisers: Robert Alsager, Thomas Edgley, John Judson, Raphe Judson.

	£	s	d
in the hall one joynt table 2 formes one lesser table with 6 stooles & 6 cushins	2	7	8
in the litle new parlour one joynt bed curtaines & vallaines with rods one arras coveringe 2 blanketts 2 bolsters one featherbed one chaffe bed & bolster & one mattress	6	13	4
one liverye Cubboard		10	0
three boxes		2	6
in the lower parlor one joynt bed with curtaynes & rods one coveringe one white caddowe one blankett three bolsters one featherbed one flockbed with foure course mattresse	6	15	0
one Court Cupboard one cheare fire shovell & tonnges		12	0
in the little chamber one standinge bed one coveringe 2 blanketts 2 bolsters one feather bed & one little table	3	16	8
in the litle upper chamber one standinge bed one paire of curtaines with rods one bolster, one pillowe one featherbed one white caddowe one coverlett	5	0	0
one presse		13	4
one table one chest of wainscott & one chaire		14	0
one gowne one peticote with greene silke silver laces	3	0	0
one cupboard cloth with silk fringe		10	0
3 boxes 5 stoole frames		8	0
all his bookes with booke frame	5	6	0
in the rowme over the hall 2 standinge bedds	1	13	8
one truckle bed with bedd cords one white caddowe one coveringe one blankett 2 bolsters one featherbedd one mattresse	4	18	6
one ioynt press		13	4
one ioynt chest 3 coffers one chaire one paire of curtaines	1	16	0
one paire of wrought vallaines & cupboard cloth with silke fringe one wrought cushin	2	0	0
3 carpetts all att	1	0	0
one bearinge cloth of stamell with lace att		10	0
2 peecs of wollen cloth att	1	16	0
some odde things in the presse		5	0
one clock att	1	0	0
in the cheese chamber one standinge bed 3 pillowes 2 coverletts one blankett 2 bolsters one chaffe bed & bolsters	2	0	0
one standinge press att	1	0	0
one bedsteed one coveringe one blankett & featherbed one chaffe bedd one bolster & pillowe all att	2	13	4
for cheese at	8	0	0
cheese frame & loose boards	1	0	0
one coffer at		6	0
rendred tallowe with other liquors att		10	0

9 paire of flaxon sheets att	5	1	0
ten pair of teare & a hempe sheets att	3	10	0
five paire of readinge sheets	1	5	0
12 paire of sheets overworne att	2	0	0
one diaper table cloth with 6 napkins att	1	0	0
7 table cloths att	1	6	8
4 dosen of napkins at		10	0
10 paire of pillowe beares att	1	0	0
6 table cloths att	1	10	0
4 flaxon towells att		6	8
one dosen of napkins att		5	0
6 yards of flaxon att		10	0
12 elne of canvas att		10	0
20 elne of canvas att	1	0	0
10 elne more att		10	0
in teare of flaxe & yarne		8	0
10 elne of cloth att		10	0
16 pounds of wooll	1	16	8
in mesures basketts wisketts Sives wheeles brakes & other implements of husbandrie att		13	4
in the buttry one ioynt bedd att		4	0
3 barrells one stoond 2 firkins att		10	0
more barrells and stoond all att		5	0
a hundred & eighte pound of pewter all att	4	16	0
in pann brasse 6 [?]at 16s.	4	6	8
in pott brasse att	2	11	0
a fornace panne one kettle one warminge pan all att	10	10	0
2 musketts one fowlinge peece 2 paire of bandileeres one cappe one sword with shott & powder & 2 girdles all att	2	13	4
in the kitchin one table 2 dressers one chaire one ioynt cradle one bacon chest one barrell with salt all att	13	4	0
in bacon 5 sides & powdred beefe all att	1	13	4
grate spitts dripyinge panns fire shovell tonngs bellies frieinge pann gobbar & landiron all att	2	0	0
one iron morter with pestill dubbinge sheeres & other implements all at		6	8
in the servants chamber 2 bedstockes three coverletts 3 blanketts with chaffe bedds & bolsters all att	2	0	0
in earthen potts all att		1	6
more Cowperie ware	1	6	8
in clout leather & 2 tandskins		10	0
in the loft over the servants chamber in yarne & towe		10	0
in Towe		5	0
in sacks winowinge sheets & hall	1	0	0
other odde things in this chamber		10	0

	£	s	d
4 barrells of vargesse & one emptie barrell at		13	0
one bedsteed with foure mattresse		4	0
in the backhowse one troughe att		2	6
in Cowperie ware att	1	0	0
in Cheese fatte saltinge basens & all other traineware		13	0
other things in the backhowse		4	0
in the kilne one haire nett cloth att		3	4
in timber broken & whole att	8	0	0
all moveable goods in the mill at	1	0	0
in cattle 14 kine att 2 £ 10s	35	0	0
4 calves & one sterke att	3	0	0
one bull att	2	10	0
2 horses whereof one for a herriott	8	0	0
3 more horses & mares att	7	0	0
2 colts att	3	10	0
all the corne in the barne	30	0	0
[hay in the] barne att	8	0	0
waines carts plowes Harrowes yokes chaines horsegeares & all other workinge instruments	6	13	4
one woemans saddle with cloth & pyllin att		10	0
for shiers & one burdnett att		10	0
one pumpe att		4	0
in mucke	1	15	0
in fewell as stocke, kidds, cole & turf all att	2	10	0
4 shoate swine att	2	10	0
in pullin		13	4
brake & byle	16	0	0
one sleadhowse valued att		13	4
stone troughes & stone tubs a grindle stone & a stone troughe	1	5	0
a sett of shookes & fellies		6	8
Corne in the house	4	10	0
12 course cushins att		5	0
all his wearinge apparell with ridinge furniture att	8	0	0

Debts Owing by Specialties March 26 1631

	£	s	d
7 bonds from Mr William Mainwaringe £4 per annum the first due	28	0	0
4 bonds from Mr Tymothie Buckley £6 per annum the first due March 25th if Sara Bromhall bee then lyvinge	24	0	0
Mr William Mainwaringe is to paye in presente att Michelmas last	14	15	0
Richard Heroold by bill due in December 1631	9	16	0

John Fisher of Aston owinge by bonnd £2 per annum for 7 yeres	14	0	0
John Beckett owinge by bonnd if Sara Bromhall bee lyvinge March the 25th	4	0	0
[ ]7 bands from Hall & Chester whereof the 3 last of £4 per annum are casualtie if Ellen Bromhall or Jane Breese die	28	0	0
owinge by Arthure Starke Esqr	3	0	0
by Richard Evanson in rent	2	10	0
Thomas Snelson owes	3	0	0
Thomas Tailer owes	4	0	0
William Wollam owes	2	0	0
Richard Spencer		6	0
Mr George Mainwaringe		11	8
Widdowe Tailer	2	0	0
James Baker owes		1	3
Thomas Loe owes	10	0	0
Thomas Stubs	4	0	0
Thomas Lowe his rent due nowe att Bartholometide last	5	2	3
Arthure Hurleston for Ashlors owinge		8	0
Widdow Buckley owes		4	3
Widdowe Preist owes	12	0	0
a lease assigned from Edward Asager to the testator whereupon was disbursed by the testator the summe of £55 13s. 4d. to enter upon the said lyvinge five yeres hence if the said Edward Alsager bee then lyvinge I saye disburse the summe of	55	13	4

Exhibitum cum protestacōne.

Endorsement: Probated 1 November 1630; administration granted to the executors named in the will.

83. RICHARD HALL OF SMEATONWOOD

S.Pr. (contested) 13 January 1630/31
Buried: 12 December 1630

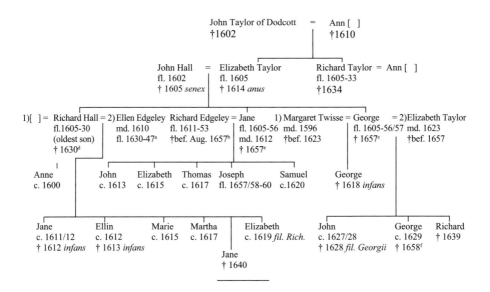

Inventory: Richard Hall of Smeatonwood.

Taken: 22 December 1630

Of: goodes and Cattells.

Prisers: George Bickerton, Richard Bickerton, John Ravenscrofte, Edward Palyne.

---

a   William Fergusson Irvine, *Chester Licences*, iv. 89: 19 November 1610 – Richard Hall and Ellen Edgeley of Wrenbury parish; at Wrenbury; the parish register shows the same date for the actual marriage. Co-executor, with her brother Richard Edgeley, for her husband, below; *Widdow* Hall paid tithe at Newhall, 1647/CRO.
b   Co-executor with his sister, Ellen Hall, for Richard Hall, below; whether he was the Richard Edgeley buried at Wrenbury in 1648 or the one in 1651 is unclear.
c   For documentation, see will of George Hall (will no. 142), note c.
d   Noted in will of his father, John Hall of Smeatonwood, pr. 1605 (will no. 22); kinsman of William Fletcher, and overseer, witness to codicil and priser for him, will pr. 1607 (will no. 23); priser for George Kemp, will pr. 1616 (will no. 50); Newhall Rentals 1625/CRO; noted in will of Andrew Cotton, made 1629, pr. 1640 (will no. 111), who held land of him in Newhall.
e   See will of Jane Edgeley of Moorehall, pr. 1657/58 (will no. 144).
f   See will of George Hall, Jr, pr. 1658 (will no. 147).

	£	s	d
in redye money	3	13	4
the Reverson of a lease from Thomas Roades of a parcell of Marbury Heys for three yeares	4	0	0
the reversion of A lease from Mr Starkey of a parte Wrenbury Woods	55	0	0
the reversion of a lease from Hughe Hopkyn for *[damaged]*			0
Two oxen	9	0	0
Two heffer oxen	7	10	0
Two steares	4	0	0
Nyne Kyne and A bull	30	0	0
Fowre incalfe heffers	9	6	8
two twynter bullockes & two heffers	4	0	0
Fowre Calves		33	4
Two mares	6	0	0
Sixe Sheepe		30	0
one Fatt hogge		20	0
Fowre yeonge shootes		16	0
Corne in the barne	16	0	0
hey in the barne	11	0	0
Cartes plowes yokes cheynes harrowes And other ymplements of husbandrye	5	5	0
plankes bordes rayles pannell and muntaynes and Carte and plowe Tymber of all sortes	8	0	0
one weetinge Combe a heare cloth brakes tutalls kneadinge trough and other thinges of huswyfferye		33	4
In bees		25	0
ladders grindellstone and fewell		5	0
powltrye ware		10	0
Corne sowed upon the ground	3	0	0
Corne and malte in the house		30	0
beeffe and bacon	3	0	0
three silver spoones		15	0
in the parler one waynescott Bested *[i.e. bedstead]* Truckell bed table presse Cheeres stooles Cushens and beddinge	5	0	0
other Romes in the house two waynscotts Beedes Fowre playne bedsteed with the Furniture of beddinge and Chistes in the same Romes	8	5	0
napperye wares sheetes table clothes napkynes and other lynnens	5	0	0
in the house tables formes cubbordes Cheares stooles waynescott and glasse		50	0
woole and Tawe		30	0
butter Cheese and bread	6	0	0
brasse and pewter	6	3	4

Cowpery vessells and other wodden vessells	45	0
a Cheese presse formes bordes and sheelves in severall Roomes	10	0
saddells brydles horse geers mattockes bills axes wedges shovells & other Iron ware belonging to husbandrye	13	3
spitts golberts, Andirons And other Iron stuffe	13	3

Some is   229   12   8
Executum cum protestacōne

Endorsement: Exhibited 13 January 1630. . . .

NOTE: Only the tiniest fragment remains of the record of contest regarding this will; it is written on both sides, but there are no complete sentences.

The Charge: The condicōn of this obligation is such that . . . doe well & truly administer all . . .
of Richard Hall late of Smeatonwood . . .
deceased accordinge to theffect of lettres of Admin[istracōn] . . .
and debts and said de . . . the . . .
goods rights Credits cattells & Chattels . . .
John Hall . . . And doe exhibite . . .
. . . a true & perfect Inventory of . .
executors of the said deceased . . .
. . . uppon the . . . doe make . . .
. . . all or other . . .
. . . of the said reverend father . . .
. . . that behalf shalbe lymitted . . .
. . . the said reverend father . . .
. . . for and concerning the . . .
. . . to bee sayd, . . .

[side 2]
. . . in the countie of Chester . . .
. . . obligating . . .
. . . two hundred pounds of good and . . .
. . . in the year of our king lord . . . Charles 1 . . .

Signature of Ellene Hall, Richard [Edgeley]

84. TIMOTHY BUCKLEY OF SMEATONWOOD, GENT.

S.Pr. 10 March 1630/31
Buried: 9 November 1630

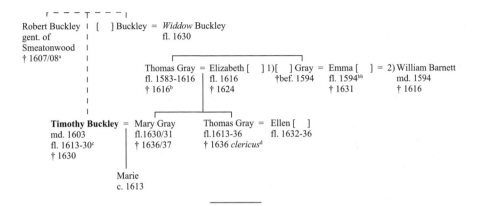

Inventory: Tymothy Bulckley of Smeatonwood, gent.

Taken: 8 December 1630

Of: goods and Chattells.

Prisers: William Maynwaring, George Mainwaring, Thomas Gray.

	£	s	d
three kine valued at	6	13	4
two clocks and a watch all ould	4	0	0
Eight payer of sheets whereof two were flaxen	2	10	0
Three payer of pillowe beeres one dozen and a halfe of napkins and two Table Clothes	1	4	8
One presse		10	0
Two Chests two trunks foure boxes		8	4
One fetherbedd one wooll bedd, five Blanketts, one Rugg, two bolsters, one pillowe, one payer of Bedstocks	5	0	0

ª See will of Robert Buckley, pr. 1607/08 (will no. 24).
ᵇ See will of Thomas Gray of Smeatonwood, pr. 1616/17 (will no. 53).
ᵇᵇ Married for the second time 1594 to William Barnett; see his inventory, 1616 (no. 52); see will of Emma Barnett, pr. 1631 (will no. 87).
ᶜ See will of Thomas Gray, 1613 (will no. 53); owed, along with George Gray (clearly a kinsman of his wife) a debt of £11 to James Brooke, 1622 (will no. 66)); owed John Bromhall £24, payable in four sums of £6 each over four years, 1630 (will of John Bromhall, will no. 82).
ᵈ See will of Thomas Gray of Aston, pr. 1636. (will no. 99).

Some siverall pieces of Brasse & Pewter		4	0
One fowling peice		13	4
Two saddles, two bridles		6	8
One table, two wheeles, one Chayre, two stooles three cushions		10	0
flaxen yarne		10	0
One bale of flax		5	0
Tow mappes		2	0
Twenty pound of hopps		8	4
One load of haye		6	8
Tooles and implements	1	0	0
Money due to him from Mr Cotton the worth of the Herriotts deducted	8	0	0
other debts, good and bad	6	6	8
His bookes	1	13	4
His wearing apparrell Ringe Sword and money in his purse	13	6	8
Summa totallis	54	4	0

Endorsement: Exhibited 10 March 1630/31; administration granted to Mary his widow.

85. WILLIAM BABINGTON OF CHORLEY, GENT.

S.Pr. 1630/31
W.T. 3 February 1630/31
Buried: 9 February 1630/31

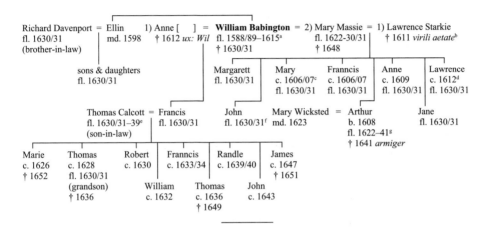

Will *[there is no traditional introduction of the testator].*

To the poore of the parishe of Wrenbury £5 to bee distrybuted by his executors or to add to the stocke already given to buy lands for the use of the same poore att the discrecōn of my executors.**ʰ** To Mary his wief his lease of his parte of

---

ᵃ Executor for his cousin William Bebbington of Chorley in the latter's will, pr. 1592 (will no. 9); as William Bebington of the Hall of Chorley, overseer of the will of Robert Tenche (will no. 45). Whether the Marie Bebington, *filia Willelmi*, who was baptized at Wrenbury in 1599, belongs to this William or to his cousin cannot be determined. Nor can the William and Thomas who died in 1599 and 1600 respectively as small boys *(pueres)* be placed. Francis thus survived as the only child of record for William and his first wife.

ᵇ See inventory of Lawrence Starkie of Wrenbury, exh. 1611/12 (no. 38).

ᶜ Ormerod, *History of Cheshire*, iii. 207, gives her husband's name as Henry *Rutter* which is better than the corrupted *Ritter* found on the Visitation pedigree of 1663; Henry was the son of Henry Rytter of *Broomhall*, not *Bramhall* as the Visitation record suggests.

ᵈ Ormerod, *History of Cheshire*, iii. 207, shows him dying unmarried.

ᵉ Made inventory for Thomas Hamnett, 1635 as Thomas Calcott, gent. (will no. 97); made inventory for William Wilson, 1639 (will no. 109); witness to will of Roger Jones, 1638/39 (will no. 110).

ᶠ Ormerod, *History of Cheshire*, iii. 207, makes him a citizen of London.

ᵍ Identified as the next of kin and heir of his grandfather, Arthur Starkey in the latter's IPM, 1622 (will no. 69)); received bequest of 20s. from William Babington, 1630/31; owed debt of 10s. to Richard Cheswis, 1632/33 (will no. 93); bequeathed 3s. 4d. in will of Elizabeth Briscoe, 1632 (will no. 103); died 1641.

ʰ This bequest is found in the 'Catalogue of such charitable gifts as have been given to the Church of Wrenbury', noted in Norwood, *Historic Notes*, no. xlii, citing Harleian MS 2176, fo. 64ᐱ.

Wrenbury Park dureing his interest herein if shee the said Mary doe soe longe lyve And after her decease to the heyres of the said William Babington. And in Case the sayd parte of the sayd Park bee not or Contynue of the cleare yearely vallue of £10 that then the executors shall pay to her yearely soe much money as shall make the sayd upp £10 yearely That in case his lease determyne dureing the lief tyme of the sayd Mary that then the Heyres of the body of the sayd William, shall after the same is ended pay to the said Mary yearely out of his tenement in Chorley dureing her lief, if the estate in the same tenement soe longe contynue £5 yearely att Michaelmas and the Annuntiacōn To Mary his wief the Remaynder of a lease of the tenement in Wrenbury which Came by her. To the Right honorable Robert Viscount Cholmondley an Elizabeth peece of gould. To John Margarett Mary Franncis Jane Anne & Lawrence Children of the sayd Mary begotten by Lawrance Starkey gentleman deceased her Former husband £5 a peece To the sonnes & daughters of Richard Davenport his brother in lawe 20s. a peece. To ~~his~~ Richard Babington my servante £5. To Frances my doughter the best bed with yt furniture in the Chamber over the howse. To his wief the seacond bedd as ytt is furnished and her owne bedd which shee brought.

[p. 2 – Top destroyed – two lines unreadable] To William Wright and Thomas his sonne 20s. a peece. To my wief the lessr silver bowle for her lief after to her sonn John Starkye. The salt & six silver spoones to my daughter. To Margarett Fleete 5s. To Anne Ackson 20s. To Thomas Calcott his grandchild his silver bowle. To his wief six silver spoones. To Arthur Starky gentleman 20s. to buy him a Ringe. To Mr Nicholls preacher of gods Word 10s. To Andrew Babingtons Children 10.s a peece. To Richard Dabers children 40s. to bee equally dyvided amongest them. To John Palin 10s. To Ellin the daughter of Richard Willson 20s. To Elizabeth Bafford 10s. To Symon Fawkever 10s. To Alie my Servante 10s. To Richard Willson preacher of gods words 20s. all my implements for husbandry to my sonninlawe Thomas Calcott. The rest of my houshould stuffe & goodes Legacies and Severall expences discharged to my wief and daughter to bee equally devided.

Inventory: William Babington of Chorley, gent.

Taken: 21 February 1630/31

Of: goods & cattells.

Prisers: William Wright, William Steele, Edward Palin, John Savage.

	£	s	d
4 oxen & 2 steers	26	0	0
14 kyne	44	6	8
3 steers 3 yeare old	7	0	0
5 twynter beastes	7		
2 heiffers & a bull	7		
2 Calves		33	4
2 horses & one mare	13	6	8

Bees		10	0
Poultrey		8	0
one Fatt Swyne & 5 rearing swyne	3	0	0
carts ploughes & all manner of husbandrye ware	6	13	1
a peece of a brick kyllne		10	0
all other bricke about the howse		20	0
stone		10	0
Fyre Fewell		10	0
mucke		10	0
Hay	15	0	0
Corne	20	0	0
corne groweinge	3	10	0
Malte	3	0	0
spokes & Fellies mountayne an parcell		33	4
boards & Reales		30	0
the best beed in the chamber over the old howse with yt furniture	7	0	0
a truckle bedd in the same chamber with ytt furniture		30	0
a Cupboard in the same chamber		5	0
hoay candles and hopes		5	0
one bed in the old chamber with yt furniture		30	0
Tables cheares stooles & one Forme in the old howse		42	0
Carpetts & Cushions		30	0
a bedd in the lyttle new chamber with ytt furniture	3	10	0
another bedd in the same chamber	2	10	0
Wollen Cloth		30	0
a Cupboard a lyttle table a truckle & some lyttle boxes		30	0
a warminge pann		5	0
pewter in the buttery with Cupps glasses & trenchers	4	10	0
brasse	8	0	0
Iron Ware in the howse		13	4
2 tables & a Forme in the new howse		8	0
one bedd in the chamber over the new howse with yt furniture	5	0	0
an other bedd in the same chamber	3	10	0
one Cupboard 4 chestes & a box		13	4
Cheeses	33	0	0
Butter		13	4
yorne & towe		20	0
wooll		23	0
Cheese boards & basketts		10	0
Lynnens	10	0	0
Bacon	4	0	0
Sacks bags a wynnoweing sheete and a hayre cloth		26	8
troughes & a Flaskett		6	8
Tymber	6	0	0
a Bybell		6	8

in Plate	11	0	0
his apparell	16	0	0
in ready money	28	8	0
a lease of ground	20	0	0
all his debtes	6	0	0
two cock sute netts and many small thinges		10	0
one fatt heiffer		1	0
[Sum	320	597	61]

exhibitum cum protestacōne &c

Endorsement: None.

86. ELLEN RAVENSCROFT OF NEWHALL, WIDOW

S.Pr. [after 11 March] 1630/31
W.T. 21 February 1626/27
Buried: 10 March 1630/31

a Homager of Newhall Manor Court, 1609; noted 1626 in will of George Dickins, pr. 1630.
b See will of Thomas Ravenscroft, pr. 1614 (will no. 43).
c Executor, 1625, and priser, 1626/27, for George Dickins (will no. 74); priser for Thomas Shrowbridge 1626/27 (will no. 75); overseer and witness for the will, and priser of the goods, of John Hall, 1635/36 (will no. 100)..
d William Fergusson Irvine, *Chester Licences*, iii. 36: 10 August 1625, Thomas Ravenscroft and Mary Taylor, spinster of Wrenbury; at Wrenbury or Audlem. Priser for George Dickins, 1626/27 (will no. 74); witness to will of John Hall, pr.1636 (will no.100).
e Made inventory for Richard Hall, 1630 (no. 83) and John Cartwright, 1634/35 (no. 96); see inventory of John Ravenscroft, exh. 1650 (no. 137).
f John Smith was related to Ellen Ravenscroft in close enough fashion to warrant a £12 legacy which she insisted was the limit of his claim on her goods; from this we may surmise that he was either the husband of a deceased daughter (the word *my* immediately preceding his name has been crossed out), or perhaps the base-born son of her deceased husband.

Will, sick.

First I give and bequeath my selfe both soule and body into the hands of Allmighty God, trustinge that I shalbe saved by the meritts and passion of my Savior Jesus Christ, and *my body to be buried in the parish Church of Wrenbury*. Item I give unto my eldest sonn John Ravenscroft the two joyned bedds standing in the Parlor, the two ioyned tables, and all the wainescott, and they shall remain earelomes to his sonn unmoveable also I give unto him five pounds in money for his Childs parte demanding noe more of my goods. Item I doe give unto his sonn Thomas Twenty shillings Item I doe give unto his daughter Anne Tenn shillings, and to his daughter Elizabeth Tenn shillings. Item I doe give unto my sonn Thomas Ravenscroft the greate fowlinge peece & twelve pence in money for his Childs parte demanding noe more of my goods. Item I give unto my sonn in law John Booth my Iron bounde Carte, with the Chaines and geeres, and all that doth belonge unto it, for I have made them all newe since my husbands decease, also my will is, that he and his wiefe Elizabeth shall have al his revercōn of yeares which I have of his house in Hankelow payeinge unto Roger Peate of Anson the sum of twelve pounds ayeare for soe many yeares that are remayning of the yeares that I am bound with him to the said Roger Peate, finding himselfe and his wife sufficiente of meate drinke and apparill, but if my sonn in law shall faile in payeing the said some of twelve pounds as above said, then my will is that my daughters Ellen Reavenscroft and Ann Ravenscroft shall have all my revercōn of yeares in his house abovesaid, payeing the said sum of twelve pounds a yeare to the said Roger Peate, and an keeping my sonn in law and his wife with sufficient of meate drinke and apparell. Item I give unto my daughter Elizabeth Booth my biggest brasse Pann. Item I doe give unto ~~my~~ John Smith twelve pounds in money demanding noe more of my goods. Item I doe give unto my three daughters Ellen Ravenscroft Ann Ravenscroft and Elizabeth Boothe all my househould goods whatsoever before unmencend to be equally devided amonge them Item I doe give and bequeath all the rest and residue of my goods and Cattells with my bills & bonds, and all obligatory matters whatsoever unto me belonginge or in anywaies appertaininge, unto my said three daughters Ellen Ravenscroft Ann Ravenscroft & Elizabeth Booth, bringinge me home and dischargeing my funeral expenses. Also my will is, that if my sonn in law John Booth either mispend his goods, or not use his wiefe as he ought to doe, that my said daughters parte of my goods shall goe forward for her owne purpose and her Childe, in my Executors: hands. And further my will is, that if God call for any of my daughters before my goods be devided, her parte shall remaine to the other two. Item I doe give unto my Godchildren 12d. a peece. Item I doe give unto the poore of Newhall Twenty shillings, whereof Robert Deverise shall have two shillings, and to Thomas Gray the elder twelve pence, and to Thomas Gray the younger two shillings, & to Margerie Morrese two shillings, and to Richard Lase two shillings, & to Mary Massie two shillings, and rest to be devided by the discrecōn of my Executor:

Executor: the testatrix's son, John Ravenscroft.

Overseer: my wellbeloved in Christ Thomas Backhouse of Newhall aforesaid yeoman.

H. & S.
Ellen Ravenscroft her marke

Witness: Thomas Graye.

Inventory: Ellen Ravenscroft of Newhall Widdowe.

Taken: 11 March 1630/31

Of: goods and cattels.

Prisers: George Halle, Lawrance Wilkinson, Thomas Backhouse and Humfrey Podmore.

	£	s	d
her wearing aparrell	5	0	0
Beddings of all sorts as feather bedds a flocke bed and other bedds with boulsters pillowes coverings blankets and curteynes	13	17	4
a peace of curteynes and wyre rods		1	6
linnen and nappery	5	19	3
six silver spounes	1	16	0
one cow called deasye	3	3	4
one cow called lee	2	13	4
one cow called cop set to gyve to John Ravenscroft till martlemas prased with the hyre	3	13	4
one cow set to gyve to Robert Whittingham til the 10th of December next with hyre	2	13	4
one cow lent John Booth till martlemas	2	10	0
one fower yeare old heffer	3	0	0
two three yeare old heffers	6	6	8
one two yeare old heffer	1	3	4
a mare	4	0	0
a swyne		9	0
corne in the barne	1	13	4
hay in the barne	2	10	0
Coles and fewell		9	6
a old combe, old heire cloth a turnell 3 spinning wheeles a reele and a brake		12	3
a packelant, old sydesadle a old packsadle & a pillin			4
all manner of tryne ware as peales turnells stounds barrels chesefatts dishes & trenchers	1	5	4
vergisse		6	0
Cheares and stooles		6	0
a Cubboard		10	0

a old ioyned bed with other bedstockes boards sheilves & formes		9	6
syves riddles basketts and flasketts		5	0
pewter in generall	1	15	6
Brasse in generall	2	2	10
an Iron pot and an Iron ketle		12	0
Iron ware of all sorts		12	8
fowre fliches of bacon	1	12	0
Corne in the house		13	4
Butter and Cheese	6	0	0
bread and beare		6	8
3 picktures ticknall ware & a grater		5	6
two Joyned bedds in the parlor & two joyned tables	3	0	0
a little Joyned table and two formes		10	0
three geese		3	0
three swyne trowes		1	0
a Iron bound carte and geares	1	5	0
mucke		2	0
a fowling peece	1	0	0
debtes oweinge by specialtyes and the remaynder of a lease from William Flecher	38	17	0
debts oweing without specialtyes	9	10	0
the rent of a feild of William Cartwright	1	23	0
money in the house	1	2	0
Chests and Coffers		9	0
Corne on the ground	3	10	0
towe and yarne sackes a winnow sheete and paynted clothes		7	0
for salte	0	0	0
[Sum	121	384	106]

Endorsement: The wrapper for the will is badly soiled, making the date of probate impossible to read.

87. EMMA BARNETT OF WRENBURY, WIDOW

S.Pr. 24 October 1631
W.T. 15 January 1630/31
Buried: [about 5] May 1631

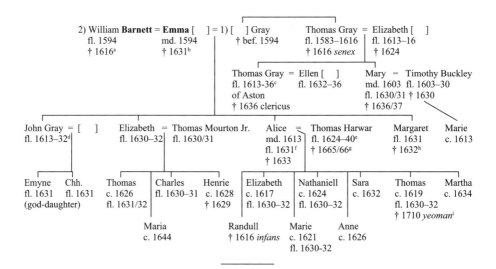

Will, sick.

First and principally I Comende my soule into the handes of allmightie God hopeing by the bloudsheedinge of Jesus Christe my alone saviour to have free pardon and remission of all my sinnes and *my body I Comitt to the earth to bee buried in the Churche of Wrenbury* aforesaid in sure and Certaine hope of a ioyfull resurrection. Item I give and bequeath unto Thomas Harware and to Thomas Mourton the younger my two mares to be equally devided betweene them. Item I give unto Emyne Graye my goddoughter one pide Cowe with a blease Down her face Item I give unto my doughter Margaret and unto my doughter Elizabeth to either of

---

a   See inventory of William Barnett, 1616 (no. 52).
b   Recorded as *Emyn* Barnet.
c   See will of Thomas Gray of Aston, pr. 1636 (will no. 99).
d   Bondsman for his sister Alice's marriage to Thomas Harwar, 1613; see below, note f.
e   Witness to will of Oliver Briscoe, pr. 1630 (will no. 80).
f   See William Fergusson Irvine, *Chester Licences*, i. 143: 23 July 1613, Thomas Harwar and Alice *Barnett* (actually) at Aldford, Cheshire; bondsman was John Grey.
g   Clerk at Wrenbury; see inventory of Thomas Harwar, pr. 1665/66/CRO.
h   See will of Margaret Graye, pr. 1632 (will no. 89).
i   If so, then he lived to be ninety years of age!

them a Cowe Item I give unto Elizabeth Harwar one Cowe Item I give unto
Nathaniell Harwar and to Marie Harwar one Cowe betweene them Item I give to
Charles Mourton one browne heiffer Item I give unto my doughter Margaret above
said one Cowe. Item I give unto my doughter Elizabeth abovesaid my best pott
Item I give unto my said doughter Margarett my seconde pott. Item I give unto
my doughter Alice Harwar my greate kettle Item I give unto Elizabeth Harwar
that pann Which came from Aston. Item I give unto my doughter Elizabeth my
greate old panne and a skimmer. Item I give unto my doughter Margarett a pann
of two gallons a little pott two little kettles and a skellet and a brasen Candlesticke.
Item I give unto Elizabeth Mourton a brasen Candlesticke. Item I give unto
Elizabeth Harwar a pewter Candlesticke. Item I give unto my doughter Margarett
my doughter Elizabeth and to Elizabeth Harwar all my pewter to be equally devided amongst them. Item I give unto my doughter Margaret my Cupebord in the
buttrye. Item I give unto Elizabeth Harwar my Cupbord in the Chamber. Item I
give unto my doughter Elizabeth my best Chest and after her time unto her sonne
Thomas. Item I give unto my doughter Margaret a Chest. Item I give unto my
doughter Margaret my doughter Elizabeth and to Elizabethe Harwar to eache of
them a silver spoone Item I give unto my doughter Elizabeth my best bedd with
all furniture belonginge to yt excepte one boulster which I give unto Elizabeth
Harwar Item I give unto my doughter Margarett a featherbedd. Item I give unto
my doughter Elizabeth a boulster and to my doughter Margarett a boulster. Item
I give all the rest of my beddinge to my doughter Margarett to my doughter
Elizabeth and to Elizabeth Harwar Item I give my bedsteed to them three amongst
them. Item I give unto my doughter Margarett Elizabeth and Elizabeth Harwar all
my Lynnens or napperie. Item I give all my Cheeses unto my doughter Margarett
my doughter Elizabeth and to Elizabeth Harwar. Item I give unto my doughter
Margarett my two best flitches of bacon. Item I give unto my doughter Elizabeth
and to Elizabeth Harwar three flitches of bacon betwixt them Item I give unto my
sonne in lawe Thomas Mourton my Carte with all thinges belongeing to yt Item
I give unto my sonne in lawe Thomas Harwar a plowe a harrowe and the plowe
Irons Item I give unto John Sproston a plowe. Item I give unto John Gray my
sonne, all my Carte timber and plowe timber. Item I give unto Mr Nicholls one
stirke of barlie. Item I give and bequeath my Corne and Haye unto my doughter
Margarett, doughter Elizabeth and Elizabeth Harwar provided allwayes that my
doughter Margaret is to take upp two bushells before the devision. Item I give to
my sonne John Grayes Children 12d. a peece Item I give unto all my godchildren
12d. a peece Item I give unto my doughter Margarett my wedley gowne and a
petticoate Item I give to my doughter Elizabeth my blacke gowne and my newe
petticoate Item I give to Elizabeth Harwar my pinke gowne and my flannell petticoate. Item I give my Corne groweinge to my doughter Margarett my doughter
Elizabeth and to Elizabeth Harwar to be equally devided amongst them provided
allwaies That Thomas Mourton shalbe considered out of the wholle for his mucke
before the devision. Item I give my Iron grate unto my doughter Margarett as
longe as shee keepes her unmarried and if shee marry then to my doughter
Elizabeth. Item the rest of my Iron ware I give to my doughter Margarett. Item I

give unto my doughter Margarett my treene ware Item I give unto my sonne in lawe Thomas Harwar 10s. Item I give unto John Graye my sonne 10s. Item I give unto my sonne in lawe Thomas Mourton 10s. Item my mynde is that my body shalbe honestly brought home out of my wholle goodes. Item I give unto my doughter Elizabeth Mourton 40s. to bee paid her out of my debtes.

Executors: the abovesaid Thomas Harwar, Thomas Mourton and the testator's daughter, Margaret Graye.

H. & S.
Emyn Barnett her marke

Witnesses: Thomas Graye, Grace Pemberton (her marke), Jane Brooke (her marke).

[A]nd my mynde is that my bedding above shalbe devided betweene my doughter Margarett and Elizabeth Harwar and that Thomas Harwar the younger shall have so much money out of the wholle as to make the price of the mare which I have given him before sufficient to buy him a Cowe.

Debtes owing to the Testator

	£	s	d
Elline Hall 20s. which I give to Elizabeth Harwar to buy her a bedd		20	0
Mr Dodd of Edge	3	0	0
Mr Warde		30	0
John Wilkinson		2	0
Mres: Bebington 7s. and for two daies ploweing which I give to my doughter Alice		7	0
William Prince 20s. which 20s. I give to my doughter Margarett		20	0
John Shrowbridg	8	0	0
John Phillippes	8	0	0

Inventory: Emma Barnett of Wrenbury.

Taken: 5 May 1631

Of: goodes.

Prisers: John Savadge, Thomas Spence, John Sproson, and Thomas Graye.

	£	s	d
seaven kyne one heffer & one sucking calfe	23	0	0
two mares	3	6	8
two younge swyne		16	0
in Poultrie		10	0

in Bees		10	0
Corne groweinge	3	0	0
Corne & Mault	7	0	0
Cheeses & Butter	6	3	4
three silver spoones		20	0
brasse & pewter	5	6	8
Bacon		40	0
beddinge linnens & Nappry	13	0	0
two Cuppords Cheste & bedstids		46	8
one Cart Cart tymber ploughes one harrowe & all other husbandry ware	3	0	0
Ironware		10	0
treene ware & Cowpie		13	4
Earthen ware		2	0
Cheares formes stooles bords shilves		10	0
fire fuell		13	4
Muck		10	0
three Cushens			12
basketts sives & spinning wheels		6	8
Lard & Honie		3	0
yarns & toe		20	0
her apparel	6	13	4
Redy money		25	6
debts oweinge her	4	19	0
a debt oweinge her by John Phillipps	8	0	0
a debt owinge her by John French	5	0	0
a debt owinge her by John Shrowbridge	3	0	0
[Sum	89	295	66]
Recte	109	10	6

Endorsement: Probated 24 October 1631; administration to Thomas Moreton and Margaret Graye two of the executors named in the said will . . . well sworn in the presence of Doughton &c.; with power reserved to the other executor when he comes.

88. JOHN CARTWRIGHT OF SHEPPENHALL, GENT.

C.(S.)Pr. 15 November 1631
W.T. 10 June 1631
Buried: 1 November 1631

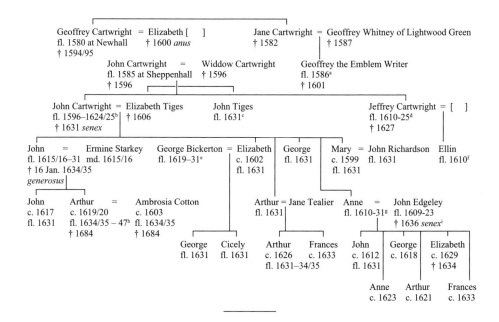

---

^a See further on Geoffrey Whitney, the Emblem Writer, above, p.xxxi.
^b Fl. 1596, 1611 gent.; CRO Newhall Manor Court Rolls. See also St George, *Visitation of 1613*: son of John Cartwright (fl. 1585, † 1596), himself the son of Geoffrey Cartwright († bef.. September 1593); juryman 1624/25 in IPM for John Wicksted, R. Stewart Brown, *Cheshire Inquisitions Post Mortem*, iii. 171.
^c Son of John Tiges of Twemlow, co. Chester; see Dugdale, *Cheshire Visitation Pedigrees 1663*, p. 25.
^d See will of James Barnett, pr. 1610 (will no. 29); CRO Newhall Rentals, 1625.
^e George Bickerton, son and heir of Roger Bickerton, aged 15 years 7 months and more on 31 March 1619, married before his father's death, and with his consent, Elizabeth, daughter of John Cartwright, gent. George and Elizabeth resided at Townley in Cheshire (see R. Stewart Brown, *Cheshire Inquisitions Post Mortem*, i. 19-20).
^f Bequeathed £1 in will of James Barnett, pr. 1610 (will no. 29).
^g William Fergusson Irvine, *Chester Licences*, i. 79: on 22 May 1610 a licence was issued to John Edgeley and Anne Cartwright, confirming their clandestine marriage.
^h See inventory and IPM of John Cartwright of Sheppenhall, 1634/35 (no. 96). Succeeded his father at age 15 in 1635; CRO Newhall Manor Court Roll.
ⁱ See will of John Edgeley of Woodcott, pr. 1637 (will no. 102).

Will, sicke & weake in body.

First I commende my soule into the hands of almyghtie god hopeinge by the merits & blodsheddinge of Jesus Christe my alone saviour & redeemer, to have free pardon & remission of all my sinnes. And *my body I commit to the earthe to be buried in the parishe church of Wrenbury* in sure & certeyne hope of a ioyfull resurrection. Item I give & bequeath unto everye one of my children Angells a peece. I give & bequeath unto John Cartwright my sonne all my bedstids, cupbords presses, tables, formes, boords, stooles, cheeares & Iron ware. Item I give & bequeath unto George Cartwright my sonne £50 out of the £100 which my brother in lawe John Tiges owes unto mee, & the remaynder of the said £100 (after my funerall expencs are discharged) I give and bequeath unto the said John Cartwright & Arthur Cartwright my sonnes to bee equally devided between them. Item I give & bequeath unto my executors hereafter named the reste of the *rie* feeld in the houldinge of Richard Hamnett to bee disposed at their discretions. Item I give & bequeath unto the worshipfull George Cotton esquire £5 to buy him a piece of plad shoo please. Item I give & bequeath unto my three daughters Anne Edgley Mary Richardson & Elizabeth Bickerton my brasse & pewter bedinge & lynannes, to be equally devided amongst them. Item I give unto John Cartwright my sonne Johns sonne £5. Item I give unto Arthur Cartwright my sonne Arthurs sonne £5. Item I give unto John Edgley my soone in law Edgleys sonne £5. Item I give unto George Bickerton my sonne in lawe George Bickertons sonne £5. Item I give unto Cicely Bickerton daughter of the said George Bickerton £5. Item I give unto Jane Brereton 10s. Item I give unto Jane Kelsall 10s. Item I give unto the other Jane Brereton 10s. Item I give & bequeath unto the poore of the parishe of Wrenbury £5 to be devided amongst them at the discretion of my executors, & the churchwardens.[a]

Executors: the testator's sons, John Cartwright and Arthur Cartwright.

Overseer: George Cotton, esquire.

Witness: Thomas Gray scribe.

John Cartwright
(signature)

Item I give unto John Richardson the yonger £5.

Inventory: John Cartwright of Shepnal, gent.

Taken: 4 November 1631

Of: goodes Cattell and Chattells.

---

[a] This bequest is found in the 'Catalogue of such charitable bequests as have been given to the Church of Wrenbury', noted in Norwood, *Historic Notes*, no. xlii, citing Harleian MS 2176, fo. 64^.

Prisers: William Cartwright, Richard Edgley.

	£	s	d
his wayring apparell prised to	8	0	0
all Bedsteds Tables formes cobbords Chests Cheres stoules and all treene ware	20	0	0
brasse and pewter	5	10	0
beding and all Linan and nappery	20	13	7
one Mare	6	13	4
one Cowe	2	15	2
all husbandrie & Iron ware		13	4
foure silver spoones		20	0
Bookes		2	0
one Muskett with furniture		15	0
monney oweinge by spetialties	191	10	0
In silver & gould	41	13	0
	[Sum 293	124	17]

Exhibited *cum protestacōne* by the executors.

Endorsement: Probated 15 November 1631; administration to the executors named in the said will.

89. MARGARET GRAYE OF WRENBURY, SPINSTER

S.Pr. 28 March 1632
W.T. 22 March 1631/32

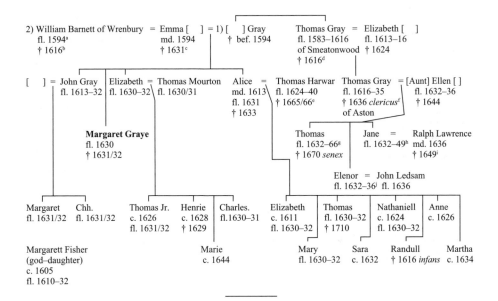

Will, sick.

First I commende my soule into the handes of almyghty God hopeinge by the bloudsheedinge of Jesus Christ my alone saviour to have free pardon of all my sinnes and *my body to be buried in the churchyarde of Wrenbury* aforesaid in sure and certayne hopeof a ioyfull resurrection. Item I give to Margarett Graye daughter of John Graye my brother £3 to buy her a cowe and to the rest of his Children

---

ª Executor of the will of James Barnett, pr. 1610 (will no. 29).
b See inventory of William Barnett, 1616 (no. 52).
c See will of Emma Barnett, pr. 1631 (will no. 87).
d See will of Thomas Gray of Smeatonwood, pr. 1616/17 (will no. 53).
e See inventory of Thomas Harwar, pr. 1666/CRO.
f See will of Thomas Gray of Aston, pr. 1636 (will no. 99).
g Executor of will of his father, Thomas Gray, pr. 1636 (will no. 99); bequeathed 5s. by Thomas Gray of Newhall, will pr. 1640 (will no. 112); married Margaret [   ].
h See bequests in will of Thomas Gray, pr. 1636 (will no. 99).
i See inventory of Ralph Lawrence of Newhall, 1648/49 (no. 133).
j Bequeathed 10s. in will of Thomas Gray, pr. 1636 (will no. 99).

10s. a peece. Item I give to my said brother 32s. beinge the use of £20 which he oweth mee Item I give to Thomas Mourton the yonger one read cowe and to Charles Mourton one farrowe blacke Cowe. Item I give to Elizabeth Harwar a blacke Cowe dam to the above said read Cowe. Item I give to Elizabeth Mourton my sister one pyed Cowe. Item I give to Thomas Harwar Nathanaell Harwar & Mary Harwar one blacke cowe. Item I give to my sister Harwar & to my sister Mourton two hoges. Item to Richard Spencer sonne of Thomas Spencer 20s. & 3d. which the said Thomas oweth mee to buy the said Richard a Calfe. Item to Margarett Sproston 10s. & John her uncle to have it to putt it fourth for her best use. Item to my sister Mourton £3 which John Sproston oweth mee. and 20s. more which he oweth mee I give to the said John. To my sister Harwar one feather bed my yarne & towe. To my sister Mourton my pewter & my lynens to be devided betweene them. To my god daughter Margarett Fisher 5s. To my uncle Thomas Graye 10s. to my Aunt Graye 12d. to Thomas Graye there sonne 12d. to Jane Graye 12d. To Elenor Ledsam 2s. To my sister Mourton a silver spoone To Elizabeth Harwar and Mary Harwar twoo brasse potes. The remaynder of my goodes (my body beinge honestly brought home) I give to my executors hereafter named . . .

Executors: Thomas Harwar and Thomas Mourton.

Margret Grayes marke
X

Debts Owing the Testator:

	£	s	d
Mr Dod oweth mee for the table of his sonne £4 10s. at May	4	10	0
Thomas Woollam		7	0
Thomas Massie the yonger		2	9
Thomas Massie the elder		2	0
Anne Hall wife of William Hall		10	0

Witnesses: John Fisher, Thomas Spencer, Elizabeth Lealande.

Inventory: Margaret Graye of Wrenbury spinster.

Taken: 26 March 1632

Of: goods and Cattells.

Prisers: John Savadge, Thomas Spencer, John Sproston and Thomas Graye.

	£	s	d
4 kyne & one heaffer	10	10	0
haye		10	0
Corne		35	0
Hemp seede		3	4
yarne & towe		25	0
Bacon		30	0

Cheeses Butter & other meate		14	4
brasse & pewter	10	0	0
beddinge & nappery	3	6	1
treene ware		10	0
Iron Ware		6	8
one Cupboard chestes addstockes cheares & stooles		20	0
poultry		4	0
bees		3	4
2 old spininge wheeles		2	0
one silver spoone		6	10
debts oweinge by specyalty	1	[ ]	4
her apparell		5	0
[Sum	24	189	35]

Endorsement: Probated 28 March 1632; administration granted to the executors named in the said will.

90. EDMUND CREWE OF NEWHALL, YEOMAN

S.Pr. 4 September 1632
W.T. 16 August 1632
Buried: 23 August 1632

John Hopkins
fl. 1553[a]

Ralph Cardiffe = Mary		Edmund Crewe = Joahne Hopkins		Elizabeth Hopkins = John Watkys
fl. 1632–41[b] fl. 1641		fl. 1580–1625[c] fl. 1632		† 1612/13
(cousin of testator)		† 1632 † 1640[d]		*virili aetate*
† 1660[e]				

Elizabeth	Ralph Jr.	Richard	Thomas		Arthur Crew	Thomas Crew
fl. 1640	c. 1628	c. 1630	c. 1633		fl. 1632	fl. 1632
fl. 1640	fl. 1640					

Will, sick.

First I comitte and comend my soule to Almighty God my Creator and redeemer by whose mercy only I confidently trust and beleeve to be saved and *my body to be buried in the Nantwich[f] Churcheyard* in the county aforsaid Item I gyve and bequeath unto Arthur Crewe of Emlenton neare London the some of £17 being in the handes of John Cartwright of Newhall due to be paid the 19th day of January next ensuinge Item I gyve and bequeath unto Thomas Crewe brother unto the said Arthur Crewe the some of £20 being in the handes of Arthur Cartwright due the 25th day of October next ensuinge If in case the said Thomas Crew be then Lyvinge or els my will is that the said £20 alsoe doe remayne and be payd unto the said Arthur Crew Item I gyve and bequeath unto Gilbert Cartwright of Nantwich the some of £10 being in the handes of Roger Wright of Nantwich afor-

---

[a] Noted in attendance at Newhall Manor Court with View of Frankpledge, 24 June 1553/CRO.
[b] Of Wolf Hall in 1640; see CRO Newhall Manor Court Roll.
[c] Survey of the Court of the Manor of Newhall, 1609/CRO, indicates that Edmund Crewe held by right of his wife, 1 messuage and 7 acres of customary and 10 pennyworth of land near Sand Pit Green, paying an annual rent of 7s. 10d. The two properties were previously in the holding of John Hopkins, who was buried at Wrenbury, leaving two daughters as heirs: Joan and Elizabeth, each with a moiety. Elizabeth married John Watkys, and on her death, her moiety (with some limitations) descended to Edmund Crewe. On 7 April 1629 Edmund Crewe, gent., and his wife surrendered for their lives the said properties to Ralph Cardiffe, gent., and his wife Mary in tail at the Newhall Manor Court. On 27 October 1641, Ralph Cardiffe, gent., and Mary his wife, surrendered 15 acres. and 8 pennyworth of customary lands, formerly held by John Hopkins of the Earl of Bath at the beginning of the reign of James I, to John Cliff (Cliff d. 1646)/CRO.
[d] See will of Joane Crewe, pr. 1641 (will no. 113).
[e] See will of Ralph Cardiffe, pr. 1660.
[f] Edmund Crewe was, however, buried at Wrenbury, as was his wife in 1640/41. We have thus counted them both among the Wrenbury testators.

said gent Item I gyve & bequeathe unto my Cosin Raphe Cardiffe the some of £20 beinge in his owne hands Alsoe I gyve unto the said Raphe Cardiffe the some of £12 due from him to mee at Mychaeltyde for his table And also the some of 40s. in money lent unto him Item I gyve and bequeath & my will is that the some of £28 being in handes of George Orpe of Lightwood in the said County of Chester due to me from the said George Orpe by bond att severall dayes shalbe by the advise & oversight of my said Cosen Raphe Cardiffe and Richard Edgeley of Newhall aforsaid their heires executors and assignes to be imployed & sett forth For the benefitt & use of a reader or mynister at Burleydam Chappell for the mayntaynance of Gods word there from tyme to tyme for ever Item I gyve and bequeath unto my wife Joahne Crew all the rest and residue of all my goodes cattell & Chattels moveable & unmoveable of what sort soever or in whose handes soever they bee or hereafter shalbe.

Executor: the testator's wife, Joane Crewe.

Overseer: the testator's cousin, Raphe Cardiffe.

Witnesses: Raphe Cardiffe, John Orpe.

NOTE (written sideways in left-hand margin): The testator doth Condicōn in regard of his gyfte unto the affor said Chappell that his whole forme may be free unto his house for ever.

Inventory: Edmund Crewe of Newhall.

Taken: 30 August 1632

Of: goodes Chattells and Cattells.

Prisers: Roger Wright, Raphe Cardiffe, Richard Edgeley and Thomas Backhouse.

	£	s	d
In the hall one Table six stooles one Cubboard wenscotte and two Cheares	1	13	4
in the Parlour one table two formes one Presse with Bason and Ewre, one Iron grate 3 pewter flower potts fyve quishions one Carpett one Bible one Service booke	4	3	4
in the kitchen one greate Combe with all other treene ware one Andiron one brasen morter one pere of golberts 3 spitts 3 pere of pothookes & chaynes with all other iron ware	3	0	0
Brasse and Pewter	8	6	8
in the best Chamber twooe Joynd bedsteddes with furniture of bedding belonging therunto	13	6	8
twooe trunkes one greate Chest twooe boxes one litle table	2	13	4
Nappery Sheetes table clothes napkins towels & pillowe beares &tc	30	0	0
Plate	5	10	0

wearinge apparrell	10	0	0
In the mydle Chamber twoe bedsteddes with furniture three Chests one litle table & forme	7	0	0
in the Cheese chamber one bed with furniture		13	4
Cheeses	20	0	0
in the kitchin chamber one bed with furniture with one Chest	2	0	0
in the store chamber Corne and malte	2	0	0
syves searches spinninge wheeles erthen potts and Ticknall stuffe Hempe flax yarne Brake & tewtawe and a hayer cloth	1	6	8
Shilves boardes trestles and fyve peeces of tymber		10	0
Fewell aboute the house	3	6	5
one hyve of Bees		5	0
in the Barnes hay	8	0	0
ladders and a wheele barrowe		2	0
mucke aboute the house	2	6	8
Poultree		6	8
fyfteene kyne	40	0	0
one mare and sadle	3	6	8
seaven swyne	6	0	0
due to the testator by bondes and bill the some of	214	0	0
other debts owinge to the testators as lent the some of	12	0	0
the entrest in a house in Nantwich called the Cocke with a feild called the Kings Ground valued at the some of	20	0	0
in the said house one Cubboard one great chest & one bedsteed	3	0	0
dyvers tryfles omitted and forgotten	1	0	0
[Total]	420	111	69

Exhibitum pro vero vero

Roger Wright
Raphe Cardiffe
Richard Edgley
Thomas Backhouse his marke

Endorsement: Probated 4 September 1632; administration granted to the sole executor named in the said will.

91. ALLIS PEXTONNE[a] OF NEWHALL, WIDOW

S.Pr. 4 October 1632
W.T. 13 April 1632
Buried: 18 May 1632

[a] Indexed and filed at CRO as Alice *PEXTOUNE.*

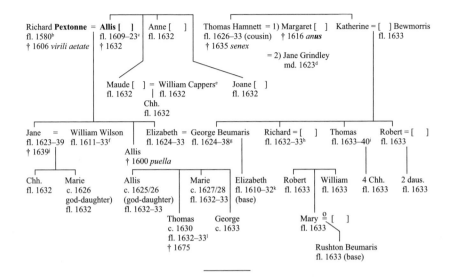

b CRO Newhall Manor Court Roll – required to scour water course between Combermere and Newhall Mill, and between Adamley Pool and Richard Shrewbridge's house.

c Survey of the Manor of Newhall, 1609, shows that Alice Pexton, widow, held 1 messuage & 1 acre and 11 p. of land in Newhall near the mill; rent is 1s. 14d. annually; listed by surname only as a tenant of Newhall, 1623/CRO.

d See will of Thomas Hamnett of Smeatonwood, gent., made 1633, pr. 1635 (will no. 97).

e Since reference is made to the children of Maude Cappers, we assume that Cappers was her married name: the most likely possibility for her husband is the William Capper who was one of the prisers of Elizabeth Pextonne's will in 1632; he is presumably also the William Capper who married Alice Woodfyne 1600 at Wrenbury (see Wrenbury Bishop's Transcripts – Marriages: 1600). Whether he is also the William Cappur of Poolecroft Heath who owed John Hall £7 in 1605 is unclear; see will of John Hall, pr. 1606 (will no. 22). A John Cappers was baptized at Wrenbury in 1614, perhaps one of the unnamed children of 1632. Undoubtedly related was the Richard Capper of Bunbury who was bondsman for the marriage licence of Marie Beumaris and Randle Cartwright 1608 at Nantwich; see William Fergusson Irvine, *Chester Licences*, i. 38.

f Noted as kinsman in will of Thomas Hamnett, 1633, and priser of his goods, 1635 (will no. 97).

g George Beumaris and Elizabeth Peckston had Chester licence dated 23 October 1624 to marry; see William Fergusson Irvine, *Chester Licences*, iii. 16; George is noted as the nephew, and executor, of Thomas Hamnett, 1633; see will no. 97, where further details on the Beumaris family are also evident (George Beumaris's mother, Katherine, was a sister of Thomas); George Beumarisse was the executor for the will of Elizabeth Briscoe, 1632 (will no. 103).

h Richard *Bumorise* was one of the prisers of the goods etc., of Allis Pextonne, 1632.

i Thomas *Bewmorres* received 10s. from Thomas Gray as the latter's god-son, will pr. 1640 (will no. 112).

j See will of William Wilson, pr. 1639 (will no. 109).

k Elizabeth *Bewmariss* (base child of George) received 40s. in codicil to will of James Barnett, pr. 1610 (will no. 29).

l Undoubtedly one of the unnamed children of Elizabeth Beumaris noted in Allis Pextonne's will.

Will, sick.

First I give and bequeath my soule to allmightye God my maker and redeemere by whose mercye I am assured of my Salvacōn and *my bodie to be buryed in the Churche or Churcheyard of Wrenburye*. First I give and bequeath a black Cowe Called silk unto my daughter Jane; Allsoe I give & bequeath a white faced Cowe called Blossom unto my daughter Elizabeth. Allsoe I give & bequeath unto my sonneinlawe William Willsons children; the bowheaded heiffer called Thrasell, and the whitefaced one cowe called Lillie. Allsoe I give and bequeath unto my sonneinLawe Georges Children the browne faced heiffer called Nightingaell and his daughter Marie more then her parte of that to have the yarre ould calfe called mowse Item I give & bequeath unto my Sister Maude Cappers Children the twynter heiffer that called att Christmas, Item I give unto my daughter Elizabeth the Feather bedd & woollbed the best blankett and and the best coverlett and one of the other blanketts, and the rest of my beddinge for my daughter Jane, and for my sheetes; and the rest to be equallye betweene my daughters. Allsoe I give and bequeath my best Tablecloth unto my daughter Elizabeth with my Napkins And allsoe I give unto my daughter Jane my Towell and I give and bequeath my best boulster & pillowes unto my daughter Elizabeth Item I give & bequeathe unto one of my daughters my greate panne, and to the other of them the greate pott, with the twoe ould pannes and the kettles for to equal the greate panne Then for the rest of my brasse and pewter to be equallie devyded betwwne them; all but one brasse Candlestick for my daughter Jane Allsoe I give and bequeath unto my daughter Jane the bedstedds in the Chamber over the kitchin with the greate Chest under the Windowe in the Chamber Item I give and bequeath unto my Daughter Elizabeths Children the best Joynde bedd in the Chamber with the Joynde table and formes and the Joynde presse in the house, yeildinge and payinge unto my sonninlawe Georges base daughter Elizabeth 20s. out of them Wainescott Comodities soe found as the Joyned them, to goe forward with her. Item I give and bequeath unto Mary Willson my goddaughter one Cheste which is the best that I have with a newe locke on itt Item I give and bequeath unto my daughter Elizabeth the other 4 Coffers Item I give and bequeath unto my daughter Jane my best gowne and my Flannell petticoate with my best Apron Item I give and bequeath unto my daughter Elizabeth my petticoate that is of Pidgeon color and my best waistcoate and my yellow petticoate and cloth to make her a petticoate of the same of my best gowne Item I give and bequeath my ould Tawney gowne to my sister Maude and my Tawney Cloake; Item I give & bequeath unto my Sister Joane my indingo Sowgoral Item I give and bequeath unto my Sister Anne my best Flaxen Smocke; Item I give & bequeath unto my Cosin Thomas Hamnett the yeoman, one hand kerchef and allsoe one to give his brother Richard Item I give and bequeath unto Marye Willson my goddaughter my best Cloake. Item I give and bequeath unto Allis Beumaris my goddaughter my Saddle, Item I give & bequeath unto my sonninlaw George my ploue and my harroue and my best newe bridle unto my daughter Jane Willson. Item I give and bequeathe unto my godchildren each one, one shillinge, Item I would have you to give unto the poore

at my buryinge one pennye to divyde; Item due unto me of Robert Harris of
Broomhall 13s. Item doe unto mee from Richard Edgley of Newhall 40s. due unto
me of Richard Plant the Cowper 10s. Item I give and bequeathe all the remainder of my goods Chattels and whatsoever is unspecified to be equallie devyded
betweene my twoe daughters Jane and Elizabeth.

Executors: the testator's sons-in-law, William Willson and George Beumaris.

Witness: Henrye Wrighte.

Inventory: Allese Peckston of Newhall.

Taken: 22 May 1632

Of: goods Cattles and Chattles.

Prisers: William Capper, Thomas Spenser, George Bate and Richard Bumorise.

	£	s	d
al her weareing Clothes	5	0	0
all Naperie as shetes Napkins & the licke	2	10	0
all Bedding and Coverings	5	0	0
all Brasse and Peuter	5	0	0
all the Silver		6	8
all Chests and Bedstockes		50	0
all Sileing one presse one Table with forms there unto belonging		50	0
all Bords and Shilfes		10	0
all trenen vessel and Earthen vessel		30	0
all Iron and husbandrie Comodities		13	0
al Corne within the house		5	0
al Corne upon the Ground sone		8	0
tow Swine		16	0
al pooulterie		7	0
~~three~~ three kine and 4 yong bests	17	0	0
one Flich of Bakon		6	8
one Chese		1	0
al the mucke		5	0
one Sadle		4	0
al ladders		1	0
al the depts dew to the late decesed Aleies Peckston	5	3	1
The some Tottall	50	1	1

Endorsement: Exhibited 4 October 1632; administration granted to the executors
named in the said will. 1632.

92. ROBERT TUDMAN OF NEWHALL, YEOMAN

S.Pr. 13 December 1632
W.T. 12 September 1632
Buried: 16 September 1632

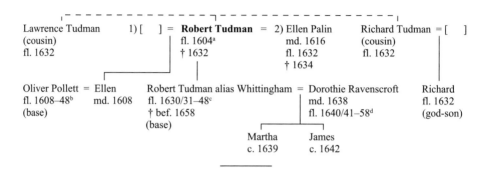

Lawrence Tudman   1) [   ] = **Robert Tudman** = 2) Ellen Palin   Richard Tudman = [   ]
(cousin)   fl. 1604[a]   md. 1616   (cousin)
fl. 1632   † 1632   fl. 1632   fl. 1632
   † 1634

Oliver Pollett = Ellen   Robert Tudman alias Whittingham = Dorothie Ravenscroft   Richard
fl. 1608–48[b]   md. 1608   fl. 1630/31–48[c]   md. 1638   fl. 1632
(base)   † bef. 1658   fl. 1640/41–58[d]   (god-son)
   (base)

Martha   James
c. 1639   c. 1642

Will, sick.

First above all things I give & Comend my soule into the hands of Almighty God that gave it mee assuredly trustinge that by the mercy & merits of Christ Jhesus my Saviour & redeemer & through faith in his blood to be one of the number of his elect & chosen Children, And *my body to be buryed in the Churchyard at Wrenbury where my ancestors lye.* Item I give and bequeath unto Ellen Tudman my wife one Incalfe Cowe called Throstle. Item I give and bequeath to Robert Tudman alias Whittingham my bastard sonne, one Pyesse of Joyned worke one table with a frame & formes belonginge to it with all boards & shelves in the house & Chambers with the glasse in the windowes, Two standinge bedstidds, one greate saltinge Turnell the best fether bedd one brasse Chaffing dish, one greate brasse Candlestick, Twoe greate peuter dishes beinge both alike touched on the brimme with these lettres R. B. Twoe large white Irish Caddowes, five silver spoones with my trunck desk & all my bookes, & all my apparrell. Item I

---

[a] Alice Blackamore owed Robert Tudman a debt of 6s. 8d. in 1604 ; see her will (will no. 20).

[b] William Fergusson Irvine, *Chester Licences*, i. 39: 2 July 1608, Oliver Pollet of Acton parish, and Ellen Tudman, of Wrenbury parish, spinster, at Wrenbury. Oliver Pollett of Baddiley appears as a juryman in the IPM for Dame Mary Cholmondeley, 24 April 1629 (R. Stewart Brown, *Cheshire Inquisitions Post Mortem*, i. 126); also for Robert Crockett 20 August 1622 (ibid., i. 147); bequeathed 2s. 6d. in George Tench's will, pr. 1648 (will no. 129).

[c] Robert *Whittingham* is noted as hiring a cow till 10 December 1631 from Ellen Ravenscroft; see will of the latter, pr. 1630/31 (will no. 86); Robert *Tudman* witnessed will of Joane Crewe, 1630/31 (will no. 113); witnessed will and made inventory for Robert Shrowbridge, will pr. 1641 (will no. 114); made inventory for Dorothy Cotton, 1647 (will no. 122); administrator of George Cotton's will, 1647 (will no. 128).

[d] Noted as cousin to Robert Shrowbridge the younger of the Royals, will pr. 1641 (will no. 114).

give & bequeath to Oliver Pollett my sonne inlawe 12d. in full discharge & satisfaccōn of all & all manner of debt bargaine or promise that ever I made him that is yett undischarged seriously protestinge before God and the world uppon my sick bedd that I have fully paid & discharged all ever I promised him with the better, or that hee can lastly demannd or Cleyme by any wayes or meanes either from mee or mine Executors. Item I give to my daughter Ellen Pollett his wife 12d. in full satisfaccōn of her Childs parte of my goods. Item I give & bequeath to my Cosen Lawrence Tudman 10s. Item I give unto John Ravenscroft whome I intreate to be one of my Executors 20s. Item I give to William Evanson my servant a yonge Cowe Item I give & bequeath to my Cosen Richard Tudman £3 6s. 8d. To my Godson Richard Tudman his sonne 13s. 4d. Item my Will & minde is, & I doe freely give & bequeath all the Rest & Residue of all my whole estate moveable & unmoveable whatsoever not devised or bequeathed to Ellen Tudman my wife And to the said Robert Tudman alias Whittingham my bastard sonne indifferently to be devided betwixt them, by the said Lawrence Tudman my Cosen and the said John Ravenscroft as equally as they Can.

Executors: the testator's wife, Ellen Tudman, and John Ravenscroft.

Overseers: the testator's cousin, Lawrence Tudman, and Richard Shrowbridge.

H. & S.

signum predicti Roberti Tudman

Witnesses: Thomas Graye 1632, Richard Shrowbridge, William Evanson.

Inventory: Robert Tudman of Newhall, yeoman.

Taken: 21 September 1632

Of: goods Cattalls and Chattalls.

Prisers: Thomas Taylor, John Fisher and Richard Shrowbridge.

	£	s	d
his wearing Apparrell	5	0	0
Six kyne	18	0	0
Twoe furrowe heffers	3	16	8
Twoe Twynter heffers	3	3	4
one Calfe		15	0
one Nagge	4	6	8
one hogge		18	0
Twoe Shotes		16	0
Corne in the feild and Barne	7	6	8
old Corne and malt in the house		10	0
Cheese in the house	6	10	0
Bread Butter and Bacon		6	8
Beddinge of all sorts	4	0	0
Twoe standinge bedstidds and other bedstidds	1	6	0
Lynnens and Napperie of all sorts	1	13	4

	£	s	d
Brasse and Pewter	3	6	8
Treenan ware and Cooperie with one Brake Tutawe and Cheespresse	1	13	4
Twoe Tables with formes Stooles cheeres, [benches] and formes and one Presse	2	0	0
one dishboard, boards, shelves, and one little peece of sileinge over the Bench		16	0
one Trunck, desk, Coffers, Chests and a paire of playinge tables		10	0
six Bookes	1	0	0
Wooll	1	0	0
hempe Flax and yarne		10	0
In Lynen Cloth Wynnow sheets, Sacks Baggs and Basketts & one old clokebagge		10	0
one Ironige panne, Sacks grate a pare of Tongues, fire shovell, a paire of Bellowes, Ironware Steele tooles, Carts a harrowe, ropes, Ladders, and all other Implements of husbandrie	1	10	0
painted Clothes and Ticknall ware		2	6
Wheeles Reeles and other Implements of huswifery		3	4
Coales Wood Tymber & Sume troughes	1	0	0
Muck and Compost		16	0
Poultrie		8	0
Five silver spoones		16	0
Silver buttons		6	8
Aples		4	0
Salt in the house and pease in the yard		10	0
[Sum	75	10	10]

Debts Owing to the Testator at the Time of His Death:

	£	s	d
owinge by Mr John Cartwright and Arthur Cartwright beinge due by specialty	17	0	0
oweinge by Arthur Cartwright beinge interest money		9	0
owinge by Thomas Palin beinge due by Bill	2	0	0
owinge by Richard Tudman	1	0	0
Readie money in the house	1	5	5
[ ]henge ?	5	6	8
ymshenes?			8

	£	s	d
Summa Totalis	96	16	10
[*recte*	112	9	1]

Exhibitum cum protestatione.

Endorsement: Probated 13 December 1632; administration granted to the executors named in the said will.

93. RICHARD CHESWIS OF WRENBURY FRITH, HUSBANDMAN

S.Pr. 10 April 1633
W.T. 24 January 1632/33
Buried: 25 February 1632/33

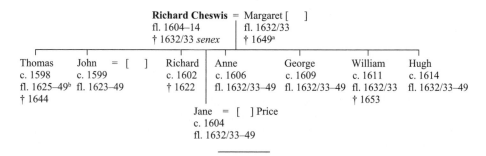

Will, 'being visited with sicknes'.

First I commend & bequeath my soule to almightie god hoping stedfastly by the meritts of the death & passion of his deare sonne our lord & savior Jesus Christe to be one of the number of the elect & *my body I bequeath to the earth to be decently buried in the Churchyarde of Wrenbury aforesaid at the Chancell and neare unto my late deceassed sonne Richards grave* And as touching the disposition of my worldly goods & substance first I give & bequeath to Anne Cheswys my daughter one Cowe called hers & one sucking Calfe Item I give & bequeath to my daughter Jane Cheswys one fetherbed conveniently furnished at the discretion of my wife Item I give & bequeath to Thomas Cheswys my sonne 10s. to be payd unto him within one yeare next after the proving of this my will in full satisfaccōn of his Childes parte of my goods Item I give & bequeath to Margarett my wife my house & tenamente in Bickerton for her life (if the terme which I have therein so long endure & continue) Item my full mynde & will is that my sonne George Cheswis shall have & enjoy the said house & tenamente in Bickerton aforesaid immediatly from & after the death of my said wife for & during all the rest & residue & continuance of my terme therein which shall be then to come & unexpyred Item I give & bequeath unto my said wife my house tenamente & grounds in Wrenbury Frith aforesaid for her life (if the terme which I have therein so long endure & continue) Item my full mynde & will is that William Cheswys my sonne shall have & enjoy the new bay of building there, the little Crofte, the

---

[a] See administration, granted 1649/50; Earwaker, *Index to Wills at Chester,* ii. 1621-50, p. 47.
[b] Thomas Cheswis of the Frith owed £1 5s. to John Cartwright of Aston; see will pr. 1630 (will no. 81).

orchard where the house standeth the ould marled feild & the barne Crofte immediatly from & after the death of my said wife for & during all the rest & residue
& continuance of my terme therein which shalbe then to come & unexpyred (if
he the said William Cheswys doe so long lyve) Item my full mynde & will is that
John Cheswys my sonne shall have & enioy the long higher feild & the shorte
higher feild immediatly from & after the death of my said wife for & during all
the rest & residue & continuance of my term therein which shalbe then to come
& unexpyred & all which said bay of building little Croft orchard ould marled
feild, barne Crofte, long higher feild & shorte higher feild are parts & parcells of
my said house [tenement?] & grounds in Wrenbury Frith aforesaid Item my mynde
& will is that my said sonne John shall remove that bay of building in Wrenbury
Frith aforesaid Wherein he now dwelleth to the said long higher feild & shorte
higher feild at his owne costs & charges & if my said sonne John be herewith
content then my will is that he shall have my whole terme & estate in my said
house tenamente & grounds in Wrenbury Frith aforesaid as the same shall severally & respectively happen after the severall deaths of my said wife & my said
sonne William but if he be not herewith content then my full mynde & will is
that he shall have no estate in my said house tenamente & grounds in Wrenbury
Frith aforesaid nor in any parte thereof & then my full mynde & will is that he
shall have 10s. to be payd unto him within one yeare next after the proving of
this my will & that then my full mynde & will is that Hugh Cheswys my sonne
shall have my whole estate in my said house tenamente & grounds in Wrenbury
Frith aforesaid as the same shall severally & respectively happen after the severall deaths of my said wife & my said sonne William Item all the rest & residue
of my goods Cattelles Chattelles & creditts whatsoever my debts legacies & funerall expenses being deducted & discharged out of the whole I wholly give &
bequeath to the said Margarett my wife & to Jane Cheswys & Anne Cheswys my
doughters & my said sonnes George Cheswys William Cheswys & Hugh Cheswys
viz the one half thereof to my said wife & the other half to them the said Jane
Cheswys & Anne Cheswys my doughters & to them the said George Cheswys
William Cheswys & Hugh Cheswys my sonnes amongst them fyve equally to be
devyded.

Executors: the testator's wife, Margarett, and his son, George Cheswys.

Overseers: George Cotton of Combermere esquire & the testator's loving friend
& landlord, John Dodd of Tussingham, co. Chester.

H. & S.
the marke of Richard Cheswys

Debts owing to the Testator:

	£	s	d
by Arthur Starkye of Wrenbury esquire		10	0
by my sonne John Cheswys	14	11	0
by John Dodd of Tussingham	20	0	0
by William Bentley	9	9	0

	£	s	d
by sonne Thomas Cheswys	21	0	0
[Sum	64	30	0]

Witnesses: Jane Cooper, Thomas Fisher.

Inventory: Richard Cheswys of Wrenbury Frith husbandman.

Taken: 7 March 1632/33

Of: goods Cattells Chattells & Creditts.

Prisers: John Fisher, John Tench, Valentyne Willdridge and John Johnson yeoman.

	£	s	d
the testators apparell		30	0
one Cowe	3	0	0
two oxen	8	10	0
three kyne & one Calfe	10	0	0
one mare		50	0
one sowe		16	0
one ould trow & some other husbandry implements with brakes & tuter & some tymber		13	4
Corne threshed & unthreshed	4	0	0
hay		10	0
poultrey		3	0
pewter		33	9
one brasse pan		46	8
one lesse pan		31	0
one greate pott		36	0
all the rest of the brasse that is pott brasse	3	0	0
one Chafing dish one warming pan & two Candle stickes		6	8
some troughes		3	4
treenware		20	0
Joyned bedstockes tables formes truckell beds other bedstockes		50	0
one Chest in the higher lofte one Cubborde in the lower chamber & one other Chest		20	0
one disheborde		8	0
Iron ware		8	0
fether beds & boulsters & the furniture to them	10	0	0
apparell that was left to the testators by his sister		40	0
Cheares Cushens shilfes stooles & all other trumpery wares		6	8
seckes & bagges		4	0
Wooll & gladdyn		24	0
leade weight a halfe hoope & strawe matts		3	4
one Chest of lynnens	3	6	8
mucke		3	4
foure kyne	9	0	0

two bulles	4	0	0
two calves	4	6	8
[?]	6	13	0
three swyne		12	0
one Coult		40	0
twelve sheepe & two skynnes		53	4
Corne threshed & unthreshed	4	13	4
hempe & flax		20	0
Cheese	10	0	0
hay	4	10	0
brasse & pewter	5	6	8
bedding & one little peece of Cloth	5	0	0
nappery		56	8
one peece of lynnen Cloth		2	8
baken beefe & butter		26	8
bedstockes formes shilfes bords Cheares & stooles with other small trumpery		40	0
Cowpery ware Coffers & Chese with a little truncke		43	4
one Carte one plough together with yokes Cheynes harrowes & other husbandry ware	3	6	8
two broches two sawes foure Iron wedges pott hookes tongues one payre of bellowes with other small Iron ware		13	4
Coles Stockes mucke & gorse		10	0
seckes bagges & wooll with a wynnow sheete		13	4

Debts oughing to the testator without specialtie:

	£	s	d
by Arthur Starkye esquire		10	0
by Raph Bostocke	10	10	9
by William Bentley	9	9	0
by John Cheswys	14	11	0

Debts oughing to the testator by specialtie:

	£	s	d
by John Dodd gentleman	21	0	0
a leas of the mesuage or tenamente in Wrenbury Firth aforesaid Wherein the testator dwelled & of the lands thereunto belonging for certeyn yeares if one life so long lyve	10	0	0

Sum totall	206	0	6
[*recte*	204	9	2]

Exhibitum cum protestacōne &c.

Endorsement: Probated 10 April 1633; administration granted to Margaret Cheswys, widow of the deceased and one of the executors named in the will.

94. JOHN BARNETT OF ASTON, YEOMAN

S.Pr. [after 26 October] 1633
W.T. 31 December 1628
Buried: 26 October 1633

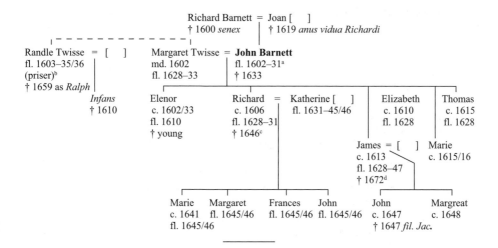

Will, sick.

First I comende my soule into the handes of almyghty god hopeinge by the merits and bloodsheedinge of Jesus Christe my alone saviour to have free pardon & remission of all my sinnes & *my bodye I committ to the earth to bee buried in the Churchyarde of Wrenbury* aforesaide: Item I give and bequeath unto my fore god Children 12d. a peece: Item I give and bequeath all my husbandry wares as plowes Carts yockes Cheanes & all Implements belonginge to husbandry to my sonne Richard Barnett & to Margarett Barnett my wife to use them betweene them: All the rest of my goodes moveable & unmoveable (my bodye beinge honestly brought home & my funerall expences debtes and legasies discharged) I give and bequeath unto Margarett Barnett my said wife dureinge her life and at her

---

[a] It is presumably this John Barnett who appears in the Newhall Manor Court Roll 15 October 1611 and 11 October 1631/CRO. He appears without connection as priser of the goods of James Barnett in 1610 and may have been the same man as John Barnett of Pillston, bequeathed £10 by James Barnett; see will of James Barnett of Aston, pr. 1610 (will no. 29).
[b] Appears as *Rauff* Twisse of Wrenbury Frith, as executor for Gilbert Woollam of Wrenbury Frith, will pr. 1635/36 (will no. 98).
[c] See will of Richard Barnett of Aston, yeoman, pr. 1647/48 (will no. 125).
[d] See will of James Barnet, pr. 1672/CRO.

descease to bee equally devided amongst my fore yonger Children: And my mynde is that my daughter Elizabeth shall have the lower Chamber dureinge her life keepeinge her selfe unmaried:

Executors: the testator's wife, Margarett Barnett, and his son, Richard Barnett.

Overseers: Arthure Cartwright and George Hall.

H. & S.
John Barnett
his X marke & seal

Witnesses: Thomas Graye (1628), Richard Shrowbrige.

Inventory: John Barnett of Aston, yeoman.

Taken: 7 November 1633

Of: goods Cattells and Chattells.

Prisers: Edward Hamnett, Thomas Taylor, Randle Twysse and Richard Shrowbrige.

	£	s	d
his wearinge Apparrell	3	0	0
Nine Kine	21	0	0
Twoe heiffers	4	13	8
Twoe Calves	1	0	0
Three mares	7	0	0
Sixteen Sheepe	2	10	0
Hey and Corne in the Barne	9	0	0
Corne in the house		13	4
Three Swyne	1	0	0
Cheese and Butter	8	0	0
Bacon in the house	1	0	0
Beddinge	6	0	0
Linnens and nappery	4	0	0
Joyned Bedd and Beddstidds	1	10	0
Brasse and pewter	3	10	0
Tables, boards, formes and shelves	1	10	0
one Presse		16	0
one Dishboard, Cheares and Stooles		10	0
Treenware and Cooperyware	1	0	0
Quishions, painted Clothes and Ticknall ware		5	0
Twoe Iron potts, Twoe broches, one paire of gobbarts and other ymplements about the fyer		13	4
Yarn Woll, hempe and flaxe	1	0	0
one paire of Scales, Spinninge wheeles, basketts and other ymplements of huswifery		6	8
Carts, plowes and all other ymplemts of husbandry	2	1	0

Tymber, plancks and boards	1	0	0
Fuell and Swyne troughes		13	4
mucke		5	0
Poultrie		6	0
Debts oweinge to the Testator by specialty	25	18	4
[Sum	102	159	32]

Edward Hamite (his X marke)
Richard Shrowbridge – 1633 -
Randle Twisse (his R marke)
Thomas Taylor (his T marke)

Endorsement: damaged; date missing; administration to Margaret his widow 1633.

95. ROBERT WADE OF WRENBURY FRITH, YEOMAN

S.Pr. 7 February 1633/34
W.T. 8 January 1633/34
Buried: 30 January 1633/34

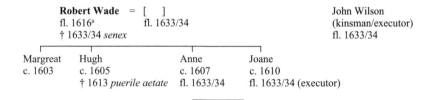

Will, sick.

First I Comend my soule into the hands of Jesus Christe my onely Saviour & redeemer, and my bodie to the earth to bee buried according to the discrecōn of my executors hereafter named, And for my worldly goods wherewith it hath pleased god to blesse mee I will & bequeath the same as followeth Firste I give

---

^a Robert Wade is noted as one of several tenants in Wrenbury of Thomas Minshull of Edswick, esq., whose IPM was taken 27 September 1616 at Middlewich (see R. Stewart Brown, *Cheshire Inquisitions Post Mortem*, ii. 207-8). Minshull held them of Sir Thomas Savage kt & bart by the moiety of a knight's fee and worth yearly (clear) £10 14s.

to every one of my Children twelve pence a peece, Item my will and desyre is, that out of my goods & Chattells my funerall expences bee satisfyed and paid which I pray may bee decent & fitting for a man of my degree & Caleinge And after my funerall expencs & legasies paid out of my estate as aforesaid I will & bequeath the rest of all my goods Cattells & Chattles to my wife, and to my daughters Anne Wade and Joane Wade to bee equally devided amongest them three.

Executors: Thomas Wilson of Chorley, Thomas Tomlynson of Cholmeley and the testator's daughter, Joane Wade.

Overseer: the testator's friend and kinsman John Wilson, Gent., one of the attorneys in the Exchequer at Chester.

H. & S.

the marke of Robert Wade

Witnesses: The marke of Magaret Croxton, Thomas Woodfen.

Inventory: Robert Wade of Wrenbury Frith.

Taken: 4 February 1633/34

Of: goods.

Prisers: Valentine Woolderidge, John Tench, Roberte Woolom, Thomas Tomlisson, Thomas Wilson.

	£	s	d
his wearinge Apparell of woolins and linnens	4	0	0
the bed which Johne his daughter did lye on to witt the under bedds & boulsters & pillow & Coverlidds & blankitts which belonges to that bed	2	6	8
his owne bedd which hee lay on beds boulsters & pillow Coverlidds and blankitts with one thrum Caddowes	4	0	0
three Chaff bedds wth some boulsters and one old Cover and a bag of Feathers		13	4
the pott brasse with two ould Chafinge dishes	2	13	4
the Pan brassed with skellitts and a brasen ladle		35	0
4 brasen Candlestickes		6	8
all the pewter dishes Candlestickes and Salts	2	0	0
for two paier of bedstidds one beinge a ioynt bedd		18	0
one Cubboard		8	0
for Iron ware plow Irons broches wedges pules horse geers axe hatchet muck yelve bills Wayers and other Implements for husbandry together with one Cart rope		30	0
for Turnills tubbs & one ould churne		10	0
for 3 Coffers & a box		6	8
one paire of ould bedstockes and a planke & some To		6	9

for butter & cheese		5	0
for one peece of new cloth		10	0
for three Coffers & one Turnill		13	4
for three flitches of Bacon		20	0
for two wheeles and a hoope and a plancke		2	0
for lynnens sheetes Table clothes and napkins	3	6	8
for two brundretts a Cressit and a puddinge pan and twoe fryinge pans a Land Iron and pottrackes		7	8
for Cowpye ware and shilves and Tresles			20
for Cheeres & Cushens		3	4
for ladders and a harrow and a Cheese presse		6	8
for oates		30	0
for barly		16	0
for hey		20	0
for five kine & a calf	15	0	0
for Poultrie		6	8
The some is	45	15	8
one mare	5	0	0
The some with this mare is Fifty pownd fifteene shillings eight pence			
[*recte*	47	3	5]

Endorsement: Probated 7 February 1633; administration granted to Joan Wade, one of the executors named in the said will, the other executors having utterly renounced the burden of execution.

96. JOHN CARTWRIGHT OF SHEPPENHALL, GENT.[a]

S.Pr. 28 August 1635
Died 16 January 1634/35
Buried: 18 January 1634/35

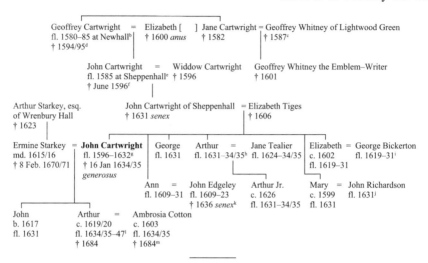

---

[a]   Dugdale, *Cheshire Visitation Pedigrees 1663*, p. 25, shows John Cartwright of Sheppenhall/Newhall with Ermin Starkey, daughter of John Starkey of Wrenbury, as his wife. See also Hall, 'Newhall Families', pp. 316–24.

[b]   CRO Newhall Manor Court Roll for 1580, 1585.

[c]   Both Geoffrey Whitney and his wife, Jane, are buried at Audlem.

[d]   Hall's assumption that he died before September 1593 fails to identify the burial entry in the parish registers.

[e]   CRO Newhall Manor Court Roll, 1585.

[f]   CRO Newhall Manor Court Roll for 12 October 1596: John is his son and heir.

[g]   Married 1616; member of the jury called for the IPM of Robert Crockett at Nantwich 20 August 1622 (see R. Stewart Brown, *Cheshire Inquisitions Post Mortem*, i. 147); referred to as the cousin of John Cartwright of Aston, May 1625; see will of John Cartwright of Aston, made 1625, pr. 1630 (will no. 81); owed jointly with his brother, Arthur, a debt of £17 to Robert Tudman of Newhall in 1632; see will of Robert Tudman, pr. 1632 (will no. 92); admitted to tenancy at Newhall Manor Court 10 April 1632; the inventory of Katherine Savage of Wrenbury, 1641/42, speaks of a £15 debt by bond which John Cartwright had owed her; Arthur Cartwright (John's brother) was co-obligant. John Cartwright also owed John Edgeley a debt of £25 in 1635, for which Arthur, his brother, was surety; see will of John Edgeley, pr. 1637 (will no. 102). John Cartwright was admitted to tenancy on 10 April 1632; see CRO Newhall Manor Court Rolls.

[h]   Owed jointly with his brother, John, a debt of £17 to Robert Tudman of Newhall in 1632; see will of Robert Tudman, pr. 1632 (will no. 92); also owed interest money of 9s. to Tudman in 1632.

[i]   Of Townley, co. Chester; see IPM for Roger Bickerton, 31 March 1619 (R. Stewart Brown, *Cheshire Inquisitions Post Mortem*, i. 19–20).

[j]   Of Tilsock, co. Salop.

Inventory: John Cartwright of Sheppenhall, gent.

Taken: 21 January 1634/35

Of: goodes cattells and Chattells.

Prisers: Hughe Whitney gent., John Cartwright gent., Thomas Brereton, Arthure Cartwright, John Ravenscrofte and Thomas Greenwollers.

	£	s	d
his apparell and two swordes	10	0	0
Three oxen seased for heriots	14	0	0
One Bullocke	4	0	0
Sixe kyne	16	0	0
One Fillie coulte & two mares	7	0	0
Sixe yonge beastes	9	0	0
Eight Calves	6	10	0
Twentye Sheepe	4	0	0
One Sowe eight pigges, & foure reareings	1	13	4
Poultry	1	0	0
Corne in the barne	13	10	0
hay and strawe	10	0	0
Carts plowes harrowes, and all other implements of husbandry	8	0	0
Saddles bridles, & horse Clothes		10	0
Boords tymber fellies & spookes	3	2	0
Coles kydes & other fuell for the fyer	3	0	0
Corne and grayne upon the grounde	4	0	0
Spyninge wheeles, a brake, a tutall, bricke & tyle, & a haire cloth		15	0
Corne in the house	2	6	8
mault	2	2	0
Brasse	4	0	0
Pewter	2	10	0
Tynn		2	0
Tryne ware and Cowperye	2	10	0
A foullinge peece , a muskett a heade peece and bandeleroes	1	11	6
All Iron ware in the house & a peare of bellowes	1	14	0
Beefe and bacon	4	6	8
Butter Cheese and bread	4	0	0
nyne silver spoones, a silver seale & a ringe	2	10	0

no. 96 footnotes continued
k   *Cheshire Visitation Pedigrees* 1663, p. 25 shows him of *Worcester*, and not of the local Edgeley family. This, however, is a very bad corruption of the local *Woodcott*, where the Edgeley family was situated.
l   Succeeded as heir at age 15 in 1635; admitted to tenancy at Newhall Manor Court 12 October 1647/CRO.
m   Several years older than her husband, Arthur Cartwright, whom she married about 1647, Ambrosia died childless. See will of Ambrosia Cartwright, dated 11 September 1684/CRO, where she describes herself as a widow and 'weak in bodye.'

In coyne	1	12	0
Tickall ware and glasses		2	0
Beddinge & bedsteds in the chamber over the kichen	7	10	0
One Chest one livery cubbord one cheare one boxe & one stoole in the same chamber	1	6	8
Beds and beddinge in the Chamber over the milk house	4	10	0
A bed & beddinge in the chamber over the entrie	1	0	0
One bedsteed & bedding one table, 3 truncks a stoole & a cheare in the chamber over the hall	5	5	0
Bedsteeds & beddinge one livery cupbord one chest one cheare one stoole and 3 carpett clothes in the chamber over the parlor	8	2	6
One bedsteed a table woollen yarne and some other implements in the Chamber over the buttrie	1	13	4
In napperye	11	14	0
Two peeces of newe lynen Cloth	2	0	0
One bed two bedsteeds a presse a drawinge table foure Cheares and eight cushions in the parlor	7	13	4
Bookes		20	0
Two tables three formes one stoole a Cheare & a peare of tables in the hall	1	10	0
Two tables formes 3 stooles 4 cheares and three cushions in the kichin	10	1	0
One bed in the stable & 2 peare of bedsteeds		10	0
One newe saddle		5	0
mucke		3	0
Baskets sives riddles bagges and a wynnowinge sheete		10	0
Sheelves and a safe		10	0
Towe and feathers		5	0
ladders		3	4
Twentie pounds in Robart Parkers handes of Nantwich	20	0	0
Salte and tallowe and goose grease		6	0
newe Iron		2	6
[Sum	233	8	10]

Hugh Whitney
John Cartwright
Thomas Brereton
Arthur Cartwright
John (X) Ravenscroft his marke
Thomas (X) Greenwollers his marke

Disbursed for funerall expenses	3	6	8
Receaved from Roger Wilkinson for rent		8	0
from Thomas Sadler for rent		15	0
from William Sadler for a payre of wheles		11	0

Exhibitum cum protestacōne[a]

Endorsement: Inventory exhibited 28 August 1635; *[no reference as to whom administration was granted].*

NOTE: The endorsement refers to John Cartwright as living at Sheping Greene, rather than Sheppenhall!

Inquisition Post Mortem for John Cartwright[b]

An Inquisition was taken 24 March 1634/5 at Nantwich to inquire into the death of John Cartwright late of Sheppenhall gent., ... The oath was taken by Hugh Whitney of Coole, gen., William Cudworth of Newhall, gen., Thomas Chester of Coole, gen., John Cheswis of Mickley, gen., Edward Hamnett of Aston, gen., [and others] . . .

They say that John Cartwright was seised in fee of 2 mess., 3 a. of land, 1 a. of meadow, in Newhall bought by him of George Cotton, esq. & so being seised by Indenture bearing date 6 February [1633/34] he conveyed the same to George Hall for a term of nine years at a pepercorn rent.

He was also seised of 4 a. of meadow & 4 a. of pasture in Newhall called Newbridge Field by heritage of his grandfather, John Cartwright.

He was also seised of 4 a. of meadow, 20 a. of pasture & . . . a. of furze & heath in Woodcote, which John Cartwright, gent., deceased . . . Arthur Cartwright, sen., gent., brother of said John Cartwright named in the writ, & Jane wife of said Arthur, & Arthur Cartwright, jun., son of the said Arthur, sen., for the term of his life, at a yearly rental of . . . .

They say the premises in Newhall are held of the King as Earl of Chester, in chief, by service of a 50th part of a knight's fee & worth yearly (clear), 12s.

The other premises are there held of the King as of his Crown of England in chief, by service of . . . & worth yearly (clear) 1s.

The premises in Woodhall *[sic! instead of Newhall]* held of George Cotton, as of his manor of Newhall in socage by fealty & rent of 5s. a year & worth yearly (clear), ...

The said John Cartwright died 16 January last past & Arthur Cartwright, gent., is his son & heir, & is aged 15 years, 2 months, 3 weeks.

---

[a] There is no surviving record of the contested documents.
[b] See R. Stewart Brown, *Cheshire Inquisitions Post Mortem*, i. 119–20 (TNA IPM 10 Chas 1, No. 4: Ches 3/102); a writ dated 26 Feb. 10 Chas I (1635) is attached; a lengthy document in poor condition. The inquisition makes no mention of Sheppenhall because IPMs only dealt with property held directly of the king; and the copyholds were held of George Cotton, who held his manor of Newhall *in capite*.

97. THOMAS HAMNETT OF THE GRANGE (IN SMEATONWOOD), GENT.

S.Pr. 26 October 1635
W.T. 11 April 1633
Buried: 6 August 1635

Editor's NOTE: The will is in beautiful condition, being comprised of four folio sheets, each with its own seal; it is tied at the top; the inventory, a separate document, is written on parchment.

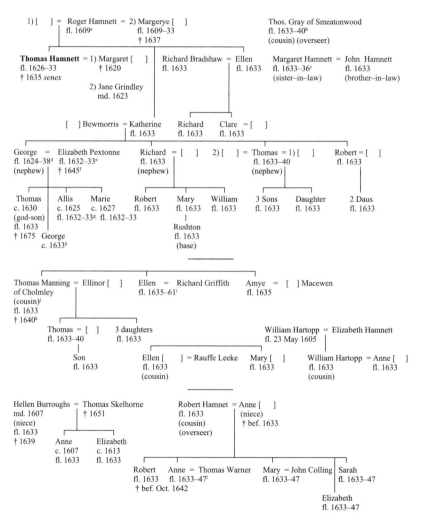

[footnotes on following page]

Will, weak and infirm.

First and principally I comend my soule into the hands of almightie god my most mercyfull creator assuredlie trustinge to bee saved by the precious death & passion of Jesus Christ my blessed and alone saviour & redeemer and to have full & free pardon and remission of all my sines And *my bodye I comitt to the earth from whence it came to bee buried in the parishe Church of Wrenbury* aforesaid at the discreacōn of my executors hereafter named. And as touchinge that worldlye estate which the lord in his mercie hath lent mee I dispose the same as followeth First my will is that my executors hereafter named shall within one yeare and six moneths after my decesse paye & deliver out of my estate the sume of £12 10s. to the right Honorable Worshipful George Cotton Esquier or his heires and the Churchwardens of the parishe Church of Wrenbury for the tyme beinge which £12 10s. my will is shall by the said George Cotton or his heires and the said Churchwardens bee either devided amongst the poore of the said parishe or bestowed upon some lands for the use of the poore & in the meane tyme the use thereof to bee yearely payd to the said poore all which I referr to the discreacōn of the said George Cotton or his heires and the said Church Wardens, Item I give to Penson widdowe whoe houldeth a tenemente under me in the longe Wolstable in Westminster if shee bee lyvinge at my death and incase shee bee dead to such person as shalbee my tenante of the said tenemente at the tyme of my death 16s. 8d. And to the rest of the poore tenants which shall dwell in the said longe Wolstable at the tyme of my death 33s. 4d. Item I give to all such householder in the parishe of Barkinge in Essex as shalbee my tenants at the tyme of my death 5s. apeece, and to the rest of the poore househoulders in the same parishe 20s. Item I give & bequeath unto the poore of the parishe of St. Gyles in the fields in the Countie of Middlesex fortie shillings in money to bee distributed at the discreation of my kinsmen Roberte Hamnett & William Hartopp or one of theim and the Church Wardens of the same parishe, Item I give & bequeith unto Thomas Cotton sonne and heire apparant of my said Landlord George Cotton my silver guilt wine boule for a token of my love. Item I give and beqeith unto my nephewe

---

^a Margery, wife of Roger Hamnett of the Grange, was bondswoman for a marriage licence granted 29 June 1609; see William Fergusson Irvine, *Chester Licences*, i. 59: Richard Kirks, of Wybunbury parish, and Alice Wright, widow, of Wrenbury parish.
^b Executor of will of Thomas Gray of Newhall, pr. 1640 (will no. 112)
^c A Margaret Hamnett was buried at Wrenbury in 1636 (see Parish Registers – Burials): probably the sister-in-law.
^d See will of Allis Pextonne, pr. 1632 (will no. 91).
^e See will of Allis Pextonne (will no. 91).
^f Parish Register entry shows *Elizabeth Morris*; likewise, the earlier baptismal entry for her son Thomas shows Thomas Mooris *filius Georgii*.
^g Both Marie and Allis are mentioned in the will of their grandmother, Allis Pextonne (will no. 91).
^h Appears in Parish Register baptism entry as George *Morris filius Georgi*.
ⁱ See will of Thomas Manning of Chorley, pr. 1640; will of Richard Griffith, pr. 1661/CRO.
^j See will of Thomas Manning of Chorley, pr. 1640.
^k See will of Thomas Manning of Chorley pr. 1640.
^l The will of Thomas Hamnett merely refers to the four daughters of Robert Hamnett, his cousin, without names. The Newhall Manor Court declared Anne Warner and Mary Colling co-heirs of their father Robert Hamnett in 1647/ CRO.

George Bewmorris my Farme called the Grange with thappurtenancs & all other my leases tackes and farmes duringe soe many yeares of my termes therein as hee the said George Bewmorris shall live, And after his decesse I give devise and bequeith the same leases tackes and farmes with thappurtenncs unto Elizabeth his wife and Thomas Bewmorris theire sonne duringe the residue of my termes therein. Item I give to the said Geoge Bewmorris tenne pownds in money and to Elizabeth his wife fifteene pownds To my godsonne Thomas Bewmorris sonne of the said George twentie five pownds and to the twoe daughters of the said George nowe lyvinge if they bee lyvinge at my death five pownds apeece and either of theim a silver spoone and if either of theim die to the sorvivor of theim tenne pownds and the said twoe silver spoones, And further I give and bequeith to the said George Bewmorris the bed wherein I use to lye with the furniture thereunto belongeinge my double silver salt one silver bowle one beaker & foure silver spoones, Item I give & beqeith unto Mr. John Snellinge of the parishe of St. Martin in the Fields Turner fortie shillings therewith to buy him a gould ringe Item I give & bequeith unto Richard Hamnett sonne of William Hamnet decessed tenne shillings in money Item I give and bequeith unto David Snellinge my late wifes godsonne tenne shillings in money Item I give and bequeith unto Gervise Partrich Citizen and Cordwayner of London twentye shillings therewith to buy him a gould ringe, Item to Richard Bratchgirdle three pownds and to his wife foure pownds and to the children of the said Richard twentie shillings apeece Item I give and bequeith to Thomas my sisters Katherins sonne tenne shillings and to her other sonne twentye shillings, Item I give and bequeith to my sister Ellen Bradshawe thirtie pownds and to her husband three pownds and to Richard her sonne and Clare her daughter tenne pownds a peece to the children of the said Clare twentie shillings a peece, Item I give and bequeith to the children of the said Richard Bradshawe fortie shillings, and to Thomas Worrall servant to the lord Needham twentye shillings Item I give and bequeith unto my neice Hellen Skelhorne tenne pownds and to Thomas Skelhorne her husband three pownds, and to their sonne at London five pownds and to theire daughter at London three pownds, Item I give and bequeith unto my Cozen Thomas Manninge of Cholmondeley[a] in Cheshire fifteene pownds a silver bowle & twoe silver spoones and to his wife fortie shillings and to his sonne Thomas I give and bequeith eighte pownds and to the sonne of the said Thomas twentie shillings, and to theldest daughter of the said Thomas Manninge the father twentie shillings and to his other twoe daughters three pownds a peece, Item I give & bequeith to theldest sonne of Alice wife of Richard Hamnett twentie shillings, and to the rest of her Children tenne shillings a peece, To Marye Rogers her twoe children tenne shillings apeece, And I give & bequeith to the children of Amy Palin tenne shillings a peece. Item I give and bequeith unto my Stepmother Margerye Hamnett sevon pownds, Item I give & bequeith unto my sister in lawe Margarett Hamnett three pownds, Item I give and bequeith unto my brother in lawe John Hamnett five pownds if hee bee lyvinge at the tyme of my death and after demannd the same, Item I give and bequeith unto my nephewe Richard Bewmorris five pownds and to his wife fortie shillings

---

[a]   This should probably read *Chorley*: see will of Thomas Manning of Chorley, pr. 1640.

and to theire daughter Marye five pownds and to theire sonne twentye shillings, And to the sonne of Marye Beckett my godsonne twentie shillings Item I give and bequeith unto my godsonne William Bewmorris eighte pownds paid of this eight poundes for the shillinges to William Bewmorris his owne hands. Item I give and bequeith unto my nephewe Thomas Beumorris five pownds and to his wife three pownds, and to their daughter fortie shillings, and to his three sonnes by a former wife I give and bequeith fortie shillings apeece, Item I freely forgive unto my nephewe Roberte Bewmorris the sume of nyne pownds which hee oweth to mee and I give and bequeith to his wife fortie shillings and to his sonne twentie shillings and to his twoe daughters fortie shillings apeece, Item I give and bequeith to my Cozen Ellen Leeke tenne pownds, Item I give and bequeith unto Marye Rauffe Leekes wives sister twentie shillings, Item I freelye forgive unto my Cozen William Hartopp the sume of twelve pownds which I lent him at the takeinge of his lese of his house and to him I give fortie shillings and to his wife my Cozen Anne Hartopp I give twelve pownds. Item I give and bequeith unto my Cozen Roberte Hamnett tenne pownds, and to Roberte Hamnett his sonne five pownds. And whereas by a former will I gave to my neice Anne Hamnett late wife to the said Roberte Hamnet and since decessed twelve pownds my will is and I give and bequeith the said twelve pownds to the four daughters of the said Roberte and Anne and fortie shillings apeece over and above the said twelve pownds, And to Elizabeth theire maid servant twentie shillings Item I give and bequeith unto Hughe Hamnett my servant fifteene pownds, Item I freelie forgive unto my fellowe James Walker all debts hee owes mee, Item I give and bequeith unto my fellowe William Shallawes tenne shillings, Item I give unto my fellowe Henrye Shepsey tenne shillings. Item I give and bequeith unto John Grimes pann keeper tenne shillings, Item I give and bequeith unto William Kampsey pann keeper five shillings, and to William Browne belonginge to his Majesty's Scullerye tenne shillings, Item I give and bequeith to my godsonne Thomas Needon twentie shillings, Item I give and bequeith to my godsonne Thomas Tacke tenne shillings Item I give and bequeith unto my godsonne Thomas Beckett five shillings, Item I give and bequeith unto my god daughter the daughter of Edward Hamnett twentie shillings. Item I give and bequeith unto everye one of my godchildren not named in this my will twoe shillings sixe pence apeece, Item I give and bequeith unto the wife of Mr. Leverett in Eastcheape in London twentie shillings and to her three children five shillings apeece, Item I give and bequeith unto Peeter Towse of Greenwich waterman his children amongst them fortie shillings if any of theim bee lyvinge at my death and to Jane Wilson my kinswoman fortie shillings and to her husband William Wilson twentie shillings and to her children twentie shillings apeece. Item I give and bequeith unto William Tench attendant about the court tenne shillings, To Thomas Burroughes of Nantwich twentie shillings to buy him a ringe, To every one that shall bee servant to the said George Bewmorris at my death twentie shillings a peece to Thomas Rogers my godsonne five shillings, Item I give & bequeith to Valentines[a] sonne my godsonne dwellinge at Barkinge aforsaid tene shillings, Item I give and bequeith to my Cozen Thomas Grey of Smeatonwood

---

[a] Quite possibly Valentine Woolrich of Wrenbury Frith, will pr. 1647 (no. 123).

fortie shilling and to Thomas Grey thelder of Aston twentie shillings. Item my mind and will is that the said George Bewmorris shall have and enioye the moytie or one halfe of all the rest and residue of my goods cattells and chattells not before herein gevon or bequeithed (excepte such plate goods and cattells as I shall give or dispose of in my life tyme) And I will that the remaynder of my estate after my legacies funerally expencs & debts paid and discharged shalbee distributed by my executors hereafter named at there discreacōns among my poorest and neer-est kindred, and my will is that all my legacies hereby gevon and bequeithed shal-bee paid and delivered within one whole yeare and six moneths nexte after my decesse.

Executors: the said Thomas Manninge thelder and my said nephew George Bewmorris.
And further my will is that my said executors shalbee allowed all theire charges which they shall spend disburse or laye out about the execucon of this my will, And that they shall deteine in their hands tenne pownds more in money or goods and dispose of the same at their discreacons.

Overseers: Thomas Graye of Smeatonwood and Robert Hamnett.

Item I give and bequeith to Ellen Griffith and Amye Macewen sisters of the said Thomas Manninge thelder fortie shillings apeece And to Thomas Grey the yonger of Aston tene shillings to Thomas Cley of my godsonne twentie shillings, Item I give and bequeith to Roberte Bewmorris sonne of Richard Bewmorris tenne shillings, and to my godsonne Thomas Wade five shillings, Item my will is and I give and bequeith to Rushton sonne of Marye Bewmorris twentie shillings Item my mind and will is & I doe give and bequeith to the said Thomas Grey and Roberte Hamnett my overseers fortie shillins apiece.

Signum Thome Hamnet testator
H

Witnesses: Thomas Burroughes, Richard Talier, Thomas Worall, Raphe Burroughes.

Inventory: Thomas Hamnett of the Grange, gent.

Taken: 20 August 1635

Of: goods, cattels and chattels.

Prisers: Thomas Calcott gent., Richard Edgley, William Wilson, William Capper yeoman

	£	s	d
In the parlor			
one bedd with it furniture & hangings	4	18	4
cheires stooles & cushions	1	10	0
one table, one carpett, one Courte cupboard one presse one			
truncke, one plate trunche, and twoe band boxes	4	18	6
in books		12	0
in plate	12	0	0
in pewter	4	2	0
a paire of tables		3	6
lynnans & nappye	1	10	0
one baskett & one little trunke		5	0
one paire of andirons		3	4
In the chamber over the parlor			
one bedd furnished	5	0	0
one warmeinge pan & one paire of andirons		10	0
one trunke & one little truncke		4	0
twoe little tables & one carpitt		6	0
a closse stoole		1	16
In the kitchin			
one longe table one farme one short table one cheire & one			
cupboard	1	0	0
in brasse	4	2	6
dreeping pannes spitts & other implements of iron		16	6
all the cooperye ware & treene ware		2	6
one lese from George Cotton Esquier for the revercōn			
in being	60	0	0
for the revercōn of a leas from Thomas Rhoads	9	13	4
debts oweinge to the testator by specialtie	492	0	0
debts oweinge to the testator without speciialtie	16	5	0
in readie money	11	10	7
his wearinge apparell	5	0	0
The Totall sume	576	4	7
[*recte*	629	150	65]

Endorsement: Probated 26 October 1635; administration granted to the executors named in the said will.

98. GILBERT WOOLLAM OF WRENBURY FRITH, YEOMAN

S.Pr. 14 February 1635/36
W.T. 19 November 1635
Buried: 23 November 1635

Gilbert Woollam = Margary [ ] = 2) Phillip Brett				Thomas Woollams = 1) Alice Woolam			
fl. 1615-22[a] fl. 1635-41 † 1641[b]				fl. 1635-41[c] md. 1602			
† 1635 *senex*				(witness) † 1607			

Richard	Raffe	Marie	Robert = Anne Burroughes	Alice	= 2) Anne Burrowes
c. 1607	c. 1610	c. 1615	c. 1619 | md. 1641[d]	fl. 1635	md. 1623
† bef. 1635	† 1635	† 1635	fl. 1635	(minor)	
			(minor)	† 1638	

Robert	Marie	Raphe	Gilbert
c. 1640	c. 1641/42	c. 1645	c. 1649 *fil. Robti*
† 1646	*fil. Robti*		

Will, sick.

Firste I give & bequeath my soule into the hands of Allmighty god trustinge throwe the merrittes of Jesus Christe my Saviour to have ffree pardon & remission of all my sinnes, & my body I Committ to the earth (whence it Came,) to bee buryed in Christian buryall, att the discrecōn of my Executors hereafter named constantly beleeveinge that it shall bee reunited to my soule att the laste day, & boeth bee made partakers of eternall blisse, by the Allmighty power of Jesus Christe, And touchinge the temporall estate, which Allmighty god of his free bounty & mercy hath giveen mee I will & dispose thereof as falloweth: Imprimis I give & bequeath unto my twoo Children twelve pennce apeece, beside what I shall heereafter bequeath unto them in this my laste will. Item I give & bequeath unto Margary Woollam my wyfe the use of all my Cartes plowes harrowes yockes Chaynes and all other my Implements of husbandrie ymmediatly after my deceasse untill such tyme as my sonne Roberte Woollam shall come to his full age of Twenty & one years, shee keepeinge the same in as good repeare as she finds them, And when my said sonne shall accomplish his said age I doe give & bequeath the same ymplements of husbandrie unto my said wyfe & sonne to bee equally devided betwixte them Item I give & bequeath unto my said sonne Roberte Woollam one peare of Joyned bedstids standinge in my parler. Item I give & bequeath unto my

[a]   Witness to will of Robert Tenche, 1615 (will no. 45); see also James Brooke's will, pr. 1622 (will no. 66), where he is recorded as owing £4 8s. to Brooke.

[b]   See will of Phillip Brett, yeoman, of Wrenbury Frith (Malpas parish), pr. 1641/CRO.

[c]   Was witness to will and made inventory for Gilbert Woollam, 1635; made inventory for George Tench, 1638 (will no. 107); William Fergusson Irvine, *Chester Licences*, iii. 182: 1 July 1623, to Thomas Woollams, widower, and Jane Yocken, widow of Wrenbury parish.

[d]   *Chester Licences*, iv. 85: 27 April 1641, to Robert Woollam, of Wrenbury parish, and Anne Burrowes, of Malpas Parish, spinster; Bondsman, Hugh Webster, of Cholmondeley; at Malpas, Wrenbury and Harthill.

daughter Allice Woollam, the bigeste Joyned bed standinge in the parler with it furneture. Item yf it shall please god to take mee out of this trancetory lyffe, before I have renewed my Lease with my woorshipfull landlord William Massie Esquier beinge nowe in motion & in parte agreede uppon betwixte us, I doe desire that my said wyfe Margary Woollam, who I doe hereafter nomenate for one of my executors shall with what Convenyente speede shee may goe one with my said landlord to renewe the same, & to putt into the same my said sonne & daughters lives with her owne, presumeinge soe farre uppon reasonable termes efecte the same, Item my will is that my said wyfe, when shee hath renewed my said Lease, shall bee stated & invested in the full moety & one halfe of my Messuage & tenemente with it appurtenancs dureinge her lyffe & in the other moety & full halfe of the same after the renewinge of my said Lease untill my said sonne Roberte Woollam shall accomplish his full age of Twenty & one yeares, for & towards the levinge & reasinge of the said Fyne & payinge of my debttes, & in regard that the said terme in the said moety of my Messuage or tenemente will bee farre to shorte, to discharge my said fyne & debttes, I doe give & bequeath unto the said Margary Woollam my wyfe, the reste & residue of All my goods Cattells & Chattells howsehould stuffe, boeth moveable & unmoveable goods of what kinde or quallitie soever the same bee of or wheresoever the same remayneeth, goeinge one with the paymente of my said fyne & debttes & dischargeinge my funerall expenncs. Item my will is that when my said wyfe hath renewed my lcase as aforesaid; that shee shall estate Assigne & Convey the same, in manner & forme fallowinge, (that is to say) the full moety & one halfe of My said messuage & tenemente, to the use & behoofe of my said sonne Roberte Woollam ymmedately after hee shall accomplish the full age of twenty & one yeares, for & dureinge the terme, which shall then bee to come & unexpired, & allsoe in the other moety & full halfe of the same after the deceasse of the said Margary Woollam my wyfe, on Condicōn that my said sonne Roberte Woollam shall well & truely Contente & paye, unto my said daughter Allice Woollam, the full Some of one Hundred & tenne pounds of lawfull English money eyther uppon the Marrige daye of him the said Roberte Woollam, or within twelve monethes after hee shall accomplish his said age of twenty & one yeares, (whether shall firste happen) yf shee the said Allice my daughter bee then liveinge, & in cause shee dye with out yssue before then the said paymente to bee voyde, Item my will is that yf it fortune that my said sonne Robert Woollam doe deceasse bofore hee shall accomplish his said age of twenty & one yeares, or bee fore his marriage, that then his estate intereste & terme in my said Messuage & tenemente (dureinge the residue of the terme) shall bee estated & invested of & in the said Allice Woollam my daughter. And in regard of the ymperfectnesse of my estate att this presente that I canne not settle the same, soe perfectly as I could havve donne, or may doe yf it please god, to lengthen the thred of my lyfe, I doe humblie intreate & desire my worshipful Landlord, to see all thinges efected accordinge to my will & desire herein before expressed. Item I give & bequeath unto every godchild I have twelve pence apeece.

Executors: the testator's wife, Margary Woollam, & 'my well beloved in Christe' Rauffe Twisse of Wrenbury Frith yeoman.

Overseer: the testator's landlord, William Massie esquire.

H. & S.
Gilbarte Woollam his X mke & seal

Witnesses: John Tenche, Thomas Woollam (his T marke), Thomas Graye clerk
1635.

Debts owed by the Testator:

	£	s	d
to Roger Podmore	100	0	0
to Richard Corke	6	0	0
to Philip Brett	7	0	0

Inventory: Gilbarte Woolam of Wrenbury, yeoman.

Taken: 7 December 1635, 11 Charles I

Of: goods Cattells & Chattells.

Prisers: Richard Corke, John Tennch, Thomas Woollames and John Barrow.

	£	s	d
his apparell	3	0	0
his Cattells & his horses	53	13	4
his shepp & swyne	40	10	0
his Corne in the barne	10	0	0
his Corne on the ground & hey	10	0	0
his Corne that is in the howse	2	10	0
his Carts plowes yockes & Chaynes & other husbandryware	4	0	0
his Coverings & blancketts	6	0	0
his beddinge boulster & pillowes	11	13	4
his Linnans & napprie	8	0	0
one peece of Cloth	1	3	4
one Wooll towe & feathers	3	0	0
his bedstids	1	6	8
his brasse	7	10	0
his pewter	2	13	4
Tables with the farmes & shilves & one presse & Cobbord	3	6	8
his Chestes & Coffers		13	4
one watringe Combe Chese tubes barrells & stonds & bookes & shilves & other trumprie	2	10	0
the dishbord & a little scileinge for abench wall		13	4
the Iron ware in the howse	1	0	0
yorne that is in the howse		10	0
the fewell aboute the howse	1	6	8
his bees of swarme		5	0
butter & Chese	5	10	0
2 flishes of Bacon		13	4

Saddles	6	8
2 silver spoones	10	0
geese & poultrie	15	0
[Sum	173 195	60]

Endorsement: Probated 14 February 1635; administration granted to the administrators named in the said will.

99. THOMAS GRAY THE ELDER OF ASTON IN NEWHALL, CLERK

S.Pr. 3 June 1636
W.T. 22 March 1635/36
Buried: 8 April 1636

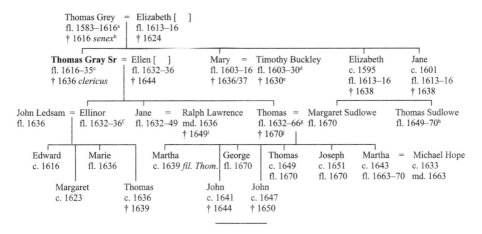

a   Witness for will of George Kemp, pr. ca. 1616 (will no. 50).
b   See will of Thomas Gray of Smeatonwood, pr. 1616/17 (will no. 53).
c   Received 20s. as bequest from Thomas Hamnett, will pr. 1635 (will no. 97).
d   Married 1603; owed John Bromhall £24, payable in four sums of £6 each over four years; see Bromhall will, pr. 1630 (will no. 82).
e   See inventory of Timothy Buckley, 1630 (no. 84).
f   For Ellinor Ledsam and her two siblings, see will of Margaret Graye, pr. 1632 (will no. 89).
g   Witness to will of Richard Dodd, pr. 1637 (will no. 101), and will of Elizabeth Briscoe, pr. 1637 (will no. 103); executor of will of Thomas Grey of Newhall, pr. 1640 (will no. 112); Thomas Gray and his wife received bequest of one half crown each in the will of Henry Griffiths, pr. 1654/55 (will no. 140).
h   Thomas Sudlowe was a priser for Ralph Lawrence, his sister's brother-in-law, 1649; see inventory of Ralph Lawrence (no. 133); executor for Edward Palin's will, pr. 1657 (will no. 143); see also will of Thomas Gray of Aston, pr. 1670/CRO.
i   See inventory of Ralph Lawrence, pr. 1649 (no. 133).
j   See will and inventory of Thomas Gray of Aston, pr. 1670/CRO.

Will, sick.

Firste I give upp willingly my soule into the hands of Allmighty god, (who firste gave it mee), trustinge throwe the merritts & passion of Jesus Christe my saviour, to have free pardon & remyssion of all my sinnes, And my body I Committ to the earth to bee buryed in Christian buryall att the discrecōn of my Executors hereafter named And Concerninge my temporall estate I will & dispose thereof as falloweth Item I give & bequeath unto every Child I have twelve pence apeece besides what I shall hereafter bequeath unto any of them by this my laste will. Item I give & bequeath unto my soninlawe John Ledsam my Cloke, Item I give & bequeath unto my daughter Ellionor Ledsam Tenne shillings. Item I give & bequeath unto Marie Ledsam my said sonneinlawe John Ledsam his daughter tenne shillings. Item I give & bequeath unto my daughter Jane Graye (over & above the porcōn I have delivered unto her & given her heereto fore in my health) one heifer Called blossome & twoo ewes & twoo lambes to bee delived unto her att the appoyntmente of my executors, Item my will & minde is that my executors hereafter named shall furnish her, after her marriage, att her goeinge to howse, out of my houwsehould stuffe, att their discrecōn. Item I give & bequeath unto my sonne Thomas Graye my sorrell Nag: Item I give & bequeath unto my lovinge wyfe Ellene Graye Tenne pounds. Item I give & bequeath unto Mr. Harwar to bye him a peare of gloves halfe a Crowne. Item I give & bequeath all the reste & residue of All my goods Cattells & Chattells of what kinde or quallitie soever the same bee of, whether moveable or unmoveable goods, or wheresoever the same remayneth (my debbtes & funerall expencs beinge in the firste place their out paid & discharged) unto the said Ellene Graye my wyfe & the said Thomas Graye my sonne to bee equally devided betwixte them.

Executors: the testator's wife, Ellen Gray, and the testator's son, Thomas Gray.

H. & S.
Thomas Graye

Witnesses: Eduard Hamnet, George Palin (his G marke).

Renunciation: Helen Gray the Relict of Thomas Gray of Wrenbury nominated an Executrix in his last will and Testamt doe renouce the proving to the sayd will and desyre that my sonne Thomas Gray the other Executor therein named may take the Execution thereof on himselfe onely. In witnes whereof I have set to my marke.

Acton May 17 1636   Helen Gray H (mark)

Inventory: Thomas Gray of Aston, Clerk of the Parish of Wrenbury.
Taken: 3 May 1636, 12 Charles I
Of: goods Cattells & Chattells.

Prisers: Edward Hamnett, George Hall and Edward Sproston.

	£	s	d
his wearinge apparell	1	13	4
Bedes boulsters & other beddinge	6	0	0
one table, bedsteds, farmes, & shilves	1	10	0
Chers & stooles		3	6
lynnans & Napprie	6	10	0
Brasse	2	10	0
Pewter & one maslin dish	1	7	0
Corne one the ground		6	0
fewell		10	0
muck		4	0
one plow, one trow, & tumbrill, Edge tooles & other small ymplements of husbandrie		6	8
twoo Coffers & a little fosett		12	0
twig basketts wiskits & strawe basketts		3	0
one Iron pott & kettle & all other iron ware		12	0
one kneydinge trow, & all other treenean ware	1	0	0
ticknall ware		1	0
Boockes		18	0
Newe Cloth	1	0	0
towe & yarne in the howse & barne	1	3	0
Bacon & meate in the howse	1	0	0
sackes Bages & quishens & one winnow shete		9	0
Foure kine & one heifer	14	0	0
one Nagge	2	13	4
Thirtine shepp	3	3	4
pwolltrie		6	0
one Cubbord & one dishbord & 2 wheles		7	0
Chese & one puddinge plate		3	0
glass in a windowe		2	0
debttes oweinge by specialty	18	10	0
in money in the howse & to come in	2	2	0
a debtt oweinge from Mr. Hamnetts executor lefte to the testator by the laste will of the said Thomas Hamnett decessed [1635]	1	0	0
a debtt from Thomas Taylor by specialty beinge remayninge unpaid in discharge of a bond		11	0
Some is	73	1	10
[*recte*	61	194	26]

Endorsement: Probated 3 June 1636; administration granted to Thomas Gray, son of the said deceased, one of the executors named in the said will.

Renunciation of Ellen Gray the other executor is included 1636: Renunciation of Ellen Gray executrix of the will of Thomas Gray formerly of the parish of Wrenbury deceased madde at Acton 17th May 1636 before Master Hunt and Jo[hn?] Bickerton in person 1636. I John Bickerton being present Above the value [i.e., over £40].

100. JOHN HALL OF NEWHALL

S.Pr. 24 June 1636
2 February 1635/36
Buried: 15 March 1635/36

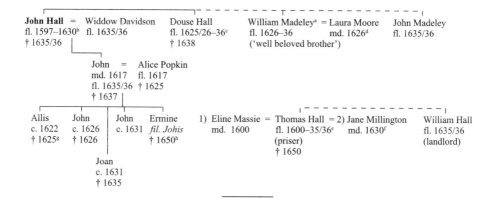

[a] The first inclination is to regard William Madeley as the brother-*in-law* of John Hall, making Hall's otherwise unnamed wife a Madeley. Given our experience with other families, however, it is more likely that John Hall's father or mother married a Madeley in a second marriage. Among the otherwise unconnected members of the family are: John Madeley, one of the recipients of a bequest from John Hall's will of 1635/36; Richard Madeley, who married Anne Woollam in 1642 at Wrenbury; Thomas Madeley, yeoman, who made the inventory of George Cudworth's goods etc. in 1624 (no. 70); and George Madeley, who married Elizabeth Twisse in 1639 at Wrenbury; Elizabeth was buried 1659 at Wrenbury as *Madele*.
[b] Witness to will of William Fletcher, pr. 1607 (will no. 23); either John Hall Sr, or his son, John Jr, was bondsman 1630 to the marriage licence of Thomas Hall of Wrenbury parish and Jane Millington of Wrenbury parish, spinster; see William Fergusson Irvine, *Chester Licences*, iii. 201.
[c] Douse Hall was owed £2 10s. by George Dickins in 1626/27; see will of George Dickins (will no. 74).
[d] William Fergusson Irvine, *Chester Licences*, iii. 73: 28 September 1626, to William Madeley and Laura Moore, Audlem, spinster; bondsman, Roger Hamnett; at Marbury or Wrenbury.
[e] Thomas Hall was a priser for the goods of Anne Kempe of Smeatonwood; will pr. ca. 1619 (will no. 57).
[f] William Fergusson Irvine, *Chester Licences*, iii. 201: 30 November 1630, Thomas Hall and Jane Millington spinster of Wrenbury parish; bondsman, John Hall; at Wrenbury.
[g] Either this child, or her mother, also named Alice Hall.
[h] Since the testator makes no mention of a daughter named Ermine, we must assume that this is the daughter of John Hall Jr.

Will, sick.

First, as before all things to be respected, I doe commend, and comitt my soule into the hands of Almighty god, and of his sonne Jesus Christ, my onely redeemer, by whose death and passion I hope, and by faith in him am assured to bee saved, & now restinge in that hopefull assurance, I doe thus dispose of my temporall goodes, and estate as followeth, I give and bequeath to my welbeloved wife, and my sonne John all my temperall goods & cattels moveable and unmoveable, to bee eaqualy devided betwixte them, Alsoe my will is that my debts & funerall expenses shall bee payd out of the whole, before it bee devided betwixt them. Debts which I owe, first I owe to my sister Douse Hall, fortie five shillings Alsoe I owe to Michill Hope fourtie shillings: Alsoe to Mr. Cotton for Rent nineteene shillings foure pence Alsoe to my brother William Madeley thirty shillings: Alsoe to John Madeley three pounds: Payd to William Hall for rent for this yeare aforehand fourtie shillings.

Executor: 'my well beloved brother' William Madeley.

Overseer: John Ravenscroft.

H. & S.
John: Hall
his X marke & seal

Witnesses: John (X) Ravenscroft, Thomas Ravenscrofte.

Inventory: John Hall of Newhall.

Taken: 21 March 1635/36

Of: goods and chattels.

Prisers: John Ravenscroft, Thomas Hall, Richard Berrington.

	£	s	d
his wearing apparel		80	0
six kine	18	6	8
one twinter heffer		30	0
one yearlinge calfe		13	4
one swine		13	4
twooe mares and a coulte	7	0	0
bedding in generall	4	13	4
linnen and napperie		30	0
brasse in generall		10	0
pewter in generall		20	0
a Iron pot and kettle		6	8
a table cuborte formes cheeres stooles and a dishboord	2	0	0
five cofferes		20	0
corne in the house		30	0

tooe and yarne		6	8
treenen ware a cheesepresse wheeles and a reele		20	0
corne in the barne and hay		20	0
cartes ploues wheeles and all Implements belonging to husbandry	3	10	0
one grate and all other Iron ware whatsoever		6	8
corne uppon grounde mucke and timber		20	0
poultry		5	0
Money which was in the house	2	19	0
things omitted		5	0
[Sum	36	382	44]

Endorsement: Probated 24 June 1636; administration granted to the sole executor named in the said will.

101. RICHARD DODD OF SMEATONWOOD, YEOMAN

S. Pr. 20 July 1637
W.T. 22 December 1636
Buried: 12 January 1636/37

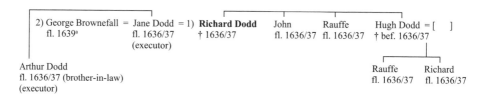

Will, sick.

First I give up willingly my soule into the hands of Allmightie God, trustinge throw the merritts & passion of Jesus Christe my saviour to have free pardon, & remyssion of all my sinnes, And my body I committ to the earth whence it came to bee decently buryed in Christian buryall att the discrecōn of my Executors hereafter named And for my temporall estate which Allmighty god of his bounty hath bestowed upon mee I will & dispose thereof as falloweth. Item I give & bequeath & Assigne over unto Jane Dood my loevinge wyfe all my terme of yeare, or yeares which I have in Marbury Hey beinge nowe in my occupacōn which I hould of

---

^a William Fergusson Irvine, *Chester Licences*, iv. 5: 15 May 1639, George Brownfall and Jane Dod, widow of Wrenbury parish; bondsman, John Proudman; at Wrenbury and Harthill.

George Bickerton of Towneley gent. Item I give, bequeath Assige & conveay unto the said Jane my wyfe, All my intereste & terme of yeares I have, in the brand peece beeing nowe in my occupacōn, which I hould of Richard Bebington of Smeatonwood aforesaid Husbandman. Item I give & bequeath unto my brother John Dood 12d. in money, and one browne Cow, called browninge. Item I give & bequeath unto my brother Rauffe Dood twelve pence in money, & one blacke Cow called Justice. Item I give & bequeath unto Rauffe Dood sonne of my Decessed brother Hugh Dood, Tenne shillings Item, I give & bequeath unto Richard Dood sonne of my said deceased brother Tenne shillings Item my will & minde is that all my debttes which of due, & wright I owe unto any man bee in the firste place trewly paid & discharged shortly after my decesse And after my said debtts & legacies herby given, & bequeathed, & my funerall expences, are well & trewly paid & discharged I doe herby give & bequeath All the reste, & residue of all my goods, Cattells, & Chattells boeth moveable, & unmoveable goods, of what kinde or quallitie soever the same bee of, or wheresoever the same remayneth unto the said Jane Dood my wife.

Executors: the testator's wife, Jane Dood, and the testator's brother-in-law, Arthure Dood of Leye in the Countie of Salop yeoman.

Overseer: the testator's landlord, George Cotton of Combermere Esquier.

H. & S.
Richard Dood
(his marke & seal)

Debttes oweinge to the testator without specialty:

	£	s	d
Rauffe Pemberton of Wrenbury Woods oweth mee		20	0
Thomas Bostocke of Whitchurch shoomaker oweth mee		28	8
Roberte Grindley of [the] Presses owe	3	0	0

And for all other that owe mee any small somes without specialty I doe freely forgive them

Witnesses: Richard Bebington (his marke), Thomas Graye, Scr. 1636.

Inventory: Richard Dodd of Smeatonwood, yeoman.

Taken: 30 January 1636/37

Of: goods Cattalles and Chattelles.

Prisers: Thomas Rowe, Richard Berrington and Raph Pemberton.

	£	s	d
Eight Kyne	20	0	0
Three Calves	2	0	0
One Mare	2	13	4

Corne in the Barne	1	6	8
One Sowe		18	0
Hay in the barne and without	1	10	0
Corne sowen in the ground	1	19	0
Corne in the house	1	17	4
Bedinge	2	0	0
Lynnens and Nappery	1	0	0
His wearinge Apparrell	1	0	0
Yarne and Towe		18	0
Brasse and Pewter	1	6	8
all Implements of Husbandry	1	0	0
One Joyned Bedd		18	0
One Cubbart and Presse	1	0	0
Twoe Joyned Tables with Formes Chayres and other tooles	2	0	0
Coffers		6	8
Wood		5	0
Mucke		2	6
All Implements belonginge to Huswifry		5	0
Bacon		15	0
Butter and Cheese		5	4
Poultry		3	4
One Heffer	1	10	0
Treenanware of all Sorts		13	4
Racks Tonges and Pothooks		1	6
A Bargaine of ground The Remainder beinge but one yeare behinde and unexpired of a Parcell of ground called Marbury Hey prised to	5	0	0
The Remainder of a Bargaine of ground called the Brand peece beinge Three yeares unexpired		20	0
One Lease for certen yeares yet to come and unexpired determinable upon one life	4	0	0

Debts owinge to the Testator without specialty

	£	s	d
Rauffe Pemberton of Wrenbury Wood oweth		20	0
Thomas Bostocke of Whitchurch Shoomaker oweth		24	8
Robert Grindley of Prees oweth	3	0	0

Summa Totalis	62	18	4
[*recte*	50	244	68]

Endorsement: Probated in the presence of Edmund Mainwaring, doctor of laws, 20 July 1637; administration to the executors named in the will. The said Arthur Downell, sojourning outside the diocese, will designate a place to summon him for [swearing the oath] in the church of Wrenbury.

102. JOHN EDGELEY OF WOODCOTT, YEOMAN

S.Pr. 26 July 1637
W.T. 1635
Buried: 21 July 1636

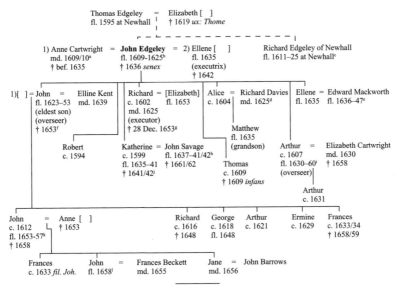

a William Fergusson Irvine, *Chester Licences*, i. 79; 22 May 1610, a licence was granted confirming a clandestine marriage between John Edgeley and Anne Cartwright; the Wrenbury parish register shows the marriage date as 12 Feb. 1609/10.
b Fl. 1609 as tenant at Woodcott; in R. Stewart Brown, *Cheshire Inquisitions Post Mortem*, iii. 81 he is noted 1623 at Newhall. Given the dates of birth for John Edgeley's older children (Robert, 1594; Katherine, 1599; Richard, 1602; Alice, 1604) it is obvious that he had an earlier (actually his first) wife than Anne Cartwright, making Ellene [ ], noted as his wife in his will, actually his third.
c Priser for Margaret Sevell, will pr. 1611 (will no. 35); Newhall Rentals 1625/CRO.
d William Fergusson Irvine, *Chester Licences*, iii. 38; 23 August 1625, Richard Davies and Alice Edgeley of Wrenbury, spinster.
e Received a bequest of £30 as a servant of George Cotton, will pr. 1648 (will no. 128); owed John Edgeley £10, see below.
f Newhall Rentals 1625/CRO; View of Frankpledge, Newhall Manor , 1649, 1651, 1653/CRO; see will of John Edgeley of Moorehall, pr. 1654 (will no. 139); Bishop's Transcript shows John Edgley *de New*: buried 30 August 1653.
g The *terminus post quem* for his death is 26 December 1653, when he first declared his will (will no. 153) nuncupatively.
h Priser of goods and chattels of John Edgeley of Woodcott, see below; executor for his wife Katherine, will pr. 1641/42 (will no. 116).
i See will of Richard Edgeley of Smeatonwood, pr. 1660/61 (will no. 153).
j See will of Katherine Savage, pr. 1641/42 (will no. 116).
k Witness to will of his father, John Edgeley of Moorehall, pr. 1654 (will no. 139); noted as John Edgeley of Woodcott, cousin to George Hall, Jr, will pr. 1658 (will no. 147); the View of Frankpledge for Newhall Manor, 11 April 1654, shows John Edgeley Sr of Woodcott surrendering to John Edgley his son.
l Appears as a juror at Newhall Manor court 1656/CRO.

Will, sick.

First I give and bequeath my soule into the hands of Allmighty god, assuredly throwe the death and marrittes of my only saviour Jesus Christe to have free pardon & forgiveness of all my sinnes and my body I committ to the earth, to bee decently buryed in Christian buryall, att the discretion of my executors, hereafter named beleeving throwe the power of my Saviour Jesus Christe, that it shall bee reased upp att the last day and beeinge reunited to my soule shall boeth bee made partakers of eternall blisse, And touchinge the temporall goods & means which Allmighty god of his bounty & mercy hath enriched mee I will & dispose thereof as followeth Imprimis I give & bequeath unto everye Childe I have twelve pence a peece, besides what I shall hereafter bequeath unto any of them hereafter in this my last will: Item I give & bequeath unto John Edgley my eldest sonne, all the anciante Earelomes that are in my howse viz the greate stone trough & one of the lesser stone troughs, the great Combe in the back howse and all the other small implements belonginge to the oven with the kneadinge trough the greate brasse panne, and the bigeste broch, immediatly after the deceasse of mee and my wyfe, for my will is that she shall have the occupation of them duringe her lyfe. Item I give & forgive unto my said sonne John Edgley one bond of Tenne pounds sixteene shillings which he stands lyable to paye to my Executors att the end of three monnethes nexte att my decease: Item my will is that my executors shall att my coste and charge free my said sonne out of all his troubles in the Spirituall Courte, if I doe not efecte it for him myselfe before my death: Item I give & bequeath unto my daughter Kathrin Edgley foursscore pounds, to bee paid her within twelve monethes after my deceasse: Item I give & bequeath unto my said daughter Kathrin one bed with it furniture which my wyffe shall appoynte: Item I give unto my said daughter one bond of twenty five pounds which Mr John Cartwright late of of [sic!] Sheppenhall deceased oweeth unto mee Arthure Cartwright his brother beinge surety Item I give & bequeath unto my sonne Richard Edgley the greate table standinge in my howse the joyned bed in the parlor with it furniture and the preesse standinge in the parlor: Item I doe give unto my said sonne Richard Edgley my stalles of bees, on condition that my wyfe have the one-halfe of the profitt of them duringe her lyffe: Item I give & bequeath unto Ellene Edgley my wyfe & the said Richard Edgley my sonne my Cartes plowes and all other my implements of husbandrie to use indifferantly betwixte them dureinge the lyffe of her the said Ellene Edgley my wyfe, And ymmediately after her deceasse I doe wholely give & bequeath the same unto my said sonne Richard Edgley: Item I doe hereby give & bequeath unto everye grandchild I have twelve pence a peece, for a remembrance: Item I doe give unto my grandchild Mathew Davies one pide heifer calfe Item I doe give & bequeath unto my executors hereafter named £10 which my daughter Ellene Mackworth oweeth unto mee towards the dischargeinge of the legaces herein bequeathed: Item my will is that all my debttes legacs and funenerall expencs shall bee paied & discharged in the firste place out of my whole estate, & after my said debttes and legaces are paid and my funerall expenses are discharged I doe give & bequeath unto the said Ellene Edgley my wyffe the rest and residue of all my goods Cattells and Chattells

Corne & howseholde stuffe both move able & unmoveable goods of what kinde or quallity soeever the same bee of or wheresoever the same remayneeth:

Executors: the testator's wife, Ellene Edgley, and his son, Richard Edgley.

Overseers: the testator's sons, John Edgley and Arthur Edgley.

H. & S
John Edgley 1635

Witnesses: Thomas Graye, Thomas Graye Jun. 1635.

Inventory: John Edgley of Woodcott, yeoman.

Taken [20/24] July 1636

Of: goods and chattels.

Prisers: John Savage, John Barrow, Robert Trickett and John Edgley.

	£	s	d
Coarne and hay and	60	0	0
for oxen and kine and younge beasts, and one mare	1	10	0
for swine	4	10	0
for plowes and Carts and all other implements belonging to husbandry	5	10	0
for Mucke	2	0	0
for straw		8	0
for Coales and [soote?]	2	10	0
for poultry aboute the house		6	8
for a Cowpre and a heare and other implements within the Backhouse	2	0	0
for 3 stone troughes		10	0
for coarne and malte within the house	7	0	0
for cheese and butter	5	0	0
for wooden ware within the house	1	10	0
for brasse and peawter	8	0	0
for Iron wares within the house		13	4
for tables and formes and stoules	2	0	0
for the bedd furnished and the presse within the parlor	6	0	0
for nappery and linnen cloathe	8	0	0
for halfe a dozen of silver spoones	1	10	0
for beddinge and bedstocks and chests standing in the lower chamber	7	0	0
for bedding and bedstocks within the lofts	5	0	0
for bakean and other household provision	2	0	0
for Cheespresse and Shilfes and loose bords	2	0	0
for wearinge Cloathes of the deseased	4	0	0
bond from John Carwright for payment of	13	10	0
a debte from Edward Mackworthe of	10	0	0

[Sum   157   107   12]
[*recte*   165   11   12]

Endorsement: *[damaged]* Probated 26 July 1637; administration granted to Richard Edgeley, one of the executors named in the said will, but with power reserved to the other executor named in the said will until he will have come.

103. ELIZABETH BRISCOE OF WRENBURY, WIDOW

S.Pr.[After 19 July 1637] 1637
W. T. 23 August 1632
Buried: 18 July 1637

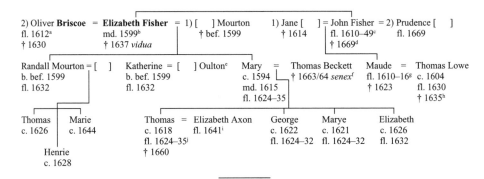

a   Randull Cowper owed Oliver Briscoe/*Bruscalle* £3 in 1612 and he was a priser of Cowper's goods and chattels; see will of Randull Cowper, pr. 1613 (will no, 40).
b   Parish Registers – Marriages: 22 July 1599, Oliver Briscoe and Elizabeth *Moorton*.
c   See will of James Barnett, pr. 1610 (will no. 29); owed £14 to John Bromhall – see debts associated with will pr. 1630 (will no. 82); made inventory for Oliver Briscoe, 1629 (will no. 80) and Robert Shrowbridge, 1641 and witnessed Shrowbridge's will (will no. 114); owed £4 10s. to Alice Buckley, will pr. 1649 (will no. 132); made inventory for Richard Barnett and witnessed his will, pr. 1647/48 (will no. 125).
d   John Fisher, yeoman of Aston, will pr. 1669/ CRO.
e   See Margaret Ankers's will, pr. 1609/10 (will no. 28) for the Oulton family; also John Anckers's will, pr. 1641 (will no. 115) for [ ] Olton and John Olton, prisers. A Robert Oulton made the inventory for Roger Jones, 1639 (will no. 110).
f   See will of Thomas Beckett, pr. 1666/CRO.
g   Bequeathed £1 by James Barnett, will pr. 1610 (will no. 29); married 1616.
h   See will of Thomas Lowe, pr. 1637 (will no. 105).
i   William Fergusson Irvine, *Chester Licences*, iv. 88: 27 May 1641, to Thomas Beckett of Wrenbury parish and Elizabeth Axon, spinster of Audlem parish; bondsman, Thomas Poole; at Wrenbury, Audlem and Acton.
j   Presumably the god-son of Thomas Hamnett who received 25s. in his will, pr. 1635 (will no. 97).

Will, sick.

First I Commende my soule and body into the handes of Almyghty god assuredly trustinge and beleevinge to be saved and made partaker both soule and body of eternall blisse and happinesse through the onely merites of Christ Jesus my alone saviour & redeemer and *my body to be buried in the churchyarde of Wrenbury* abovesaid in sure and Certayne hope of a ioyfull resurrection. Item I give and bequeath unto Randall Mourton my sonne £4 in full satisfaction of his Childes parte of all my goodes. Item I give and bequeath unto Katherine Oulton my daughter 40s. in full satisfaction of her Childes parte of all my goodes. Item I give and bequeath unto Marye Beckett my daughter 40s. Item I give and bequeath unto Thomas Beckett the yonger my grandchilde one Cowe and £9 Item I give and bequeath unto George Beckett my grandchilde £7 Item I give and bequeath unto Elizabeth Beckett my grandchilde £10 Item I give and bequeath unto Marye Beckett the younger my grandchilde 20s. Item I give unto the worshipfull Arthure Starkey esquier 3s. 4d. to buy him a peare of gloves. Item I give unto John Cartwright of Sheppenhall gent 3s. 4d. to buy him a peare of gloves desyreinge & requestinge them both not to see my grandchildren above named wronged & yf any man wronge them to doe there best to right them. All the rest of my goods moveable & unmoveable & the reversion of the lease of my house unexpired (my body beinge honestly brought home & my funcrall expences discharged) I give & bequeath unto Marye Beckett above said my daughter & to Thomas Beckett her husbande.

Executors: ~~the above said Marye Beckett~~ John Fisher, the testator's brother, and George Beumarisse.

H. & S.
Elizabeth Briscoe
her E marke

Witnesses: Thomas Harwar, Thomas Graye ~~1632~~.

Inventory: Elizabeth Briscoe of Wrenbury.

Taken: 19 July 1637

Of: goods Chattells & Chattells.

Prisers: Thomas Spencer and Ranndle Weaver.

	£	s	d
her weareinge apperrell		13	4
In beddinge	2	10	0
In Linnannes & Napperie	1	0	0
Linnan Yarn		10	0
In Pewter	1	0	0
In Brasse	2	6	8

Twoo peare of bedsteds, tables, formes, quaffers & shilves	1	0	0
In Iron ware		4	0
In Cowperie ware	1	0	0
Cheres & stooles		3	4
In treene ware		2	0
In ticknill ware		1	6
One Cowe	2	10	0
In redy money in the howse	3	0	0
One Lease for Yeares in Reversōn	13	6	8
debbtes oweinge by speciallty	24	0	0
debbtes oweinge without speciallty	9	0	0
Somme totale	62	4	6

Endorsement: There is none.

104. WILLIAM COWPER THE ELDER OF SOUND, YEOMAN

S. Pr. [After 13 October] 1637
W.T. 2 October 1637
Buried: 13 October 1637

Editor's NOTE: Both the original will and a copy are extant at the CRO; both have seals of the testator.

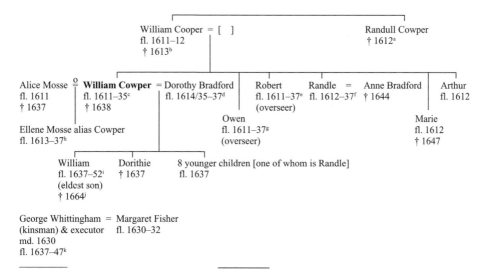

George Whittingham = Margaret Fisher
(kinsman) & executor   fl. 1630–32
md. 1630
fl. 1637–47ᵏ

ᵃ See will of Randull Cowper of Wrenbury, pr. 1613 (will no. 40).
ᵇ See will of William Cowper of Sound, made in 1611, pr. 1613 (will no. 42).
ᶜ Witness to will of John Bromhall of Sound, pr. 1630 (will no. 82); witness to will of Thomas Lowe of Sound, ?1635 (will no. 105).
ᵈ William Cowper of Wrenbury parish had a licence dated 20 February 1614/15 to marry Dorothy Bradford of Wrenbury parish at St. Oswald's, Chester; see William Fergusson Irvine, *Chester Licences*, i. 179.
ᵉ See will of William Cowper (will no. 42); overseer of his brother's will, below.
ᶠ Randall Cooper from Wrenbury parish had a licence dated 1 May 1612 to marry Anne Bradford of Baddily parish at Wrenbury; see *Chester Licences*, i. 119; bondsman was Arthur Cooper, his brother. Anne Bradford appears to be the sister or kinswoman of the Dorothy Bradford who married William Cooper in 1614/15. Randle is noted as the *kinsman* of William Cowper when named as his executor in 1637 (see below).
ᵍ See will of William Cowper of Sound pr. 1613, made in 1611 (will no. 42); overseer of his brother's will, below.
ʰ See will of William Cooper of Sound, pr. 1613, wherein Ellin is noted as 'the supposed daughter of my eldest sonne William Cooper begotten on Allice Mosse'. Ellen was given a sum of £10 within a year of the demise of William's wife, Ellen.
ⁱ In 1652 William Cowper recently held £9 belonging to Henry Griffiths Sr, but was now in the hands of Henry's son Robert Griffiths; see will of Henry Griffiths, made 1652, pr. 1658 (will no. 145).
ʲ See inventory of William Cowper, pr. 1664/CRO.
ᵏ Noted 1647 in will of John Tenche of Wilkesley/ CRO.

Will, sick.

Firste I give & bequeath my soule into the hands of Allmighty God who firste gave
it mee trustinge throwe the merrittes & passion of Jesus Christ my Saviour to have
free pardon & remission of all my sinnes, And my body I Committ to the earth
whence it came to bee decently buryed in Christian buryall att the discrecōn of my
Executors hereafter named And touchinge my temporall estate which allmightie
god of his bountie & mercie hath bestowed upon mee, I will & dispose thereof as
followeth: Item I give & bequeath unto Dorathie Cowper my loevinge wife the use
of all my weanescoth tables formes & shelves in my howse wherein I live & the
joyned bed standinge in the higher parler, the bigeste brasse pott, & the bigeste
brasse panne, with the Cubbords & presses in my howse, dureinge her naturall life,
Condicon that shee remove non of them out of my house And ymmediately after
her deceasse I doe give & bequeath the same unto my eldeste Sonne William
Cowper & to the heires of his body to remayne as earelomes unmoveable Item I
give & bequeath unto my said Wyfe the use of all my Cartes plowes & ymplements of husbandrie dureinge her naturall life (& keepeinge her selfe in my name)
& att her death or marriage whether shall firste happen I give & bequeath the same
unto my said sonne William Cowper, shee leveinge the same in as good repeare
as shee nowe finds them Item I give & bequeath unto my said wife the use of ~~my~~
all the reste of my householld stuffe beinge within my house as beds beddinge
Chestes, brasse pewter & such lyke dureinge her naturall life & keepeinge her selfe
in my name And att her death or marriage (whether shall first happen) I doe give
& bequeath the same unto my Eight yonger Children to bee equally devided amon-
geste them Item I doe give & bequeath unto my sonne Ranndle Cowper the beste
Cowe I have Item I give and bequeath unto my said wife Dorathie Cowper the use
of all the reste & residue of all my kine, Calves, horses or mares & yonge Cattell
during her naturall life & keepeinge her selfe in my name and ymmediately after
her death I doe give & bequeath the same unto my said Eight yonger Children or
att her marriage whether shall Firste happen to bee equally devided amonngeste
them Item I doe give & bequeath unto everye Childe I have 12d. apiece on & above
what I have heretofore or shall hereafter bequeath unto any of them by this my last
will Item my will is that my said base daughter Ellene Mosse, alias Cowper shall
have the some of £10 paid her with which I was intrusted by my father for her
Item I doe give & bequeath unto my said base daughter £3 6s. 8d. Item in regard
that my yonger Children are yet by yonge my will & minde is & I doe hereby
devise that after my debttes legacies, before bequeathed & funeral expences shall
bee paid & discharged that my said eldeste sonne William Cowper by & with the
aide & assistance of my executors hereafter named shall take all the reste & resedue of all my goods Cattels & Chatelles, (which I doe reserve for and toward the
porcons of my said Eight yonger Children respectively) for & towards the
reneweinge of my Lease of my howse & tenemente wherein I doe nowe live, (presumeinge soe farre, that my honorable landlord Roberte lord Viscounte
Cholmondeley will renue the same upon reasonable Consideracon & upon the
surendringe of my ould Lease for my said wife Dorathie Cowper Life my said

sonne Williams life & my said sonne Ranndles Cowper their three lives. Condicōnally that my said sonne & executors shall goeaboute the renueinge of my said Lease with What Conveniente speede the maye after my decease and that my said sonne shall putt into the Said lease (if it bee obteyned) my said wives life my said sonnes life & my said sonne Ranndle Cowpers life, And one this Condicon allsoe & further my will is that after my said sonne William Cowper & my Executors shall have renued my said Lease, as aforesaid, that my Said sonne William Cowper shall make my said Wife Dorathie Cowper a good estate for terme Of her life, & keepeinge her selfe sole & unmarried of & in the full moetie of my said Whole messuage, & tenemte wherein I doe nowe live & in the full moetie of all the meadows Leasowes & pastures thereunto belonginge with thappurtenancs shee mentayninge my Children Until the shall bee able for them seles and in cause shee doe happen to marrie, then To pay unto her £5 a yeare out of the same & to take the Children from her ~~until the shall~~, & to keepe them until the shall bee able for them selves And one this Condicōn allsoe, that my said sonne William Cowper within the terme of Sixe monethes nexte after the renueinge of the said Lease shall make unto my Executors hereafter named aswell out of the other moetie & full halfe of my messuage & tenemente before mencōned wherein I doe nowe live as allsoe out of my lease which I have from Mr Mynshull of Erdswick Esquier of the Hobfields scituate lyine & beinge in Wrenbury Frith within the said Countie a good sure & undefeasable estate or of soe much of boeth of them, as shall bee well worth the yearely value of twentie pounds a yeare, for the terme of twelve yeares then nexte & ymmediatly ensuinge & fully to bee compleate & ended yf the termes therin soe longe Continue The which some of twentie pounds a year For the said terme of twelve yeares, I doe intruste with my Executors hereafter named, To bee sett forth & ymployed as it comes in, for the use & behoofe of my afore Said Eight yonger Children in lewe of the remainder of my estate which I have devided to be imployed as aforesaid. Item I doe hereby give & bequeath & devise that my said Executors shall paye unto my said Children the some of £30 a peece as they & every of them severally shall attayne their full ages of twentie & one yeares & not before out of the said yearely somes of £20 a yeare to bee levied in twelve year- es as aforesaid, & in case any of my said Children doe dye (as god it defende) that then when my yongeste Childe shall accomplish it full age of twentie & one year- es his or her porcon soe deceasinge as allsoe the surplus of the said some of £240 & the geane, or, intereste that shall bee made by the ymploymente of the same to bee by my said Executors hereafter named ~~to bee~~ equally devided amonngeste my said Eight yonger Children or soe many of them as shall fortune to bee then liveinge Item I doe hereby give & devise unto my said sonne William Cowper & his heires, all my Lands, tennements & hereditaments which I have by inheritance within the Realme of England or els where for ever.

Executors: the testator's wife, Dorathie Cowper, and his kinsmen George Whittingham and Ranndle Cowper yeomen.

Overseers: the testator's brothers, Owen Cowper and Robert Cowper.

H. & S.
William Cowper

Witnesses: John Wright, John Barnett (his marke), Thomas Graye, clerk.

Endorsement: All that remains of the endorsement is the date at the bottom – 1637.

105. THOMAS LOWE OF SOUND, HUSBANDMAN

I?Pr. 1637
W.T. (before 4 June 1635)
Buried: 4 June 1635

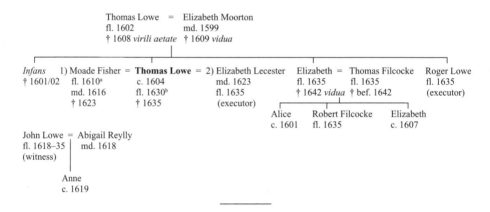

Will, sick.

First I give and bequeath my[ ] soule unto almighty God my maker and Redemer hoping by Christ death to have Remission for all my Sines *And my body to be buried in the parish Church or Church yard of Wrenbury* Imprimis I give and bequeith unto my espoused wife my house and all my whole estate moveable and unmoveable during her life if she keepe her selfe soule and unmaried paying and discharging all my detes and funerall expenses discharged and if shee the sayd widdow chance to mary any other man to meake her Choyse whether shee will take £10 with in the yeare or all the good the Cubwart the bedstockes the table

---

ᵃ Bequeathed £1 by James Barnett, will pr. 1610 (will no. 29).
ᵇ Thomas Lowe owed John Bromhall £10 and was also £5 2s. 3d. in arrears of rent, due the previous Bartholomewstide, in debts recorded 1631; see will of John Bromhall (will no. 82).

the siling the glase excepted and to avoyd plesanly out of the house and grounde and it is my mind that Robart Filcockes my sisters Sonne shall after the decease of my wiffe and my brother Roger Looe shall Have this my house and ground yelding and paying to the rest of all my sisters Children the some of £10 equally to bee devided amongs them With in the yeare.

Executors: the testator's wife and his brother, Roger Looe.

Signum per Thomas Looe

Witnesses: Roger Looe, William Coowper, Jonne Jooe.

Endorsement: Thomas Lowe of Sound 1637.

106. EDWARD BOWDON OF CHORLEY

S.Pr. 18 April 1638
Buried: 15 April 1638[a]

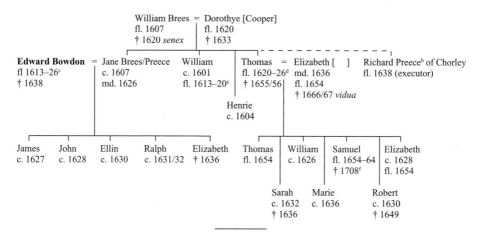

---

[a] The day of the month is obscure in the Parish Registers, but the Bishop's Transcript gives it clearly as 15 April.
[b] Clearly related to Raphe Preece, yeoman, who owed Roger Jones of Chorley £2, will pr. 1639 (will no. 110) and was priser of the inventory of John Woodfen of Chorley, 1642 (no. 118).
[c] Received bequest from Humphrey Rylands of Chorley 1613; will pr. 1613.
[d] See will of William Brees of Broomhall, pr. 1621 (will no. 64); Thomas Brees churchwarden, 1636.
[e] William Brees was bequeathed 3s. 4d. as the god-child of William Cooper of Sound, will pr. 1613 (will no. 42). This suggests that his mother was a Cooper, in which family the name Dorothy was prominent.
[f] Samuel Brees was churchwarden at Wrenbury, 1664; will of Samuel Brees of Broomhall, yeoman, pr, 1708/CRO.

Inventory: Edward Bowdon of Chorley.

Taken: 23 April 1638, 14 Charles I

Of: goods and Cattells.

Prisers: John Sparrow gent., John Woodfaine, William Rogers, John Pattrick and William Millington.

	£	s	d
One mare and a colt	4	0	0
one Cowe prized for a herriott	4	0	0
one Twynter beast	3	10	0
two Calves	2	13	4
one Swyne		7	0
one gander & a goose			16
Two ducks			12
three hennes			18
In hay		6	8
in hempe			12
one payre of wheeles		2	6
one Cart bodye			6
all the fewell		8	8
one Bedsteed		6	0
all the Threstles plancks boards and shelves		6	0
one Chest and one Coffer		5	0
one flockbed and Two boulsters		4	0
one payre of Swaddles			6
Three Coverlets Two blankets and two pillowes		26	0
fyve sheetes and one Table cloath		11	0
for Corne		12	0
hempseede			12
in wooll		16	0
in Tow and yarne		6	0
one pillow			12
Two kettels and a skellet			18
in pewter		4	0
in Bacon		2	0
one braspot		10	0
in gretes			18
Two Remnants of woollen cloath			18
stockcards			18
Ashen			12
All the Cowperye and Trynnware		13	0
Ropes a Coller and a brydle		2	0
Rakes and Staves			4
Leaden weights and a beame			12

All the Iron ware		6	0
one Sword and a dagger		2	0
one Chayre and fower stooles		18	0
All the earthen ware		2	0
all the Mucke		4	6
for a truckle Bedstead			4
all his Apparell		13	4
In Silver or ready money		10	11
In feathers		5	0
one Bonnd of a specaltie debt for forgotten goods	10	10	0
in other debts [without specialtie]　Thyrtye three shillinges and fower pence			

Summa totalis	36	17	3
[*recte*	40	16	11]

Endorsement: Exhibited 18 April 1638; administration granted to Richard Preece of Chorley. The same day tuition of the children of the said deceased was granted to the feodary for B. 1638.

[NOTE: The feodary is an officer of the Court of Wards and the tuition is not granted to a named individual].

107. GEORGE TENCH OF SMEATONWOOD, YEOMAN

S.Pr. 11 May 1639
Nuncupative will (Before 19 July) 1638
Buried: 19 July 1638

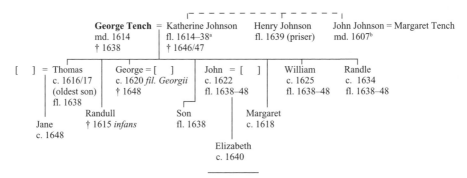

Will, sick.

George Tench of Smeatenwood in the countie of Chester yeoman haveing his wife and most parte of his family visited with sicknes and takeinge into his consideracōn the Incertainety of life, as also feeling hymselfe some what dis[impid or dilimpid?] and not in very good health and misdoubtinge the approchinge of his owne ~~death~~ insuinge death: desired Thomas Taylor of the same Towneship that in case god had determined to take hym away at that tyme he would (as formerly he had don) stand a good freind to his wife & childryn and for the further orderinge and settlinge of his estate delivered his will and meaninge in hise ~~he~~ words or ~~he~~ to this effect following viz: First That he conceived his best goods he had to be his yonge bay mare which he desired accordinge (as he said) he was bound in dutye, should be delivered to his Master and landlord Mr. George Cotton of Combermere Esquier in leiw and consideracōn of an herriott doe at his decease. Item He left all his goods cattell and chattels whatsoever for the payment and discharging of his debts, and with the said goods wanted to the dischardinge of the said debts his ~~tenemt~~ tenement in Smeatonwood aforesayd to be sett and the profitts issuinge theire from to be converted towards the payment and dischardinge of the remaynder of his debts undisharged Item That afterward his debts more fully satisfied and discharged he left £10 A yeare to be issuinge out of his tenement aforesd to be paid to seaven of his yonger children for their better preferment by equall portions, (if the lease of the said tenement ~~shall~~ should so longe ~~to~~ continue) begininge at the eldest and so descend and end at the yongest And afterward that

---

a   William Fergusson Irvine, *Chester Licences*, i. 164: 8 July 1614, to George Tench of Wrenbury parish and Katherine Johnson of Malpas parish; at Nantwich.
b   *Chester Licences*, i. 28: 14 November 1607, to John Johnson of Malpas parish and Margaret Tench, spinster of Wrenbury parish; at Malpas.

all the said debts and Legasies weare discharged the reversion of the lease duringe the whole terme thereof to returne to the refund profitt of Katherine Tenche his ~~wfe~~ wife, and to Thomas Tench his eldest son At the makinge of his verball will the said George Tenche told the aforenamed Thomas Taylor that in case he found hym selfe grown weaker that he would send for hym againe, and take fyrther course theirein which accordlingly he did, And Thomas Taylor cominge unto hym and fyndinge him selfe much weaker he cold not exprese hym selfe (through the extremitie of his sicknes) what further he intended should be don but only said that according to his former speeches he would have all things performed.

Inventory: George Tench of Smeatonwood.

Taken: 23 July 1638

Of: goods and debts.

Prisers: Thomas Taylor, Edward Palin, Thomas Wollam and Henery Johnson.

	£	s	d
Corne and hay at	11	0	0
4 Steeres at	11	0	0
4 Cowes at	10	0	0
4 twinter beastes at	7	0	0
6 Sterkes at	8	0	0
5 weaninge calves at	2	10	0
1 mare at	4	0	0
3 swine at	7	13	4
Poultrie at		10	0
Ploughs cartes and other husbandrie ware	3	0	0
mucke at		8	0
brasse and Pewter ect	7	0	0
Corne in the howse		16	0
Cheese at	4	0	0
beddinge & napperie ware at	10	0	0
4 silver spoones at	1	0	0
tables, formes, beddstockes chaires and stooles	2	0	0
1 cubboard & Coffers at	1	10	0
2 colmes with other wooden or trynen ware	2	0	0
taw within the house and groweinge on the ground	1	0	0
golberth, broches, with other Iron ware in the howse		8	0
Cushions at	3	4	0
2 sword & 1 muskett		10	0
3 wheeles brakes with other such things		4	0
bees at		10	0
his apparraile	3	0	0
bookes, Saddles, and boots with other things unknowne		3	0
Summa totalis	93	9	8
[*recte*	102	6	4]

Endorsement: Exhibited 11 May 1639; since noone was named executor in the nuncupative will, administration was granted to Katherine Tench, widow of the said deceased.

108. THOMAS HARE OF CHORLEY

S.Pr. 2 June 1639
Buried 20 January 1638/39

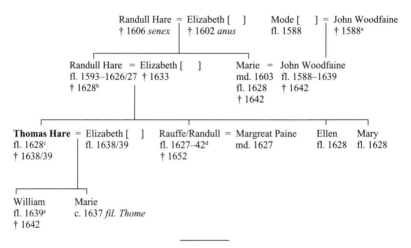

Inventory: Thomas Hare of Chorley.

Taken: 22 January 1638/39

Of: goods Cattalls and Chattells.

Prisers: Richard Millington, Richard Hassall, John Hassall and Thomas Willson.

	£	s	d
For the best Bedd beinge a featherbed with one Boulster and two pillowes one blankett and one Coveringe	2	0	0
For the secend Bed being two Cases two blanketts two boulsters and one Coveringe		20	0
For the third Bedd		10	0
All the linins, sheetes, and other napperies	2	0	0
For all the Brasse		2	0
For all the Pewter		12	0

ª See will of John Woodfaine, pr. 1588 (will no. 7).
ᵇ See will of Randull Hare, pr. 1628 (will no. 76).
ᶜ See will of Randull Hare (will no. 76).
ᵈ Rauffe, Ellen and Mary are noted as siblings of Thomas in their father's will (will no. 76); Randle made the inventory for John Woodfen, 1642 (no. 118).
ᵉ Made inventory for Roger Jones, 1639 (will no. 110).

For three pece of Bedstocks		13	4
For the best table and A Cubbord & a little table	2	0	0
For all the Cowpperie ware		20	0
For all the Earthen vessell		2	0
For one pott of honney		2	0
For the tooles for Joyninge		14	4
For the husbandry tooles		10	0
For one beame and skales		2	0
For one peece of netosea *[some sort of cloth?]* and A peece of linsty wolsty		12	0
For Cheese and Butter		37	0
For Bred Corne		9	0
For two Barrells of vergis		6	8
For three sacks and wyndow sheete		5	0
For two wheeles and A Reele		3	0
For one hetcheloe and two pare of Cartes			18
For 3 Baskets A flaskett and A peck		3	0
For stooles and Cheares & Cushins		2	0
For broch and galborks and potthoockes tonges and bellies & grate		6	0
For Bacon		30	0
for one bible		5	0
For all his waringe apparell	3	6	8
For unthresht Corne and unwinowed		20	0
For heay	2	0	0
for Corne upon the grownd	3	10	0
For five kyne and one Calfe	20	0	0
for one ould mare	2	0	0
for one plowe with the plowirons		4	0
two Carts with 2 pare of chenes 2 pare of hornes 2 ould saddles one harrat one packsaddle		26	8
For fewell		13	4
for foure hives of bees		20	0
for one grindlestone one Stoinetrough			6
for two ladders	10	3	0
for one Cheesepres one brake			18
for Eaight fellowes and a plow beame		2	0
for two geese two Cocks two hennes		4	0
For foure pickles		2	0
for A throwinge bench and planeinge bench		1	0
For one debt owinge me		20	0
Totall	56	46	8
[recte	66	0	6]

Endorsement: Exhibited 2 June 1639; administration granted to Elizabeth, widow of the deceased.

109. WILLIAM WILSON OF WRENBURY FRITH, GENT.

S.Pr. 8 June 1639
W.T. 23 March 1638
Codicil: 12 April 1639
Buried: 30 May 1639

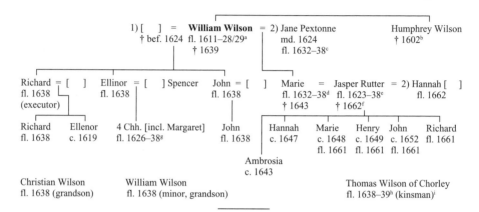

Will, beinge in health.

First I give and bequeath up willingly my soule into the hands of Allmighty God who firste gave it mee, not doubtinge by throwe the merritts of Jesus Christe my Saviour to bee received into his glorious kingdome, And my body I committ to the earth from whence It came, to bee decently buryed in Christian buryall, att the discrecōn of my Executors hereafter named, And touchinge my worldly estate, I will and dispose thereof as falloweth: Imprimis I give and bequeath unto every Childe I have Twelve pence apeece in full discharge of their parte and porcōn: Item I give and bequeath, unto my wyfe Jone Wilson the house in Wrenbury wherin Margarie

---

^a William Wilson priser for inventory of Lawrence Starkie, 1611 (no. 38); for Robert Tenche, 1615 (will no.45); overseer of will and priser for William Wicksteed Sr , will pr. 1629 (will no. 77); priser for William Wicksteed Jr, will pr. 1629 (will no. 78).
^b See will of Humphrey Wilson, pr. 1602 (will no. 16).
^c Daughter of Allis Pextonne of Wrenbury; see the latter's will, pr. 1632 (will no. 91).
^d Born ca. 1626/27, Marie Wilson was the god-daughter of Alice Pextonne; see the latter's will, pr. 1632 (will no. 91).
^e Jasper Rutter fl. 1646–48 as tenant.
^f See will of Jasper Rutter, pr. 1662/CRO.
^g The will of Randle Starkie, 1624, pr. 1626/27 (will no. 73), notes that Margaret Bromhall, the daughter of *Elline* Spencer, received a bequest of 3s. 4d. The fact that both the 1624 will and the present will refer only to Elline/Ellinor Spencer argues that her husband was dead by 1626.
^h Witness to the will of Roger Jones of Chorley, pr. 1639 (will no. 110).
ⁱ Thomas Wilson was one of the prisers of the inventory, below; he also produced the inventory for Thomas Hare, 1638/39 (will no. 108).

Barlowe widdowe nowe dwelleth, and the grownde thereunto belonginge, and the goods therein, And allsoe all the grounds I heretofore held by Lease, of Peter Mynshull of Erdswick in the said Countie Esquire (the said Lease beinge yett in beinge) For the terme of Threescore yeares after my deceasse nexte and ymmediatly fallowinge, (yf my said wyfe doe soe longe live, and my Lease, thereof doe soe longe Continue and endure, and in case my said wyfe doe deceasse within the said terme then ymediatly from and after her deceasse, to the use and behoofe of my sonne Richard Wilson dureinge the residue of the said terme of threescore yeares then unexpired yf hee doe and shall soe longue live and the said Leases soe longe Continue, And in case hee dye before the expiracōn of the said terme, then to the use and behoofe of my grandchild Richard Wilson my said sonne Richard Wilsons sonne dureninge the said terme, (yf hee bee then liveinge) & in case hee dye before then to the nexte yssue male of my said sonne Richard Wilsons that shall then bee liveinge dureinge the residue of the said terme of threescore yeares, then unexpired, yf the said Leases doe soe longe Continue Item I give and bequeath unto the poore inhabetors of the parish of Wrenbury Foure Pounds to bee distributed amoungeste them, att the discrecon of my Executors hereafter named Item I give and bequeath unto my daughter Ellionor Spencer, her three youngeste Children Foure Pounds to bee equally devided amoungeste them and to her sonne my beste suite of Clothes; Item I give and bequeath unto my grandchild Christian Wilson one Joyned bed furnished. Item I give and bequeath, unto Mr. Pearetree preacher of Wrenbury 10s. Item I give and bequeath unto my kinsman Thomas Wilson of Chorley 20s. Item I give and bequeath unto Thomas Gray Clarke of Wrenbury 2s. 6d. Item I give and bequeath unto my sonn John Wilson and his heires All my terme and intereste in my woods Lands wherein my barne standeth dureinge the terme of thermes exceptinge onely and rezerveinge, unto my said wyfe six waynes lodes of Torves yearley out of the Mosse dureinge her naturall liffe Item the Three pounds Rennte yssuinge out of the woods and the Lease thereof, I give unto my said sonne Richard Wilson dureinge the terme. Item I doe hereby give & Assigne unto my said grandchild Christian Wilson my house in Wrenbury, wherein my sonneinlawe Jasper Rutter nowe dwelleth and all the buildings and grounds thereunto belonginge For the terme of twentie yeares after the deceasse of my daughter Marie Rutter (yf shee the said Christian soe longue live) And all the reste and residue of my terme, or termes therein I give and bequeath unto my grandchild John Wilson my said sonne John Wilsons sonne. Item I doe hereby give and bequeath all the reste and residue of all my goods Cattells, and Chattells boeth moveable and unmoveable goods, of what kinde or quallitie soever the same bee of or wheresoever the same remayneth, (my debbts, legacs, and funerall expencs beinge in the Firste place thereout paid & discharged) unto my said wyfe Jone Wilson.

Executors: the testator's wife, Jane Wilson, and his son, Richard Wilson.

Overseer: Mr Pearetree, preacher at Wrenbury.

William Wilson
his marke & seal

Witnesses: Henry Rutter, the marke of **X** Thomas Massie, Thomas Gray ~~1638~~.

Codicil: 12 April, 14 Charles I [1639].

Be yt knowen unto all men by these presents that I William Wilson of Wrenbury Frith in the County of Chester gent beinge weake in body, by the visitation of God by of sound memory and haveing lefte some thinges undesposed of my further will and pleasure is And by, by thise presents I doe give grante and confirme unto my grandchild William Wilson and his heires the free inherritance of all that lande scytuat lyinge and beinge in Wrenbury Frith aforesaid with that appurtences Commonly caled by the name of the Barcson Crofts Withyng Crofts and Green Crofts now in the tenure houldinge or occupacons of Randle Weaver and Margery Barlowe when hee the said William Willson shall come to his age Item I leave to my grandchild Richard Willson Ten pounds Item I leave to Mary Bennion twenty shillinges Item to I leave to Margeret Twisse ten shillinges Item I leave to all all the rest of my servants six shillinges apeece In wittness weherof I have heare unto set my hande and Seale the daye and yeare Above written.

William Wilson
his marke & seal

Witnesses: Anne Sutton her marke, Henry Rutter.

Inventory: William Wilson of Wrenbury Frith, gent.

Taken: 4 June 1639

Of: goods Cattells and Chattells.

Prisers: Richard Davenport, Thomas Calcott, Jasper Rutter and Thomas Willson.

	£	s	d
For Fifteene kine	47	0	0
For three Calves		30	0
For the Fitches & otes with them		30	0
For the residue of the otes		10	0
For the barly	10	0	0
For Foure oxxen	20	0	0
For a mare	4	0	0
For the wheate	8	0	0
For the munck corne	4	0	0
For the hay att the house	2	0	0
For the 2 Calfekitts	1	13	4
For unthrasht wheate	4	0	0
For three hodgges	3	0	0
For three Carts waine, Muck cart & marle Carte	2	0	0
For 2 harrowes		5	0

For plowes with their Irons		10	0
For Inch bords in the hayhouse	1	0	0
For laddars		10	0
For Foure hengled yokes, one horse geres, 2 Chaines, one Cops			
& a peare of ould horse Chaynes		10	0
For Carte & plowe tymber		10	0
For turfe	1	0	0
For hay att the hyer barne	1	6	8
For Foure Carte blades		5	0
For three Roules		3	0
For planks & other lose tymber		10	0
For Strawe		3	4
For Bils and axes		3	0
For three Cuttinge Irons		3	0
For one Male & 4 wegges		4	0
For twoo Sawes		2	0
For Naugers Chissels reapeinge hookes & other small tooles			
for husbandrie		3	0
For Sixe pikells		3	0
2 mattocks & gorse axe		3	0
For 2 shoos & 3 muck yelves		4	0
For hayhookes one muckhack twoo hallockrakes & & garden			
rake Iron head		1	8
For 2 Cartropes		6	0
For one Saddle bridle & pillin		5	0
For one Combe with it stole in the backhouse		5	0
For one Chese presse		3	4
For one brake & spinninge wheiles		3	4
For one Iron wheele			6
For 2 yokes 4 boes & a tuter		2	6
For Fewill		10	0
For Muck		13	4
For a grindlestone			6
For bees in the garden			6
For 2 logs of timber & some broken tymber	[ ]	4	0
For poulterie		3	4
For one bed in the parlor with all its furniture	8	0	0
For one Faire presse with a Cubbord	1	13	4
For one table and 2 farmes	1	0	0
For 5 Cheres		8	0
For one warminge pan		3	4
For 3 Carpitts & 16 quishins	2	0	0
For one basin & ure		6	8
For a deske, one Coffer & boxes		5	0
For plate	10	0	0

For pottells, Cups, glasses, & painted dishes		3	0
For one Iron grate		3	0
For wheate, Rye and barly in the parlor lofte	4	0	0
For Cheese	5	0	0
For meale		10	0
For nue Cloth & yarne		13	4
For tubes, Flaskits, Cespits, and Baskits		10	0
For Cheseframe & Chesebords		10	0
For yarto handles *[sic!]* & reeles		1	0
For a wayinge beame & scales		1	0
For hops		2	0
For one lanthorne & scerch			6
For a tallowe cake & greese		2	0
For 4 sackes		3	0
For Juges, glasses, & other little things		1	0
For In the lofte over the house 9 flaxen sheets	4	0	0
For 4 table Clothes & a towell	1	0	0
For 5 pillowes beeares, 2 tawels & a napkin	1	0	0
For 32 peare of Sheetes	10	0	0
For 3 dosen of Napkines	1	4	0
For eight table Clothes		16	0
For 4 pillowes Beares		4	0
For one Still		10	0
For one coshen & one forme		6	0
For the bed with the greene Curteynes	5	0	0
For the bed with blewe Carteynes	5	0	0
In the Clossett one s[?]yer lofe, a table, baskett, glasses & Cuppes	1	10	0
In the Cocklofte, for ots, mault with 2 Flaskitts	1	10	0
For a scervants bed	[1?]	0	0
For stockcards & heckes		4	0
In the howse for tables & stooles with a sett of drawe boxes	1	0	0
In the little butterie, for pewter	4	0	0
For dishes and trenchers, pattells & barrells and Judges		13	0
For bookes		5	0
For a bed, a presse, a heirecloth, bords and all other things att the house in Wrenbury	1	10	0
In the kichen for Bras	4	10	0
For puddinge plate, dreepeinge pan & apple pan		4	0
For broches, golbarts, Fire shovell & tonges, brandrede, potthookes, gridiron land Iron, pottrackes, with other small Iron ware in the kichin		10	0
For Treenean ware		10	0
For Salte, & Salte quoffer		3	4
In the lower Chamber, for kneadinge turnell, Saltinge turnell			

and all other Comodities in that roome	1	0	0
In the lower butterry one Safe with treenean & earthen ware		13	4
For beefe & Backon	2	10	0
In the Mault Lofte for Mault	4	0	0
For winnowe sheete & a sack & other things in higher kitchin lofte	1	10	0
For grote & other things in the kichin Clossett	1	0	0
For 3 Beds with their appurtenancs	7	0	0
For 3 Coffers with other things		10	0
For one little sword		6	8
For his weareinge apparrell	5	0	0
In redy money	13	0	0
For Armor	1	0	0
For a Lease of £3 per anum for 21 yeares	25	0	0
For another Lease of 2 lives	13	0	0
For another Lease in reverson	10	0	0
Twoo bonds of £10 apeece	20	0	0
Money laid out for seaven yeares	60	0	0
Summa totalis	367	5	10
[*recte*	368	6	2]

Endorsement: Probated 8 June 1639; administration granted to Richard Wilson, one of the executors named in the same will, the other executor named in the same having totally renounced taking upon himself the burden of execution of the same.

110. ROGER JONES OF CHORLEY

S.Pr. 2 July 1639
W.T. 15 January 1638/39
Buried: 5 June 1639

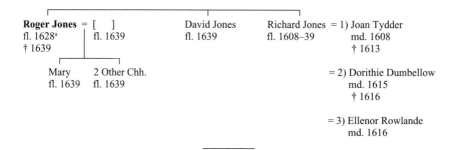

Will, 'beinge by the hand of God vissited in body'.

First I Commend my sole into the hands of Almighty God from whence I ferst receivd it in Full assureance of a joyfull resurrextion at the Last day and *my bodye to the earth from Whence it came and to be buryed at Wrenbury in such place of the Churchyard as shall be thought convenient* It my will is that my goods moveable & Unmoveable within and without shal be equally Devyded betwixt my wife and three children Provyded that £10 out of the whole shall be Given to my daughter Mary if that shee marry as now shee is in motion my funeral expences beinge ferst taken out.

Debts owing to the Testator:

	£	s	d
my Brother Daved Jonnes oweth	7	0	0
my Brother Richard Jones	2	0	0
Olliver Parker for Chese	5	0	0
John Bradshaw	4 with use		
Edward Kedrope	2	2	0
Raph Prees	2	0	0

Memorandum: that I have paide thaforesaid Raph £3 alredy for the Eller Meadow.

Lent Mr Sporrow	10	0
Lent Thomas Bathow	6	0
Widow Meekin	6	10
John Pattrick	3	1

---

[a]   Owed Randull Hare of Chorley a hundred[weight?] of wheat and was priser of his goods; see will of Randull Hare, pr. 1628 (will no. 76).

Executors: the testator's brother, Daved Jones, and the testator's wife.

Witnesses: Thomas Calcott, Thomas Wilson and Richard Jones.

Inventory: Roger Jones of Chorley.

Taken: 13 June 1639

Of: goods and Chattells.

Prisers: William Hare, John Woodfenn, John Bradshaw and Robert Oulton.

	£	s	d
Eleaven kyne and one calfe praysed to	40	0	0
one heffer one bollocke and two stirkes	9	0	0
two Colts	5	6	8
two ould mares	4	0	0
sheepe	3	10	0
Swyne	2	0	0
two weaninge calves	1	3	4
Geese		4	0
hens and Chickens		2	0
Bees		15	0
Corne sowed upon the grownd	2	8	8
Oates sowed upon the grownd		16	8
hempseed sowed upon the grownd and beanes		4	1
one horse Carte	2	6	8
one muckcart one ould weanes body And a plowgh sleade		10	0
one Swyne trough			8
plowes and plowirons and harrows		6	0
one ould payre of wheeles & ould carte body		1	0
three payre of horse Chaines and Other furniture for 3 horses to drawe in		6	0
heay and strawe		8	0
waynetimber for Carts and plowes Three brakes and one grindle-stone with The trow and one wheele plowe		4	0
yoakes for oxen		3	0
ladders and fewell		6	0
two cart ropes ould iron and other necessaries for husbandree		4	0
one Caboard table, frame Bench formes and bench cloath	1	0	0
Brasse and Pewter	4	15	0
sheetes and all napperie	4	0	0
Wearinge apparell	2	0	0
Beddinge	5	0	0
Corne	2	13	4
Woole and woolen cloath	1	0	0
towe and linen yarne	1	0	0

Oates		10	0
Cheese	2	0	0
Three Spininge Wheeles		2	0
dishboarde bedsteads Chaires and Stooles		6	8
one winnow sheete and sackes for corne		3	4
Bacon and other victuals		6	8
three coffers one Cheese presse two Tornells, treeneware and other Household stuff	1	0	0
lente money to my Brother Richard Jones	2	0	0
to John Bradshaw	4	0	0
Raphe Preists	2	0	0
Thomas Bathow	3	0	0
John Pattrick		3	1
Paide for A meddowe afourehande	3	0	0

The whole sume	116	16	3
[*recte*	116	5	10]

Endorsement: Probated 2 July 1639; administration granted to the executors named in the said will.

111. ANDREW COTTON OF COMBERMERE, GENT

S.Pr. 21 October 1640
W.T. 1629
Buried: 6 September 1640

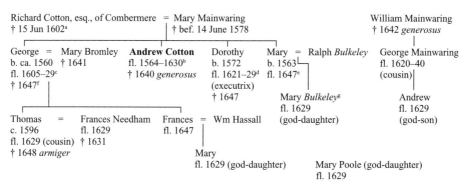

Richard Cotton, esq., of Combermere = Mary Mainwaring
† 15 Jun 1602ᵃ   † bef. 14 June 1578

William Mainwaring
† 1642 *generosus*

George = Mary Bromley   **Andrew Cotton**   Dorothy   Mary = Ralph *Bulkeley*   George Mainwaring
b. ca. 1560 † 1641   fl. 1564–1630ᵇ   b. 1572   b. 1563└   fl. 1620–40
fl. 1605–29ᶜ   † 1640 *generosus*   fl. 1621–29ᵈ fl. 1647ᵉ   (cousin)
† 1647ᶠ   (executrix)
                                                        † 1647   Mary *Bulkeley*ᵍ   Andrew
                                                                      fl. 1629   fl. 1629
Thomas   =   Frances Needham   Frances = Wm Hassall   (god-daughter)   (god-son)
c. 1596   fl. 1629   fl. 1647
fl. 1629 (cousin) † 1631
† 1648 *armiger*   Mary
                                                fl. 1629 (god-daughter)   Mary Poole (god-daughter)
                                                                            fl. 1629

ᵃ See IPM for Richard Cotton, esq., of Combermere, taken 6 April 1605 at Sandbach (R. Stewart Brown, *Cheshire Inquisitions Post Mortem*, i. 146).
ᵇ Noted in the will of John Cartwright of Aston in Newhall, pr. 1630 (no. 81).

Will *(parchment)*, sick *(a lengthy preamble shows deep degree of piety)*, good health.

I cheerfully surrendre up my Soule to the hands of him that gave it, as to a faith-full Creatour, who (beeing god allsufficient) is able, and (beeing freely gracious) wilbe willing to keep in safety that which is remitted to him unto the day of our Lord Jesus Christ, who of his owne free will took on him our fraile nature, was wounded for our transgressions, bruised for our iniquities, and by his all sufficient sacrifice & oblacion made once for all, hath satisfyed for all our sinnes; now sit-ting att the right hand of his Father in heavenly places making request for us; that when we shalbe disburdened of this masse of earth, he may receive us into ever-lasting habitacions Wherefore abandoning (as strong delusions) all supposed mer-itorious workes of sinfull men; all fayned intercessions of Saints or Angells, or what else may derogate from that ever effectuall worke of our redemption, I repose myself onely upon the sufferings of my Lord and Saviour Jesus Christ, who by his most precious blood shead upon the crosse hath sealed my Quietus est. *My body likewise I bequeath thither whence it was originally derived, earth to earth; and if it shall please my good God to call me from this place where now I live, or from these neere adjoyning quarters, my desire is to be convayed to Wrenbury,* the particular place I referre to the discretion of my surviving Friends, making no difference for conscience sake (for the earth is the Lords and all that therein is) and he that will, I hope, lay me downe in peace, will free me from the power of the grave, and rayse me up in his owne power (perfiting that which concerneth me) tho I were cast into the Bottome of the Sea for I know that my Redeemer liveth and that he shall stand the last upon the earth; and though after my skinne wormes destroy this body, yet in my flesh shall I see God, whom myne eyes shall behold though my reynes be consumed within me. Now concerning the things belonging to the occasions of this life, whether leases, or moneyes, cattells or Chattells, apparrell, or houshold stuffe or what else of what name or nature soev-er I doe by this my last will and Testament dispose of them in manner and forme following. First I doe willingly, as of due belongs, give up to my most worthy Brother Mr George Cotton, or to his heyres & succesours whatsoever shall in his or their estimacōn be accounted the best of my goods in liewe of an herriott: and in as much as I have allready given him a small ring for a remembrance, in my

---

111 footnotes continued

c   The IPM for his father (noted above) declared that in 1605 George Cotton was his son and next heir and at the time forty years and more in age.

d   William Fergusson Irvine, *Chester Licences*, ii. 154: 13 February 1621/22, William Massey, esq., and Dorothy Cotton, spinster, at Audlem or Wrenbury; the marriage obviously never took place, as Dorothy Cotton died 1647 a spinster.

e   While Andrew Cotton's will simply refers to Mary *Bulkley* as his god-daughter (she was bequeathed 20s. in his will), she is clearly one of those children of Mary Bulkley noted in the will of Dorothy Cotton, pr. 1647 (will no. 122).

f   See will of George Cotton of Combermere, pr. 1648 (will no. 128).

g   This is undoubtedly the Mary Gray, wife of Timothy *Buckley* of Smeatonwood, noted in the latter's will, pr. 1630 (will no. 84).

life time, I doe further by this my will give unto him three pownds, six shillings eight pence to buy him a scarlett wastCoate. Item I give to my worthy good Sister Cotton his now wife as much to buy her a Furred peticoate; and to them both joyntly my larger bedd with all things therto belonging: with request (wherof I make no doubt) that they will suffer it to remaine to the Howse as an Heyreloome. Item I give to my loving Cosin Mr Thomas Cotton all my latine Bookes, and to his wife Mrss Frances Cotton his new wife my large English Bible in confidence that shee will dayly bestowe some time in reading and serious meditating thereon, and I further give joyntly to them both my lesser bedd with all the Furniture therto belonging for the use if it so please them of their eldest daughter to be placed neere to them. Item I give to my Brothers daughters that shall be unmarried att the time of my decease to everyone of them 20s. to buy them rings and this to be payed to them when they have bought them according to their severall affections. Item I give to Mr Nicholls Forty shillings a yeare issueing out of that interest I have in Richard Halls Land in Newhall to be yearely payed to him or to his 20s. att the Feast of Saint Michaell, and 20s. att the Lady Day imediately after my deceasse so long as I shall have any interest there; and that to continue whether he continue att Wrenbury or elsewhere for I confesse that chiefly (if not onely) by his paynefull and in itself powerfull ministry the Lord giving a blessing, and his good Spiritt assisting, I have attayned to that measure of knowledge, and good affection to the best things that my weakenes was capeable of. Item I give to George Leicester in token of acknowledgement of his love to me a 20s. piece who if he be in health & of ability att the time of my death will make one to place me in my bedde of rest. Item I give to my godsonne Andrewe Mainwayring 20s. & to my god daughter Mary Hassall 20s. & to my god daughter Mary Bulkeley 20s. & to my god daughter Mary Poole 10s. Item I give to my Servant that shalbe att the time of my deceasse all my wearing apparrell if the sayd Servant have continued with me the space of three yeares or more, if lesse then I referre the proportion to the discretion of my executour, to deale with him according as shee hath found him respective to her selfe and me And if he that is now my my servant, John a Pova, continue with me to the time of my death and that I fortune to dy before the expiracion of the terme that we have in his fathers Tenement: my request to my sayd executour is that upon his good behaviour to us both in the meane time, that shee will bestowe on him for his further preferment out of the proffitt of the eight yeare the sume of ten pownds, provided that there be no arrereages of rent but that shee be first fully satisfyed of twenty pownds per annum for the space of seaven yeares past: and shee beeing thus fully satisfyed and the ten pownds abovementioned so given, my further request is that shee will bestowe the overplus of the eight yere if any be, upon John a pova the Father to the behooffe of his Daughter Anne Now for the time of my Funerall the things concomitant & subsequent I propose this course as chiefly affected but injoynd it not as inviolable. I would be convayed to the place assigned the first evening with conveniency after my deceasse as soone as it may be termed night accounting that silent time the fittest season for a worke of that nature; my selfe having had my sorrowes redoubled att the solemnities of worthy Friends, through the confused clamours of the unruly multitude that usually presse upon such assemblies and as I have desired to live with the love of all so to dy without just aspersion from any & that I be not censured to dislike the custome of Doles meerely for saving of what is then none of mine, I doe hereby give as by my last will and testament 40s. yearely to the parish of Wrenbury issueing out of the interest I have in Richard Hall's land in Newhall to be payed so long as I have any estate therein att the foure quarter Comunions or att the times that they usually are by ten shillings a quarter to ten poore of the Parish, five of theym beeing poore Householders and five single persons such as have lived so all their lives in good fame, the choyce I referre to Mr Nicholls for his time, or to his successour, if any such be, during the time of this payment. If none be then after him to Mr George Mainwaring of Baddington Mr Richard Egerton, John Bromhall, Edward Palin or any two of theym, and my desire is that choyce be made of such as be of note for constant & withall conscionable [reserters] to holy dutys & if any assigned to this number of ten shall by my foresayd Friends be noted to growe remisse, or in any sort scandalous, my will is they be exempted and that a fitt choyce be made. And whereas I Doe hereby chiefly ayme att the drawing of those poore Comunicants to the enjoying of a farre more excellent portion then this poore allottemt: of 12d. & that the Parish shall have no cause to complaine that, ther groweth any charge to it by this number I doe farther for every one of the foure Comunions assigne 12d. to the Clarke for the time beeing, to make provision for that number, yf the Churchwardens shall so farre presse it, yf not then to his owne use Item I give to six that shalbe thereto assigned 2s. 6d. a piece by course to convay me to the place of Buriall of the distance by a myle, or more & for avoyding of repining, £5 to the ringers and if it maybe of use to the living that ther be a warning peale to all within distance that ly upon their bedds of security, that they deferre not their repentance lest death come sodeninely unawares, lett them ring, to me it will neither be proffitt nor anoyance and thus I Andrew Cotton beeing in good health, and perfect memory, not feeling sicknesse, nor fearing death, nor weary of my life, such are the Lords mercys towards me, have with my owne hand, after my owne forme, in a plaine & intelligible phrase sett downe this my Last will and Testament: wherein if any thing shall seeme of a doubtfull sence I referre the expression to my loving Cosin Mr George Mainwayringe with whom I have most familiarly conversed herein.

Executor: Mistris Dorothey Cotton, the testator's sister.

If it shall please the Lord to take from me part of that which is wholly his, ther must be a proportionable abatt: and if I shall finde my selfe able to a farther remembrance of any of my Friends that shalbe comitted to her in some private note apart onely what is here expressed is all wherewith shee shall stand changeable in Lawe. To my knowledge I owe nothing to any man but what I owe to all men love. I can freely forgive and because I remember nothing from any as an injury and I hope I may challenge the like from all because I am conscious of wronging one beyond this conpasse of [?]s reconcilemt: I have desired to live att

peace with all but familarly to converse with a fewe: I desire the charitable cen-
sure of all but chiefly of those few who are therefore the most competent Judges,
ause best acquainted with my wholl course If they have observed in me anything
of a better nature: Lett that be their modell wherby to frame to themselves a more
substantiall Anchore the many things they have seene amisse lett their wisdome
to reforme themselves & this I take for the best use that is to be made of a poore
departed Friend. The last but chiefest request to my sayd executrix is that shee
mourne not for me as one without hope nor be inconsolate [*badly damaged
bottom portion of the will*] selfe as one left destitute of Friends they who had their
afections devided betwixt us will redouble them. I hope upon her seeing they shall
finde no want of me so long as they injoy her most useful presence What ever is
any [*damaged*] only to them that truly serve him.

1629 Andrew Cotton

Witnesses: John Bramhall [?]

Inventory: Andrew Cotton of Combermere, gent.
Taken: 14 September 1640, 16 Charles I
Of: goods, and Chattells.

Prisers: William Massye, George Mainwaring, William Tenche, George [Godfrey]
and John Tenche.

	£	s	d
in ready money, Debts and leases for yeares yet to come, to the valew in all, of about	240	0	0
in wearing apparrell to the valew of	20	0	0
his bedding & lynnens	13	6	8
his Books	20	0	0
his watch, & Plate	6	0	0
his Truncke, Deskes, tables, Chaires, stooles, Boxes, Hangings, and other Implements	10	0	0
His two Horses, Saddles, and other Furniture in his stable	17	0	0
Divers utensils in a little roome under his mans chamber	1	10	0
his Hay & Corne for his Horses	2	3	4
Sum Total	330	0	0

Endorsement: Probated 21 October 1640; administration granted to his sister
Dorothy Cotton the sole administrator named in the said will.

112. THOMAS GRAY OF NEWHALL, YEOMAN

S.Pr. 1 December 1640
W.T. 16 February 1639/40
Buried: 12 March 1639/40

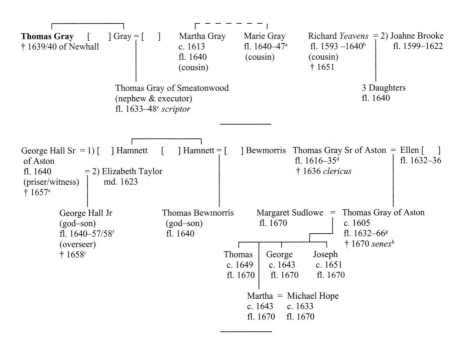

---

a Both Martha Gray and Marie Gray are witnesses for the will of John Cheswis, pr. 1648 (will no. 127).

b Richard *Evans* married Marie Povall 1593 at Wrenbury (Wrenbury Bishop's Transcripts – Marriages: 1593). See note a, will no. 66, for further documentation of Richard *Evans*, also known as Richard *Yeavanson* and Richard *Evanson*.

c Thomas Gray of Smeatonwood, cousin, bequeathed 40s. and overseer for will of Thomas Hamnett, pr. 1635 (will no. 97); landlord of William Taylor of Smeatonwood and executor, witness and priser; see will of William Taylor, pr. 1649 (will no. 134).

d See will of Thomas Gray the elder of Aston in Newhall, clerk at Wrenbury, pr. 1636 (will no. 99).

e See will of George Hall of Aston, pr. 1657 (will no. 142).

f Both George Hall Jr and Thomas Bewmorris had Hamnett mothers: see will of Thomas Hamnett of the Grange, pr. 1635 (will no. 97).

g Witness to wills of Richard Dodd, pr. 1637 (will no. 101) and Elizabeth Briscoe, pr. 1637 (will no. 103); recipient of bequest of 5s. from Thomas Gray, and also witness to his will (see below).

h See will and inventory of Thomas Gray of Aston, pr. 1670/CRO.

i See will of George Hall of Aston, pr. 1658 (will no. 147).

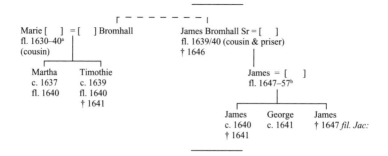

Will, sick.

Firste I yeld up willingely my Soule into the hands of allmighty god who firste gave it mee, thrustinge throwe the mirritts & death of Jesus Christ my Saviour to have free pardon & remission of all my sinnes, and my body I Committ to the earth to bee decently buryed in Christian buryall att the discrecion of my executors hereafter named: And as Concerninge my temperall estate wich allmighty god hath enriched mee with all I will and dispose thereof as Followeth: Firste I give unto Lawrance Fisher my second peare of breeches. Item I give unto William Hardinge my third peare of breeches. Item I give & bequeath unto Henry Griffyth of Wrenbury my worste dublett & Jerkin. Item I give unto my godchildren George Hall the younger & Thomas Bewmorres 10s. a peece. Item I give unto all the reste of my godchildren 2s. 6d. a peece. Item I give & bequeath unto my Cosen Richard Yeavans three daughters 2s. 6d. a peece Item I give and bequeath unto Thomas Gray of Aston 5s. Item I give unto George Hall of Aston £5. Item I give & bequeath unto Avis Wigin my maid 5 marks (if shee bee dweling with mee att my deceasse) Item I give and bequeath unto my Cosen Martha Gray & Marie Gray £10 a peece. Item I give and bequeath unto my Cosen Marie Broomehall £4 & to her sonne Tymothie 10s. & to her daughter Martha 10s., and to my Cosen James Broomehall thelder 2s., All which legacs, & my debtts I doe desire may bee discharged with the moneyes which I doe hereafter intende to charge my Lands with all. Item I give & bequeath unto the said Martha Gray & Marie Gray one Cowe cald whitefoote. Item I give and bequeath unto my loevinge Nephewe Thomas Graye of Smeatonwood all the reste and residue of all my goods Cattells & Chattells, boeth moveable & unmoveable goods of what kinde or quallity soever the same bee, or wheresoever the same remayneeth, payinge my debtts & dischargeinge my funerall expences.

<hr />

[a] [?] Daughter of John Bromhall; see will pr. 1630 (will no. 82).
[b] William Taylor leased six parcels of land from James Bromhall at annual rent of £10 5s.; see inventory of William Taylor, will pr. 1649 (will no. 134); James Bromhall owed George Cotton £4 13s. in 1647 (will no. 128) and witnessed will of Edward Palin, pr. 1657 (will no. 143).

Executor: the testator's nephew, Thomas Gray of Smeatonwood.

Overseer: the testator's god-son, George Hall.

H. & S.
Thomas Gray

Witnesses: George Hall, George Chester (his marke), Thomas Gray Scr.

Inventory: Thomas Gray of Newhall, yeoman.

Taken: 14 March 1639/40, 15 Charles I

Of: goods Cattells and Chattells.

Prisers: Edward Palin, George Hall, James Broomhall and George Reeve.

	£	s	d
Foure kine and one Mare	17	0	0
Carrtes, plowes, Harrowes some plowe and Carte timber, Saddles, Yeookes, Chaynes and other ymplements of husbandrie	4	6	8
hay, strawe, Corne in the barne, in the howse, and in the ground	1	14	0
Fewell and Muck		10	0
Shovells, Sawes, Bills, Axes and other small edge twooles	1	0	0
Spitts, goulbetts, andians and all other Iron ware	1	0	0
In Poulterie		6	8
Artillerie	1	3	4
In Bedstids, beddinge and Napperie	10	0	0
Tables, quoffers Cheeres, Stooles, Formes and Shilves and twoo Cubbords	4	0	0
Brasse and Pewter	5	10	0
In bookes		13	4
In treenean ware	1	10	0
In tickenall ware		2	6
Towe and yearne		18	0
one spininge Whele and some other small ymplements and things in the howse		5	0
In Gould plate and redy money in the howse	6	6	8
a debtt oweinge by specialty from George Tennch	2	12	0
his weareinge apparell	4	10	0
in Cheese and Bacon	1	0	0
Somme is	64	8	2

Endorsement: Probated 1 December 1640; administration granted to Thomas Gray sole executor named in the said will.

113. JOANE CREWE OF NEWHALL, WIDOW

C.(S.)Pr. 8 April 1641
Original will made 10 February 1639/40 (lost)
Memorandum: March 1639/40
Died: Monday, 1 March 1639/40
Buried: Thursday, 4 March 1639/40

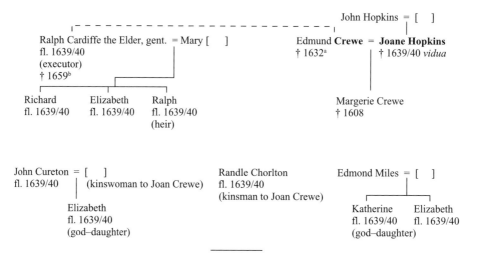

John Hopkins = [   ]

Ralph Cardiffe the Elder, gent. = Mary [   ]   Edmund **Crewe** = **Joane Hopkins**
fl. 1639/40   † 1632[a]   † 1639/40 *vidua*
(executor)
† 1659[b]

Richard   Elizabeth   Ralph   Margerie Crewe
fl. 1639/40   fl. 1639/40   fl. 1639/40   † 1608
(heir)

John Cureton = [   ]   Randle Chorlton   Edmond Miles = [   ]
fl. 1639/40   (kinswoman to Joan Crewe)   fl. 1639/40
(kinsman to Joan Crewe)

Elizabeth   Katherine   Elizabeth
fl. 1639/40   fl. 1639/40   fl. 1639/40
(god–daughter)   (god–daughter)

Will, 'weake in body but otherwise in health'.

Firstly, I give and bequeath my soule into the hands of Allmighty God whoe gave
it and unfaignedly trustinge through the death passion and merits of our Lord and
Savior Jesus Christ to be one of the number of gods elect *And my body I bequeath
to the earth from whence it came to be buryed in Christian buriall in the Church
or Churchyard of Wrenbury* Item as touchinge my personall Estate goods cattalls
and chattalls I give devise and bequeath in manner and forme following: I give
and bequeath unto Thomas Miles of Nantwich gente the some of Tenne pounds
Item I give and bequeath unto Elizabeth Arcall widdowe the Some of tenne
pounds. Item I give and bequeath unto Elizabeth Miles and Katherine Miles daughters of Edmund Miles of Nantwich gente to either of them the some of five pounds
a piece. Item I give and bequeath unto Richard Cardyfe one of the sonnes of Ralph
Cardyfe gent The Some of Twenty Pounds Item I give and bequeath unto Elizabeth
Cardyfe daughter of the said Ralph Cardyfe the Some of Twenty pounds Item I

[a] See will of Edmund Crewe of Newhall, pr. 1632 (will no. 90).
[b] See registered copy of the will of Ralph Cardiffe of Woldhall, Cheshire, TNA PCC 1659/prob
     11/301. Sig 242.

give and bequeath unto Ellen Bate wife of Rowland Bate The Some of Three pounds to buy her a cow Item I give and bequeath unto Ralph Cardyffe sonne and here apparent of the said Ralph Cardyffe All and singuler frames formes stooles chayres cubbarts chests truncks coffers and all treenen whatsoeve in or about the house wherein I now live, And alsoe I give and bequeath unto the said Ralph Cardyff the sonne the best covering in the house to the use and behoof of him and his heires for ever Item All the rest and residue of all my personal Estate goods cattalls chattalls utensils and implements of husbandry and all other goods of what nature soever in and about the house or elswhere whatsoever I doe here by freely and absolutely give devise and bequeath unto the said Ralph Cardyffe thelder To thonly *[i.e. the only]* proper use and behoofe of the said Ralph and of his children for ever . . . Item I doe hereby except out of the said last mencōned goods the Some of Twenty Pounds to mee due and owinge by Randle Chorlton of Nantwich which some of Twenty Pounds I doe give and bequeath in manner and forme followinge: that is to Say I give and bequeath the Some of Tenne pounds percell of the same last mencōned some of Twenty Pounds I doe give and bequeath unto Elizabeth Cureton daughter of John Cureton of Nantwich And the Some of Tenne Pounds being residue of the said some of Twenty Pounds I give and bequeath unto the said Randle Chorlton in lieu and full satisfaction of all or any Clayme and demand of hime the said Randle Chorllton of in to or out of all or any of the rest and residue of all or any of my goods cattals and chattalls what-soever Item I doe except alsoe out of the said severall personal Estate lastly bequeathed to the said Raphe Cardiffe the Elder the Some of Twenty shillings which Twenty shillings I doe give and bequeath unto Margaret Hassall daughter of Richard Hassall of Wilkesley yeoman.

Executor: Ralph Cardyffe thelder.

H. & S.
Joahne Crewe
The mark of (X) the said Joahne Crew

Witnesses: Randle Hardinge, The mark of Richard Hassall, John Bateman, Robert Tudman.

Allegation: 11th day of March AD (in English Style) 1640/41.

A matter of the proving of the testament of Joane Crewe, deceased, formerly of Newhall within the Chapelry of Wrenbury, parish of Acton, in the diocese of Chester.

On which day Master Russ[ell], his Proctor, appears and exhibits in writing in behalf of Ralph Cardiff senior, concerning the same to all effects of law and fact and to the lasting memory of things, he says, alleges and in these writings pro-pounds jointly severally and articulately as follows:

1. Firstly, namely he says and alleges that the aforesaid Joane Crewe being, whilst she lived, of sound mind and perfect in her memory, in or about the month of March in the fifteen year of the reign of King Charles, by the grace of God of England, Scotland, France and Ireland &c AD 1639[/40] composed, made and declared her Testament of her last will in writing and signed and sealed the same and recognised it for her testament containing in it her last will in the presence of several trustworthy witnesses; and afterwards departed this life. And he propounds jointly severally and concerning whatsoever.

2. Item That after the death of the said deceased her aforesaid last will and Testament was delivered into the handes of Randle Harding Clarke by him to bee carried to the Consistory Courte att Chester on the behalfe of the Executor therein named to procure a Comission of the execution thereof & administration of the goods & chattles of the said deceased unto him accordinge to the said last will & Testament. *Et ut supra* (And as above).

3. Item That the said Mr Hardinge havinge received the will [of Joane Crewe the] aforesaid did casually loose the same and the same is lost and cannot bee found. *Et ut supra.*

4. Item That Raphe Cardiffe of Newhall aforesaid the elder gent was appointed sole Executor of the said will and aforesaid Randle Hardinge Clarke, Richard Hassall, John Bateman and Robert Tuddman were wittnesses to the makinge sealinge signinge and deliveringe of the same and do very well remember the contents thereof, *Et ponit ut supra.*

5. Item That the schedule hereunto annexed (which this party regards and wills to be regarded as if here read and inserted in so far as it explains itself) doth containe the substance and effect of the said last will & Testament of the aforesaid Joane Crewe deceased and doth agree with the same to all intents and purposes and the aforesaid wittnesses can and will depose upon them oathes that the aforesaid Joane Crewe deceased did in her last will and Testament aforesaid soe [declare] as aforesaid will devise give and bequeath severall legacies & appoint the same Executor as in and by this schedule affixed as aforesaid is contained.

6 Item That all and singular the premises were and are true, public, well known &c Wherefore proof being made this party prays right and justice and for the value of this document containing the last will of the said deceased [&c], And right [&c] which all and singular he propounds jointly and severally &c not obliging &c.

Endorsement: Allegation with document attached, containing the testament or last will of Joane Crewe on behalf of Ralph Cardiffe gentleman, against Randle Chorlton and others.

Memorandum That about the month of March in the year of Our Lord and in the 15th year of the reign of Charles king of England 1639 Joane Crew late of Newhall in the Countie of Chester widdowe now deceased beinge Then livinge and in good and perfect remembrance & In the presence of us whose names are subscribed and others did make her last will and Testament and publish the same in writeinge under her hand and seale wherein and whereby shee the said Joane Crewe did dispose of all her worldly goods, personall Estate, cattalls and chattalls whatsoever in manner and in effect as followeth:

The said Joane Crew did by her said last will and Testament give and bequeath to Richard Cardiffe one of the sonnes of Raph Cardiffe of Wolfhall in the said Countie gent the Somme of Twentie Pounds To Elizabeth Cardiffe daughter of the said Raph Twentie pounds To Thomas Miles Tenne Pounds To Elizabeth Arcall widdow Tenn Pounds, To her goddaughter Katherine Miles and to Elizabeth Miles daughters of Edmond Miles to either of them Five Pounds a peece To Ellen Bate wife of Rowland Bate Three pounds to buy her a Cowe, Alsoe whereas there remaines 20s. in the hands of Randle Chorlton without Specialtie which hee receaved from Cholmoneley Salmon gent The will and minde of the said Joane Crew by her said last will was that the said Randle Charlton should pay 10s. of the said 20s. to Elizabeth Cureton daughter of John Cureton her goddaughter The other 10s. residue of the said 20s. the said Joane gave and bequeathed to the said Randle Chorlton Item All and singular Tables with frames Formes Cheeres Stooles Bedstidds and utensills and alsoe the best coveringe for a bedd She the said Joane did give and bequeath unto Raph Cardiffe sonne & heire apparant to the said Raph Cardiffe Gent All the rest and residue of her personall Estate debts goods Cattalls and Chattalls whatsoever moveable and unmoveable within the house and with-out shee the said Joane did give and bequeath soly and wholy unto the said Raph Cardiffe the elder and to his children except that out of the said personall Estate her will and minde was and by her said last will and Testament shee did give and bequeath to Margret daughter of Richard Hassall 20s.

Executor: Raph Cardiffe the elder.

Witnesses: Randle Hardinge Clerk, the marke H of Richard Hassall, John Bateman and Robert Tudman.

18 March 1640/41: Ralph Cardiff vs Randle Chorlton and John Cureton

On which day Russell in the name of Proctor and as lawful Proctor of Master Ralph Cardiff, with a mind of declaring and of specifying in more detail, the Allegation otherwise exhibited on behalf of his said Client together with a Schedule containing the last will of Joan Crew deceased, to all effect of law and fact, says, alleges and in these writings in law propounds and exhibits the Original Testament or Last Will of the said Joan deceased, affixed to these presents. And he states jointly, severally and concerning whatsoever.

1. Inprimus that the aforesaid Joane Crew being sicke in body but of sound and perfect Memory did make this her last will and testament in writing hereunto annexed (which this party wishes to be regarded as if here read and inserted) and did name the Pl[ain]t[iff] Raphe Cardiffe gent her Executor and did give devise and bequeath her goods and Chattles as in the same is conteyned in the presence of the wittnesses thereunto subscribed, And This was and is the <Originall> last will and Testament of the said deced[en]t Joane Crew Sealed Signed and Subscribed as is therein Conteyned Et ponit con[uncti]m div[isi]m et de quoli[be]t (And he states jointly, severally and concerning whatsoever).

2. Item that this will doth to all effects and purposes agree with the Schedule heretofore exhibited on the behalfe of the said Raph Cardiffe whereupon the Plaintiff hath produced sworne and examined wittnesses And was casually lost but since the examinacōn found againe, and is proved by the deposicōns of the aforesaid wittnesses to all Intents & purposes *et ut supra* (And as above.)

3. Item that all and singular the premises were and are true, public, notorious, manifest and in like manner reputed and of and concerning the same public voice and fame have been troubled and in the present are troubled. Wherefore with the proof lawfully required in this regard being made this party prays right and justice and the fullness of justice in and concerning the premises to be done and to be administered with effect And for the value and force of the said testament of the said deceased affixed to these presents to be pronounced and declared &c Which all and singular this party propounds jointly and severally not obliging himself to proving all and singular nor to the burden of a superfluous proof but in so far as he shall have proved in the premises he may obtain in the petitions &c

Endorsement: Allegation with Testament annexed of Joan Crew, lately whilst she lived of Newhall, deceased annexed on behalf of Ralph Cardiff Executor of the said deceased against Ralph Chorlton and John Cureton, dated and exhibited 18 March (in English style) AD 1640/1.

Interrogatoria (Questions), ministered and to be ministered on behalf of and by the party of Randle Chorlton and John Cureton to all and singular pretended witnesses in one way or another produced and being produced on behalf of Ralph Cardiffe pretended Executor of the pretended Testament of Joan Crew widow deceased in a certain business of proving the said pretended Testament, follow.

Firstly, let the peril of perjury and the penalties for false witness be explained to each of the pretended witnesses aforesaid, and let him be questioned concerning his origin, age, occupation and situation, and for how long he has known the said deceased before her death, and the litigant parties in this suit; and let him be questioned and let it be done jointly and severally and concerning whatsoever.

2. Item, Let each of them be asked whether doe you knowe beleeve or have Credibly heard that the sayde Joane Crew deceased did make a will certen yeares before her death in wryteing, being in health & of good memory and thereof did make the sayd Randle Chorleton one of her Executors; have you at any tyme seene any such will and when and where and upon what occasions, declare the truth; and let it be done as above.

3. Item, Let each of them be asked whether you knowe beleeve or have credibly heard, that the wife of the said Randle Chorleton, and hee the sayd John Cureton were neare a kinne to the sayd Joane Crew, and neerer to her in degree then the sayd Raph Cardiffe or Mary his wife and soe reputed and taken and did the sayd deceased love them well in her lyfe tyme, declare the truth, And let it be done as above.

4. Item, Let each of them be asked whether were you a wittness to any pretensed last will of the sayd Joane Crew deceased the Contents whereof are pretended to bee sett down in the schedule whereupon you are examined; were you presente at the making thereof, and did you subscribe your name as a wittness thereunto or did any other subscribe your name, & whoe, & by whose meanes & procurement; declare the truth at large; And let it be done as above.

5. Item, let each of them be asked Whoe writt the pretensed will now controverted; what day of the weeke & month & what tyme of the day or night and in what particular Chamber Roome house & place was the same written, and whether was the pretensed will written all at one tyme & in one place, or at severall tymes & in severall places; and at what tymes, & in what places; and whether in or out of the presence of the sayd deceased; declare the truth particulerly & at large; And let it be done as above.

6. Item, Let each of them be asked whether was the sayd Joane Crew, sicke or in health, in her bed, or out of her bed; whether was shee sitting, lyeing, or standinge, wakeing, or sleepeing, at the tyme of the makeing & writeing of the sayd pretensed will? And whether were any persons then presente, saving such as are subscribed as wittnesses to the said will? Declare the truth; And let it be done as above.

7. Item, Let each of them be asked whether were you with the said deceadent immediately before the makeing of the sayd will alleged, and upon what occasion, and whoe procured you to be present? Whither did you then or at any other tyme heare the s[ai]d deceased affime that shee had not made her will or settled her estate; And did shee say or expresse that shee was desyrous to make a will and to settle her estate? Did the s[ai]d deceased send for the wryter of the s[ai]d will, and by whome, and when? or whoe sent for the sayd wryter & whoe was sent, and whoe procured the sayd wryter to wryte the sayd will? And what had hee, or what hath bene promised unto him for the wryteinge thereof? Declare the truth particulerly at large; And let it be done as above.

8. Item, let each of them be asked whether did the writer of the sayd pretensed will receive Instruccōns imediately from the mouth of the sayd deceased for the making of the sayd pretensed will, or did he receive instruccōns of and from the sayd Raph Cardiffe the partie producent or from any other, and of whome, and whether in or out of the said deceaseds presence were the sayd instruccōns given and received. And in case any such pretensed instruccōns were received and had of and from the sayd deceased (then let him be asked and he will pronounce) whether did the said deceased voluntarily and upon her owne accord deliver and declare her will and mynd? did shee of herselfe, name and expresse the particuler legataries and legacies mencioned in the sayd pretensed will, did shee alsoe signifie that it was her mind to revoake or reverse all former willes <and did shee name the said Raph Cardiffe sole executor> or whether was the sayd pretensed Instruccōns taken and the will made by and at the persuasion and Interrogacōn of some persons or person present, whoe asked and urged her from from pointe to poynte what to give and to whome? and whether did the writer at first write the will at large, or did hee take briefe notes for his instruccōns & afterwardes extend the same? declare the truth particulerly & at large; And let it be done as above.

9. Item, Let each of them be asked whether after the sayd pretensed will was written was it playnely and distinctly read out to the s[ai]d deceased in your presence? did shee give eare thereunto and understand the same and approve thereof? and what wordes did shee utter imparting her lykeing and approbacōn of the s[ai]d pretensed will? did shee of her owne accord signe, seale, acknowledge, and deliver the same? or was shee moved urged & procured soe to doe? was her hand taken & held & moved by some other or others there to sett to her seale and make her marke? was the sayd will putt into her hand and was shee told that shee must deliver the same for her last will, and by whome or whose meanes were these things soe done and urged upon the sayd deceased? declare the truth particulerly & at large; And let it be done as above.

10. Item, Let each of them be asked whether did the s[ai]d deceased intreate and desire you to bee a writtnes to the sayd pretensed will, or at whose intreatie and procurment were you a wittnes thereunto? and did you write your name or whoe did write your name as a wittnes to the said will and did the s[ai]d deceased knowe or take notice that you were a wittnes in this behalfe? declare the truth particulerly & at large; And let it be done as above.

11. Item, Let each of them be asked to whose handes or Custodye was the sayd pretensed will comitted and deliverd after the same was written, and where did the same remaine afterwardes untill the death of the sayd Testatrix? whether did you ever read the sayd will, or heare the same read after the making thereof before the death of the sayd deceased? And how often have you read or heard the same read, and when, where, and in whose presence, and upon what occasion? declare the truth particulerly & at large; And let it be done as above.

12. Item, Let each of them be asked when and how longe since did the sayd deceased depart this lyfe, upon what day did shee dye, and upon what day was shee buryed? declare the truth; And let it be done as above.

13. Item, Let each of them be asked whoe writt the pretensed Schedule annexed to the Allegacōn whereupon you are examined, where was the same written & contrived, and whoe were present beside your self at the wryteing and contriving thereof, and what day, and where was the same done; And whoe were Assistants for the doeing thereof? declare the truth; And let it be done as above.

14. Item, let Randle Harding, one of the pretended witnesses and each of the others intending to depose concerning the pretended lost original will of the said deceased, be asked when, and where, and by whome was the said pretensed originall will delivered unto you how many howers, and how longe after the death of the sayd deceased and whether before, and how longe before her buriall was the same delivered unto you, & in whose presence, and to what purpose or effect? And did you read the sayd will wholie over after that you had received the same, & where, and whoe heard you read the same? declare the truth at large; And let it be done as above.

15. Item, Let the said Randle Harding be asked if he has deposed concerning the pretended Testament lost by him whether were you sent to any Clerke or other officer of thise Courte about the probacōn of the said pretensed will, and to whome? And whether did you goe to any such person & to whome? what day did you come to this Citty, and when did you departe? in how many and what howses were you dureing your aboad or stay in this Citty, and whoe were in your Companye? whether did you come and returne the same way, and in or att what howses or places did you stay in your comeing & returning; declare the truth; And let it be done as above.

16. Item, Let the said Randle Harding be asked where did you receive the said pretensed originall will when you were sent about the probacōn thereof? where and how did you putt upp the sayd pretensed will to bee kept? when, and where, did you loose the same, or when, and where, did you first misse the same; and where & of whome have you enquired & what manner of inquirie have you or the partye producent made for the finding thereof? declare the truth; And let it be done as above.

17. Item, Let each of them be asked whether was the pretensed will aforesayd written and contrived by the direccōns and procurement of the sayd Raph Cardiffe or any other or others and by whome? was it wholy written out of the s[ai]d deceasedes presence & prepared & made readye before the same was brought unto her? whoe did bringe and tender the sayd will first unto the sayd deceased?

was it sayd unto her by the sayd partie producent or some others or other and by whome, that there was a will made for her, and that shee must seale it, or sett her hand and seale unto the same? did shee answeare and say that shee had made her will allready, and that it was at Nantwich, or to that effect? And what meanes were used to procure and make the sayd deceased to approove, and to signe, seale, and acknowledge the sayd pretensed will, in case it were soe done; and what answeares or answeare did the s[ai]d deceased make; declare the truth; and let it be done as above.

18. Item, [Let] each of them be asked whether was the s[ai]d pretensed will sealed & signed by the s[ai]d deceased, declare the truth yea or noe; And let it be done as above.

19. Item, Let each of them be asked whether was the s[ai]d Joane Crewe deceased a very aged woman & 80 [LXXXty] yeares old at her death or thereabout, and soe reputed and taken? had shee bene very sicke & weake, & much decayed in understanding & memory by the space of two yeares, at least one whole yeare next before her death, And was shee soe farre spent with age and weakness of body & mind before and att the tyme of the makeing of the s[ai]d pretensed will that shee was not able of herselfe to dispose of her estate with goode reason & discrecōn? nor was indeed of a disposeing memory or fitt to make a will, and soe reputed and taken? And doe you beleeve, and are you perswaded in your Conscience that the s[ai]d pretensed will was made & contrived by the sayd Raph Cardiffe, and some other or others without the direccōns of the sayd deceased, declare the truth; And let it be done as above.

20. Item, let Robert Tudman, one of the pretended witnesses aforesaid, be asked whether did you assist the sayd Raph Cardiffe in and about the makeing & contriving of the s[ai]d pretensed will, and alsoe in & about the wrytinge of the schedule exhibited? what hath hee given or promissed to give you, in case the pretensed will alledged doe prove goode; whether have you directed & assisted him the sayd Raph in this cause, have you written any notes or note for execucōn of the Citacōn which yssued forth in this cause, have you Conferred with the Proctor of the sayd Raph and with any other of your Contests about your Examinacōns or other the proceedings in this cause, and what was theffect of your sayd Conference; declare the truth; And let it be done as above.

21. Item, Let each of them be asked whether did you live in howse with the s[ai]d deceased, or were a neere neighbor unto her for diverse or some yeares, and how longe before her death? whether was her memory soe decayed, that shee has forgotten her rent dayes, and the times which shee ought to receive her moneys, And after shee had received her rents or moneys, hath shee not alsoe forgotten the receipt thereof and doe you knowe or can you mencōne any particuler instance in this kind? declare the truth at large, so farre as you knowe beleeve or have credibly heard; And let it be done as above.

22. Item, Let each of them be asked and he will render the true reasons of his knowledge in everything. And let it be done as above.

Endorsement: Questions [Interrogatoria] posed to Randle Chorlton and John Cureton against the testimony of Raph Cardiff in the Cause of the Will of the said Joane Crew widow deceased, sworn 11 March AD 1640/1.

Depositions: Statements of witnesses examined and taken 11 March 1640/1 before the venerable Edmund Mainwaring Doctor of Laws, lawfully upheld Official Principal of the Episcopal Consistorial Court of Chester, concerning an Allegation and Testament affixed to the same of Joan Crew widow deceased.

Robert Tudman of the parish or chapelry of Wrenbury, 29 years of age or thereabouts, having known well the parties litigant and also the deceased before her death.

To the first article of the allegations he saith that in or aboute the moneth of March last save this present moneth of Maerch & in the year 1639 arlate *[i.e. articulate]* this deponent did write the deceadents will according as the deceased had given direccōns and after this deponent had finished the same he did read the same plainely & distinctely over unto her the deceadent & shee being a then of good & perfectt sence memory & understandinge & in reasonible good health for any thinge this deponent Conceaved thereof to the Contrary approved thereof and lyked the same will and did freely and of her owne accord seale signe and acknowledge ye same will for her last will & testament present alsoe at the premises his contests Randle Hardinge clarke Richard Hassall & John Bateman whose names were subscribed to the said will as wittnesses, and alsoe divers others, and afterwards shee departed this life otherwise he knows nothing to certainly depose.

To the 2nd and 3rd articles of the allegations he knows nothing to depose except from the report of others.

To the 4th and 5th article and to the schedule or writing, mentioned in the same, he saith that the ar[ticu]late Mr Raphe Cardiffe was named sole executor of the will pretensed, and saith the schedule annexed to the said allegacōns doth containe the true substance and effectt of the said will to all intents & purposes & in every particuler legacie & the value & qualitie or sume of the same without adiccōn or diminucōn as hee is verily persuaded in his conscience and saith he doth beleeve & is verily persuaded that all the legacies that were contayned in the said will soe sealed signed & acknowledged by the said deceased are expressed & sett downe in the said schedule or wrytinge annexed to the said allegacōn whereupon hee this deponent is examined and seeinge & perusinge the said schedule at the time of his examinacōn in this cause saith it doth containe the true substance & effect of the said will in all points by him predeposed as hee verily beleeveth in his consideracōn otherwise hee knows nothing certainly but refers himself to the things predeposed by him which are true.

To the last he says that the things predeposed by him are true.

Robert Tudman

Randle Hardinge Clerk of the parishe or chapelry of Wrenbury, 33 years of age or thereabouts, having known well the parties litigant and also the deceased before her death

To the first article of the *[crossed out]* allegacōne he saith that in or aboute the moneth of March in the yeare 1639 ar[ticu]late the deceadent Joanne Crewe beinge minded & disposed to make her will desyred this deponent livinge in house with her to sett downe in wrytinge what particuler legasies shee would give & dispose by her will which this deponent did & some shorte space soone after shee sent for his precontest Robert Tudman to make her will and hee came unto her and writt her will & after he had finished the same accordinge to the said note writt by this deponent as he has in part predeposed, & the residue thereof accordinge to her the deceadentt direccōns unto him, *[something crossed out]* hee read the same plainely & distinctely over unto her the deceadentt in the presence of this deponent & his contests Richard Hassall & John Bateman *[something crossed out]* whose names were subscribed to the said will as wittnesses, & divers others and shee the deceadent beinge then of good & perfectt sence memory & understandinge lyked the same will & approved thereof & did freely & of her owne accorde seale signe & acknowledge ye same for her last will & testament & afterwards departed this life otherwise he knows nothing certainly to depose.

To the 2nd & 3rd articles he saith yt since the deceadentes death the said will was delivered to this deponent by Mr. Raphe Cardiffe sole executor nominated in the said will to the end that this deponent should fetch him a comission from this Courte to take his oath for the execucōn of the said will accordinge to lawe & saith this deponent hath since lost the said will & canot by any meanes finde ye same Otherwise he knows nothing to depose.

To the 4th & 5th and to the schedule or writing mentioned in the same he says that this deponent veweinge and readinge over the wrytinge or schedule annexed to the allegacōn whereupon hee is now examined at the time of his examinacōn saith it doth containe the whole substance & effectt of the same will which shee the said deceadent soe sealed signed & acknowledged for her last will & testament & saith that the legasies expressed in the said wrytinge or schedule are the same legasies without any alteracōn addiccōn or dimunicōn that were contayned in the same will which this deponent lost as he has predeposed for hee very well doth remember the Contents thereof Otherwise he does not know anything except as above to which he refers himself.

To the last he says that the things predeposed by him are true.

Randle Hardinge

Richard Hassall of the parishe or chapelry of Wrenbury 48 years of age or there-abouts, having known the parties litigant and also the deceased before her death.

To the first article he saith that this deponent was present about the beginninge of March in the yeare 1639 ar[ticu]late when the deceadent haveinge caused her will to bee written, his precontest Robert Tudman did reade the same will plainely & distinctely over unto her the deceadent and shee the deceadent beinge of good & perfectt sence memory & understandinge did approve thereof and lyked the same well & did freely & of her owne accorde seale signe & acknowledge it for her last will & testament Present alsoe at the premises his contest John Bateman & his precontests Randle Hardinge clerke & Robert Tudman & divers others & saith this deponent did put his marke to the said will as a wittness & saithe the said deceadent is since dead, Otherwise he knows nothing certainly to depose.

To the 2nd & 3rd he knows nothing to depose except from report.

To the 4th article hee says yt the ar[ticu]late Mr. Raphe Cardiffe was named sole executor of the said will Otherwise hee knows nothing except as above to which he refers himself.

To the 5th article of the allegacōn and to the schedule or wrytinge mentioned in the same he says that this deponent haveinge the said wrytinge or schedule read unto him at the time of his examinacōn in this cause saith it doth containe in it the effectt & substance of the said will soe sealed & acknowledged by the said deceadent as hee hath deposed, & saith hee is verily persuaded in his conscience that the legasies contayned in the said schedule are the very same legasies with-out alteracōn addiccōn or diminucōn which were given & bequeathed by the said deceadent in her said will, soe by her sealed signed & acknowledged for her last will and testament as he has predeposed for hee well remembered the contentes thereof Otherwise he knows nothing except as above to which he refers himself.

To the last he says the things predeposed by him are true.

sign of Richard Hassall

John Bateman of the parishe or chapelry of Wrenbury 33 years of age or there-abouts having known well the present litigants also the deceased before her death.

To the first article of the allegations he saith that this deponent as alsoe his pre-contests Richard Hassall & Randle Hardinge clerke were present aboute the begin-ninge of March in the year 1639 ar[ticu]late when his preconteste Robert Tudman did reade a will which the deceadent had then made plainely & distinctely over unto her the deceadent & shee the deceadent beinge then of good & perfect sence memory understandinge approved thereof & lyked the same well & did freely &

of her owne accorde seale signe acknowledge the will exhibited for her last will & testament & since then is departed this life Otherwise he knows nothing certainly to depose.

To the 2nd & 3rd articles hee knows nothing to depose.

To the 4th hee saith yt the ar[ticu]late Mr. Raphe Cardiffe was named sole executor in the said will, & saith persons ar[ticu]late there named were subscribed to the said will as wittnesses as is ar[ticu]late Otherwise he knows nothing certainly to depose.

To the 5th article and to the Schedule or wrytinge mentioned in the same he saith that this deponent haveinge the schedule or wrytinge exhibited shewed unto this deponent & hearinge the same reade unto him at the time of his examinacōn in this cause saith it doth containe in it the full substance and effectt of the will predeposed and saith hee is verily persuaded in his conscience that the legasies therein contayne are the selfe same without alteracōn addicōn or diminucōn which were given & bequeathed by the said will soe by the said deceadent sealed signed & acknowledged as he has predeposed for hee well remembreth the Contents thereof Otherwise he knows nothing certainly to depose.

To the last he says that the things predeposed by him are true.

John Bateman

Robert Tudman *ad Interrogatoria* [Answers to the Questions]

To the first question he respondeth hee is a yeoman & did knowe the deceadent 3 or 4 yeares before her decease & hath knowen Randle Chorleton & Mr. Raphe Cardiffe for ye time & the Inter[rogate]³ John Cureton hee knoweth by sutch onely Otherwise it has been explained.

To the 2nd hee respondeth that hee hath heard that the deceadent Joane Crewe did make a will certen yeares agoe & that the Inter[rogate] Randle Chorleton was named executor therein Otherwise hee knows nothing to respond.

To the 3rd: hee respondeth that hee hath heard that the wife of the said Randle Chorleton, & the said John Cureton were a kinne to the deceadent Otherwise hee knows nothing to depose.

---

³· The Latin *Interte* is anglicized as *interrogate*, and is used as an adjective (in the same way as 'said' and 'aforesaid') to qualify any person, place, thing, fact, date and so forth which has been referred to in the Articles or Interrogatories respectively. Its use is so widespread, frequently without contraction, that it might properly be considered as a word in its own right.

To the 4th & 5th: hee respondeth that this respondent did write the deceadents will pretensed aboute six of the Clocke in the eveninge all at one time, but saith that some part thereof was written in a parlor of the deceadents house where out of his presence shee died accordinge to a note delivered unto him by his Contest Randle Hardinge & the rest thereof hee writt in the deceadents fire house & in her presence & accordinge to her direccōns & saith yt this respondent haveinge written & finished ye said will & when the deceadent had sealed signed & acknowledged ye same as he has predeposed hee this respondent of his owne accorde put his hand thereunto as a wittnes as other Clarkes are accustomed to doe to any wrytinges they make Otherwise hee knows nothing except as predeposed to which he refers himself.

To the 6th: hee respondeth yt the deceadent sittinge by the fireside in her house when the will predeposed was made, & saith shee was then in good health & pleasant for any thinge this respondent Conceaved to the Contrary & saith divers persons were present at the sealinge & acknowledgeinge of the will pretensed besides those who subscribed there names thereunto as wittnesses Otherwise hee knows nothing except as above to which he refers himself.

To the 7th: hee respondeth yt the partie producent sent for this respondent in the deceadents name to come to make her the deceadents will, & after this respondent came unto her shee tould this respondent that shee was desyrous to make her will & settle her estate, & saith the partie producent gave this respondent 2s. 6d. & noe more for his paines in makeinge the said will but saith the deceadent would have paid him and the partie producent would not suffer for her Otherwise hee knows nothing except as above to which he refers himself.

To the 8th: hee respondeth that this respondent received instruccōns in part from the said Randle Hardinge for the makeinge of the said will & the rest from the deceadents owne mouth, and saith shee did freely & voluntarily name the legatories & legasies therein mentioned, of that part of the will which this respondent received in instruccōns for from her owne mouth, without the persuasion or intreatie or any saveinge that shee would have given but 12s. a peece to her kinsfolkes in Nantwich meaneinge the deponentes in this sute but that the partie producent persuaded her to leave them some more whereupon shee gave them the severall legasies expressed in the said schedule or wrytinge whereupon hee hath bine examined, and saith the deceadent did of her owne accord nominate the Inter[roga]te Mr. Cardiffe executor of her said will, & did alsoe of her owne accorde say that shee did revoke all former will or wills by her made Otherwise hee does not know anything except as predeposed to which he refers himself.

To the 9th: hee respondeth that this respondent did read the will exhibited plainely & distinctely over unto her the deceadent after hee had finished ye same & she gave eare there unto & did understand the same, & said it was well & according to her mynde & shee thanked god shee had settled her estate or to that effectt & saith shee did of her owne accorde & with her owne hand without the helpe or assistance or persuasion of any put her marke to the said will & sealed the same & delivered it without the direccōn or persuasion of any Otherwise hee knows nothing except as above to which he refers himself.

To the 10th: hee respondeth that the deceadent did take notice that this respondent was a wittnes to the said will Otherwise hee refers himself to the things predeposed by him.

To the 11th: hee respondeth yt after ye said will was soe writen sealed signed & acknowledged as he has predeposed ye said will was delivered into the Custodie & keepinge of the partie producent who kept the same till the deceadents death as hee beleeveth & saith hee did never read the same or heare the same reade since the deceadent sealed and acknowledged the same as predeposed Otherwise hee knows nothing except as above to which he refers himself.

To the 12th: hee respondeth yt the deceadent died upon Monday or Tuesday last save one, & was buried upon Thursday followeinge Otherwise hee knows nothing.

To the 13th: hee respondeth yt this respondent did write the schedule Inter[rogate] at his owne house, but saith his conteste Mr. Hardinge & this respondent had before at the deceadents house & considered to gether & put one an other in mynde of the legasies given in & by the will predeposed & this respondent had there drawne a note or briefe thereof, & shewed & read The same to Richard Hassall & John Bateman two wittnesses who were subscribed to the said will and they approved thereof & concluded that, that briefe or brieffes was the whole substance of the deceadents will, whereupon this respondent writ the s[ai]d schedule as he has predeposed and they all subscribed there names thereunto Otherwise he knows nothing except as predeposed to which he refers himself, savinge the partie producent was present when the said first draught was drawen, & saith both the said first drawght, & ye schedule predeposed were writt on Friday last.

To the 14th: hee knows nothing to respond.

To the 15th: hee knows nothing to respond.

To the 16th: hee knows nothing to respond.

To the 17th: hee responds yt at the time the deceadent sealed signed & acknowledged the will predeposed as he has predeposed, shee said that shee had made an other will which was at Nantwich, & earnestly desired the partie producent to send for both that and all other her wrytinges there with all speed, that shee might Cancell the s[ai]d will Otherwise hee knows nothing except as predeposed to which he refers himself.

To the 18th: hee refers himself to the things predeposed by him, Otherwise hee knows nothing.

To the 19th: hee respondeth yt the deceadent was an aged woman at the time shee made the will predeposed but saith shee was of good & perfectt sense & memory & fitt & able to dispose of her estate when shee made the same, Otherwise hee knows nothing except as predeposed to which he refers himself.

To the 20th: hee respondeth that hee did never assiste the inter[rogate] Cardiffe in makeinge the deceadents will predeposed & saith the said Mr. Cardiffe to this respondents knowledge had noe hand or was acquainted either with the makeinge of the said will or draweinge the schedule inter[rogate] untill after the same were finished & saith hee hath neither given nor promised to give this respondent any thinge for his assistance or paines in & aboute ye same, but saith a note beinge sent from this courte for direccōns of *[something crossed out]* the execucōn of the citacōn which issued out in this cause this respondent writt a nother note by the same note, Otherwise hee knows nothing except as predeposed to which he refers himself.

To the 21st: hee respondeth yt this respondent lived aboute a miledistant from the deceadent Otherwise hee does not know anything except as above to which he refers himself.

It has been explained as far as explained.

Robert Tudman

Richard Hassall's Responses to the Interrogatories:

To the first question: hee replies hee is a yeoman and hath knowen the parties Interrogate a dozen years & upwards Otherwise it has been explained.

To the 2nd: hee does not know anything to reply.

To the 3rd: hee replies that hee hath heard that ye wife of the Interrogate Randle Chorleton & the said John Cureton were a kinne to the deceadent Otherwise hee knows nothing to reply.

To the 4th: hee replies yt this respondent was a wittness to the will by him predeposed & saith this respondent did heare the said will read over unto the deceadent & did see her seale signe & acknowledge the will predeposed as he has deposed & afterward did put his marke to the said will as a wittnes & saith the other wittnesses subscribed to the schedule whereupon hee hath bine now exhibited did alsoe subscribe there names & the said will as wittnesses, as he verily beleeveth, Otherwise hee knows nothing to respond for certaine.

To the 5th: hee replies that the will predeposed was redd as he has deposed by the aforesaid Roberte Tudman *[crossed out]* & was sealed & acknowledged by the decedent as hee hath deposed in the evening Otherwise hee knows nothing except as he has predeposed to which he refers himself.

To the 6th: hee replies yt the said deceadent was in good & perfectt sense & memory & in good health for any thinge this respondent perceaved to the Contrary & was fitt & able to dispose of her estate at the time shee soe sealed signed & acknowleged her will as he has deposed & was then sittinge by her fire in her owne house and saith there were severall persons besides the wittnesses subscribed to the said will present at the same time Otherwise hee knows nothing certainly except as above to which he refers himself.

To the 7th he does not know anything except as predeposed to which he refers himself.

To the 8th he does not know anything to reply except as above to which he refers himself.

To the 9th he replies yt the will predeposed was plainely & distinctly read over unto the deceadent in this respondents presense at the time shee sealed signed & acknowledged the same & shee did understand the same & lyked it well & did freely & of her owne accorde without the aide persuasion or direccōn of any & with her owne hand without any holdinge or guidinge the same did put her marke to the said will & sealed & delivered the same as he has deposed otherwise he knows nothing certainly except as he has predeposed to which he refers himself saveing hee doth not remember what particuler wordes the deceadent uttered inporteinge her approbacōn & lykeinge of the said will.

To the 10th he replies yt the deceadent did knowe that this respondent was a wittness to the said will, but whether shee requested him to bee a wittnes thereunto or noe hee canot remember Otherwise he knows nothing except as before to which he refers himself.

To the 11th he replies that this respondent did never see the will predeposed nor heare the same redd after the deceadent soe sealed & acknowledged the same as he has deposed, neither doth hee knowe who had the keepeinge thereof, Otherwise he knows nothing except as before to which he refers himself.

To the 12th he replies yt the deceadent died upon Munday or Tuesday night last save one as hee beleeveth & was buried upon the the Thursday next followinge.

To the 13th he replies that the Schedule Interrogate was read unto this respondent & John Bateman by the said Robert Tudman after the same was written & drawen by the said Robert Tudman as he beleeveth, Otherwise he knows nothing certainly except as predeposed to which he refers himself.

To the 14th / 15th & 16th hee knows nothing to respond.

To the 17th he does not know anything to reply except as he has predeposed to which he refers himself.

To the 18th he refers himself to the things predeposed by him..

To the 19th he replies yt the deceadent was a very aged woman at the time shee made the will predeposed & was some times sickely but this respondent did never knowe heare or perceave that shee was any way decayed in her sence memory or understandinge at the time shee made the will predeposed, Otherwise he does not know anything except as predeposed to which he refers himself.

To the 20th it does not concern this respondent.

To the 21st he replies that this respondent was a neere neighbour to the deceadent severall yeares before her death but did never heare or knowe that shee was soe forgettful as not to remember her rente daies or when shee ought to receive her moneys, nor that shee did forgett any money shee had received, Otherwise he knows nothing except as above to which he refers himself.

To the last it has been explained as far as explained.

John Bateman['s Responses] to the Questions (Interrogatories):

To the first question he replies yt hee is a smith by trade & hath knowen the persons Interrogate a dozen yeares & upwards, Otherwise it has been explained.

To the 2nd question he replies yt this respondent hath heard that the deceadent severall yeares before her death made a will & made Randle Chorleton Interrogate one of her executors, Otherwise it has been explained.

To the 3rd he replies yt hee hath heard yt ye wife of the Interrogate Randle Chorleton & the Interrogate John Cureton were a kinne to the deceadent, Otherwise he knows nothing to respond.

To the 4th he replies yt this respondent was a wittness to the will by him predeposed & did put his name thereto as a wittnes & saith his contestes Roberte Tudman & Randle Hardinge Clerke writt there names & his conteste Richard Hassall put his marke to the said will as wittnesses, otherwise he knows nothing certainly to respond saveinge he beleeveth that the deceadent did not wishe this respondent or any of the rest of the wittnesses to bee wittnesses to the same will.

To the 5th he replies yt hee beleeveth his contest Robert Tudman writt the will predeposed, Otherwise he knows nothing to respond.

To the 6th he replies yt the deceadent was in good health as he beleeveth at the time shee sealed signed & acknowledged the will predeposed as predeposed & did then sitte in her owne house by the fireside, & saith divers persons were then alsoe presente besides the wittnesses whose names were subscribed to the said will, otherwise he knows nothing except as above to which he refers himself.

To the 7th he replies that this respondent lived in house with the deceadent when the will predeposed was sealed & acknowledged as hee hath deposed & saith a little girle of his this respondent came unto him to fetch him to bee a wittness to the will but who sent for him he canot answere, otherwise he knows nothing certainly to respond.

To the 8th he knows nothing to reply except as above to which he refers himself.

To the 9th he replies that the will predeposed was plainely and distinctly read twice over to the deceased after the same was written & shee did give eare to the same & did understand it & said shee lyked it well or it was accordinge to her mynde or to that effectt, & then did with her owne hand without the helpe of any put her marke to the same & sealed it & did freely & of her owne without the p[er]suasion or direccōn of any other acknowledge the same for her last will & testament, otherwise he does not know anything except as he has predeposed to which he refers himself.

To the 10th he replies yt this respondent did write his owne name to the said will as a wittnes, & the deceadent did take notice that this respondent was a wittnes thereunto, otherwise he knows nothing except as he has predeposed to which he refers himself.

To the 11th he replies that the will predeposed was delivered unto the partie producent after ye same was sealed & acknowledged & saith hee did never since see the same or heare it read, otherwise he knows nothing except as above to which he refers himself.

To the 12th he replies yt ye deceadent died upon Monday or Tuesday at night last save one, & was buried the Thursday followeinge, otherwise he knows nothing except as above to which he refers himself.

To the 13th he replies that his contest *[something crossed out]* Robert Tudman did write the Schedule Interrogate & after hee had writt the same hee did read it over unto this respondent & the said mr Hardinge & Richard Hassall & they findinge the substance thereof & the legasies therein specified to Concurre with the will predeposed did subscribe there names thereunto as they had formerly done to the said will, otherwise he knows nothing except as he has predeposed to which he refers himself.

To the 14th, 15th and 16th *[almost whole line crossed out]* he knows nothing to respond.

To the 17th he knows nothing to respond in anyway except as he has predeposed to which he refers himself.

To the 18th he refers himself to the things predeposed by him otherwise he knows nothing.

To the 19th he replies yt the deceadent was a very aged woman at the time of her decease & by reason of her age was sometimes sicklie but saith shee was *[something crossed out]* of good & perfectt memory & fitt to make a will & able to dispose of her estate both at the time shee made the will predeposed & longe before & after, otherwise he knows nothing certainly to respond except as above to which he refers himself.

To the 20th it does not concern this respondent.

To the 21st he replies yt hee lived in house with the said deceadent fower or five yeares before her death, but saith yt hee did never knowe or heare that her memory was soe decayed that shee did forgett her rent daies or the times that shee was to receave any money, neither that shee did ever forgett the receipt of any moneys shee had received, otherwise he does not know anything to reply except as predeposed to which he refers himself.

To the last it has been explained as far as explained.

John Bateman

Randle Hardinge['s Responses] to the Interrogatories.

To the first question he replies yt he is a minister & hath knowen all the parties Interrogate two yeares or thereaboute, otherwise it has been explained.

To the 2nd: hee replies yt hee hath heard that the deceadent made a will certaine yeares before her death, & named the Interrogate Randle Chorleton one of the executors thereof, otherwise he knows nothing certainly to respond.

To the 3rd: hee hath heard that the Interrogate Randle Chorleton his wife, & John Cureton were a kinne to the deceadent otherwise he knoweth nothing to respond.

To the 4th: hee replies yt hee was present when the will by him predeposed was made & written & did subscribe his name thereunto as a wittnes & the deceadent desyred this respondent to bee a wittnes thereof, otherwise hee knoweth nothing certain to respond.

To the 5th he replies that his contest Robert Tudman writt the will predeposed some part in a parlor of the deceadents house out in her presence & the rest in the house it selfe where the decead[en]t then was, & saith the same was all written at one time & about the eveninge, otherwise he knows nothing certainly to respond.

To the 6th he replies yt the decedeant was somewhat sickely at the time the will predeposed was made, & was sittinge by the fyre in her owne house, & saith there were other persons present when the said will was made, besides the wittnesses which were thereunto subscribed, otherwise he knows nothing except as above to which he refers himself.

To the 7th he replies yt this respondent lived in house with the deceadent at the time of the makeinge of the will predeposed and saith the said deceadent two or three daies before shee made her will predeposed intreated this respondent to sett downe some legasies in wrytinge which shee intended to give in her will for the more readines to the wryter & shee desired this respondent to bee present at the makeinge of her will, & said shee was desyrous to make her will & to settle her estate & saith the partie producent by the deceadents direccōns did send for the said Robert Tudman to make her will, & after hee had made it as he has predeposed the deceadent would have paid him for his paines but the said partie producent would not suffer her to pay him, but hee did give him 2s. 6d. & noe more as hee beleeveth, otherwise he knows nothing certainly to respond except as above to which he refers himself.

To the 8th he replies yt the wryter tooke direccōns for soe much of the will as hee writt in the parlor of the deceadents house out of & from the note which this respondent had taken & sett down accordinge as the deceadent directed him, & saith hee receaved direccōns for the makeinge of the rest thereof from the deceadents owne mouth as he has predeposed and saith the decedent did freely & of her owne accorde without the direccōn or intreatie or persuasion of any Saveinge that shee would have given but 12s. a peece to her kinsfolkes in Nantwich in respectt they had taken some of her goods perforce from her as shee said, but that shee was persuaded to give them better legasies by the partie producent & this respondent whereupon shee was contended & did give them the legasies contayned & expressed in the schedule predeposed whereupon hee hath bine examined & saith the deceadent said of her owne accorde that shee would make all former wills by her made void, & did of her owne accord without the persuasion or direccōn of any, nominate the partie producent sole executor of her said will, otherwise he knows nothing except as above to which he refers himself.

To the 9th he replies yt after the will predeposed was written it was plainely & distinctely read over unto her the deceadent as hee hath deposed, in his presence, & shee did give eare to the same & did understand it, & did approve thereof, & saw it was accordinge to her mynde & shee did give god thankes that shee had finished the same & settled her mynde or to yt effectt, & saith shee did of her owne accorde without the helpe aide or persuasion of any put her marke to the same did seale, acknowledge & deliver the same for her last will & testament, otherwise he knows nothing in anyway except as predeposed to which he refers himself.

To the 10th he replies yt ye deceadent did take notice that this respondent was a wittnes to the said will, otherwise he knows nothing in anyway except as predeposed to which he refers himself.

To the 11th he replies yt ye deceadent delivered the will predeposed to the partie producent, & saith that hee did keepe the same till the deceadents death, as hee beleeveth & saith hee did never to his now remembrance see the same or heare it reade after it was delivered unto the partie producent until after the deceadents death, otherwise he knows nothing except as above to which he refers himself.

To the 12th he replies yt the deceadent died upon Monday night last save one, & was buried upon the Thursday then next followinge.

To the 13th hee replies that the first draught of the schedule Interrogate was writen by the said Robert Tudman at the house where the deceadent died upon Friday last in the presence of this respondent the partie producent, & saith this respondent & the said Robert Tudman did assiste one an other in there memories for the particuler legasies given by the deceadent & after the said first draught was drawne the same was read to Richard Hassall & John Bateman who did both acknowledge that the same draught was the full same & substance of the said deceadents will predeposed & saith they would sweare to the truth thereof, & saith the said Robert Tudman did write the schedule Interrogate whereupon hee hath bine examined otherwise hee knows nothing certainly to respond except as above to which he refers himself.

To the 14th hee replies yt ye will predeposed was delivered to this respondent by the partie producent at the deceadents house the next morninge after the deceadent died, & aboute ten or twelve howers after her death, & two daies before her buriall, with an intent yt this respondent should fetch a Comission from this courte to take his oath for the execusōn & performance thereof, & saith hee did not read it over after hee received it, otherwise hee knows nothing certainly except as deposed above to which he refers himself.

To the 15th hee replies yt hee was sent to noe Clarke by name to procure the said comission, but to the Clarke in generall, & saith he came to this Cittie upon Tuesday last save one & returned late the same day & saith hee was first in the house of Robert Cappur scituate in this Cittie and did there soe soone as hee came into the house, looke for the said will in his pockett where hee did verily beleeve hee had put the same, but could not find it, & there was the first place that he missed the same & perceaved that he had lost it & saith there was noe company then with him when hee first missed the same but him selfe, & saith hee was afterwards in Mr Chancellors house with Mr Chancellor & Mr Brian Pretious & Edward Hall in his Company, & alsoe in Mr Bickertons house with him & in John Wright the Barbers Shoppe & hee did come & goe backe on & the same day, & saith hee did call as he came to Chester at Francis Saunders his house in Whitchurch but staied there but a shorte space & afterwards called there as hee went backe to see if hee had left the said will there & did not call or stay any where else by the way either comeinge or goeinge, otherwise hee knows nothing except as above to which he refers himself.

To the 16th hee replies yt hee sought for the said will at the said Francis Saunders his house & enquired of all in ye house aboute the same & of all others who hee did Conceave might by any meanes come to knowledge thereof or finde the same by any possibilitie, otherwise hee knows nothing except as predeposed to which he refers himself.

To the 17th hee replies that the said will was made accordinge to the deceadents direccōns & not by the procurement of the partie producent & saith that after the said Robert Tudman had finished the same hee tould her hee had made an end thereof but saith hee did heare noe such words uttered as is Interrogate, otherwise hee knows nothing to respond except as predeposed to which he refers himself.

To the 18th he refers himself to those things predeposed above, otherwise he knows nothing.

To the 19th hee replies yt ye deceadent was a very aged woman at that death & saith shee was somewhat sickely by reason of her age but was of very good memory & understandinge & able to declare her will & dispose of her estate when shee made the will predeposed & both at the time shee made the will predeposed & longe before & after, otherwise hee knows nothing except as predeposed to which he refers himself.

To the 20th it does not concern this respondent.

To the 21st hee replies that hee lived in house with the said deceadent at the time of her death & two yeares before, but did never heare or knowe that shee did ever forgett any of her rent daies, nor forgett the time when shee had any money due, neither that shee did ever forgett any money yt shee had received, otherwise hee knows nothing except as above to which he refers himself.

To the last it has been explained as far as explained.

Randle Hardinge

Endorsement: Probated 8 April 1641; administration to Ralph Cardiff, sole executor named in the will who must produce an Inventory by 23 June next ensuing.

114. ROBERT SHROWBRIDGE THE YOUNGER OF ROYALS,ª YEOMAN

S.Pr. [October?] 1641
W. 13 February 1640/41
Buried: 27 September 1641

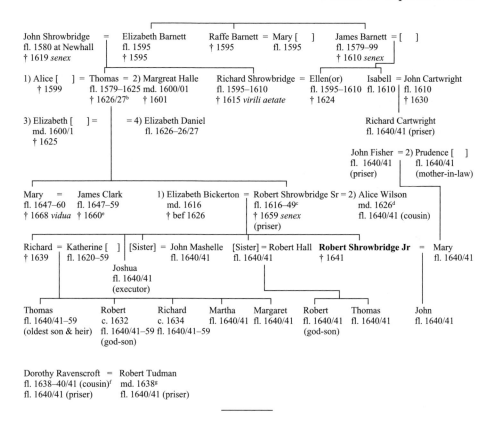

ª See note regarding The Royals in connection with Robert Shrowbridge Sr, will pr. 1659 (will no. 150).
ᵇ See will of Thomas Shrowbridge of Newhall, yeoman, pr. 1626/27 (will no. 75).
ᶜ Priser for John Ravenscroft, 1649 (no. 137).
ᵈ William Fergusson Irvine, *Chester Licences*, iii. 56: 15 April 1626, to Robert Shrowbridge and Alice Wilson, at Wrenbury or Audlem.
ᵉ See will of James Clark, pr. 1660 (will no. 152).
ᶠ Dorothy Tudman, née Ravenscroft, was the wife of Robert Tudman, one of the witnesses of Robert Shrowbridge's will and a priser of his moveable goods.
ᵍ What was apparently a clandestine marriage was certified 15 May 1638 in Wrenbury Parish Register.

Will, sick.

First, I give and bequeath my soule unto the hands of Almighty god who gave it mee and *my body I bequeath unto the earth freely wherein it came to be buried in Christian burial in the churchyard of Wrenbury* according to the direction of my executors hereafter named. And or to using the disposal of my worldly estate I give devise and bequeath the same manner and forme followinge: First I give and bequeath unto Robert Shrowbridge, Richard Shrowbridge, Martha Shrowbridge, and Margret Shrowbridge four yonge children of my late brother Richard Shrowbridge deceased to each of them foure the sum of £5 apeece. Item I give and bequeath unto Thomas Shrowbridge eldest son and heire aparent of my said brother Richard the sum of 13s. 4d. to buy him a pott with when he shall keepe house. Item I give and bequeath unto my godson Robert Hall 10s. Item I give and bequeath unto Thomas Hall yonger son of my brother in law Robert Hall 5s. Item I give and bequeath to Sarah Mashelle daughter of my brother in law John Mashelle 5s. Item I give and bequeath to my mother in law Prudence Fisher, my cosen Alice Shrowbridge and my cozen Dorothy Tudman to each of these three women the sum of 2s. 6d. apeece. Item I give and bequeath to my servant Margrett Higgison the better of my tow black twinter heifers *[insert in margin]* according to the desireing of my said executors hereafter named Item I give and bequeath unto my brother Joshua Shrowbridge the sum of 10s. to buy him a shott: Item I give and bequeath to Mr. Peartree Minster of God's worde at Wrenbury[a] aforesaid 10s. to preach a funerall sermon after my decease at my buriall. Item I give devise bequeath and assigne over unto my executors hereafter named and ther executors and assignes all my estate right tithes and interest which I have of in and to the one half of the messuage tenements lande and premisses conteyning by estimation Tenne Acres of customary lande of ye mannor of Newhall and now in the tenner *[i.e. tenure]* or occupation of mee the said Robert or my assignes to have and to hold the same with all and every there appurtaining remeners *[i.e. remainders]* to my said executors hereafter named and there executors and assignes for and during all the rest and residue of ye tearme of myne yeares yet to come and unexpired, according as they are mentioned expressed in a certen leases thereof to me made by my said late brother Richard Shrowbridge in his also time as by the said lease, relative thereunto entry, but more at large appeareth. They the said executors of myne hereafter named yet beinge, doinge, accomplishinge and performing enjoying and disposing of all the said premisses according to the true entent and meaning of every Article and clause of the said lease: Item all the rest of my goods cattells, and chattels moveable and unmoveable whatsoever after my debts and funerall expenses are discharged, I give devise and bequeath unto my loving wife Mary Shrowbridge provided alwayes, and my will and mening is yt if my said wife shall and doe att the ende and terme of seavon yeares next ensuing the date of this my last will and testament well and trully satisfie and pay unto John Shrowbridge my son the summ of £30, if he the said John shalbe then living: But if it happen that my said son

---

[a]   William Peartree served several years as pastor at Wrenbury and ended his days at St Mary's Church, Chester. He was succeeded by Henry Griffith, who signed the Cheshire Attestation of Presbyterian Ministers in 1648 as *minister* at Wrenbury.

shall not be living at the ende of the said terme of seaven years, then my will and meaninge hereby is yt my said wife Mary shall have £20 of the said £30 and the residue then being £10 I give and bequeath and my will is that my godson Robert Shrowbridge one of the sons of my said brother Richard shall have £5 thereof and then other £5 residue of the last £10 I give and bequeath to my brother Joshua Shrowbridge aforesaid and to Thomas Richard Martha and Margaret, children of my brother Richard with each of them 20s. apeece. Item my will & meaning is yt as touching the said £20 herein before bequeathed to Robert Richard Martha and Mary the said foure children of my said brother Richard yt my executor hereafter named shall pay and discharge the sum in manner aforesaid imedeatley after thee end and expiration of foure yeares next ensuing the date therof and not before

H. & S.

Executors: the testator's wife Mary Shrowbridge, and his brother, Joshua Shrowbridge.

Witnesses: Robert Tudman, John Fisher, Robert Shrowbridge Thelder.

Inventory: Robert Shrowbridge the Younger of Royals, yeoman.

Taken: 22 September 1641, 17 Charles I

Of: goods Cattells and Chattells.

Prisers: Richard Cartwright, John Fisher, Robert Shrowbridge Senur and Robert Tudman.

	£	s	d
his wearing apparell	2	0	0
six kine and one heifer at 50s. apeece	17	10	0
3 stirkeheifers at 23s. 4d. a peece	3	10	0
3 calves at 10s. a peece	1	10	0
one Hogg and one mare the nagg £3 6s. 8d., the Mare comp att and lame at £1 3s. 4d.	4	10	0
two hoggs and two shots	1	8	0
three sheepe		4	0
Corne in the barne as followeth Rye and wheate	10	2	6
Oats	6	3	4
Barly	8	6	8
hey in the barne	3	6	4
maulte in the house		11	0
cheese in the house	2	3	4
brasse of all sorts	1	9	0
two Iron potts		11	0
Pewter of all sorts	1	3	4
bedding of all sorts with pillows bolsters and coverings thereunto belonging	4	10	0
lynnens and napery of all sorts	2	6	8

all coffers of all sorts old [trye] two corne baskets	1	2	0
one other old coffer two old other baskets and one little turninge table		6	8
Treeneware and Cowpery ware of all sorts	1	6	8
brakes Tutawes and spinnge wheeles	1	10	0
flaxs and towe of all sorts within house and without	1	6	8
bread (?) butter and bacon		14	8
Ticknallware		2	0
one payre of Iron bounde wheeles	1	10	0
Iron ware of all sorts whatsoever and Implemts of husbandry		6	8
poultry of all sorts		8	6
sacks and baggs		3	4
fire woode and cooles		14	0
mucke and compost		13	4
all Quishines		3	4

of the Testators goods at the other house at Aston Heath as foloweth

3 payre of bedstids 3 hetchells and loose boards in the loft 3 chayres and 3 stooles and certen loose boards in and about the Premices one payre of pottracks and shills and 2 larders	1	1	4
one presse and Table with a frame and forms	1	0	0
Ready money in the house	2	10	0

Debts owing to the Testator:

	£	s	d
John Wade by specialty		4	
		with interest	
Thomas Sadler by specialty	2	10	
		with interest	
John Plante		2	6
Thomas Seavell		2	6
Ellin Buckley widow		6	0
Mr. Fulkes without specialty	3	16	0

X The marke of Richard Cartwright
The marke of John Fisher
Robert Tudman

Endorsement: Testamentum Roberti Shrowbridge 1641.

Wrapper: Inventorium Roberti Shrowbridge 1641.

115. JOHN ANCKERS OF BROOMHALL, YEOMAN

S?Pr. 24 January 1641/42
W.T. 2 December 1629
Burial: none recorded at Wrenbury, Audlem or Acton

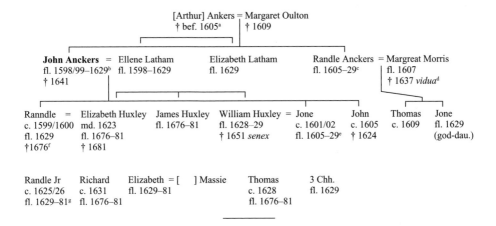

Will, weak in body.

Firste I give and bequeath my soule in to the hands of allmightie god, trustinge, by the merritts of and passion of my saviour Jesus Christe to have full pardon and forgivenesse of all my sinnes, and *my bodye to bee buryed by my predecessors, in the parish Church yarde of Wrenbury*: Item I give and bequeth unto my brother Ranndle Anckers, 5s. Item I give Jone Ankers my god doughter 5s. Item I give and bequeth unto Ranndle Anckers my sonne 5s., and to either of his Children 12d. a peece: Item I give and bequeth unto my doughter Jone Huxley 5s., and to theire three Children 12d. a peece: Item I give, and bequeth unto all

a   For both Arthur Ankers and Margaret, his presumed wife, see will of Margaret Ankers, pr. 1609/10 (will no. 28).
b   See will of Margaret Ankers, made 1605; pr. 1609/10; beneficiary, witness and priser. Made inventory for William Heighfield, 1620 (will no. 62).
c   Beneficiary of and executor of will of Margaret Ankers.
d   Buried at Acton; see Parish Register/CRO.
e   Noted 1605 as *Johan* daughter of John in will of Margaret Ankers; married at Wrenbury, 1623.
f   See will of Randle Ankers, pr. 1676/CRO.
g   See the will of Randle Anckers (pr. 1676/CRO), and the will of Elizabeth Anckers (pr. 1681/CRO).

the reste of my god Children before unnamed 12d. a peece; Item I give and bequeth unto Elezabeth Latham my sister in Lawe 2s. 6d. Item I give and bequeth, my Carts plowes, yokes, Chaines, and all other Implements of husbandrie what soever unto Ellene Anckers my wife and Ranndle Anckers my sonne to bee equally devided, betwixte them, And my will is that dureinge the lyfe of my wife they shall bee used, all to gether as the have bine heere to fore: Item I give and bequeth unto Ellene Ankers, my wife, all the reste and residue of my goods, and Cattels obligacōns, bills, or bands whatsoever, and all the remainder of my goods both movable and unmovable to mee belonginge or in anie waies appertaineinge and before unmentioned, payinge my detts and discharginge my Funerall expences.

Executors: the testator's wife, Ellene Anckers, and the testator's son-in-law, William Huxley.

Overseer: the testator's brother, Ranndle Anckers.

Witnesses: Ranndle Anckers, Thomas Gray.

John Anckers
his X marke

Inventory: John Anckers of Broomhall, yeoman.

Taken: 3 November 1641

Of: goods Chattels Cattels.

Prisers: Robert Heath, Randle Bekett, [Robert][a] Olton and John Olton.

	£	s	d
his weareing Clothes	*[the right-hand edge of the*		
one yocke of Oxen	*inventory is gone completely;*		
	no values have been preserved]		

one mare price
Five kyne price
tow sterke bullocks
two Calves price
Eight sheep
one Swyne
Fower measures of Rye sowed
sixteene thraves of Rye
barly Oates pease and French wheate and barly in the barne
Corn and malt in the house

[a] Robert Oulton made the inventory of the goods etc. of Roger Jones in 1639 (will no. 110): he is thus a likely candidate for this otherwise unidentifiable person in 1641.

Hey, straw and other Fodder
Bedding Nappery ware and all other Lynneins
Bedsteds and Chests
Cubbart Tables Cheres stooles & shelves
stones, bonkes & al manner of trene ware
Brasse & pewter
Bacon chese & other provission
Carts plowes yokes chaynes Iron ware and all other husbandry ware
wood & cooles and other fuell
poultery ware
Bees
in money that was lent fourth

Endorsement: *[damaged]* Probated 24 January 1641; administration granted to the executors named in the said will.

[*Obverse of will*: John Ankers, his will].

116. KATHERINE SAVAGE OF WRENBURY

S. Administration granted 16 March 1641/42
Buried: 10 February 1641/42

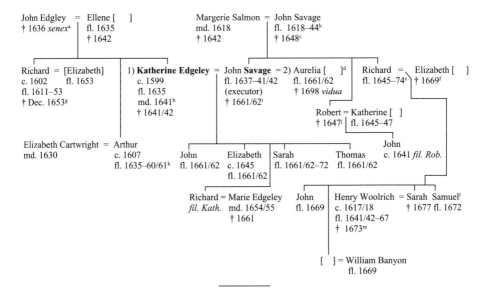

Inventory: Katherine Savage, late wife of John Savage of Wrenbury.

Taken: 15 March 1641/42, 17 Charles I
Of: goods Cattells and Chattells.

Prisers: Thomas Taylor, Arthure Hurleston, Thomas Gray and Lawrence Fisher.

---

a   See will of John Edgeley, pr. 1637 (will no. 102).
b   See will of Richard Culliner alias Comber, pr. 1644 (will no. 119).
c   See administration papers for John Savage, 1648 (no. 131).
d   Aurelia Savage married for the second time, 1 October 1662 at Chester, to Richard Savage.
e   As brother of Robert Savage, overseer of his will, pr. 1647 (will no. 124); priser of the moveable goods of John Savage of Wrenbury; see will, pr. 1661/62; Newhall Manor court records, 1672–74/CRO.
f   See will of Elizabeth Savage, widow of Richard Savage, pr. 1669/CRO.
g   See will of Richard Edgeley of Smeatonwood, pr. 1660/61 (will no. 153).
h   William Fergusson Irvine, *Chester Licences*, iv. 87; to John Savage of Wrenbury and Catherine Edgeley of Wrenbury, spinster; at Wrenbury, Acton or Marbury.
i   See will of John Savage, pr.1661/62.
j   See will of Robert Savage, pr. 1647 (will no. 124).
k   Arthur and Richard Edgeley mentioned in inventory of Katherine Savage, below; they were her brothers, all in turn the offspring of John Edgeley of Woodcott, will pr. 1637 (will no. 102) and his wife, Ellene [   ]. Further, see will no. 153, note k.
l   Newhall Manor court records/CRO.
m   See will of Henry Woolrich of Wrenbury, yeoman, pr. 1673/CRO.

	£	s	d
A Lease of Certaine grounds from Arthure Edgley for 13 yeares In beinge	92	16	0
A debtt due unto her from Richard Edgley without specialty acknowledged by him before Wittnesse	16	16	0
A debtt due by bond from John Cartwright of Sheppenhall deceased & Arthure Cartwright	15	0	0
One bed with it furneture bequeathed unto her by her fathers laste will & detained from our vewe may well bee worth in valewe out of that house	6	13	4
her weareinge apperrell detained From our vewe may bee worth	6	13	4
her Truncke & Cheste by relacōn well furneshed with Linnans A peece of newe Cloth & other things but detained from our vewe may bee well worth	20	0	0
Some totall	157	18	8

Endorsement: Exhibited 16 March 1641; administration granted to John Savage, husband of the deceased.

117. ROWLAND SALMON OF COOLE LANE, YEOMAN[a]

S.Pr. 21 April 1642
W.T. 21 February 1641/42
Buried: 23 February 1641/42 at Audlem

```
┌─────────────────────────────┬──────────────────────────────────────┐
Rowland Salmon = Allice Luftkyn[b]   Chumly Salmon = Elizabeth Whitney   William Salmon
  † 1641/42    │ fl. 1641/42          fl. 1610–41/42[c]  md. 1616/17       fl. 1618–41/42[d]
┌─────────────┴──┐
John          George    =   [    ]     4 siblings
fl. 1641/42–64[e]  fl. 1641/42–58          fl. 1641/42
(executor, 1658)   † 1664 of Coole Lane
              ┌────────┬────────┬──────────┐
           Rowland  George    Mary    Elizabeth
           fl. 1658  fl. 1658  fl. 1658  fl. 1658
```

Will, sick.

Firste I give & bequeath my soule into the hands of Almighty god who firste gave it mee trusting throwe the mirritts of the death & passion of my saviour Jesus Christ to have free pardon & remission of all my sinnes & my body I committ to the earth from whence it came: & for the temporall estate which god of his bounty & mercy hath enriched mee with all I will & dispose thereof as falloweth: Firste my will is that all such debtts which of right I owe unto any man bee in the firste place paid & discharged and alsoe my funerall expences by my executors hereafter named out of my whole estate, & after my debtts and funerall expences are paid & discharged: I doe heerby give and bequeath the full moety & one halfe of all my goods Cattells & Chattells boeth moveable & unmoveable of what kinde or quality soever the same bee, unto Allice Salmon my loveinge wife, And I doe hereby alsoe give & bequeath the other halfe & full moety of all my said goods cattells & Chattells boeth moveable & unmoveable unto my Sixe

---

[a]   Although Rowland Salmon is noted as a resident of Audlem parish at the time of his marriage and is buried at Audlem, it is clear from the wording 'Coole Lane within the parish of Wrenbury' that he was regarded as a resident of Wrenbury parish at the time of his death. Other members of the Salmon family living at Coole, though participants in Newhall Manor Court activities, identified with Audlem parish.

[b]   Marriage recorded 24 June 1614 at Audlem.

[c]   Elizabeth Whitney of Wrenbury parish, Cholmondeley Salmon of Audlem parish; see William Fergusson Irvine, *Chester Licences*, i. 82 (7 July 1610) at Wrenbury as *Salmond*; also *ibid.*, ii. 23 (21 Jan. 1616/17) at Wrenbury or Audlem, licence to Mr William Prince, curate at Wrenbury parish; Parish Registers – Marriages: 22 January 1616/17 Chomeley Salmon and Elizabeth Whitnay.

[d]   A William Salmon fl. 1618 as priser for Robert Massie (CRO).

[e]   The will itself only refers to Rowland Salmon's *six* children: it is obvious from the will of George Salmon (pr. 1664/CRO) that John was alive in 1641/42.

Children to bee equally devided amonngeste them & my will is that if any of my said Children doe die before the come to their severall ages (as god it defend) that the survivors shall enioye his or their porcōn soe deceasinge.

Executors: the testator's wife, Allice Salmon, and Roger Cumberbach of Nantwich.

H. & S.
signum Rawland Salman
his X marke and seal

Witnesses: Roger Cheswis, Chumly Salmon, William Salmon and Thomas Gray.

Inventory: Rowland Sallmon of Coole Lane.

Taken: 8 March 1641/42

Of: goods Cattell and Chatells.
Prisers: Roger Cheswis Gent., John Hill, Robart [ ] and [Lawrence?] Fisher.

	£	s	d
by bond dew	145	4	11
without specalltie	6	0	0
in redy monays		15	0
in a chatell beafe	80	0	0
22 kine	60	0	0
Ten yonge beasts	17	10	0
Three mares	9	6	0
in hay and Straw	10	0	0
in Corne	4	0	0
in hempe and flaxe		2	0
one shepe		1	0
Potree ware		10	0
Tow Swine		13	4
in husbandree ware	2	0	0
in Chesses	22	0	0
in Beafe & Bacon	2	0	0
Bedinge and Bedstocs	5	0	0
in naperey ware and yorne	5	0	0
in Brasse and Pewter	5	0	0
in Treen ware	1	0	0
in Coffers bards Cheers and Stooles	1	0	0
hemp seed and Linseed		1	4
in dressoe toe		6	8
in waring Apparell Sadell & bridel	4	0	0
in Bookes Iron ware & other things		10	0
Some is	382	0	3

Endorsement: This Inventory was exhibited as genuine by one of the executors named in the will of the said deceased; to whom was granted the letter of administration on 21 April 1642, with power to add and take away etc.

[**Endorsement on back**] Will with inventory of the goods of Rowland Salmon deceased of *Cow Lane* exhibited and probated 21 April 1642; administration and execution to Alice Salmon widow of the said deceased, one of the executors named in the said will, the other executor named in the will having renounced the burden of execution in person.

118. JOHN WOODFEN OF CHORLEY, YEOMAN

S. Administration granted 19 January 1642/43
Buried: 22 December 1642

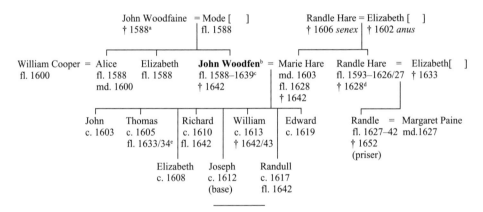

Inventory: John Woodfen of Chorley, yeoman.

Taken: 27 December 1642

Of: goods Cattell and Chattells.

Prisers: Raphe Preece yeoman, Thomas Willson yeoman and Randle Hare yeoman.

ᵃ See will of John Woodfyn, pr. 1588/CRO.
ᵇ Without further data, we can only surmise that the John Woodfen of 1642 is the son of the John Woodfaine of 1588.
ᶜ Priser for Roger Jones of Chorley, will pr. 1639 (will no. 110).
ᵈ See will of Randull Hare, pr. 1628 (will no. 76).
ᵉ Witness to will of Robert Wade, pr. 1633/34 (will no. 95).

	£	s	d
Cheeses fourescore and seventeen	6	0	0
One Joyned bed one featherbed two feather Bolsters one Covering one blankett one wooll bed One Chaffe bed & two Chaffe bolsters	3	10	0
One featherbed one Chaffe bed three blanketts one Covering two fetherbolsters two Chaffe bolsters With the bedstede	2	10	0
One bed with it appertenances	1	10	0
One standing bed & a wheele bed	2	0	0
Three payre of flax sheets & seventeen payre Of Coorse sheets six tableclothes five Pillowbeers six napkins & two towells	6	10	0
Three potts foure kettles three panns two Skelletts and one Chafeing dish	3	6	8
pewter of All sorts	1	13	4
Two brasse Candlesticks & one brasse morter		4	0
five Coffers and two boxes		13	4
stooles and Chayres		10	0
flax and hempe	1	10	0
One Cupboard and one table with benches	1	0	0
One dishboard		10	0
Tubbs stooles Barrells and Churnes		18	0
Two straw flasketts		5	0
shelves tressles with Earthen potts		8	8
All kind of Iron ware		12	0
Two oxen and two horses	12	0	0
six kyne	18	0	0
Three Bullocks & two heyfers	9	0	0
One calfe	1	0	0
henns and geese with one swine		14	0
Corne and malt	7	8	0
hey and straw	5	0	0
Bacon	2	0	0
Saddle and bridle		2	0
One wayne with tumbrell body	2	13	4
harrowes ploughes yokes & muck Copps		10	0
Two payre of horse geers [gont?] Cartrope		8	0
Two sleads three Ladders with brakes		6	4
One muckhook with other ymplemts of Husbandry		1	6
Bookes		8	0
More shelves and tressles		10	0
stockcards woollcards & one hetchell		4	0
scales and measures		2	4
Baggs sives & Basketts		10	0
Cheese fatts & Cheese pa[nui]ells		6	0
Turnells and salting basons		3	0

Bowks Canns piggans dishes & trenchers		5	0
Bees		14	0
spininge wheeles		3	0
feathers and flocks		5	0
weareinge Apperrell	2	0	0
more small Lynnens	1	2	0
[Sum	88	283	42]

Endorsement: Exhibited 19 January 1642; administration granted to Ranulph and Richard Woodfen, the natural and legitimate sons of the aforesaid deceased, desiring the same to begin with, in due form etc. . . .

Bond & Condition:

NOTE: Only a half to two-thirds of this document survives. On the obverse (bond) the RHS of the text, and on the reverse (condition) the LHS of the text, is missing.

Bond:

NB. Text in [   ] brackets has been supplied from common form.

Know all men by these presents that we Ranulph Woodfen, cobbler of the city of Chester in [the county of Chester and Richard Wright of Nant]wich . . . [do promise] to John, through divine providence Bishop of Chester, in the form of £100 in good and lawful coinage of England, to be paid to the same Reverend Father or to his appointed Attorney, or his successors, to the proper & honest payment of which we oblige ourselves jointly & severally on our own behalf in respect of the whole sum and, immutably, in its entirety, our heirs, executors & administrators through the present document, sealed with our seals, issued on the 18th day of January in the year of the reign of our lord Charles by the grace of God of England Scotland [France and Ireland] and in the year of the Lord (in English Style) 1642.

Sealed and delivered in the presence of *[signatures too faded to be read].*

Condition: The condicōn of this obligation is . . . *[damaged].*

. . . [the] within named Randle Woodfen and Richard Woodfen doe well and trule administer . . .Cattalls and chattells of John Woodfen late of Chorley in Wrenbury [chapelry in the diocese of Chester] . . . [ed] according to the effects of Letters of Administration granted unto them in that behalfe
. . . [ed] att the tyme of his decease soe farr as the same goods rights credits in
. . . extend & as the law in that behalfe will charge them And doe exhibite in
. . . administer a true & perfecte Inventory of the goods rights credits cattells & Chattells
. . . full and just accompte unto the within named reverend father his vicar generall

. . . when and as often as they shalbee thereunto lawfully called or required And also

. . . thoes rights credits cattells & Chattells as shalbee found due and remaining upon

. . . shall distribute and dispose as by the discretion of the said reverend father his

. . . that behalfe shalbee limited and appointed And finally doe att all tymes

. . . Reverend father his vicar generall and all other his officers and ministers for and

. . . of Administration Then this obligacion to bee voyd and of none effecte of bee

. . . virtue.

119. RICHARD CULLINER ALIAS COMBER[a] OF WRENBURY FRITH, LABOURER

C.(S) Pr. 29 October 1644
Nuncupative will 20 October 1644
Burial: none recorded at Wrenbury or Marbury

Brethren	Richard Culliner alias Comber	George Culliner of Elsud'
fl. 1644	fl. 1644	fl. 1644

Will, sick.

The last will and testament of Richard Culliner alias Comber of the parish of Wrenbury in the County of Chester laborror published and declared by word of mouth before the wittnesses hereafter named the 20 day of October 1644. First: In regard of the paines and Charges that John Wilkinson the yonger hath had with mee, in my longe time of disseases & sicknes I doe give and bequeath unto the said John, the some of £10 which hee oweth unto mee by Specialty. Item In regard of houseroome, bedroome and other certifies I have received & had from Thomas Woollam of the parish abovesaid in my longe time of sicknes and Disseases I doe I doe [*sic*] give and bequeath unto the said Thomas £10 I have in John Savages hande & George Flechers due unto mee by Specialty. Item I doe give unto the said Thomas Woollam £4 which I have in Katherine Tennches hande due unto me by Specialty. Item one Condicōn that Randle Weaver of Wrenbury shall helpe mee with Some presente moneyes in my necessity & allowe somethinge to be payde to bringinge mee honestly whome, I doe give & bequeath unto him the £5 hee oweth mee by Specialty. Item If my Souerion Richard Massie deale honest-

---

[a] Filed as COMBER at CRO.

ly with mee, & as hee ought my will is that hee shall have 20s. Item I give unto Katherine Pemberton servante to the said Thomas Woollam & Ellioner Daughty 22s. which Mr Roger Broome oweth unto mee to bee equally devided betwixte them. Item I doe give & bequeath unto my breethren 12d. apeece.

Executors: John Wilkinsson and Thomas Woollam.

And I doe give & bequeath unto them the remaynder of my moneyes (if it will be gotten) to bee equally devided betwixte them.

Witnesses: Margarett Smyth her marke, Kathrine Pemberton her marke, Ellionor Daughty her marke.

Inventory: Richard Culliner alias Comber of Wrenbury Frith.

Taken: 23 October 1644

Of: goods Cattells & Chattells.

Prisers: Thomas Spencer, John Twisse, Randle Weaver and John Wilkinson, thelder.

	£	s	d
his wearinge apprell		6	8
Twoo little heoffers		1	6
Widdowe Tench of Smeatonwood due by bond	4	0	0
Randle Weaver of Wrenbury due by bond	5	8	0
John Savage of Wrenbury due by bond	10	16	0
George Culliner of Elsud' [*Elson, Shropshire?*] due by bond	1	19	0
Richard Hitley by bond of due	10	16	0
John Wilkinson by bond due	10	0	0
Some totall	43	17	2

Thomas Spencer his marke
John Twisse John Twisse
Randle Weaver his marke
John Wilkinson senior his marke

Exhibited as true 29 October 1644

Endorsement: Exhibited 29 October 1644; administration granted to the executors named in the said will.

120. RALPH MALKIN [MEAKIN] OF NEWHALL, YEOMAN

I? Pr. PCC 10 October 1645
W.T. 16 January 1644/45
Burial: none recorded at Wrenbury [no entries 1644–45 at Audlem]

Ralph Malkin^a = [ ]	Margery Malkin of Adderley

Ralph Malkin^a = [ ]
fl. 1614
† 1645

Raffe
c. 1614 *fil. Rad.*
† 1622/23

Margery Malkin of Adderley
fl. 1644

Douce Malkin
fl. 1644

Will, sick.

Firste I comend my soule into the hands of God my faithfull Creatour and Redeemer. And my body to the earth whence it was taken. And after my funerall expences discharged I bequeath to Thomas Hamnite of thaforesaid Newhall in the said countie of Chester All that is mine wearing apparrell goods, Cattles and chattles moveable and unmoveable, all monies that are due to me, both that which I have bonds for, and 53s. more that William Mullenders borrowed of me that I will him to pay to Thomas Hamnite mine Atturney when he shall call for it, Excepting onely (notwithstanding all aforesaid) one bible that is in the dwelling house of Margery Malkin of Adderley my sister which I bequeath to Douce Malkin the daughter of thabovesaid Margerie.

Executor: Thomas Hamnite of Newhall.

Overseer: Richard Hamnite the elder, yeoman of Newhall.

H. & S.
The marke of Ralph Malkin

Witnesses: John Palin 1644, George Hamnite, Matthew Jenkyn.

Endorsemeent: Probated at London before Nathaniele Brent, knight, doctor of laws, 10 October 1645; administration granted to Thomas Hamnett, one of the executors named in the said will.

---

^a That the PCC – *Malkin* – is most likely incorrect is suggested by the Parish records which contain several entries for *Meakin*, including that of Raffe, *filius Radulfi* in 1614.

121. EDWARD HAMNETT THE ELDER OF ASTON IN NEWHALL, YEOMAN

Pr. PCC 18 June 1646
W.T. 18 June 1645
Buried: 21 June 1645

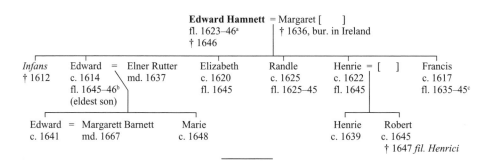

Will, sick.

Firste I give bequeath and yeild up willinglie my soule into the hands of Allmightie God trusting and beleiving by the merits of the death and passion of Jesus Christ my savior to have free pardon & remission of all my sins. And my bodie I comitt to the earth to be decentlie buried in Christian buriall at the discrecōn of my Executors hereafter named. And for the temporall estate which Allmightie God of his great bountie and mercie hath enriched me withall I will and dispose therof as followeth. First I give and bequeath unto my eldest sonne Edward Hamnett 12d. Item I doe give & bequeath unto my sonne Henrie Hamnett £10 out of the sum of forty poundes which my said sonne Edward Hamnett oweth unto me by specialtie Item I doe give & bequeath unto my sonne Randle Hamnett £10 out of the said sum of £40. Item I doe give & bequeath unto my two daughters Francis Hamnett & Elizabeth Hamnett £10 a peece being the remainder of the said sum of £40 Item I doe give & bequeath unto my said two daughters Frances and Elizabeth £35 a peece out of the sum of £100 which Lewis Nightingale of Coole Lane oweth unto me. And my will & mind is that my said two daughters shall receive the use and interest that shalbe due for their said severall porcōns from

---

a CRO Newhall Manor Court Roll 1623; CRO Newhall Rentals, 1625.
b It is Edward Hamnett the younger who was a priser of the goods of Richard Barnett of Aston in Newhall on 5 June 1646 (will no. 125), since Edward the elder was already dead.
c Whether this is the same Francis Hamnett who married Hugh Loyde in 1669 at Wrenbury (see Parish Register, 1669) is not certain, but it is a reasonable assumption.

the feast of St Michaell Tharchangell last past before the date of theis presents during my life for and towards the encreasing and augmenting of the same. Item I doe give and bequeath unto my said two daughters either of them a guilded silver spoone Item I doe give and bequeath unto my said two daughter all my insett or household goods as bedding, naperie, Linens, brasse, pewter, bedsteds, tables, cupboards, chestes, & such like to be equallie divided betwixt them. Item moreover I doe give & bequeath unto my said two daughters five of my kine called by the names of Silke, Starr, Pettock, Filbooke, & the winter cowe, to be equallie divided betwixt them, & my will & minde is that if any of them shalbe seized upon for my herriott that in liew thereof they shall make their choice out of the rest of my Cowes. Item I doe give & bequeath unto my said sonne Randle Hamnett £6 13s. & 4d. out of the abovesaid sum of £100. Item I doe give and bequeath unto my said sonne Henrie Hamnett one silver spoone Item I doe give & bequeath unto my said sonne Henrie Hamnett the remainder of the said sum of £100 20s. of interest due unto me for the same at our Lady day last past & also all the rest & residue of all my goods, corne, cattles & chattells pay-ing my debts and discharging my funerall expences. Item my will is that if it hap-pen that anie of my said fower younger children doe decease (which God it defend) before they receive their said severall porcōns that his or her porcōn soe deceased shalbe equallie divided amongst the rest that survive.

Executors: the testator's son, Henrie Hamnett, and his 'welbeloved in Christ' Robert Hassall of Newhall yeoman.

I doe give & bequeath unto the said Robert Hassall towards his paines herein to be unpleged 10s.

H. & S.
Edward Hamnett his marke.

Witnesses: George Hall, Thomas Gray.

Endorsement: Probated at London before Nathaniele Brent, knight, doctor of laws, 18 *[originally given as 8]* June 1646; administration to Henry Hamnett son of the deceased and one of the executors named in the said will. Robert Hassall, the other executor named in the said will, having since died.

122. DOROTHY COTTON OF COMBERMERE, SPINSTER

S.Pr. 5 June 1647
W.T. 16 April 1646
Buried: 7 April 1647

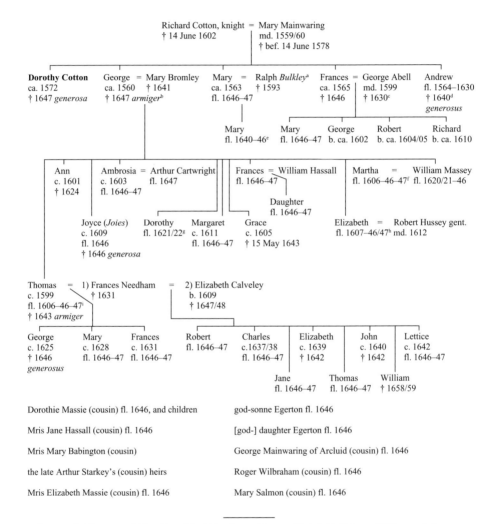

Dorothie Massie (cousin) fl. 1646, and children

Mris Jane Hassall (cousin) fl. 1646

Mris Mary Babington (cousin)

the late Arthur Starkey's (cousin) heirs

Mris Elizabeth Massie (cousin) fl. 1646

god-sonne Egerton fl. 1646

[god-] daughter Egerton fl. 1646

George Mainwaring of Arcluid (cousin) fl. 1646

Roger Wilbraham (cousin) fl. 1646

Mary Salmon (cousin) fl. 1646

---

[a]   Ormerod, *History of Cheshire*, iii. 211, shows him as Ralph Bulkley of Woore, Salop., not *William* as in St George, Visitation Pedigrees 1613, p. 66.

[b]   See will of George Cotton of Combermere, pr. 1648 (will no. 128).

[c]   See *International Genealogical Index*, Church of Jesus Christ of Latter-day Saints, ver. 5.1; also *Ancestral File* AFN: FKK6-X1, showing place of burial as Hemington Parish, Leicestershire.

Will, sick.

First I comend my soule into the hands of the Allmighty, my most mercifull Lord, and Saviour, in full assurance of the pardon of all my sins, and of an Inheritance in the Heavens, of his [meere] mercy, in Christ Jesus, who shall change this my vile body, that it may be fashioned like unto his glorious Body according to the mighty working whereby he is able to subdue all things unto himself, In assured hope of which most blessed change, *I desire that my Body maybe interred, as neere as may be to the body of my late deare Brother Mr. Andrew Cotton.* As touching these worldly goods wherewith it hathe pleased almighty God yet to trust mee, First I give and bequeath to my ever honoured Deare Brother Mr George Cotton above-named one piece of gold of sixe pounds; To my Cousin Mistris Martha Cotton 20s., To my Cousin, Mistris Ambrosia Cotton, 20s. To my Cousin Joyce Cotton £5, to my Cousin Margrett Cotton £5, my Feather bedd that is plaine without blew Inkle?, my Bolster, pillowes, and my white mantle, To my good Cousin Mr. William Massie of the Mosse £15, my great silver spoone, and all my English Bookes which I have usually kept in my new Cupboard. To my Cousin Dorothey Massie £5 pounds, my Rubie ring, my Corall Bracelett, my great Cabinett and Spice Boxe, my Trunke that contaynes my best linnens, with halfe the linnens therein, the other halfe of my best linnens, usually kept in the sayd Truncke, I give to my Cousin Mary Abell. To my deare Cousin Mr. George Cotton I give and bequeath my great Silver Can, and to my Cousin his wife my great silver dish; To my cousin Mary Cotton my great silver spoone, and £5 in moneys, To my Cousin Francis Cotton £4, To my Cousin Robert Cotton £4. To my Cousin Charles Cotton £4 To my Cousin Lattice Cotton £4. To my sister Bulkeley I give & bequeath 40s., To every one of her Children 20s. a piece, To each of my Cousin Massies Children I give £4, To my Cousin Mistris Jane Hassall I give my gilt Bolle, To my Cousin Mistris Mary Babington I give 40s. yearely during my lease of parte of the Lands belonging to the Hall of Wrenbury, if shee so long lives; The two last yeares of my Terme in the sayd Lands in Wrenbury I give and bequeath to the right heyres

---

[d] See will of Andrew Cotton, pr. 1640 (will no. 111). Robert and Richard Abell appear both to have emigrated to America, thus accounting for their absence from the Cotton wills of the 1640s.

[e] The will of Andrew Cotton (will no. 111) refers to Mary Bulkley, who was to receive 20s., as his god-daughter; she was clearly Mary's daughter. The will of Dorothy Cotton refers simply to the children of 'my sister Bulkeley'.

[f] Bequeathed £20 in will of Robert Buckley, pr. 1607/08 (will no. 24).

[g] CRO ZCR 72/2/1 contains a marriage indenture between William Massie and Dorothy Cotton, daughter of George Cotton of Combermere, made 1 March 19 James I: parties to the agreement were George Cotton of Combermere, William Massie of Audlem; a £600 marriage portion was pledged by Massie; reference is made to manors, messuages, lands, tenements and hereditaments of Massie in Audlem, Denfield, Wrenbury, Wrenbury Frith, and elsewhere in the county of Chester. A licence to marry was issued 13 Feb. 1621/22 to William Massey, esq., and Dorothy Cotton, and the Wrenbury Parish Register contains a marriage entry for 4 March 1621/22.

[h] Bequeathed £20 in Robert Buckley's will (will no. 24).

[i] Bequeathed £10 in Robert Buckley's will.

of my late deceased Cousin Mr. Arthure Starkey, they paying therfore, £4 yearely to my executores or their assignes, to be distributed among the poore of Wrenbury Parish, such as shall be thought fitt objects of Charity by my Brother Cotton or his heyres. To my Cousin Mistris Elizabeth Massie I give £10, and my Damaske gowne To my Cousin Mary Abell £5 in money, the rents and proffits of Thomas Steele of Leighton his Howse and lands for the two yeares next after my decease, my best safeguard, and my best saddle Cloth; To my Sonne Egerton of Christleton £5, To my daughter Egerton 20s., To my Cousin Mary Salmon 40s., To my Cousin Frances Hassall 20s., and to her eldest daughter 20s. to buy either of them a ring, To Mr Harwar 20s., To Thomas Graye the Clerk 10s., To Thomas Steele of Leighton aforsayd the last yeare of the terme I have in his house and the lands therto belonging, To Mr Chambres of Betton the last £10 Ive to be payed from him to me, and to Thomas Orton the last yeare of the terme I have in the terme his Tenement, To my Brother Cotton's servants, men and mayds, to be divided as my Cousin Massie shall think fit among them, I give £5, whereof my will is that Margery Robinson shall have the largest share To my Cousin George Manwaring of Arcluid £5. I give to my sayd cousin George Manwaring To his wife 40s., and the Can of Silver which was my brother Andrewes [?] To Mistris Nicholls £5, To Randull Walton £5, To the poore of Wrenbury Parish, I meane such poore as my Brother Cotton or his heyres shall comend to be of lowest conversation, £4 yearely during all my terme in Wrenbury grownds aforesayd, saving the two last yeares thereof, for which two last yeares, I have herein, before limited the same to be payed by the heyres of my Cousin Starkey, out of the proffitts of the sayd lands which for the two sayd last yeares I have upon that Condicōn, hereby bequethed to them. To my Cousin Mary Babington my two best and largest linnen shifts, and one Apron, To my Cousin George Manwaring aforesayd, Mr. Perkins works in 3 volumes Mr Grantam's workes, the Doctrine of the gospell, Two of Dr. Prestons Bookes & Mr. Balls treatise of faith;[a] To Margery Barlowe 10s., To Alice Weaver 5s. If hereafter I shall thinke of any farther legacy to any of my Friends, and expresse the same under my hand writing before two or more sufficient witnesses, I doe hereby appoynt such writing to be taken as part of this my will. The rest of my goods, and Chattells I give to my under named executors to be equally divided between them then if ther be any remayning after the payment of debts, & legacies, my owne and late deare Brother Andrews, and the erecting a small monument for him to the valew of Twenty markes or thereabouts, if which I desire may be donne when God shall restore an happy peace in the Land To my Cousin Mris Elizabeth Cotton late the wife of my deare cousin [Thomas] Cotton 20s. To my worthy Cousin Mr Roger Wilbraham 20s. To William Bennett besides his part in the £5 above mentioned I give 10s. To Joane Massie 10s.

Executors: the testator's cousins above named, Mr. William Massie of the Mosse and George Mainwaring.

H. & S.
Dorithy Cotton

---

[a] On the more exact nature of Dorothy Cotton's books, see above, Introduction, pp. xxxvi–vii.

Witnesses: David Ridgeway, William Benett.

Inventory: Dorothy Cotton of Combermere, spinster.
Taken: 22 April 1647, 23 Charles I

Of: goods cattells and Chattels.

Prisers: Robert Tudman, William Bennett, George Cooke, and Francis Moore

	£	s	d
One Assignement from Thomas Steele of a Messuage and Lands for one and Twentie yeares whereby there is a reservacōn of 24 per annum; of which sayd Terme there remaines five yeares unexpired The last of which yeares but 14 charged to Steele	50	0	0
Another assizement from Thomas Orton of a Tenement and lande for 21 yeares wherein there is referred £12 per annum of which sayd Terme ther remaines 8 yeares unexpired	60	0	0
Five lands from Mr. Arthure Chambre for the payment of the yearely sume of Twenty pounds att Michaelmas, and the annunciation by equall porcōns The last payment whereof become due att the annunciation 1646 whereof received £36 13s. 4d., remaines	73	7	8
In ready gold	14	5	0
In ready silver	12	11	0
One Bond of £40 more	40	0	0
Lynnens, and Nappery of all sorts	2	6	8
Three Trunckes, one Cabinett, one Chest, Seven Boxes in her Chamber	2	16	0
One Chest more, a close stoole, five Boxes, a looking glass and foure Basketts	1	5	4
foure Chaires, and foure Cushions		16	0
Brasse and Pewter of all sorts and a warming panne	1	9	0
One Paire of Bellowes, Anndirons, three fire Shovles, and other Iron ware of all sorts		10	0
Her Bedding, pillowes, and Bolsters, Curtaines and Valence, coverings, and other appurtanances therto belonging	5	6	8
Her Bookes	3	6	8
Her plate	8	5	0
Her Diamond Ring	2	13	4
Glasse bottles, Glasses, vialls, Earthen potts, a burning glasse a Standish, and all small Boxes, and other Small Comodities as they now stand in her Closett, and not before mencōned	1	13	4
Her wereing Apparrell	30	0	0
Debts and Arreres due from severall persons to the decedent both good and badd	74	0	0
Sum total	374	6	8

Robert Tudman
George Cooke
William Bennett
Francis Moore

Exhibited as true 5 June 1647.

Endorsement: Probated 5 June 1647; administration granted to the executors named in the said will.

123. VALENTINE WOOLRICH OF WRENBURY FRITH, YEOMAN

S.Pr. 26 October 1647
W.T. 26 January 1641/42, 17 Charles I
Buried: 3 February 1641/42

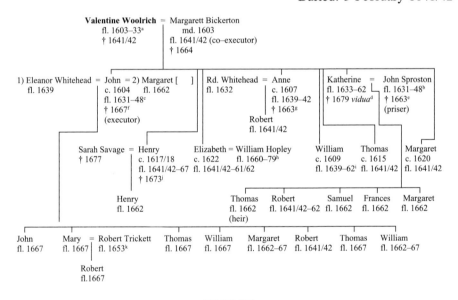

[a]   Valentine Woolrich was an appraiser of the property of Robert Tenche, 1615 (will no. 45); an appraiser for the estate of Robert Wade, 1633/34 (will no. 95); also did inventory for Richard Cheswis, 1632/33 (will no. 93). According to the IPM for Thomas Minshull of Erdswick, taken 27 September 1616 at Middlewich (see R. Stewart Brown, *Cheshire Inquisitions Post Mortem*, ii. 207), Valentine *Woodrich* was one of several tenants at Wrenbury Park in Wrenbury on lands belonging to Minshull.

Will, sick.

First I give and yeld up willingly my soule into the hands of Almighty God who first gave it mee to frytly beleevinge throwe the merritte only and death of Jesus Christ my saviour to have free pardon and remyssion of all my sinnes, and *my body I committ to the earth from whence it came to bee decently buryed in Christian buryall in the parish Church yard of Wrenbury*, att the discrecōn of my executor hererafter named; And for the temporal estate which Almighty God of his bounty andmercy hath inriched mee withall I will and dispose therof as followeth: First I doo give and bequeath unto Mr. Peartree preacher att Wrenbury tenne schillings to preach att my funerall. Item I doe give and devise and bequeath all the right revercōn and intereste I have reserved in all my Lande Tenemente and hereditamente situate lyinge and beinge in Wrenbury Frith with in the said County, in my owne power yett to dispose of, (as by one deede or Feaffemente beareinge date the Seaventh day of November in ther fifteenth yeare of the raigne of our said sovigne Lord kinge Charles of England etc. for the defaulte of the heires males of the body of my eldeste sonne John Woolrich, lawfully begotten or to bee begotten, to the use and behoofe of my sonne Henry Woolrich and the heires males of his body lawfully begotten or to bee begotten, And for default of such yssue, to the use and behoofe of my sonne William Woolrich and his heires males of his body lawfully begotten or to bee begotten, And for default of such yssue, the use and behoofe of the yssue male of the body of my sonne Thomas Woolrich (in case hee have twoo sonnes) beinge lawfully begotten or to bee begotten; And for default of such yssue to the use and behoofe of my grandchildren Roberte Sproston sonne of John Sproston of Wrenbury aforesaid, And Roberte Whitehead sonne of Richard Whitehead of Aston Mondrom in the said county, & to the onely use and behoofe of their heirs and assignes for evermore, the said Henry Woolwich & his heires & every other person and persons, to whom the said Messuage Lande & Tenemente & hereditamente shall happen to e[?] and

---

b Priser for Emma Barnett, will pr. 1631 (will no. 87); priser for Margaret Graye, to whom he owed £3 20s., and noted as uncle of Margaret Sproston in Margaret Graye's will, pr. 1632 (will no. 89); married 1633; witness and priser for Randle Sproston, will pr. 1648 (will no. 130).

c John Woolrich had £20 belonging to Henry Griffith Sr in 1652; see will of Henry Griffith, pr. 1658 (will no. 145). William Fergusson Irvine, *Chester Licences*, iv. 27: 20 November 1639, John Woolrich and Elleanor Whitehead, of Acton, at Acton and Wrenbury.

d See will of Katherine Sproston, widow, pr. 1679/ CRO.

e See will of John Sproston, yeoman of Wrenbury, pr. 1663/ CRO.

f See will of John Woolrich, yeoman of Wrenbury Frith, pr. 1667/ CRO.

g See will of John Sproston, yeoman of Wrenbury, pr. 1663/ CRO.

h Married 1660; made inventory for John Woolrich 1667; noted in will of Katherine Sproston, pr. 1679/CRO.

i William Fergusson Irvine, *Chester Licences*, iv. 7: 10 June 1639, William Woolldridge, of Wrenbury parish, and Matilda Heath, spinster; at Wrenbury and Malpas. She died 1658/59 (buried as *Maudlin*).

j See will of Henry Woolrich of Wrenbury, yeoman, pr. 1673/ CRO.

k Copy-holder at Newhall; see CRO Newhall Manor Court Rolls.

come (by force of Presents yeldinge payeinge performingeing and doeing all such some and somes, acte and actes, thinge & thinges as the said messuages Lande Tenemente and hereditamente, by vertue of the said deede or Feoffemente, stand lawfully charged withall: Item I doe give and bequeath unto my said sonne Henry Woolrich in full satisfaxton of his childes parte and of such somes of money as I stand indebtted unto him my ffoure steeres, one whitefased heifer, and all my tooles that belonge to my occupacōn or trade of a plummer, & all the mettells as pewter & lead yt att the time of my death shall bee in my hande to use in anay of my tradeinge: Item I doe give and bequeath unto my loevinge wife Margarett Woolrich, all my Corne and graine, boeth one the ground, and in my house and barne towarde her house keepinge. Item I doe give and bequeath unto my said sonne John Woolrich my bay nagg. Item I doe give and bequeath unto my said sonne William Woolrich my lesser black Calfe. Item I give and bequeath unto my said sonne Thomas Woolrich 12d. Item I doe give and bequeath unto my daughter Katherine Sproston 12d. Item I doe give and bequeath unto my daughter Anne Whitehead my greate brasse kettell & three pewter dishes. Item I doe give and bequeath unto all my grandchildren 6s. 8d. apeace. Item I doe hereby devise, give, and bequeath, all the reste residue & remaynder of all my goods, Cattells and Chattells, boeth moveable and unmoveable goods of what kinde or quality soever the sime bee or wheresoever the sime remayneth, my debtts beinge therout firste paid, & my funerall expenses being discharged, unto my said wife Margarett Woolrich, and to my two youngeste daughters Margarett Woolrich & Elizabeath Woolrich, to bee equally devided amongste them.

Executors: the testator's wife, Margarett Woolrich, and his son, John Woolrich.

H. & S.
Signed Valentine Woolrich
His Vmarke

Witnesses: Henry Rutter, John Sproston, Richard Burrowes his marke and Thomas Gray.

Inventory: Valentine Woolrich of Wrenbury Frith, yeoman.

Taken: 14 February 1646/47

Of: goodes Cattels & Chattels.

Prisers: John Heath, John Tench, John Savich and John Sproson.

	£	s	s
Eaight cowes	26	13	4
Five yong beafe	13	0	0
Six yong beafe	9	0	0
One nagge	3	0	0
One mare	3	10	0

Tow calfes	1	15	0
For heay	3	6	8
Corne sone and vnsone	18	0	0
Cartes plowes and all towles for hosbandrie	6	13	4
Bras	6	0	0
Pewter	6	13	4
Dreeping panes grates and such iron ware	1	10	0
Puter leade and all the towles belonging to the trad or profechtion of a plummer	13	6	8
Bed and beding	13	0	0
Bed stockes	1	15	0
Linenes yarne and toe	10	0	0
Cofferes		15	0
One pres one table and formes	2	0	0
Boordes and shilfes and a chese prese with tow little cobboordes And a table	1	0	0
Varyes *[various]*		13	4
Corne basketes and sackes for corne		10	0
Trene ware	1	0	0
Chese and butter	1	0	0
Beefe and bacon	1	10	0
Soote trey		6	8
Swill and mucke		10	0
Cheres and stowles chochinies		10	0
Three powndes of moneay	3	0	0
Wearing apparil	5	0	0
[Sum]	154	18	4

Endorsement: Probated 26 October 1647; administration granted to the executors named in the said will. The inventory was exhibited by the executors *cum protestatōne* on 26 October 1647.

124. ROBERT SAVAGE OF WRENBURY, YEOMAN

S.Pr. 29 October 1647
W.T. 6 May 1645
Burial: none recorded at Wrenbury

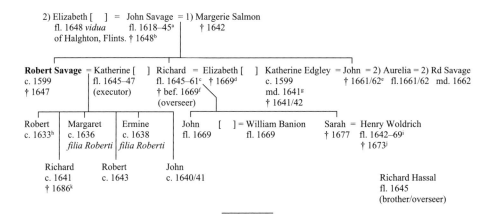

Will, sick.

Firste I give & bequeath my soule to Almightie god my heavenly father who made heaven & earth & hope through the merritts of Jesus Christ his sonne my Redeemer he will have mercie on my soule & pardon my sinnes and for my bodie I committ to the earth from whence I came and to be buried & brought home at the descretion of my wife & overseeers Alsoe I give and bequeath nigh my goods Chattells Leases debts and whatsoever ells in this world I have inioyed unto my Loveinge wife Katherne Savage trusting that she will provide to bringe up my

---

^a Made inventory for John Edgeley, will pr. 1637 (will no. 102); owed Richard Culliner alias Comber £10 16s. 1644 (will no. 119); owed Robert Savage debts of £10 and £110 in 1645.
^b See administration of John Savage, 1648. (no. 131).
^c See will of John Savage of Wrenbury, pr. 1661/CRO.
^d See will of Elizabeth Savage, widow of Richard Savage, pr. 1669/ CRO.
^e See will of John Savage, pr. 1661/62/CRO.
^f See will of Elizabeth Savage, widow of Richard Savage, pr. 1669/ CRO.
^g William Fergusson Irvine, *Chester Licences*, iv. 87: 8 May 1641, to John Savage of Wrenbury and Katherine Edgley, spinster of Wrenbury; bondsman, Godfrey Leigh; at Wrenbury, Acton and Marbury.
^h Wrenbury Bishop's Transcripts – Baptisms: 1632, 1633, 1636. These are quite clearly Robert's children, and his will clearly states that he had but three. The Frances, c. 1630, and [ ] c. 1631, are thus presumably the children of John Savage and Katherine Edgley.
ⁱ See will of Valentine Woolrich, made January 1641/42, pr. 1647 (will no. 123).
^j See will of Henry Woolrich, yeoman of Wrenbury, pr. 1673/CRO.
^k See will of Richard Savage of Newhall, yeoman, pr. 1686/CRO.

Chilldrne with fear of God & keep them with all mentaynnance as she is able But in case my said wife Marrie then my said will is that desire that my wife shall with the advise of my overseers sett a parte one halfe of my estate which I shall if please God at the day of my death leave for the advancement of my Three Children to be devided in Equall proportions to be sett out; & the other halfe I freely & willingly give to my Wife my debts & buriall discharged.

Executor: the testator's wife, Katherine Savage.
Overseers: the testator's brother, Richard Savage, and his brother, Richard Hassall[a].

(signature)
Robart Savage

Witness: Richard Wicksteed.

Inventory: Robert Savage of Wrenbury, yeoman.

Taken: 29 October 1647

Of: goods Cattells & Chattells.

Prisers: Richard Davenporte gent., Roberte Heath, William Hassall, John Sparke and Richard Hassall yeomen.

	£	s	d
his weareinge apprell	3	6	8
Bedsteds quoffers tables, one presse one Cubbord, stooles formes & shilves	3	10	0
in Beddinge	7	0	0
in Brasse	3	10	0
in Pewter	2	0	0
Linnens & Napprie	4	0	0
one Iron pott one grate & all other Ironware in the house		15	0
Twoo Cheese tubbes one Cheese presse turnills & all other treeneanware	2	0	0
Straw basketts ticknallware and all other trumperie in the house		10	0
in muck & fuell aboute the house	1	0	0
in hay and Corne in the house in the barne & in & upon the ground	3	10	0

---

[a] As will be noted elsewhere in this volume, the wording of this phrase 'my brother Richard Hassall', identical with 'my brother Richard Savage', allows several possible explanations: 1) Richard Hassal was the brother of Robert Savage's wife, Katherine, and was technically his brother-in-law; 2) Robert Savage's father, John Savage († 1648) had a previous wife to Margerie, and this first wife was the mother of Robert Savage and his siblings, while Margerie was mother to Richard Hassall; 3) John Savage († 1648) remarried following Katherine's death in 1641/42, and this unidentified second wife was the mother of Richard Hassall.

Carts plowes harrowes yoakes Chaynes plowtimber & other ymplements of husbandrie	4	0	0
Foure reareinge swine	1	0	0
provission in the house	1	0	0
in redy money in the house & in his owne purse	2	10	0
Twenty Seaven kine & one Bull	60	[ ]	0
Fifteene yonge Cattell	18	0	0
one lame Nagg		4	0

In debtts oweinge by specialty

from John Savage of Wrenbury	110	0	0
In debtt oweinge by the same John Savage without specialty	10	0	0
In debtts & redy money some by specialty & some in the testators hands & in freinds hands	100	0	0
A debtt oweinge by John Cheswis of Mickley gent	10	0	0
Totall	347	15	8

Endorsement: Probated 29 October 1647; administration granted to the sole executor named in the said will.

NOTE: Mistakenly 1645 at end of endorsement became filing/catalogue date – proved 1647.

125. RICHARD BARNETT OF ASTON IN NEWHALL, YEOMAN

S.Pr. 18 January 1647/48
W.T. 28 February 1645/46
Buried: 20 May 1646
Renunciation: 18 January 1647/48

```
                    Richard Barnett = Joan [    ]
                    † 1600 senex    | † 1619 anus vidua Richardi
            ┌──────────────┐
    Randle Twisse      Margaret Twisse = John Barnett
    fl. 1603–35/6ᵃ     md. 1602       | fl. 1602–31ᵇ
    † 1659ᶜ            fl. 1628–33ᵈ   | † 1633ᵉ

  Ellenor    Richard Barnett = Katherine [    ]   Elizabeth    James = [    ]   3 younger Chh.
  c. 1602/03   c. 1618     fl. 1631–45/46         c. 1610      c. 1621         fl. 1628
  fl. 1610     fl. 1628–31 (executor)             fl. 1628     fl. 1628–47
               † 1646                                          † 1672ᶠ
                                                               (executor)
      Richard                Thomas    Marie    James            Margaret   John
      c. 1613                c. 1615   c. 1615/16 † 1618 infans    c. 1622    c. 1623/24
      † 1613 infans          fil. Joh.                            † 1622 infans

  John        Marie      Margaret    Frances            John         Margaret
  fl. 1645/46 c. 1641    c. 1643     fl. 1645/46        c. 1647      c. 1648
  (oldest child) fl. 1645/46 fl. 1645/46                † 1647 fil. Jac.
```

Will, sick.

Firste I give bequeath & yelde upp Willingly my soule into the hands of Almighty god who firste gave it mee, trustinge & stedfastly beleeveinge by the merritts of the death & passion of Jesus Christe my saviour, to have free pardon & remission of all my sinnes, and my body I remmitt to the earth from whence it came, to bee decently, buryed in Christian buryall, att the Discrecōn of my executors hereafter named, And for that temporall estate, Which Almighty god of his bounty & mercy hath enriched mee with all, I will, & Dispose theereof as followeth: Imprimis I give and bequeath unto every Child I have twelve pence a peece besides What I shall heereafter bequeath unto any of them by this my laste Will Item I Doe give & bequeath unto my sonne John Barnett all the husbandrie ware, as

---

ᵃ Priser for John Barnett of Aston, 1633 (will no. 94)..
ᵇ See CRO Newhall Manor Court Rolls, 1611, 1631.
ᶜ Buried as *Ralph* Twisse.
ᵈ See will of husband, John Barnett, made 1628, pr. 1633 (will no. 94). The John Barnett who married Catherine Cheswis 1605 at Wrenbury appears to have been a different individual.
ᵉ See will of John Barnett of Aston, pr. 1633.
ᶠ Yeoman of Aston; see nuncupative will, pr. 1672/CRO.

Carts plowes harrowes, & such like as shall bee att my howse after the decease of Kathrine Barnett my wife. Item I give & bequeath unto my daughter Marie Barnett, my presse: Item I give & bequeath unto Margerett Barnett my daughter my joyned Cheste: Item whereas I am confidente that my said wife Kathrine Barnett will bee a loveinge & kinde mother unto my Children, & bee carefell to bringe them upp, I Doe give & bequeath unto my said wife the full moety & one halfe of all my goods Cattells & Chattells & house hould Stuffe, boeth moveable & unmoveable, whatsoever the same bee or wheeresoever the same remayneth: Item wheereas I am indebtted to the value of threescore pounds or theere abouts, I Doe heereby give devise and, bequeath unto my executors heereafter named the other halfe and full moety of all my goods Cattells & Chattells househould Stuffe, & goods moveable & unmovable Whatsoever, to bee by them imployed, for and towards the payment of my said debtts soe farre as the somme Will extend, & wheereas I ham Doubtfull, that the said laste mencōned moety of my said estate, will bee twoo shorte, for to Dishcharge my said debtts: I Doe heereby demyse, give, grannte, devise & bequeath unto my said executors heereafter named the one halfe, & full moety of all my Messuage & tennements wherein I live & of all howses Edifice buildings, lands Tennements Meadowes leasowes & pastures to the same belonginge or appertaineing, with all & singular thappertenances, emediatly from & after my decease for & dureinge the tearme of three Yeares from thence nexte & ymediatly followinge & soe from three yeares to three yeares nexte & imediatly ensuinge, one after an other unto the full ende & tearme of nine yeares according to the Custome of the Mannor of Newhall, & my will & minde is, & I doe heereby devise that my said executors hereafter named, shall converte & imploye, soe much of the yssues & Asetts, that shall be reased out of the same, for & toward the paymente of soe much of my said debtts, as shall bee Wantinge in the said moety of my said goods: And after my said debtts are payed & discharged, my will & mind is that my said Executors heereafter named, shall converte & imploye, the said moety of my said Messuage lands & premisses to the beste use for & towards the reasinge of porcōns for my three yonger Children Marie Barnett Margarett Barnett & Frances Barnett dureinge all the said severall tearmes: & further my will & minde is, & I doe repose so much truste in my said executors, that they shall converte & ymploye, all such some or somes of money soe rayesed of the said moety of my said Messuage lands & premisses, for the use of my said three yonger Children unto the beste use & benefite untill my said three yonger Children & every of them shall attayne their severall ages of 21 yeares, & then the same by my said executors to bee equally devided amoungeste them, & if any of my said three yonger Children doe decease before shee or they doe attayne their severall ages, (as god it defends) that her or their porcōn soe deceaseing, shall bee equaly devided, amoungeste those that survive: Item I doe give & bequeath unto my said sonne John Barnett my swoord; Item my will & minde is & I doe heereby devise & ordayne that my said sonne John Barnett after thend & expiracōn of the said tearms of Nine Yeares, shall have his mayntenance & keepeinge, out of the said moety of my said Messuage lands & premisses, untill hee shall attayne the full age of twenty & one yeares; And that my said executors heereafter named shall converte & ymploye the overplus theereof, dureinge all that time for & towards, the mayntenance bringinge upp, or augmentacōn of the porcōns of my said three yonger Children, soe & in such force as to my said executors heereafter named shall bee thought moste meete & conveniente, with out accompt guidinge unto my said sonne John Barnett for, the same; And although I doe conceive, that I have by aformer estate by mee made of my Lands & tennements disabled my selfe for the chargeinge of my said sonne, with any parte or portions, for my said yonger Children, (which oversight now very much troubleth mee) yett I doe desire, & my will & minde is that my said sonne, shall att his marriage, or att his enteringe upon his whole meanes, (whether sall firste happen) paye unto my said three yonger Children, or soe many of them as shall bee then liveinge, twenty Markes apeece, for & towards the augmentacōn of their severall porcōns, Item my will & minde is that my Executors heereafter named shall bee payed & discharged their expences out of my estate . . . & I doe give unto my said brother twenty shillings in money for his paynes heerein to be ymployed; And my will & minde is that if my said sonne doe refuse to paye unto my said yonger Children the above said Somes of twenty Markes a peece, that my Executors shall sall any Woods, or timber groweing upon my lands & the same to sell & rayse moneyes for the paymente of the Same.

Executors: the testator's wife, Kathrine Barnett, and his brother, James Barnett.

H. & S.
Signed Richard Barnett
His R marke

Debtts oweinge to the testator without Specialty:

	s	d
Thomas Taylor of Smeatonwood	20	0
John Edgley of Woodcott surety for William Grosvenor	14	0
Roberte Hassall of Newhall	4	0
Widdowe Seavell of Newhall	13	6
Thomas Sale of Newhall		16

Signed Richard Barnet
his R marke

Witnesses: John Fisher his x marke, John Chedley his marke, Thomas Gray:

Renunciation: Whereas I James Barnett was left ioynte executor with my Sisterinlaw Catherine Barnett of the last will and testament of my brother Richard Barnett deceased these are to certifie all whom it may concern that I the said James Barnett doe renounce my executorship and leave it wholy to my said sister in law as written my hand.

James Barnet

Witness: Richard Wilson.

Inventory: Richard Barnett of Aston [in] Newhall.

Taken: 5 June 1646, 22 Charles I

Of: goods cattels and Chattels.

Prisers: John Jenkes, John Fisher, Edward Hamnett, William Whitcombe, Edward Whitcombe and Thomas Gray.

	£	s	d
his weareinge apparell	2	10	0
In Beddinge	4	0	0
Linnens & Napprie	1	13	4
In Brasse	1	0	0
In Pewter		13	4
In Bedsteeds tables formes Stooles & Shilfes	3	6	8
In Cheste quaffers & one Trunck		10	0
In Ironware		10	0
In Treenean ware	1	13	4
In Beefe and Bacon		10	0
In Corne and Mault in the house	2	10	0
one Presse		3	4
one Heare Cloth		6	8
In Sacks bagges & one winnow shett		1	6
In Ticknall Ware			6
In Cheese & meate in the hause		3	4
In Basketts Flasketts & all other true napery in the house		2	0
In Poultrie		5	0
Twoo reareinge swine		13	4
In Muck		6	8
In timber plankes, wastetimber ould timber & fuell	2	0	0
In Carts plowes harrowes and all other ymplements of husbandrie	2	0	0
Eight kine one winter heifer & Foure Stirkes	28	0	0
Two Naggs	2	0	0
Corne one the ground	6	6	8
In Bookes		6	8
one Coult taken for a harriott	4	0	0
In redy money in the house	3	0	0
one sword & one peece		6	8
In debtts due without specialty	2	12	10
A lease of the moety of the Messuage for 9 yeares, £6 13s. 4d. per annum	60	0	0
[Sum]	131	1	10

John Jenkes his X marke, John Fisher his X marke, Edward Hamnet, William Whitcombe, Edward Whitcombe, Thomas Gray:

Endorsement: Exhibited as true by Katherine Barnett 18 January 1647/48, the other executor having utterly renounced [the burden].

126. ELIZABETH COTTON OF COMBERMERE, WIDOW

S.Pr. 29 July 1648
Buried: 14 February 1647/48

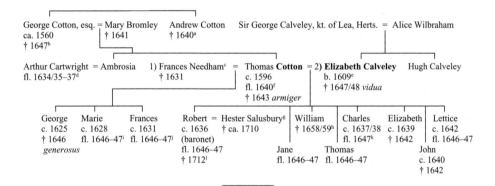

a   See will of Andrew Cotton of Combermere, pr. 1640 (will no. 111).
b   See will of George Cotton of Combermere, pr. 1648 (will no.128).
c   Daughter of Robert (Needham), 1st Viscount Kilmorey.
d   For both Arthur Cartwright and his wife, Ambrosia Cotton, see note n., inventory and IPM for John Cartwright of Sheppenhall, 1634/35 (no. 96).
e   Ormerod, *History of Cheshire*, iii. 211, shows her birth as 1 August 1609, her marriage as after 1631.
f   Noted as the *cousin* of Andrew Cotton in the latter's will, pr. 1640 (will no. 111); he was Andrew's nephew.
g   Daughter of Sir Thomas Salusbury of Llewenny, Bart, and sister and heiress of Sir John Salusbury, who died without issue in 1684.
h   Ormerod, *History of Cheshire*, iii. 211, has William as married, but without issue; the Bishop's Transcripts entry seems to fit, but it is speculative.
i   Became wife of Captain Mainwaring of Nantwich.
j   Became wife of Colonel Richard Fletcher of Morley, Cheshire.
k   Became a colonel in the Coldstream Guards; see Ormerod, *History of Cheshire*, iii. 211.
l   Died 17 December 1712, aged 77 years; second son and heir of Thomas; created baronet 29 March 1677; MP for Cheshire for 36 years: see Ormerod, *History of Cheshire*, iii. 211.

Inventory: Elizabeth Cotton of Combermere, Wyddow.

Taken: 2 March 1647/48, 23 Charles I

Prisers: Arthur Swanne, Thoms Steele, Hugh Webster, and John Larden.

	£	s	d
for 6 oxen	40	0	0
4 kyne & one bull	21	13	4
10 sheepe	3	15	0
25 bushell of seed barley	25	16	8
4 bushell of munkcorne	4	0	0
9 measures of rye	3	0	0
20 bushell of malte	22	0	0
18 bushell of Oates	10	16	0
500 weight of	7	4	0
all the treene ware in the Cheese chambre	2	10	0
all the iron ware there		10	0
for hempe & yarne		10	0
hoppes		14	0
all the plancks & boards in the Cheese chambre		16	0
all the treenen ware in ye dairy howse with a double Cheesepresse	2	10	0
brasse in the dairy howse a pescell, iron morter, & iron kettle	2	10	0
in the kylne, 5 whitches, one greate Colme, & a hairrecloath	3	0	0
all the brewinge vessells	3	0	0
10 Swyne	7	0	0
two little pyggs		5	0
all in the dyneinge roome	3	0	0
two longe tables in the hall	4	0	0
in the greene & white chambre furyture [*sic*]	5	0	0
furniture in ye yellow Chambre	3	0	0
in ould Mr Cottons Chambre apayr of bedstocks, Curtayns & valence		15	0
the furniture in the nursery	6	13	4
in ye Cocklofte over		1	0
in the mayds Chambre ye furniture	1	15	0
in the Cap room in furniture	1	0	0
all the husbandry ware	8	0	0
7 fflyches of Bacon	3	10	0
one Jacke with thapurtenances	2	10	0
brasse in the kytchin & other things	5	0	0
the treenen ware, & the safe in the Larder	6	8	0
all the Pewter	4	0	0
two horses	4	10	0
all in the little Closett	2	0	0
the lynnens boughte of William Bennett	4	0	0
Mistres Cottons owne nappery	11	0	0

the bedd & furniture in here owne Chamber	13	0	0
her pyllin, Cloath & furniture	2	0	0
one greate Herball	1	13	4
her wearinge lynnens	5	0	0
her wearing apparell	30	0	0
in the guilded boxe things to the value	3	6	8
in the Cookes Chamber	1	0	0
in a little longe blacke boxe to the value	1	10	0
tenne hoggsheads	1	13	4
all belonging to ye Butter	1	10	0
the ffurniture in in mr Mackwoods Chambre	2	0	0
28 frames for stooles & Cheares	1	12	0
in the howse in money	10	0	0
for Coales	1	10	0
for Clyfts & shovell trees	0	2	0
receaved of debts	40	0	0
6 kyne at Bellahill at £4 3s 4d a peice	25	0	0
5 twynters at £2 3s 4d a peice	10	16	8
7 Calves at £2 a peice	14	[1]0	0
two twynters more	4	6	8
two Calves	1	6	8
in money from Wilialm Dyckson	2	0	0
in money from John Stockton	0	14	0
hey	6	13	4
from wyddow Allen	0	3	4
Coales, Turffes, & other fewell	2	0	0
6 bushells of Barley	6	0	0
5 bushell of mongcorne	7	0	0
2 measures of barley & wheate	0	10	0
4 payre of Course bedstockes a Cheese presse	0	10	0
4 iron wedges & one iron Crow	0	6	8
one Jacke, Coardes, weights & pullaces	0	10	0
plow tymber, & Carte tymber	0	8	0
a Tumbrell draught & two Sleads	0	12	0
one spyning wheele	0	1[?]	4
2 tables & one tresse	0	5	0
wheate uppon ye grownd	2	10	0
one peice of Tymber square	0	6	8
two [c]addowes, one blankett one [ ] bedd boulster a pa[ ]	1	0	0
two Swyne troughes	0	1	0
for strawe	0	6	0
[Sum	433	14	8]

Endorsement: This inventory was exhibited as true by William Steele sole executor named in the said will the 29th of July AD 1648.

James Bennett
Notarius Publicus

Endorsement on back: The true perfect and particuler Accompt of William Steele sole Executor of all the Goods Cattels and Chattles of Elizabeth Cotton late of Combermere in the County of Chester widow deceased made by virtue of this date, the 22nd day of August Anno domini 1648.

	£	s	d
This accomptant chargeth himself with the whole summe of the inventory exhibited and remaining upon record which ammounteth to the summe of	433	14	8

Out of which he chargeth allowance of the severall summes following as necessarily paid for the use of the decedent.

	£	s	d
paid unto Robert Tudman and William Bennet Administrators of the goods of George Cotton Esq. a debtt due by the decedent	179	0	9
paid to Mris Mary Grosvenour a debtt due by the decedent	48	0	0
to Jone Brereton of Barrell a debtt due by the decedent	31	12	0
to Widow Chryichlee a debtt due by the decedent at her death	14	0	0
to Thomas Moore a debtt due by the decedent at her death	12	0	0
to William Hall of Wrenbury a debt due by the decedent at her death	40	0	0
to the Lord of Lemster *[Leominster]*for a debtt due by the decedent at her death	8	10	0
to George Guest for going to Lyine		3	4
paid to Mris Lettice Lee a debtt due by the decedent at her death	50	0	0
paid to John Watson a debtt due by the decedent at her death	10	8	0
to the Smith		3	0
to Mris Lettice Cotton of Chaisling Money which her mother owed her	6	0	0
to Mris Venables a debtt due by the decedent at her death	7	0	0
for funerall charges	14	1	8
to Mrs. Parry a debtt due by the decedent at her death	5	0	0
paid unto the servants belonging to the decedent at her death	8	18	4
to *[blank]* Guest for digging the hopyer		8	0
for proving the will		8	0
paid a debtt due for shues hatte and other necessaryes	3	1	0
to *[blank]*Barnett a debt due by the decedent at her death	6	3	2
to the Smith		6	6
to Mr. Golborne his attorney or fee		2	6
to Mr. Russell his Advocates fee		10	0
paid to the Lord Ch[olmondeley] an other debt due by the decedent	50	0	0

~~Suma totalis 496~~

for drawing these Accompts and for engraving them for a ring	16	4

Suma totalis	497	0	0

So ~~th~~ that this Accomptant hath disbursed £63 5s. 11d. over and above the charges of the Inventory this sume of 63. 5; 11. Whereupon he desires to be dismissed from further Accompt or Chardge towching his executor ship and the Administracōn of the decedents estate.

127. JOHN CHESWIS OF MICKLEY, GENT.

C.Pr. 28 August 1648
W.T. 21 May 1625
Buried: 22 March 1647/48

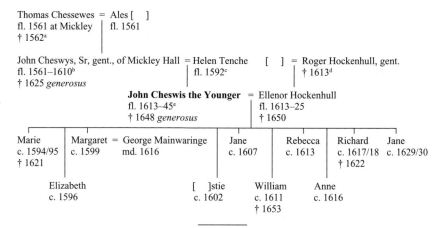

---

a See will of Thomas Chessewes of [Mickley Hall], Wrenbury, pr. 1562 (will no. 3).
b John Cheswis of Mickley was one of the IPM jurymen called 6 April 1605 for Richard Cotton, esq., of Combermere (see R. Stewart Brown, *Cheshire Inquisitions Post Mortem*, i. 146); see also note on John Cheswis the elder in connection with the will of Richard Cheswis, pr. 1633 (will no. 93).
c See will of her father, Robert Tenche, pr. 1594 (will no. 11).
d See will of Roger Hockenhull, pr. 1614 (will no. 44).
e John Cheswys was a member of the IPM jury for Roger Bickerton 1619 (see R. Stewart Brown, *Cheshire Inquisitions Post Mortem*, i. 17; he also served in the IPM jury for John Cartwright 1634/35 (see *ibid.*, i. 119; the name is incomplete in the transcription, but it clearly fits; he owed Robert Savage £10 in 1645 (see latter's inventory, will pr. 1647, will no. 124). Juryman for IPM for Dame Mary Cholmondeley 24 April 1629 (*Cheshire Inquisitions Post Mortem*, i. 126); also for Robert Crockett 20 August 1622 (*Cheshire Inquisitions Post Mortem*, i. 147); also served on the IPM for Hugh Massie of Denfield, gent., taken at Nantwich 4 January 1620/21 (see *ibid.*, ii.184); also for Robert Massie, taken at Nantwich 31 March 1619 (see *ibid.*, ii. 190); also for John Wicksted 18 January 1624/25 (see *ibid.*, iii. 171).

Will, sick.

Firste I comend my soule into the hands of Allmighty God assuredly trusting by the death and passion of my Lord & Savior Christ Jesus to have free remission of all my sinnes; and my body to the earth wherof it was made. Item whereas I by my deed Indented bearing the first day of May in the yeare of the late King of famous memory James King of England the one and twentieth made betweene me the sayd John Cheswis, by the name of John Cheswis the yonger of Mickley in the County of Chester gen, upon the one parte, And George Mainwaringe of Badington in the sayd County gen and Richard Wicksteed of Nantwich in the sayd County of Chester gen upon the other parte, did Covenant and grannt to and with the sayd George Mainwaring and Richard Wicksteed their heyres & assignes That I the sayd John Cheswis should, and would, before the Ferst day of the Nativity of our Lord God next insueing the date of the sayd deed Indented acknowledge and levie one fine *sur Cognizans de droyt, come ceo que il ad de son done*[a] to the sayd George Mainwaring, and Richard Wicksteed, and the heyres of the one of them or the survivour of them, and his heyres before his Majesties Justices of Chester, of all my Messuages lands, tenementes and hereditaments in Mickley, Henhull, Broomhall, and Church Coppenhull in the said County of Chester, or elsewhare within the same Countie In and by which sayd deed Indented It was Covenanted, declared, and agreed That the sayd Fine so then to be levied should be, and so for ever therafter should be adjudged, construed, and taken to be; And that they the sayd George Mainwaring, and Richard Wicksted, and their heyres, and the survivour of them, his and their heyres should stand & be seised of and in all my messuages lands Tenementes and hereditaments to and for such uses, behooffes intents & purposes, out of such person and persons, and for such estate & estates of Inheritance Freehold, or otherwise and in such sort, manner, quality & forme either absolutely, limitably or Condicōnally as I should att any time or times during my naturall life, by any my deed, or deedes to be by me sealed, or delivered in the presence of three wittnesses att the least, or by my last will, and Testament in writing to be by me published in the presence of three wittnesses at the least, absolutely, limitably, or Condicōnally, declare, limitt, convay, will, or appoynt, As by the sayd deed Indented amongst other things therin contayned more att large, it doeth and my appeare; Which sayd fine was had, and levied accordingly. I doe by this my last will, and Testament in writing declare, limmitt, convaye, will and appoynt all my messuages, lands, Tenements & hereditaments for Ellenor my wife, her heyres, and assignes for ever, To the use of her, her heyres, and assignes for ever, absolutely to dispose of without any Condicōn or other limitacōn whatsoever. Item I give and bequeath to every one of my Children which shall be unpreferrd att the time of my decease £5 of lawfull money of England, in lewe recompense and full satisfaction of all such Childs parte, and

---

[a]   A fine upon acknowledgment of the right of the cognizee, as that which he hath of the gift of the congnizor. See *Blackstone's Commentaries*, Book the Second, Chapter the Twenty-first: Of Alienation: § 2: Fines, p. 352.

filiall porcōn as they or any of them shall, or may challenge, clayme or have of or out of all or any my goods, Cattells, or Chattells in any wise. Item my debts, legacies, and funerall expenses beeing payd and discharged, the rest and residue of all my goods, Cattells, & Chattell I give and bequeath to the sayd Ellenor my wife.

Executor: the testator's wife, Ellenor Cheswis.

H. & S.
John Cheswis

Witnesses: George Mainwaring, John Bromhall, Thomas Burroughes, Robert Burroughes, Thomas Bowker.

This writing contayning the last will and Testament of the within named John Cheswis was read to him and he approved therof, as he declared this Fiffeteenth day of June 1647 in presence of Randle Whittingham, Roger Williams, Thomas Powell, Martha Gray, Mary Gray.

Endorsement: Probated at Tar[porley] 28 August 1648; administration granted to the executrix named in the said will.

128. GEORGE COTTON, ESQUIRE, OF COMBERMERE[a]

S.Pr. 21 September 1648
W.T. 3 May 1647
Buried: 1 December 1647

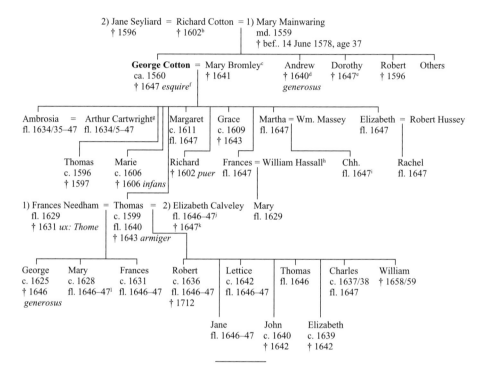

a   Earwaker, *Index to Wills at Chester, Vol. III, 1621–50*, p. 53, lists him as George Cotton of Comberbach.
b   See IPM, dated 6 April 1605; R. Stewart Brown, *Cheshire Inquisitions Post Mortem*, i. 146.
c   Daughter of Sir Thomas Bromley of Halton, Salop., chief justiciar of Cheshire; see Ormerod, *History of Cheshire*, iii. 211.
d   See will of Andrew Cotton, pr. 1640 (will no. 111).
e   See will of Dorothy Cotton, pr. 1647 (will no. 122).
f   Ormerod, *History of Cheshire*, iii. 211, incorrectly places date of death as 1649.
g   Of Sheppenhall, gent.
h   William Fergusson Irvine, *Chester Licences*, iii. 15: 1 October 1615 to Frances Cotton of Wrenbury parish; William Hassal of Audlem parish; at Wrenbury or Audlem. In Ormerod, *History of Cheshire*, iii. 211, he is given as being of Hankelow, co. Chester.
i   See will of Dorothy Cotton, pr. 1647 (will no. 122): included Dorothy and Elizabeth.
j   Bequeathed 20s. as *cousin* of Dorothy Cotton (will no. 122).
k   See inventory of Elizabeth Cotton, 1648 (no. 126).
l   Mary Cotton and her siblings are noted as the *cousins* of Dorothy Cotton (will no. 122).

Will *[very large parchment]*, sick.

First I comend my soule into the hands of God my Creator and Redeemer in full assureance that when it shall please him to put an End to this my transitory life hee will of his free grace and mercy through Faith in the bloud of that immaculate Lambe Christe Jesus receive it into Comunion with himselfe in his heavenly Kingdome my body I comitt to the Earth whence it was in assured hope of a blessed Change at the resurrection of the Just The Care of my Funeralls I leave to my undernamed Executor. And as touchinge my worldly estate not otherwise already settled I give dispose and bequeath in manner and forme following Whereas by one Indenture Tripartite bearinge date the Sixth Day of November in the Two and Twentith Yeare of the Raigne of our late soveraigne Lord Kinge James of famous memory over his then Realme of England made betweene mee the said George Cotton of the first parte and the Right honorable the Lord Viscount Killmorrey by his then name of Robert Nedham Esquire sonne And heire apparent of Sir Robert Nedham of Shavington in the county of Salop Knight upon the second parte And Sir Edward Bromley Knight then one of the Barons of his Majesty's Court of Exchequer Sir Richard Wilbraham Knight and Barronet Sir Robert Vernon and Sir Rowland Cotton Knight upon the third parte, As alsoe by one other Indenture bearinge date thee forrth day of March in the Tenth yeare of the Raigne of our said soveraign Lord Kinge Charles over England &c made betweene mee the said George Cotton and Thomas Cotton gent my then brother of the second parte And Peter Venables Esquier Baron of Kinderton in the said county Sir Hugh Calveley knight Sir Thomas Wilbraham Baronett and Sir Thomas *[damaged]* by the hand of Hugh Calveley of Lea in the said county Esquire Thomas Wilbraham Esquire sonne and heire apparent of Sir Richard Wilbraham of Woodhey in the said County Knight and Baronett and Thomas Wolrich of Dudmaston in the county of Salop Esquire. It was and is amongst other things contayned in the said Indentures provided and agreed by and betweene the said partyes to the said Indentures That all and every the estate and estates to be raised created and made by Feoffment Fine or other assureances of, in, or upon the Manors Mesuages Landes Tents and hereditaments in the said Indentures menconed Except those limited to the use of Mary my late wife and of Elizabeth now the widdowe and relict of my late sonne Thomas Cotton now deceased dureinge their severall estates therein should be from and ymediately after my death for the levyinge and raisinge of One Thousand pownds of lawfull money of England To be payd over to my executors or to such other person or persons and in such manner and forme as I the said George Cotton by any Act by mee to be done or executed in my life tyme or by my last Will and Testament in writeinge should limitt and appoynt the same to be payd As in and by the said Indentures more fully and at large it doth and may appeare And whereas alsoe sithence the date of the said Indentures I have made and executed a Feoffment and other assurances accordinge to the said Provisoes and Limitacōns in the said Indentures expressed, Now I the said George Cotton doe hereby limitt and appoynt and my Will and meaninge is That the said Some of One Thousand pownds shall be payd to my executors assoon as by force of the said Deeds and other assurances the same can or may be levyed or raised out of the said Mannors Mesuages Landes Tentes and hereditaments therewith charged or had and receaved and by my said executors paid over to my Three Daughters Martha, Ambrosia (now wife of Arthur Cartwright gent) and Margret the survivors and survivor of Them within Three yeares next after my decease To be equally divided amongst them the survivors and survivor of them Moreover I give and bequeath to my daughter Martha all such moneys as shee converted to her owne use in her mothers lifetime Two hundred Pownds for which I have suffered her to take Bonds and Specialtyes in her owne name from Mr. Jonathan [P]owley of Shrewsbury £100 of lawfull money of England out of my personall estate, and £100 more which was in the hands of Mr. Richard Leicester of Poole and now secured in her owne name And to my said daughter Ambrosia I give and bequeath £200 The Specialtyes for which from Mr. Tannat of Braxton in the said County of Chester shee hath in her owne keeping £30 due to mee from Mr. Roger Hamnet, £20 which was lent to my sonne Cotton, and £100 more in the hand of my sonne Massy which is secured in her owne name and £100 more of like lawfull money of England out of my personall estate, And to my daughter Margret I give and bequeath £150 due by Specialtyes in her Keeping from George Davyes of Burghall and Thomas Rannshall of Hinton in the County of Salop and Richard Hamnet of the Fields £50 which she hath receaved from Robert Gryndley and £100 accordinge to my deceased daughter Grace her request The Specialty for which from John Burscough shee hath in her owne hands, Moreover I doe further give and bequeath to my said daughter Margret £230 due by severall Specialties from the said Mr Massye and Thomas Gray £50 whereof shee hath already receaved The Specialties for which shee hath in her owne hand And £100 more of lawfull money of England out of my personnall Estate Furthermore my Will is that all such arrerages as shall be due and oweinge unto mee by all or any of my Tenants whatsoever I doe give and bequeath unto my said three daughters (Martha, Ambrosia and Margret) To be equally divided amongst them the survivors and survivor of them And to my daughter Elizabeth Hussey I give and bequeath £80 out of my personall estate And to my daughter Cotton I doe hereby as a finall remembrance of my Love bequeath 20s. in gold To my Grandchildren Mary, Frances, Robert, Charles and Lettice beinge each of them (I hope) competentlie provided for out of me estate I give 20s. a peece, To Francis Moore my servant whome I have allready otherwise preferred 20s. To Beniamine Moore £3 6s. 8d. To George Cooke £6. To Margery Cooke £10. To Jane Bromhall £20. To William Bennet £25. To my servant Edward Mackworth £30. To George Ravenscrofte £5 6s. 8d. Furthermore my desire is That with my Nephew Cottons and his mothers good approvall my daughters may keepe together at Combermere where they and I now lodge till they shall be preferred in marriage or otherwise provided for to their better Content What further Legacyes I shall hereafter give to any or what other Clause in writeinge I shall at anie time dureing my life add or annex hereunto further to inlarge and expresse my minde touchinge the further disposinge of my estate under my hand accordinge as things shall alter or happen shalbe taken as parte of this my last Will And I doe hereby give and bequeath all the rest and residue of my goods Cattalls and Chattalls whatsoever my debts and funeralls beinge discharged To my said Three daughters Martha Ambrosia and Margret equallie to be divided amongst them or given to the survivors and survivor of them Provided allways That if either of my said Two daughters Martha or Margret doe marry without the Consent of my executors or the greater number of them shee shall loose the one halfe of her Legacyes here by above bequeathed to her and the same to be given to such of my other daughters that have not maryed or hereafter do not marry without such Consent to be equally divided amongst them.

Executors: the testator's friends, Roger Wilbraham of Derfold in the County of Chester Esquire, William Masey of the Mosse in the same County, Esquire, Thomas Bromley of Hampton in the same County Esquire, Richard Whitall of Doddington in the County of Salop gent., the testator's cousin, George Mannwaringe of Arcluid in the same County of Chester gent.

I doe hereby give and bequeath unto my daughter Massey [Martha] and my daughter Hassall [Frances] whome I have not herein before mencioned and to everyone of their Children that shalbe liveinge at the time of my decease To such of them 20s. a peece as a small remembrance of my Love unto them, And to my Said executors to every one of them 40s. a peece, And to my daughter Hussey [Elizabeth] over and above that which I have formerly bequeathed unto her, £80 and to each of her children £5.

H. & S.
George Cotton

Memorandum that the word (the) was interlined betwixt the Sixth and Seventh lines, and these words the said Mr. (Massey) and these words (one hundred pownds more of lawfull money of England out of my personall estate) were interlined betwixt the two and thirtith and three and thirtith lines And the word (Thirty) written upon a rased place in the beginninge of the three and thirtith lines, And the word (thirty) upon a rased place in the thirthy ninth line. And these words (and his mothers) betweene the thirty ninth and Fortith line of this present will.

Witnesses: George Mainwaring, Francis Swan, William Poole, William Bennett and Robert Tudman.

Memorandum That whereas I George Cotton of Combermere in the County of Chester Esquire in and by my last Will and Testament bearing Date the Third Day of May last past before the Date hereof Reserved power in my selfe at any time thereafter to add unto, alter or otherwise determine of the same and dispose of all or any of my personall estate according as things should alter or happen And whatsoever I should hitherunto should be taken as parte and parcell to my said last Will and Testament Therefore my Will and meaninge is And I doe by these presents further give and bequeath out of my personall estate unto Rachell Hussey one of the daughters of my daughter Elizabeth Hussey The Some of One Hundred marks of lawfull money of England And I doe hereby further declare and my Will is That these presents be and shalbe taken to be as parte and parcell of my said last Will and Testament And I doe intreat my executor therein named to performe this my said guifte and bequest together with and as parte and parcell of my said Last Will according to my said true intent and meaninge.

Witnesses: George Cooke, William Benett and Robert Tudman.

This is to certifie all that it may concern that wheras George Cotton late of Combermere esquire made his last will & testament and dyed in which he named me, Roger Wilbraham, together with William Massie Thomas Bromley esq. George Manwaringe and Richard Whitall gent his Executors all which for sever-all reasons have refused the execucon of the said wyll, and by the consent of the daughters of said Mr Cotton who are chiefly interested in the estate of the said Mr Cotton do desire that Robert Tudman and William Bennet may be admitted to administer the said estate accordinge to law and the true meaning of the said Mr Cotton expresed in his wyll In witnes wherof I in the name of the [aforesaid daughters] [do] witnes this under my hands this 18th of Januarie 1647.

Witness: Roger Wilbraham.

Know all men by these presents that we Robert Tudman of Newhall Park in the county of Chester yeoman, William Benett of Combermere in the same county of Chester yeoman and Arthur Cartwright of Sheppenhall in the county of Chester, gent., are held and firmly bound to Edward Mainwaring doctor of laws and prin-cipal official of the Consistory Court of Chester lawfully constituted in £2000 of good and lawful (gold) money to be paid to the said Edward Mainwaring or his certain attorney or successors for this purpose for well and truly making which payment we bind ourselves and each one of us for himself wholly and jointly our heirs and administrators firmly by these presents Sealed with our seals and given the 3rd day of January AD 1647/48.

This obligacōn is such that if the above bounden Robert Tudman and William Benett doe well and truly administer all and singuler the goods Cattells Chattells Credits and debtes of George Cotton late of Combermere Esquier deceased accordinge to the effects of Letters of administracōn to them in that behalf grant-ed vizt: pay all the debts the said deceacedent owed at the time of his decease [so far foryh as] the said goodes Cattells Chattells and debts will thereunto extende and as the lawe in that behalfe charge them and likewise faithfully performe the said deceadents will and doe exhibite into the Consistory Courte of Chester a true and perfecte Inventory of all and singuler the said goods Cattells Chatells and debts at or before the first day of July next ensuinge and of and upon the same doe make a true and perfecte accompte unto the above named Edward Manwareinge or other Judge Competent in that behalfe when and as often as they shalbe thereunto lawfully called or required them this present obligacōn to be voyd and of none effect or els the same to be and remayne in full power force and vertue.

Robert Tudman
William Bennett

Witnesses: John Benett, Arthur Cartwright.

Inventory: George Cotton of Combermere, esquire.

Taken: 14 December 1647, 23 Charles I

Of: goods Cattells & Chattells.

Prisers: John Massye, John Ravenscrofte, John Watson, John Edgley, George Hall and William Bickerton.

	£	s	d
His wearinge apparrell	30	0	0
One and Twenty milch kyne and one Bull at £4 13s. 4d. a peece	102	13	4
Twelve draught Oxen at £15 10s. paire	93	0	0
Three fatt Oxen at £10 an oxe	30	0	0
Three fatt kyne at £5 6s. 8d. a peece	16	0	0
Five Twynter heifers at £2 8s. a beast	12	0	0
Two three yeare old heifers at £4 a beast	8	0	0
Sixe Calves at £2 a peece	12	0	0
Tenne Sheepe at 7s. 6d. a sheepe	3	15	0
Two & Twenty Swyne	21	12	0
One geldinge & one mare	9	0	0
Barley thrashed & unthrashed and mault	100	0	0
Oats	13	6	8
Rye & wheate	33	6	8
Tenne measures of course pease	2	0	0
Haye	40	0	0
Carts plowes Harrows & a slead	13	10	0
Foure Ladders	1	0	0
Yoakes Chaynes, plow timber Cart timber and all the implements of husbandry	6	10	0
Corne on the ground	36	0	0
In the Newhall Mills			
One tugge Chaine and great hamer and eight parts	1	10	0
Three windinge ropes two horseheld Two barrells & a mill Chizell	1	0	0
Two Tall arks	1		
a measureinge hoope one half measure & a peck		3	4
Timber about the mill	1	0	0

In Brooks mill

a measure a peck, Tenne pecks a Crow of Iron a hammer one windinge rope a horshead & one Iron pinne, Timber framed & unframed	4	0	0

In the Kyll

One great Combe & two Whitches & old haire cloth	3	6	8
Wood & Coales	16	0	0

In the Brewhouse

A Cooler and a little Trough over it	3	10	0
Foure Combes or brewinge salts and one old Combe	3	10	0
One little Ringe Two little Barrells and two little stounds		7	0
Sixteene Hogsheads one other little stoand and slopes	3	6	8
Foure old tubbes		6	0

In the day house & Milkhouse

Boards Shelves and Cheese presse	3	10	0
Treenan & Coopery ware of all sorts belonginge to the same	1	15	0

In the Larder

Tubbes Turnells and other Coopery ware	1	16	4
Item Shelves Dressers, one Cubbart & safe	1	10	0

In the Two Kitchins

Boards & Shelves		7	6
Brasse of all sorts, one little brasse morter & one Iron morter	9	0	0
One Jack	1	10	0
Racke, potracks, hooks & other Iron the reste belonginge, Spitts gobbarts & two fryinge pannes	2	3	4
Three dreepinge pannes Two Axes Shreadinge knives & other Iron ware not particalayized		13	4
Boards in the garden		15	0
One planke at the neare side		5	0
Two boats	1	0	0
Coggs & rounds in the barne	1	10	0
Two Grindlesones		5	0

In the Storechamber

Hoppes groats Sixe tubbes ould hampers Towe & other trumpery and one Iron pott	5	4	0

In the Cheese Chamber

Tenn Hundred weaght of Cheese and a halfe	15	10	0
Skales & weights planks and Tressells & one brasse pott	2	6	8

In the Greene & white Chamber

One Joyned bedd one fetherbedd one boulster one blankett

one Coveringe al the appurtenances	2	0	0
One other bedd one fether bedd one Flockbedd Two blankets, Two bolsters	2	10	0

In the Day house Chamber

One Joyned bedd one trucklebedd Two fether bedds a matt & an old forme	3	3	0
One fether bedd one wallbedd one boulster two blanketts, one blacke Coveringe one old Joynd stoole frame & one grate	1	13	4

In Mr. Andrews Chamber

One Joynd bedd Curtains & valens one fetherbedd, one boulster, one blankett & an old greene rugge	4	16	8
One fether bedd & mattresse, one boulster: Two blankets & one Coverlett	1	10	0
One Presse one old Cheste one paire of Anndirons, a fireshovle & a paire of Tongues	1	10	0

In the Servants Chamber

Beddstidds beddclothes & formes	1	0	0

In George Cooks Chamber

A fetherbed two boulsters Two double Coverings	2	0	0

In other servants Chambers

Beddinge there	1	15	0

In the Gatehouse Chamber

One Joynd bedd with Curtaines & padds, two fether bedds, one boulster, one pillowe Three Coverings one Livery Cubbart, One Chayre Two paire of Tongues, one paire of bellowes, & in the gallerye one table, and paire of beddstidds and one pair of bedd stidds in the Chamber over head	5	0	0
Brasse in the Day house and Brewhouse	7	6	8
Twelve Gallons of butter	3	0	0
Two Gallons of Lard		8	0
150 Gallons & halfe a barrell of *Bacinice*	3	0	0
Pursnetts		5	0
Beddinge in other Servants Chambers	1	10	0
Bacon & *brawne*	5	0	0
Salte		13	4

In the Decedents olde Chamber

One Joynd bedd one Truckle bedd and Curtaine, one fether bedd, Two boulsters three Coverings, one table one Livery Cubbarte	5	3	4

In the maids Chamber

One bedd with Coverings, one Chest, Two paire of Beddstidds over the same, one Presse & one great Chest in the little roome by	2	3	4

In the Nursrye

One high bedd, one Truckle bedd Two fether bedds, Three boulster, foure Coveringe one old bedd, one fether bedd, one flock bedd Two boulsters, Three Coverings one grate, one fireshovle and a pair of tongues	8	5	0

In the Courte Chamber

One Joynd bedd Curtains & valens a flockbedd, one boulster, Three Coverings & a fether bedd	7	13	4
A truckle bedd, Two fether bedds, a flockbedd, Two pillowes one blankett	4	0	0
Another Canopy bedd & Curtaine one fether bedd one woolbedd three boulsters three Coverings	4	6	8
One little Table, one Chaire, one Trunck & three Quishions	1	0	0

In the Corner Chamber

One fether bedd one wollbedd one boulster foure Coverings & a redd rugge & one Chest	4	6	8

In the blew Chamber

One Joynd bedd Cartaines & radds & Cover and fether bedd, one Mattresse one wollbedd one boulster three pillowes foure blanketts, one Covering, one Chaire Two stools, a Livery Cubbart one paire of Annirons, a fire shovle & a pair of tongues	10	13	4

In the best Chamber

One Joynd bedd an imbroydered Cover Silke Curtaines & imbroydered valens radds Two Fetherbedds, Two boulsters a wollbedd Two pillowes foure blanketes a redd rugge one imbroydered Chayre, foure quilt back stooles, one greene Chayre Twelve greene Covered stooles, Two little stooles, one livery Cabbarte & Cloth a paire of Anndirons a pair of tongues, Two window Curtaine & two rodds, one picture & a little Curtaine to it	20	0	0

In the Gardaine Chamber

One pair of beddstidds, Three fether bedds a flockbedd two boulsters, two blanketts & a Coveringe, Two white blanketts & a rugge, one pillow, one Cubbart, a little table & three stooles	7	18	4

In the yellow Chamber

One Joynd bedd Curtaines & valens one fether bedd one wallbedd, one boulster two pillowes, foure blanketts, one Coveringe one other fether bedd, two pillowes, one mattresse, three blanketts one livery Cubbarte, one wrought Cubbart Cloth one Chaire, two stooles one paire of Anndirons, a fire shovle & a paire of tongues	11	10	0

In the Joyners Chamber

One Joyned bedd a truckle bedd, one fether bedd one blankett, one Coveringe one other Joynd bedd one Coveringe one Livery Cubbarte, Two tables one farme foure stooles, two old truncks, one Chest, one Coffer & Candles	9	0	0
the best Carpett & Cubbart Clothes & the best Coveringe	8	0	0

In the dyninge roome

One great drawinge table and frame & one green Carpett, one other drawinge table & Carpet, one Liverye Cubbarte, Two formes, another frame with Originales Cover, fourteene Joynd stooles two Covered Chares three Covered stooles, three backstooles, Six Quishions, a fire shovle, a fire slicer one little backstoole, one window Curtaine & radd	10	3	4

In the Hall

One longe table & frame two Joynd formes one other longe table & a farme one little table & frame one Curtiane radd, Three brass & Trine Candlesticks	4	17	4
Pewter	13	0	0
Lynnens & Napperye of all sorts	6	13	4

In the Buttrey & Sellers

Sacks bottles Trenchers, a leaden Cisterne, a little Iron grate, one table one presse for lynnens and shelves Beare & Ale	2	6	0
Some small plate leste, & one sugar spoones & other things in the Chest belonging to the dyninge roome	3	14	0

In the Decedents Closett

One Chaire, books Shelves and boxes	2	0	0
Pictures mappes Boxes Ticknall ware wheeles & all other trumperye of all sorts not before particularly menconed	1	0	0
Swanns, Capons, Hennes and other Poultrye		10	0

Debts owinge to the testator by Specialtye

George Davyes	20	0	0
Robert Wilson	104	0	0
Mr Tannatt	200	0	0
Richard Boote	20	0	0
desperate Item John Claye	5	0	0
desperate Item John Burscough	100	.0	0

Without Specialtye

Mr. Cartwright	10	0	0
George Bickerton	10	0	0
James Bromhall	4	13	0
George Bickerton	13	0	0
Arrears of rent from severall persons [ware]	145	14	0
desperate It The Administratrix of Richard Edgleye	5	0	0
desperate It The Administrator of Arthur Starkey Esqr deceased	3	0	0
desperate It Mrs. Babington	1	10	0
Mr. Peartree	1	0	0
from Mr. Thomas Cotton deceased in money lent	300	0	0
more from him by covenant	100	0	0
[Sum	1072	03	0]

Debts without spetialty due to the deseased.

	3	11	8

Exhibitum cum protestacōne de Addendum et subtrahendum [   ] &c 21ˢᵗ of September 1648.

Be it known by these presents that we Robert Tudman of Newhall Park and William Benet of Combermere in the county of Chester yeoman having been bound and duely sworn by Edward Mainwaringe doctor of laws and principal official of the Consistory Court of Chester &c. *[A repeat of the earlier statement].*

Endorsement: Exhibited 21 September 1648; *[reference to administrators is not visible].*

129. GEORGE TENCH OF WRENBURY

S.Pr. 14 October 1648
W.T. 1 May 1648
Buried: 5 May 1648

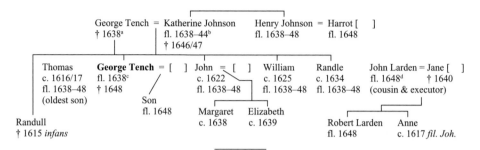

Will, sick.

I bequeath my soule to almightie god that gave it *and my bodie to bee buried at the parish Church of Wrenbury* & for my temporall goods I bequeath them after this manner First I give to *[several words crossed out]* my son & my Ladie either a 20s. peece to bye them Rings to wear for my sake & to Mr. Stanley Burroughs & his wife either of them ten shillings for the like use to Mistres Susan Andrews a 40s. & to Mary Andrews a great peece of silver in my trunk and 10s. in money besids Item I Doe give to Mr William Domvill Mr. John Coldecote Gregory Ambrose John Richardson John Abram John Croxton John Pouall Richard Metles Hugh Webster of Bickley & Hugh Webster of Cholmondeley & Richard Metles Junior Oliver Pollett William Griffith & William Sound every one of these heare named 2s. 6d. a peece. Item I Doe give to my brother John Tench my new gray suite & to my brother William Tench I give my black suite and colored Cloack and Friz gerkin and for the rest of my Clothes & wearinge aperrell goods & moneys *[interlined]* shalbee disposed of by my executors heareafter named. Item I doe give to my brother Randle one Cow and a Calfe that my brother Thomas *[interlined]* hath. Item I Doe give to little Robert Larden 20s. Item I doe give to the

---

ᵃ See will of George Tench of Smeatonwood, yeoman, pr. 1639 (will no. 107). Reference to Henry Johnson in 1638 as one of those who made George Tench's inventory, and to Henry *Johnston* in 1648 (see below) as the uncle of the testator, allows the conclusion that the two Henries are identical, and that the George Tench of 1639 was father to the George Tench of 1648.
ᵇ Mentioned both as Katherine Tench and as *Widdow* Tench of Smeatonwood in the will of Richard Culliner alias Comber, pr. 1644 (will no. 119): she owed Comber a debt of £4.
ᶜ The children of George Tench Sr are mentioned without name in 1638; see his will, pr. 1639 (will no. 107).
ᵈ John Larden was also a priser of the goods of Elizabeth Cotton, 1647/48 (no. 126).

poore ten pound & to Mr. Griffes the minister at Wrenbury 20s. and to My uncle Henrie Johnston & my Aunt Harrot either of them 2s. 6d. Item I Doe give to Mr. Holland 10s.

Executors: the testator's cousin, John Larden & Hugh Webster Senior.

George Tench

Witnesses: William Domville, John Caldecott, Gregory Ambrose.

Inventory: George Tench of Wrenbury.

Taken: 20 June 1648

Of: goodes.

Prisers: Gregory Ambrose, Richard Nettles.

	£	s	d
his wearinge apparrell	5	0	0
his Bookes		10	0
one Cowe and Calfe	3	10	0
in Money oweinge him	67	0	0
Some	76	0	0

Endorsement: Probated 14 October 1648; administration to John Larden, one of the executors named in the will.

130. RANDLE SPROSTON OF NEWHALL, HUSBANDMAN

S.Pr. 24 October 1648
W.T. 1 May 1648
Buried: 3 May 1648

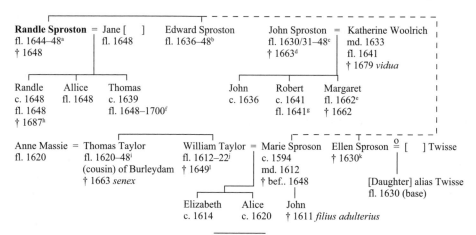

Will, sick.

First I give & bequeath my soule into the hands of Almighty god who firste gave it mee, trustinge by the Death & merritts of Jesus Christe my Saviour to have free pardon & remission of all my Sines & my body I committ to the earth to bee decently buryed in Christian buryall att the discrecōn of my Executors heerafter named & for that small temporall estate which almighty god of his bounty &

---

a Fined at Newhall Manor Court, 1644/CRO.
b Made inventory for Thomas Gray, will pr. 1636 (will no. 99).
c Priser for the goods of Ellen Sproson, 1630/31; received a bequest of a plough from Emma Barnett, will pr. 1631 (will no. 87); made inventory of Margaret Graye's goods, and owed her £4, will pr. 1632 (will no. 89). Margaret Graye also made a bequest of 10s. to Margaret Sproston, administered by her uncle, John Sproston. He was also witness and priser for Valentine Woolrich, will pr. 1647 (will no. 123).
d See will of John Sproston, pr. 1663/CRO.
e See will of Margaret Woolrich, pr. 1662/CRO.
f See Backhouse inventory, 1700/CRO.
g See will of Valentine Woolrich, made 1641/42; pr. 1647 (will no. 123).
h See will of Randle Sproston of Audlem, pr. 1687/CRO.
i Marriage 1620; made inventory for George Tench, will pr. 1639 (will no. 107). Owed 20s. to Richard Barnett, will pr. 1647/48 (will no. 125). Received bequests from his brother, William Taylor, of Smeatonwood; will pr. 1649 (will no. 134); also noted as the cousin of Randle Sproston of Newhall (below), as Thomas Taylor of Burleydam.
j Made inventory for William Barnett, 1616 (no. 52); witness to will of James Brooke, pr.1622 (will no. 66).
k See will of Ellen Sproston of Newhall, pr. 1630.
l See will of William Taylor, pr. 1649 (will no. 134).

mercy hath bestowed upon mee I will & dispose thereof as falloweth: First, for that small Cottage garden & yarde which I have scituate lyinge & beinge in Wrenbury within the said County for certayne yeares yett to come, & unexpired; I doe heereby give devise Assigne & bequeath the same unto Jone Sproston my loevinge wife for & duringe soe many of the yeares mencōned in my Assignemente, as my said wife shall happen to live & lives mencōned in the Firste lease made of the said Cottage garden & yarde to Randle Maurice Carpenter or any of them alsoe Doe & shall soe longe continue & endure, And Ymediatly from and after the Death of the said Jone Sproston my said wife I doe hereby give devise Assigne & bequeath the said Cottage garden & yarde with their appurtements unto my sonne Randle Sproston his executors, Administrators & Assignes Dureing all the reste & residue of my whole terme therein: Item I doe heereby give and bequeath unto my sonne Thomas Sproston Three shillings and Foure pence current money claymeinge noe more of my goods. Item I give and bequeath unto my godsonne Randle Stubbes twelve pence: Item I doe heereby give and bequeath all the rest and residue of all my goods Cattells & Chattells boeth moveable and unmoveable goods quick & Dead of what kinde or quallitie soever the same bee of or where soever the same remayneth my Debttes legacies and funerall expences beinge theere out payd and discharged, unto my said wife Jone Sproston & my said sonne Randle Sproston and Aillice Sproston my Daughter, the full moyetie and one halfe theereof to the said Jone Sproston my said wife, and the other halfe and full moyetie to my said sonne Randle Sproston & my said Daughter Allice Sproston to bee equally devided betwixte them.

Executors: the testator's wife, Jone Sproston, & his 'lovevinge Cosen' Thomas Taylor of Burledam.

H. & S.

Debts owing to the testator:

I the said Randle Sproston have a debtt of Fifteene pounds oweinge unto mee by the executors or Administrators of John Cooke of Childs Ercall in the County of Salop yeoman Deceased which I lente unto the said John Cooke in Market Drayton before his death in the presence of William Poole & John Mosse & he was to allowe mee intereste for the same whilste hee kepte it.

Signed Randle Sproston
his X marke & seal

Witnesses: William Taylor his X marke, John Sproston his X marke, Thomas Gray 1648.

My brother ~~Randle~~ Edward Sproston oweth unto mee the testator £6 & if I dye att this time my will is that payinge to my executors the one halfe theereof I will forgive him the other halfe in the presence of the wittnesse heere named.

Witnesses: William Taylor, John Sproston, Thomas Gray.

Inventory: Randle Sproston of Newhall, Husbandman.

Taken: 12 June 1648 (24 Charles I)

Of: goods cattells and Chattells.

Prisers: John Shawe, John Sproston, Thomas Clay ~~the younger~~ & Thomas Gray.

	£	s	d
his wearinge apprell		13	4
Corne in the house and on the ground	2	17	0
Linnens and Napprie	1	0	0
Bedinge	2	0	0
Cheese		18	0
Pewter		13	4
Brasse		17	[ ]
one Joyned Cheste quoffers, bedstids farmes & Shilves	[ ]	[ ]	[ ]
one Iron Pott or frying pan & all other Iron ware		11	[ ]
Treenen ware	1	0	[ ]
Edge tooles		5	[ ]
Ticknall ware		1	[ ]
Towe & yarne in the house & one the Ground		14	[ ]
Basketts Flaskett & all other tru naperie	[ ]	[ ]	[ ]
Twoo Pigges		6	8
one Cock 2 hens & 4 yonge geese		2	0
Sackes bagges & one Cartrope		6	0
In muck		3	0
2 Spinninge Wheeles		2	6
Sixe Milk Kine	23	0	0
one Bullock one heifer & one sterke	7	0	0
A Chattell lease of 2 pcells of land from John Sproston for 8 yeares In beinge	30	0	0
A Debtt Ive by bond from Thomas Backhowse	20	16	0
one Chattell lease from John Savage of a Cottage in Wrenbury	9	13	4
one Debtt due by bond from John Sproston	12	8	0
one Debtt due from the said John Sproston by bond	10	16	0
A Debtt oweinge from the executors or Administrators of John Cooke with out Specialty	15	0	0
a Debtt oweinge by Edward Sproston with out Specialty	3	0	[ ]
Some total	145	12	[0]

John Shawe his X marke
John Sproston his X marke
Thomas Cley
Thomas Gray 1648

Exhibitum cum protestacōn.

Endorsement: Probated 24 October 1648; administration to the executors named in the will.

131. JOHN SAVAGE OF WRENBURY

S?Administration granted 10 November 1648

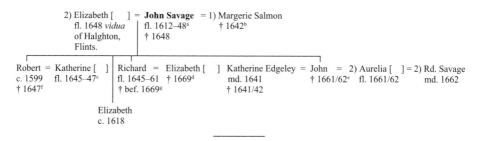

Charge: Know all men by these presents that we Elizabeth Savage of Halghton in the county of Flint widow and Thomas Hughes of Hanmer in the said county of Flint husbandman are held and firmly bound to Edmund Mainwaring doctor of laws legally appointed official principal of the Consistory Court of Chester in £100 of good and legal English money to be paid to the same Edmund Mainwaring or his certain attorney for this purpose, or his successors for well and truly making which payment we bind ourselves and each one of us for himself wholly and jointly our heirs, executors and administrators firmly by these presents Sealed with our seals & given the 10ᵗʰ day of November in the 24ᵗʰ year of the reign of Charles by the grace of God of England, Scotland, France & Ireland & in the year of the Lord 1648.

The Obligation: The Condicōn of this obligacōn is such That if the above bounden Elizabeth Savage doe well and truely administer all and singuler the goodes Cattells Chattells Credits and debtes of John Savage late of Wrenbury deceased according to the effecte of lettres of administracōn to her in that behalfe granted,

---

a   See inventory of Katherine Savage, pr. 1641/42 (no. 116); John *Savich* made inventory for Valentine Woolrich, see will of Valentine Woolrich, pr. 1647 (will no.123); John Savage owed Richard Comber £10 16s. in 1644; see will of Richard Culliner alias Comber, pr. 1644 (will no. 119); Randull Cowper of Wrenbury owed John Savage 44s. and was owed 20s., see will of Randull Cowper, pr. 1613 (will no. 40); he was also one of the prisers of Randull Cowper's goods in 1612. He owed Robert Savage debts of £10 and £110; see will pr. 1647 (will no. 124). The inventory of the goods etc. of Randle Sproston of Newhall, dated 12 June1648, indicates that Sproston had a chattell lease of a cottage in Wrenbury from John Savage, valued at £9 13s. 4d. (will no. 130).
b   Burial entry in Wrenbury Parish Register shows *Margaret Savage*.
c   Executor of her husband's will, 1647 (will no. 124).
d   See will of Elizabeth Savage, widow of Richard Savage, pr. 1669/CRO.
e   See will of John Savage, pr. 1661/CRO.
f   See will of Robert Savage, pr. 1647 (will no. 124).
g   Overseer of his brother's will; see will of Robert Savage. Also see will of Elizabeth Savage, widow of Richard Savage, pr. 1669/CRO.

videlicet: pay all the debtes the said deceadent owed at the time of his decease so farr forth as the said goodes Cattells Chattells Credits and debtes will thereunto extend and as the lawe will charge her and doe exhibite in writinge into the Consistory Courte of Chester a true and perfecte Inventory of all the said goods and thereof doe make a true and perfecte accompte unto the above named Edmund Mainwaringe or other Judge Competent in that behalfe when and as often as she shall be thereunto lawfully called or required and all such parte and portion of the fore said goodes and Chatteles as shalbe found due and remaininge upon her And accomples examined and alowed shall distribute and dispose as by the discrecōn of the said Edmund Mainwaringe or other Judge Competent in that behalfe shalbe by him designated and appointed then this present obligacōn to be voyd or els the same to be and remaine in full power and virtue.

Signature of the said Elizabeth Savage

Sealed and delivered:
in ye presence of
Tho: Humphreys Signature of the said Thomas Hughes

132. ALICE BUCKLEY OF WRENBURY, SPINSTER

Pr.C. 28 April 1649
W.T. 30 December 1646

Alice Buckley[a]	William Buckley	James Baker $\overset{o}{=}$ [ ] Buckley
c. 1621	fl. 1646 (kinsman)	fl. 1646 fl. 1639
† 1647/48		
		Elizabeth Baker *alias Buckley*
		c. 1639
		fl. 1646

Will, sick.

I give my soule unto god Almightie my heavenly father trusting through the merits of Jesus Christ hee will pardon & forgive me all my sins and a Joyfull resurection in the kingdome of heaven *I give my bodie to the Earth from whence I came and to be buried in the Church yard in Wrenbury*. And to be brought home at the love and discretion of my Mistres and my executor Kathern Horseman whome I

[a] In referring to her Mistress, Alice Buckley is indicating that she is a servant girl or domestic for Katheren Horseman of Wrenbury.

give all what at the time of my death I have whatsoever as that foure pounds ten shillings John Fisher oweth mee by bill forgiveing him all the interest shee discharging my buriall And giveinge unto my kinsman William Buckley one shilling unto Elizabeth daughter of James Baker six pence unto Anne the maid servant in my Mistres house four pence unto Arthur Fisher foure pence And all this beinge discharged I give unto my good freind Kathern Horseman the residue

The marke of Alice Buckley

Witness: Richard Wicksteed.

Endorsement: Probated 28 April 1649; administration to Raphe Ware, executor of the said deceased.

133. RALPH LAWRENCE OF NEWHALL, HUSBANDMAN

Administration Bond dated: 14 June 1649
Buried: 10 December 1648

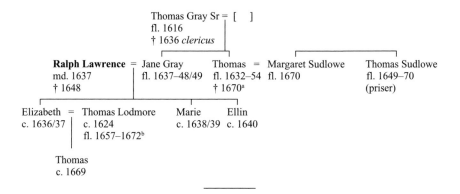

Inventory: Ralph Lawrence of Newhall, husbandman.

Taken: 6 January 1648/49

Of: goods Cattells & Chattells.

Prisers: Thomas Gray sen., Thomas Gray Junior and Thomas Sudlowe.

---

^a See will of Thomas Gray, pr. 1670/CRO.
^b See will of Edward Palin, pr. 1657 (will no. 143); see administration. of Thomas Lodmore, 1672/CRO.

	£	s	d
his weareinge apprell	1	0	0
Bedstids tables farmes & shilves		18	0
In Beddinge	2	13	4
In Brasse	3	0	0
In Pewter	1	0	0
In Lynnans and Napprie	1	10	0
quoffers Cheeres & Stooles	1	0	0
In Iron ware		6	4
In Treeneanware		13	4
In Ticknall ware		1	6
Sackes bagges & a old winnow sheette		1	6
one dishbord spininge wheeles and all other trumperie in the house		13	4
Corne in the house and all other meate ware		10	0
In Edge twooles		6	8
one ould plowe & harrowe & a ould packsaddle		3	4
hay & Corne in the barne	1	0	0
In Poultrie		3	0
one heifer and one Calfe	3	10	0
debtts oweinge by specialty	33	10	0
debtts oweinge without specialty by widdowe Sale	2	0	0
by *[blank]* Broster without specialty	1	0	0
by Roberte Treckkett without specialty	1	0	0
In redy money	14	17	4
In Muck & fuell		5	0
one debtt by Hugh Corser with out specialty	1	5	6
one debtt by Richard Cartwright	1	0	0
Soma totallis	73	8	2

Thomas Gray Junior
Tho: Gray Senior 1648
Thomas Sudlowe his T marke

Exhibitum pro vero per viduam relictam 19 die Januarij Anno 1649.

Charge: Know all men by these presents that we Jane Lawrence of Newhall in the county of Chester widow and Thomas Grey of Aston in the said county of Chester yeoman are held and firmly bound to Edmund Mainwaringe doctor of Laws legally appointed official principal of the Consistory Court of Chester in 100 pounds of good and legal English money to be paid to the same Edmund Mainwaring or to his certain attorney for this purpose, or his successors for well and truly making which payment we bind ourselves and each one of us for himself wholly and jointly our heirs, executors and administrators firmly by these presents Sealed with our seals & given the 14th day of June in the year of our Lord 1649.

The Obligation: The condition of this Obligacōn is such that if the above bounden Jane Lawrence doe well & truly Adminyster all and singuler the goods and Chattalls of Raph Lawrance laite of Newhall in the County of Chester Deceased to have the Administracōn of all & singuler the goods rights Creddits Cattles & Chattles of the sayd deceased according to the effecte of lettres of administracōn to her in that behalfe granted & doe truly Administer the same accordingly to law *videlicet* doe pay all the deceased: debts soe farr as the goods will extend & the law Charge And also doe exhibit unto this Court. or other Judge Competent in that behalfe a true & perfect Inventory of all the deceased goods rights Creddits Cattles & Chatles And of the said doe make & exhibit into the sayd Court or other Judge Competent in that behalfe a true & perfect accompte when & as often as shall be there unto lawfully called or required And lastly doe save & keepe harmelese the sayd Consistory & all other of his officerse & ministers in that behafe for granntinge the sayd lettres of Administracōn that then this present obligacōn to be Voyd & of now effect or else to remayne in full power & vertue.

Signature of Jane Lawrence
I (Seal)

Witnesses: Thomas Bickerton,   Thomas Gray
                          (Seal)   (Seal)

Endorsement: Letters of administration granted to Jane Laurence, widow of the said deceased, 14 June 1649.

134. WILLIAM TAYLOR OF SMEATONWOOD, HUSBANDMAN

S.Pr. 29 June 1649
W. 20 December 1648 (24 Chas. I)
Buried: 26 December 1648

1) Marie Sproson =	**William Taylor**	= 2) Elizabeth [ ]	Randle Taylor	Thomas Taylor =	Anne Massie
c. 1594	fl. 1612–22[a]	fl. 1648	fl. 1648	fl. 1620–48[b]	md. 1620
md. 1612	† 1649	† 1663	† 1649	† 1663 *senex*	† 1647
† bef. 1648					

Elizabeth	John	Margaret	Alice
c.1614	c. 1615	c. 1617	c. 1620
	† 1627	† 1617/18 *infans*	

[a] William Fergusson Irvine, *Chester Licences*, i. 118: 24 April 1612, to William Taylor, of Audlem parish, and Mary Sproson, of Wrenbury; at Wrenbury.
[b] See will of George Tench, pr. 1639 (will no. 107), also priser, 1638; owed 20s. to Richard Barnett, will pr. 1647/48 (will no.125).

Will, sick.

First I doe give and bequeath unto Elizabeth Taylor my wife all my househould stuffe as brasse pewter bedinge Napperie Corne hay Bacon and all my [insett?] goods whatsoever exceptinge such as shall heerafter bee mentioned. Item My will and mind is that the said Elizabeth my said wife shall have the use of all my kine and yonge cattell which I have for the nexte yeare onely, to use the ground withall which I have already taken for the same yeare to discharge the rente withall, and my will is and I doe give and bequeath all my said kine and cattells unto my said wife, and unto my brothers Thomas Taylor and Randle Taylor to be devided att the end of the yeare in manner & forme following (that is to say) Twoo equall parts thereof I doe give and bequeath unto my said wife, and the third equall parte thereof I doe give and bequeath unto my said brother Thomas Taylor, & my will & mind is that my said brother Randle Taylor shall have one heifer out of my said brother Thomas his third parte of my said cattell And if any of my said Cattell shall be sould within the said yeare my will is that my wife shall have twoo parts of the money & my said brother Thomas Taylor the third parte thereof: And my will is that my debts & funerall expences shall bee payd out of the whole estate. I doe give and bequeath my horse and carte unto my landlorde Thomas Gray, onely my will is that my wife shall have the use of them for the nexte yeare onely. I doe give & bequeath unto my said brother Thomas Taylor all my wearinge apparell except my worste[d] suite which I doe give unto my said brother Randle Taylor, And I doe give and bequeath unto my said brother Thomas Taylor my plowe my little gunne & my mattocke.

Executor: the testator's landlord, Thomas Gray.

Witnesses: Edward Palin, Thomas Gray, William Tench.

Inventory: William Taylor of Smeatonwood in the parish of Wrenbury, husbandman.

Taken: 20 January 1648/49 (24 Charles I)

Of: goods, Cattells and Chattells.

Prisers: Richard Cartwright, Edward Palyn, Thomas Gray and John Barker.

	£	s	d
His wearing apparell	3	6	8
Bedstide and Beddinge	4	0	0
In Brasse		5	0
In Pewter		5	0
Linnens and Napperie	3	0	0
quoffers boxes & stooles		10	0
one Iron pott one Fryinge pan & all other Iron ware		10	0

In treenean ware		12	0
Basketts sives & all other trumperie		2	0
Ticknall ware		1	6
Twoo spinninge wheeles		5	0
one Bracke		2	0
one Chese presse		3	0
In Poultrie		10	0
Fore rereinge Swine	1	8	0
In Chese Bacon & meate ware in the house	8	13	4
In muck & fuell		10	0
In Edge tooles one groome one pistoll and one sword		13	4
hay and corne in the house & in the barne	13	13	4
Carts and plowes	2	6	8
Thirteene kine	48	0	0
Nine yonge beasts	18	0	0
Five calves	4	0	0
a debt oweinge by Richard Lewis without specialty	1	0	6
one horse	5	0	0
a debtt oweinge by Thomas Skelhorne without specialty		2	0
A bargeninge by Artickles of Sixe parcells of ground from			
James Broomhall for one yeare yett in beinge	10	5	0
Summa totalis	127	4	4

Richard Cartwright His marke
Edward Palyn
Thomas Gray
John Barker His marke

Endorsement: Probated at Chester 29 June 1649; administration to the executor named in the will.

Endorsement on inventory: This inventory was exhibited in the Consistory Court of Chester by the sole executor named in the will.

135. GEORGE BARNETT OF SOUND

I. Administration granted 8 February 1649/50
Burial: None recorded at Wrenbury or Audlem[a]

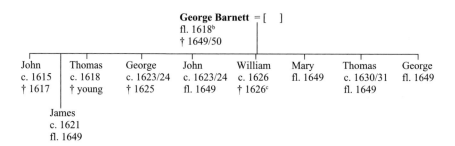

Administration:

The true and just accompte of John Steventon of Botton in the Countie of Salop the comadministrator of the goods and Chattells of George Barnet late of Sounde in the Countie of Chester deceased of and Concerninge the administracōn of the goods and Chattells of the said deceased rendered and Made by vertue of his Corporall oath taken the eight day of Februarie in the yeare of our Lord God accordinge to the Computacōn of the Church of England one thousand six hundred fourtie and nyne.

	£	s	d
Firstly, is this Accomptant doth Charge himselfe with the totall sume of the Inventarie taken of all and singuler the goods and Chattells of the said deceased extending to the sume of Two hundred thirtie and two pound seaventeene shillings and six pence of lawfull money of England which Inventary is hereto affixed beinge:	232	17	5

Payments and disbursments made by this Accomptant whereof hee desireth allowance as followeth:

---

[a] There is a burial entry for one George Barnet, 4 May 1641, at Wrenbury. If this is in fact the above-noted testator, then he presumably died intestate and his estate (which exceeded £230) required several years to sort out, perhaps because of the various children for whom legacies had to be paid out. If he did in fact die in 1641, then the majority of his children would have been minors at the time, thus accounting for the arrangements made for their upkeep.

[b] Priser for Peter Walton of Sound (CRO).

[c] Wrenbury Bishop's Transcripts – Baptisms: 1626; Burials: 1626.

paid unto Mary Barnet daughter of the said deceased the sume of Threescor and seaventeene pounds of lawfull money of England as it doth fully appear by her acquittance under hand and seale forth and sume of:	77	0	0
paid to Thomas Barnet one of the said deceased sonnes the sume of threescore and one pounds three shillings of lawfull money of England:	61	3	0
for tabling James Barnett the said deceadents sonn for two years and a quarter the sume of:	12	5	0
paid for James Barnets apparill	2	10	0
paid unto the same James Barnetts Master when he was found an apprentice and for his apparell the sume of	21	19	0
paid more for James & Thomas aforesaid the sume of	1	6	0
paid for George Barnets table for two years	11	0	0
paid for George Barnets apparell	2	0	0
paid for binding the said George Barnet to bee an apprentice	10	0	0
for his then apparrell	2	0	0
for a Bible for the said George		6	0
paid for the funerall expenses of the said George Barnett	1	16	0
paid to Thomas Fisher for Mucke and for avoiding from the house	5	0	0
expenses in Law against John Barnet of Pilstonn	4	17	0
paid more unto the said James Barnet	23	8	0
paid more unto the said James Barnet the sume of three-score & one pound whereof fortie four pounds was parte of the said George Barnets porcōn to be divided betwixt him the said James and his sister Marie Barnet the other seaventeene was in full of his owne in the whole	61	0	0
paid for John Barnets tabl and for his Cloaths for two years	13	6	8
paid more amongst the said Children	20	0	0
Suma Inventory	232	17	5
Summe of expenses	330	16	8
In surplusage	98	0	3

Endorsement: Accompte of John Steventon . . . administrator of the goods of George Barnett formerly of Sound deceased rendered and made the 8th day of February in the year of our Lord 1649/50.

136. MARGARET CHESWYS OF WRENBURY FRITH, WIDOW

Administration granted 5 March 1649/50
Burial: None recorded at Wrenbury

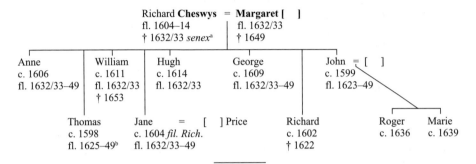

The Charge: Know all men by these presents that we Jane Price of Wrenbury Frith in the County of Chester John Wilson of the City of Chester gentleman and John Taylor of the same city barber are held and firmly bound to Edward Russell deputy rural dean of the rural deanery of Middlewich lawfully constituted in 40 pounds of good and legal English Money to be paid to the same Edward Russell or his certain attorney for this purpose or his successors for well and truly making which payment we bind ourselves and each one of us for himself wholly and jointly our heirs executors and administrators firmly by these presents Sealed with our seals and given the 5th day of March AD 1649.

Obligation: The condition of this obligacōn is such that if the above bounden Jane Price doe well and truly administer all and Singuler the goods Cattells Chattells Credits & debts of Margaret Cheswys late of Wrenbury Frith deceased according to the effect of lettres of administracōn to her in that behalfe that is to say doe pay all the debts the said decedant owed at the time of her decease soe far forth as the said goods Cattells & Chattells will thereunto extend and the Law in that behalfe will Charge her And doe exhibit in writing into the Office of the Rigister of the said Dean Russell a true and perfect Inventory of all and Singuler the foresaid goods Cattells & Chattells of the said deceased at or before the first day of July next ensueing and of and upon the same doe make a just and perfect accompt to the above named Edward Russell or other Judge competent in that behalfe when and as often as Shalbe thereunto Lawfully called or required Then this present obligacōn to be void and of none effect or els the same to remaine continue & be in full force & virtue.

ᵃ See will of Richard Cheswis, pr. 1633 (will no. 93). He was buried at Wrenbury 25 February 1632/33, a fact which argues for Margaret's burial there as well.
ᵇ 1630, Thomas Cheswis of the Frith owed debt of £1 5s to John Cartwright of Aston; see above, no. 81, p. 242.

Signed by Jane Price (seal)

Witnesses: Thomas Humphreys, John Wilson (seal), John Taylor (seal).

Endorsement: Letters of administration were granted of the goods of Margaret Cheswys formerly of Wrenbury Frith deceased to Jane Price natural daughter and executrix of the aforesaid deceased for good etc sworn in person 5th March AD 1649 Save always justly etc.

137. JOHN RAVENSCROFT OF NEWHALL

Pr.C. 2 July 1650
I. 20 November 1649
Buried: 4 November 1649

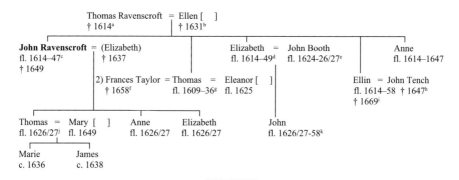

a　See will of Thomas Ravenscroft, pr. 1614 (will no. 43).
b　See will of Ellen Ravenscroft of Newhall, widow, pr. ca. 1631 (will no. 86).
c　John Ravenscroft was a priser for John Backhouse, will pr. 1620 (will no.61); executor and priser for George Dickins of Newhall, will pr. 1626/27 (will no. 74); overseer, witness and priser for John Hall of Newhall, will pr. 1636 (will no. 100); see also will of John Tench, pr. 1647/CRO.
d　Elizabeth Booth is noted in the will of her father, Thomas Ravenscroft, pr. 1614 (will no. 43) and in that of her mother, Ellen Ravenscroft, pr. ca. 1631 (will no. 86). She married John Booth in 1624 at Wrenbury. She owed £2 to her brother, 1649 (see below).
e　John Booth received bequest from Ellen Ravenscroft, will pr. ca. 1631 (will no. 86) 1626/27.
f　See will of Frances Ravenscroft, pr. 1658/59 (will no. 148).
g　William Fergusson Irvine, *Chester Licences*, iii. 36: 10 August 1625, to Thomas Ravenscroft and Mary [?] Taylor, spinster; at Audlem or Wrenbury; priser for George Dickins, will pr. 1626/27 (will no. 74); witness for John Hall, will pr. 1636 (will no. 100).
h　See will of John Tench of Wilkesley, pr. 1647/CRO.
i　See will of Ellen Tench, widow of Wilkesley, pr. 1669/CRO.
j　Thomas and his sisters, as well as their cousin John Booth Jr, are noted in the will of their grandmother, Ellen Ravenscroft, pr. ca. 1631 (will no. 86).
k　Appointed overseer of the estate of Frances Ravenscroft, will pr. 1658/59 (will no. 148).

Inventory: of John Ravenscroft of Newhall, yeoman.

Taken: 20 November 1649

Of: goods Cattells and Chattells.

Prisers: William Poole Richard Hassall Robert Shrowbridge and Richard Berrington.

	£	s	d
His wearinge apparrell	5	6	8
Seaven Cowes at £2 16s. 8d. a Cowe	19	16	8
Sixe Bullocks at £7 a paire whereof Two were taken for herriotts	21	0	0
Two Twynters at 29s. a peece	2	18	0
Three Calves at	2	17	0
a barren heifer at	2	3	4
a bay nagge	3	6	8
a little roane nagge	2	3	4
Foure Lambs —		10	6
Carts, ploughes, harrowes, Chaines, yokes plow timber, Cart timber & all implemets of husbandry	5	14	6
Corne in the barne	10	8	0
a fatt hogge	1	8	0
Hey in the barne and in the feilds	6	16	8
Rakes, pikeyelves, Tooles, a ripple combe Billes, axes shovles, a stock sawe and other small implements not before mencōned		10	0

In the Kill

	£	s	d
A weeting Combe, a whitch & a hair Cloth		16	8
Malt	1	16	0
Coales wood & other fuell	1	0	0
Corne in the ground	1	0	0
Muck		10	0

In the Storechamber

	£	s	d
Cheeses	7	13	4
Yarne & towe		13	4
Shelves and skales		7	10

In the Chamber over the house

	£	s	d
Item One pair of beddstidds and beddinge for Servants		17	0
Item one Fetherbedd wth Coverings and boulsters	2	10	0
Item Three Coffers one boxe & one old Cubbart and a shelfe		5	0

In the Parlor

	£	s	d
Two Joyned bedds Two Fetherbedds with boulsterss and blanketts one Coveringe one rugge, Two pair of Curtains, one paire of vallens with all appurtenncs	7	6	8
Lynnens and Nappery and one peece of Ticke	4	6	8
One Presse	1	0	0
Five Chests	1	0	0
One table with a frame & two formes		13	4

In the Chamber over the Kitchin

	£	s	d
One Joynd bedd, beddinge thereto, One little side table & a little Coffer	1	4	0

In the Chamber over the Kitchin buttry

	£	s	d
One old Joynd bedd and Beddinge thereto		7	6

In the Buttry

	£	s	d
Pewter of all sorts	2	5	0
Shelves		1	8

In the Kitchyn & Kitchin Buttry

	£	s	d
Brasse of all sorts and one Iron pott & one Iron kettle	3	10	6
Spitts gobbarts racks, potracks, fireshovle tongues & one Iron grate, Anndirons, drippinge panns a paire of bellows and all other Iron ware not before mencōned		13	4
a fowling peece		6	8
Treenan ware of all sorts	1	2	4
Two longe Spinninge wheles a sittinge wheele & an ald reele		5	4
Baggs, Sacks, a mym[ ] wth eete sives and riddles		8	8
Bacon, butter, larde & other provision in the house	2	1	6
Poultry of all sorts		9	8
Ticknall ware of all sorts and all other trumpye in and about the house not particalerly mencōnded		6	6

In the house

	£	s	d
One longe table & frame & two formes	1	0	0
one little table		5	0
Cheeres and Stooles		5	4
Quishions		5	0
One rideinge saddle		5	0
a lookeinge glasse			8

At Newhall Park house

	£	s	d
One Joynd bedd, a table a Tressell & foure shelves		10	0

Debts owinge to the decedent:

	£	s	d
Ready money in the house	10	1	6
Elizabeth Booth oweth	2	0	0
Mary Ravenscrofte	2	6	8
Mr. Cotton in amounts for suits	2	0	0
Robert Clare		3	6
Robert Furbur		5	0
[illegible]	16	16	8
Tot	149	5	6

Prisers: William Poole, (H) Richard Hassall his mark, Richard (RB) Berringtons marke, The marke (X) of Robert Shrowbridge

Endorsement: Inventory of the goods &c. of John Ravenscroft deceased, while he lived, of Newhall 1650.

Exhibitum cum protestacōne 2 July 1650.

138. THOMAS WOOD OF NEWHALL

PCC: Administration granted: 31 August 1653
Burial: None recorded at Wrenbury or Audlem

```
┌──────────────────────┐
Thomas Wood             George Wood
† 1653                  fl. 1653
        ────────────
```

August 1653. Thomas Wood the 31ᵗʰ day a comission issued forth unto George Wood the naturall and lawfull brother of Thomas Wood late of Newhall in the county of Chester deceased to administer the goodes chattells & debts of the said deceased he being first legally sworne truely to administer.

Inventory exhibited 1 October 1653.

139. JOHN EDGELEY OF MOOREHALL, YEOMAN

S? Pr. PCC 13 August 1654
W.T. 25 August 1653
Buried: 30 August 1653

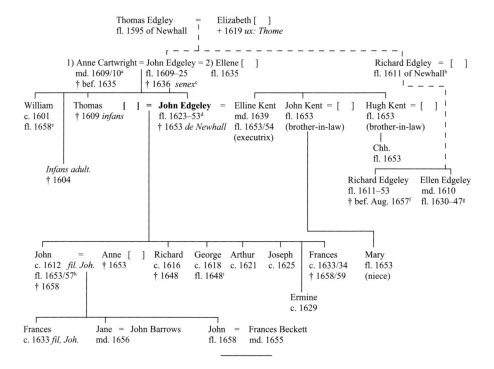

a   See will of John Edgeley of Woodcott, pr. 1637 (will no. 102), note a.
b   Priser for Margaret Sevell, will pr. 1611 (will no. 35).
c   For documentation, see will no. 102, note b.
d   Appears as a tenant of Woodcott Farm, 1636, held under Richard Wilbraham; flourished 1648 at Moore Hall as a tenant of Newhall/CRO.
e   Married Dorothy Heighfield, 1658 at Wrenbury.
f   See no. 83, note b; married Jane Hall, daughter of John Hall (d. 1605) at Wrenbury, 1612.
g   See no. 83, note a; married Richard Hall 1610 at Wrenbury.
h   Witness to will of his father, John Edgeley of Moorehall, below; noted as John Edgeley of Moorehall, a copyholder about Dods Green, 1653/CRO (Hall's Notes, p. 179); mentioned by George Hall, Jr as his cousin John Edgeley of Woodcott, will pr. 1658 (will no. 147).
i   Newhall Manor Court Records, 1648/CRO: appeared as George Edgley, gen.

Will, sick.

First I Gyve and yeeld upp my soule into the hands of Almighty God who First Gave itt mee trustinge and stedfastly beleevinge by the death and only Merritts of Jesus Christ my Saviour to have free pardon and Remission of All my Sinnes And my body I Committ to the Earth to bee decently buryed In Christian buryall att the descrecōn of my Executors hereafter named And for the temporall Estate which Almighty God of his free bounty and Mercy hath inriched mee withal I will and dispose thereof as followeth First I Gyve and bequeath unto my neece Mary Kent Tenne Poundes in money Alsoe I doe Gyve and bequeath unto my brother in Law John Kent his Children Tenne shillings a peece in money Alsoe I doe Gyve and bequeath unto my brother in law Hugh Kent his children Tenne shillings a peece in Money Alsoe I doe gyve and bequeath unto all my God children that shalbee lyvinge att my decease Two shillings a peece Also I Doe Gyve and bequeath unto my two Servants John Whittingham and Elizabeth Rabone either of them one Lambe Also I doe heerby give & bequeath unto My lovinge wife Elline Edgley All the rest and residue of all my goods Cattells And Chattells both moveable and unmoveable goods quick and deade of what Kinde or quality soever the same bee of, or wheresoever the same remayneth My debts legacyes and Funerall Expences beinge in the first place thereout Payd and discharged.

Executrix: Elline Edgley my said wife.

H. & S.

Witnesses: John Edgley George Hall William Fletcher Thomas Gray 1653.

Endorsement: This will was proved att Westminster the One and Thirtieth day of August In the yeare of our lord 1654 Before the Judges for Probate of Wills and grantinge of Administracōns Lawfully Authorized By the Oath of Elline Edgley the Relict and Sole Executrix named in the said Will To whom was Committed Administrator of All and singuler the goods Chattells and debts of the said deceased shee Beinge by vertue of a Commission first sworne truly to Administer the same.

140. HENRY GRIFFITHS OF BROOMHALL, CLERK

S? Pr. PCC 18 January 1654/55
W.T. 1654
Buried: Nantwich?

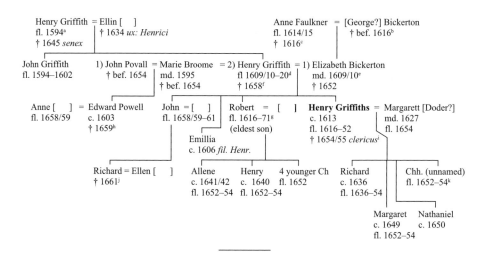

---

a   Henry *Garfferth* and his son John owed £6 to Humphrey Bickerton, will pr. 1594 (will no.
    12)); in 1602, John Griffith owed ca. £4 to Humphrey Wilson, will pr. 1602 (will no. 16).
b   The most likely candidate for Elizabeth's unnamed father is George Bickerton, who was
    buried in 1596. Humphrey Bickerton, who was buried in 1594, left a will (will no. 12) in
    which he named his wife, namely Ales Renshaw. He is equally explicit that he has but three
    children, none of whom is Elizabeth. He is thus eliminated as a possibility.
c   Anne Bickerton is noted as sister to Thomas Faulkner; see latter's will, pr. 1615 (will no.
    47). See also will of Anne Bickerton, pr. 1616. (will no. 49).
d   Witness for John Wilkinson, will pr. 1615 (will no. 46); executor for William Heighfield, his
    neighbour and bequeathed 5s. 6d., will pr. 1620 (will no. 62). Henry Griffith had tenure of
    land in Wrenbury parish as noted in R. Stewart Brown, *Cheshire Inquisitions Post Mortem*,
    ii. 207, for John Chetwoode.
e   William Fergusson Irvine, *Chester Licences*, i. 74: 10 February 1609/10, to Henry Griffith
    of Nantwich and Elizabeth Bickerton, spinster of Wrenbury; bondsman John Taylor of
    Chester, ironmonger; at Wrenbury or Nantwich.
f   See will of Henry Griffiths the elder, pr. 1658 (will no. 145).
g   Henry *Griffies* and Robert *Griffies* are noted as grandsons of Anne Bickerton, will pr. 1616
    (will no. 49); Robert noted 1632 as god-son of William Bebington of Nantwich (see latter's
    will/CRO); Henry and Robert executors for his father's will, pr. 1658 (will no. 145). Robert
    and John Griffiths were bequeathed 40s and £5 respectively as the brothers of Edward Powell,
    will pr. 1659 (will no. 149). Robert Griffith made inventory for Thomas Dickin 1671/CRO.
h   See will of Edward Powell, pr. 1659 (will no. 149).
i   Incumbent at Wrenbury 1646–54. Henry Griffyth of Wrenbury noted in will of Thomas Grey,
    pr. 1640 (will no. 112), and in tithe 1647.
j   See will and inventory of Richard Griffiths Sr, pr. 1661/CRO.
k   The will of Henry Griffiths Sr, made 1652, pr. 1658 (will no. 145) mentions three unnamed
    children of Henry Jr.

First, I Commend my soule into ye hands of my Creator trustinge through the mercy of God and ye Merritts of my Savior Jesus Christ to Receive free pardon of all my Sins And a blessed resurrection unto Eternall life and my body I Committ to the Earth to bee decently buryed att the discrecōn of my Executors heerafter named And my minde and Will is And I doe heerby nominate appoint and declare that Margarett my deare and lovinge shalbee the sole Executrix of this my Last Will and Testament and that shee shall have the tuicōn & educacōn of all my Children until such tyme as they shalbee severally able to make Choyce of lawfull Guardians for themselve, & for the temporall Estate which the Lord Almighty hath bestowed upon mee after my just debts and funerall Expences bee paid and discharged I doe heerby dispose thereof as followeth First I doe give and bequeath unto every one of my Children each of them an In calfe Cow and an Ewe and a Lambe to bee sett forth for them by my said Executrix within the space of one whole yeare next after my decease And my desire is that shee will bee very carefull to see the profitt of the said Cattle and sheep imployed and Continued forth for the best benefitt of my said Children And Concerninge all the rest of my Personall Estate And alsoe Concerninge my two houses & Tenements thereunto belonginge in Broomhall aforesaid my minde and will is that my said Wife shall have the whole Profitt and use both of the said personall Estate & Tenements with their Appurtenanncs duringe her naturall life if after my decease shee remayne soe longe sole and unmarried shee maintayninge all my said Children with meate drinke and apparrell and other necessaryes accordinge to her owne discrecōn But if shee happen to Contract Matrimony with any other man after my decease Then my minde and will is and from thenceforth I doe devisse and bequeath unto her only one third parte of my said personall Estate And all that my mes-suage and Tenement in Broomhall aforesaid wherin Thomas Saunders doeth now Inhabitt for and duringe her naturall life And alsoe Fyve Markes a yeare to bee paid her by my eldest sonne out of that Messuage and Tenement in Broomhall aforesaid wherein I doe now Inhabitt and dwell upon every first day of March duringe her Naturall life if the Terme I have in the said Tenement shall and doe soe longe Continue And the other two third parts of my personall Estate I doe then gyve & bequeath unto my younger Children to bee equally divided amongst them And alsoe after the marriage and death of my said wife whether shall first happen my minde & will is And I doe Gyve grannt devise and bequeath unto each of my said younger Children Twenty markes a peece to bee raysed out of the Rents & Profitts of my said Tenements in Broomhall and to bee paid unto them as they are in Seniority or priority of birth one before another And after ye said severall summes are paid and discharged I doe heerby give grant Assigne and bequeath all the rest residue & Remaynder of my Estate Title Interest Tennant Right Clayme and demand of and the said Two houses and Tenements unto my eldest sonne.

Sealed subscribed and Published and before the sealinge heerof I doe hereby fur-ther Publish and declare this my Will and minde is And I doe and I doe further *[sic!]*give and bequeath unto my daughter Margarett Griffiths Twenty Nobles to bee paid her out of my Tenements in Broomhall to make her porcōn out of the said Tenements Twenty pounds And I doe Gyve unto my lovinge Friends to Allen Griffiths Ellen Ranshall and to Thomas Gray and and Margarett his wife and to every of them as a remembrance of half Crownes a peece and to all my servants that are dwellinge with me att my decease Twelve pence a peece.

Henry Griffiths Minister

Witnesses: John Ravenshaw Thomas Gray 1654.

Endorsement: Proved at Westminster 18 January 1654/55 (English Style) before the Judges for Probate of Wills; administration to Margarett Griffiths relict of the deceased and sole Executrix named in the said will.

141. THOMAS BREES OF BROOMHALL, YEOMAN

S.Pr.PCC 8 March 1655/56
W.T. 1 November 1654

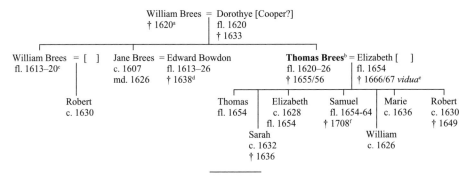

Will, sick.

I committ my soule into the hands of my Creator trustinge through the mercy of God the father and the meritts of Christ my Savior to receive free pardon of all my sinnes and a blessed resurreccōn unto Eternall life And my body I Committ

---

[a] See will of William Brees of Broomhall, pr. 1621 (will no. 64).
[b] Executor of the will of his father William Brees of Broomhall (will no. 64).
[c] William Brees was bequeathed 3s. 4d. as the god-child of William Cooper of Sound, will pr. 1613 (will no. 42). This suggests that his mother was a Cooper, in which family the name Dorothy was prominent.
[d] See inventory of Edward Bowdon, 1638 (no. 106).
[e] Wrenbury Bishop's Transcripts – Burials: 1666/67 Elizabeth Breese *vidua*.
[f] Samuel Brees churchwarden at Wrenbury 1664; Samuel Brees yeoman of Broomhall † 1708; see will/CRO.

to the Earth from whence itt came to bee decently buryed at the discrecon of my Executor heerafter named Item I Gyve and bequeath unto my sonne Thomas Brees Tenn shillings of lawfull money of England [in full satisfacton of his] [ch]ildes part of all my personall Estate Item I Gyve and bequeath unto my daughter Elizabeth Brees One hundred poundes of like lawfull money [which is] owinge unto mee and due by specialty from my Said Sonne Thomas Item I Gyve and bequeath unto my sonne Samuell Breese all my bookes [ ] and all my standinge Goods as Bedsteads Tables Boards [?] shelves and such like and all my husbandry ware of what kinde & quality soever And alsoe I doe Gyve grant devise assigne and sett over unto my Said Sonne Samuell Breese the Moyetye as one halfe of my Messuage and Tenement in Broomhall aforesaid wherin I doe now Inhabite and dwell and the moyetye or one halfe of all houses Edifices buildings barnes Stables kilnes Backe houses Outhouses Lands Tenements Meadowes Leysowes pastures woods wayes waters Commons profitts & Commodityes thereunto belonginge or therewith usually granted [?]oyed or enjoyed with their and only of their appurtenances to have and to hould the said Moyetye or one halfe of the said Messuage and Tenement houses Edifices buildings lands Tenements Meadowes Leysowes pastures and premisses with their and every of their appurtenances unto the said Samuell Breese his Executors administrators and assignes Imediatly from and after the decease of mee the said Thomas Breese for by and duringe and untill the full end and terme of Threescore yeares if Elizabeth Breese now wife of the said Thomas Brees shall and doe soe longe lyve to all such and the like uses as I the said Thomas Breese coulde or might have held or enjoyed the same Hee the said Samuell Breese yeelding payinge & performinge all Rents dutyes and Services due and payable for the Moyety or one halfe of the Messuage &Tenement afore-said Item I doe Gyve and bequeath all the rest & residue of my Goods Cattells and Chattells quick and dead of what kinde or quality soever after my debts are payd and funerall Expences discharged, to my lovinge wife Elizabeth Breese and my Said Sonne Samuell Breese to bee equally divided betwixt them.

Executor: the testator's son, Samuell Breese.

H. & S.
Thomas Brees

Witnesses: Thomas Massie Ellen Massie.

Endorsement: Probated at London 8 March 1655/56; administration to Samuell Breese, son and sole executor named in the will.

142. GEORGE HALL OF ASTON, YEOMAN

S?Pr.PCC 29 September 1657
W.T. 3 February 1656/57
Buried: 25 August 1657
Buried: at Wrenbury, 1657

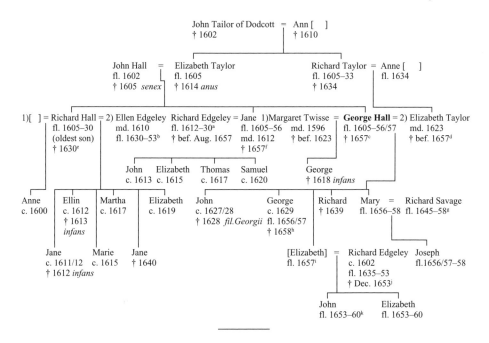

^a Co-executor with his sister, Ellen Hall, for Richard Hall, 1630/31 (no. 83).
^b Co-executor with her brother, Richard Edgeley, for her husband (see previous note); *Widdow* Hall paid tithe at Newhall, 1647/CRO.
^c For ancestry, see will of John Hall of Smeatonwood (will no. 22); bequeathed 12d. as god-son of George Kemp, will pr. 1616 (will no. 50); noted 1634 as son-in-law of Richard Tailor of Dodcott, will pr. 1634/CRO; noted 1653 as a freeholder of Newhall Manor/CRO.
^d While there is no mention of George Hall's wife in his will, an Elizabeth Hall, widow, appears in 1658 at Aston, suggesting that she was in fact still alive /CRO.
^e See inventory of Richard Hall of Smeatonwood, 1630 (no. 83), and note d.
^f See will of Jane Edgeley of Moorehall, pr. 1657/58 (will no. 144).
^g Overseer of the will of his brother, Robert Savage, pr. 1647 (will no. 124).
^h See will of George Hall, Jr, pr. 1658 (will no. 147).
ⁱ See will no. 153, note k.
^j See will of Richard Edgeley of Smeatonwood, pr. 1660/61 (will no. 153).
^k John Edgeley and his sister Elizabeth are referred to in this will, as well as those of George Hall, Jr , pr. 1658 (will no. 147) and Richard Edgeley, pr. 1660/61 (will no. 153).

Will, *[no statement regarding health]*.

First I give and bequeath my soule into the hands of Almighty god my only saviour and Redeemer *And my body to the earth To be buried in the Church yard of Wrenbury aforesaid* Item I give unto Richard Savage my sonne in lawe five pounds and unto Mary Savage his wife tenne pounds to be paid her in Gould Item I give unto John Edgley to Elizabeth Edgley and to Joseph Savage my three grandchildren five pounds a peece And to her daughter Elizabeth Edgley*[sic]*one cowe now in the possession of John Hassell Item I give unto John Wade Humphrey Deekes Thomas Wright and Anne Wade my olde servant tenne shillings a peece Item I give and bequeath unto my sonne George Hall the house wherein I now dwell the land and buildings with theire appurtenances and all things belonging thereto. But if it please god he dye sole and not marryed Then I bequeath it to John Edgley and to his sister Elizabeth Edgley the said sonne John Edgley to give his sister for her parte one hundred pounds Item I give unto my sonne George Hall all the rest and residue of all my goods Cattell and Chattells of what sorte or manner soever they bee as ready money in the house debts oweing by specialty or without or of what sorte or kind soever they bee.

Executor: the testator's son, George Hall.

H. & S.
George Hall

Witnesses: John Fischer (his marke) Edward Hamnett.

Endorsement: This will was proved at London before the Judges for probate of willes and granting administracōns lawfully authorized the twenty nyneth day of September in the yeare of our Lord one Thousand six hundred fifty seaven by the oath of George Hall the sonne and sole executor named in the said will to whome administration of all and singuler the goods Chattells and debts of the said deceased was committed He being first by commission sworne truely to administer the same.

143. EDWARD PALIN OF SMEATONWOOD, YEOMAN

I?Pr. PCC 2 October 1657
W.T. 12 August 1657

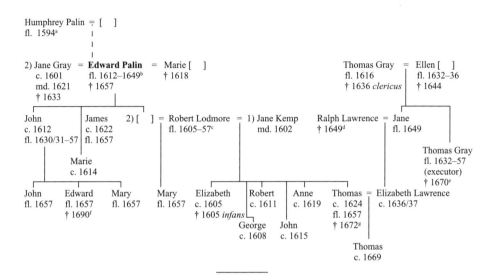

Will, sick.

First I yield upp Willingly my Soule into the handes of Almighty God who First gave itt mee trustinge therefore in the Merritts and death of Jesus Christ my Saviour To have free pardon and Remission of All my Sinnes and my Body I Comitt to the Earth to bee decently buried in Christian burial att the discretion of my Executors here After named And as Concerninge my Temporall Estate which Almighty God hath Inriched mee withal I dispose as followeth Inprimis All my debts being first dis Charged and payd I give and bequeath unto my Sonne John Palyn £6 13s. 4d. To be duely payd unto him or his assignes yearely Soe long as the Lease which I the said Edward Palyn had granted to me by George Cotton

ᵃ Owed Humphrey Bickerton 5s. 4d., see will of Humphrey Bickerton, pr. 1594 (will no. 12).
ᵇ Edward Palin made inventory for George Tench 1638 (will no. 107); paid tithe in 1647; see also will of John Tenche, 1647/48; made inventory for William Taylor, will pr. 1649 (will no. 134).
ᶜ Owed a debt to James Brooke; see will of James Brooke, pr. 1622 (will no. 66).
ᵈ See inventory of Ralph Lawrence of Newhall, husbandman, 1648/49 (no. 133).
ᵉ See will and inventory of Thomas Gray of Aston, pr. 1670/CRO.
ᶠ See will of Edward Palin of Smeatonwood, pr. 1690/ CRO.
ᵍ Thomas Lodmore married Elizabeth Lawrence 27 December 1668 at Wrenbury. See will, pr. 1672 /CRO.

late of Combermere deceased doth or may Continue and endure To be payed att Two severall payments (That is to say) £3 6s. 8d. Att the feast of St. Michaell Tharchangell and £3 6s. 8d. upon the Twenty Fift day of March next Followeinge in the manner aforesaid I give and bequeath unto my Sonne James Palyn £3 of Currant English money to bee payd unto him or His Assignes att Michaelmas next after the debts are discharged, and the said Payment of £3 to continue yearely soe long as the above menconed Lease doth or maye Endure Item I give unto my Grandchild Mary Lodmore £10 Item I give and bequeath unto my Grandchild Mary Palin £10 Item I give And bequeath unto my Grandchild John Palin £6 13s. 4d. Item Itt is my desire and I will and appoint That my Sonne in Lawe Robert Lodmore shall Take unto him att May next my Grandchild Edward Palin And him to keepe Until hee bee One and Twentye yeares of Age If hee soe long live with Sufficient meate Drinke Cloth keepinge him to some Convenient Learneing And in case That the debts and Legacyes with the above said Tenement doth stand Charged with bee cleerely quitt and dis Charged by Then the said Edward Palin come to the yeares of one and Twenty That then the Aforesaid Edward Palin Sonne to John Palin shall have hold Occupie and enjoye All the Said messuage and Tenement Together with one parcel of groundes known by the name of The Little Gersly Loddiate; The said Edward dischargeinge All rents dutyes and Taxacōns Together with such Annueties as the Tenement may be Charged with or any way due; And In case the said Edward Palin dye and departe this life before the Lease that is now a foote Be Expired That then the revercōn of the Lease to fall to John Palin younger brother to the said Edward And in case the said John Palin dye and departe this life before the said Lease be Expired That Then the revercōn To belonge to Thomas Lodmore Sonne to Robert Lodmore dischargeing as aforesaid.

Executors: Thomas Gray of Smeatonwood and Robert Lodmore of Erge, both in the Countye of Chester.

Overseer: John Swan, Parson att Baddiley.

Edward Palin
S.

Witnesses: George Brownefall of Smeatonwood[a] (His marke), Elizabeth Gray, James Bromall.

Endorsement: Probated at London 2 October 1657; administration to Thomas Gray and Robert Lodmore, executors named in the will.

---

[a] See will of George Brownefall of Smeatonwood, pr. 1666/CRO.

144. JANE EDGELEY OF MOOREHALL IN NEWHALL, WIDOW

S?Pr. PCC 5 January 1657/58
W.T. 4 August 1657
Buried: 11 August 1657

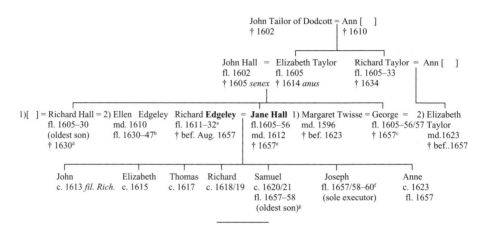

Will, sick.

I doe hereby bequeath my soule to The Allmighty who gave it, And and after death *my body to be buried in the Church or Churchyard of Wrenbury* at the discrecōns of my Children & friends And after funeral expences and debtes beinge discharged as followeth Item I give And bequeath to my eldest sonne Samuel Edgley four shillings Item I give And bequeath to my other sonne Joseph Edgley

---

^a Priser for Margaret Sevell, will pr.1611 (will no. 35); married 1612 at Wrenbury; noted in will of Edmund Crewe and acted as priser, will pr. 1632 (will no. 90); churchwarden at Wrenbury, 1636. Jane Edgeley was already a widow when she made her will on 4 August 1657.

^b Co-executor, with her brother Richard Edgeley, for her husband, 1630/31 (no. 83); *Widdow* Hall paid tithe at Newhall, 1647/CRO.

^c See will of George Hall, pr. 1657 (will no. 142).

^d See testamentary papers of Richard Hall, 1630/31 (no. 83).

^e For ancestry, see will of John Hall of Smeatonwood, pr. 1606 (will no. 22); on 16 October 1657, at the View of Frankpledge of Newhall Manor Court, Jane Edgeley is noted as being deceased; the heriot due was one cow/CRO.

^f Challenged appointment of Arthur Edgeley of Poole as guardian of minor children of Richard Edgeley of Smeatonwood; see his will, pr. 1660/61 (will no. 153); noted 1664 in occupation of Hall's Fields at Newhall/CRO.

^g On 6 November 1658 Samuel Edgeley was recognized as the brother and heir of John Edgeley, deceased; see Newhall Manor Court records/CRO. The fact that he was noted as Jane Edgeley's 'oldest son' in 1657 indicates that John, Thomas and Richard - his older brothers - had all predeceased him.

foure paire of bed hookes One standinge bed in the parlour one pair of bed stack-es in the little chambr Two paire in the left over the house the two tables in the house the Presse and the Chest standinge in the parlour three feather beds and three Chaffe beds foure paire of Sheetes foure boulsters Item I give and bequeath To my daughter Anne Edgley one featherbed the best in the house fyve Boulsters tow pillows three paire of sheetes two pillowbeers six napkins two Blankets and one shillinge and one table Cloth Item I give and bequeath to My daughter Elizabeth Edgley two paire of bedstockes one paire in the parlor And the other in the Loft over the parlor one feather bed one Chaffe Bed five paire of Sheetes of those nine paire in the Chest beinge Amongst them there all disposed of and the foure paire of sheetes that goe About in the house two of the best boulsters after Anne hath hers and One of the best pillows Alsoe one table Cloth one table Standinge in The kitchin one great comnpe and a heare beinge in the kill Item I give bequeath more to my sonne Joseph two pillowbeers and as fourth Blankets and coverlets gyt be undisposed of to be equally decided betwixt him And his sis-ter Elizabeth And alsoe all Coffers tubbs barrels, booukes, and all Such house-hold stuffe as brasse pewter and the like to be equally devided betwixt The said Joseph and Elizabeth Alsoe I give and bequeath sixe silver spoons To be equal-ly devided betwixt Joseph Elizabeth and Anne And alsoe for corne Haye knifes and all other goods undisposed of (after funeral expences & debtes Beinge dis-charged) to be equally devided betwixt the said Joseph and Elizabeth And alsoe I give and bequeath to my daughter Elizabeth all my hempe and flaxe.

Executor: Joseph Edgley, son of the testator, as sole executor.

H. & S.

The marke of Jane Edgeley

Witnesses: The marke of Michaell Harris, William Fletcher.

Endorsement: Probated at London 5 January 1657/58; administration to Joseph Edgley, the natural son and sole executor of the deceased.

145. HENRY GRIFFITHS THE ELDER OF BROOMHALL, GENT.

S.Pr. PCC 2 July 1658
W.T. 24 December 1652
Buried: No record at Wrenbury or Audlem

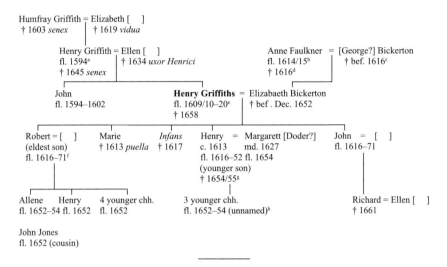

Will, 'beeing very aged and weake in body'.

First I give and yeld up willingly my soule into the hands of allmighty God my Creator, who first gave it mee, Trusting by the onely merits of the death and pas-

---

[a] Henry *Garfferth* and son John owed £6 to Humphrey Bickerton; see latter's will, pr. 1594 (will no. 12); in 1602, John Griffith owed ca. £4 to Humphrey Wilson, will pr. 1602 (will no. 16).

[b] Noted as sister to Thomas Faulkner of Chorley in his will, pr. 1615 (will no. 47).

[c] See will no. 140, note 'b' for arguments supporting identification of Anne's unnamed husband with George Bickerton, who was buried at Wrenbury in 1596.

[d] See will of Anne Bickerton, pr. 1616 (will no. 49).

[e] William Fergusson Irvine, *Chester Licences*, i. 74: 10 February 1609/10, to Henry Griffith of Nantwich and Elizabaeth Bickerton, spinster of Wrenbury; bondsman, John Taylor of Chester, ironmonger; at Wrenbury and Nantwich. Henry was a witness for John Wilkinson, will pr. 1615 (will no. 46); executor for William Heighfield, his neighbour, will pr. 1620 (will no. 62). Henry Griffith had tenure of land in Wrenbury parish as noted in the inquisition post mortem for Thomas Minshull; see R. Stewart Brown, *Cheshire Inquisitions Post Mortem*, ii. 207.

[f] Robert and Henry Griffes are noted as the grandsons of Anne Bickerton will pr. 1616 (will no. 49); Robert Griffith is noted as the oldest son in his father's will, and served as executor thereof (below); made inventory for Thomas Dickins 1671/CRO.

[g] Noted 1632 as god-son of William Bebington of Nantwich; see latter's will (CRO); see will of Henry Griffiths of Broomhall, pr. 1654/55 (will no. 140).

[h] Undoubtedly includes Richard (fl. 1636–54) and Margaret (fl. 1651–54).

sion of Jesus Christ my Saviour to have free pardon and remission of all my sinnes, and my body I Comitt to the Earth to bee decently buryed in Christian buriall at the discretion of my Executor hereafter named, and for that temporall Estate wherewith Allmighty God of his free bounty and mercie hath enriched mee withall I will and dispose thereof as followeth First I give and bequeath grant and convey unto my Grandchild Allenne Griffiths all that my Burgage or Tenement with it appurtenances scituate in Nantwich within the sayd County of Chester now in the holding or occupacōn of the widow Gandie together with an annuall rent of Eight shillings a yeare due to mee out of the Chantry lands in Nantwich, and allso a rent charge of twenty pence a yeare due to mee from Mr Wilbraham of Nantwich abovesaid for, by and during the Terme and unto the full end and Terme of ffower score yeares next ensuing after my decease (if hee the sayd Allene doe and shall soe long live) Allso I give grant, enfeoffe and Confirme unto my Eldest sonne Robert Griffiths all my Right and Inheritance of and in three severall messuages, Burgages or tenements with the yards Gardens and lands thereunto belonging with their appurtenances scituate, lying and beeing within the liberties of the towne of Nantwich abovesaid and now in the occupacōn of the said Widdowe Gandie John Simcock and Jane Hammnete Together with the Remainder and remainders of the said yearely rents of Eight shillings a yeare and twenty pence a yeare to him and his heires forever Alsoe I doe give and Bequeath unto my said sonnes Robert Griffyths his five younger Children the some of nine pounds which I had lately in William Cowpers but now in my said sonne Roberts hands to bee equally devided amongst them Alsoe I doe give and bequeath unto my Servant Margarett Griffyths the bedd where on I ly with its furniture and one Coffer Alsoe I doe give and bequeath unto my Grandchild Nathaniell Griffyths one weanescott Trunck Alsoe I doe give and bequeath unto my Grandchild Henry Griffyths my said Sonne Roberts Sonne all my Carts Ploughs yokes Chaynes and Implements of husbandry and alsoe all the rest and residue of all my insett or household goods remaineinge and beinge in my house wherein I doe now live Alsoe I doe give and bequeath unto my younger sonne Henry Griffyths my younge Mare and I doe alsoe give and bequeath unto my said Sonn Henry his three children two kine and one heifer Calfe to bee Equally devided amongst them Alsoe I doe give and bequeath unto my said servant and kinswoman forty pounds in money whereof Randle Ranshall oweth mee tenne pounds Mary Wilkinson: £5: Thomas Tench: £5: & John Taylor: £20: Alsoe I doe give unto her one Cowe called Tye or Browning on Condicōn shee shall bestowe her selfe in Marriage with the approbacōn of my said Sonne Henry Alsoe I doe give and bequeath unto Mary Davies the elder of Salop Mary Davies the younger Elizabeth the wife of John Hanton and the wife of Robert Brittaine Edward Ambler all of Salop above said five shillings a piece to buy them gloves Alsoe I doe give unto Jane the wife of William Higgins to Robert Brittaines Daughter and to Richard sonne of Mary Davies late Daughter of Robert Brittin five shillings sixe pence a piece to buy them gloves and I doe alsoe give and bequeath unto my servant Mary Davies two shillings and to Alice Bedward two shillings Alsoe I doe give and bequeath unto my said sonne Robert Griffiths my gray Mare Towards the payment of my Cozen John Jones his debt which hee oweth him Alsoe I doe give and bequeath unto my said sonne Robert Twentie pounds in mony being in John Woolrich his hands Alsoe I give and bequeath unto my said sonn Henry Griffiths twenty pounds in mony being in Mr. Cartwright's hands.

Executors: the testator's two sons, Robert Griffith and Henry Griffith (and if there shalbee any remainder of my estate my Legacies above bequeathed and funerall Expences discharged That they shall loveingly devide the same betwixt them).

H. & S.

Witness: Thomas Gray.

Memorandum: the day and yeare formerly written, these things were omitted as followeth and before the Ensealing hereof by the Testator corrected and amended Legacy vizt Martha the wife of Richard Farrin 5s. 0d. Money lent Item in the hands of William Higgin of Ightfield gent £2 0s. 0d. Legacie. Item to Katherine Murray an old servant, whose name is mistaken in the will and Mary Davies put falsely for it £2 6s. 6d. There is likewise a mistake in my will, for my mind is That Allene daughter to my Eldest sonne Robert is not to have those certaine sumes within specified of Eight shillings & five Groats annually, but onely the howse, where the widdow Gandie liveth with the appurtenances.

Endorsement: Probated at London 2 July 1658; administration to Robert Griffiths, the son and surviving executor named in the will.

146. ROBERT DAVIES OF COMBERMERE, YEOMAN

S.Pr. PCC 20 October 1658
W.T. 15 September 1658
Buried: 20 September 1658

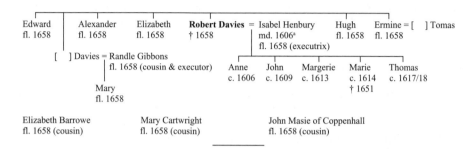

Will, sick.

First I give and yield Upp my soule into the hands of Almightie God trusting by the Free merritts of Jesus Christ my Saviour to have free pardon and remission of all my sinnes. And my bodie I Comitt to the earth to be decently buried in Christian buryall at the discrecōn of my Executors hereafter named And for my temporall estate I dispose thereof as followeth: First I give And bequeath to my brother Edward Davies twentie pounds, And to my Brother Alexander Davies twentie And to my brother Hugh Davies twenty pounds, And to my sister Elizabeth Davies twentie pounds, And to My sister Ermine Tomas, twentie pounds, Also I doe give and bequeath unto my neece Mary Gibbons, fiftie pounds And to little Mary Davies tenn pounds in money, Also I give and bequeath unto my Cosen Elizabeth Barrowe tenn pounds, And to my cosen Mary Cartwright, tenn pounds in money; Also I give and bequeath unto all my servants as they be dwelling with me At my decease, twentie shillings a peece Also I give and bequeath unto my Cosen John Masie of Coppenhall tenn pounds in money; Also I doe give and Bequeath all the rest and residue of all my goods Cattells, and Chattells, My debts, legacies, and severall expences being thereonto, in the first place Paid and discharged unto my loveing wife Isabell Davies.

Executors: the testator's wife, Isabell Davies, and his cousin, Randle Gibbons of Welsh Roe.

H. & S.
Robert Davies his marke

---

^a Wrenbury Parish Register marriage entry shows *Elizabeth Henbury*.

Witnesses: Martha Tudman, Thomas Gray 1658.

Debts oweing to the testator:

	£	s	d
Without specialty Thomas Maynaling of Nantwich gent	3	0	0
John Hall of Newhall		20	0
Richard Pemberton			6
Robert Brownefall		4	0
Anne Hassall		10	0
George Chester		3	8
Arthur Swan		9	0
Roger Bentley		5	3

Endorsement: Probated at London 20 October 1658; administration to Isabell Davies the relict and Randle Gibbons Executors named in the will.

147. GEORGE HALL, JR, OF ASTON, YEOMAN

S.Pr. PCC 27 October 1658
W.T. 31 July 1658
Buried: 7 September 1658

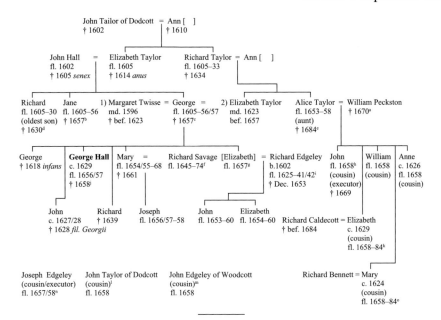

ᵃ See will of William Peckston, pr. 1670/CRO.
ᵇ See will of John Hall of Smeatonwood, pr. 1606 (will no. 22); md. Richard Edgeley, 1612
  at Wrenbury; see will of Jane Edgeley, pr. 1657/58 (will no. 144).
ᶜ See will of George Hall of Aston, pr. 1657 (will no. 142).
ᵈ See inventory of Richard Hall of Smeatonwood, 1630 (no. 83).
ᵉ Noted in will of Richard Edgeley, pr. 1660/61 (will no. 153); see will of Alice Peckston, pr.
  1684/CRO.
ᶠ Overseer of will of his brother Robert Savage, pr. 1647 (will no. 124); married at Wrenbury,
  1654/55.
ᵍ See will of Richard Edgeley (will no. 153), note k.
ʰ John *Peckston* also appears in Newhall Court records 1651–54 as John *Penckston*/CRO.
ⁱ See will of Richard Edgeley, pr. 1660/61 (will no. 153).
ʲ See will of George Hall of Aston, pr. 1657 (will no. 142).
ᵏ See will of Alice Peckston, pr. 1684/CRO.
ˡ John Taylor of Dodcott, noted as a cousin of George Hall, Jr in 1658 (see below), was
  undoubtedly the son of an unnamed brother of George's mother, Elizabeth Taylor Hall, and
  of his aunt, Alice Taylor Peckston, and as such a descendant of John Tailor of Dodcott, will
  pr.1602/CRO.
ᵐ John Edgeley of Woodcott, noted as a cousin of George Hall, Jr in 1658 (see below) was the
  son of John Edgeley of Moorehall, with pr. 1654 (will no. 139).
ⁿ Joseph Edgeley, son of Richard Edgeley and Jane Hall Edgeley, was executor of his mother's will, pr. 1657/58 (will no. 144).
ᵒ See will of Alice Peckston, 1684/CRO.

Will, sick.

First I give and yield upp willingly my soule into the hands of Almighty God my Creator, trusting by the only merritts of the death and passion of Jesus Christ my Saviour to have free pardon and remission of all my sins *And my bodie I comitt to the earth from whence it came to be decently buryed in Christian buryall at the discrecōn of my Executors hereafter named in the parish Church yard of Wrenbury as neere to my late deceased Father as conveniently may be* And for the temporall estate which Almightie God of his free bounty and mercy hath enriched me withal I will and dispose thereof as followeth First I give and bequeath unto my brother in lawe Richard Savage of Smeatonwood twenty pounds in money, And to my sister Mary now his wife twentie pounds in money. And to their sonne Joseph Savage twenty pounds in money. Also I doe give and bequeath unto my nephewe John Edgley And to my neece Elizabeth Edgley sonne and daughter of my late deceased brother in lawe Richard Edgley Threescore pounds in money, to be equally devided betwixt them And my will and mind is, that my said legacies to bequeathe to the said John Edgley and Elizabeth Edgley shall be by my Executors here after named, paid into such person or persons as the lawe shall elect for their Gardians within the time and space of one yeare next after my decease for their use and benefitt; And also to be by their Gardians imployed for their use until they shall attaine the full age of twentie and one yeares; And then the said summe with the benefitt that shall accrewe by the imployment of the same to be equally devided betwixt them. And also that if either of them shall decease before the shall attaine to their full ages of twentie and one yeares the whole shall be paid to the survivor, And further my will is, That the tenn pound legacie lefte to the said Children by my late deceased father being yet in my hands; shall also by my Executors hereafter named be paid unto such Gardians for their use, out of the first monyes that shall come into their hands; Also I doe give and bequeath unto the said John Edgley and Elizabeth Edgley the longe table standing in my house at Aston, the ioyned bedd, in the parlor and all the standing shelves in the same house; Alsoe I doe give and bequeath unto my sister Mary Savage, and to the said John Edgley; and Elizabeth Edgley; all the Brasse, pewter, and linnans, and naperie that I have to be equally devided amongst them, Also I doe give and bequeath unto my Aunte Alice Peckston of Wrenbury tenn pounds in money, And to my Cosen John Peckston forty pounds in money: And to my Cosen William Peckston five pounds in money; And to my Cosen Mary Barnett five pounds, And to my Cosen Anne Peckston five pounds in money, And to my Cosen Elizabeth Caldecott five pounds in money, Also I doe give and bequeath unto my Cosen Joseph Edgley twentie pounds in money, Also I give and bequeath unto my cosen Elizabeth Edgley tenn pounds in money; Also I doe give and bequeath unto my Cosen William Poole of the Northwoods five pounds in money; Also I doe give & bequeath unto my cosen Elizabeth Swetnam five pound in money; Also I doe give and bequeath unto my Cosen John Taylor of Dodcott, five pounds in money, And to my Cosen John Edgley of Woodcott fifty shillings in money Also I doe give and bequeath unto the poore of the parish of Wrenbury five pounds in money,

And my will and mind is, that the said sume of two pounds shall be paid in by my Executors hereafter named to the then present Churchwardens and overseers of the poore of the same parish, to be by them sett forth and imployed to the best benefitt, to the use of the poore aforesaid from time to time, And that the use and interest thereof shall be yearely distributed amongst the poore aforesaid, every St. Thomas day by the guarding Charchwardens, and overseers of the poore of the same parish as other charitable givfts formerly have bin; Also I doe give and bequeath unto Humfrey Deaks Thomas Wright, Anne Wade, my late father's servant, Raphe Hassall, Katherine Chedley widow, and George Woollam five shillings a peece; Also I doe give and bequeath Unto John Bromhall of Newhall my finest Cowe, now in the hands of Ann Hassall widdow; Alsoe I doe give unto my said Aunte Alice Peckston the ould Cowe now in her possession.

Executors: the testator's cousin *[actually, his nephew]*, Joseph Edgley, and John Peckston (his cousin).

I alsoe (after my funerall expences, debts, and legacies are paid and discharged out of my estate) doe give unto them the remainder (if any exist) to be devided betwixt them, And I doe desire my said kinsmen John Taylor of Dodcott, and John Edgley of Woodcott, to see the disposeing of my said Newphewe John Edgley and my said neece Elizabeth Edgleyes estate and to be ayding, and assisting to such as shall be come their Gardians.

H. & S.
1658: George Hall

Witnesses: William Fisher, Thomas Gray.

Endorsement: Probated at London 27 October 1658; administration to Joseph Edgley and John Peckston, executors named in the will.

148. FRANCES RAVENSCROFT, WIDOW

S.Pr. PCC 21 January 1658/59
W.T. 6 December 1658
Buried 15 December 1658

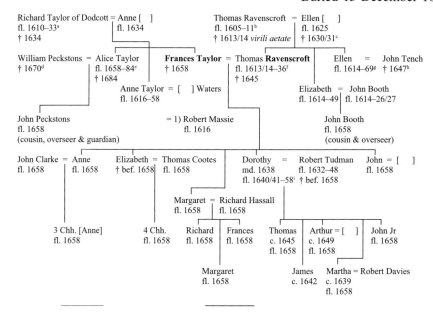

Will, sick.

First I give and yeild upp willingly my soule into the hands of Almighty god which first gave it mee trustinge by the onely merritts of the death and passion of Jesus

ᵃ The reference by Frances Ravenscroft to John Taylor of Dodcott, her executor, as her cousin suggests a connection to the family of Richard Taylor of Dodcott who died in 1634, and to the earlier Taylor (1602). The only caveat is the fact that Richard does not refer to any of his assumed daughters in his will; he does, however, refer to George Hall as his son-in-law, and the will of George Jr, pr. 1658 (will no. 147) leaves no doubt that George Sr's wife was the sister of Alice Peckstons. George Hall Jr refers to John Taylor of Dodcott as his cousin, adding more certainty to our conclusions.

ᵇ Appears as a churchwarden at Wrenbury, 1605; tenant of Newhall Park 1609; in 1611 as afferer in CRO Newhall Manor Court Rolls.

ᶜ See CRO Newhall Rentals, 1625; will of Ellen Ravenscroft, pr. ca. 1631 (will no. 86).

ᵈ See will of William Peckston, pr. 1670/ CRO.

ᵉ See will of Alice Peckston of Wrenbury, pr. 1684/ CRO.

ᶠ William Fergusson Irvine, *Chester Licences*, iii. 36: 10 August 1625, Thomas Ravenscroft and Mary [Frances?] Taylor, spinster; at Audlem or Wrenbury; CRO Newhall Rentals, 1625; priser for George Dickins, will pr. 1626/27 (will no.74); witness for John Hall, will pr. 1636 (will no. 100).

ᵍ See will of Thomas Ravenscroft, pr. 1614 (will no. 43); also will of Ellen Tench, widow, of Wilkesley, pr. 1669/ CRO.

ʰ See will of John Tenche of Wilkesley, pr. 1647.

ⁱ Bequeathed 2s. 6d. as cousin to Robert Shrowbridge, will pr. 1641 (will no. 114).

Christ my savioiur to have free pardon and remission of all my sinnes And my body I Commytt to the earth from whence it came to bee decently buried in Christian buriall at the discretion of my executors heereafter named And for the temporall estate which Allmighty god of his free bounty and mercy hath enriched mee with-all I will and dispose thereof as followeth first where as I have oweing unto mee from George Pugh of Stockton in the County of Chester husbandman the summe of twentie and eight pounds due to bee paid unto mee my executors or administra-tors by foure pounds a yeare in seaven yeares next ensueing to witt every five and twentieth day of July as by seaven severall bonds beareing date the two and twen-tieth day of July one thousand six hundred fyfty and seaven It doth moreffully appeare I doe heereby devise give and bequeath unto my sonneinlaw Mr John Clarke to and for the onely use and behoofe of his wife and three Children as the same shall fall to bee due and to bee first raised out of the said bonds the summe of twen-ty pounds in money to bee equally divided amongst them Alsoe I doe give and bequeath unto my sonne in Law Mr Thomas Cootes and to his wife and to his foure Children which hee formerly had by his first wife Elizabeth my late daughter deceased to bee next raised out of the said bonds after the afore mentioned legacies are discharged Twenty shillinges a peece to buy every of them a ringe withall. Alsoe I give and bequeath unto my sister Anne Waters twenty shillinges in money to buy her a ringe to bee next paid her as the same shall bee raised out of the said bonds And whereas I have oweing unto mee by Richard Eddowe of Iscoyde in the County of Flint yeoman the summe of one hundred sixty and ffive pounds payable unto mee my executors or administrators by an Annuall rent or summe of Thurty pounds a yeare upon every foure and twentieth day of June and five and twentieth day of december yearely by even and equall portions As by his deed Indented beareing date the fyfth day of November in the yeare of our Lord god one thousand six hun-dred fyfty and five more at large may appeareth I doe heere by devise give and bequeath unto my executors heere after named to pay my debts and discharge my funerall expences withall the first fyfteen pounds due unto mee upon the five and twentieth day of december next ensueing out of the said Annuall rents Alsoe I doe heereby devise give and bequeath unto my sonne in law Richard Hassall out of the said Annuall rents the sume of Three score pounds in money Thirty pounds where-of to be paid unto him out of the said annual rents upon the fower and twentieth day of June and five and twentieth day of December in the yeare of our Lord god one thousand six hundred fyfty and Nyne and the residue of the said summe at such daies and tymes as heereafter in this my last will is mentioned and expressed Alsoe I doe give and be queath unto my sonne the summe of twenty pounds in money out of the said Annuall rents Tenne pounds thereof to bee paid unto him in the yeare of our Lord god one thousand six hundred and sixty and the residue of the said summe at such tymes as heereafter in this my present will is mentioned and expressed Alsoe I give and bequeath unto my daughter Dorothy Tudman widowe the summe of twenty pounds in money out of the said Anuall rents Tenne pounds therof to bee paid unto her in the said yeare of our Lord god one thousand six hundred and sixty and the residue of the said summe at such tymes and daies as heerein after shall-bee mentoned and the other tenne pounds due in the last mentioned yeare to bee paid to my sonne in Law Richard Hassall in more of his abovesaid legacie Alsoe I doe devise give and bequeath my said yearely rents fallinge or bee due in the yeare of our Lord god one thousand six hundred sixty and one and one thousand six hundred sixty and two as followeth To witt To John Ravenscrofte the younger sonne to my said sonne John the elder Tenne poundes in money and to Richard the sonne of my said sonne in Law Richard Hassall Tenne pounds in money And to Margarett and Frances daughters of the said Richard five poundes a peece in money And to Martha the daughter of my said daughter Dorothy Tudman Tenne pounds in money And to Thomas and Arthur sonnes of my said daughter Dorothy Tudman five poundes a peece in money And my will and mynde is that the said legacies as the same shall become due shall bee by my executors heereafter named received and by them to be immediately paid over into the hands of my Cosen John Booth of Hankelow yeoman and John Peckston of Wrenbury yeoman whom I doe desire and appointe to bee overseers and guardians to my said grand children for theire said severall legacies to bee by them sett forth and imployed to the best use and benefitt untill such tyme as every such Childe shall attaine theire full age of twenty and one yeares And then to bee paid unto them with such use and benefitt that shall arise by the imployement of the same And further my will and mynde is that if any of my said grandchildren doe decease before they shall attaine theire full age of twenty and one yeares that then the portion of him or her soe deceaseinge shall bee equally devided amongst the rest of the Children of the same familie And I doe heereby give and bequeath unto my said Cosens John Booth and John Peckston towards theire paines heerein to bee imployed Three pounds a peece in money Alsoe I doe further devise that the yeares rent fallinge due in the yeare of our Lord god one thousand six hundred sixty and three shall bee paid tenne poundes thereof unto my said sonne John Ravenscrofte in full of his before mencioned legacie And tenne pounds therof unto my said daughter Dorothy Tudman in full of her before mentioned legacie And the other Tenne pounds the residue of the said yeares rent unto my said sonne in law Richard Hassall in more of his legacie Alsoe I doe give and bequeath unto sister in Law Ellen Tennch twenty shillinges to buy her a ringe Alsoe I doe give and bequeath unto my Neece Anne Clarke daughter of John Clarke my gould ringe Alsoe I doe give and bequeath unto my said daughter Dorothy Tudman my best petticoate Alsoe I doe give and bequeath all the rest and residue of all my estate both moveable and unmoveable goodes Cattles and Chattles quicke and dead of what kinde or quallitie soever the same bee of or wheresoever the same remaineth unto my daughter Margarett Hassall now wife of my said sonne in Law Richard Hassall.

Executors: the testator's son-in-law, Richard Hassall, and her cousin, John Tailor of Dodcott, gent.

And I doe give unto my said Cosen John Taylor towards his paines heerein to bee imployed Three poundes in money if hee shall ioyne with my said sonne in Law.

H. & S.
Frances Ravenscroft her marke.

And before the sealeinge and delliveringe heereof I doe give for a remembrance unto my sister Alice Peckston and Anne Hassall widowe five shillinges a peece.

Witnesses: William Dickin his marke Thomas Grey. 1658.

Endorsement: Probated at London 21 January 1658/59; administration to Richard Hassall and John Taylor, executors.

149. EDWARD POWELL OF NEWHALL, MILLINER

I.Pr. PCC 26 May 1659
W.T. 5 February 1658/59
Buried: 26 March 1659

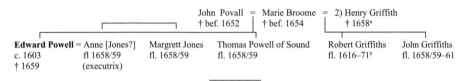

Will, sick.

First I give and yeild upp willinglie my Soule into the handes of Almightie God which first gave it mee Trustinge by the onely merritts of the death and passion of Jesus Christ my Saviour to have free pardon and remission of all my sinnes And my bodie I Comitt to the earth from whence it came to bee decentlie buryed in Christian buriall at the discrecōn of my Executix hereafter named, And for the temprall estate which Almightie God of his free bountie and mercie hath enriched me withall I will and dispose thereof as followeth first I doe give and bequeath unto my brother Thomas Powell Fortye shillings in money Alsoe I doe give and bequeath unto my brother Robert Griffiths Forty shillinges in money Alsoe I doe give and bequeath unto my brother John Griffiths five poundes in money Alsoe I doe give and bequeath unto my sister in lawe Margarett Jones Twenetie shillings in money Alsoe I give and bequeath unto my said brother Thomas Powell my Coate my best doublett and my best hatt And I doe give and bequeath all the rest of my wearinge apparrell unto my said brother John Griffiths Alsoe my will and minde is That my Funerall expences my debtes and the legacies before mencōned and by me heretofore given and bequeath shall in the first place by paid & discharged out of my estate And after my said debtes legacies and Funerall Expences are soe paid and discharged I doe hereby give and bequeath all the rest and residue of all my goodes Cattells & Chattells both moveable and unmoveable goods debts and sumes of money and estate whatsoever quicke or dead whatsoever the same

---

[a] See will of Heny Griffiths, Sr, pr. 1657 (will no. 145).
[b] Reference to Robert Griffiths and John Griffiths as Edward Powell's *brothers* can imply that they were half-brothers or brothers-in-law. If the latter, then both Anne Powell, Edward's wife, and Margaret Jones, her sister, were siblings to Robert and John.

be or where soever the same remayneth unto my loveinge wife Anne Powell to heer sole and onely use and behoofe.

Executrix: the testator's wife, Anne Powell.

H. & S.

Edward Powell his marke and seale

Witnesses: William Fletcher. Thomas Graye Scr, 1658.

Endorsement: Probated at London 26 May 1659; administration to Anne Powell, relict and sole executrix named in the will.

150. ROBERT SHROWBRIDGE OF ROYALS[a] IN NEWHALL, YEOMAN

S?Pr. PCC 8 June 1659

W.T. 26 April 1659

Buried: 28 April 1659

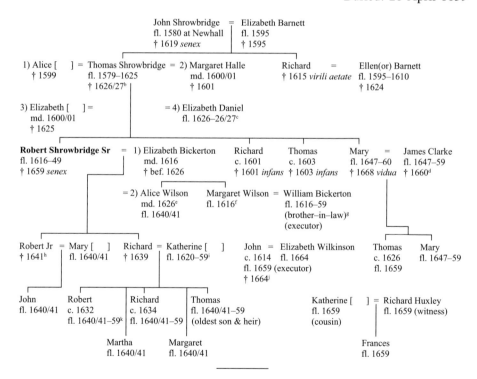

[footnotes on following page]

Will, sick.

First I give and yeeld upp willinglie my soule into the hands of Almightie God my Creatour hoping by the onlie meritts of the death and passion of Jesus Christ my Saviour to have free pardon and forgivenes of all my sinns And my Bodie I Committ to the Earth from whence it came to be decently buried in Christian buriall att the discretion of my executors hereafter named And for the Temporall Estate which almightie God of his free bountie and mercy hath enriched mee withal I will and dispose thereof as followeth First I doe give and bequeath unto my Grandchild and heire apparent is Robert Shrowbridge eldest sonne to my late deceased sonne all the bedsteads in my house together with all the Tables formes silieng ioyned Chaires and ioyned stooles in my house and alsoe all the joyned presses Cupboards greate Coffers that were his Grandmothers and my Truncke and all that is in it and the Featherbedd Boulsters Curtaines and Vallance and other bedding being upon the bedd wherein I doe now lie to remaine to him and his heires unmoveable Alsoe I doe give and bequeath unto my daughter in Lawe Katherine Shrowbridge Five pounds in monie Alsoe I doe give and bequeath to my Grandchildren the said Robert Shrowbridge Richard Shrowbridge and Thomas Shrowbridge Thirtie pounds in monie to be equallie devided amongst them and my will and minde is That the same shall be sett forth and ymployed by my Executors hereafter named to and for the best benefitt untill the said Children shall obtaine their severall ages of Twentie and one yeares and then the said Legacies with the benefitt that shall accrue by the improvement of the same shall be paid unto them And alsoe that if anie of the said Children doe decease before the shal

---

a   In 1610 John Chetwoode, gent., paid three shillings eight pence to the Earl of Bath for *The Royals*. John had inherited possessions in Newhall in 1598 after the death of his mother. The Royals House was then in his tenure, whether he lived there or not, and he paid the customary annual Court fee. The Royals House was sold by the Chetwoodes to Robert Shrowbridge, Esq., about 1638. See Norwood, 'Historic Notes', no. xxxix. Robert appears 1625 in CRO Newhall Rentals; made inventory for John Ravenscroft, 1649 (no. 137).

b   See will of Thomas Shrowbridge, pr. 1626/27 (will no. 75).

c   William Fergusson Irvine, *Chester Licences*, iii. 73: 29 September 1626, to Thomas Shrobrick and Elizabeth Daniell, spinster of Wrenbury; bondsman John Fisher; licence to Mr. Andrew Wright, clerk. Although there is no marriage entry at Wrenbury, she is noted as his wife at time of death.

d   See will of James Clarke, made 1647, pr. 1660 (will no. 152).

e   William Fergusson Irvine, *Chester Licences*, iii. 56: 15 April 1626, to Robert Shrowbrich and Alice Wilson, spinster; at Wrenbury or Audlem. Alice is noted as *cousin* to Robert Shrowbridge the younger , will pr. 1641 (will no. 114) – technically his step-mother.

f   *Chester Licences*, ii. 16: 30 September 1616, to William Bickerton, of Wrenbury parish, and Margaret Wilson, spinster of Audlem parish; licence to Mr Robert Sandford, clerk.

g   Whether the executor William Bickerton's status as Robert Shrowbridge's brother-in-law stems from Robert's first wife, Elizabeth Bickerton, or from his second, Alice Wilson, remains undetermined; perhaps it was a double relationship.

h   See will of Robert Shrowbridge of Royals, pr. 1641 (will no. 114).

i   Owed debt of £2 11s. to William Breese; see will of William Breese, pr. 1621 (will no. 64).

j   See will of John Bickerton of Newhall, yeoman, pr. 1664/CRO.

k   Appears as Robert Shrowbridge *junior* as witness to will of James Clarke, made 1647, pr. 1660 (will no. 152).

attaine their said ages his or theire portion soe deceasing shall be paid to the Survivour Alsoe I doe give and bequeath to my loving freinds Randle Hare Richard Huxley William Bickerson John Bickerton and Thomas Gray whoe are all now present with mee five shillings a peece to buy every of them a paire of Gloves Alsoe I doe give and bequeath unto my Sister Mary Clarke two shillings expence in monie Alsoe I doe give and bequeath unto Thomas Clarke and Mary Clarke sonne and daughter to my said sister Twelve pence a peece Alsoe I doe give and bequeath unto Francis Huxley Two shillings sixpence in money Also my will and minde is that my debts legacies before given and hereby bequeathed and my funerall expences shall be in the first place paid and discharged out of my whole Estate And after my said debts legacies and funerall Expences are soe paid and discharged I doe hereby give and bequeath all the rest and residue of all my Goods Cattells chattells housholdstuffe both moveable and unmoveable goods quick and dead of what kind or qualitie soever the same be of or wheresoever the same remayneth unto my said daughter in Lawe Katherine Shrowbride and to my said Grandchildren Richard Shrowbridge and Thomas Shrowbridge to be equallie devided amongst them excepting all the Carts ploughes and other implements of husbandrie which I solely give to my said daughter in Law Katherine Shrowbridge and Eighteene pence in monie to my Cousin Katherine Huxley.

Executors: William Bickerton of Newhall, yeoman, brother-in-law of the testator, and John Bickerton, his son, cousin to the testator.

H. & S.
Robert Shrowbridge (his marke and seale)

Witnesses: Randle Hare Richard Huxley his marke Martha Woodcock her marke Joane Rabone her marke Ellen Robinson her marke Tho: Gray Scr: 1659.

Endorsement: Probated at London 8 June 1659; administration to William and John Bickerton, joint executors named in the will.

151. RALPH TWISSE OF WRENBURY FRITH, YEOMAN

S?Pr. PCC 25 June 1659
W.T. 8 February 1643
Burial: None recorded at Wrenbury or Audlem

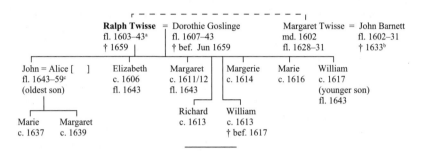

Will, sick

First I give and bequeath my Soule into the hands of Almightie God whoe first gave it mee trusting by the meritts of the passion of Jesus Christ my Savior to have free pardon and remission of all my sinns And my bodie I Committ to the Earth to be buried in Christian buriall att the discretion of my Executors hereafter named and for my Temporall Estate I will and dispose thereof as followeth First whereas I have an Estate of all my Messuage or Tenement wherein I doe now live together with all houses Edifices Buildings lands Tenements Meadowes Leasowes pastures and premisses with the Appurtenances to the same belonging by vertue of one lease or Deed indented under the hand and Seale of my Worshipfull Landlord William Massey of the Mosse in the said County Esquire bearing date The Two and twentieth day of November in the Seaventeenth yeare of the raigne of our said Soverainge Lord King Charles for the Terme of fourscore and nineteene yeares next ensueing after the date of the said rented & indented if I the said Ralph Twisse John Twisse my sonne and Alice his wife or anie of us doe or shall soe long live for and under the yearely rent of 26s. of lawfull monie of England as by the said Rented deed in dented more att large appeareth I doe hereby give bequeath assigne and Convey over all my said Messuage and Tenement Barnes buildings meadowes Leasowes pastures and all other the premisses with Thappurtenances in the said recited deed indeted mentioned and contained unto my loving wife Dorothie Twisse and my eldest sonne John Twisse whoe I doe intend to nominate Executors in this my last Will for the terme of five yeares next after my decease if the Tearme mentioned in the said recyted deed

---

[a] Appears 1633 as *Randle Twysse*, priser for John Barnett (will no. 94); as *Rauffe* Twisse as executor for Gilbert Woollam, will pr. 1635/36 (will no. 98).
[b] See will of John Barnett, pr. 1633 (will no. 94).
[c] Priser for estate of Richard Culliner alias Comber, 1644 (will no. 119).

indented soelong Continue for ye payment and dischargeing of all my debts which of right I owe unto anie man And my will and minde is that if there be anie over-plus made or raised out of the same over and above the payment of my said debts that the same shall be equallie and lovingly devided betwixt them for and towards their maintenance Item after thene and expiration of the said Terme of five year-es I doe hereby give bequeath and assigne over unto my said wife Dorothie Twisse and her assignes the one halfe and full moyetie of all my said Messuage or Tenement Houses Buildings meadowes Leasowes pastures and of all other the premises for soe manie yeares of the said Terme of four score and nineteene year-es as the said Dorothie my said wife shall live if the Terme in the above said Lease soe long continue and after the decease of the said Dorothie my wife my will and minde is And I doe hereby assigne and devise the said Moyetie of my said Messuage unto my younger sonne William Twisse and my daughter Margarett Twisse for soe manie yeares of the said Terme of fourscore and nineteene year-es as they shall be in leavying and raising the summe of £30 for and towards theire severall portions if the terme in the said Lease soe long continue whereof I doe give and bequeath unto my said sonn William £10 and the other £20 to my said daughter Margarett Item after the said summe of £30 shall be leavyed And raised of the moyetie of my said Messuage Land and premisses as abovesaid I doe hereby give bequeath assigne and convey the same moyetie and all other the premisses unto my said sonne John Twisse and his assignes during all the rest and residue of the said Terme of ffourscore and nineteene years then to Come and unexpired if the terme in the said lease soe long continue Item I doe hereby give bequeath and assigne unto my said sonne John Twisse and his assignes after thend expiraton of thabovesaid Terme of five yeares The other halfe of all my said mes-suage and Tenement Lands Tenements Meadowes Leasowes pastures and pre-misses for and during all the rest and residue of the said Terme of fourscore and nineteene yeares then to come and unexpired (if the Terme in the said Lease soe long continue) they and everie of them paying dischareing and doeing such Rents duties and services as are due for the same severallie and respectivelie for soe much and soe long as they or anie of them shall enjoy the same Item I doe here-by give and bequeath all my Goods Cattells and Chattells both moveable and unmoveable Goods of what kinde or Qualitie the same be of, or wheresoever the same remaineth my funerall expences being discharged out of the whole The one halfe unto the said Dorothie my wife And the other halfe unto my Three Children William Twisse Margarett Twisse and Elizabeth Twisse to be equallie devided amongst them.

Executors: the testator's wife Dorothie Twisse and his son John Twisse.

H. & S.
Ralph Twisse (X)

Witnesses: John Cheswis (X), Tho: Gray.

Endorsement: Probated at London 25 June 1659; administration to John Twisse, son and surviving executor named in the will.

152. JAMES CLARKE OF SOUND (IN THE PARISH OF WRENBURY), YEOMAN

S?Pr. PCC 16 July 1660
W.T. 11 November 1647
Buried: Not recorded at Wrenbury or Audlem

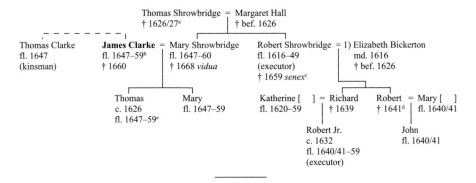

Will, sick.

First I give and bequeath my Soule into the handes of Almighty God hopeing assuredly through the merritts Death and passion of my Lord and Saviour Jesus Christ to bee made partaker Of his Heavenly Kingdome and to receive pardon and Remission of all my sinnes And my body I give to the earth Whereof it was first made and as for my Worldly estate which God hath lent mee in this life I give and dispose of The same in manner and forme following And first I give and bequeath And assigne overall that Tenement wherein I now live and dwell to my Deare and Loveing wife Mary Clarke to hold and enioy for and durein [*sic*] the terme of her naturall lyfe and from and after her decease I give and assigne over the same to my loveing sonne Thomas Clarke during all the residue of the said Lease Item I give to my oldest daughter Mary Clarke twenty poundes To bee paid to her the said Mary by my sonne Thomas Clarke out of the said Tenement the First tenne poundes within the space of one yeare next after my said sonne shall enter in and upon the said Tenement and the other tenne poundes within the space of two yeares next after his first entering and in default of payment the said sumes at the time aforesaid then my daughter Mary shall enter in and upon the one halfe of the said Tenement and to hold and enjoy the same untill the said sume of twen-

---

a   See will of Thomas Shrowbridge, pr. 1626/27 (will no. 75).
b   Noted as the brother-in-law of Robert Shrowbridge, whose will was pr. 1659 (will no. 150).
c   See will, pr. 1659 (will no. 150).
d   See will of Robert Shrowbridge of Royals, pr. 1641 (will no. 114).
e   Thomas and Mary Clarke were bequeathed 12d. each by Robert Shrowbridge (will no. 150).

ty poundes shalbe raised and paid out of the said Tenement to her the said Mary Item I give to my daughter Mary [a] Cow which her mother shall thinke good, and alsoe my best standing bedstead Item my debts legacies and funeral expences Being first paid and discharged out of the whole and my heriott being paid I give all The rest of my goods Cattell and chattel moveable and unmoveable quicke and dead Of what nature or kind soever the same be to my Loveing wife for and during the Terme of her naturall life and at her decease she to dispose the same to my said Sonne and daughter as she shall thincke best and fitt save onely all my Carts Ploughes and all other my implements of husbandry the which I give and bequeath After my wifes death to my sonne Thomas Clarke.

Executors: the testator's wife, Mary Clarke, as sole Executrix.

Overseers: the testator's brother-in-law, Robert Shrowbridge, and the testator's kinsman, Thomas Clark.

H. & S.
James Clarke

Witnesses: Robert Shrowbridge, Nicholas Willson, Robert Shrowbridge Jun.

Endorsement: Probated at London 16 July 1660 before William Merick, Doctor of Laws, Keeper of Commissary of the Prerogative Court of Canterbury; administration to Mary Clarke, relict of the deceased and sole executrix.

153. RICHARD EDGELEY OF SMEATONWOOD

S.Pr. 10 January 1660/61
Nuncupative will made: 26 December 1653
Buried: 28 December 1653

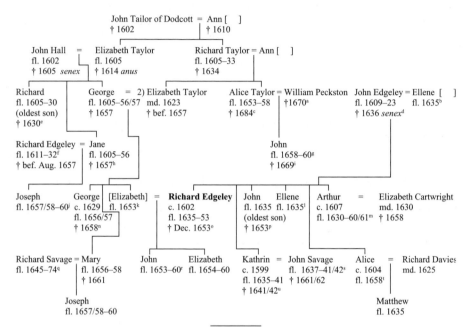

---

a   See will of William Peckston, pr. 1670/CRO.
b   See will of John Edgeley of Woodcott, pr. 1637 (will no. 102), note b.
c   Bequeathed £10 in will of George Hall, Jr, pr. 1658 (will no. 147); see will of Alice Peckston, 1684/CRO.
d   See will of John Edgeley of Woodcott, yeoman, pr. 1637 (will no. 102) and note b; 1609 tenant at Woodcott; in R. Stewart Brown, *Cheshire Inquisitions Post Mortem*, iii. 81 he is noted at Newhall in 1623.
e   See inventory of Richard Hall, 1630 (no. 83).
f   Priser for Margaret Sevell, will pr. 1611 (will no. 35); married 1612 at Wrenbury; noted in will of, and priser for, Edmund Crewe, will pr. 1632 (will no. 90); Churchwarden at Wrenbury 1636; Jane Edgeley was already a widow when she made her will on 4 August 1657.
g   Bequeathed £40 in will of his cousin George Hall, Jr and co-executor with Joseph Edgeley, will pr. 1658 (will no. 147).
h   See will of Jane Edgeley of Moorehall, widow, pr. 1657/58 (will no. 144).
i   As John *Penckston*.
j   Bequeathed £20 in will of his cousin George Hall, Jr and co-executor with John Peckston, will pr. 1658 (will no. 147).
k   The wife of Richard Edgeley, daughter of George Hall of Aston (will no. 142) is nowhere mentioned by name; our speculation is suggested by the name given to their only daughter.
l   Married Edward Mackworth, fl. 1636–47.

Memorandum: January 1660/61

That upon or about the Sixe and Twentieth daye of December in the yeare of our Lord God One thousand Sixe hundred Fiftie three Richard Edgeley of Smeatonwood in the Parish of Wrenbury being sicke in bodie but of perfect minde and memorie and having a desire to make his last will and Testament did Nuncupatively and by word of mouth saye and declare as followeth or did utter the wordes to the same effect viz: Brother Arthur (meaning and speakinge unto his Brother Arthur Edgeley of Poole whom that day hee had sent a special messenger for) I desire you to bee my Executor and to take the care and Tuition of my Childe. As alsoe my father Hall (meaninge George Hall of Aston his wifes father) if hee please and I doe give unto my child Alcocks Feilds in peaceable possession As also I doe give unto him £100, £50 whereof is in Alice Peckestons hand and what of my parcell of cheese and yoke of Oxen come shorte of the other £50 for my childe the same shall bee raised out of the remainder of my goods And all the rest of my goods to bee equallie devided betwixt my wife and Childe And if my Childe dye before hee comes to age my will is it shall goe to the nexte of kinne *And I desire to bee buried in the Church or Church yard of Wrenbury* which words or the like in effect the sayde Richard Edgeley did spake and declare the sayd Sixe and Twentieth daye of December One Thousand Sixe hundred fiftie and three att severall other times afterward and before his death in the presence & hearinge of the sayed Arthur Edgeley John Vernon and others and did alsoe send divers times for a clarke to committ the same to writinge though none could bee received before hee dyed.

153 footnotes continued

[m] Co-overseer with his brother John of will of his father John Edgeley of Woodcott, pr. 1637 (will no. 102). Appointed guardian for his brother Richard's minor children in 1653, an arrangement challenged by his cousins Joseph Edgeley and John Peckston; see legal dispute below.

[n] For all documentation of George Hall Jr's ancestry, see his will, pr. 1658 (will no. 147).

[o] Beneficiary, and co-executor (with his mother Ellene) of his father's will; administration granted to him alone, will pr. 1637 (will no. 102); owed debt of £16 16s. to Katherine Savage, his sister; see her inventory, 1641/42 (no. 116); referred to as *my late deceased brother in lawe* by George Hall, Jr, will pr. 1658 (will no. 147).

[p] Beneficiary of will of his father John Edgeley of Woodcott, co-overseer with his brother Arthur and priser of his father's goods, will pr. 1637 (will no. 102); see also his own will, pr. 1654 (will no. 139).

[q] Overseer of will of his brother, Robert Savage, pr. 1647 (will no. 124).

[r] John Edgeley and his sister Elizabeth are the subjects of the legal dispute recorded below, and are mentioned in the wills of George Hall of Aston, pr. 1657 (will no. 142) and George Hall, Jr, 1658 (wil no. 147).

[s] Priser of the goods and chattels of John Edgeley of Woodcott, will pr. 1637 (will no. 102); granted administration of estate of his wife Katherine, 1641/42 (no. 116).

[t] No mention is made of her in her father's will, pr. 1637 (will no. 102), but her son Matthew is noted.

[u] Noted as Kathrin Edgeley in will of her father John Edgeley of Woodcott, pr. 1637 (will no. 102); married 1641; see inventory of Katherine Savage, 1641/42 (no. 116).

Letter Appointing Brother As Executor, dated 26 December 1654:

Brother Arther I doe desire you to bee my Executor of my goods and for my
Child, and my father Hall if he will: first I give my Child Alcocks Fields in pea-
sible possession first I give my child one hundred and 50 pounds in Ales Pexton
hands all my Cheese and a good yoke of oxen to sel I will have yt maide out in
goods or mony one hundred pounds for my Child and the rest of my goods equally devided betwixt my wife and my Child and if my Child doe dye before he shall
come to his age it shall goe to the next akinn it must goe forward and can nott
come backe againe to my wife I will be buried in the Church or Churcheyard
wherever they will December 26th 1654.[a]

Endorsement: Probated 10 January 1660/61; administration to Arthur Edgeley,
the executor named in the will.

Allegations:

21 February 1660/61
Edgeley and Peckston vs Edgeley

On which day Wilson adding to an allegation given and exhibited previously by
him in this cause and with a mind of pleading in a cause whereby Letters of Tuition
of the person and property of John Edgeley a minor in this cause, otherwise his
client, granted and under the seal of this Court are bound to be ratified and con-
firmed and returned into his hands, Alleges that the said Arthur Edgeley his client
was natural, lawful and only brother of the said Richard Edgeley deceased and
for such and as such was and is commonly said, held and had, &cr and therefore
Tuition of the person and property of the said minor, belongs and pertains to the
aforesaid Arthur Edgeley, uncle and next of kin of the said minor according to
law and the process of this Court, referring himself &c

21 February 1660/61
Joseph Edgeley and John Pickston vs Arthur Edgeley
Wilson
Williamson

On which day appeared the party John Edgeley natural and lawful son of Richard
Edgeley late of Smeatonwood deceased and alledged himself to have been and to
be constituted in the minority of his age, in fact to have attained eight years of
age, not yet to have arrived at the twenty first year of his age and therefore neither to have managed or to manage properly the administering and caring for his
means, property and business nor [to be] a fit person of acting, defending or standing in judgement, wherefore he seeks to procure for himself as guardians the

---

[n] It is clear from the Wrenbury Parish Register that Richard Edgeley made his will on 26
December 1653, and that he was buried on 28 December 1653. It is thus a scribal error which
places the appointment of his brother Arthur on 26 December 1654, both for the heading and
for the date in the body of the text.

aforesaid Joseph Edgeley and John Pickston as Guardians to the aforesaid John Edgeley to the effect aforesaid with a Bond executed beforehand according to the demands of law and form of the registry; In the presence of the said John Peckston accepting for himself the burdens of this office.

Interrogatories:

Questions, ministered and being ministered on behalf and by the party of Joseph Edgeley and John Peckston to all and singular pretended witnesses in whatever manner produced and being produced on behalf of and by the party of Arthur Edgeley in a business of revocation of pretended Letters of Tuition of the person and property of John Edgeley a minor, being moved and prosecuted, follow:

1. Firstly, let the peril of perjury and the penalties of false witness be explained to each of the pretended witnesses aforesaid and let it be asked of him concerning his age, work, origin, condition and lifestyle and how long he has known the parties litigant, and let him be asked and let it be done jointly, severally and concerning whatsoever.

2. Item, whether any of the pretended witnesses aforesaid have been pressed to depose concerning any pretended testament or pretended last will of Richard Edgeley, first let it be asked of the said minor and he will express, whether did the decedent of himself give Instruction for the pretended will whereupon you have been examined or whether did hee speaks such wordes at the importunity and solicitation of yourself or others and who (?) whether is the Note hereto affixed in all things both as to time and other Circumstances the truth, and have you soe acknowledged: *Ac fiat ut Supra* - And let it be done as above.

3. Item when where and in whose presence was the pretended Nuncupative will made, what day And year and who was present beside your selfe, *Ac fiat ut supra*.

4. Item whether was the deceased at the pretended time of his makinge of the will of good and perfect memory & understanding and how long did he continue alive after speaking thereof, *et ut supra*.

5.Item let him declare who is next of kinne or shallbe heire in Remainder to the Child the Minor for whose Tuicōn and Government this suite is, or he knows, beleeves or hath heard. *Et ut Supra*.

6. Item was the pretended will made as he Remembers in December 1654 and who were present besides himself. *Et ut [supra]*.

7. Item hath he heard or doth not he beleeve that the Tuicōn and Government of the aforesaid minors John and Elizabeth was in a Judicial hearing in the Exchequer Ordered unto the parties Interrogant upon good Security for answearing their

porcōns when the said Children should come to age of 21 years. And was the same served accordingly. *Et ut supra.*

8. Item of what Age are the said Minors as he knows or beleeves at this tyme of your produccōn. *Et ut supra.*

9. Item whether is the said Minor John Edgeley educated in the Protestant Religion and Disscipline of this Church in the Christian faith according to the Rule and Lawes of the Church. *Et ut supra.*

10. Item when did he see Arthur Edgeley at his parish Church to heare divine service upon Sondayes or Holidayes and how oft hath he observed him there within theis 12 moneths? and hath he bene Conformable to the Church Disscipline? Or otherwise Schismatically affected and hath he not perversely practiced and Lied & Ruled and done against the King, the Church and his Neighbours in many things and is he not for such a Man notoriously accompted reputed and taken and therefore unfit to take Care and Educacōn of Children. And as above.

Deposition:

Statements of witnesses taken 15 February 1660/1 in a certain business concerning the revocation of Letters of Tuition of the person and property of John Edgeley, a Minor, son of Richard Edgeley deceased concerning a certain Allegation and Nuncupative Testament of the said deceased in the same cause given and exhibited on behalf of Arthur Edgeley against Joseph Edgeley and John Peckston.

John Vernon of Baddiley in the County of Chester, yeoman, aged 55 years or thereabouts, a witness examined and with prior knowledge of the parties examined, says that he has known all the parties litigant in this cause a long while and also he knew well Richard Edgeley, the deceased.

[Concerning the Allegations and Testament aforesaid, examined he says] that upon a Sunday at night being the same night that the decedent dyed this deponent hearing that he was very ill went to visitt him, whom when he came he found very sicke and at his request staid some houres with him till the time of his death during which time hee was very desirous to have his will made, and caused a Clarke to be sent for for that purpose and asked severall times whether the Clarke was come or noe but none could be procured in time so that the said decedent declared his will by word of mouth to be to the effect following vizt. he desired his brother Arthure Edgeley, one of the parties in this cause who was then present to be his executor, and to take the care and tuicion of his children as alsoe his father Hall if he pleased, And he said that he would give to his said Childe Allcocks Feilds and an hundred poundes, whereupon this deponent asked him how or where it should be raised to which the deceased answeared that there was fiftie poundes of it in Alice Peckstons handes, then there was all his cheese to sell and a good yoke of oxen and the rest to be made good out of his other goods, and all the rest of his goods & estate he gave to his said childe and wife to be equally divided betwixt them. And if his childe dyed before he came to age it should goe to the next of kin for it must goe forward it could not goe backward to his wife, And he desired to be buryed in the Church or Churchyard whether they would and presently after a Clarke came and began to frame a will to the effect as before but before he could neare finish it the said Richard was deprived of his senses & within an houre after dyed. And this deponent is the more certaine to depose therein for that presently after he came to his owne house he caused his sonne to make a note for his better remembrance of the words spoken by the deceased at the time abovesaid which was to the same purpose as it about deposed by him.

John Vernon *[mark]*

The same to the questions

To the first it has been satisfied

To the 2nd hee replies that the note now showed unto him is the same in effect with a note that this respondent caused to be made for his better memory concerning the words spoken by the deceased as it predeposed by him and for the rest mentioned in this question he refers himself to the things predeposed by him concerning the Allegation and Testament exhibited in this cause.

To the 3rd that the words predeposed by him to be spoken by the decedent were soe spoken the same night and not many hours before he dyed but he did not see any other person there at that time save the said Arthur Edgeley as he remembers and otherwise hee knows nothing.

To the 4th hee replies that not long before the decedent uttered the words predeposed by him purporting his will, he did speak some idle words, And otherwise referring himself to the things predeposed by him concerning the aforesaid Allegation and testament, he knows nothing to depose.

To the 5th he replies that Arthur Edgeley the party produceing him was brother to the deceased and he doth not know of any other that is nearer or soe neare of kinn to the said Minor except a sister that he has that was borne after the decedents death and he believes that that child is next heir in remainder to the said John her brother the minor in this cause & the next of kin to him.

To the 6th hee refers himself to the things predeposed, and otherwise knows nothing.

To the 7th hee replies that the security put into the Exchequer about the tuicōn of the Minors Interrogate was very good as he hath heard say & doth believe.

To the 8th that John Edgeley is about 8 years of age as he believes & and that Elizabeth was borne about halfe year after his decedents death.

To the 9th hee knows not what to reply.

To the last that he this deponent lives not in the same parish with the said Arthur Edgeley nor hath he seen him at any Church here 3 or 4 years. He further saith that the said Arthur was imployed in the late time of troubles as a *Sequestrator* as he hath heard but how he behaved himselfe he knows not haveing never any thing to doe with him concerning that business, And otherwise referring himself to the law he knows nothing to depose.

John Vernon *[mark]*

GLOSSARY

In addition to the more widely-used vocabulary found in the *Oxford English Dictionary*, there are now many regional and even local glossaries which enable us to assess usage of such Cheshire places as Stockport and Bowdon, as well as neighbouring areas such as southern Lancashire (i.e. Bolton) and Derbyshire. In our glossary of Wrenbury chapelry wills and inventories we have drawn on such word-lists wherever possible. Occasionally a word appears which - if transcribed correctly - defies definition. Often the meaning may be inferred from context, where, e.g., items related to textile manufacturing or animal husbandry may be grouped together, or where items of similar construction or material may be lumped together. This was obviously not always the case, however, since even a casual reading of the inventories suggests that items were appraised as they were brought before the prisers, and/or as the prisers encountered them during their perambulations about the house and property.

Even commonplace objects apparently had no agreed-upon orthography, for, in the days before standardized spellings, the scribe wrote what he heard, and this could result in a half-dozen variations in a single document: e.g., *board, borde, boward, boyrde, burd, bowrde, burde*, or the even more varied *brandrede, brendert, brunderd, brand rate, brandart, brondrett, brendreth, brundrett*. Rather than list all such variants, we have chosen the most significant forms and leave it to the reader to extrapolate from there.

Reference Works
Bolton & District Family History Society, *Of Good & Perfect Remembrance: Bolton Wills & Inventories 1545 to 1600, Surnames A to M* (Bolton, Bolton & District Family History Society, ca.1987).
Campbell, Mildred, *The English Yeoman Under Elizabeth and the Early Stuarts* (London, The Merlin Press, 1960).
Clarke, H.A., *The History of the Ancient Parish of Wrenbury (Including Combermere Abbey)*(Wrenbury, n.d. [1962/1989]).
Groves, Jill, *Piggins, Husslements and Desperate Debts: A Social History of North-east Cheshire Through Wills and Probate Inventories, 1600 - 1760* (Sale, Cheshire, Northern Writers Advisory Service, 1994).
Hole, Christina, *English Custom & Usage*, 2nd ed., rev. (London, B.T. Batsford Ltd, 1943).
Milward, Rosemary, *A Glossary of Household, Farming and Trade Terms from Probate Inventories*, 3rd ed., rev. and extended (Chesterfield, Derbyshire Record Society, 1986).
Moore, J.S., *The Goods and Chattels of Our Forefathers: Frampton Cotterell and District Probate Inventories 1539–1804* (London, Phillimore, 1976).
Oxford English Dictionary.
Phillips, C.B. and J.H. Smith, eds, *Stockport Probate Records, 1620–1650*, RSLC, cxxxi (1992).

acre	a measure of land; the Cheshire acre was 10,240 square yards; the statute acre 4,840 square yards
ale borde	ale bench: a bench in or before an ale-house
alias	otherwise called or named; another name; an assumed name
amare, aumare	early type of large cupboard with doors, usually for food, but later used for books, linen, clothes, etc.
ambry	see *amare*
angell	English coin, so called for having as its device the Archangel Michael; value varied from 6s. 8d. to 10s.
annuity	a yearly allowance of income
apparel	dress or external habiliments; clothing
applgrate	small cradle of iron to contain apples for roasting over a fire; also called an apple iron
appurtenance	an appendage, minor property, right or privilege belonging to another and passing with it
arke	a chest, coffer, close basket with domed lid; especially in the north, a bin for meal or bread ; also used in the house for clothes
arras work	superior type of tapestry fabric originating from Arras in Flanders
assigns	those appointed to act for another or to whom a right of property is transferred
axell tree	the fixed bar or beam on the round ends of which the opposite wheels of a carriage, etc revolve
bacinice	meaning unknown
backhouse	a subsidiary house or building which lies behind the main house
backstoole	single chair without arms
bandileere	broad belt, worn over the shoulder and across the breast, by which a wallet might be suspended at the side
bargaine of ground	a small land-holding
base	born out of wedlock; illegitimate
bason, basen	a bench with a plate of iron or stone flag fitted into it, and a little fire underneath, on which (before the introduction of machinery) the first part of the felting process was performed
beaker	a large drinking vessel with a wide mouth; an open cup or goblet
beck, beake	a large shallow vessel or tub, used in brewing, dyeing etc.
beddcase	see *bedstead*

bed hengynges	see *hilling*
bedstead	the framework of a bed; the sides and ends were perforated with holes, through which strong cords were drawn to form a tight net on which was placed a woven rush mat, other mattresses and feather beds
bed stocke	see *bedstead*
beeffe coume	a scumming comb used in a brew-house
beeff tubb	used together with beef comb in brew-house
bellies	bellows
benche clothe	decorated cloth or thin cushion for a bench
berddinge pise, *birding peece*	long-barrelled gun for sporting purposes, e.g., shooting wild fowl
bill, byll	long bladed implement used for pruning, cutting etc.
billowe	pillow
binge	implement for beating bark for the tanning industry
board, boyrde, *burd, bowrde*	board: flat wooden planks used as tables, supported on trestles but not fixed to them
boes	a plasterer's tray or hod; a seat of straw; a hassock
bole	bowl
bolsterre, boulster	applied to various things of the nature of a pad; used to obviate friction or chafing, or pad out hollows or deficiencies, etc.; especially in furniture
bordcloth, *burde cloth*	a dressed, double width cloth made from fine English wool
boucke	a wooden pail with upright handle; whence, *bucket*
boullinge pipe	meaning not found
bounde-whelles	wheels with iron rims
brake	toothed instrument for breaking flax or hemp
brandart, brand rate, *brendreth, brondrett*	a gridiron, tripod or trivet for a pot or pan, placed over or in front of an open fire; also, an iron tripod on which to hand cooking vessels over the fire
brasen dustbox	resembling brass in colour; or, made of brass
brawne	the muscle or flesh of animals as food; more specifically, a boar
bread grater	a scraper to use on bread
breches	breeches: a garment covering the loins and thighs: at first perhaps only a 'breech-cloth', later reaching to the knees
brend iron	see *brandart*
brickyudar	meaning unknown
broche	a spit, a piercing instrument, a chisel
brooke grasse	broken glass?

broth, broythe	see *broche*
bruinge coumes	see *beef coume*
bruing pann	large, kettle-like container used in brewing process
bryne	salt-water or brine
buckett irons	iron straps to bind a wooden bucket
buckler	a small round shield; in England usually carried by a handle on the back, and used not so much for a shield as for a warder to catch the blow of an adversary, but sometimes it was larger, and fastened by straps to the arm
buffett stooles	1) one of a set of stools for use at a long table; 2) high or low stools; foot stools, often with three legs
burning glasse	a lens, by which the rays of the sun may be concentrated on an object, so as to burn it if combustible
buttrie	a store room, originally for liquor but later for general provisions
buz	a sort of measurement for grain
cadow, caddowe	rough woollen bed covering
calfekitts	circular wooden vessel made of hooped staves, bound with iron bands, for containing milk, butter and other foods: in this case, apparently used to help feed young calves
Candlemas	2 February: Feast of the Purification of the Virgin Mary, or the Presentation of Christ in the Temple
cappon	capon (a castrated cock)
capulle	a horse
carde	implement used for parting, combing out and setting in order the fibres of hemp, wool etc. before spinning
carre	wood or grove on moist soil; any hollow place or marsh
cartropp	cart-rope
cather, cader	a cradle
certey	see *suertie*
chaff bedd	a bed or mattress stuffed with chaff instead of feathers
chaffe	a collective term for the husks of corn or other grain separated by threshing or winnowing
chaffyng dyshe	small enclosed brazier containing hot coals or burning fuel, for heating food and drink
chandler	a candle-maker; also, a candlestick
charger	large flat dish or plate
cheespresse, chist press	apparatus for pressing the curds in cheese-making
cheese ladder	structure for standing cheeses on while curing or ripening; cheese bridge
cherabet	meaning unknown

chesfatt	mould in which the curds are pressed and the cheese shaped
chipping knife	a knife used for 'chipping' bread
church warden	an officer of the parish, elected to assist the incumbent in the discharge of administrative duties and to manage various parochial offices as by custom
ciles	see *scileinge*
cisterne	an artificial reservoir for the storage of water; esp. a water-tight tank in a high part of a building, whence the taps in various parts of it are supplied
clappery ware	see *cowpery ware*
cliespitt	meaning unknown
clifte tymber	split wood for fuel
clokebogg	cloak bag, used for protection during storage or travel
close bowk, closse bouke	washing-tub
closes	enclosures about or beside a building
closse stoole	commode
cloute	cloth
cocke	male domestic bird; a rooster
codicil	a supplement to a will
coffer, quoffer	a small box or chest
coggs	a mechanical arrangement, consisting of pieces of wood attached by mortices, or notches cut out of the substance of the wood, which, in revolving, catch the rungs or trundles of a lantern-wheel
colander, culender	a perforated container used for straining (Milward)
coles, coolles	coals
coller	a leather-covered roll made to fit over the lower part of the neck of a horse or other draught animal, forming that part of the harness through which the power is directly exerted
combys	combs
commons	the undivided land belonging to the members of a local community as a whole; hence, the patch of unenclosed or 'waste' land which remains to represent it
compas	compost: a mixture of various ingredients for fertilizing or enriching land
computus calculus	[Latin:] account calculation
consistory	of or pertaining to Church government, as e.g., the Consistory Court of the Bishop of Chester
coope	cup: a small open vessel for liquids, usually of hemispherical or hemi-speroidal shape, with or without a handle; a drinking-vessel; the common form of cup (e.g., a tea-cup or coffee-cup) has no stem, but the

	larger and more ornamental forms (e.g., a wine-cup or chalice) may have a stem and foot, as also a lid or cover; in such case cup is sometimes applied specifically to the concave part that receives the liquid
cop, coppe	the moveable frame attached to the front of a wagon or farm cart, or projecting all round its sides, so as to extend its surface when carrying a bulky load, as of hay, corn, copsewood, or the like
copery, cop-ware	see *cowpery ware*
coppe yock, cupp yoke	the beam placed between a pair of oxen; how it differed from a draught yoke (often listed with it) is not clear, unless it was the local name for the yoke across the necks of the oxen
coppine, copp pyn	the wooden pin which fixes the copsole in place
copsole, capsoule, copsow	a wedge for keeping the coulter of an old-fashioned wooden plough in its place at a proper angle to the beam
corne	grain
corstet, corslet	1) a garment (usually tight-fitting) covering the body as distinct from the limbs; 2) a piece of defensive armour covering the body
coulte	colt (a young, male horse)
coulter	the iron blade fixed in front of the share in a plough; it makes a vertical cut in the soil, which is then sliced horizontally by the share
counterfett	a likeness or portrait
course (e.g., *pease*)	ordinary, common, mean (in the depreciatory sense of these epithets); base; of inferior quality or value; of little account
court cupboard	a movable sideboard or cabinet used to display plate, etc.
cousin	child of aunt or uncle: sometimes used for nephew, niece, or even a great friend
coverlidd, coverlette	the uppermost covering of a bed; a counterpane, quilt
coverpane	see *coverlidd*
cowmpe, comnpe	comb
cowpery ware	wooden vessels such as barrels, tubs, kits and looms, made of staves and hoops by a cooper
crab troughe	possibly a local name for crab press, used for making verjuice from crab apples
cratche	a rack used to hold fodder for cattle and horses
cresselt, cresset	vessel, usually of iron, to hold materials to burn for light, usually mounted on a pole, hung from the roof, or sometimes attached to the fire irons

crofte	a piece of enclosed ground, used for tillage or pasture: in most localities a small piece of arable land adjacent to a house
croscloth, crostcloathe	1) a linen cloth worn across the forehead; 2)a knitted kerchief
crosse	see *cresselt*
crowne	a unit of English coinage; five shillings
cubbart	cupboard: a side table with one, two or three shelves for displaying silver, pewter or earthenware; before the seventeenth century it had no doors
curleyes	meaning unknown
dame	the 'lady' of the house; the mistress of a household; a housewife
diall	1) an instrument serving to tell the hour of the day, by means of the sun's shadow upon a graduated surface; 2) a watch or compass
diapre	a twilled linen cloth woven with diamond patterns, used for napkins, towels and tablecloths
diggs	meaning unknown
dishcrate	dishcradle: wooden rack for drying dishes
dobnett	a close-fitting body-garment, with or without sleeves, worn by men from the fourteenth to the eighteenth centuries
doublet	close-fitting body-garment, with or without sleeves, worn by men and sometimes women, from the fourteenth to the eighteenth centuries
dower	1) the portion of a deceased husband's estate which the law allows to his widow for her life; 2) the money or property which the wife brings to the husband
drale	Meaning unknown
dripinge pan	a pan used to catch the 'drippings' from roasting meat
droppers	meaning unknown
dubbing shers	meaning unknown
dubble duckett	a gold coin of varying value, formerly in use in most European countries; that current in Holland, Russia, Austria and Sweden being equivalent to about 9*s*. 4*d*.
dysheboarde	dresser for displaying dishes and plates
edge toules, edgtoomes	in early use, any implements with sharp cutting edges, as knives or swords
elne	a measure of length varying in different countries: the English *ell* = 45 in.
enfeoffed	invested with a fief; to be put in possession of the fee-simple or fee-tail of lands, tenements, etc.

eshenn, ashen	an ash pail or shallow tub, often used for milk
ewer	pitcher with a wide spout, used to bring water to the table for washing hands, before and after meals
fawcett, fosett	a peg or spigot to stop the vent-hole in a cask or in a tap; a vent-peg
Feast of St Bartholomew	24 August
Feast of St Martin	11 November
Feast of St Michaell Tharchangell	1) Michelmas or 29 September: the feast of St Michael and all Angels, one of the quarter days in England, Ireland, and Wales; 2) a period or season around this date
Feast of St Thomas	23 December (Winter Solstice)
fellyes, fellowes	rim or part of rim of a wheel
fellts	a kind of cloth or stuff made of wool, or of wool and fur or hair, fulled or wrought into a compact substance by rolling and pressure, with lees or size
filches	see *fliche*
fipes	a crop of some sort?
fire forke	a fork-shaped instrument used for stirring up the fire, putting on fuel, etc.
firegrate, fireshoo	a frame of metal bars for holding fuel in a fireplace or oven; hence, the fireplace itself
firesclicer	fire shovel used particularly for getting the ashes out of a baking oven; the end was shaped like a spade or paddle
fir kine	firkin: small cask for liquids
flagen	a large bottle for holding wine or other liquors; in early use sometimes especially a metal bottle with a screw top, such as was carried by pilgrims
flaxkerchers	handkerchief made of flax
fleshmeate	flesh, as opposed to fish and vegetables, as an article of food
flesh forke	a fork for removing meat from the pot
fliche, fletche, fittche	flitch: side of an animal, usually beef or bacon, salted or cured and commonly hung from the roof
flocke bed	bed made from coarse tufts and refuse of wool, etc.
forme	a bench
fother, fodder	a load; a cart-load (of hay, turf, wood, etc.)
fowling peece	see *berddinge pise*
framinge sawe	a thin saw stretched in a frame which gives it sufficient rigidity in its work
french wheat	a species of *Polygonum* (*P. fagopyrum*), a native of Central Asia, whence it was introduced into Europe by the Turks about the thirteenth century; the seed is used in Europe as food for horses, cattle, and poultry;

	in N. America its meal is made into 'buckwheat' cakes, regarded as a dainty for the breakfast-table
frish	frieze: a coarse woollen cloth with a nap on one side
fussian	fustian: formerly, a kind of coarse cloth made of cotton and flax
futhers, fythers	feathers
gaffe	an iron hook; a staff or stick armed with this
gallepott	small earthen glazed pot
gaorge, gourge	chisel with a concave blade
gelbart, golberte, gobard	the iron rack in the chimney that supports the pot hooks
geldinge	a castrated horse
gladdyn	meaning unknown
glade nett	a net used for snaring birds in a glade
gobiring	see *gelbart*
goyst	joist
gratte, grote	see *firegrate*
grid irone, gryd iren	a cooking utensil formed of parallel bars of iron or other metal in a frame, usually supported on short legs, and used for broiling flesh or fish over a fire
gryndlestone	a disc of stone of considerable thickness, revolving on an axle, and used for grinding, sharpening, or polishing
gylt salte	a gilded salt cellar
haircloth, heyre clothe	coarse open cloth or fabric made of hair, used in drying malt, hops or the like, in the kiln
hallockracke	meaning unknown
handyron	large fire-dog or cobiron, having hooks at various levels, from which cooking spits were supported over a fire
harde corne	a general name for wheat and rye
harness	equipment associated with military weapons, such as the belt and scabbard of a sword; armour
harriot, heriot, heryote	tender of the best live beast or dead chattel of a deceased tenant due by legal custom to the lord of the manor
harrowe	a heavy frame of timber (or iron) set with iron teeth or tines, which is dragged over ploughed land to break clods, pulverize and stir the soil, root up weeds, or cover in the seed; sometimes made in two halves, and then locally called *the harrows*
hatchone	meaning unknown
head peace	helmet
heath sheep	sheep living on the open heath or down

hecke	heckle: an instrument for combing or scutching flax or hemp
heireloomes	chattels that, under a will, settlement, or local custom, follow the devolution of real estate; hence, any pieces of personal property that have been in a family for several generations
herball	a book containing the names and descriptions of herbs, or of plants in general, with their properties and virtues; a treatise on plants
herbriche	herbage
hereditament	anything that in the absence of a will descends to the heir at common law
hetchill, hechele	an instrument for combing flax or hemp
hilling	covering, mainly applied to beds, or sometimes tables
hogeshead	a large cask for liquids, etc.; especially one of a definite capacity, which varied for different liquids and commodities
hoope	measure of varying capacity
hoppette	a basket, especially a small hand-basket
horse comb	a curry-comb
horse gears	harness or riding equipment or tack; also referred to as horse or riding furniture
horse pavemente	road surface, in this case probably cobblestones
horseheld	possibly, a horselock or hobbles, a device to prevent a horse from straying; or horse *hillings*?
hossen	stockings, or *breeches*
husbandrey	the business or occupation of a husbandman or farmer; tillage or cultivation of the soil (including also the rearing of live stock and poultry, and sometimes extended to that of bees, silkworms, etc.); agriculture, farming
Imprimis	[Latin]: in the first place
incalf	pregnant [of a cow]
inch boards	board an inch thick
indenture	deed between two or more parties, the copies having their edges indented
inkle	linen tape
in toto	[Latin] all together; all combined
ioyned	of furniture, made by a joiner: hence, with parts joined or fitted together, as distinguished from items of more clumsy workmanship
issue, yssue	heirs of the body
jack	machine for turning the spit

jerkin	close fitting jacket or short coat
jill	mentioned in connection with pewter ware - refers to a vessel of the capacity of a *gill*, or half a pint?
kersie	coarse narrow cloth woven from long wool and usually ribbed
kiddes, kydes	bundles of sticks, gorse etc., used for heating bread ovens and other purposes
kleeuer	cleaver
kneadinge turnell	tub in which curds were kneaded to squeeze out the whey; trough or tub in which to knead dough
knedinge troughe	see *kneadinge turnell*
knight's fee	the amount of land for which the services of an armed knight were due to the sovereign
koo	cow
kyne	cattle; cows
kyschynes	cushions
landirons	see *handyron*
lanthorne	lantern
leads	leaden vats for brewing, sometimes only lined with lead
leaseowes	leases
legacies	sums of money, or specified articles, given to another by will; bequests in a more general sense
lenten seedenes, *lynseed*	the seed of flax, well known as the source of linseed oil, and as a medicament
lintsy wolsty	linsey wolsey: cloth made of a mixture of wool and linen
liverie cubboard	cupboard in which food and drink was kept; usually had pierced doors
livery table	a table on which 'liveries' or rations were put; hence, a side table
London pynte	meaning unclear
longnette	longette or longart: the tail end or board of a cart
loockinge glasse	a mirror
lynbeck	limbeck: a still for making liquor such as aqua vitae
mark	unit of account equal to 13s. 4d.
markeinge ireon	1) a branding iron; 2) an implement for incising or inscribing marks
marle, marled field	of land or soil: manured or improved with marl (OED); marl: an earthy deposit, typically loose and unconsolidated and consisting chiefly of clay mixed with

	calcium carbonate, formed in prehistoric seas and lakes and long used to improve the texture of sandy or light soil
Martinmas	see *Feast of St Martin*
mastulyn, maselen, masin	a shiny yellowish alloy of copper resembling brass (perhaps a form of the copper-zinc alloy now called *brass*); in later use (especially attributed): such a metal as used for making pots, pans and kettles
mattock	a tool similar to a pick but with a point or chisel edge at one end of the head and an adze-like blade at the other, used for breaking up hard ground, grubbing up trees, etc.
maulte, malt	barley or other grain prepared for brewing, distilling or vinegar-making, especially by steeping, germinating and kiln-drying
mazer cupp	mazer: maple or other fine-grained hardwood used as a material for making drinking vessels
meat cloyth	a table-cloth
meedinge, myddinge	midden, a dunghill or dung heap; a refuse heap; also, a domestic ash-pit
melding burd	moulding board; 1) board on which dough or paste was kneaded or shaped; 2) board or metal plate in a plow which turns over the furrow slice
milling podege dishes	some sort of pewter ware: pottage dishes
moiety, moytye	a half, one of two equal parts
montans, muntanes	in panelling, the central vertical piece of wood between two panels
morris pike	a weapon, known also as a 'brown bill' because of the brown finish of its blade, originally an agricultural implement which evolved into a tool of war; the bill consisted of a leaf-shaped, or hook-shaped, steel head, with a cutting edge on the concave side, mounted on a shaft of about six feet, which aided close-quarter fighting; it was well-known in the sixteenth century, as attested by Shakespeare's reference in Act IV, Scene III of *Comedy of Errors*, and by George Silver's *Paradoxes of Defense*, published in 1599; as with the Morris Dance, the name is a corruption of 'Moorish'
morter	a receptacle of a hard material (e.g. marble, brass, wood, or glass), with a cup-shaped cavity in which ingredients used in pharmacy, cookery, etc., are pounded with a pestle
mortuarie	customary gift formerly claimed by the incumbent from the estate of a dead parishioner for burial

muck(e)	dung, excrement, especially the dung of farm animals used for manure (often mixed with vegetable matter, usually straw); farmyard manure
munkcorne, mongcorne	a mixture of different kinds of grain (usually wheat and rye), especially when sown together
musterd mill	a mill for grinding mustard seeds
musterilly wherler, musterd whirle	see *musterd mill*
Mychelmas	see *Feast of St Michaell Tharchangell*
mylne stonne	either of a pair of circular stones which grind corn by the rotation of the upper stone on the lower (or nether) one
nagge, nadge	a saddle or riding horse
nappery(e) ware	linen used for household purposes
nawger, nagare, noger	carpenter's tool for boring holes in wood or an instrument for boring in the earth.
Needle woorke, nidlework Purle	work done with a needle; especially the art or practice of sewing or embroidery; also, sewn or embroidered items collectively
netosea	meaning unknown
noggen	small drinking vessel; a mug, cup or ladle
nother	another
outer	other or another
outhouse	a subsidiary building in the grounds of or adjoining a house, as a barn, shed, etc.
overpluse	that which remains over; an amount left over from the main amount, or from what is allotted or required; an additional or extra quantity; a surplus
packelant, packlent, packillant, parkelant	meaning unknown
pannell, pannell & muntanes	originally: a piece of cloth, especially a piece placed under a saddle to protect the horse's back; a saddle pad (obsolete). Later: the padded underpart of a saddle
parce	a part, portion, or division *of* something (material or immaterial), considered separately as a unit; a small part
partelit	a ruff or band worn by both sexes, but latterly only by women, when it became a neckerchief, covering the neck and shoulders
pattell	a shallow pan or dish

peck, peake	a unit of capacity for dry goods equal to a quarter of a bushel
pettecote	1) a man's tight-fitting undercoat, usually padded and worn under a doublet and over a shirt; (also) a padded jerkin worn under armour for protection; 2) a skirt, as distinguished from a bodice, worn either externally or showing beneath a dress as part of the costume (often trimmed or ornamented); 3) an outer skirt; 4) a decorative underskirt; freq. in plural: a woman's or girl's upper skirts and underskirts collectively
peuter, peauvter	a grey alloy of tin, originally with about 20 per cent lead (and sometimes other elements) but now with about 10 per cent antimony and a small quantity of copper, used chiefly for ornaments and (especially formerly) utensils
peynyte cloyth	a cloth or hanging decorated with images or text executed in paint (formerly also embroidered or woven in colours)
pickellant	see *packelant*; see also *pykelle*
pickle	a pitchfork or hay-fork
pillin, pyllin	pad or cushion attached to the hinder part of an ordinary saddle, to carry a second person, usually a woman
pillowe beeres	pillow cases
pinsorre	pincer: a tool for tightly grasping or nipping anything, consisting of two limbs pivoted together, forming a pair of jaws with a pair of handles or levers by which they can be pressed tightly together
plane	a tool, used by carpenters and others, for levelling down and smoothing the surface of woodwork by paring shavings from it
plate	silver plate - utensils for table and domestic use, ornaments, etc.
plate coatt	corselet of leather on which were sewn a number of small plates of iron or steel
ploughtes	ploughs
plow beam	the central longitudinal beam or bar of timber or iron in a plough, to which the other principal parts are attached
ploweirons	any iron parts of a plough, especially the coulter and share
plowe timber	see *plow beam*
powke, poake	applied to a bag of any material or description, but usually smaller than a *sack*
pol axe	a kind of axe formerly used as a weapon of war, a battle-axe

polayens	piece of defensive armour covering the knee
porcōn	that part of the personal estate of a deceased person which by law or custom descends to wife or children
possnett, pursnett	a small metal pot or vessel for boiling, having a handle and three feet
pot hoycke, pothocke	a hook suspended over a fireplace, for hanging a pot or kettle on; a crook; an iron rod (usually curved) with a hook at the end, for lifting a heated pot, stove-lid, etc.
pottynger	bowls of silver, pewter or earthenware for soup or porridge
powtry, pulterye ware	poultry as a marketable commodity
preese, pras	a large cupboard with doors and usually shelves, for keeping clothes, linen, books etc; sometimes placed in a recess in a wall
presinge bord	table with a cupboard beneath
priggen, piggen	small wooden vessel made in the manner of a half barrel, with one stave longer than the rest to form a handle
pullen	poultry
pyde	pied: marked, dappled, speckled with a colour or, in extended use, some other thing
pykelle	pike
quarrel bricks	the stone or other material obtained by quarrying
quiches	see *qyssion*
quietus est	[Latin]: acquittance
quyer	choir: the east end of the church or chapel; often where prominent members of the parish were buried
qyssion, cushine	cushion
rayles	bars of wood, fixed in a horizontal position for hanging things on, or for other purposes; or, forming part of the sides of a cart
readinge sheets	readings: a course sort of cloth
reapinge hook	a scythe with a curved steel blade about eighteen inches long with a serrated edge
revercion	the return of an estate to the donor or grantor, or his heirs, after the expiry of the grant; an estate which thus returns to the donor or his heirs
riddle	a coarse-meshed sieve, used for separating chaff from corn, sand from gravel, ashes from cinders, etc.; the most usual form has a circular wooden rim with a bottom formed of strong wires crossing each other at right-angles

rippon or *ripple come*	an implement toothed like a comb, used in cleaning flax or hemp from the seeds
round, rowne	a tooth or stave of a trundle
ruff, ruffle band	a circular outstanding frill on the sleeve of a garment; a ruffle
rydinge furniture	see *horse gears*
rylle	a small stream; a brook, runnel, rivulet; especially a small trickle of water formed temporarily in soil or sand after rain or tidal ebb
ryngers	those who ring the bells in connection with a funeral
sackhouse	sack is white wine imported from Spain; hence, a wine-cellar
salting basyn	receptacle used for salting meat
saltceller, sallet, salt parcell	small vessel placed on table for holding salt
saltinge pye	salt pyche: a salt box, or a container of earthenware, for use in the kitchen
salt meate, sault flesh	meat that has been salted to preserve it
sarcenett	see *sarche*
sarche, scerch	a sieve or strainer
sattlerye	articles made or sold by a saddler; saddles and other articles pertaining to the equipment of a horse, especially of one used for riding
sauffe, saffe	a ventilated chest or cupboard for protecting provisions from insects and other noxious animals; a meat-safe
sawinge tymber	sawn timber
sawser	saucer: a small pan or platter in which sauce is set on the table
scileinge, seylinge, sileing, scylinge	panelling or wainscoting
scullerye	the department of a household concerned with the care of the plates, dishes and kitchen utensils; also the room or rooms in which the work of this department is carried on
searser	a sieve
Service Book	a book containing the procedure for Divine Service
setts	stitched or embroidered work
seve	sieve
seysed	seised, or in possession of
shafeing dish	see *chaffyng dyshe*
sheets of readings	see *readinge sheets*
shertyship	see *suertie*

shette, schete	a napkin, cloth, or towel; a broad piece of linen or cotton stuff, canvas, or the like, for covering, swathing, protecting from injury, etc.
shilves, shilfes	shelves
shoate	a young weaned pig
shookes	a set of staves and headings sufficient for one hogshead, barrel, or the like, prepared for use and bound up in a compact form for convenience of transport. Boards for boxes prepared or fitted for use and packed in the same way bear the same name
shules	shovels
skance	sconce: 1) a lantern or candlestick with a screen to protect the light from the wind, and a handle to carry it by; 2) bracket candlestick fixed to the wall
skellett	a cooking vessel of various metals, with three feet and a long handle, to stand over a fire
skimmer	scummer, perforated ladle
sleade	sled or sledge
smocke	probably a shift (women's wear)
snett	sneck: a latch
snuffer	an instrument used for snuffing, or snuffing out, candles, etc.
socage	the tenure of land by certain determinate services other than knight-service
specialties	contracts, obligations or bonds expressed in a written instrument under seal
spit	a cooking implement consisting of a slender sharp-pointed rod of metal or wood, used for thrusting into or through meat which is to be roasted at a fire; a broach
splents	two pieces of armour to protect the elbows, formed of plates or strips of overlapping metal
sploid	meaning unknown
square	an implement or tool for determining, measuring, or setting out right angles, or for testing the exactness of artificers' work, usually consisting of two pieces or arms set at right angles to each other, but sometimes with the arms or sides hinged or pivoted so as to measure any angle; especially one used by carpenters or joiners
standinge bed	a high bedstead, as distinguished from a truckle-bed or one fixed against a wall, with corner posts, tester, curtains and valances, usually decorated with embroidery, rich materials, or painted cloths

standerd	1) a tall candlestick; 2) large or small chest with domed or gabled lid, used for travelling; the larger were carried on carts, the smaller on sumpter horses; 3) a tree that stands alone, or above the underwood
standish	a stand containing ink, pens and other writing materials and accessories; an inkstand; also, an inkpot
stands of beese	colonies of bees, or beehives
staves	each of the thin, narrow, shaped pieces of wood which, when placed together side by side and hooped, collectively form the side of a cask, tub or similar vessel
steeping comes	steeping means to soak: apparently related to brewing
sterke, styrke, stearke	a young bullock or heifer, usually between one and two years old
still	an apparatus for distillation, consisting essentially of a close vessel (alembic, retort, boiler) in which the substance to be distilled is subjected to the action of heat, and of arrangements for the condensation of the vapour produced
stockbedd	see *bedstead*
stocke card	a large wool-card fastened to a stock or support
stock sawe	a saw used in a stock-gang
stoke, stocke	a colony of bees
stole, stoyle	stool
ston	stone: a measure of weight, usually equal to 14 pounds avoirdupois, but varying with different commodities from 8 to 24 pounds. The stone of 14 lb. is the common unit used in stating the weight of a man or large animal
stone bowe	an arch of stone *or* a kind of cross-bow or catapult used for shooting stones
stoond, stounde	wooden vessel in which small beer was put
stracōn cheyr	meaning not found
straine flaskett	see *seve*
stricke, stryke	a measure of capacity for corn, coal, etc.; also the measuring vessel
stuere, steere	young ox
stuff	cognate with German: Stoff - 1) new draperies; 2) worsteds, without nap or pile
suertie	surety: person who offers security of contract, right, or possession on behalf of another
suyte	lawsuit
syling nails	see *scileinge*

tacke	1) tenure or tenancy, of land, benefice, etc.: especially leasehold tenure, e.g. of a farm, mill, or the like; the period of tenure; 2) hired or leased pasture for horses, cows, etc.
teare, the	seed of a vetch: usually in reference to its small size
teith, tithe	one tenth (of one's goods, earnings, etc.), given for the support of the Church
tenement	land or real property which is held of another by any tenure; a holding
tertern, tenter	stone or wooden post with beams for stretching cloth
tester, testern	canopy over a bed
tewtawe, tutall, tutave, tutuwe	tewtaw: to beat or break, as with flax or hemp; hence, a device for doing this.
thrave, thrawe	a measure of corn, straw etc., consisting of two 'stooks' of twelve sheaves each
thrivin worke	thrown: of wood, turned on a lathe; of pot, shaped on a potter's wheel; of silk, cleaned and prepared for spinning
throck	in full, *plough-throck*: the share-beam
throwed cheyre	a chair turned on a lathe
throwinge bench	bench used for supporting a lathe
thrum	thrumbed: cloth or cushions with tassels, or a fringe of threads left at the edge
ticke	the case or cover containing feathers, flocks, or the like, forming a mattress or pillow; also, from the sixteenth century, applied to the strong hard linen or cotton material used for making such cases
ticknals, ticknall ware	pottery of a coarse, common kind, made at Ticknall (South Derbyshire) from the reign of Elizabeth I
timbrelle, tumbrell	a farm cart, especially a heavy cart used for manure; a wagon
tole	tool
tooe, towe, tawe	flax or hemp before spinning; more strictly, the shorter fibres
torves	see *turffes*
tounges	tongs
tournell, turnill	a large oval, shallow tub, especially one used for salting meat or scalding pigs
treene, trayne, trinde ware	wooden, made of wood; usually thrown rather than sawn
trencher	wooden or pewter plate or dish
tressel	frame or support of a table
trowe	trough
trumpery	something of less value than it seems; hence, something of no value; trifles; worthless stuff, trash, rubbish

trunklebed, trocle bed	a low bed running on truckles or castors pushed beneath a high or standing bed when not in use
tubb	an open wooden vessel, wide in proportion to its height, usually formed of staves and hoops, of cylindrical or slightly concave form, with a flat bottom
tugge chaine	a chain trace; also a short chain by which a leather trace is attached to the splinter-bar
tuggs	see *tugge chaine*
turfe spade	a spade for cutting turf or peats
turffes, turves	peat, blocks of peat, pieces of cut turf used for fuel
turninge dishe	turning: the action of shaping or working something on a lathe; the art of shaping things by means of a lathe; hence, a lathe-produced dish
tuter	see *tewtawe*
twenters, twinters	sheep, cattle or colts two years old
twige chayre	a chair made out of twigs (i.e., small branches), plaited or woven
twilshetes, twyll schetes	a woven fabric characterized by parallel diagonal ridges or ribs, produced by causing the weft threads to pass over one and under two or more threads of the warp, instead of over and under in regular succession, as in plain weaving
ure	see *ewer*
valans, valens, valse	valance: a border of drapery hanging from the canopy of a bed, and from the mattress to the floor; a deep frill
venic glasses	Venice glass
vergisse, vergis	the acid juice of green or unripe grapes, crab-apples, or other sour fruit, expressed and formed into a liquor; formerly much used in cooking, as a condiment, or for medicinal purposes
vicar	a person acting as priest in a parish in place of the parson or rector, or as the representative of a religious community to which the tithes had been appropriated; hence, in later use in the Church of England, the incumbent of a parish of which the tithes were impropriated or appropriated, in contrast to a rector
vicualles	victuals: whatever is normally required, or may naturally be used, for consumption in order to support life; food or provisions of any kind
videlicett, vizt.	[Latin]: that is to say; namely; to wit - used to introduce an amplification, or more precise or explicit explanation, of a previous statement or word

vircle	meaning unknown: a silver *vircle* mentioned in connection with a sword
voyder	table basket for dishes, knives etc.; pail-like article of wood or wicker into which bones etc. are shelved or thrown during a meal
wainscote, wenscott	a superior quality of foreign oak imported from Russia, Germany, and Holland, chiefly used for fine panel-work; logs or planks of this oak; oak boarding for panel-work
Walkers Erth	fuller's earth: a hydrous aluminium silicate, used in cleansing cloth
wastcoate	a garment forming part of ordinary male attire, worn under an outer garment (a doublet, later a coat, jacket, or the like), and intended to be partly exposed to view when in wear
wayne	a large open, four-wheeled vehicle or wagon, drawn by horses or oxen, for carrying heavy loads, especially of agricultural produce
wayninge beam	wagon-tree
weddley gowne	wedding gown
weeting malte combe	used in the kiln-drying process of malting
wegges	wedge: a piece of wood, metal, or other hard material, thick at one end and tapering to a thin edge at the other; chiefly used as a tool operated by percussion (or, less frequently, pressure) applied to the thick end, for splitting wood, stone, etc., forcing apart contiguous objects, dilating a fissure or cavity, tightening or securing some part of a structure, raising a heavy body, and other similar purposes. (OED)
wemtell	horse's belly band
whirl	the fly-wheel or pulley of a spindle
whitche, which	salt
whytmeate	foods prepared from milk; dairy produce (occasionally including eggs); *or* certain white or light-coloured flesh foods
wichhouse	place for drying brine for salt
wimble	see *nawger*
windinge ropes	ropes used for winding, hoisting or hauling, by means of a winch, windlass, or the like
windowe sheete	sheet or sack over an unglazed window to keep out the cold
wiskett	local name for a basket, of various kinds and uses
woodwaint	see *wainscote*
worthyng yelve	dung or manure fork

wrecking iron	crowbar
wrought cover	worked iron covering of some sort
wuulsted	worsted: superior woollen fabric made from well-twisted yarn of long staple wool, originally made at Worsted in Norfolk
wynter corne	corn sown in winter, or in autumn and remaining in the ground through the winter
yarto hindles	meaning unknown
yeoman	a social ranking above that of husbandman
yelve, yelue	a dung- or garden-fork
ymshene	meaning unknown
yt, ye	that; the

BIBLIOGRAPHY

Unpublished Sources

Cheshire Record Office (CRO)

'Boke of the Tithe Calves of the Parish of Wrenbury AD 1574'
Cheshire Composition Papers, ca. 1650 [1]
Greenwood Map 1819 .... DM 13/10C
James Hall, 'Introduction to a History of Combermere
    and Newhall' .... D 4059/15
James Hall, 'The Manor of Newhall in Wrenbury Parish' ...... D 4059/23
James Hall, 'Newhall Families' .... D 4059/27
James Hall, 'Newhall Manor Court Rolls 1538–1545' .... Mf 283/178
James Hall, 'Newhall Manor Court Rolls - Extracts' .... D 4059/29
James Hall, 'Notebook containing draft history of
    Combermere estate' (pages numbered 1–27; see 16–19); translation of
    account roll (Computus Roll) of Newhall Manor, 1387–88
    and History of Newhall Manor in C15th and C16th ...... D 4059/23, 24,
                                                     25, 27, 30

Wrenbury Bishop's Transcripts 1593–1684
Wrenbury - Notes on History by John Hewitt .... D 4348/1
Wrenbury Parish Registers 1593–1684 .... Mf 156/1–3
Wrenbury Tithe Map - Apportionment .... EDT 445/1
Wrenbury-cum-Frith Tithe Map .... EDT 445/2

The National Archives (formerly Public Record Office) (TNA)

Ches 3/65 Inquisition Post Mortem 20 Henry VIII for Thomas Starkey of Wrenbury, esq.
Ches 3/68 Inquisition Post Mortem 34 Henry VIII for John Starkey, gent.
Ches 3/73 Inquisition Post Mortem 2 Elizabeth for Mary Cotton.
Ches 3/80 Inquisition Post Mortem 23 Elizabeth for Thomas Starkey.
Ches 3/561 Inquisition Post Mortem 19 Henry VII for Richard Cotton.
Ches 15/1/127 Bill of debt brought by Thomas Pexstons and his wife Elizabeth, against Roger Parleby.
HL/PO/JO/10/1/138 Petition from Sir Edmond Wright, alderman of the City of London, 1642.
PCC 1659/prob 11/301 sig 242 [?] Registered copy of the will of Ralph Cardiffe of Woldhall, Cheshire.

---

1 Cited in *Cheshire Sheaf,* 3rd ser., ix. 75.

Published Sources

Sir George J. Armytrage, ed., *Allegations for Marriage Licences Issued by the Dean and Chapter of Westminster 1558–1699*, Harleian Society Publications, 23 (1886).

George Baker, *The History and Antiquities of the County of Northampton,* vol. I (London, J.B. Nichols and Son, 1822).

John Ball, *A Treatise of Faith: Divided Into Two Parts* (London, pr. George Miller for Edward Brewster, 1632).

J.H.E. Bennett and J.C. Dewhurst, compilers and editors, *Quarter Sessions Records, with Other Records of the Justices of the Peace for the County Palatine of Chester 1559–1760*, RSLC, xciv (1940).

Sir William Blackstone, *Commentaries on the Laws of England*.

Mary Bodfish, ed., *Probate Inventories of Smethwick Residents 1647–1747* (Smethwick, Smethwick Local History Society, 1992).

Bolton & District Family History Society, *'Of Good & Perfect Remembrance': Bolton Wills and Inventories 1545 to 1600, Surnames A to M* (Bolton, Bolton & District Family History Society, 1987).

Burdett, P.P., *A Survey of the County Palatine of Chester*, 1777 edition, reprinted in facsimile with an introduction (and text) by J.B. Harley and P. Laxton, Historic Society of Lancashire and Cheshire, Occasional Series, vol. 1 (London, Lund Humphries for the Society, 1974).

Calendar of the Patent Rolls, Edward VI, vol. III: 1549–51; vol.V:1547–53 (London, HMSO, 1925, 1926).

Calendar of the Patent Rolls, Philip and Mary, vol. I: 1553–54; vol.II: 1554–55; vol.III: 1555–57; vol. IV: 1557–58 (London, HMSO, 1937, 1936, 1938, 1939).

Calendar of the Patent Rolls, Elizabeth, vol. IV: 1566–69; VIII: 1578–80; IX: 1580–82 (London, HMSO, 1964, 1986, 1986).

Mildred Campbell, *The English Yeoman*, paperback ed. (London, Muhu Press, 1982).

Cheshire Countryside and Recreation, *Cheshire Churches – Church of St. Margaret, Wrenbury,* Cheshire County Council (privately printed, 1988).

Cheshire Federation of Women's Institutes, *The Cheshire Village Book* (Newbury, Berkshire, Countryside, 1990).

Cheshire Federation of Women's Institutes, *Cheshire Village Memories*, Vol. 1, ed. D. Haworth and W.M. Comber, vol. 2, ed. W.M. Comber, L. Gibson and D. Haworth (published by Tilston Court, 1952, ?1961)].

H.A. Clarke, *The History of the Ancient Parish of Wrenbury (Including Combermere Abbey)* (Wrenbury, n.d. [1962/1989]).

Jack Cockroft, transcr., *Transcripts of Nantwich Wills and Inventories 1603–1688* (Crewe, South Cheshire Family History Society, 1999).

George Edward Cokayne, ed., *The Complete Baronetage*, reprint (Gloucester, Alan Sutton, 1983).

Domesday Book, vol.26: Cheshire, ed. Philip Morgan (Chichester, Phillimore, 1978).

William Dugdale, esq., Norrey King of Arms, *Cheshire Visitation Pedigrees 1663*, ed. Arthur Adams, Harleian Society Publications, 93 (1941).

J.P. Earwaker, *East Cheshire: Past and Present, or A History of the Hundred of Macclesfield in the County Palatine of Chester*, 2 vols (London, pr. for the author by Wyman & Sons, 1877–80).

J.P. Earwaker. ed., *An Index to the Wills and Inventories Now Preserved in the Court of Probate at Chester*, Vol. I, 1545–1620 (including wills printed by the Chetham Society); Vol. II, 1621–50; Vol. III, 1660–80, RSLC, ii, iv, xv (1879, 1881, 1887).

Jeremy S.W. Gibson, *A Simplified Guide to Probate Jurisdictions: Where to Look for Wills,* 4th ed. (Birmingham, Federation of Family History Societies, 1994).

Robert Glover, Somerset Herald, *The Visitation of Cheshire in the Year 1580...With Additions and Continuations, Including Those From the Visitation...in... 1566[etc]*, ed. J.P. Rylands, Harleian Society Publications, 18 (1882).

Stephen R. Glynne, *Notes on the Churches of Cheshire*, Chetham Society, new.series, 32 (1894).

Jill Groves, *Piggins, Husslements and Desperate Debts:a Social History of North-east Cheshire Through Wills and Probate Inventories, 1600–1760*, Between the Bollin and the Mersey Series, vol. 1 (Sale, Cheshire, Northern Writers Advisory Service, 1994).

James Hall, ed. & transl., *The Book of the Abbot of Combermere 1289–1529 [Begun 1524 by John Massie, Sub-Prior]*[transl. from the original in the possession of Lord Combermere], in *Miscellanies Relating to Lancashire and Cheshire*, vol. II, RSLC, xxxi (1896).

James Hall, *A History of the Town and Parish of Nantwich or Wich Malbank in the County Palatine of Chester* (Nantwich, printed for the author, 1883).

James Hall, *Notes and Queries*, s9 IV: no. 91 (1899).

B.E. Harris, A.T. Thacker [and others], eds, *A History of the County of Chester*, vol. 1 (1987), vol. 3 (1980), Victoria History of the Counties of England (Oxford, Oxford University Press for the Institute of Historical Research, 1979-).

Mark D. Herber, *Ancestral Trails: The Complete Guide to British Genealogy and Family History* (Stroud, Sutton in association with the Society of Genealogists, 1997).

N.J. Higham, *The Origins of Cheshire* (Manchester, Manchester University Press, 1993).

A. Hughes, ed., *Seventeenth Century England: a Changing Culture*, vol. I - Primary Sources (Milton Keynes, Open University Press, n.d.)

International Genealogical Index [Electronic resource] (Salt Lake City, Utah, Church of Jesus Christ of Latter-Day Saints).

William Fergusson Irvine, ed., *A List of the Clergy in Eleven Deaneries of the Diocese of Chester 1541–42*, in *Miscellanies Relating to Lancashire and Cheshire*, vol. III, RSLC, xxxiii (1896).

William Fergusson Irvine, ed., *An Index of the Wills, Inventories, Administration Bonds, and Depositions in Testamentary Suits Now Preserved at the Diocesan Registry, Chester, from 1487 to 1620 Inclusive*, in *Miscellanies Relating to Lancashire and Cheshire*, vol. III, RSLC, xxxiii (1896).

William Fergusson Irvine, ed., *Marriage Licences Granted Within the Archdeaconry of Chester in the Diocese of Chester, 1606–1700*, vols I-V, RSLC, liii, lvi, lvii, lxi, lxv (1907, 1908, 1909, 1911, 1912).

Giles Jacob, *New Law Dictionary:Containing the Interpretation and Defination of Words and Terms Used in the Law*, 6th ed. (London, pr. Henry Lintot for R. Ware [and others], 1750).

Daniel King, *The Vale Royal of England* (London, pr. John Streater, 1656).

David Knowles, *Bare Ruined Choirs: the Dissolution of the English Monasteries* (Cambridge, Cambridge University Press, 1976).

Frank A. Latham, ed., *Acton (near Nantwich): the History of a Cheshire Parish and its Seventeen Townships* (Whitchurch, Shropshire, Local History Group, 1995).

John Leland, *Antiquities* (1634–43).

John Leland, *Itineraries* (1610).

Letters and Papers, Foreign and Domestic, of Henry VIII, 2nd ed., revised and greatly enlarged by R.H. Brodie (original ed. London, HMSO; reprint, Vaduz, Kraus, 1965).

Thomas Malbon, *Memorials of the Civil War in Cheshire*, ed. James Hall, RSLC, xix (1889).

Henry Melville, *Ancestry of John Whitney* (New York, De Vinne Press, 1896).

Rosemary Milward, *A Glossary of Household, Farming and Trade Terms* (Derby, Derbyshire Record Society, 1986).

J.S. Moore, *The Goods and Chattels of our Forefathers: Frampton Cotteral & District Probate Inventories 1539–1840* (Phillimore, Chichester, 1976).

F.W. Norwood, 'Historic Notes', *The Wrenbury Church Monthly (1900–1905)*, collected by John Parkin, Newhall Mill Farm, Aston, Nantwich.

George Ormerod, *The History of Cheshire 1819*, 2nd ed., 3 vols, revised and enlarged by Thomas Helsby (London, Routledge, 1882).

Alfred Neobard Palmer, *History of the Thirteen County Townships of the Old Parish of Wrexham* (Hughes and Son, 1903; facsimile reprint Wrexham, Bridge Books, 1983).

'The Parishioners of Wrenbury', *Cheshire Sheaf,* 3rd series, 10 (February 1913).

William Perkins, *The Whole Treatise of the Case of Conscience, Distinguished Into Three Books* (Cambridge, T. Pickering, 1606).

C.B. Phillips and J.H. Smith, eds, *Stockport Probate Records, 1578–1619* and *1620–1650*, RSLC, cxxiv (1985) and cxxxi (1992).

The Rev. G.J. Piccope, ed., *Lancashire and Cheshire Wills and Inventories From the Ecclesiastical Court, Cheshire*, Portion II, Chetham Society, 51 (1860).

Paul B. Pixton, ' Wrenbury, Cheshire, and the Pixton Family', *Journal of the South Cheshire Family History Society,* 19, 20 and 22 (1995).

John R. Pound, 'St. Margaret's Church, Wrenbury: a Brief Account of this 900 Year Old Churchyard' [typewritten] (1993).

John Preston, *The Brest-Plate of Faith and Love* (London, pr. R.Y. for Nicholas Bourne, 1634).

John Preston, *Life Eternall: a Treatise of the Knowledge of the Divine Essence and Attributes* (London, pr. E.P. for Nicholas Bourne and Ralpha Harford, 1634).

Paul C. Reed, 'Whitney Origins Revisited: John Whitney of Watertown, Massachusetts and Henry Whitney of Norwalk, Connecticut', *The American Genealogist,* 69 (1994).

Raymond Richards, ed., *Old Cheshire Churches, With a Supplementary Survey Related to the Lesser Old Chapels in Cheshire*, revised ed. (Didsbury, Manchester, E.J. Morten, 1973).

Richard St George, esq. , Norroy King of Arms and Henry St George, *Pedigrees Made at the Visitation of Cheshire, 1613*, ed. George J. Armitage and J.P. Rylands, RSLC, lviii (1909).

S.A. Smith, comp., *Index of Wills Proved in the Prerogative Court of Canterbury, vol. 4: 1584–1604*, The Index Library, 25 (London, 1901, repr. 1968).

R. Stewart Brown, *Cheshire Inquisitions Post Mortem: Stuart Period, 1603–1660*, 3 vols, RSLC, lxxxiv, lxxxvi, xci (1934, 1935, 1938).

William Tunnicliff, *A Topographical Survey of the Counties of Stafford, Chester and Lancaster* (Nantwich, pr. E. Snelson, 1787); repr. 1982 by Neil Richardson, Manchester.

William Urwick, ed., *Historical Sketches of Nonconformity in the County Palatine of Chester by Various Ministers and Laymen in the County* (London, Kent & Co., 1864).

Geoffrey Whitney, 'Geoffrey Whitney's "To Richard Cotton, of Combermere": an Early English Country-House Poem', *JSTOR: Review of English Studies*, new series, 28 no. 112 (November 1977).

Jonathan Wilshere, ed., *Glanfield Probate Inventories 1542–1831*, paperback ed. (Leicester, Jonathan Wilshere Publications, 1983).

Rodney Horace Yale, *Yale Genealogy and History of Wales* (Beatrice, Neb., pr. Milburn and Scott, 1908).

INDEX OF NAMES

Despite our efforts to identify those individuals noted in the text of the edited wills as part of larger family and kinship groupings, we have purposely avoided a similar approach in compiling this Index. It is quite simply an Index of Names, rather than an Index of Persons. We leave it to the reader to decide which specific individual is associated with any given reference. We have not attempted the even more complex and daunting task of indexing the genealogical charts and their notes. Titles such as yeoman, gentleman, esquire (armiger) or husbandman have also been detached from all names, as have all occupational or administrative designations. Page numbers with an asterisk (*) indicate more than one appearance of the name.

Varied spellings of a surname have been combined, with the alternatives listed in parentheses for both surnames and Christian names: hence . . . *Mainwayring* (Mainwaring), Randle (Randulphe).

[?], Alie, 260
[?], Anne, 430
[?], Edward, 39
[?], Elizabeth, 301
[?], Eve, 39
[?], John, 60
[?], Katheryn, 39
[?]. Margaret, 177
[?], Marye, 301
[?]esons, William, 9
a Pova see Pova, a
Abell, Mary, 391–2
Abram, John, 423
Ackson (Acson, Axson),
    Anne, 261
    James, 77
    John, 131*
    Nicolas, 11
    Oliver, 77–8
    Richard, 77, 242
Alcock (Alcocke),
    John, 32–3
    Thomas, 32–3
Allen (Allin, Allyn),
    Elizabeth, 152
    Richard, 95
    William, 114, 186
    Wyddow, 407
Allixanders, Jone, 39
Alsager (Asager, Alseger),
    Edward, 253*
    Margreate, 28

    Raffe, 28
    Robert, 199, 247*, 248*, 249*
Alstanteston,
    Agnes de, xxii, xxiii
    Thomas de, xxii
    William de, xxii
Aluric, x
Ambler, Edward, 455
Ambrose, Gregory, 423, 424*
Anckers (Ankers),
    Ellene, 376*
    Johan (Joan, Jone), 73–4, 375
    John, 73–4, 172, 375, 376*, 377
    Margaret, 73–4
    Ranndle, 74, 375*, 376*
    Raphe, 138
Andrews, Mary, 423
Arcall, Elizabeth, 348, 351
Archdeacon Matthew, 36
Aston, John, 149
Audley (Audeley),
    Constance de, xxv
    Elizabeth, xxvi
    family, x, xxii*
    James de, xxiv–xxv
    Lord, xxviiin.*
    Nicholas de, xxiv–xxvi
Austen, William,, 149

Backhouse (Backhowse),
    John, 60–1, 110, 137, 168, 170
    Margreate (Margrette), 168, 169*

Thomas, 48, 95, 97, 168–9*, 199, 230, 264*, 277–8, 427
Bafford, Elizabeth, 260
Baker,
 Elizabeth, 430
 James, 233*, 253, 430
 Thomas, 35
Ball, John, xxxvi, 392
Bancnes (Bankes),
 Robert, xiii, xiv, xxxiv
Bancroft, Richard, 175
Barker,
 John, 433–4
 Mr, 148
 Thomas, 229
Barkley, Mr, 203
Barlowe, Margerie
 (Margery), 332–4, 392
Barnes,
 John, 28–9
 William, 56, 220
Barnett (Barnet, Barnitt, Bernett),
 Ales (Alice), 77–8, 268
 Elizabeth, xxxviii*, xxxix*, 77*, 82–6, 88, 91, 93, 266, 267*, 290
 Ellen, 34, 77
 Ellenor (Eleanor), xxxviii*, xxxix*, 77
 Emma, xlii & n., 266, 268
 Emyn, 268
 Frances, 402
 George, xxxvii, 161, 435* & n., 436*
 Humphrey, xxxv, xxxviii*, xxxix*, 77*, 80–1, 83–4, 86–9, 92–3, 120, 132, 161
 Isabel, xxxiii, xxxv
 James, xxxv, xxxvi, xxxviii*, xxxix*, xl*, 33, 35–6, 76–8, 81, 84, 92, 403*, 436*
 Johan (Joan), 77
 John, 7, 34, 35, 46, 50, 77*, 78, 81, 83, 91, 119*, 289, 290*, 324, 401, 402*, 436
 Kathrine (Catherine), 402*, 403*, 405
 Margaret (Mawde), 77, 266, 267*, 268*, 289*, 290–1, 402*
 Marie (Mary), 35–6, 402*, 436*
 Raffe (Raphe), 26, 34
 Richard, 29, 77, 289–90, 401, 403*, 404
 Robert, 34–5
 Thomas, xxxv, xxxix*, 2–3, 34–5, 58, 77*, 80, 83, 86, 89–90, 436*

William, xliin., 34–5, 77*, 78, 81, 89–90, 99, 111, 132, 151
Barrow, John, 317
Baskervilde (Baskerville, Baskerfild, Baskervild),
 Anne, 157
 Edward, xliin., 116, 117*
 Elizabeth, xliin., 118, 157
 Ellen, 157
 Margarett, 157
 Richard, 157
 Thomas, 149, 157
 William, 157
Bate (Bates, Batte, Bett),
 Ellen, 349, 351
 George, 281
 Margaret, 15
 Richard, 48, 94, 96–7
 Rowland, 230, 349, 351
Bateman, John, 349–51, 357–60, 362, 364–5, 367, 369
Bath, Earl of, 467n.
Bathoe (Bathow, Bathowe),
 Edward, 133
 Randle (Randull), 46
 Richard, 242
 Thomas, 338, 340
 Widow, 77
 William, 120, 220*
Baxter, William le, xxiv
Bebbington (Bebington, Babington, Bebingtone, Bebyngton, Bebenton, Bebinton, Bebbyngton),
 Amye, 19
 Andrew (Andrewe), 190, 197, 233*, 260
 Anne, 77, 79
 Edward, 26
 Ellen, 19, 22*, 39
 Frances, 260
 George, 143
 Henry, 17, 75
 Hugh, 19
 John, 19, 22*, 39, 113, 115*, 157, 179, 190
 Margaret, 79, 101
 Margery, 79
 Marsellon, 19
 Mary, 259, 260*, 391–2
 Mres, 268, 422
 Rafe, 22

Randle (Randulphe), 19, 22, 134
Richard, 22, 32–3, 260
Thomas, 17*, 22*, 57, 101, 103*, 143*, 154, 157*, 163*, 185–6, 220, 222
William, xv*, 18*, 20*, 21, 22*, 26*, 27*, 39, 53*, 55, 101*, 130, 134–5, 140*, 151*, 157*, 179, 202, 220, 259, 260*
Beckett (Becket, Bekett, Beeckett),
   Elizabeth, 318
   George, xv, 113, 232, 318
   James, 78, 161
   John, 113, 120, 253
   Marie (Mary), 233*, 234, 318*
   Randull (Randle), 79, 376
   Thomas, 233*, 234, 301, 318*
Bedward, Alice, 455
Beecham, Robert Joseph, xxn.
Belingham, William, 6*, 7*
Bellot (Billot),
   Mary, xix
   Roger, 190, 198
   Thomas, xix
Bennett (Bennet, Benett),
   John, 64, 417
   William, 392, 393*, 394, 406, 408, 414–15, 416*, 417, 422
Bennion, Mary, 334
Bentley,
   Roger, 458
   William, 286, 288
Bernard, John, xxiv
Berrington,
   Anne, 167
   Richard, 167*, 311, 313, 439, 441
Beston, Roger de, xxiv
Beumaris (Beaumaris, Beumarrisse, Bewmarris, Bumorise, Bewmorris),
   Allis, 280
   George, 280*, 281, 300*, 301, 302*, 318
   Elizabeth, 78, 280*, 281
   family, xl
   Marie (Marye), 280, 301–2
   Richard, 281, 300, 302
   Roberte, 301–2
   Rushton, 302
   Thomas, 301, 346
   William, 301*
Bickerton (Bikerton, Bicarton, Bickerson),
   Anne, xv, 96–7, 134, 139*, 140
   Cicely, 271

Dorothie, 137*
Edmund (Yedmond), 26–7, 107, 113* & n., 114, 117, 159, 160*, 161
Edward, 3
Elene (Ellin), 32, 46–7, 137*, 139, 160*, 161–2
Elizabeth, 137*, 139, 271
George, 64, 254, 271*, 313, 422*
Harry, 160
Humphrey, 31–2, 47
John (Johannes), 32, 50*, 61, 64, 95, 110, 113* & n.*, 114, 136*, 137*, 234, 243, 310*, 468*
Margaret (Moade), 32, 137, 139, 140*
Mr, 370
Richard, 19, 33, 160*, 161*, 162, 254
Thomas, 32, 432
William, 136*, 137*, 417, 468*
Birch, Thomas, 80
Bird,
   Anne, xxvi
   Richard, xxvi
Birtles, Laurence, 175
Bishop Gastrell, xvii
Bishop John of Chester, 384*, 385
Blackamore (Blackmore),
   Alice (Alles), 49–50, 77, 80
   Hughe, 50
Blackhurst,
   Randle, 114
   William de, xxiv
Blantoone, John, 66
Blease, Ralph, 229
Blooer, William, 202
Bodall, James, 138
Boden (Bowden),
   Anne, 204, 205*
   Edward, 325–6
   John, 148
   Raphe, 204, 205*
Body, Johanna, xxiv
Bolton,
   Good wiff, 9
   Randull, 9
Bonde, Malyn, xxiv
Bonham, William, xiii
Booth (Boote),
   Elizabeth, 263*, 441
   John, 263*, 264, 464*
   Richard, xiii, xv * & n., 422

Bostock (Bostocke),
  Adam, xxvi
  Elizabeth, 98
  Margaret, xxvi
  Rauffe (Raphe, Ralph), 134, 149, 288
  Thomas, 313–14
Bottoms, Margery, 22
Bowker, Thomas, 177, 411
Bowyer, Richard, 57
Bradford,
  Edward, 25–7, 53
  George, 229
Bradshawe (Bradshaw)
  family, xl
  James, 149
  John, 338–40
  Richard, 300*
Braye, Oliver, 131*
Brees (Breese, Bressie, Bressye, Breesse),
  Dorothye, 176*
  Edward, 144, 146
  Elizabeth, 447*
  family, xxv
  Jane, 176*, 177*, 253
  John, 177*
  Samuell, 447*
  Thomas, xxv, xxxvii, 131, 172, 176*,
    177*, 446–7
  William, 120, 126, 140, 164, 165*, 171–2,
    176*, 177*, 178
Brent, Nathaniele, 387, 389
Brereton (Bruerton),
  Jane (Jone), 271, 408
  Randell, 138
  Robert, xxv
  William, 198
Brester (Broster),
  Mr, 431
  Richard, 165
  Thomas, 9
Brett, Philip, 305
Bridgeman, John, xx
Briscoe (Bruscalle, Burscoe, Burscough),
  Elizabeth, xlii & n., 232*, 234, 318*
  John, 414, 422
  Oliver, xliin., 115*, 232–3, 234*
Brittaine (Brittin), Robert, 455*
Broghton, Ralph, xxvii
Bromley,
  Edward, 413

Thomas, 415–16
Brooke (Brocke, Brok),
  Agnes, (Anne), xxvi & n.
  Charles, 67
  Dorothie, 181
  James, 180, 181*
  Joan (Jane), 180, 181*, 183, 268
  John, xxvin.
  Margaret (Margery), 180, 181*
  Richard, 181*
  Roger, 2, 181*
  Thomas, xxvin., 66, 148–9
Broome (Broime, Brome),
  Elizabeth, 52
  Hughe, 52–3
  Margarett, 52
  Richarde, 224
  Roger, xvi, 22, 32–3, 40, 42, 51, 53,
    386
  Thomas, 52–3
  Ursalae, 224
  William, 52
Broomhall (Bromhall, Bromehall, Bromhall,
    Bromall, Bromhale, Broumale),
  Elizabeth, xxv, 246, 248*
  Ellen, 246*, 249, 253
  family, xxv
  James, xxiii, 347, 422, 434, 451
  Jane, 414
  John, 3, 78, 117*, 126, 164, 177*,
    245–6, 247*, 248*, 249*, 343, 411,
    461
  Margaret, 207
  Marye, 246*
  Sara, 246*, 249, 252–3
  Roberte, 249
  Thomas, 246*, 247, 248*, 249*
Brown (Browne),
  Robert, 66
  William, 67
Brownefall,
  George, 451 & n.
  Robert, 458
Bryan (Bruin, Bryne),
  Piers, of Tarvin, xxvi
  Ralph, 149
  Randull, 155, 177
Buckley (Bulckley, Bucley, Boucley),
  Alice, 429–30
  Elizabeth, 155

Ellin, 374
Mary, 258, 342, 391
Raffe (Rafe), xiv, xv & n., 64
Randall (Randle), 35, 58
Richard, 64
Robert, 63–4
Thomas, 138
Timothy (Timothie, Tymothie), 153–5,
    183, 252, 257*
Widdow, 253
William, 430
Burgen, George, 44
Burrowes (Borrowes, Burroughs,
    Burroughes, Barrowe, Barrow),
Elizabeth, 457
family, xl
George, 67
Hugh, 233
John, 305, 317
Raphe, 302
Richard, 216*, 217, 396
Robert, 411
Stanley (Standley), 134, 152, 423
Thomas, xxxv, xxxix, 77, 80–4, 86–8,
    90–1, 93, 134–5, 301–2, 411
Burton,
Andrew, 229
John, 39–40
Butcher (Bucher),
Ellis the, 138
Richard, 212
Bynse, Homfrie, 9

Caldecott (Calcott, Coldecote),
Elizabeth, 460
John, 423–4
Thomas, 260*, 302, 334, 339
Calles (Callye),
Thomas, 66
William, 220
Calveley, Hugh, 413*
Capper (Cappur),
George, 138
Maude, 180*
Robert, 369
William, 57, 281, 302
Cardiffe (Cardiff, Cardyfe),
Elizabeth, 348, 351
Mary, 353

Ralph (Raphe), xvii, 66, 277*, 278,
    348*, 349*, 350*, 351*, 352*, 353,
    354*, 355, 356*, 357*, 358–61, 363*,
    370
Richard, 348, 351
Carter,
James, 61
William, 50
Cartwright (Cartwrighte,
Ales, 26
Ambrosia (née Cotton), 391, 414*
Arthur, 242*, 271*, 276, 284, 290, 316,
    379, 414, 416–17, 422
Edward, xxix
Elene (Ellen), 45–6, 77
Elizabeth, xxix, xxxii, 77–8, 239
family, xxix, xxxn., xxxii
Francis, 46, 77–8
Geoffrey (Jeffrey), xxxi, 30, 35, 47, 77
George, 271
Gilbert, 276
Hugh, xxix
Isabell (Isabel, Ezabell), xxxviii*, xxxix,
    34, 77–8, 83, 236–7, 239
Joan, xxxi
John, xiii–xvi, xxviii, xxix*, xxx, xxxi*,
    xxxii, xxxv*, xxxvii–xxxviii, xxxix,
    29, 32–5, 45–7, 77–80, 93, 105, 109,
    138, 146, 152, 181, 198, 233, 235,
    237. 238*, 240, 241*, 242*, 243*,
    271*, 276, 284, 294 & n., 316–18,
    379
Marcie (Marcye), 242*
Margaret, xxxn.
Mary, 457
Mr, 456
Nicholas (Nicholas le), xxiv, xxxn.
Nicolas, 79
Randle, 74
Richard, xv, xvi, xxix, xxxi, xxxv, 45–6,
    79, 155–6, 217, 237, 240*, 241*, 242,
    373–4, 431, 433–4
Sara, 239
Shakerley, 242* & n.
Thomas, xxix, 35
William, xxix, xxxn., 46, 50, 181, 190,
    236, 265, 271
Carver, Mawde, 14
Chambers (Chambre), Arthur, 392–3
Chancellor, Mr, 370*

Chantler, Edward, 44
  Edgar, 44
  William le, xxiii
Chapman,
  Edward, 95–6
  William, 220
Charles I, King, 229*, 256, 308, 326, 334,
    344, 350–1, 373, 378, 384, 395, 404,
    406, 413, 417, 427–8, 433, 469
Charles II, King, xxxi
Cheaddocke, John, 147
Chedley,
  John, 403
  Katherine, 461
Chester,
  George, 347, 458
  Joan, 49
  John, xxxii, 49*, 50*
  Margaret, xxivn., 50
  Richard, 50
  Robart, 49–50
  Thomas, 49, 50*, 78, 200
  William, 15
Cheswis (Chessewes, Cheswys, Chesswess,
    Chessewis, Cheswise, Chessewess,
    Chesewes),
  Ales, 8*, 9*
  Alixander, 125
  Anne, 285, 286*
  Cisely, 125
  Elisabeth, 8–9, 125
  Ellenor, 125*, 410, 411*
  family, xxxii*
  George, xxxviii, 285, 286*
  Helen, 28, 30
  Hugh, xxxviii, 9, 286*
  Jane, 125, 285, 286*
  John, xiii–xiv, xxvii, xxxii* & n., xxxviii*,
    8–9, 28–9, 105, 125*, 126*, 127, 144,
    149, 188, 286*, 288, 400, 409, 410*,
    411*, 470
  Margaret (Margarett), 8, 125, 285, 286*,
    288, 437*, 438
  Mary, 126
  Rebecca, 125
  Richard, xxxviii*, 285*, 286–7
  Roger, 125*, 126, 182, 381*
  Thomas, xiv, xxxii, xxxviii*, 2, 8*, 9,
    242, 285, 287
  William, xxxviii, 285, 286*

Chesworth, Katheryne, 63
Chettwood (Chetwoode, Chitwoode),
    family, 467n.
  John, 467n.*
  Thomas, 108, 160
Cheynie,
  Raphe, 157
  William, 157
Cholmondeley, (Chomley, Cholmodeley,
    Chomdley, Chomondley,
    Chomondleye),
  Hugh, 25–6, 37
  Lady, 202
  lords of, xxii
  marquis of, xxii
  Mr, 220
  Richard, xxviiin.
  Robert, 260, 322, 408
  Thomas, 201
Chorlton (Churlton),
  Mary, 220, 222
  Randle (Ralph), 349*, 350, 351*, 351*,
    352*, 353*, 357, 360*, 363, 365*, 367*
Chryichlee, Widow, 408
Church,
  John, 133
  William, 26
Clarke
  Anne, 464
  Rev. H.A., xxxiv
  James, 471–2
  John, vii, xix, 463–4
  Mary, 468*, 471*, 472*
  Mr, 134
  Richard, 113
  Thomas, 468, 471*, 472*
Clarre (Clare),
  Allen, 48
  Robert, 441
Claye (Cley, Clay),
  John, 422
  Thomas, 302, 427*
Clayton (Cleaton), George, 133
Clubb, Richard, 160
Clutton,
  Richard, 46, 150
  Thomas, xxvii
Colfall, William, 44
Collines (Colenso, Collin)
  family, xl

John, 48
William, xxiii
Colyer (Colly),
    James, xx
Comber, Richard *see Culliner*, Richard alias
    Comber
Combermere, Lords of, xxiin.
Coneway (Conway),
    John, 202
    Thomas de, xxiv
Connyes, Robert, 53
Cooke,
    Ane, 98
    Elizabeth, 47–8
    George, 393–4, 414, 416, 419
    Isabell, 40
    John, 48*, 426*, 427
    Margery, 414
    Richard, 48, 95, 109, 169
    Thomas, 26, 48*, 49, 170
Coole, Roger, xxiii
Cooper (Cowper, Cowpers, Couper),
    Arthur, 115
    Dorathie, 322*, 323*
    Ellen, 119*, 120*
    Jane, 287
    Mary (Marie), 115, 119
    Owen, 119*, 323
    Randull (Randle, Ranndle), 114, 115*,
        120, 322, 323*
    Richard, 114
    Robert, 119*, 323
    William, xvi, xxxvi, 78, 115, 118, 119*,
        120*, 161*, 207, 210, 249, 321, 322*,
        323*, 325, 455
Cootes,
    Elizabeth, 463
    Thomas, 463
Corbet, Robert, xxvii
Corey, Thomas, 114
Corke,
    Richard, 305*
    Robert, 181*, 183*
Cotgreve, Randall, 13
Cottingham, John, 227*
Cotton,
    Ambrosia, 414–15
    Andrew, viii, xvii, xxii, xxxvi*, xxxvii*,
        238*, 239, 241*, 340, 343, 344*,
        391–2

Arthur, xxii
Charles, 391, 414
Dorothy (Dorothey, Dorithy), viii, xx,
    xxin., xxii, xxxvi, xxxvii, 343–4, 390,
    392 & n., 393
Edward, 149–50
Elizabeth, xxii, 64, 392, 405, 406*, 408,
    413
family, xix, xx, xxi, xxiin., xxxii, xxxv
Frances, xxii, xxxvi, 342, 391
George, viii, xx* & n., xxi* & n.*, xxii,
    xxx, xxxiii, 45–6, 56, 78, 123*, 146,
    198, 237, 238*, 239, 241*, 242, 258,
    271*, 286, 297n., 299, 303, 311, 313,
    328, 341, 391–2, 408, 412 & n., 413*,
    415*, 416*, 417, 441, 450
Grace, 414
Jane, 56
Joyce, 391
Lettice (Lattice), 391, 408, 414
Margaret (Margret), 391, 414*, 415*
Martha, 64, 391
Mary, xx* & n., xxi* & n., xxii, 342, 391,
    413–14
Mr *see* Cotton, George
Richard, viii, xx, xxi* & n.*, xxii*, xxvii,
    xxviii & n.
Robert, xxiin., 391, 414
Rowland, Sir, 413
Thomas, xxxvi, 63–4, 342, 392, 406,
    413*, 422
Winifred, xxii
Coxsie (Coxie, Coxsey, Cocksee),
    Alane (Allen), 57–8
    George, 46–7, 57
    Roger, 46
    Thomas, 11
Crewe (Crue, Crew),
    Arthur, xxxv, 276*
    Edmund, xvii, xxxv, xxxvi, xxxvii, xliin.,
        276 & n., 277
    Joane, xxxix*, xl, xliin., 276n., 277*, 348,
        349*, 350*, 351*, 352*, 353*, 356,
        357*, 358, 360
    Mathilda de, xxiv
    Thomas, 276*
Crosby, Raphe, 95
Croxton (Coxton),
    James, 32–3
    John, 423

Margaret, 292
Randle, 135
Cudworth (Cudwerth, Cudworthe),
  George, xv, xxxii, xxxiii, 28–31, 163,
    199* & n.
  Margerie (Margery), 28, 30–1
  Robert, xv
  William, xxxii
Culkin, Hugh, 185
Culliner,
  George, 386
  Richard alias Comber, xxxv, 385* & n.,
    386
Cumberbach, Roger, 381
Cureton,
  Elizabeth, 349, 351
  Joane, 351*
  John, 349, 351*, 352*, 353, 357, 360*,
    363, 365, 367
Curriar, Richard, 156

Dabers, Richard, 260
Dainton, Mr, 220
Dale (Dalle),
  Anne, 44
  Hugh, 66
  John, 160
Damold, Ellen, 202
Danyell, Peter, 198
Darlington,
  Gorge, 67
  Margerye, 67
  Robert, 169
Daughty, Ellioner, 386*
Davenport (Davemport, Damport),
  George, 134
  Raphe, 22, 53*
  Richard, 53, 55, 101, 129*, 220, 260, 334,
    399
Davies (Davyes, Davie),
  Alexander, 457
  Alice, 109
  Edward, 457
  Elizabeth, 457
  George, 414, 422
  Hugh, 457
  Isabell, 457–8
  Margaret, 129
  Margery, 148
  Mathew, 316

May, 169, 455*, 456–7
Owen, 242
Richard, 99, 455
Robert, 457*
Thomas, 129*
William, 108–9
Dawson, Randle, 202
Daykin, Nicholas, xxiv
De[?]oe,
  James, 25
  William, 25
Deaks (Deekes, Deakes, Dikes),
  Ellen, 22
  Humfrey (Humphrey), 449, 461
  Thomas, 144
Deane, Thomas, 149
Desley, John, 2
Deverise (Deavorise, Deveres),
  Elizabeth, xviin.
  Frances, xviin.
  Robert, xvii & n., 263
Dickins (Dickin, Dyckson),
  George, 211*, 212*
  Joan (Joanna, Johane), 211*, 212*, 213
  John, 211*, 212
  Roberte, 212
  William, 26, 211*, 212, 407, 465
Dodd (Dood, Dod, Dode),
  Arthure, 313
  Ellis, 202
  Hugh, 313
  Jane, 123, 312, 313*
  John, xx, 286*, 288, 313
  Mr, 268, 274
  Phillip, 97, 166* & n.*
  Rauffe, 313*
  Richard, 312, 313*
  Robert, 202*
  Thomas, 3
  William, 138
Dolten (Doughton), Mr, 2, 269
Domvill (Domville), William, 423–4
Downe (Doonne, Dune),
  Richard, 19–20, 22, 42
Downell, Arthur, 314
Downes, Phillip, 149
Dutton, Peter, xxviiin.

Eaton, James, 156
Eccles, Robert, 43

Eddowes (Eddowe),
 Ellenor, 180
 Richard, 463
Edgley (Edgeley, Eggeley, Egley),
 Anne, 271, 453*
 Arthur, xxxvii*, 474*, 475* & n., 476,
  477*, 478*, 479*
 Elizabeth, xxxvii, 449*, 453*, 460*, 461,
  476, 479
 Ellen (Elena), 29, 31, 316*, 317, 443*
 George, 130, 249
 Jane, xxxvii, xliin., 452
 John, xvii* & n., xxxvii*, 3, 79, 190, 217,
  271, 315, 316*, 317*, 403, 417, 442–3,
  449*, 460*, 461*, 475*, 476*, 477*,
  478–9
 Joseph, xxxvii, 452, 453*, 460, 461*,
  475*, 476, 477
 Kathrin (Kathrine), 316*
 Richard, xvii, xxxvii*, xliin., 29, 72, 92,
  95–6, 108, 137*, 215–17, 256, 271,
  277*, 278, 281, 302, 316*, 317–18,
  379, 422, 460, 473, 474*, 475* & n.,
  476, 477*, 478
 Samuel, 452
 Thomas, xxxii, 50, 72, 77, 80, 83, 86, 91,
  95–6, 123, 137, 249
Edric, ix
Edward I, King, x, xxivn.
Edward III, King, xviii
Edward VI, King, xxvii, xxviiin.
Edward the Confessor, King ix, x
Egerton (Eggerton, Egynton),
 Elizabeth, xxviii, 150, 185
 family, xxiin.
 George, 185*, 186
 John, xxxii, 184, 186
 Raffe (Rauffe), 185, 241*
 Richard, xxiv, 185*, 247*, 248*, 249*,
  343
 Thomas, xxii
Elcocke, Widdowe, 242
Elizabeth, Queen, xxi & n., xxii, xxvii, xxviii,
 xxxi, xxxviin., 14, 28, 31, 37
Ellen, poor, 14
Emeswouth, Richard, 185
Erasmus of Rotterdam, xxn.
Evanson (Evans, Yeavan, Evanns),
 Humfrey, 57
 John, 57, 113, 115, 183

 Mary, xv, xvi
 Richard, 57, 78, 253, 346
 Thomas, 78
 William, 29, 283*

Falkener (Faulkner, Falkner),
 Edward, 44
 family, 43n.
 Francis, 134*
 Henry, 134–5
 Richard, 134
 Simon, 260
 Thomas, 133, 135
Farington, Agnes, 26
Farres (Ferrer),
 John, 50
 Martha, 456
 Richard, 456
 Thomas, 188
Felton, Thomas, 242
Filcock (Filcocke, Fillcocke)
 Alles, 19
 Margret, 48
 Robart, 325
*Findelaye (*Finnie),
 John, 26
 Richard, 22
Fisher (Fischer, Fysher, Fyssher),
 Arthur, 430
 Clemence, 242
 Ellin, 8
 John, 77, 111, 133, 155, 215, 216*,
  217–18, 233, 243, 253, 274, 283, 287,
  318, 373*, 374, 403–5, 430, 449
 Lawrance, 346, 378, 381
 Margarett (Maud), 77, 274
 Prudence, 216*, 217, 372
 Richard, 26
 Robert (Robart), 50, 381
 Thomas, 287, 436
 William, 461
 William le, xxiv
Fitzwarren, William, Lord, xxii
Flavell,
 Edward, 43
 Ellen (Ellyn), 43
 family, 43n.
 Margaret, 43
Fleet (Fleete, Flite),
 Margaret (Margarett), 208, 260

Robert, 37
Rondull, 32
[   ], 134
Fletcher (Flecher, Fleccher),
   Anne, 59, 97
   Edward, 118
   Elizabeth, 60
   Ellen, 59, 109*, 110
   George, 385
   Joane, 32
   John, 14
   Katherine, 2
   Lawrence, 60
   Margaret, 59–61
   William, 59*, 60*, 61, 137, 169*, 265,
      443, 453, 466
Fouleshurst, William of, xxiii
Foundelynge, Richard, 39
French (Frenche),
   John, 269
   Thomas, 205, 220*
Fryth, Richard del, xxiv
Fulkes, Mr, 374
Furbur, Robert, 441
Fyndlowe, Edward, 174

Gandie (Gandye, Gandy),
   Ellen, 148
   Hendrye, 67
   Hugh, 147
   Widow, 455*, 456
Garrett, Randull, 2
Gascoyne, Mr, 148
Gibbons,
   Mary, 457
   Randle, 457–8
Gilbert, William, 66
Glover, John le, xxiv
Godfrey, George, 344
Golborne, Mr., 408
Good, William, 134
Gorstilowe (Goosteloe),
   Richarde, 183
   Roger, 108
Goughe, Elizabeth, 186
Gouldsmith (Gouldsmithy, Goldsmyth)
   George, 95, 181
   Nicholas, 8
Grantham (Grantam), Mr, xxxvi,
   392

Gray (Graie, Graye, Grey, Graye),
   Alice, 129
   Aunt, 274
   Elizabeth, 153–4, 451
   Ellen (Ellene, Helen), 308*, 310*
   Emyne, 266
   family, xl
   George, 123, 137, 153, 183*
   Jane (Joan), 154, 274, 308
   John, 151, 267–8, 273
   Margaret (Margret), 268–9, 273*, 274*
   Marie (Mary), 346, 411
   Martha, 346, 411
   Philip, 6*, 7*
   Thomas, xxxv, xxxix, 11, 26–7, 77*, 78,
      80–2, 86, 88–9, 115, 129, 133, 143,
      152, 153*, 154*, 155, 163, 181, 207,
      210, 233, 257, 263*, 268*, 271, 274*,
      283, 290, 301*, 305, 307, 308*,
      309–10, 313, 317*, 318, 324, 333–4,
      345, 346*, 347*, 376, 378, 381, 389,
      392, 396, 403–5, 414, 426*, 427,
      430*, 431*, 432, 433*, 434, 443,
      446*, 451*, 456, 458, 461, 465–6,
      468*, 470
Greatbatch, Josua, 134
Greene (Grene),
   Edmund (Edmond), 172*
   John, 48, 230
   Robert, 183
   Rondull, 170
   Thomas, 113*
Greenowlers,
   John, 126
Greson, Christopher, 220
Griffith (Griffiths, Griffin, Griffithes,
      Greffith, Greffeth, Griffies, Garfferth,
      Griffin, Griffes, Griffyn, Griffine,
      Gryffith),
   Bertram, xxiv
   Ellen (Allen, Allenne, Ellenne), 302, 446,
      455–6
   family, xxiv, xl
   Geoffrey, xxiv
   Henry (Henrye), 32–3, 133, 140*, 172,
      188, 243, 346, 372n., 424, 444–5, 454,
      455*, 456*
   Hugh, 8
   James, 9
   John, 32–3, 42, 465*

Margarett, 445*, 446, 455
Nathaniell, 455
Robert, 140*, 454*, 455*, 456*, 465
William, 423
Grimes, John, 301
Grindley (Gryndley, Grinley, Grendeley,
    Grindleye),
Ales (Alis, Alice), 2, 205*
Margerie, 98
Marrie, 48
Phillipp, 165
Richard de, xxiv
Robert (Roberte), 165, 313–14, 414
Thomas, 15, 48, 95–7, 156, 163, 183
Grovener (Grosvenour, Grosvenor),
Mary, 408
Mr, 79, 148
Thomas, 79
William, 403
Grymsdich, Thomas, 149
Guest (Gest, Gueste),
George, 408*
Raphe (Raph), 32–3
Richard, 212

Hall (Halle)
[?], 41
Anne, 274
Douse, 311
Edward, 370
Elizabeth, 56
Ellene (Elline), 256, 268
George, xvi, 143, 217, 264, 290, 308,
    346*, 347*, 389, 417, 443, 448, 449*,
    459, 461, 474*, 475, 477
Hugh, 78
James, xxxiv, 47
John, 17, 42, 55–7, 60*, 256, 310, 311*,
    458
Jone, 79
Richard, 11, 66, 137, 143, 183, 186, 254*,
    256, 342–3
Robert, 108, 110, 372*
Thomas, 17, 163, 311, 372
William, 202, 274, 311, 408
Hallywell, John, xxx
Hamnet (Hamnett, Hamlet, Hamlett,
    Hamnite, Hammnete, Hampnet,
    Hamblett),
Anne, 301*

Edward (Eduard), 95, 97, 140, 290–1,
    301, 308–9, 388*, 389, 404–5, 449
Elizabeth, 388
family, xl*
Francis, 388*
George, 387*
Henrie, 388, 389*
Hughe, 301
Jane, 455
John, 3, 11, 95–7, 155
Randle, 388–9
Richard, 48, 95, 166*, 280, 387, 414
Roberte, 301*, 302*
Roger, 56, 58, 414
Thomas, xvi, xxxii, xxxv*, xl, 199, 230,
    280, 302*, 309*, 387
William, 95*, 96
Hampton (Hanton),
Elizabeth, 455
Hugh de, xxxiv
John, 148, 173, 455
William, 35, 113
Harcourt, Robert of, xxiii
Harding (Hardinge),
Randle, 349, 350*, 351, 355*, 357, 358*,
    359*, 361*, 362, 365–7, 370
William, 346
Hare,
Elizabeth, 64, 331
Ellen, 219*
John, 219*
Mary, 219*
Ralph (Rauffe), 6,* 7*, 204, 219
Randull (Randle, Rondull), xxxvi, xxxvii,
    26, 40, 173, 205*, 219*, 220, 382,
    468*
Thomas, xxxvi, 219, 330
William, 5, 6*, 7, 205, 219, 220, 339
Harper, Annis, 2
Harrington, James, xxxivn.
Harris,
Michaell, 453
Robert, 281
Harrould (Heroold),
Richard, 252
William, 249
Hartropp,
Anne, 301
family, xl
William, 301

Harwar (Harware),
Alice, 267
Elizabeth, 267*, 268*, 274
Marie (Mary), 267, 274*
Mr *see Harwar*, Thomas
Nathaniell, 267
Richard, 52
Thomas, 208, 233, 266, 267, 268*, 274*,
308, 318, 392
Hassall,
Anne, 458, 461, 464
Frances, 392, 414–15, 464
Jane, 391
John, 330, 449
Margaret, 349, 351, 464
Mary, 342
Raphe, 461
Richard, 230, 330, 349*, 350, 351*,
357–8, 359*, 362–3, 365–6, 368, 399*
& n.*, 439, 441, 463*, 464*, 465
Robert, xxvn., 389*, 403
William, 53, 399
Hasselwalles, John, 185
*Healinshows*e, Henry, 52
Heath,
Elizabeth, 201*
Greffen, 33
James, 180
John, 396
Robert (Roberte), 165, 172, 376, 399
Roger, 201*
Thomas, 172*
Heighfield (Heighfeilde, Heifeild, Heifilld,
Heyhfeild, Highfield),
Anne, 172*, 173, 177
Elizabeth, 171*, 172
Ellen, 172
Henry, 43
Homfrey, 172
Richard, 171
Thomas, 171, 172*
William, xxxvi, xxxvii, 67*, 123*, 171,
172*
Henberrie (Henbere, Henbury, Henberie),
Margarett, 78
Raffe (Raph), 11, 80
Robert, 35, 50
Henry II, King, x
Henry VII, King, vii, xxvi, xxix
Henry VIII, King, xx, xxiv, xxxii, 6

Higson (Higgson, Higgins, Higginson,
Higgison, Higgenson, Hickson),
Anne, 50
Ellinor (Elenore), xxxv, 36, 37
Hugh, 138
Jane, 455
John, 56
Margrett, 372
Richard, 56
Thomas, 37, 50
William, 56, 140*, 455–6
Hill (Hyll, Hilles),
John, xx, 140*, 141, 381
Thomas, 99
Hinnes, Edward, 25 & n.*
Hitley, Richard, 386
Hockenhull (Hocknell),
Hamon, xxvi
Margaret, 126*, 127
Richard, xxvii, 149
Roger, 50, 79, 125–6
Hoffeld (Hofeld), David, 2–3, 11
Hoggedoghter, Agnes, xxiv
Holbrook, Randle, 186
Holford (Hollford), Robert, 202, 229
Holland, Mr, 424
Holy Company in Heaven, 19, 21
Hooline (Holline),
Anne, 180
Elizabeth, 181
Margret, 98
Raphe, 181
Hope, Michael (Michell, Michill), 79, 165,
311
Hopkin (Hopkuyn), Hughe, 57, 255
Horobin, Margret, 160
Horry,
Richard, xxiv
William, xxiv
Horseman, Kathern, 429, 430
Horton, Richard, xxvn.
Howe, Edmund, 149
Hugh Lupus, Earl of Chester, ix
Hughes,
Charles, xixn.
Thomas, 428–9
Hughet, Thomas, xxiv
Hughson, William, 138*
Humphreys,
Mr, 215

Thomas, 429, 438
Hunt, Master, 310
Hurlebutt (Hurlbutt),
    Thomas, 22
    William, 78
Hurleston (Hurleton, Hurdluston),
    Anne, 2
    Arthure, 233, 253, 378
    Margaret, 26
    Thomas, 26, 37, 111, 133, 152
    William, 11, 120
Hussie (Hussey),
    Arthur, 109
    Elizabeth, 414–16
    Rachell, 416
Hutton, James, 134
Huxley,
    Francis, 468
    Jone (née Anckers), 375
    Katherine, 468
    Richard, 468*
    William, 177, 376

Jackson, John, 46
James I, King, xiii, 149, 413
Janyon, Edward, 3
Jenkinson (Jenkes, Jenkyn),
    George, 200
    John, 404–5
    Matthew, 387
    Thomas, 200
John, King, xxii
J*ohnston* (Johnson, Joneson, Joynson),
    Arthur, 229
    Harriot, 424
    Henery (Henrie), 329, 424
    John, 287
    Richard, 46
    Thomas, 26
    William, 29, 35, 79
Jonnes (Jones, Johnes),
    Daved, 338–9
    John, 67, 455
    Margarett, 465
    Richard, 338–40
    Robert, 202
    Roger, 220, 223, 338–9, 376n.
Judson,
    John, 157, 181, 242*, 243*, 245, 249

Raphe, 249
William, 241–2
June, Raf (Randle), 2*

Kampsey, William, 301
Kedrope, Edward, 334
Kelsall (Kelsoe, Kelso, Kelsey),
    Jane, 271
    Thomas, 35
    William, 14*
Kempe (Kemp),
    Anne, xliin., 143*, 162–3
    George, xvi, xliin., 58, 142*
Kent,
    Hugh, 443
    John, 443
    Mary, 443
Kettle, Richard, xliii, 49, 51, 72
Killmorrey, Lord Viscount, 413
King, The, xxi, 150, 230
Kinge, William, 249
Kinsey (Kinsie),
    Catherine, 168
    Edwarde, 181
    Elizabeth, 180
Kniveton, Edward, 227
Knolle,
    John del, xxiv
    William atte, xxiv

Lacy,
    Humfrey, 220
    Richard, 220
Ladie Saynt Mare, see Mary, Saint, the
    Blessed Virgin
Lane, Richard, 32–3
Lanmarke, Thomas, 26
Lapworth, Edward, 112
Larden,
    John, 406, 424*
    Robert, 423
Lase, Richard, 263
Latham, Elezabeth, 376
Lawrence,
    Jane, 431, 432*
    Ralph (Raph), 430*, 431
Lawton, John, 181
Lealande, Elizabeth, 274

Ledsam (Ledsame),
  Elenor, 274
  John, 308
  Peter, 212
Lee (Leay, Leey, Lye, Lyes),
  Jone, 224
  Lettice, 408
  Richard, 71, 146
  Roger, 44
  Thomas, 224
  William, 118
Leeke (Leek),
  Ellen, 301
  family, xl
  Rauffe, 301
Leftwich,
  Richard, 161*
  Widow, 118
Leicester (Lester),
  George, 63–4
  Richard, 414
Leverett, Mr, 301
Lewin, ix
Lewis, Richard, 434
Lingart, Randulph, 175
Linghame, William, 66
Llewellyn, Thomas, 202
Lloyd, Margaret, 190, 197*
Lodmore,
  Jane, 143, 163
  Mary, 451
  Mr, 123
  Robert, 96, 183, 451*
  Thomas, 451
Lord John [   ] *see* Bishop John of
    Chester
Lovell, John, xxiv
Lowe (Looe, Loe),
  John, 67, 100, 325
  Katherine, 100
  Roger, 325*
  Thomas, 99, 253*, 324, 325*
Lucas, William, 57

Macewen,
  Amye, 302
  family, xl
Mackworth (Mackwood),
  Edward, 317, 407, 414
  Ellene, 316

Maddocke,
  Margaret, 180
  Ralph, 229
  Randall, 180*
Madeley,
  John, 311
  Thomas, 199
  William, 311*
Mainwayring (Mainwaring, Mainwaringe,
    Manwaring, Maynwaring,
    Maynwaringe, Manwering),
  Andrewe, 342
  Edmund, 314, 357, 428*, 429*, 431*
  Edward, xliii, 416*, 422
  family, xx
  George, 57, 177, 247*, 248*, 249*, 253, 257,
    343*, 344, 392*, 410*, 411, 415*, 416
  Henry, xxi, 149
  Hugh, 160, 229
  Humphrey, xxivn.
  Katherine, xvii–xviii
  Mary, xxii
  Richard, xix*, 2
  Thomas, 60–1
  William, 2, 154, 252*, 257
Maisterson (Maistersonne, Maystersonne),
  Thomas, 2*
Malbanc
  family, xx
  Hugh de, xviii
  William de, ix
Malbane (Malbon),
  Thomas, 66
  William, xxiv
Malkin (Meakin, Meekin),
  Douce, 387
  Margery, 387*
  Ralph, xxxvii, 387*
  Richard, 170, 212
  Widow, 338
Maninge (Manninge),
  Ellen, 64
  family, xl
  John, 134
  Thomas, 300* & n., 302*
Marmion, Shakerly, xxx
Mary, Saint, the Blessed Virgin, 1, 9, 238
Mashelle,
  John, 372
  Sarah, 372

Mason, John, 242
Massie (Massey, Masy, Massye, Massy,
    Masie, Massy),
  Ales, 160
  Dorothey, 391
  Edward, 148
  Elizabeth, 25n., 26, 146*, 147*, 392
  Ellen, 447
  Hugh, xxviii, 146*, 147*, 148, 150
  Jane (Joane), 71, 147–8, 392
  John, xiv, xix, xxxvii, 13, 15, 26, 33, 72,
    78, 173, 417, 457
  Margaret, 16
  Marie (Mary), xix & n., 26, 263
  Martha, 414*, 415*
  Richard (Rychard), xxxvii, 13, 14, 26, 385
  Thomas, 15, 25n., 26, 58, 113, 133, 160,
    177, 274*, 334, 447
  William, xxxvii, 13–14, 227, 305–6, 344,
    391–2, 414, 415*, 416, 469
Maurice, Randle, 426
Maynaling, Thomas, 458
Maynart (Maynerde),
  Alice, xxiv
  John, xxivn.
Meddens, Thomas, 156
Meredith,
  Elizabeth, 82*, 85–6, 88*, 91, 93
  John, xxxviii*, xxxix, 77*, 78*
Merick, William, 472
Meyre, John, 14
Miles,
  Elizabeth, 348, 351
  Katherine, 348, 351
  Thomas, 348*, 351
Millington (Myllington),
  Ellen, 164
  John, 74, 101, 164*, 165*
  Randull, 101
  Richard, 101, 330
  William, 164, 326
Mills,
  Jane, xxxivn.
  William, xxxivn.
Minshall (Minshull, Mynshull),
  Edward, 41
  Godfraye, 15
  Mr, 134, 323
  Peter, 333
  Richard, xix, 202

  Thomas, 25, 32–3, 46
Molocke, David, 3
Monckas,
  Lawrence, 66
  Thomas, 66
More (Moore),
  Arthur, 35
  Beniamine, 414
  Francis, 393–4, 414
  Thomas, 408
Mores (Morrese, Morres, Morris),
  Jone, 156n.
  Lawrence, 224
  Margerie, 156n., 263
  Richard, 15, 50
Morrey,
  John, 35
  Margarett, 156 & n.*, 202
Moseley, Robert, 14
Mosse,
  Allice, 119
  Ellene, 322
  Francis, 239
  John, 115, 426
  Richard (Richardus), 239, 241, 242*,
    243*, 245
Motterham, Widow, 53
Mottersthed,
  Edwarde, 174
  John, 174
  Marie, 179
  Thomas, 179
Moulson, John, 150
Mourton (Moreton),
  Charles, 267, 274
  Elizabeth, 268, 274*
  Randle, 233, 319
  Thomas, 266, 267*, 268–9, 274
Moyle, Thomas, 32, 33
Mullenderr, William, 387
Mulward, Richard le, xxiv
Mundew, Robert, 183*
Murray, Katherine, 456

Needham (Needon),
  Lord *see* Thomas
  Robert, 413
  Thomas, 140–1, 242, 301
Neild, Thomas, 229
Netles (Nettles), Richard, 423*, 424

Newhall, Mr, 148
Newton, John, 9
Nicholls,
    Mistris, 392
    Robert, xxxi, 202, 241, 260, 267, 342–3
Nightingale, Lewis, 388
Noden, Thomas, 249
Norbury, Margaret, 44

Olton (Oulton),
    John, xixn., 74, 376
    Katherine, 74, 233, 318
    Margaret, xixn.
    Raphe, 74
    Robert, 339, 376 & n.
Onley,
    Mary, xx
    Peter, 35
Orpe (Orp),
    George, xvii, 277*
    John, 30, 138, 157, 277
    Thomas, 118*, 138, 157
Orten (Orton),
    Joan (alias Wyen), 132
    Margery, 148
    Raphe (Rauff), 101, 220
    Thomas, 392–3
Orwele, Henry, 175
Osmer, ix–x
Oswin, x
Oteley (Otley), Elizabeth, 125, 127*

Page, Humphrey (Humfrey), 144n., 146,
    147*, 149
Paget, Rauf, 8–9
Palin (Pallin, Palyne, Paline, Palen),
    Edward, 254, 260, 329, 343, 347, 433*,
        434, 450*, 451*
    Elen (Ellen, Elyn), 39, 101
    Elizabeth, 39
    George, xiii, xiv* & n., xv & n., xxxiv,
        202, 308
    Henry, 202
    Humphrey, 32
    James, xiii, 202*, 229, 451
    John, 39, 260, 387, 450–1
    Margaret (Margerit, Margrete), 39
    Mary, 451
    Richard, 202*
    Robert, 78

    Thomas, xvi, 130*, 156n.*, 201–2, 284
    William, 38–40, 163
Paltonne, Peter, 120
Paraphet, John, 99
Parker,
    John, 78
    Margerie (Margery), xxiv, 107
    Olliver, 338
    Robert, 181
    Thomas, 108, 160
Parkes,
    Elizabeth, 74
    Ellen, 74
    Margaret, 74
    William, 74
Parr, Thomas, 134
Parry, Mris, 408
Pattrick (Pattricke, Patrick, Paterick),
    Anne, 39
    Dorothie, 101, 204, 205*
    Elizabeth, 38, 40, 43, 95, 203*, 204*, 205,
        223
    Ellen, 39–40
    Humphrey (Homnmfre), 39, 41
    Issabell, 39–40
    John, 39, 41, 42*, 53, 55, 101*, 138,
        203*, 204*, 205*, 206*, 233, 326,
        338, 340
    Margrete, 39*, 40*
    Maria (Mary), 204*, 205*
    Richard, 39, 101, 204*, 205*
    Roger, 39, 101
    William, 17, 39–42, 100–1, 204, 205*,
        206
Pearetree (Peartree), William, 333*, 372 &
    n., 395, 422
Peate, Roger, 263*
Peckston (Pexton, Pextonne, Pickston),
    Alice (Ales, Allis, Aleies, Allese), xvi,
        278 & n., 281*, 460–1, 464, 474–5,
        477
    Anne, 460
    Antony, 11
    Dorothie, 68
    Edward, ix, xii, xiv, xxxiv, 11
    Elisabeth, 11
    family, vii, xl, 10n.
    John, xxxvii, 460, 461*, 464*, 475*,
        476*, 477
    Richard (Rychard), 11

Thomas, 10 & n., 11
William, 11, 32, 460
Pemberton,
Grace, 268
Katherine, 386*
Margaret, 74
Rauffe (Raph), 313*, 314
Richard, 458
Penket, Margrete, 39
Perkins, William, xxxvi, 392
Phillipps,
John, 58, 152, 268–9
William, 26
Pichford,
Alice, 185
John, xxviii, 105, 144, 186
Mr, *see Pichford*, John
Pickmeare, Henry, 229
Pigitt, Richard, 197
Plante,
John, 374
Richard, 94–7, 281
Plenkett, Thomas, 179
Podmore,
Elizabeth, xv
Humfrey, 264
Robert, 67, 200
Roger, xv, 305
Pollett (Pollet, Pollit, Pollitt),
Ellen, 282–3
Oliver, 283, 423
Thomas, 40
Poole,
Kathren, 58
Mary, 342
Thomas, 57
Widowe, 9
William, 58, 415, 426, 439, 441, 460
poor Ellen *see* Ellen, poor
poor of Audlem, xv, 140*
poor of Baddiley, xvi, 25
poor of Marbury, xv, xvi, 25
poor (power) of Nantwich, xvi, 67
poor of St Giles-in-the-
Fields, xxxv, 299
poor of St Martin-in-the-
Fields, xxxv
poor of Wrenbury, xv, xvi, xvii, xxx, xxxi,
25, 28, 35, 52, 59, 73, 97, 119, 123,
140*, 142, 299

poor within Newhall quarter, xxxviii, 77
Pova, a
Anne, 342
John, 342
Powell (Powall, Povall, Pouall, Powfall,
Pownall)
Anne, 466*
Edward, xxxv, 465–6
Elizabeth, 25, 26
Isabel, 101
James, 25
John, 52, 53*, 423
Margerie, 25 & n.
Marie (Marye), 25n., 26, 52–3
Randle (Randulphe), xvi*, 15, 22, 25 &
n.*, 73, 83
Raphe, 25, 170
Robert, 25, 83, 117
Thomas, 411, 465*
William, 25, 83
Powley, Jonathan, 414
Pownall, Margaret, 40
Poystok, Hugh, xxiv
Praers, William de, xxiii
Preane, Raphe, 42
Prees (Preece, Price, Priese, of the
Preses),
Henry, 17–18
Jane, 437*, 438
Jasper, 50
Raphe, 338*, 382
Richard, 327
Thomas, 157
Preists (Priest),
Raphe, 340
Widdowe, 253
Prestlande, John, 119*
Preston,
John, xxxvi & n., 392
Margery, 175
Pretious, Brian, 370
Prince (Prynce), William, xv, 41–2, 53, 57,
80, 101–3, 109, 126, 137, 140, 152,
186–8, 268
Prowdman (Proudman),
John, 48
Thomas, 170
Pugh, George, 463
Puleston, Roger, xxi
Pullfords, Thomas, 185

Pursell, Thomas, 200

Queen, The *see* Elizabeth, Queen

Rabone,
  Elizabeth, 443
  Joane, 468
Rall, Margerie, 101
Ravenscroft (Ravenscrofte, Ranschrofte),
  Anne, 122*, 263*
  Elizabeth, 122*, 263*
  Ellen (Elene), xvi, xvii & n., xliin., 122*,
    156n., 173, 262, 263*, 264
  Frances, 462, 464
  George, 414
  James, 123
  John, 77, 80, 122*, 123*, 149, 169, 172,
    212*, 217, 243, 246, 263*, 264, 283*,
    311*, 417, 438–9, 441, 464*, 467n.
  Margerie, 171
  Mary, 441
  Randle (Randulphe), 95–6
  Rauffe, 172
  Robert, 77
  Thomas, xvi, xxii, xliin., 56, 121, 122*,
    123, 212*, 263*, 311
Reade, Joane, 26
Readings, Edward, 224
Redbert, William, xxiv
Reeve, George, 347
Reiffe, William, 67
Renshaw (Ranshall, Ranshawwe, Ravenshaw,
    Rynshawe, Ranshawe),
  Alis, 3
  Elizabeth, 180
  Ellen, 446
  John, 32, 66, 446
  Randle, 455
  Thomas, 2–3, 32–3, 80, 414
  William, 32–3
Rhodes (Roades, Rodes),
  Anne, 162
  Frances (Francis), 134, 143, 162*
  Thomas, 162, 255, 303
Richard II, King, xviii, xxii, xxv
Richardson,
  John, 271, 423
  Mary, 271
  Robert, 202
Ridgeway, David, 393

Robinson,
  Ellen, 468
  Margery, 392
Rogers (Rodgers),
  Matilda, 179
  Richard, 22, 40, 53, 55, 101, 135,
    178–9
  Thomas, 301
  William, 179, 326
Rowe (Roe),
  Hughe, 134
  James, 6–7
  Thomas, 313
Royley, Edward, 174
Ruffe, William, 67
Russell, Edward, 349, 351, 408
Rutter (Rudders),
  Henrye (Henrie), 126, 165, 177*, 188,
    334*, 396
  Jasper, 150, 333
  Kathrin, 132
  Mary (Marie), xxviii, 333–4
  Thomas, xxviii, 149, 202
  Widdow, 148

Sadler,
  Roger, 97, 156
  Thomas, 374
Saint Margaret of Antioch, xii
Sale (Sales),
  John, 34, 80, 137–8, 156
  Thomas, 403
  Widdowe, 431
Salmon (Sallman),
  Allice, 380–2
  Cholmoneley (Chomeley, Cholmeley,
    Chumly), 351, 381
  family, 380n.
  Mary, 392
  Richard, xxiv, 32–3
  Rowland (Rawland), 380 & n., 381–2
  William, xv, xxviii, 66–7, 105, 140,
    381
Sanders (Saunders),
  Francis, 370*
  Thomas, 14, 445
Sanemp, Richard, 113
Sanford, Marie, 101
Savage (Savadge, Savich),
  Alles, 48

Edmund, xx
Elizabeth, 428*, 429
John, xviiin.*, xlii, 115*, 260, 274, 317, 378–9, 385–6, 396, 399n.*, 400*, 427, 428*
Joseph, 449, 460
Katherine, xlii, 378*, 398 & n., 399 & n.*
Margerie, 399n.*
Mary, 449, 460*
Richard, 399 & n., 449, 460
Robert, 398, 399* & n.*
Simon, 32
Thomas, 198
Seavel (Seavell, Sevill, Sivill, Sewell, Seyvil, Seyvell, Sevell),
Elizabeth, 107
Elline, 71–2, 107
John, 2, 17, 26, 32, 137, 177
Katherin, 137
Margaret, 71
Margerie, xliin., 107–8
Richard, 132
Thomas, 26, 32–3, 99, 212, 374
Widdowe, 403
William, xliin., 71–2
Sefton (Safton),
Elizabeth, xxiii & n.
family, xxiiin.
Thomas, 66
Sergant (Sergeant),
Thomas the, xxii, xxiii*
William, 246
Serle,
Katherine, xxvi
Vivian, xxvi
Shael, John, xxiv
Shakerley, Marmion, xxx
Shallowes, William, 301
Shawe,
John, 13, 14, 427*
Richard, 48, 98
Sheen (Sheeine), John, 138, 233
Shepherd, Henry, xxiii
Shepsey, Henrye, 301
Shingleton, Anne, 140
Shore, Richard, 156
Shrowbridge (Shrobridge, Schrowebridge, Shrewbridge),
Alice, 216–17

Eleanor (Ellenor, Ellen), xxix, xxxviii*, xxxix*, 215–17
Elizabeth, 34, 215*, 216*, 217*
family, xxv
Jasper, 216*, 217
John, xxix, 26, 35, 152, 268, 372*
Joshua, 372–3
Katheren (Katherine), 178, 467–8
Margret, 372–3
Martha, 372, 373*
Mary, 215, 216*, 217*, 372*, 373*
Randle, 35
Richard, xxxv, xxxix*, 2, 34–5, 47, 78, 80, 215*, 216*, 217*, 283*, 290*, 291, 372, 373*, 467, 472
Robert, xxv, 30, 79, 215, 216*, 217*, 371 & n., 372*, 373*, 374*, 439, 441, 466, 467* & n.*, 468, 472*
Thomas, 3, 34, 79, 214*, 215*, 216*, 217, 372, 467–8
Widow, xxv
William, 216*, 217
Simcocke (Symcocke, Simcock),
Arthur, 229
John, 455
Simcone,
John, 42–3
Elizabeth, 212
Skelhorne,
family, xl
Hellen, xxxv
Thomas, 434
Skelton, James, 79
Slade, John, 148
Slare, Katrin, 2
Smith (Smyth),
Edward, 2
John, 37
Margarett, 386
Robert, xxv
Thomas, 67
Snellinge, John, 300
Snelson, Thomas, 253
Sound, William, 423
Sparke,
John, 399
Margret, 160–1
Mr, 185
Roger, 79
Thomas, 79, 115, 161

Sparrow (Sporrow), John, 326, 338
Spencer (Spenser, Spence),
    Alice, 132
    Elline, 207
    Ellionor, 333
    Margerie, 26
    Richard, 220, 253, 274
    Thomas, 151, 229, 268, 274*, 281, 318,
        386*
    William, 26, 131
Spragg, Thomas, 220, 222–3
Sproston (Sproson),
    Aillice (Allice), 426*
    Edward, 309, 426–7
    John, 267–8, 274*, 395, 396*, 426*, 427*
    Jone, 426*
    Katherine, 396
    Margarett, 274
    Randle, 425, 426*
    Roberte, 395
    Thomas, 425
Stanley, Richard, 8, 9
Stapely, Peter de, xxiii
Starkey (Starkie, Starke, Starker, Starky,
        Starkye, Sterkye),
    Anne, xix, 260
    Arthur, xviiin., xix, xxxv, xxxvii, 60, 189,
        190*, 197, 198*, 242, 253, 260, 286,
        288, 318, 392, 422
    Elenor, xixn.
    Elizabeth, 207*
    Ermin, 294n.
    family, xviii & n., xix* & n., xx, xxxii,
        xxxv
    Frances (Franncis), xix, 260
    Henrie, 122
    Hugh, xxviiin.
    James, xixn.
    Jane, xix, 260
    John, xviii & n.*, xix & n.*, xxxii, xxxvii,
        1*, 3, 60–1, 260*, 294n.
    Joseph, 207
    Lawrence, xix* & n.*, 25, 111*, 198,
        260*
    Margaret (Margarett), xix, 2*, 260
    Margerie, 3
    Mary, xix*, 2, 3, 190, 198*, 260
    Mr, 255
    Randle, 207–8
    Richard, 2

    Thomas, xviii & n.*, xix & n.*, xxviii,
        xxxv, 2*, 3, 57, 60, 79, 126, 138
    William, 3
Steele,
    Thomas, 392*, 393, 406
    William, 260, 407–8
Stenton,
    Ellin, 19
    John, 20
Steveton, John, 435–6
Stockton,
    Hugh, xxiii
    John, 407
Stofford, Thomas, xliii, 214, 234*
Stoke,
    John, 128*
    Randle, 128
    Sara, 129
    Thomas, 128
Stondeley, Hugh, 17
Stringer, Elene, 115
Strongitharm,
    family, 43n.
    John, 43
    Thomas, 44
Stubbes (Stubs),
    Randle, 426
    Thomas, 253
Sudlowe, Thomas, 430–1
Sutton,
    Anne, 334
    Thomas, 37
Swane (Swan, Swann, Swanne, Swaine),
    Aleys (Alles), 43, 97
    Arthur, 406, 458
    Edward, 44
    Elene, 94
    family, 43n.
    Francis, 415
    Henrie, 43
    John, 94
    Randulff, 43
    Roger, xvi, 94, 95
    Thomas, 29, 43–4, 126, 143, 163*,
        451
Swetnam, Elizabeth, 460

T[?], Richard, 32–3
Tacke, Thomas, 301
Tannat (Tannatt), Mr, 414, 422

Tarbock,
  Dorothy, xxin.
  Edward, xxin.*
  Mary, xxin.
  Thomas, xxin.
Tarnher, John, 67
Tatnall, George, 18
Taylor (Tailor, Taillior, Tealor, Tayeller),
  Elene, 46
  Elizabeth, 433
  George, xxxiii
  Jane (Jone), 59, 181*
  John, 14, 57–8, 63–4, 95, 97, 123, 437–8,
      455, 461, 464*, 465
  Joshua, 27, 220*, 222
  Randle, 433*
  Richard, 57, 80, 123, 302
  Richard le, xxiv, 26, 48, 249
  Robert, 59
  Thomas, xv, 73, 79, 94, 95*, 96, 97*,
      140*, 208, 210, 212*, 217, 243, 253,
      283, 290–1, 309, 328, 329*, 378, 403,
      426, 433*
  Widdowe, 253
  William, 39, 46, 66, 151, 174*, 181, 426*,
      432–3
Tenche (Tench, Tennch, Tentch),
  Anne, 129*
  Ellen, 455, 464
  George, xvi, xxxvii, 328*, 329*, 347, 423,
      424*
  Joan (Joane, Joahne), 28–9, 129
  John, xxxv, 2, 9, 11, 29–30, 70–1, 79,
      129*, 131*, 224*, 225, 227, 287, 292,
      305*, 344, 396, 423
  Katherine, 329–30, 385
  Margaretta (Margaret), 30–1
  Raffe (Ralph), 9, 28, 129
  Randle, 33, 423
  Richard, xxiv
  Robert, xxxv, 9, 11, 27–33, 66–7, 70, 79,
      128, 129*, 131, 137, 199n.
  Thomas, 11*, 79, 329, 423, 455
  Widow, 386
  William, 29, 123, 130, 200, 301, 344, 423, 433
Tervell, Lady, 2
Thyrlwynde, Isabell (Elizabeth), 39
Tiges, John, 271
Tomas (Tomise, Thomise),
  Ermine, 457

  Raphe (Rauff), 183*, 242
Tomlinson (Tomlynson),
  Thomas, 292*
Touchet (Tuchett),
  family, xxii
  John, xxviiin.*
Towers, Bartholomew, 100
Towse, Peeter, 301
Tracy, Richard, xxx
Trickett (Treckett), Robert, 317, 431
Tudman (Tuddman),
  Arthur, 464
  Dorothy, 372, 463, 464*
  Ellen, 282, 283*
  John, 200
  Lawrence, 283*
  Margarete, 22
  Martha, 458, 464
  Richard, 283–4
  Robart (Robert), 50, 282*, 283*, 349–51,
      356–7, 358*, 359*, 360, 363, 364*,
      365*, 366, 368, 369*, 370, 373*, 374,
      393–4, 408, 415, 416*, 417, 422
  Thomas, 464
Tunnall, Randall, 181
Turner (Torner),
  Henry, 134
  Richard, 78
  Thomas, 78*, 80
Twisse (Twise, Twiss, Twysse),
  Alice, 46, 469
  Dorothie, 469, 470*
  Edward, 3
  Elizabeth, 470
  John, 8, 15, 386*, 469*, 470*
  Margaret, 334, 470*
  Ralf (Raphe, Rauffe), 131, 202, 305,
      469*, 470
  Randle, 290–1
  William, 131, 183, 470*
Twyford (Twyfforde, Twyfort),
  John, 234
  William, 79
  [?], 46

Venables,
  Hugh, 149
  Mris, 408
  Peter, 413
  Ralphe (Raphe), 66–7

Randull, 3
Richard, xxivn., 32, 33
Thomas, 66
William, 149
Vernon (Vernhone, Vernan),
    Cattren (Kathrane), 65*
    family, xviii
    Henry, xvi, 67
    Hughe, 65–6
    John, 65*, 66–7, 474, 477–9
    Oliver, 149
    Raphe, 65
    Robert, 413
Vicaers, Margaret del, xxiv

W[?]ge, John, 134
Wade,
    Anne, 292, 449, 460
    Jane *see* Williams[on], Jane
    Joane (Johne), 292*
    John, 374, 449
    Randul, 69
    Robert, 291, 292*
    Thomas, 302
Walker,
    James, 301
    John, 175
Walthall, Roger, 8
Walton (Wolton),
    Peter (Peeter), xxiii, 117–18
    Randull, 392
Warburton,
    Douce, xviii, 1
    John, xviii, 1
Warde, Mr, 268
Ware, Raphe, 430
Warner family, xl
Waters, Anne, 463
Watkys, John, 150
Watson,
    Henry, 246
    John, 117, 408, 417
Weaver (Weever, Weyver),
    Alice, 392
    Randle (Randull, Ranndle), 133, 207, 210,
        220, 222, 318, 334, 385, 386*
    Richard, 134
    Robert, 134
Webb (Weebe),
    Eustace, 238*

    Thomas, 48, 238*
    Walter, 238*
Webster, Hugh, 406, 423*, 424
West, Joanna, 68
Westbroke, Rauff, 2
Weston, Thomas, 181
Weytfelde, Rychard, 69
Whild, John, 138
Whininge, John, 134
Whitcombe,
    Edward, 404–5
    Richard, 415–16
    William, 404–5
Whitehead,
    Anne, 396
    Richard, 395
    Roberte, 395
Whitesyde, Elizabethe, 39
Whitney (Whytney, Whytne, Whitnaye,
        Witnaye),
    Anna, xxvii
    Elizabeth, xxvi, xxviii, 106, 146*, 173,
        180, 185
    family, xxv, xxix
    Geoffrey (Geffrey), xxvii & n., xxxi
    George, xxvi
    Howell de, xxv–xxvii
    Hugh, xxviii, 104–5, 146, 148, 150
    Jone, 156n.
    Margaret, xxv, 64
    Margary, 64
    Mary (Marie), xxviii & n., 138, 144* &
        n.*, 146*, 147*, 148, 150, 156
    Michael, 64n., 155 & n., 156n.
    Mr, 148
    Robert (Robart), xxv, xxvi, xxvii* & n.*,
        xxviii, xxix, 66–7, 78, 126, 146*, 147*,
        149*, 150*
    Thomas, xxvi
    William, xxvi
Whittingham,
    Edward, 187–8
    Elizabeth, 34, 77
    George, xv, 323
    Homfrey, 187
    John, 35, 48, 77, 187, 443
    Margerie, 187–8
    Mary, 119
    Randle (Randall), 135, 187, 411
    Richard, 229

Robert, 67, 109, 264
Thomas, xxxiii, 187*, 188*
Whytycars, Thomas, 44
Wicksteed (Wickstead, Wickstide,
    Whicksteed, Wicksteede, Wixsted),
  Alice, 229*
  Anne, 227*
  Elizabeth, 224, 226*, 227*, 229*,
    230
  Hugh, 229
  Jasper, 161
  John, xix, 26, 129
  Margaret, 224, 225*, 226, 229
  Margerie, 224, 229
  Mary (Marie), xix, 227*
  Mr, 220
  Randle (Randull), 150
  Richard, 242, 399, 410*, 430
  Thomas, 224, 242*
  William, xxxii, 73, 130*, 161*, 223* &
    n.*, 224*, 225*, 226, 227*, 229*,
    230*, 237, 238
  Winfraite, 226
Wigin, Avis, 346
Wilbraham,
  Mr, 455
  Ralph, xxi
  Richard, 198, 237, 241*, 247, 413*
  Roger, 392, 415–16
  Thomas, 413*
Wilkinson,
  Anne, 132
  Henrie, 132
  John, 132*, 133, 168, 385*, 386*
  Lawrence, 264
  Margaret, 132
  Mary, 455
  Roger, 183
William I, King, the Conqueror, ix
Williams (Williamson),
  Amy, 180
  Jane, 207
  Joseph, 207
  Roger, 411
Wilmsley, George, 6
Wilson (Willson, Wylson),
  Christian, 333*
  Elizabeth, 41
  Ellin, 260
  Humphrey, *see Pattrick*, Humphrey

Jane (Jone), 280*, 281, 301, 332, 333*
John, 292, 333*, 437–8
Lawrence, 224
Randle, 241*
Richard, 260*, 333*, 337
Robert, 422
Sara, 101
Thomas, 220, 292*, 330, 333–4, 382
William, xvi, 41, 111, 130, 133, 224–5,
  227, 233, 280–1, 301–2, 332, 334*,
  339
Witter,
  Margaret, 71, 107
  Robert, 71, 107
Wodecot, Robert de, xxiii
Woleftodfen, John, 205
Wolley (Woll, Woolley),
  Ellen, 148
  John, 163–4
  Margaret, 207
Wood (Wode),
  George, 441
  John the, xxii, xxiii*
  Thomas, 441*
Woodcock (Woodcocke),
  Martha, 468
  Thomas, 149
Wooddall (Woodealle),
  James, 134, 222
Woodfaine (Woodfen, Woodfyne,
  Woodfenn),
  Ales, 17
  Edward, 75
  Elizabeth, 17
  John, 17* & n., 18, 53, 179, 205, 220,
    326, 339, 382, 384
  Joseph, 75
  Mary, 220
  Maude (Mode), 17
  Randall (Ranulph), 75, 384*
  Richard, 75, 384*
  Thomas, 75, 292
Woodlaye, Hugh, 66
Woodward, Robert, 3
Woollam (Wollam, Wollen, Woollom,
  Woollames),
  Allice, 305*
  George, 461
  Gilbert (Gilbarte), 130, 304–5
  Margerie (Margery), 304, 305*

Roberte, 292, 304*, 305
Thomas, 152, 222, 305*, 329, 385*, 386*
William, 32–3, 253
Woolrich (Woolriche, Woolderidge, Wouldrich, Willdridge),
Elizabeth, 396
Henry, 395*, 396
John, xxxiii, 395, 396*
Margarett, 396*
Thomas, 395–6, 413
Valentine, 130, 224, 227, 287, 292, 301 & n., 394, 396*
William, 395–6
Worall, Thomas, 302
Wordhull, Thomas de, xxiv
Wrenbury,
family de, xviii
John, xixn.
John de, xviii
Richard de, xviii, xxiii
Wrench, Randall, 229
Wright (Wrighte, Wryght),
Ales, 49
Catherine, xxxivn.
Edmund, xxxiv* & n.*, xxxv
Ellen, 35, 78

family, xxxiv* & n., 43n.
George, xiii, xxxiv, 19–20
Henry, 281
Isabell, 231
Jane, xxxivn.
John, xxxiv, 46, 49, 163, 230*, 324, 370
Lawrente, 30
Margret, 160
Mr, 145
Randull, xxxiv
Rebecca, xxxivn.
Richard, 8, 384
Robert (Robart), xxxix, 35, 72, 77–8, 83–4, 86, 91, 107–8
Roger, 242, 276–8
Thomas (Tomas), 44, 260, 449, 461
William, 19, 183*, 260*
Wylls, John, 220
Wyn, Fardinand, 134
Wynyngton (Winington),
John, 229
Paul, 229
Wyrvyn, John, xxiv

Yale, David, xliii, 20, 36, 37, 102, 146n., 147
Yure, Hankyn, 2

INDEX OF PLACES

Unless indicated or unless it is otherwise obvious, it can probably be safely assumed that the places noted in this Index lie within the County of Chester. When the more specific location of certain parcels is known, it is noted in brackets ( ). Ancient spellings which are not easily recognizable have been italicized, with the reference *see* etc. Page numbers with an asterisk (*) indicate more than one appearance of the place.

Acsones ground, 79

Acton, 43, 113 & n., 310 *and see* parish of Acton

Adderley, 387

Alcocks Feilds (Allcocks Fields), 474–5, 477

Aldelem see Audlem

Alkinton, Salop, 53

Allerton [Ollerton], 66*, 149

Allstocke, 149

Alsager, 247

Alvastbury, xxiii

Anson, 263

Apsdall, 77, 79

archdeaconry of Chester, 7

Arcluid, 392, 415

Ashlors, 253

Aston, 149

Aston (in Newhall), x*, xi, xxii, xxiv–xxvi, xxix, xxxn.*, xxxv*, xxxviii*, 35, 45, 47, 57–8, 76, 78, 80, 149, 180–1, 235, 236*, 237, 243, 253, 289–90, 297, 302*, 307–8, 346*, 388, 401, 404, 431, 448, 459–60, 474

Aston Hall, xxix, xxxi

Aston Heath, 374

Aston Lane, xxix

Aston (iuxta) Mondrom, 395

Audlem, xx–xxi, xxvn.*, 3, 380 & n., 435, 441 *and see* parish of Audlem

Awdelem see Audlem

Aynho, Northants., xxxi

Baddiley, 22, 76, 249, 451, 477

Baddiley Lane, 129

Baddiley Park, 202

Badeley see Baddiley

Badington, 247, 410

Barcson Crofts (Wrenbury Frith), 334

Barkinge, Essex, xxxv, 301 *and see* parish of Barkinge

Barne Crofte (Wrenbury Frith), 286

Barton, 198

Batherton, xxiv

Beggars Fields (Coole), 150

Bell, Ye, Nantwich [public house], 8

Bellahill, 407

Berches, 229

Betton, 392

Beverley, Yorkshire, xxxiv

Bickerton, xxxviii, 2, 285*

Bickley, 423

Birmingham, Warwickshire, 249

Blackhurst, 53, 129*

Bloxham, xxxi

Bostocke, xxvi

Boston, Lincolnshire, xxxiv

Botton, Salop, 435

Brand peece, the, 314

Brasenose College, Oxford, xxxi

Braxton, 414

Brooks mill, 418

Broomhall, ix, x, xxix, xxxii, 9, 13, 73–4, 95–6, 99*, 123, 125–6, 139–40, 149, 164, 171–2, 176–8, 187–8, 281, 375–6, 410, 434, 444, 445*, 446–7, 454

Brunhalda see Broomhall

Buerton, 67*, 152

Bunbury *see* parish of Bunbury

Burghall, Salop, 414

Burleydam (Burledam), xvii, 48*, 426

Burleydam Chapell, xvi, 67, 277*

Butterly Hey, 60

Calvers Croft (Coole), 150

Canfeth Green, 48

Canterbury, Prerogative Court of *see* Prerogative Court of Canterbury

Capellhouse (Chapell house), 48, 95, 97

Cardon, 198

Catesby, Northants, xx

Cauden, 185
Cerele see Chorley
Chaisling, 408
Cheshire *see* county of Chester
Cheshire Record Office (CRO), vii, ix, xxiin., xxv, xxx, xli, xliii*
Chester, vii, viii, xviii, xxvi, xxxv*, xxxviii, xliii, 2, 9, 37, 146n., 148, 185, 220, 252, 370, 384, 434, 437* *and see* Consistory Court of Chester; Court of Exchequer of Chester
Chester Castle, 91
Chester Cathedral, xviiin
Childs Ercall, Salop, 426
Cholmondeley (Cholmondley, Cholmeley), 37, 81, 89, 134, 220, 292, 300, 423
Chorley, ix, x, xvii, xxii & n., xxiii, 22*, 38, 40–1, 43, 51, 53, 101, 130–1, 133, 135, 174*, 175, 178–9, 203, 205*, 206, 219–20, 259, 260*, 292, 300n.*, 325–7, 330*, 333, 338–9, 382*, 384
Chorley Hall, 39, 130
Christleton, xxiin., 185*, 392
Church Coppenhall, 410, 457
Churchulme, 149*
Church of Wrenbury, xii*, xiii*, xiv*, xv*, xxiii, xxxii, xxxiv, 1, 6, 7, 34, 38, 41, 125, 128, 136, 139, 143, 160, 168, 187, 207, 223, 236, 263, 266, 271, 299*, 314, 324, 423
Churton, 198
City, The *see* London
Clutton, 198
Clyff (lands), xx
Cocke, The [public house in Nantwich], 278
Combermere, viii, xxi* & n.*, xxii*, xxx, xxxii, 71, 123*, 237–8, 241, 286, 313, 328, 340, 344, 390, 393, 405–6, 408, 412, 414–15, 416*, 417, 422, 451, 457
Combermere Abbey, xviii & n.*, xx & n.*, xxv, xxxii, xxxvii
Consistory Court of Chester, xxxvii, xxxix*, xliii, 147, 214, 218, 316, 350, 416*, 422, 428–9, 431, 432*, 434
Coole (Coule, Covlle), xxii, xxv* & n., xxvi*, 104–5, 134, 144* & n., 146–7, 149*, 150*, 297*, 380n.
Coole Lane (Coolane), xxiv & n.*, xxvn., 9, 15, 65, 67, 95–6, 140, 380 & n., 381, 382, 388

county court, *see* Court of Exchequer of Chester
County of Chester, vii*, viii*, x, xiii, xvii, xviiin., xixn., xxv*, xxvi*, xxviii & n., xxxi*, xxxii, xxxiv, xxxv*, 113, 256
County of Flint, ix, 428*
County of Middlesex, 299
County of Shropshire (Sallopp, Salop), ix, 113, 455*
County of Stafford, 113–14
Courte, le, Newhall, xxviiin
Court of Exchequer of Chester, 66, 146, 292, 478
Court of Wards and Liveries, xxin.
Cow Lane *see* Coole Lane
Cuddington (Codington), 198*

Darley, 122*
deanery (rural) of Middlewich, 437
deanery of Nantwich, 18
Dee [River], xxviiin.
Denfield, 146–7
Denton, 44
Derfold, 415
Deverton Dayth, 186
Dodcott, ix, 26, 461, 464
Doddington, Salop, 67, 415
Dodds Green (Newhall), 94–5, 146–7
Dorfold Hall, xxvin.
Dovehouse Fields (Coole), 150
Duckington, 220
Duddon, xxviin.
Dudmaston, Salop, 413
Dunnes Tenement (Wrenbury Frith), 227, 237

Eagle Hall (Newhall), 184
Eastcheap (London), xxxv, 301
Eleven Acres (Wrenbury Frith), 229
Eleven Acres Lane (Wrenbury Frith), 229
Eleven (Leaven) Acres Meadow (Wrenbury Frith), 229*
Eller Meadow, 338
Elsud, Salop, 386
Emlenton, near London, 276
Emmanuel College, Cambridge, xxxvi
Erdswick, 32, 323, 333
Erge, 451
Essetune see Aston (in Newhall)
Evesham, Worcestershire, xxn.

Farndon, 198

Fields (Felles, Fellees), The, 48, 414
Finny (Fenny) Wood, 122*, 123
Flintshire *see* County of Flint
Frith, The *see* Wrenbury Frith

Gainsborough, Lincolnshire, xxxiv
Gardiners Fields, Coole, 150
George Claytons feild (Wrenbury), 208
Grange, The (Smeatonwood), xxxv, 298, 300, 302
Great Eleven (Leaven) Acres, (Wrenbury Frith), 229*
Great Mosse [common pasture] (Coole), 105–6, 150*
Green Crofts (Wrenbury Frith), 334
Greenwich, London, xxxv, 301
Grindleyes Feeld (Newhall), 30
Grindleys Green, 48*

Halghton, Flintshire, 428
Hampton, 415
Handley Park, 242
Hankelow (Hanckeloe), 263, 464
Hanley, 198
Hanmer, Flintshire, 428
Harringay Parish, Middlesex, ix, xiv
Henhull, 410
Hinton, Salop, 414
Hitchins Field (Wrenbury Frith), 49
Hobbfeildes (Hobfields) (Wrenbury Frith), 119, 323
Holden [*county?*], xxxiv
Hollford, 202
Hollinlane house and ground, 80
Hospellstreet (Nantwich), 160
Hoult, Derbyshire, xixn.
Hulse, 229
Hurdemans Feild (Coole), 150

Ightfield, Salop., xxiin., 456
Inillon, 48
Iscoyde, Flintshire, 463

Kiddington, xxxviii*, 77
Kinderton, 413
King's Bench prison, London, xxxiv
Kingesley, 149
Kitchin Croft (Wrenbury Frith), 229

Lankhayder in Kynnierch, 190
Lea, 413

Leftwich, 229*
Leighton, xxvin., 148–9, 392*
Lenton, Nottinghamshire, xxxiv
Leye, Salop, 313
Lightwood Green, 73, 94, 96, 277
Lincoln, Lincolnshire, xxxiv
Lincolnshire, xxviii
Little Casy Meadow (Wrenbury), 198
Little Croft Orchard (Wrenbury Frith), 286
Little Gersly Loddiate (Smeatonwood), 451
Little Lane (Wrenbury Frith), 229
Little Weever Meadow (Coole), 150
Littull Hashall, 66
Lodmore Lane, 94, 146
Lolegrove, xxiii
London, xxxiv*, xxxv*, xxxvii, 2, 64, 66, 220*, 276, 300*, 387, 389, 447, 449, 453, 456, 458, 461, 465–6, 468, 470, 472
Long Higher Feild (Wrenbury Frith), 286*
Long Woolstable of Westminster, xxxv
lordship of Newhall *see* manor of Newhall
lordship of Whitchurch *see* manor of Whitchurch
Lostocke Gralam, 229
Lower End of the Lane (Coole), 150
Ludgate prison, London, xxxiv
Lutterworth, 77, 89
Lyine [Lyme?], 408
Lynn [King's Lynn, Norfolk?], xxxiv

Madeley, xxiv
Malpas *see* parish of Malpas
manor, ix, x, 413–14
manor of Newhall, xxii* & n., xxviiin.*, 237*, 238, 240*, 297, 372, 402
manor of Stretton, 198*
manor of Whitchurch, Salop, 237–8, 240*
manor of Wrenbury, xviiin.*, 198*
Marbury, 229
Marbury Hey, 255, 312, 314
Margaret Wolls Crofte (Wrenbury), 208
Market Drayton, Salop, xx, 138, 426
Marley, 58, 249
Mickley, 8, 149, 297, 400, 409, 410*
Mickley Hall *see* Mickley
Middle Field (Wrenbury Frith), 229
Middlesex *see* County of Middlesex
Middlewich, 37, 149* *and see* deanery (rural) of Middlewich
Milne Feild (Wrenbury), 208

Minshull Hall, xix
Minshull Vernon, 2
Moore (More) Hall, xviin., 216–17, 442, 452
Morton, 9
Mosse, The, 392, 415, 469
Moulton, 149, 229

Nantwich, ix, xixn., xxxiv*, 2, 29*, 67, 80,
129*, 148, 160*, 198, 202*, 220, 243,
245, 249, 276*, 296–7, 301, 348*,
349*, 356, 361–2, 368, 381, 384, 410,
444, 455*, 458 *and see* deanery of
Nantwich
Nantwich churchyard, 276
Nesten, at le, 227
Newbridge Field, 297
Newgate prison, London, xxxiv
Newhall, ix, x*, xi*, xii, xxiin., xxivn.,
xxviiin.*, xxxn., xxxiv, xxxv*, xli, 9,
28, 30*, 31, 36, 47–8, 56, 59*, 61,
64n., 71–2, 82, 86, 88, 93, 107–10,
121–3, 136, 137*, 155*, 163, 168–9,
186, 199, 211–12, 214*, 215–17, 230*,
247, 262, 264*, 276*, 277*, 278, 281*,
282–3, 294n., 297* & n., 310–11,
342–3, 345, 347–52, 387*, 389, 403*,
425–6, 430*, 431–2, 438–9, 441*, 452,
458, 461, 465, 467n., 468 *and see*
manor of Newhall
Newhall Manor Court, xxxiin., xli, 380n.
Newhall Mills, xxviiin., 417
Newhall Park, xxii, xxviiin., 28, 29*, 30*,
122–3, 416, 422, 440
New Lands (Lownes) (Coole), 149–50
New Ridding (Wrenbury), 198
Northwich, 229

Ocleston, 149
Office of the Register, 437
Orchard Croft, 229
Ould Marled Feild, 286*
Over, 229*
Oxford University, xxn.
Ox Meadow, Newhall, xxviiin.

parish of Acton, ix & n., xi, xii*, 349
parish of Audlem, xxiv & n., 140*, 380n.*
parish of Barkinge, Essex, 299
parish of Bunbury, 9, 185
parish of Malpas, 80, 88
parish of Sandbyge [Sandbach], 66

parish of St Giles in the Fields, Middlesex,
xxxv, 299
parish of St Lawrence, London, xxxiv
parish of St Martin in the Fields [London?],
300
parish of St Olave Jewry, London, xxxiv
& n.
parish of St Peter near St Alban's, London,
xxxiv
parish of Tilston, 185
parish of Wrenbury, ix, x, xi, xv*, xxiiin.*,
xxiv* & n., .xxxiv*, xxxv, xxxvi*, xl*,
xlii, 50, 82, 84, 86, 90, 93, 103, 123,
140, 149, 167, 202, 204, 212, 216*,
217, 230, 259, 271, 308, 310, 333,
343*, 349, 357–8, 359*, 380n.*, 384,
385*, 392*, 433, 460, 461*, 474, 477,
479
parochial church of Wrenbury *see* church of
Wrenbury
Pencrage, 220
Pillston (Pilstonn), 77, 83, 131, 134, 436
Poole, 414, 474
Poolecroft Heath, 57
Povlle (?), 134
Preece (Prees, Presess, Preses), Salop, 44,
157, 313–14
Prerogative Court of Canterbury, xxxiv,
xliii*, 64, 472
Puddington, 227, 230*
Pulleston, 143
Purgath feelde, 106

Ridlington, xxxivn.
Rostherne, 64
Rough Croft(s) (Wrenbury Frith), 229*
Rowton, 185
Ryalls (Royals) in Newhall, xxviiin., 371 &
n., 373, 466, 467n.*

St Giles in the Fields [Church of] *see* parish
of St Giles in the Fields, Middlesex
St Lawrence [Church of] *see* parish of St
Lawrence, London
Saint Margaret's Church, Wrenbury *see*
Church of Wrenbury
St Martin in the Fields [Church of] *see* parish
of St Martin in the Fields, [London?]
St Mary's Church, Chester, 372n.
St Olave Jewry [Church of] *see* parish of St
Olave Jewry, London

St Peter [Church of] *see* parish of St Peter
Sandbach *see* parish of Sandbyge
Sandy Croft (Wrenbury), 208*
Scrateley, 153
Shavington, Salop, 413
Sheppcroft (Coole), 150
Sheppenhall (Shepnal), xxxiin., 270–1, 294 &
    n., 295, 297* & n., 319, 379, 416
Shetton, 190*
Shipbrooke, 229*
Shorte Higher Feild (Wrenbury Frith), 286*
Shrewsbury, Salop, 414
Shropshire *see* County of Shropshire
Shurlach, 229
Smeatonwood, ix, xxxvii*, 55, 57, 63*,
    142–3, 153–4, 254*, 256, 257*, 301–2,
    312–13, 328*, 329, 346–7, 386, 403,
    432–3, 450, 451* & n., 460, 473–5
Sound, ix, x, xxii & n., xxiii*, xxxviii*, 113*
    & n., 114, 116, 117*, 118–20, 130–1,
    157*, 159–61, 245, 247, 249, 321,
    324–5, 435*, 436, 471
Spiritual Court *see* Consistory Court of
    Chester
Springyard man feelde, 106
Sproston, 149
Spurstowe, 40
Staffordshire *see* County of Stafford
Stanthorne, 149
Stockton, 407, 463
Stretton, xixn., 198
Sucknales (name of a piece of ground), 79
Sutton, 91
Synsmedowe, 29
Synswood (Sins woodde), 29*, 30

Tarporley, 411
Tearton, 185
Tereth see Wrenbury Frith
Tilston *see* parish of Tilston
Tofte, 149
Tottenhall [*i.e. Tattenhall*], xxviiin.
Towneley, 313
Tussingham, 286*
Two Barn Crofts (Wrenbury Frith), 229

Walke, The (Newhall), 94
Walkerton, 67*, 122
Wardes Fields (Coole), 149, 150*
Warenberie see Wrenbury
Wareton, 229

Warmundestrou, x
Weaver (*Wyvere*) River, xxiii
Welsh Roe, 457
Westminster, Middlesex, 443, 446 *and see*
    Long Woolstable of Westminster
Westo wylond, xxiii
Wettenhall, 238, 239*
Whitchurch, Salop, ix, 26, 202*, 313–14, 370
    and see manor of Whitchurch, Salop
Wich Malbank see Nantwich
Wich Malbank, barony of, xxii, xxiii
Wilkesley, 130, 349
Wimbaldsley, 149
Withington, 149
Withyng Crofts (Wrenbury Frith), 334
Wolfhall, 351
Woodall, 297
Woodcott (Woodcote), ix, 198*, 297, 315,
    317, 403, 460–1
Woodhey, 237, 413
Woodhouses, 48
Woodsfields (Coole), 106, 159
Wrenbury, ix*, x*, xvn., xviin., xviiin.*,
    xxiin., xxviii & n., xxxii, xxxiv*,
    xxxv*, xxxviii, xli, 1, 2, 10n., 43 & n.,
    58, 86, 97, 108*, 111*, 112, 113 & n.*,
    114–15, 129, 131, 132*, 133, 151*,
    166* & n., 167, 189, 190*, 198*, 202,
    207–8, 232–4, 260, 266, 268, 273–4,
    276n.*, 286, 294n., 308, 318–19, 332,
    333*, 336, 341–2, 346, 372* & n.*,
    378*, 385, 386*, 387, 391–2, 395*,
    398–400, 408, 423, 424*, 426–7, 428*,
    429, 435 & n., 437, 441, 460, 464 *and*
    see Church of Wrenbury; parish of
    Wrenbury
Wrenbury Frith ix, x*, xxxviii, 31–2, 47–9,
    70*, 119, 128, 130, 132*, 201–2, 223,
    225–7, 229*, 237, 242, 285*, 286*,
    287–8, 291–2, 304–6, 323, 332, 334*,
    385–6, 394–6, 437*, 438, 469, 475n.
Wrenbury Hall, 391
Wrenbury Park, 260
Wrenbury School, xivn., xvn.
Wrenbury Woods, 255, 313–14
Wylkesley, xxivn.
Wyncull Grange, xx
Wynnall, 77, 89

Yerdshaw (Eardsall), 149*
York Province, ix

INDEX OF SUBJECTS

In order to simplify this Index as much as possible, we have eliminated formulaic and highly-repetitive words which comprise the testamentary vocabulary – e.g., will, testament, inventory, *summa totalis* or sum, endorsement, administration, units of money (pounds, shillings, pence), phrases regarding physical and/or mental state, moveable and immoveable property (goods, cattles and chattels), regnal years, rest and residue, prised value, and the like. We have also deleted phrases which express some eternal reward for a life well-lived, as well as instructions for the manner and place of burial. The various spellings of words have been noted as completely as possible, except where the difference from modern orthography is so slight that any misunderstanding seems improbable; where we have included the item in the Glossary, the spelling found in the Glossary comes first in the Index.

acre, 2, 30
Act of Dissolution, xx
addstocke, 275
aisle, xxxiii, 13
akarrea see acre
alabaster, 191
ale, 421
ale borde, 39
allegation (allegacōn), xxxviii, xl, 80, 91,
    102, 203–5, 214–15, 216*, 217*, 218*,
    349–50, 352, 357*, 358–60, 475*
almshouse, xxxiv
amare (aumare, ambry), 1, 4
andiron (andian, anndiron, anniron), 256,
    277, 303*, 347, 393, 419, 420*, 421,
    440
angell, King Henry, 25, 45, 125
Anglican Church *see* Church of England
anniversary (anniversarie), 3
annuity (annuetie), 140, 238, 239*, 240*,
    451
apparel (apparell, apparill, apperell), 1, 3, 11,
    16, 18, 20, 24, 30, 33, 35, 40, 42, 44,
    46–7, 49–50, 55, 58, 66, 69, 72, 74,
    78, 80, 96, 98, 100, 102, 105, 108,
    110, 112–13, 116–17, 120, 123, 127,
    130, 133, 135, 138, 141, 143, 145, 148,
    151, 154, 156, 158, 161, 163, 165–7,
    169, 174, 177, 179, 185*, 186, 188,
    193, 200, 202, 206, 210, 212, 218, 222,
    224, 227, 230, 234, 237, 243, 252, 255,
    263*, 264, 269, 272, 275, 278, 281–3,
    287*, 290, 292, 295, 303, 306, 309,
    311, 314, 317, 319, 327, 329, 331, 337,

339, 341–2, 344, 347, 373, 376, 379,
    381, 385–7, 393, 397, 399, 404, 407,
    417, 423*, 424, 427, 431, 433*, 436*,
    439, 445, 451, 465
apple pan, 336
applgrate, 196, 209
apron, 280, 392
arable, 30, 238
arke (ark), 39, 200, 417
armour (armor), 28, 125, 127, 185, 196, 200,
    337
arras carpett, 193
arras coveringe, 260
arras cushon, 193
arras (bedd) hylling, 191–2
arrerages (arrears) of rent, 291, 342, 422
artilery (artillerie), 200, 347
ashen *see* eshen
asset, 204, 215
assignment (asseyment), 29, 426
assize, xxxiii
augmentacon, 403*
axe (ax), 4, 24, 30, 35, 53, 101, 131, 173,
    195, 209, 221, 231, 255, 292, 335, 347,
    418
axell tree (axeltrei, axletree), 102, 197, 222

bacinice, 419
backhouse (backhowse, bakehouse,
    backhowes), 68, 123, 244, 252*,
    316–17, 335, 447
backstoole, 421*
bacon (bacone, bakon, baken, bacen, backon,
    bakean), 20, 36, 44, 58, 61, 74, 79, 96,

98, 102, 105, 109, 112, 117, 124, 127,
131, 135, 138, 141, 152, 154, 156, 161,
165, 170, 173, 178, 186, 187–8, 200,
206, 212, 218, 231, 244, 251, 255, 261,
265, 267, 269, 281, 283, 288, 290, 293,
295, 306, 309, 314, 317, 326, 331, 337,
340, 347, 377, 381, 383, 397, 404, 406,
419, 433–4, 436, 440
bacon chest, 251
bagg (bagge), 58, 74, 130, 218, 231, 261,
284, 287–8, 296, 309, 383, 404, 427,
431, 440
bag of feathers, 292
ballance (scale), 228
balle (bale) of flax, 69, 258
band (i.e., bound) box, 303
bandileere(bandeleroe), 251, 295
baren heifer, 439
bargaine (bargayne) of ground, 79, 169, 245,
314*
barh, 102
barley (barlie, barle), 4, 12, 30, 141, 145,
158, 208*, 222, 267, 293, 334, 336,
373, 376*, 407*, 417
barlie malt, 24
barly seede, 222, 406
barn croft (barne crofte), 229, 286*
barne, 24, 68, 145, 150, 160, 169, 187, 197,
229, 236, 238, 264*, 278, 290, 295,
309, 333, 373, 399, 418, 434, 439, 447,
469
barran (barraine) cowe, 68, 78
barrel (barrell), 4, 23, 124, 197, 209, 221,
251*, 252, 264, 306, 331, 336, 383,
417–18, 453
barrel of varyies *[i.e., odds & ends]*, 69
barrell frame, 193
Bartholomew Day (Bartholomewtide), 26, 253
base-born, 8
baskete (baskett), 68, 74, 127, 141, 145, 156,
200, 209, 218, 251, 261, 265, 269, 284,
290, 296, 303, 309*, 331, 336*, 383,
393, 404, 427, 434
bason (basen, basin, basyn, bassen), 3, 194*,
208, 277, 335
bass, 197
bastyng dish, 4
bay of building, 285, 286*
beaker, 300
beam (beme), 187, 326, 331

beaner, 194
beans (beanes), 99, 339
bearing cloth, 250
beast, 417*
beck, 200
bed (bead, beed, bedd, bad), 1, 3–4, 13–15,
39–40, 43, 45, 47, 49, 52, 69, 85,
87–8, 90, 92–3, 98, 103, 145*, 215–17,
225, 243, 244*, 251, 260*, 261*, 264,
267–8, 278*, 292*, 296*, 300, 303,
309, 316–17, 322, 335, 336*, 337,
342*, 343, 353, 383*, 397, 407, 419,
420*, 455, 467
bedcase (beddcase), 4, 9, 191, 192*, 193,
194*, 196, 330*
bedchamber, 137–8, 140, 142
bedcloth, 200, 419
bed coveryng (coveringe), 4, 250, 352
bedd cord, 260
bedd furnished, 303
bedd furnishings (furniture), 236, 244*, 255,
278*, 300, 316, 342
beddyng (beadinge, beddinge, bedding), 11,
16, 18, 20, 36, 40, 44, 47, 49–50, 52,
54–5, 72, 74, 79, 96, 98, 100, 102,
105, 108–9, 116–17, 120, 124, 126,
130, 133, 135, 138, 141, 143, 145*,
154, 156, 158, 161, 163*, 165–7, 170,
173, 178–9, 186, 188, 200, 206, 212,
218, 224*, 228, 231, 236, 255, 264,
267–9, 271–2, 275, 280–1, 283, 288,
290, 296*, 306, 309, 311, 314, 317,
319, 322, 329, 339, 344, 347, 373, 377,
381, 389, 393, 397, 399, 404, 419*,
427, 431, 433*, 439, 440*, 467
bed hengyng (hanging) *see* bedhilling
bedhilling, 12, 192–3, 246*
bedhooke, 453
bed panne, 101
bedroome, 385
bedstave, 228
bedstead (bedsted, bedstidd, bedstydde,
bedestede, bedstedde, bedstid,
bedsteedd, badd stead, bed steide), 12,
22–3, 39–40, 42, 44, 47, 54, 57, 61,
68, 71–2, 74, 79, 96, 98, 108–9, 112,
116–17, 119–20, 126, 130, 133, 135,
138, 141, 143, 145*, 156, 158, 161,
163, 165, 173, 178–9, 186–7, 192,
195–6, 200, 206, 208, 212, 218, 221*,

bedstead (bedsted, bedstidd, bedstydde,
bedestede, bedstedde, bedstid, bedsteedd,
badd stead, bed steide) continued
    222–4, 227, 236, 246, 250–2, 257, 265,
    267, 269, 271–2, 278*, 281, 283*,
    287–8, 290, 292*, 296*, 306, 309, 317,
    320, 324, 326, 331, 340, 347, 352, 374,
    377, 383, 389, 397, 399, 404, 407,
    419*, 420, 427, 431, 433, 439, 447,
    453*, 467
bedstock (bedstocke, bedstack, bedstoc) *see*
    bedstead
beefe (befe, beeffe, bife), 72, 74, 79, 105,
    117, 124, 127, 138, 161, 173, 178, 186,
    200, 218, 244, 255, 288, 295, 337,
    381*, 397, 404, 406
beeffe coume, 196
beer (beare), 265, 421
beere barrell, 193
bees (beehive), 9, 30, 49, 58, 117, 120, 127,
    130, 154, 158, 161, 163, 200, 244, 255,
    261, 269, 275, 278, 306, 316, 329, 331,
    335, 339, 377, 384
bell, xii, xiii, xv, xxxii, xxxiv, 191
bellies (bellowes, bellows), 105, 131, 191,
    194, 210, 222, 228, 251, 284, 288, 295,
    331, 393, 419, 440
belt, 228
benche, 39, 52, 54, 69, 73, 141, 170, 187,
    284, 383
benche cloth, 24, 339
bench formes, 339
berddinge (birding, burding) pise (piece) *see*
    fowling piece
bevylling bill, 9
Bible (Bybell, also King James or
    Authorized), xxxvi* & n.*, 120, 173–4,
    222, 234, 261, 277, 331, 387, 436
bill (bille, byll, byl, bile, byle), 3, 12, 22, 24,
    30, 101, 131, 173, 178, 209, 221, 225,
    228, 231, 244, 252, 256, 292, 335, 347,
    439
bill of debt, 14, 66, 94, 106, 137, 148, 163,
    200*, 213, 239, 252, 263, 278, 284, 376
binge, 192
birdnet (burdnett), 252
blanket (blancett, blanckett, blanquett), 4, 14,
    23, 39, 42, 56, 101, 130, 163, 191*,
    192*, 193*, 194*, 197*, 208, 221*,
    231, 246*, 250*, 251, 257, 264, 280*,

    292*, 306, 326, 330*, 383*, 407, 418,
    419*, 420*, 421*, 440, 453*
board (bord, boird, boy[r]ed, boyrde, bourde,
    boorde, brde, boward, bard), 1, 3, 5, 9,
    12, 18, 23–4, 36, 39, 42, 44, 51, 54,
    57, 60–1, 68, 72–4, 79, 96, 100, 106,
    108, 116, 119, 126, 130, 133, 138, 141,
    143, 165–7, 169*, 178–9, 200, 209*,
    212, 215–18, 225*, 228, 231, 236,
    255–6, 261, 265, 269, 271, 281–2, 284,
    288, 290–1, 295, 326, 336, 381, 397,
    406, 418*
board (burde, bourd) cloth, 1, 3, 23, 68, 72,
    162, 173
boat, 418
bolsterre (bolester, boulster, bowelster,
    bolster), 4, 12, 22–3, 39, 46, 101, 130,
    145, 162–3, 191, 192*, 193, 194*,
    197*, 208, 221*, 225, 228*, 231, 243,
    246*, 250*, 251, 257, 264, 267*, 280,
    287, 292*, 306, 309, 326, 330*, 373,
    391, 393, 407, 418, 419*, 420*, 421,
    439–40, 453*, 467
bonde (bonnd, bound, band, bonde)
    [financial], 94, 106–7, 137, 148, 200*,
    239, 252*, 253*, 263, 277–8, 309, 316,
    327, 337, 376, 379, 381, 384*, 386*,
    393, 414, 427*, 476
bonnet (bonete), 3
bookeframe, 250
book of accompts, 46
books (bouks, bookes), xvn., xxxvi*,
    xxxvii*, 13, 112, 125, 127, 135, 167,
    192, 206, 224, 227, 250, 255, 272, 282,
    284, 296, 303, 306, 309, 329, 336, 344,
    347, 377, 381, 383–4, 392* & n., 393,
    404, 421, 423, 447, 453
bootts (bootes), 134–5, 174, 329
bord *see* maintenance
border (cottager), ix, x
bore, 1
bottle, 210, 221, 393, 421
boucke, 72
boullinge pipe, 209
bow (and arrows), 1, 3, 9, 335
bowl (bolle, bole, boule), 23, 135, 209, 243
boxe (box), 54, 112, 135, 145, 163, 191,
    200, 206, 208*, 250*, 257, 261*, 277,
    292, 296, 335, 344, 383, 393*, 407,
    421*, 433

boye, 4
brake (bracke, brak, borak, brace), 68, 75,
    101, 130, 158, 170, 196, 210, 213, 221,
    251–2, 255, 264, 278, 284, 287, 295,
    329, 331, 335, 339, 374, 383, 434
brandart (brendart, brunderd, brundet,
    brundret, brandrate, brendreth, brondet,
    bradart, brondrett, brandrede), 4, 12,
    39, 54, 102, 165, 179, 191, 195, 210,
    221, 293, 336
brand peece, 314
brass (brasse, brase), 16, 18, 20, 23, 36,
    39–40, 42, 47, 49, 54, 58, 61, 69, 72,
    74, 79, 96, 98, 105, 108–9, 112, 115,
    117, 120, 126, 130, 133, 135, 138, 141,
    143, 145, 154, 156, 158, 161, 163*,
    165–7, 169, 173, 178, 186, 188, 194,
    212, 218, 225, 231, 236, 244, 255, 258,
    261, 265, 269, 271–2, 275, 277, 280–1,
    287–8, 290, 295, 303, 306, 309, 311,
    314, 317, 319, 322, 329–30, 336, 339,
    347, 373, 377, 381, 389, 393, 396–7,
    399, 404, 406*, 418–19, 427, 431,
    433*, 440, 453, 460
brasse baster, 195, 200
brasse (brasen) case, 191
brasse chafing dish, 282
brasse (brasen, brazen) chamdler
    (candlestick), 193, 195*, 222, 267, 280,
    282, 292, 421
brasse (brasen) dustbox, 191
brasse kettell, 195
brasse (brazen) ladle, 195*, 292
brasse morter and pestell, 208, 222, 277,
    383, 418
brasse pane (pann, panne), 98, 101, 129,
    137*, 168, 187, 228*, 263, 287, 316,
    322
brasse (brase) pott, 101, 119, 129, 185, 187,
    194, 197, 208, 219*, 222*, 274, 322,
    326, 418
brasse pott lidd, 194
brasse (brasen) skalles, 208
brasse verdelt (?), 124
brasse weights, 191
brawne, 419
bread, 255, 265, 283, 295, 374
bread grater, 195
breches (breeches), 135, 187–8, 346*
bred corne, 331

brend iron *see* brandart
brew house, 196*, 418–19
brewing (bruinge) coume, 196
brewing (bruing) pan (pann), 194, 197, 406
brewinge salts, 418
brewinge vessel *see* brewing pan
brick (bricke), 106, 124, 196, 261, 295
brick kyllne, 261
brickyudar, 3
bridle (brydle, bridel), 68, 120, 131, 135,
    138, 152, 256, 258, 280, 295, 326, 335,
    381, 383
brissil, 194
broche (broach, broache, broythe), 1, 4, 12,
    39, 54, 62, 69, 129, 131, 135, 138,
    188, 221, 225, 228, 236*, 288, 290,
    292, 316, 329, 331, 336
broken tymber, 58, 335, 404
brons waight, 196
brooke grass *[broken glass?]*, 112
brushe, 112, 194
bryne Wallinge, 160*
buckett irons, 196
buckler (buclere, bucler), 3, 9, 55
buffett stoole, 192*, 196
building, xxiii, 402, 447*, 449, 469*, 470
bull (bulle), 1, 42, 57, 120, 123, 151, 160,
    186, 197, 199, 243, 252, 255, 260, 287,
    400, 406, 417
bull calf, 25, 115
bullock (bullocke), 20, 24, 32, 40, 57, 61,
    68, 99, 117, 130, 145, 158, 161, 169,
    177, 197, 220, 243, 295, 339, 383, 427,
    439
burgage, xxvii, 455*
burial vault, xix
burning glasse, 393
bushell, 30, 57, 209
bushell of barley (barlie), 44, 99, 138
bushell of malt, 79
bushell (boshell) of oates (otes), 68, 78, 138
bushell of rye, 44, 53, 78, 99
bushell of wheat, 79, 197
butter, 4, 22, 29, 36, 40, 42, 50, 54, 58, 74,
    96, 101, 105, 117, 120, 124, 127, 131,
    135, 154, 162, 165, 170, 186, 212, 218,
    231, 244, 255, 261, 265, 269, 275, 283,
    288, 290, 293, 295, 306, 314, 317, 331,
    397, 407, 419, 440
butter pote, 69

buttrie (buttery, butterie, buttrye), 39, 54, 105, 192, 225*, 244, 246, 251, 261, 265, 296, 336, 421, 440*
buz, 24

cabinett, 391, 393
cadow (caddowe), 130, 194, 221, 246*, 250*, 292, 407
calf (calfe, cawefe, caulffe), 5, 18, 24, 32–3, 37, 44, 52–3, 57, 68, 99, 106, 112, 115, 117, 120, 123, 126, 145, 151, 158, 161*, 169, 177, 179, 186, 199, 208, 213, 215*, 216*, 217*, 220–1, 229, 243, 252, 255, 260, 274, 280, 283, 287–8, 290, 293, 295, 311, 313, 322, 326, 331, 334, 339, 373, 376, 396–7, 407*, 417, 423–4, 431, 434, 439, 445, 455
calfekitt, 334
Calvinism, xxxvii
candle, 261, 287, 421
Candlemas (Candilmas, Candellmas), 3, 79, 242
candlestick (candlesticke*), 23, 39, 124, 206, 208, 228, 292, 383
canepey, 192
cann (canne, can), 191, 195, 209, 221
can of silver, 392
canonical sanctions, 6
canopie bedd, 215–16, 420
canvas (canvis, canvers, cannvres), 3, 44, 251*
canvas shete (shite), 4, 39, 68
cappe, 251
cappon (capon), 50, 421
cap room, 406
capule (capulle), 5, 12
carde, 141, 210
carpet (carpett), 4, 55, 186, 192*, 250, 261, 277, 304*, 335, 421*
carpett clothe, 296
carpett of broadcloth, 193
carpett of hoom worke, 193
carre, 96
carriage, 134, 220*
cartblade, 335
carte (cart, cort), 1, 4, 12, 20, 33, 42, 52, 56, 58, 73–4, 78, 99, 101, 105, 116, 120, 124, 127, 129, 130–1, 137–8, 141, 145, 154, 161, 165, 173, 178, 185, 187–8, 200*, 206*, 209, 218, 221–2, 225, 228, 231, 234, 236, 244*, 252*, 255*, 261, 267, 269, 274, 284, 288–90, 295, 304, 306, 312, 316–17, 322, 329, 331, 335, 339*, 347, 376–7, 383, 397, 400, 402, 404, 417, 433–4, 439, 455, 468, 472
carte body (bodye), 4, 24, 197, 326, 334, 339
carte waine *see* carte body
carte wheel, 197
cartropp (cart rope, cartrop, carte rope), 102, 206, 209, 225, 228, 292, 335, 339, 383, 427
cart timber (carttimber, cart tymber), 24, 54, 130, 206, 267, 269, 347, 407, 417, 439
carucate, ix, x, xxiv
cather, 158
cattle (cattail), 12, 18, 20, 24, 30, 33, 35, 40, 42, 51, 53, 57, 60–1, 67, 74, 78, 95, 97–9, 101, 105, 108, 112, 115, 117, 120, 123, 126, 133, 135, 137*, 141, 145, 151, 154–5, 161, 163*, 165*, 169, 177, 179, 186, 188, 197, 199, 208, 213, 215*, 216*, 217*, 225, 229, 231, 236*, 243, 252*, 255, 257, 260, 268, 278, 281, 283, 287*, 290, 293, 295, 306, 309, 311, 313, 322*, 331, 334, 339, 347, 373, 376, 381, 389, 400*, 404, 406, 417, 433*, 434, 445, 455
certey *see* surety
certified representative, 416
chafbolster, 221
chaff bedd (chaffbed), 57, 221, 250*, 251, 292, 383*, 453*
chaffe (chefe), 188, 197
chaffe bolster, 383*
chafing (chaffing, chaffyng, shafeing, chaffen, chafeinge) dish (dyshe), 4, 12, 23, 39, 71, 194, 208, 222, 228, 287, 292, 383
chain (cheyne, chene, chayne, cheane), 4, 12, 24, 39, 42, 54, 56, 58, 68, 73, 78, 101, 105, 120, 124, 129, 131, 138, 154, 161, 169, 173, 185, 187, 225, 231, 236, 244, 252, 255, 263, 277, 288–9, 304, 306, 331, 335, 347, 376–7, 400, 417, 439, 455
chair (cheyre, cheare, cher, cheer, cheire, cheeare), 12, 16, 23, 62, 69, 72, 74, 79, 100, 105, 116–17, 124, 126, 130, 133,

135, 138, 141, 145, 156, 158, 161, 163, 165, 167, 170, 178–9, 186, 187, 190, 192*, 193, 196–7, 200, 206, 210, 212, 222, 231, 236*, 250*, 251, 255*, 258, 261, 264, 269, 271–2, 275, 277, 284, 287–8, 290, 293, 296*, 303*, 309, 311, 314, 320, 327, 329, 331, 335, 340, 344, 347, 349, 352, 377, 381, 383, 393, 397, 407, 419, 420*, 421*, 431, 440

chamber (chambre), xxxii, 52, 54–5, 68, 85, 87, 92, 105, 145*, 150, 185, 187, 192*, 194, 196, 215–17, 243, 244*, 246, 250*, 251, 260, 261*, 265, 277, 280*, 282, 287, 296*, 303, 393, 406*, 407*, 418, 419*, 420*, 421*, 439, 440*, 453

chamberpott, 194

chamber roome, 353

chancel (chancell), xvi, xix, 1, 285

chandler (chandeller, chandelerre), 4, 12

chantry lands, 455

charge, 121, 256, 302, 316

charger, 4

charitable givfts, 461

cheese (chese, cheyse, cheise), xxxv, 4, 20, 22, 29, 36, 40, 42, 44, 50, 54, 58, 61, 68, 74, 96–8, 101, 105, 112, 117, 120, 124, 127, 131, 135, 141, 154, 156, 162, 170, 173, 178–9, 186, 188, 206, 209, 212, 218, 220*, 221–2, 228, 231, 242, 250*, 252, 255, 261, 265, 267, 269, 275, 278, 281, 283, 288, 290, 293, 295, 306*, 309, 314, 317, 331, 336, 338, 340, 347, 373, 377, 381, 383, 397, 404, 418, 427, 434, 439, 474–5, 477

cheese bowel, 206

cheese chamber, 278, 406*, 418

cheese frame, 250, 336

cheese ladder, 221

cheese pa[nui]ells [?], 383

cheesestone, 222

cheese tubbe, 399

chees (chist) presse, 54, 75, 130, 138, 141, 158, 170, 196, 206, 209, 244, 256, 284, 293, 312, 317, 331, 335, 340, 397, 399, 406–7, 418, 434

cheestandler (ashins), 195

cherabet, 3

cheseboard, 130, 261, 336

chesefatt dishe, 264

chesefork, 209

chesfatt, 383

Cheshire Attestation of Presbyterian Ministers, 372n.

Cheshire Composition Papers, xvii–xviii

chespitt (cespit), 209, 336

chessmen and chess table, 191*, 209, 284

chest (chiste, cheist), 23, 42, 45, 52, 54, 61, 72, 79, 92, 98, 101, 109, 112–13, 117, 124, 127, 129–31, 135, 138, 145*, 157–8, 161–2, 163*, 166–8, 170, 174, 179, 185, 186, 187, 188, 192, 196, 200, 206, 236, 243, 244*, 246, 251, 255, 257, 261, 265, 267*, 269, 272, 275, 277, 278*, 280*, 281, 284, 287*, 296*, 306, 322, 326, 349, 377, 379, 389, 393, 404, 419, 420*, 421*, 440, 453*

chickens, 221, 339

chikin trough, 196

child's (childes) part or portion, xxxviii*, 8, 11, 17, 22, 28, 46, 52, 60–1, 65, 73–4, 77, 101, 125*, 137, 139, 143*, 153–4, 160*, 161*, 162, 164, 171, 212, 224, 239, 263*, 283, 285, 308, 319*, 396, 410, 447

chipping knife, 192

chisell (chissel, chessel), 4, 209, 335

choir (quyre), 13

Christian faith, 477

Christmas, xv, xvi, xxii, xxx, 123, 128, 176, 410

Church disscipline, 477*

Church of England, xxxvii, xlii, 435

churn (chorne), 16, 23, 68, 195, 209, 221, 292, 383

churne staffe, 195, 209

chymneys harth, 193

Cistercians, xviii & n., xxn.

Civil War, xxxvii

clappery ware *see* cowprieware

clifte (clyft) tymber, 169

clipp, 209

clipping knife, 192

cloak (cloake), 169, 280*, 423

clock (clocke), 3, 250, 257

clokebagge, 284

close (clause, clausure), 198, 238, 291, 353, 414

close [clothes] *see* apparel

close bowk (bouke), 23, 209*

closepress, 186

closett, 191–2, 336–7, 393, 406, 421

closetubb, 221

closse (close) stoole, 303, 393

cloth (clothe, cloath), 3, 13, 96, 98, 193, 216–17, 250, 288*, 293, 306, 309, 407, 420

cloth breches, 134

clothe lese, 208

cloth now in the makeing, 107

cloth stockings, 134

clout leather, 251

coarde, 407

coat (cote), 28, 465

coat-of-arms, xxiv

cock (cocke), 24, 50, 99, 102, 212, 331, 427

cocklofte, 336, 406

cock sute nett, 262

codicil (codicell), xxxviii*, xxxix, 60, 83–5, 88–9, 91*, 92, 93*, 241, 242n., 334

coffer (coffre, quaffer, quoffer), 1, 4, 5, 9, 11, 16, 36, 39, 47, 49–51, 57, 61, 69, 71, 74, 96, 98, 100, 102, 105, 108, 116, 127, 133, 138, 141, 143, 154, 156, 165, 167, 170, 173, 178, 206, 208, 218, 221*, 222, 224, 227, 231, 250*, 265, 280, 284, 292–3, 306, 309, 311, 314, 320, 326, 329, 335–6, 340, 347, 349, 381, 383, 397, 399, 404, 421*, 427, 431, 433, 439–40, 455, 467

cogg, 418

colander, 194

coles (coals, cooles), 96, 123, 161, 173, 178, 252, 264, 284, 288, 295, 317, 374, 377, 407*, 439

coller, 135, 141, 209, 231, 326

colt (coulte, coolt), 52, 55, 68, 112, 135, 137, 145, 154, 158, 165, 169, 171, 177, 199, 217, 236, 243, 252, 288, 295, 311, 326, 339, 404

combys (combe, comp, come, colme, comnpe, cowmpe), 4, 12, 24, 68–9, 101, 170, 196, 263, 277, 316, 329, 335, 406, 418*, 446, 453

comissary, 90

commodities (commodityes), 175–6, 185, 337, 393, 447

commons, 119, 160, 447

compas, 105, 284

comunion, 343*

conye [fur?], 12

cookes chamber, 407

cooler, 196, 418

coorse sheets, 383

cop (coppe), 52, 335, 383

cop pynne (cop pinn, coppine, copsowe pin, copp pyn), 39, 52, 196, 225, 228

cop solle (copsole, copsoule, copsow, cop sowe, coppsole, capsoule), 4, 12, 24, 39, 52, 54, 196

coppe yock (cupp yoke), 39, 52, 222

coppie of recognizature, 148

copyhold (or customary) messuage, 236–7, 240, 372

corall bracelett, 391

corne (growing or sowen on grounde, being bladdes), 40, 44, 49, 54, 61, 74, 100, 102, 105, 108–9, 116–17, 121, 124, 126, 129*, 130*, 131, 135, 138, 165, 169, 178–9, 208*, 236, 243, 255, 261, 265, 267, 269, 281, 283, 295, 306, 309, 312, 314, 317, 329, 331, 339, 347, 396, 399, 404, 417, 427, 431, 434, 439

corne (in house, i.e., harvested), xxivn., 16, 18, 20, 24, 40, 42, 51, 54, 61, 74, 95, 101, 105, 108–9, 117, 121, 124, 126*, 129, 131, 133, 135, 141, 143, 145, 151, 154–6, 158, 161*, 165, 169, 173, 178–9, 186*, 187, 188*, 200, 206, 212, 217–18, 229, 231, 236*, 243, 252*, 255*, 261, 263, 265, 267, 269, 274, 278, 281, 283*, 287–8, 290*, 295*, 306*, 311–12, 314*, 317, 326, 329, 331, 339–40, 344, 347, 373, 376, 381, 383, 389, 396, 397*, 399, 404, 427, 431, 433–4, 439, 453

corne baskett, 68, 206, 397

corne unthreched, 117, 288

corstet (corslet), 117, 127, 158, 170, 243

cotage (cottage), 9, 198, 427

cottage garden, 425*, 426*

cotton (cloth), 12

coulter, 195

counterfett (counterfeit, conterfett), 4, 39–40, 228

course pease, 417

court cubboard, 250, 303

courte chamber, 420

cover, 209, 228, 292, 420*, 421

covered chare, 421

covered stoole, 420–1

covering (coveringe, coveryng, cowering), 4*, 14, 124, 163, 208, 225, 228, 243, 246, 250*, 264, 281, 306, 330*, 373, 383*, 393, 419*, 420*, 421*, 439–40

coverlidd (coverlett, couerlett, coverlet), 4*, 11–12, 22–3, 39, 42, 45, 98, 101, 130, 167, 192, 194*, 221, 231, 250*, 251, 280, 292*, 326, 419, 453

coverpane, 14

cow (cowe, kow, koo), 11, 17, 37, 39, 43–4, 48, 52–3, 56–7, 95, 97–8, 101, 108–10, 113, 117, 123–4, 143*, 158, 187, 197, 215–17, 220, 264*, 266, 267*, 268, 272–3, 274*, 280*, 283, 287, 313*, 319, 322, 326, 329, 346, 349, 352, 389*, 396, 417, 423–4, 427, 439*, 445, 449, 455, 461*, 472

cowe heir (hire, hyer), 113, 212

cowprieware (cowpryware, coperie, couperie, cooperie, cowpre), 36, 40, 44, 108–9, 127, 133, 135, 138, 145, 156, 161, 179, 188, 200, 206*, 218, 236, 251–2, 256, 269, 284, 290, 293, 295, 303, 317, 320, 326, 331, 418

coyffe (quoffe), 3*

coyne *see* readie money

coyrkr [cookerie?], 1

crab troughe, 75

crache (cratche) to set in chieses, 68, 74

craddle (cradle), 170, 251

cresselt (cresset, cressit), 5, 44, 209, 293

crofte (croft), xxiii*, 30, 52, 208*, 285

cropwod, 102

croscloth, 160

crossbowe (crossebowe), 55, 135, 200

crowne of gould [money], 185

Crown of England, 297

cruell *see* needle woorke

cup (cupp, coope, cupe), 20, 54, 63, 112, 141, 241, 261, 336*

cupboard (cupbord, cubbard, cubbord, cuppord, cubboard, cubord, cupborde, cubbarte, cobbard, cobbord, cupebord, cupboord, cobbord, cuborte, cubwart, caboard, cobboorde), 1, 3–4, 23, 46, 49, 51, 54, 57, 61, 69, 72, 79, 96, 109, 117, 119, 129, 133, 154, 156, 158, 161, 166, 173, 178–9, 186, 191*, 192*, 196, 200, 206, 212, 221, 223–4, 227–8, 236, 244, 246, 255, 261*, 264, 267*, 269, 271–2, 275, 277–8, 287, 292, 303, 306, 309, 311, 314, 322, 324, 329, 331, 335, 339, 347, 349, 377, 383, 389, 391, 397, 399, 418, 420, 439, 467

cupboard cloth, 193, 196, 250, 421*

curleyes, 192

currant money of England *see* lawfull money of England

curtain (curteyn, curten, curtayne, curtiane, carteyne, cartaine), 191, 192*, 193, 194, 208, 228, 243, 246, 250*, 263*, 336*, 393, 406, 419*, 420*, 421*, 440, 467

curtain rod (iron), 191, 250*

curtain rod rings, 191

curtilage, xxiii

cushion (cusshyn, cushen, quishen, cushine, chusshens, cushione, cushon, cushin, coshen, chochinie), 4, 24, 55, 62, 69, 74, 116, 124, 126, 138, 145, 170, 173, 186, 193*, 196, 206, 210, 213, 218, 228, 231, 250, 252, 255, 258, 261, 269, 277, 287, 290, 293, 296*, 304, 309, 329, 331, 335–6, 393, 397, 400, 420–1, 440

customary land *see* copyhold

cutrye, 69

cuttinge irons, 335

cuttwork, 52

dagger (dagar), 3, 46, 55, 134*, 135, 209, 327

dairy howse, 406*

damaske gowne, 392

day house, 196, 418–19

day house chamber, 419

Day of St John the Baptist *see* Feast of Saint John the Baptist

deed, 198*, 237, 247*, 248*, 249*, 395–6

default, 248, 414

demesne, ix, x

deposition (deposicōn), 80, 81, 84

deske (deaske), 112, 192, 193, 196, 208, 282, 284, 335

diamond ring, 393

diaper table cloth, 251

diapre, 246

diggs, 62

diocese of Chester, ix, 7, 147, 190, 314, 349, 384

dish (dyshe, dysh), 23, 39, 191, 209*, 221, 264, 336

dishboard (dysheboarde, dishborde), 16, 36, 72, 179, 187, 206, 210, 284, 287, 290, 306, 309, 311, 340, 383, 431

dishcrate, 209, 221

Dissolution [of the monasteries], xx

divine service, 477

dobnett, 195

Doctrine of the Gospel, xxxvi, 392

dole *[i.e., charity]*, 342

Domesday Book, ix, x, xiin.

double covering, 419

doublet (dublet, doublett), 1, 3, 129, 134, 465

dower, 150

downe featherbed, 191

dowrie, 9, 32

drale, 221

draught yock (yoke), 39, 52, 102, 222

drawe boxe, 336

drawen beasts, 57

drawing knyfe, 101

drawing table, 190, 296, 421

dress, 226

dresser, 251, 418

drink (drynke, drinke), 3, 185

drinkingpot, 100

dripinge panne (drepynge panne, drippinge, dreping, dreeping pan), 4, 39, 54, 124, 195*, 209, 225, 228, 251, 303, 336, 397, 418, 440

dropper, 195

drought oxen, 5 *and see* ox

drum, 196

dubbinge shers (sheeres), 191, 251

ducks, 12, 116, 326

dyneinge (dyninge) roome, 406, 421*

earth *see* ground

earthen pott (erthen) *see* earthenware

earthenware (erthen ware), 23, 50, 54, 191, 200, 206, 209, 221, 251, 269, 278, 281, 327, 331, 337, 377, 381, 383, 393

Easter, 220

edgetoule (toole, twoole), 36, 165, 309, 347, 427, 431, 434

edgtoome *see* edgetoule

edifice *see* building

education (educacōn) and bringinge upp, 125, 445, 477

Elizabeth peece of gould, 260

elne, 251*

enfeoffment, 198

English Bible, xxxvi, 342

Englishe books, 391

English Church *see* Church of England

English Style (of calculation), 384, 446

entry (entrye, entrie), 145, 244, 296

eshen (eshenn, ashen), 124, 209, 326

Established Church *see* Church of England

ewe (yooe) lambe, 25, 164

ewe (yewe) sheep, 18, 35, 161, 179, 187, 308, 445

ewer (ewre, ure), 3, 194, 208, 277, 335

eyrie, ix, x

facer, 4

faire presse, 335

farme, 239*, 300*, 303, 309

farme lands, 122

farrowe (furrowe) heaffer, 143, 283

fatte, 252

fawcett (fosett), 236, 309

fealty, 198

Feast Day of Easter *see* Easter

Feast of Christmas *see* Christmas

Feast of Saint John the Baptist, 79

Feast of Saint Mychell Tharchangel *see* Michaelmas

Feast of Saint Thomas the Apostle before Christmas, 73, 461

Feast of the Annunciation (anunciacōn, annuntiacōn), xvn., 9, 79, 238, 260, 393*

Feast of the Nativity of our Lord God *see* Christmas

feather (father, fether, fidder) bed, 4, 14, 23, 39, 42, 56–7, 68, 137*, 163, 192*, 193*, 194*, 197*, 200, 208, 221*, 228*, 243, 246*, 250*, 257, 264, 267, 274, 280, 282, 285, 287, 330, 383*, 391, 418, 419*, 420*, 421*, 439–40, 453*, 467 *and see* downe featherbed

featherboulster, 221, 383

feathers, 296, 306, 327

feather waighes, 221

fee, 30, 149, 198, 229, 297, 408*

feelde of gresse (grass), 106, 174
fellye (fellie, fellow), 52, 197, 252, 261, 295, 331
fene, 24
feoffement (feaffemente), 237, 395–6, 413*
fief *see* fee
field (feild), 229, 265, 278, 439
fier (fyre) fuell *see* firewood
filial portion *see* child's part
fillye (filly, fillie, philly), 57, 67, 95, 147, 197, 295
finchte, 25
fipe, 152
firefork, 131, 196
firegrate, 54
fire sclicer, 421
fireshovel (fersholle, fire shovell, fire shoo, fire shovle), 69, 105, 124, 190, 192, 209, 228, 251, 284, 336, 393, 420*, 421*, 440
firewood (fyrewoodde, fyrrewood), 24, 68, 79, 96, 112, 120, 124, 127, 130, 133, 138, 155, 165, 210, 218, 223, 244, 269, 374, 377
fir kine (firkin), 209, 251
fisheries, xxviiin.
fishmonger, xxn.
flannell petticoate, 267, 280
flasket (flaskett), 221, 261, 265, 331, 336, 404, 427
flaxe, 20, 58, 127, 138, 141, 145, 154, 156, 179, 210, 228, 278, 284, 288, 290, 381, 383, 453
flaxe dress, 173
flaxen (flaxson) sheete (shet), 13, 23, 68, 98, 162, 193, 246, 251, 257, 336*, 383
flaxen smock, 280
flaxen towell, 162–3, 251
flaxen yarn, 222, 258
flaxon reeding sheet, 246
fleshe, 116
fleshfork, 195
fleshmeate, 120, 129
fletch (fliche, flitch, flyche) of bacon, 23, 29, 54, 69, 110, 158, 179
fletch of beffe, 23, 54
fliche (filche, fletch), 83, 163, 211, 233, 282, 319, 335
flocke bed, 23, 68, 191, 221*, 246, 250, 264, 326, 419, 420*

footplough (foot plowe), 68, 102
forfeyture, 238
forgotten goods, 327
forke *see* muck yelve
forme (form, fourme, foorm), 1, 3–4, 12, 16, 18, 23, 36, 38–40, 42, 44, 52, 54, 57, 61, 69, 72–4, 79, 100–1, 105, 108–9, 112, 116–17, 120, 126, 129, 131, 133, 135, 138, 141, 143, 156, 158, 161, 163, 179, 185–6, 190, 195, 200, 206, 209*, 212, 218–19, 221, 223, 224*, 225, 227*, 228, 231, 233, 236, 246, 250, 255–6, 261, 265*, 269, 271–2, 277–8, 280–2, 284*, 287–8, 290, 296*, 311, 314, 317, 320, 322, 329, 339, 347, 349, 352, 374, 397, 399, 404, 419*, 440*, 467
fother (fodder), 165, 377
fowling piece, 124, 134–5, 251, 258, 262, 265, 295, 440
fox fur, 14
frame (farme), 52, 54, 131, 167, 179, 191*, 192*, 195*, 200, 208, 209*, 236, 282, 335, 339, 349, 352, 374, 407, 419, 421*, 427, 431, 440*
framed ioynt stoole, 190
framed stoole, 190, 193
framingtawe, 101
freehold, 410
french wheate, 108, 141, 376
friche (frish), 99
frieng (frying, fryeing, frine, frieinge) panne, 4, 12, 39, 69, 102, 170, 195, 197, 209, 221, 225, 251, 293, 427, 433
fuel (fewel, fewell, fewal, foole), 61, 74, 106, 154, 158, 165, 169, 173, 176, 188, 200, 206, 222, 231, 234, 252, 255, 261, 264, 278, 291, 295, 306, 309, 326, 331, 335, 339, 347, 377, 404, 407, 434, 439
funeral sermon, 372
furlong, ix
furnace, 196*
furnace (fornace) panne, 119, 251
furniture, 24, 56–7, 78, 135*, 155, 200, 260–1, 267, 272, 287, 305, 316*, 335, 379, 406*, 407*, 455
furniture for a horse (tack), 138
furred peticoat, 342
furze, 297
fussian (fustian), 3, 45, 129, 134–5

gabardine, 3
gaffe, 55
gallan (gallon), 39
gallepott (gallepottlpott), 194*
gandar (gander), 99, 326
gardaine chamber, 420
garden, 160*, 237–8, 335, 418, 455
gardenrake, 335
gardiner, 129
garnett, 28
garret, 192
gatehouse chamber, 419
geare (geere), 52, 263
geese (gysse, gise), 12, 40, 50, 62, 99, 116,
    145, 166, 177, 221, 265, 307, 326, 331,
    339, 383, 427
gelbart (gobbarch, gobart, gobbart, gobbar,
    gobbert, goberde, gobert, golbert,
    goulboard, golboard, golborde, goulbert,
    gobete, goubbort, goulbett), 1, 4, 12,
    39, 44, 54, 69, 101, 105, 124, 129, 135,
    188, 209, 221, 225, 228, 236, 244,
    251, 256, 277, 290, 331, 336, 347,
    418, 440
geldinge, 229, 417
gelt (tax), ix, x
gilt bolle, 391
girdell (girdle), 2, 251
gladdyn, 287
gladenett (glade nett), 224, 228
glass (ware), 52, 54, 112, 141, 185, 191*,
    192*, 228, 246, 261, 282, 296, 325,
    336*, 393*
glass bottle, 210
glass charger, 54
glerio tymber, 4
glese bill, 9
gloves, 134, 308, 319*, 455, 468
goat, 161
gobiring *see* gelbart
Gods Word, 260*
godyche, 1
gold (gould), 2, 56, 152, 171*, 173, 239,
    272, 347, 391
good and lawful money of England *see*
    lawfull money of England
Good Friday, xxxviii, 119, 131, 172
goose grease, 296
gorse, 288
gorse axe, 209, 335

gould ringe, 120, 134, 300*, 464
gould weights, 191–2, 208
gourge, 209
gowne (gown, goune), 1, 3, 13–14, 37, 107,
    140, 267*, 280*
goyst (joist), 169
grain *see* corne
grate (grete), 69, 170, 251, 284, 312, 326,
    331, 397, 399, 419–20
grater, 265
grave, 285
graven ringe, 134
greese, 336
greesehedd, 39
grid (gryd, gridd) iron (yrone, ieren, ireon),
    5, 12, 23, 39, 69, 195, 209, 336
gridle, 102
grindstone (grindleston, gryndle stone,
    grindle stan, grinding stone), 75, 102,
    116, 206, 222, 231, 252, 255, 331, 335,
    339, 418
groat (grote), 337, 418
groome, 434
ground (grounde, grounds), 24, 26, 29, 129,
    146, 154, 156, 168, 181, 185, 187, 210,
    212, 215, 222, 225, 230, 235, 256, 262,
    280, 285, 286*, 287, 290, 299, 320,
    325*, 331, 333, 343, 346, 357, 379,
    427
ground chamber, 243–4
guilded boxe, 407
gunne *see* pistoll

hacking knife (knyfe), 195, 209, 221
hacknaye sadle (hacknye saddle), 68
haircloth (heirs, heyre, here, hayre, hayer,
    hairre) clothe (cloth, cloath), 58, 75,
    117, 130, 178, 244, 255, 261, 264, 278,
    295, 336, 406, 418, 439
haire (heare, heyre, harh, heyr), 102, 124,
    170, 177, 196, 200, 317, 404, 453
haire nett cloth, 252
hair sieve (heir sive, hayre sive), 102, 221
halfe hoope, 287
hall (hawle, haule), 3–4, 13, 104, 145*, 193,
    195, 224*, 227, 250*, 251, 277, 296,
    406, 421
hallockrake, 335
halter, 209
hammer (hamer), 24, 54, 209, 417–18

hamper, 418

hand kerchef, 280

handle, 102

hand sawe, 209

handyron (iron), 23

hanginge bord, 209

hanging candlestick, 222

hangying (hengyng), 1, 4, 344

harness (harnes, harneis), 1, 9, 28

harriot (heriot, herryott, harryot, harrat, heryote), 44, 46, 72, 78, 95, 108, 117*, 130, 137, 143, 156, 158, 179, 223, 236, 246, 258, 326, 328, 331, 341, 389, 404, 439, 472

harrowe, 1, 4, 24, 42, 52, 54, 56, 58, 68, 74, 78, 96, 99, 101–2, 105, 116, 120, 127, 129, 131, 135, 138, 141, 154–5, 161, 185, 187–8, 209, 222, 225, 228, 244, 252, 255, 267, 269, 280, 284, 288, 293, 295, 304, 334, 339, 347, 383, 400, 402, 404, 417, 431, 439

hat (hatt, hatte), 37, 173, 178, 408, 465

hatchet (hatchat, hatchett), 4, 24, 30, 134, 209, 292

hatchowe, 62

hay (haye, hey, heye, haie), 12, 16, 20, 24, 29, 33, 40, 42, 51, 61, 68, 96, 98–9, 102, 105, 112, 117, 124, 126*, 131, 133–5, 143, 145, 151, 154–5, 161, 165–6, 169, 174, 186, 188, 200, 208, 213, 217, 220, 223*, 229, 231, 234, 236, 243, 252, 255, 258, 261, 264, 267, 274, 278, 287–8, 290, 293, 295, 306, 312, 314, 317, 326, 331, 334–5, 339, 344, 347, 373, 377, 381, 383, 397, 399, 407, 417, 431, 433–4, 439, 453

hayhooke, 221, 335

hay sowen, 74

haystack, 174

hay unsowen, 74

heade peece (headpiece), 55, 295

heath, 297

heath sheepe, 125

hecke, 336

heehowes (hay house), 68, 335

hefer (heffer) calfe, 15–16, 137, 316

hefferre (heifer, heaffer, heyfer, heoffer), 12, 18, 24, 30, 32–3, 43–4, 52, 57, 68, 99, 115, 117, 126, 130, 143, 155, 169*, 199, 217, 220, 225, 231, 243, 260, 262,

264*, 267–8, 274, 280, 290, 308–9, 339, 373, 383, 396, 404, 427, 431, 455

heffers in caulfes, 5, 123, 137, 255, 282, 314

heffer oxen, 255

heireloome (heir lombe, heirloom, earlome, earelome, heyreloome), 1, 3, 120, 236, 263, 314, 322, 342

hemp, 20, 453

hemp (growing), 54, 58, 127, 138, 141, 145, 148, 154, 210, 222, 290, 326, 381, 383

hempe and yorne spone in the howse, 108, 173, 179, 278, 284, 406

hemp seede, 124, 274, 326, 339, 381

hemp shete (hempe sheet), 23, 246, 251

hemp unbrak, 222

hengled yokes, 335

hens (hennes), 24, 40, 50, 62, 99, 102, 116, 133, 145, 166, 177, 213, 221, 326, 331, 383, 421, 427

'her and her grasse' *[sic]*, 129

herball, 407

herbriche of the grounds [herbage], 97

hereditament (heredytamts), 28, 60, 119, 236, 237*, 238*, 247, 248*, 323, 395*, 396, 410*, 413–14

heritage, 297

hettchill (heichowe, hetchell, hetshall, hechele), 68, 141, 210, 222, 331, 374, 383

hide (of land), ix*

high bedd, 420

higher feild, 286*

hoe (how), 4, 68

hogeshead (hog's head, hoggshead, hogshead), 193, 407, 418

hogg (hodgge) *see* pig; swine

hogge in salte, 40

holy gospels of God *see* Bible

honie (hony, honney), 154, 158, 269, 331

hook, 221, 418

hoope (hoop, hoppe, hope), 102, 127, 210, 221, 261, 293, 406, 418

hoope of barley, 39, 156

hoope of corne, 39

houpe of ottes, 44

hoope (hope) of wheat, 29, 68–9

hopps (hops), 58, 258, 336

hoppette on wheel, 221

hopyer, 408

hornes, 331

horscheynes (horse chaynes), 196, 335, 339

horse, 1, 33, 74, 155, 161, 165, 177, 225, 236*, 243, 252, 260, 306, 322, 339, 344*, 383, 406, 433–4

horse cart, 339

horse clothes, 295

horse comb, 209

horsefleshe, 186

horse furniture, 339, 344

horsegear (geare, geer), 116, 178, 209, 223, 244, 252, 256, 292, 335, 383

horseheld (horshead), 417–18

horse pavemente, 129

hossen (hose), 1, 3, 25, 32

house (housse, howse, howes), 9, 24, 36, 38–9, 43, 52, 54, 57, 60–1, 63, 66, 69, 72, 81, 85, 92, 119, 122, 124, 129*, 154, 156, 160*, 169, 185*, 187*, 188*, 190, 200, 206, 212, 215*, 216*, 217, 219*, 223, 225, 226*, 227, 229, 236*, 237–8, 246*, 255, 260, 261*, 265, 277, 278*, 280, 282, 284*, 285*, 286*, 290*, 295*, 306*, 308, 316, 317*, 319, 322*, 325*, 329*, 332–4, 336*, 347*, 349*, 352–3, 368*, 369*, 370*, 372, 373*, 374, 379, 387, 392*, 399*, 400*, 402*, 404*, 407, 427, 434, 436, 439, 440*, 441, 445, 447, 449*, 453*, 456, 460*, 467*, 469–70

household stuff (goods, ware, provisions), 18, 72, 78, 82, 85, 88, 93, 110, 112, 129, 161, 236, 260, 263, 283*, 305, 308, 317, 322, 340–1, 377, 389, 400, 402, 433, 440, 453*, 455, 468

houseroome, 384

howline cloth in the soo, 69

huswyfferye things *see* implements of huswifery

hulse, 229

husbandry (husbandtree) ware, 18, 20, 32–3, 36, 42–4, 56, 58, 60–1, 71–2, 74, 81, 99, 101, 109, 116–17, 120, 124, 126*, 127, 129*, 131, 137–8, 143, 145, 148, 154, 158, 165, 168–9, 173, 179, 185*, 187*, 188, 200*, 215–18, 236, 244, 251, 255–6, 260–1, 269, 272, 281, 284*, 287–8, 289*, 290, 292, 295, 304*, 306, 309, 312, 314, 316–17, 322, 329, 331, 335, 339, 347, 349, 376–7,

381, 383, 397, 400–1, 404, 406, 417, 429, 439, 447, 455, 468, 472

hyer (higher) barne, 335

hyve of bees *see* bees

imbroydered chayre, 420

imbroydered cover, 420

imbroydered valens, 420

implement (impellment) *see* tool

implements (ymplements) about the fyer, 290

implements belonginge to the oven, 316

implements (ymplements) of husbandry *see* husbandry ware

implements (ymplements) of huswifery, 255, 284, 290, 308, 314

implements of iron *see* iron ware

imprisonment *see* ymprisonment

incalfe cowe *see* heffers in caulfes

incalfe heffer *see* heffers in caulfes

inch bord, 335

in chief (*in capite*), 297

indenture, 28, 229*, 238*, 247, 413*

inkle (inckle), 246*, 391

inquisition post mortem, xviiin.*, xxxn., 30, 149, 198*, 229*, 297*

instrument of husbandry *see* husbandry ware

interest money, 284, 323

ioyned (ioynt, joyned) bedd, 215–17, 224*, 227–8, 250, 263, 265*, 280, 287, 290, 292, 305, 314, 316, 322, 333, 383, 418, 419*, 420*, 421*, 440*, 460

ioyned (ioynd) bedsted (bedsteed), 52, 54, 78, 162, 219, 277, 304

ioyned bedstocke *see* ioyned bedd

ioyned cheare (cheere), 206, 224, 227, 467

ioyned forme, 224, 228, 421

ioyned (joynt) stoyle (stool), 54, 208, 222, 419, 421, 467

ioyned (ioynt) table, 200, 250, 263, 265*, 280, 314

ioyned work, 282

ioynt chest, 250, 402, 427

ioynt press (ioyned presse), 250, 280, 467

Irish cadow (caddowe), 193, 282

iron (yron) *see* iron ware

iron barr, 195*

iron (yron) bound (bond, bounde) cart or weane, 4, 12, 20, 54, 68, 135, 179, 244, 263, 265

iron bound wheele, 24, 200, 374
iron cheyns, 196, 221
iron crow, 407, 418
iron grate, 190, 192, 194, 267, 277, 336, 421, 440
iron hooke, 191
iron kettle, 265, 406, 440
iron ladle, 192
iron morter, 251, 406, 418
iron pinne, 418
iron pott, 50, 265, 290, 309, 311, 373, 399, 418, 427, 433, 440
iron rake (rack), 195*, 221
iron ringe, 191
ireon rodd, 208
iron snett, 196
iron (iorn) spitt, 196
iron (iren, irone) ware, 16, 18, 24, 32, 36, 40, 44, 50, 58, 61, 69, 72, 74, 78, 96, 98, 109, 112, 116–17, 120, 124, 127, 129, 131, 133, 135, 138, 141, 143, 145, 154–5, 158, 161, 166–7, 170, 179, 186, 187–8, 200, 206, 212, 218, 221, 231, 244*, 256*, 261, 265, 267, 269, 271–2, 275, 277, 281, 284, 287–8, 292, 295, 303, 306, 309, 312, 317, 320, 327, 329, 336, 347, 374, 377, 381, 383, 393, 397, 399, 404, 406, 418*, 427, 431, 433, 440
iron (ireon) wedge, 30, 195, 209, 222, 407
iron wheele, 335
iron work *see* iron ware
ironige panne, 284

jack (jacke), 407, 418
jacket, 1, 3
jerkin (gerkin), 346, 423
jewel, 161
jill, 194
joyne tree, 222
joyners chamber, 421
judge (jug), 336

kersie, 200
kettle, 39, 194, 222, 251, 267*, 280, 309, 326, 383, 396
kidde, 179, 252
kiln (kilne, kylln, kylne, kyll, kill), 196, 236, 244, 252, 406, 418, 439, 447, 453
kine (kyne, keyne) *see* cattle; cow

King's ground, 278
King's writ, 149, 229
kitchen (kitchine, kytchen, kichen), 145, 150, 186, 194, 225, 244*, 251, 277, 280, 296, 303, 336*, 406, 418, 440*, 453
kitchin butterie (buttry), 244, 440
kitchin chamber *see* kitchen
kitchin croft, 229
kitchin lofte, 224, 228, 337
kleeuer, 195
kneading turnell (turnill, tournel), 102, 209, 221, 336
knedinge (kneydinge) trough (trow), 24, 196, 209, 309, 316
knife, 453
knight's fee, xxviiin., 30, 150, 230, 297
knight's service, xviiin.*, 30, 198

ladder (laddar, ladre), 24, 54, 62, 74, 106, 133, 155, 161, 206, 210*, 221, 278, 281, 284, 293, 296, 331, 335, 339, 383, 417
ladle (leydl), 1, 192
Lady Day, 342, 389
lamb (lambe), xviin., 18, 30, 32, 68, 105, 141, 161, 179, 187*, 221, 308, 439, 445
land (lands), xixn., xxin., xxviiin., 28, 31, 59–61, 119, 123, 136, 149, 160, 190*, 198, 226*, 227, 229, 236, 237*, 238*, 240*, 247*, 248*, 249*, 259, 288, 297, 333, 342–3, 391*, 392*, 393, 395*, 396, 403, 410*, 414, 447, 449, 455, 469–70
land iron, 192, 195*, 209, 251, 293, 336
lantern (lanthorne), 130–1, 195, 221, 336
lard (larde), 59, 198*, 269, 419, 440
larder, 406, 418
larder chest, 192, 195
larder cheyr, 192
latine (Latin) bookes, xxxvi, 342
lawfull money of England, 22, 60, 73*, 177, 207, 305, 384, 410, 413, 414*, 415, 416*, 425, 428, 431, 435, 436*, 437, 447*, 451, 469
leade (leaden) weight, 287, 326, 396–7
leaden cisterne, 421
leaden diall, 191
leaden standish, 191
lease, 70, 79, 106, 138, 154, 185, 190, 227*, 238*, 245, 248–9, 253, 255, 259, 262, 265, 288, 300*, 303*, 305*, 314,

lease continued
  319, 320, 322*, 323*, 328–9, 333*,
  337*, 341, 344, 379, 391, 398, 404,
  426, 427*, 469–70
lease goods, 154
leasehold, 28, 119, 160
leasowe (lessowe, leysow, leysowe), 59, 323,
  402, 447*, 469*, 470
least heaffer, 224
leather, 190*
leatherbill, 101
leathern box, 194
leaved table, 190
lent (lint), 194
lente money, 340, 377, 456
letter of acquittance or quittance (*quietus
  est*), 149, 175
letter of adiuration, 201
letter of administracōn (administration),
  144n., 146, 190, 204, 206, 256, 382,
  384, 416, 432*, 437–8
letter of attorney, 67, 220, 475
letter of tuition, 475–7
liberties, 455
licke, 281
lidd, 194
linen shifts, 392
linnan yarn, 319, 339
linnen (lynene, linan, lynnen) clothe, 44–5,
  105, 108, 148, 193, 200, 212, 261, 284,
  296, 317
linnens (lynnens, linans, linnannes, linneins,
  linenes), 42, 52, 57, 68, 112, 124, 143,
  148, 224, 228*, 236, 246*, 255, 264,
  267, 269, 271–2, 274, 283, 287–8, 290,
  292–3, 303, 306, 309, 311, 314, 319,
  330, 344, 373, 377, 379, 389, 391*,
  393, 397, 399, 404, 406–7, 421*, 427,
  431, 433, 440, 460
lintsy wolsty, 331
liverie cubboard (cupboord, cabbarte), 186,
  192*, 250, 296*, 419*, 420, 421*
livery table, 190
locke, 209, 280
lodging, 185, 237
loft (lofte), 39, 54–5, 68–9, 129, 150, 191–2,
  209, 215, 224*, 225, 227, 244, 251,
  287, 317, 336*, 337, 374, 453
logs, 335
lond ireones, 209

London pynte, 14
longnette, 195
loockinge glasse (looking glass), 112, 193,
  228, 393, 440
loome, 196
loose boards (lose tymber), 250, 317, 335
lower butterry, 337
lower chamber, 54, 290, 336
lower parlor, 250
lynbeck, 196
lynen cupboord, 193
lynseed (linseed, lenten seedenes), 124, 381

maids (mayds) chamber, 406, 420
Maie Daie, 95
maintenance (mentaynnance), 2–3, 37, 66,
  185, 237, 263*, 399, 402–3, 436*, 445,
  451, 470
male [maul], 335
malt (molte, maulte, mallte), 36, 54, 57, 99,
  102, 105, 109, 117, 129, 131, 156, 158,
  169, 173, 178, 218, 255, 261, 269, 278,
  283, 295, 317, 336, 337*, 373, 376,
  383, 404, 406, 417, 439
malter, 228
mans chamber *see* servants chamber
mansion (mantion) house, 190, 226
mantle, 391
mappe, 258, 421
marbull, 3
mare (marre), 18, 20, 24, 33, 36, 42, 44, 51,
  53–4, 57, 60–1, 68, 74, 95, 99, 105,
  112, 115, 117, 120, 124, 126, 130, 135,
  138, 151, 155, 158, 161, 174, 177, 179,
  188, 199, 208, 213, 215–16, 217*, 221,
  231, 233, 236, 242–3, 252, 255, 260,
  264, 266, 268, 272, 278, 287, 290,
  293*, 295, 311, 313, 322, 326, 328–9,
  331, 334, 339, 347, 373, 376, 381, 396,
  417, 455
mark (marke) [money of account], 11, 55, 92
markeinge ireon, 209
marle carte, 334
marled feild, 286*
mariage portion *see* dowrie
marriage, 8, 30, 32, 61, 134*, 136, 137*,
  149–50, 160, 236, 305*, 308, 322*,
  403, 445*, 455
Martinmas (martlemas), 26, 37, 46, 65, 152,
  263*

maselon (masslen, maselen) basin (bason), 3, 12, 23, 131, 309

mastin (mastulyn) panne *see* maselon basin

matrimony *see* marriage

matt, 419

mattock, 4, 24, 131, 209, 231, 244, 256, 335, 433

mattres (mattress, mattrasse, matteres, matres, mattres, mattresse), 4, 11, 14, 22, 45, 54, 250*, 419–21

mattresse bed, 57

mazer cupp furnished with silver & gould, 125

meadow (medowe, meddowe, meadowe, ix, x, 2, 28, 30, 59, 119, 149, 198*, 229, 238, 297*, 322, 340, 402, 447*, 469*, 470*

meale, 336

measure, 141, 200, 210, 251, 383, 417*, 418

measure hoppes, 210

measure of corne, 140

measure of rye, 138

measure of wheat, 97

meat (meate), 274, 309, 404, 431, 434

meatborde, 98

meat clouth (cloth), 12

meate and dryncke *see* maintenance

meatware *see* meat

medicine, 175

melding bard, 24

messuage *see* tenement

mettell, 396

Michaelmas (Michaellmasse, Mychelmas, Michelmas), 8, 9, 26, 55, 80, 226, 252, 260, 277, 342, 389, 393, 451*

midsummer, 65

milch kyne *see* cow

military service *see* knight's service

milke basen, 209

milk heffer, 68

milk house, 150, 209, 296, 418

mill, xviiin.*, xxviiin., 198, 252 *and see* watermill

mill chizell, 417

milling podege dishe, 194

moitie (moyete, moytie, moietye, moyetye), 28, 56, 137, 150, 160*, 176*, 226, 228*, 248, 302, 305*, 323*, 380, 402*, 404, 425, 447*, 470

money in the purse *see* readie money

montans (muntanes, muntaynes), 106, 169, 255, 261

morris pike, 9

morter and pestell (pestle), 195, 206, 208, 228, 251

mortgaug, 237, 245

mortuarie, 1

moug pots, 20

Mr Andrews [Cotton] chamber, 419

muck (mucke, mock), 16*, 20, 54, 62, 68, 79, 100, 102, 116, 120, 133, 138, 143, 152, 161, 165, 173, 178–9, 200, 206, 210, 213, 218, 231, 234, 244, 252, 261, 265, 267, 269, 278, 281, 284, 287–8, 291, 296, 309, 312, 314, 317, 327, 329, 334–5, 347, 383, 397, 399, 404, 427, 434, 436, 439

muck cart *see* muck wayne

muckfork *see* muck yelve

muckhack, 335

muckhook, 383

muck tumbrel *see* muck wayne

muck wayne (muckwain), 4, 24, 54, 68, 209, 244

muck yelve (muckyelfe), 209, 225, 228, 292, 335

muckyule, 12

mug *see* moug pots

munck corne (mongcorne), 334, 406–7

musket (muskett), 154, 200, 251, 272, 295, 329

mustardmill, 141

musterd whirle (musterilly whirler), 24

Mychaeltide *see* Michaelmas

myddinge (meeding), 165, 173

mydle chamber, 278

nagge (nag, nadge), 17, 61, 68, 99, 102, 105, 115, 124, 137, 145, 169, 187–8, 199, 208, 217, 220, 236, 243, 283, 308–9, 396, 400, 404, 439*

napkin (napken, napkine) *see* nappery ware

nappery (naperie, napry, nappye) ware, 1, 3, 16, 18, 20, 36, 40, 42, 44, 47, 49–50, 54, 57, 68, 72, 74, 96, 98, 100, 105, 108–9, 112, 116–17, 120, 124, 126, 130, 133, 135, 138, 141, 145*, 154, 156, 158, 161, 163*, 165–7, 170, 173, 179, 188, 200, 208, 218, 222, 224, 230, 236, 244*, 246*, 251*, 255, 257, 264, 267,

nappery (naperie, napry, nappye) ware
continued
269, 272, 275, 277*, 280, 281*, 283,
288, 290, 293, 296, 303, 306, 309, 311,
314, 317, 319, 329–30, 339, 347, 373,
377, 381, 383, 389, 395, 399, 404*,
421, 427, 431, 433*, 440, 453, 460
nawger (nauwger, nagar, nagare, noger), 12,
24, 101, 173, 209, 225, 228, 335
neatherd (neatherherd), ix, x
necessaries of husbantrie *see* husbandry
ware
needle woorke (nidlework), 190*, 193
nele (nail?) parsell, 4
netosea, 331
newe iron, 296
noble (money), 44, 84
noggin, 209
Norman period, ix, x
nue cloth, 336, 379
nuncupative testament (will), xxxvii, xlii,
203*, 206, 214*, 215*, 216*, 330, 385,
476–7
nursery (nursrye), 406, 420

oates, 57, 99, 141, 145, 169, 208*, 222, 293,
334, 336, 339–40, 373, 376, 406, 417
oath, 91, 103, 174, 229, 297, 314
oatmalt, 24
orchard (orachard), 160, 237–8, 286
other od things, 101
ould iron, 191, 200, 339
Our Ladie Day *see* Feast of the
Annunciation
ou[r]sted *see* worsted
outhouse, 447
over see [i.e., imported] dishe, 228
ox (oxen, oxxen, ox sone), 4, 18, 20, 24, 33,
42, 67, 78, 99, 120, 123, 126, 130*,
144, 151, 169, 179, 186, 188, 199, 236,
255, 260, 287, 295, 317, 334, 339, 376,
383, 406, 417*, 474–5, 477

packelant (packillant, packlent), 152, 206,
209, 231, 264
packet, 148
pack saddle (pacsadell), 61, 67–8, 213, 231,
264, 331, 431
padd, 419
pail (peale), 264

painted (paynted, pented, peynted, pinted)
clothe, 4, 12, 24, 36, 39–40, 52, 55, 58,
62, 69, 72, 74, 79, 108, 124, 127, 133,
141, 152, 170, 173, 188, 218, 231, 265,
284, 290
painted dishes, 336
painted hangyng, 39
pane brass, 44, 101, 179, 206, 251, 292
panne (pan, pane), 1, 4, 12, 23, 28, 39, 50,
71, 94, 124, 131, 194–5, 208, 222, 236,
267*, 280*, 287, 383
pannell, 106, 169, 255
panning morter, 191
pan pott, 28
pantry, 192*
parcel, 185, 255, 261, 314
parlor (parloure), 1, 4, 39, 45, 78–9, 93,
145*, 185, 190, 191*, 192*, 223, 224*,
227*, 228, 243, 244*, 250, 255, 263,
265, 277, 296*, 303*, 304, 316*, 317,
322, 335–6, 368, 440, 453*, 460, 471
parsell of barly in the barne, 68
partelit, 107
past piele [compost pile], 195
pasture (pastur), 28, 30, 59, 119, 150, 153,
160, 198*, 229*, 238, 297*, 323, 402,
447*, 469*, 470*
pattell, 336
peck (peake), 102, 331, 417, 418*
peece of silver, 423
pees (pes, pease), 99, 158, 208, 218, 284,
376
pegon, 23
penne, ink and paper, 80, 83, 86, 91, 103,
134, 136, 139, 143, 241
pension (pencōn), 13–14
peppercorn rent, 297
pettecoate (peticote, petticote, petecote), 37,
98, 107, 140, 250, 267*, 280*, 464
peuter (pewter, peauvter, puter), 3, 12, 14,
16, 18, 20, 23, 36, 39, 42, 44–5, 50,
54, 58, 61, 69, 72, 74, 96, 98, 100–1,
105, 108–9, 112, 115, 117, 120, 124,
126, 133, 135, 138, 141, 143, 145, 148,
154, 156, 158, 161, 163*, 165–7, 169,
173, 178–9, 186–8, 194, 200, 206, 208,
212, 218, 225, 228, 231, 233, 236, 244,
251, 255, 258, 261, 265, 267, 269,
271–2, 274–5, 277, 280–1, 287–8, 290,
292, 295, 303, 306, 309, 311, 314, 317,

319, 322, 329–30, 336, 339, 347, 373,
377, 381, 383, 389, 393, 396, 397*,
399, 404, 406, 421, 427, 433*, 440,
453, 460
pewter candlesticke, 267
pewter dishe, 101, 197, 219, 282, 396
pewter flower pott, 277
pichforke, 178
pickel (pickle, pikel, pikell, pykel, pykelle),
24, 102, 228, 331, 335
picklife, 68
picture (pickture), 55, 124, 191, 194, 228,
265, 420–1
pig (pigge, pidge), 143, 295
and see swine
pike, 225
pikeyelfe, 439
pillin (pyllin), 209, 264, 335, 407
pillow (billowe, pillowe, pilloe), 4, 22–3, 39,
98, 130, 152, 163, 191–2, 208, 221,
228, 246*, 250*, 251, 257, 264, 280,
292*, 306, 326*, 330*, 373, 391, 393,
419, 420*, 421*, 453*
pillowbeere (bare, beare), 23, 162, 163*,
193, 208, 246, 257, 277, 336*, 383,
453*
piltt, 209
pinsorres (pincorr), 4, 209
pipe, 4
pistoll/gunne, 433–4
plad shoo please, 271
plane, 209
planeinge bench, 331
planke (plank, plancke), 158, 197, 209, 255,
291–3, 326, 335, 404, 406, 418*
plate, 126, 141, 154, 161, 163, 194, 262,
277, 302, 335, 344, 347, 393, 421
plate (ware), 163, 194, 213, 262, 277
plate coatt *see* armour
platter, 194
playing table *see* chessmen and chess table
playne bedsteed, 252
plough (plowe, plooe), 4, 33, 42, 54, 56, 58,
74, 78, 96, 99, 101, 105, 116, 120,
124, 127, 129, 131, 137–8, 141, 154–5,
161, 165, 169, 173, 178, 185, 187–8,
196, 200, 206, 209, 218–19, 222, 236,
244, 252, 255, 261, 267, 269, 280,
288–90, 295, 304, 306, 309, 312,
316–17, 322, 329, 331, 335, 339, 347*,
377–8, 383, 397, 400, 402, 404, 417,
431, 433–4, 439, 455, 468, 472
ploughbeam *see* plough timber
plough (ploe) timber, 54, 101, 130, 197, 200,
210, 244, 255, 267, 331, 335, 400, 407,
417, 439
plough wheele, 197
plow form *see* plough timber
plowgh sleade, 339
plughe (plough, plowe) iron (ireon, irorn,
iorn), 4, 135, 209, 225, 267, 292, 331,
335, 339
polayen, 55
pole, 229
poleax (pole axe, pol axe, pollux, pollox,
pullace), 3, 62, 209, 407
porche, 243
possnett (possenet, posnet, pursnett), 4, 194,
208, 228, 419
pot (potte, pott, pote, poughte), 1, 4, 9, 12,
23, 39, 50, 73, 94, 100–1, 124, 131,
228, 236, 267*, 280, 287, 331, 372,
383
pot (potte and panne) brass, 44, 100–1, 179,
206, 251, 287, 292
pothanger, 165
pot hoyck (pothook, pot hocke, pathooke,
potthook, 12, 23, 39, 129, 197, 209,
225, 277, 288, 314, 331, 336
potrack (pot racke, pottrak), 23, 69, 102,
131, 154, 170, 179, 197, 209, 221, 225,
228, 293, 336, 374, 418, 440
pottell, 336
pottell pott, 14
pottery (pottree) ware *see* earthenware
pott hengulle, 4
potting stick, 221
pottlidd, 195, 210
pott of butter, 234
pottynger (pottinger, potynger), 4, 39–40
poultry (pulterye, poultrie, pultrie, poulterie,
powltry, powtry), 16, 18, 20, 36, 40,
54, 58, 72, 74, 79, 96, 106, 108–9,
112, 116–17, 120, 124, 126, 129–30,
135, 138, 141, 143, 151, 154–5, 158,
161, 165, 167, 170, 173, 179, 186–8,
199, 206, 208, 218, 244, 255, 261, 268,
275, 278, 281, 284, 287, 291, 293, 307,
309, 312, 314, 317, 329, 335, 347, 374,
377, 404, 421, 431, 434, 440

poultryware *see* poultry
powdred beefe, 251
powkes *[bags?]*, 24
pownd stones of lead, 196
preferment, 65
presinge bord, 209
presse (pres, pras, press, preese), 57, 116–17,
　129, 131, 145, 158, 168, 170, 179,
　193–4, 196*, 206, 250*, 255, 257, 271,
　277, 281, 284, 290, 296, 303, 306, 314,
　316–17, 322, 336, 374, 397, 399, 402,
　404, 419–21, 440, 453
presser, 221
priggin, 209
priority of birth, 445
proctor's fee, 175*
Protestant religion, 477
protestation, 192
provisions for house *see* household stuff
pudding pan, 293
pudding plate, 221, 309, 336
pules (pulleys), 292
pullen (pulyn, pullin, pyllin, pulleyne), 44,
　199, 236
pumpe, 252
purse, 24
pyed cowe, 274
pye plate, 194
pynt, 194

quarrel bricks, 196
quart pott, 194
quarter of wood, 106, 138
quern, 18
quiche (quyssion, quishene, quishion) *see*
　cushion
quick cattail, 236
quilt back stoole, 420
quyer *see* choir
quylte, 13

racke (rack, rake), 3, 9, 67, 105, 209, 314,
　326, 418, 439–40
rack and iernes, 124
racke rent, 81
radd *see* rod
rayle (reale, rail), 58, 106, 197, 261
readie (reddye, redy) money (monaye), 2,
　24, 58, 69, 95, 97, 102, 110, 113, 119,
　125–7, 138, 152, 154, 162, 173, 218,

255, 303, 320, 327, 337*, 344, 347,
　374, 377, 381, 391, 393, 397, 400*,
　402, 403*, 404, 407*, 408, 423–4, 433,
　441, 449, 455, 456*, 457*, 460*, 463*,
　464*
readinge sheet, 251
ready gold, 393
ready silver, 393
reaming hook, 221
reapeinge hooke, 335
rearing swyne (rereinge swine), 261, 400,
　434
reele, 210, 264, 284, 312, 331, 336, 404,
　440
remainder (remaynder), 31, 260, 271
remnant, 112, 326
rent (rental), xxi, 2, 29, 30, 42, 46, 66–7,
　122, 131, 148, 152, 160*, 185, 198*,
　220, 230, 237*, 238*, 239–40, 242*,
　247*, 248*, 252*, 265, 296*, 297,
　309*, 333, 356, 367, 370, 445, 455*
renunciation, 27, 43, 80, 243, 308, 310*,
　403, 463*, 464*, 470
reparation (repare), 32, 39, 41, 236*
reservacōn, 238, 240, 393
reversion (revercōn, revertion), 26, 79, 138,
　174, 255, 263*, 303*, 320, 329, 451
riddle (riddl), 102, 133, 156, 265, 296, 440
rideinge saddle, 440
riding coate, 134
ridinge (rydinge) furniture, 200, 252
rie feeld, 270 *and see* rye
ringe (ring), 143, 202, 222, 241*, 258, 301,
　341–2, 392, 418, 423, 463*, 464
ripplecome (combe), 62, 192, 210, 439
rod (rodd), 4, 420*, 421*
Roman Catholicism, xxxvii
roome (rowme), 145, 250, 255*, 256, 344,
　420
rope, 284, 326
rope crease, 141
roule, 335
round napkin, 246
rounds, 418
round sheet, 246
round towell, 246
rubie ring, 391
ruffe band (ruffband), 202*
rug (rugge), 257, 419, 420*
rydinge stirropp, 208

rye (rie), 4, 57, 141, 158, 208*, 218, 373, 376*, 406, 417
rye in the barne, 68
rye uppon the grounde, 30

s[?]yer lofe, 336
sack (sacke), 39, 58, 68, 100, 130, 145, 162, 179, 188, 206, 210, 218, 222, 224, 228, 251, 261, 265, 284*, 287–8, 309, 331, 336–7, 340, 374, 397, 404, 421, 427, 431, 440
saddle (sadle, seddell, settell), 60, 117, 120, 131, 134–5, 152, 158, 179, 206, 218, 221, 256, 258, 278, 281, 295–6, 307, 329, 331, 335, 344, 347, 381, 383
saddle cloth, 392
safe (saffe, sauffe), 141, 156, 296, 337, 406, 418
sallet dishe *see* saltcellar
salt *see* saltcellar
saltcellar, 1, 3, 4, 9, 22, 94, 186, 194*, 208, 260, 265, 284, 292, 296, 336*, 419
salt flesh *see* salt meat
salting basyn (basen), 195, 228, 252, 282, 336, 383
saltinge turnell *see* salting basyn
salt meate, 4, 33
salt pork *see* hogge in salte
salt set *see* saltcellar
sarcenet *see* sarche
sarche (search, searche, scerch, sarch), 3, 127, 221, 229, 278, 336
sartane hee, 122
saten (satten, satin), 3
sattlerye, 153
sawe, 60, 68, 225, 228, 288, 335, 347
sawser (saucer), 23, 194*
sayd (sawed, sawinge) bords & other tymber, 5, 58, 116, 169
scales (skales), 191, 290, 292, 331, 336, 383, 418, 439
scall barrs of iron, 194
schoolmaster, xv & n.
scileing (seylinge, syleing, syling, sileinge, siling, silieng, ceiling), 119–20, 168, 200, 206, 219, 222, 281, 284, 306, 325, 467
scoch, 221
screne *[screen]*, 3
scythe (seithe, sycthe), 68, 102, 209

seale ring, 63
searser, 191
seat, 190
securetye *see* surety
seed, 75, 328
seised in fee, 30
servants (scervants) beade, 225, 336
servants chamber, 251*, 344, 419*
Service Booke, xxxvii, 277
seve (sieve, sive, syve, seive), 74, 130, 133, 141, 156, 162, 178, 183, 186, 195, 200, 208, 214, 222, 232, 237, 251, 265, 269, 278, 296, 383, 434, 440
shede, 68
sheepe (schepe, shipe, shepe, shepp), xxxv, 9, 12, 18, 30, 36, 42, 46–8, 54, 57, 61, 68, 78, 105, 115, 117, 120, 126, 130, 141, 165, 177, 188, 217, 221, 243, 255, 288, 290, 295, 306, 309, 339, 373, 376, 381, 406, 417*, 445
sheet (sheat, shete, schete, shette, shite), 3, 4, 12, 14, 20, 39, 68, 102*, 105, 117, 124, 163*, 173, 188, 208, 233, 244, 251, 255, 257, 281, 326, 330, 339, 453*
shelfe (shilfe, shilefe, shillvfe, shylfe, sheelfe, sheilfe), 39–40, 47, 54, 58, 60–1, 69, 74, 79, 96, 98, 108–9, 116, 124, 130, 133, 135, 138, 141, 156, 161, 167, 170, 178, 187, 191, 193, 196, 200, 206, 208, 209*, 212, 215–17, 221, 231, 233, 236, 244, 256, 265, 269, 281–2, 284, 287–8, 290, 293, 296, 306*, 309, 317, 320, 322, 326, 347, 377, 383*, 397, 399, 404, 418*, 421*, 427, 431, 439*, 440*, 447
shertyship *see* surety
shiers, 252
shipinge of yearne, 68
shire (shier), 41
shirt, 107
shoate (shoett, shoot, shot, shote, shott piggs (pidges), 16, 40, 99, 109, 126, 135, 251–2, 255, 283, 373
shoe (shooe, showe, shue), 2, 3, 61, 62, 127, 187, 335, 408
shooke, 252
shott & powder, 251
shovel (showell, shovell, shule), 23–4, 68, 78, 209, 221, 231, 244, 256, 347, 429

shovel tree, 407
shreadinge knife, 209, 418
sidesaddle (sydesadle), 264
silke curtaines, 420
silke fringe, 250*
silke silver laces, 250
silver (sylver), 1–3, 9, 272, 281, 327
silver boule (bowle), 125, 260, 300
silver bucle, 134
silver button, 200, 284
silver cupp, 206, 246*
silver dish, 391
silver salt (double), 300
silver salt parcell guilt, 125, 246
silver seale, 295
silver spoon (spone, sponne), 58, 105, 112, 120, 124, 125*, 129, 131, 143, 145, 152, 154, 161, 162*, 163, 173, 186, 200, 206, 215*, 216*, 217*, 218, 228, 244, 246*, 255, 260, 264, 267, 269, 272, 274–5, 282, 284, 295, 300*, 307, 317, 389, 391*, 453
silver spoone (gilded), 389
silver wine boule (guilt), 299
sitting wheel, 440
skellett (skillet, skellete), 4, 39, 187, 195, 208, 222, 228, 267, 292, 326, 383
skimmer (skimer), 194, 228, 267
skinner, 208
skolle (school), 66
skynnes, 288
sleade, 74, 154, 197, 222, 383, 407, 417
sleade vumade (?), 75
sleadhowse, 252
slope, 418
smocke, 107, 280
snike (sneck), 24
snuffer, 191
socage, 198, 297
sokinge pipe, 68
soote trey, 397
sowe, 287, 295, 314
sowgoral, 280
spade (spad), 24, 225, 228
spice boxe, 391
spinninge wheel (spynnynge whele, spining while, spyninge wheele, spyns wheel), 16, 39, 54, 75, 117, 124, 130, 133, 156, 162, 165, 167, 170, 195*, 206, 210, 228, 264, 269, 275, 278, 290,

295, 335, 340, 347, 407, 427, 431, 434, 440
spit (spitt, spytt), 105, 124, 135, 138, 141, 154, 179, 195, 197, 231, 244, 251, 256, 277, 303, 347, 418, 440
splente (splenet), 3, 9, 22, 76
sploid, 24
spoak (spoke, spooke), 24, 52, 261, 295
spoakeshave (spoycks schayff), 4, 209
spoaks for wayns, 197
spone (spoon), 1, 154, 208
spures (spuirres, spurres), 134*, 135
square, 209, 407
squared tymber, 200
square table, 190, 196–7, 209
stable, 296, 447
stack, 228, 243
standing beddcase, 196
standinge bedd, 85, 93, 105, 124, 208, 243, 250*, 383, 453
standinge bedstidd (bedstead), 282, 472
standinge cuppord, 209
standinge goods, 447
standinge press, 250
standing shelves, 460
standish, 393
stares (stairs), 95, 195, 250
starnell with lace, 250
Statute of Wills, xlii
stave, 200, 326
steeping come, 196
steer (stuere, steare), 11–12, 20, 33, 39, 78, 99, 199, 255, 260*, 396
sterk bullock, 376
sterkebeast *see* stirk
stex [sticks], 68
still, 195
stirk (stirke, sterk, styrk, steark, sterke), 5, 12, 33, 35, 53, 78, 95, 108, 145, 155, 177, 199, 221, 252, 329, 339, 404, 427
stirke calf, 137, 206
stirke (sterke) heffer, 22, 61, 123, 208, 213, 373
stirropp *see* rydinge stirropp
stockbedd *see* bedstock
stocke, 68, 75, 79, 252, 259, 288
stocke card (stockcard), 62, 221, 326, 336, 383
stock sawe, 244, 439

ston (stone, stonne), 158, 196, 209, 261, 377
stone bowe, 135, 200
stone troughe (stoinetrough), 145, 252*,
  316*, 317, 331
stone tub, 252
stoole (stowel, stoyle, stole), 9, 36, 57, 74,
  96, 100, 105, 116, 126, 130, 133, 135,
  138, 141, 143, 145, 156, 161, 170, 179,
  186–7, 190, 200, 212, 218, 224–5,
  227–8, 231, 233, 236, 244, 250, 261,
  264, 271–2, 275, 277, 284, 287, 290,
  296*, 309, 311, 317, 320, 327, 329,
  331, 335, 340, 352, 374, 377, 381,
  383*, 397, 399, 404, 407, 420*, 421*,
  431, 433, 440
stool frame, 250, 255*, 258, 336, 344, 347,
  349
store chamber, 244, 278, 418, 439
storinde, 4
stound (stonde, stoinde, stownde, stoonde,
  stande), 16, 39, 68–9, 72, 93, 98, 124,
  170, 221, 251*, 264, 306, 418*
stounde with eares, 39
stracon cheyr, 192
straine (strayne) flaskett, 224, 228
straw (strawe), 61, 102, 105, 155–6, 161,
  169, 295, 317, 335, 339, 347, 377, 381,
  383, 407
straw baskets, 105, 170, 231, 309, 399
straw flaskett, 383
strawe matt, 287
street, 160
stricke of barlie, 50
strike of malt, 138
stryke *[read stirke?]* calf, 20
stryke of corne, 112
stub ox, 137
sucking calfe *see* weaning calf
sugar spoone, 421
suite (sute) *[clothing]*, 46, 134, 333, 423
surety (suertie, shewerty), 14, 65–6, 156,
  220, 476
surplus (surplusage), 215, 436
sute (suyte) *[legal action]*, 89, 91, 202*
swaddle, 326
swann, 421
swill, 397
swine (swyne), 18, 20, 24, 33, 36, 42, 44,
  54, 57, 61, 69, 74, 78, 96, 98, 101,
  106, 108, 112, 117, 120, 124, 129–31,

  135, 137, 141, 145, 151, 165, 169, 173,
  177, 179, 186, 188, 199, 206, 208, 217,
  221, 229, 231, 233, 236, 243–4, 252,
  264, 268, 274, 278, 283, 288, 290, 311,
  317, 381, 383, 406, 417, 439, 460
swine troughe (trowe), 54, 74, 102, 130,
  143, 152, 196, 218, 261, 265, 291,
  306, 326, 329, 334, 339, 373*, 376,
  407
sword, 1, 3, 9, 55, 114, 134*, 135, 138, 200,
  228, 251, 258, 295, 327, 329, 337, 339,
  402, 404, 434
swyne tob *see* swine troughe
syled bed, 200
syling nayles, 197
syting chere, 54

table, 16, 23, 52, 54, 69, 105, 109, 117, 120,
  131, 135*, 145*, 154, 156, 161, 163,
  167–8, 173, 185, 186–7, 192–3, 195–6,
  206, 208, 209*, 215, 222*, 223*, 224*,
  227*, 228, 231, 233, 244, 246, 250*,
  251, 255, 258, 261*, 271–2, 274, 277*,
  278, 281–2, 284, 287, 290, 296*, 303*,
  306, 309, 311, 316–17, 320, 322, 324,
  329, 331*, 335, 336*, 344, 347, 352,
  374, 377, 383, 389, 397*, 399, 404,
  406–7, 419*, 420*, 421*, 431, 440*,
  447, 453*, 467
table and cloaths *see* maintenance
table and table men *see* chessmen and chess
  table
tableboard (boarde), 129, 168, 170, 236
tablecarpett, 206
tablecloth (table cloathe), 13, 39, 124, 163*,
  193*, 208, 244, 246*, 251*, 255, 257,
  277, 280, 293, 326, 336*, 383, 453
table napkin, 23, 193
tabling *see* maintenance
tacke (tack) of ground, 44, 80, 96, 239*,
  240*, 300*
tacke of one howse in Wrenbury, 112
tallowe (rendered or cake), 250, 296, 336
tandskin, 251
tax, 247
teare of flax and yarne, 251
tearme of yeares, 154
tenement (tenemente), xxiii, xxxv, 9, 28,
  30–1, 59–60, 87, 92, 119, 122*, 130,
  149–50, 153–4, 160*, 185*, 198, 227,

tenement (tenemente) continued
229, 237*, 238*, 239*, 240*, 247*,
248*, 249*, 260*, 285*, 286*, 288*,
297, 299, 305*, 322, 323*, 328, 342,
372*, 392–3, 395*, 396, 402*, 403–4,
410*, 413*, 414, 445*, 447*, 451*,
455*, 469*, 470*, 471*, 472
tenure (tenner), 119, 372
term of lease, 153, 160
tester (testern), 163, 194
tewtawe (tutall, tutawe, tuter), 255, 278, 284,
287, 295, 335, 374
Thanunciacion of our ladye, *see* Feast of the
Annunciation
third parte, 8, 9, 11, 32, 40, 65, 241
thrave of rie, 145
thrawe of oates, 197
thrivin worke, 193*
throck, 210
throwed cheyre, 190, 192–3
throwinge bench, 331
ticke, 228, 440
ticknal *see* ticknallware
ticknallware, 54, 209, 212, 218, 231, 265,
278, 284, 290, 296, 309, 320, 347, 399,
404, 421, 427, 431, 434, 440
tie, 251
timber (tymber), 1, 62, 79, 116, 120, 138,
145, 154, 156, 169*, 197, 206, 218,
251, 261, 278, 284, 287, 291, 295, 312,
335, 403, 404*, 417–18
tin (tynn), 295
tin (tyein) chandler, 195
tinn cofers, 208
tithe (teythe, teith), xxivn., 2, 30, 185*, 372
tithe (tyeth) calfe, 148
tithe dues *see* tithe
tithe (tythe) terme, 29
toe cloth, 61
toe growing upon the ground, 62
tongs (tongues, tonges, tonngs, tonnges), 23,
69, 102, 105, 124, 131, 170, 188, 190,
192, 195, 209, 225, 228, 244, 250–1,
284, 314, 331, 336, 419*, 420*, 421,
440
tool (tole, tewel, toole), 54, 96, 115*,
116–17, 127, 145, 206, 236, 251–2,
258, 284, 288, 296, 314, 331, 344*,
347, 349, 352, 396–7, 439*
tools of husbandrie *see* husbandry ware

tornt (turned) forme, 197
tournell (tornell, turnell, turnill), 23–4, 39,
69, 94, 168, 195–6, 209, 264*, 292–3,
340, 383, 399, 418
towe (toe, to, tawe) *see* yarne and towe
towel (towelle, tawel, tole), 3, 12, 23, 39,
72, 173, 193, 246, 277, 280, 336*, 383
towne, 90
Treatise of Faith, 392
treene (trene, trine, terrene, treenen, trennen,
treyne, tryne, trayne, trein, traine,
treenean, trinde, trillene) ware, 4, 12,
18, 20, 36, 42, 44, 47, 54, 58, 61,
68–9, 72, 74, 96, 98, 100–2, 105, 109*,
112, 116–17, 120, 124, 127, 130, 133,
135, 138, 141, 143, 145, 154, 156, 158,
161, 163*, 165–7, 170, 173, 178–9,
186, 187–8, 195, 200, 212, 218, 225,
228, 231, 236, 244, 252, 256, 264, 268,
272, 275, 277, 281, 284, 287, 290, 295,
303, 309, 312, 314, 317, 320, 326, 329,
336–7, 340, 347, 349, 377, 381, 397,
399, 404, 406*, 418, 427, 431, 434,
440
trees in Wrenbury Wood, 106
trencher, 23, 191*, 193, 221, 228, 261, 264,
336, 421
tressel (tressle, trestle, tristelle, tresle,
threstle, trestelle), 12, 23, 40, 167,
209*, 221, 225, 228, 278, 293, 326,
383*, 407, 418, 440
treyses, 135
trine candlestick, 421
trough (troughe. trow, trowe), 145, 155, 208,
252, 261, 284, 287*, 309, 339, 418
trovell (tryfle), 209, 278
trucklebed (trocle bed, trucklbedd, truckle
beed), 14, 54, 105, 192–3, 194, 224,
228, 250, 255, 261*, 287, 419*, 420*,
421
truckle bedstead, 327
trumpery (trumprie) ware, 287, 306, 399,
418, 421, 431, 434
tru naperie, 427
trunk (troncke, truncke, trunche), 105, 112,
134–5, 193, 200, 228, 257, 277, 284,
288, 296, 304*, 344, 349, 379, 391*,
393, 404, 420–1, 423, 455
tub (tubb, tube), 54, 195, 124, 292, 306, 336,
383, 418*, 453

tugg, 209
tugge chaine, 417
tuition (tuicōn), 327, 445, 474–8
tumbrell body, 383
tumbrill (tumrel, tunbrell), 4, 197, 309, 407
tun, 4
turbary, 198
turfe (turve, torve), 54, 335
turfespade, 209, 221
turkie, 145
turninge dishe, 209
twill (twyll, twell, twil) shete (shet), 4, 12, 22–3, 179, 188
twinter (twynter, twynter) beast, 5, 35, 53, 57, 78, 126, 135, 143, 179, 260, 326, 329, 407*, 439
twinter bull, 78
twinter bullock, 99, 151, 206
twinter coulte, 78
twinter (twenter, twynter) heffer, 20, 25–6, 115, 137*, 151, 177, 187, 280, 283, 311, 372, 417*
twynter fillie, 155
tyle, 295

under cloth, 4
upper chamber, 250
utensills *see* tool

valans (valen, valence, valan, vallaine, vallens, vallance), 3, 196, 250, 406, 419–21, 440, 467
vallaines rod, 250
velvet, 3
venic glasses, 191
vergisse (vergis), 264, 331
viall, 393
victualles (victuals), 173, 188, 236, 340
videor (?), 4
view of frankpledge, xxxiin.
virgate, ix, x
visitation, xixn., 2–3
voyder, 194

wage, 2, 3, 29–30, 148
waien whiels, 102
waights, 124, 206, 208
wain (weyne, wayne) *see* carte
wain (wayne) body (bodie) *see* carte body
wain (wene) rope, 69

wainscoat (wainescote, waynscoat, waynscot, wenecotte, weanescoth, weanescott), 119, 141, 178, 185, 191, 192*, 193, 197, 246, 250, 255, 263, 277, 280, 322, 455
walkers erth, 79
wallbedd, 419, 421
walnutt tree, 208
wanne timber *see* cart tymber
warming (warminge, warmeinge) pan (pann), 193, 251, 261, 287, 303, 335, 393
washne dishe, 54
wastcoate, 342
wastetimber *see* broken timber
watch, 257, 344
watermill, xxviiin., 198*
waters, 160, 447
watringe combe, 306
wax candle (candell), 191, 194
wayers *see* scales
waye [*i.e., path or lane*], 447
wayers *see* scales
wayinge beame, 336
wayne and plowe tymber, 200, 339
waynelode, 333
waynescott bested, 255
waynscotts beede, 255
weaning (wayning, waineinge, whynynge, weininge, weyninge) calf, 12, 20, 35, 61, 78, 99, 109, 130, 135, 137, 268, 285, 329, 339
weapon, 125
wearinge apparel or cloths *see* apparel
weavers loome, 200
wedge (wegge, wigge), 68, 101, 225, 228, 256, 288, 292, 335
wedley gowne, 267
weeting (malt) comb (comnpe), 102, 140, 236, 255, 439
weight, 407, 418
wellcard, 62
wemtell, 39
wheat (whette, whaete), 4, 57, 158, 229, 334, 336, 373, 407, 417
wheate in the barne, 68
wheate upon ye grownd, 407
wheel (whele, whelle, wheele), 4, 23–4, 78, 145, 178, 196, 251, 258, 284, 293, 296, 309, 312*, 326, 329, 331, 339, 421
wheele bed, 383

wheel (whiell) plowe, 68, 339
wheel plow of iron, 196
whele borowe (wheele barrowe), 130, 278
whele plowe without wheels, 39
whitch (whitche), 406, 418, 439
white (whyt, whit) meate, 16, 109, 129, 145,
    200
whitton crest, 131
wichhouse, 185
wicker baskett, 193
wicker hamper, 191
wicker skreene, 196
wife's portion *see* third parte
wildriges ground, 131
wimble (wembell), 4, 24, 39
wimble bitt, 209
windinge rope, 417–18
window curtaine, 421
window cushin, 193
windowe, 100, 193, 280, 282
wine glass, 191, 309
winow (winnowe, winowinge, wynoweing,
    window) sheet (shett), 102, 231*, 251,
    261, 265, 284, 288, 296, 309, 331, 340,
    404, 431
wintercorne, 24
wiskett (wisket), 251, 309
witacōns *see* visitation
wodden vessel *see* treene ware
wodden ware *see* treene ware
woemans saddle with cloth & pyllin, 252
wolstable (wool staple), 299
wood (wodde, woad), 20, 50, 54, 74, 145,
    161, 178–9, 222, 229, 242*, 284, 314,
    377, 418, 439
wood (woods), 59, 120, 147, 149, 160, 198,
    333*, 403, 447
wooden waights, 210
woodenware *see* treene ware
wood for fier *see* firewood
wood Rowines, 160
woodwaint, 38
wool (wooll, wole, wolle, woole), 36, 54, 72,
    117, 120, 127, 129, 131, 173, 218, 228,
    230, 244, 251, 261, 284, 287–8, 290,
    306, 326, 339
woolbed (wolbede, woolbedd, wooll bedd),
    98, 145, 163, 193, 221, 257, 280, 420*

woolen (wollen) cloth, 54, 79, 96, 98,
    116–17, 200, 206, 244, 250, 261, 326,
    339
woolen yarne, 210, 228, 296
woolins, 292
wooll wheel *see* spinninge wheel
word of mouth, 477
workinge instruments *see* tool
worsted, 13, 101
worste dublett, 346
worste suite, 433
worst sheets, 193
worthinge *see* muck
worthyng yewe *see* muck yelve
wountye, 213
wreking iron, 196
writ, 297 & n.
writing style of the English Church, 214
wrought cushin, 250
wrought vallaines, 250
wuulsted stockings, 134
wyne, 202
wyne chest, 193

yard (yord, yarde), 237, 284, 426*, 455
yarne (yarn, yorne, yearne) and towe, 22*,
    51, 54*, 61*, 98, 100–1, 117, 124, 127,
    145, 156*, 158*, 165, 170, 173, 178–9,
    188, 206, 210, 212, 218, 228, 230, 236,
    244, 251, 255, 261, 265, 269, 274*,
    278, 284, 290, 292, 296, 306, 309, 312,
    314, 326, 329, 336, 339, 347, 381, 397,
    418, 427, 439
yarto handles [?], 336
yelfe, 68
yerelinge calves, 130, 179
yewe sheepe *see* ewe sheep
yewer *see* ewer
ymprisonment, 37
ymshene, 284
yocke (youke, yoke, yoak, yeooke), 4, 12,
    24, 42, 54, 56, 58, 68, 73, 78, 105,
    120, 127, 129, 131, 161, 169, 173, 185,
    187–8, 200, 219, 225, 228, 236, 244,
    252, 255, 288–9, 304, 306, 335, 339,
    347, 376–7, 383, 417, 439, 455
young beast (yong best), 42, 74, 120, 141,
    229, 236, 281, 295, 381, 396, 433*, 434